Praise for

GATEKEEPERS

"Iacovetta's title *Gatekeepers* puts it just right because it tells us that the immigrants were to a large extent manipulated or managed into a pattern of conformity set by groups that wanted to 'Canadianize' them in certain ways. Her text is replete with excellent examples of these kinds of top-down attempts to control the immigrants to make them 'fit in.' She's used everything I know about and lots more to provide a rich, scholarly, and compelling work."

—Jerry Tulchinsky, History, Queen's University

"Iacovetta sheds light on the importance of ethnicity in the context of post-World War II immigration. Her comparison of the experiences of different ethnic groups makes an original contribution. She develops a valuable discussion of the dynamics of citizenship and nation-building from the perspectives of both gatekeepers and newcomers."

—Frances Swyripa, History, University of Alberta

FRANCA IACOVETTA

GATEKEEPERS

Reshaping Immigrant Lives in Cold War Canada

BETWEEN THE LINES

TORONTO

Gatekeepers

© 2006 by Franca Iacovetta
First published in 2006 by
Between the Lines
720 Bathurst Street, Suite #404
Toronto, Ontario   M5S 2R4
Canada
1-800-718-7201
www.btlbooks.com

LIBRARY AND ARCHIVES CANADA CATALOGUING IN PUBLICATION

    Iacovetta, Franca, 1957-
       Gatekeepers : reshaping immigrant lives in cold war
    Canada / Franca Iacovetta.
    Includes bibliographical references and index.
    ISBN 1-897071-11-6
    1. Immigrants–Canada–History–20th century. 2. Europeans–Canada–History–
    20th century. 3. Immigrants–Canada–Social conditions–20th century. 4. Europeans–
    Canada–Social conditions–20th century. I. Title.
    FC104.I29 2006   305.9'06912097109045   C2006-905898-9

Cover and text design by David Vereschagin, Quadrat Communications
Printed in Canada

Between the Lines gratefully acknowledges assistance for its publishing activities from the Canada Council for the Arts, the Ontario Arts Council, the Government of Ontario through the Ontario Book Publishers Tax Credit program and through the Ontario Book Initiative, and the Government of Canada through the Book Publishing Industry Development Program.

For my brother Dave

Contents

Preface and
Acknowledgements

AS A STUDY OF A TRANSFORMATIVE ERA in Canadian nation-building, this book aims to shed new light on connections between the political, social, gender, sexual, and immigrant history of early Cold War Canada and the politics of citizenship in a postwar capitalist democracy. I hope that I have conveyed something of the complex dynamics that shaped the many encounters between Canadian gatekeepers and European newcomers, and that I have provided readers with useful analytical tools and interpretations for understanding how postwar Canada became both a more decidedly multi-ethnic nation and a national security state. As a historian who appreciates the power of storytelling, I also hope that I have captured both a sense of the human drama that unfolded in these years and the mix of optimism, fear, and sense of urgency that marked the period.

Given the emphasis in *Gatekeepers* on controversial or unflattering features of postwar reception and citizenship work, and the critique of the modest and hypocritical form of cultural pluralism that developed in those years, it might seem odd that I begin my acknowledgements by noting the multicultural features of my own personal history. Yet by doing this I want to underscore the significant distinction between a state- and elite-driven policy of what would eventually be called multiculturalism, and the reality that many Canadians live multiracial lives – and that they, like me, have found this experience to be enriching.

In addition to being the first Canadian-born, and eldest, daughter of six children born to now deceased Italian parents who came to Canada in the early 1950s, I, like all my siblings, partnered outside our culture. My large family now includes four sisters-in-law: one, the daughter of a Mohawk father and white mother, has official Native status; another is the adopted child of Polish Jewish survivors recruited from the displaced persons camps to work at Tip Top Tailors; and a third is an "Easterner" who grew up in a number of small towns in New Brunswick, Nova Scotia, and Prince Edward Island before her family headed "down the road" to Toronto. The family also includes an Irish-Catholic brother-in-law from Northern Ontario, my own partner, the son of an English immigrant father and Scottish-Canadian mother who grew up in an almost exclusively Wasp middle-class planned community. It includes his kind-hearted sister (my fourth sister-in-law) and a gang of nieces, nephews, and their various partners. While none of the children of the different unions can speak Italian, Yiddish, Irish Gaelic, or Mohawk, a multicultural world is what they know and value.

The same is true of the bright and energetic undergraduate students whom I have taught for the last decade and a half at the University of Toronto's Scarborough campus, where the student body is more not-white than white. Teaching them has been an exciting and empowering experience. I have also greatly benefited – personally, intellectually, and politically – from working with a large and diverse group of brilliant Canadian graduate history students.

As this book makes abundantly clear, however, celebrations of multiculturalism, however defined, are not enough. As a left feminist anti-racist, I am not content with simplistic notions of liberal pluralism or self-congratulatory rhetoric about how, these days, everyone gets to join the ever-expansive Canadian "family." We must also be prepared to fight racism in whatever form it takes and to challenge the grim realities of a Canada that, notwithstanding important accomplishments, remains in many respects a vertical mosaic in which privilege and opportunity still arise according to class-based, racist, and sexist, including heterosexist, criteria. While the backlash against multiculturalism, from both left-wing and conservative critics, reveals much misunderstanding, gross oversimplification (as in the misplaced assumption that anti-racist critics fall into the category of liberal multiculturalists), and muddled politics, my professional historical community remains overwhelmingly white – so there is much work still to be done.

I could not have completed this book, or the articles published from this research over the past few years, without the help of many people and institutions. I am delighted to be able finally to thank them. I want to acknowledge the financial support of the Social Sciences and Humanities Research Council of Canada, the Department of Canadian Heritage (and the Multiculturalism fellowships program), and the Department of History (St. George) and the Division of Humanities (Scarborough) at the University of Toronto. In addition to the much appreciated funds, which allowed me to hire research assistants at different stages in what became an ever-expanding project, the SSHRC Thérèse Casgrain Fellowship and the University of Toronto's senior Connaught Fellowship gave me the most precious thing of all – the time to write in more than fits and starts between teaching and many other pressing responsibilities.

I very much appreciated the help of archivists and librarians at various institutions, including Library and Archives Canada, Ontario Archives, City of Toronto Archives, Multicultural History Society of Ontario, and Acadia University Archives, and the John Robarts and Thomas Fisher libraries at the University of Toronto.

This book might still be in the works had I not been encouraged by Paul Eprile at Between the Lines, and freelance editor Beth McCauley, to stop writing. Both of them convinced me that there was already a real book lurking in the massive and rambling one-thousand-plus-page draft I had written by the winter of 2004. For Beth's excellent suggestions for transforming long and cumbersome chapters sure to annoy readers, or put them to sleep, into more focused and lively chapters of reasonable length, I remain truly grateful. I also want to express my appreciation to the editorial committee and staff at Between the Lines for the interest they showed in my work and for inviting me to join their Canadian social history series. I owe Paul a special thanks for his constant support and enthusiasm, including during a particularly difficult winter, and for the sushi lunches and drinks on Bloor Street. I thoroughly enjoyed working with Lynn McIntyre, whose skills as a photo researcher and communicator saved me a great deal of time and headache. My thanks to Jennifer Tiberio and David Vereschagin for handling the photographs. I could not have had a more skilful, engaged, and respectful copy-editor than Robert Clarke, whose careful work on the manuscript, and probing questions, helped to make this a better book.

For their fine research skills and valuable insights, my heartfelt thanks to a number of fine scholars who as graduate students or recent graduates transcribed interviews that had been taped in different languages or worked on collections in the Robarts or at the Ontario Archives: Andrew Boyd, Renata Brun, Lykke de la Cour, Stephen Heathorn, Martha Ophir, Cecilia Morgan, Mona Pon, Cheryl Smith, Jane Thompson, Robert Ventresca, and Barrington Walker. Another graduate of the Toronto Ph.D. program, Deborah Van Seters, cut her teeth on the academic editing of some earlier and unwieldy chapters and gave me excellent advice.

I thank the colleagues and graduate students who invited me to present papers based on this research and offered me excellent feedback. I had the privilege of trying out my material in History, Women's Studies, Labour Studies, and Graduate departments at the universities of British Columbia, Victoria, Winnipeg, Montreal, Manitoba, Toronto, Queen's, Carleton, York, and New Brunswick as well as at the University of Bremen, Bowling Green State University, and University of Pittsburgh. My friends in the Toronto Labour Studies Group have grown accustomed to my long drafts (they don't even complain anymore) and I to their wisdom, sage advice, and support. They have yet to fail me. Various conference venues in North America and Europe yielded valuable feedback, as did my graduate and undergraduate seminars.

As Ph.D. students at the University of Toronto, and then as colleagues, Catherine Carstairs, Marlene Epp, Valerie Korinek, Katrina Srigley, Ruth Percy, and Barrington Walker were important reminders that the academy can be more than an ivory tower but also a place where we can combine research, debate, comradery, emotional support, and friendship. I am similarly indebted to a network of academic friends whose compassion, respect, and scholarly input helped to sustain me through several years of tragic loss and painful grieving. They include Bettina Bradbury, Ramsay Cook, Karen Dubinsky, Luca Cordignola, Donna Gabaccia, Julie Guard, Seth Wigderson, Sean Hawkins, Rick Halpern, Craig Heron, Lynne Marks, Wendy Mitchinson, Rex Lingwood, Jim Naylor, Ruth Pierson, Angelo Principe, Bruno Ramirez, Roberto and Yvonne Perin, Gabe and Cathy Scardellato, Arthur Sheps, David Blewitt, Linda and Greg Kealey, Veronica Strong-Boag, Frances Swyripa, Mariana Valverde, Maggie Redmonds, and Cynthia Wright. The support and generosity of colleagues on the planning committee of the labouring feminism conference, especially Eileen Boris, Ardis Cameron, Sue Cobble, Jennifer Guglielmo, Alice Kessler-Harris, Nancy Hewitt, and Karen Hunt, made it possible for me to keep writing the book while organizing the conference. Several friends and colleagues generously read parts or all of earlier versions of the manuscript: my thanks to Larry Hannant, Richard Cavell, Modris Eksteins, Christiana Harzig, Rhonda Hinther, Greg Kealey, Jim Mocheruk, Larissa Stavroff, and Jennifer Stephen. I also took full advantage of the exceptionally insightful and helpful reports of my confidential reviewers. My oldest and dearest friend, Tracy Stewart, was simply there for me. So, too, was Ian Radforth, who, as always, offered me the things I value most – respect, support, intellectual debate, political solidarity, and, most of all, uncompromising love.

As regards terminology, I adopt a wider definition of the term "gatekeepers," which normally refers to those authorities who determine admission requirements and regulations for a country or institution. I do this in order to cover the wide array of reception, citizenship, and regulatory activities under scrutiny. Unless the context requires it, I use the terms "refugee" and "displaced persons" interchangeably – both refer to people who are uprooted, homeless, and stateless – and I refer to Holocaust survivors as refugees, DPs, and survivors. In the West the administrative term "displaced persons" generally referred to the millions of dislocated East Europeans, including those who came under UNRRA's mandate (and were temporary sheltered in DP camps while the Allies oversaw their repatriation to the East) and, later, the IRO's mandate. Most of Canada's DPs fell within the IRO mandate and signed labour contracts for specific industries. Their family members often came along later. The term DP quickly developed negative connotations, and I have used it throughout because it effectively conveys how the refugees were stigmatized, even by sympathetic gatekeepers. To distinguish the DPs from the later-arriving refugees from Communist regimes who, following a wait period in the West (two years), entered Canada, I call the latter group Iron Curtain or East bloc refugees. When I use "Hungarian 56ers," or "56ers," I am drawing on common parlance. Unless necessary, I use the term "newcomers" interchangeably with "Europeans," "immigrants," and "refugees." Unless otherwise specified, I use the term "old Canadian" to refer to Canadian-born Canadians who belonged to the Anglo majority in English Canada, and "ethnic Canadian" to refer to Canadian-born or Canadian-reared people of European descent. I use phrases such as "democratic decency" and "Cold War democratic culture" with intended irony meant to highlight the hypocrisies and corruption of democratic ideals. When I use words like "reds" and "pinkos" I am simply echoing my sources.

My decision to deal with the complex and difficult subject of mental illness was not made lightly. Moreover, given that in some cases I am writing about people who may still be alive (though I have masked their identities), or whose children may come upon this book, I think it only fair that I acknowledge my own family history of mental illness and suicide. Recently I have written, for mostly academic audiences, about this history and its impact on my professional scholarship; with one or two exceptions, my colleagues and readers have appreciated my willingness to write vulnerably. This book is not an exercise in personalized scholarship – I do not weave together my historical research and my own family history – but I acknowledge that it is nonetheless a product of my personal history as well as my professional training.

I dedicate the book in the loving memory of my brother David – and also in the continuing anger with which I remember the horrific and debilitating mental illness against which he did such heroic battle for more than a decade of the thirty-three years of his short life. I do not believe in the meaningless clichés about closure, silver linings in black clouds, or that someone's death might simply be for the best. The only saving grace is that although the bad memories never go away, with time some of the good ones do come back. Among his many siblings, Dave was the brightest, the most athletic, the most charming, the funniest, the most stubborn, and the most popular. He also endured the greatest pain, one that the rest of us could barely fathom. When I first began this research, I did not know that mental health would emerge as such a powerful theme, both in the final pages and in my brother's life and hence my own. This irony is no source of comfort, but it has influenced how and, ultimately, why, I knew that I had to finish writing this book.

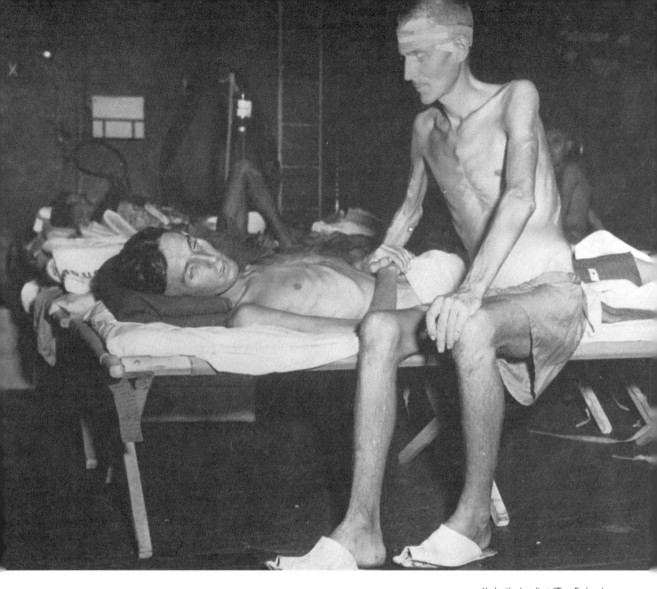

Under the heading, "They Endured Jap Starvation Tactics, Pacific," this U.S. Navy photo of two English prisoners of war liberated from a Japanese prison by the U.S. Pacific Fleet appeared in various newspapers, including the Toronto *Telegram* 14 Sept. 1945. (YUA, Toronto Telegram, ASC Image 1200, ACME, New York Bureau, SS 771689)

Mass Immigration and the Remaking of the Postwar Nation

1

IN THE YEARS IMMEDIATELY AFTER THE SECOND WORLD WAR, far removed from the carnage and chaos, Canadians could follow events in Europe as they had the war: they could read newspapers and news magazines, listen to radio broadcasts, and watch American newsreels at movie theatres. As the years went by, more and more of them could witness events on their small black and white TV screens.

The mass media of the day captured snapshots of the confusion and sense of desperation that reigned in liberated Europe. Audiences saw graphic images and descriptions of disoriented soldiers released from prisoner-of-war camps, bloated bodies floating in canals and rivers, and the many malnourished people in feverish flight. The daily papers featured news of the bombed-out rubble of London streets, of German cities with dead bodies littered amid mountains of debris, and of Polish towns and Italian villages in disarray. Film footage showed miles of churned-up countryside, destroyed bridges and viaducts, and the remnants of French, Belgium, and Dutch farms. The most ghastly images were of emaciated survivors captured on film by camera crews as the Allied forces liberated the Nazi death camps. The footage also revealed the piled-up corpses, huge open graves, and grounds covered in the vomit and excrement of inmates left to suffer from dysentery and starvation. Canadians also came face to face with similar bleak images in *Life* magazine, which featured the work of photojournalist Margaret Bourke White.

Abroad a range of Canadian workers were hired, along with Europeans and Brits, as United Nations administrative staff and relief workers in displaced persons (DP) camps in Germany, Austria, France, and Italy. The Canadian personnel included social workers, welfare administrators, dietitians, and Canadian Red Cross medical officers. In the pages of English-language dailies and mass-circulation news magazines, and in their professional journals and government reports, the Canadians provided a glimpse of the daunting challenges facing the Balts, Jews, Ukrainians, Greeks, Italians, and others who had survived the trauma of war and dislocation. Canadian relief workers commented on the desperate and displaced people, some with large bundles, others with handcarts piled high with household goods, who waded through rivers and sunk in mud as they tried to make their way home or into the liberated cities. The refugees included nearly ten million ethnic Germans (*volksdeutche*) expelled from Eastern Europe – many of whom, though not part of the United Nations' refugee mandate, were relocated in Germany or repatriated to their countries of origin. Also on the move were Latvians, Estonians, Lithuanians, Poles, and other East Europeans. Having toiled in Nazi factories, hospitals, and private quarters under the German occupation of their countries, they now saw their liberation by the Red Army as a return to Soviet occupation, an equally horrifying prospect – and those who had collaborated with the Nazis had all the more reason to fear Soviet revenge. Both the innocent and guilty used whatever means necessary – lies, bribes, falsified papers – to get out and head for the U.S. and other Western, hence safe, military zones of influence.[1]

A principal welfare officer at an Austrian camp near Salzburg, veteran Canadian social worker Ethel Ostry Genkind, wrote about the eerie presence of the Jewish survivors who streamed into the DP camps: "sunken-eyed ragged adults and children with outstretched arms, begging hands and rickety bare legs, their chest bones sticking out from thin tattered bits of clothing."[2] Among the many so-called child orphans were Jewish teenagers who at war's end had emerged from the woods, where they had been hiding in the ruins of bombed-out houses and underground bunkers and living off stolen food or scraps offered by resistance fighters or charitable strangers. German and other youths had also taken refuge in the forests, and they, too, had to be identified, processed, and resettled. Other Canadian workers measured out food supplies, gathered clothing for children, and staffed the registry offices that were trying to locate missing family members. They noted the thin war widows and children who lined up at the crowded food depots or scrambled into already picked-over farmers' fields in hopes of scratching up a few remaining potatoes or turnips. They reported on the weak and diseased and called on Canadians and the world to help.

In the fall of 1945 the Western Allies estimated that they were taking care of nearly seven million refugees, and the Soviets said they were doing the same for roughly the same number in Eastern Europe. The United Nations Relief and Rehabilitation Administration (UNRRA), to which Canada belonged, had assumed responsibility for the repatriation of the East European displaced persons. Under the terms of the Yalta Agreement of 1945, UNRRA and the Allies participated in the forced repatriation of millions of DPs to their homelands, which were now

Communist-controlled and where, it soon became known, they were categorically denounced as collaborators and traitors. Many of them were persecuted, tortured, sent to Siberian labour camps, or killed. By 1946 nearly one million remaining DPs refused repatriation to Soviet-controlled homelands. Although dubbed hard-core anti-Communists, many of them had become so only while in the camps, in part because of the news of Stalin's slaughter of compatriots who had returned home. Their growing resentment against the Soviets also reflected the influence in the camps of a small but well-organized minority of highly militant anti-Communist leaders, some of whom belonged to the governments-in-exile. Amid the growing animosity between Stalin and the Western Allies over the remaining DPs, UNRRA was shut down in 1947, and its successor, the International Refugee Organization (IRO), which the Soviets did not join, was

In the displaced persons camp, relief workers and the refugees themselves organized activities. Biruta Eksteins, second row, centre, was a Girl Guide leader. (Courtesy of Modris Eksteins)

given the task of resettling these homeless and stateless people – attempting to do so in nations such as Canada and Australia.

The hundreds of DP camps were hastily built out of every possible facility, including warehouses, air-bombed railway stations, schools, movie theatres, anchored ships, tourist houses, village housing, stables, and even former Nazi concentration camps. Canadians were among the Allied and United Nations staff who ran the orientation classes, administered food and supplies, and pre-selected residents for possible admission to Canada. In their reports home, these staffers noted the crude conditions of the camps and the continuing challenges of feeding and keeping the camp residents healthy. A veteran Toronto social worker, Edith Ferguson, told *Saturday Night* magazine readers that the living quarters in the camps usually consisted of one small room, where families slept and women cooked on electric plates or "Quebec-style" heater stoves and had few utensils to use. Ferguson reported that anti-Semitism was hampering relief efforts in the camps. The Canadian selection teams that were recruiting able-bodied DPs for Canadian jobs, she noted, were discriminating against Jews (on Ottawa's instructions), and she urged Canadians to do their democratic duty and pressure Ottawa to admit more survivors.[3]

All of these many people – the Canadian overseas relief workers, along with the staff of Canadian embassies and visa offices and the Canadian journalists posted

The original caption: "Lonely little figure on an European dockside, standing out from the bustle of workers behind her, is this small girl, her eyes toward the New World. Protectingly she holds her younger brother." Children such as these found a haven in Canada thanks to the Canadian Jewish Congress. *The Telegram* (Toronto) 20 Dec. 1949.
(YUA, Toronto Telegram, ACS Image 1293)

overseas – were among the first Canadian gatekeepers encountered by the postwar Europeans. The overseas workers included French Canadians and Anglo-Celtic, Jewish, and ethnic Canadians of European descent. In the camps, Canadian officers used the Eaton's or Simpsons catalogues as well as films to teach the Europeans English and orient them to a modern and affluent Canada. They were among those who counselled women about nutritional standards, organized the exercise classes and sports, and tried to comfort those still looking for lost family members. Later, back in Canada, many of these same Canadians would run a variety of reception and citizenship programs for immigrants or staff the social agencies and government offices that dealt with an increasingly large newcomer clientele. Edith Ferguson and Nell West, a senior social welfare administrator in the Ontario government who also did a stint with UNRRA, would both work with the International Institute of Metropolitan Toronto, the city's largest immigrant aid society.

As the Europeans travelled from refugee camps or from home to Canada, they met more Canadian gatekeepers along the way, including ship chaperones, train escorts, and welcome visitors. One group of enthusiastic port and train visitors belonged to the United Church of Canada's Women's Missionary Society (WMS), which offered gifts to the arrivals and shared their encounters with the newcomers in their church reports and publications. The *United Church Observer* featured Dutch and other families with children who happily accepted a gift of a doll and children's Bible (with "gaily coloured pictures"). One WMS worker wrote about the "thrill" of meeting the ships at Halifax and of never knowing how many "cranky," "confused," "anxious," "helpless," or "penniless" newcomers would need help. Her colleague in Montreal, an ethnic Canadian, relayed her encounter at the train station with a "deadly sick" Italian mother who had four children, including twin babies "bare up to their armpits." She found yellow jersey pants for the babies to wear. Travellers' Aid groups at Toronto's Union Station and other stops told similar stories. In these reports the arrivals were always "gracious in their thanks," but whether they felt embarrassed or diminished by the gift-giving encounter that so boosted these religious gatekeepers' morale was rarely considered.[4]

The early arriving DPs included Jewish Holocaust survivors from across the continent as well as the anti-Communist Baltic and Slavic groups and other East Europeans recruited from the DP camps. Most of the DPs came as labour recruits to fill "bulk orders" for contract workers in Canadian industries, with the remainder of them being family members sponsored by earlier arrivals. In recruiting DPs as labour power, Canada was acting in concert with other nations in what was in essence a worldwide labour relocation program. Of the 165,000 DPs who arrived between 1947 and 1953, the largest groups were Poles (23 per cent) and Ukrainians (16 per cent), followed by Germans and Austrians (11 per cent), Jews (10 per cent), Latvians (6 per cent), Lithuanians (6 per cent), Hungarians (5 per cent), Czechs (3 per cent), Dutch (3 per cent), and Russians (4 per cent). They also included smaller numbers of volunteer or independent immigrants from West Germany (a number of whom were the *volksdeutsche*), Holland, Greece, Italy, and Portugal. A final group was the Iron Curtain or Eastern bloc refugees who had escaped from Communist states such as Poland and Czechoslovakia and then made their way to Canada.

A child refugee in Greece.
Telegram, undated.
(YUA, Toronto Telegram, 1533)

An important source of labour, DP recruits wore personal tags that indicated their status and intended placement, such as the sugar-beet industry in Alberta. (J.G. Corn Photographs, 1938–73, MHSO Photo Collection, F1405 10-2, MSR 0074)

In the wake of the early arrivals, by 1965 nearly 1.5 million continental European newcomers had come to Canada. Although some of these, too, were refugees – notably the more than 37,000 Hungarian refugees of the failed 1956 revolt against the Communist regime – the great majority were volunteer immigrants – people moving to a different country mainly to seek a better life for themselves and, usually, their children. The immigrants came from all over Europe, with the largest numbers coming from Germany and impoverished regions such as rural Italy and the fishing villages of the Azores in Portugal. These Europeans, too, were the targets of the gatekeepers' attention. They, too, were viewed as people needing assistance in adjusting to their new situation, finding work, accessing social services, adapting to Canadian gender roles and family models, and absorbing Canadian democratic values. This mass influx of Europeans coincided with another major development that would deeply influence the character of postwar Canadian nation-building and society, the rise of the Cold War.[5]

The Newcomers

The Europeans were an early and numerically significant presence among the postwar newcomers to Canada.

Approximate Totals of Immigrants to Canada, by National Origin, 1946–67

Britain, more than 800,000
Italy, more than 400,000
Germany, almost 300,000
United States, more than 240,000
The Netherlands, 165,000
Poland, more than 100,000
France, more than 80,000
Greece, about 80,000

Portugal, about 57,000
Austria, about 54,000
Hungary, about 52,000
China, almost 47,000
Belgium, West-Indies-Antilles,
Denmark, Australia, Yugoslavia,
Republic of Ireland,
Switzerland, more than 20,000,
in descending order

With an average age of 24.9, the newcomers tended to be youthful. Before 1955 male arrivals outnumbered female, but by the mid-1960s the sex ratio for many groups, including the Europeans, was even or close to it. Among the European groups, women represented a significant percentage of the adults, with the proportions hovering between 47 and 56 per cent. Although not all women migrated for family reasons, many of them had children, raised children, and experienced the double day of domestic and paid labour. In Toronto foreign-born women, both single and married, were significantly involved in the labour force: about one-third of the Metropolitan Toronto labour force in 1961 was of European origin.[6] In 1961 a larger proportion of Canada's foreign-born women were married (71.5 per cent) compared with Canadian-born women (65.6 per cent). Several groups, including Ukrainians, Italians, and Portuguese, were youthful populations with many young parents and small children.

By 1965 more than half of Canada's newcomers had come to Ontario, with 727,011 Europeans representing almost 60 per cent of this total. While most women arrived through the family classification scheme (sponsored by close kin), others came as contract workers. They had landed immigrant status but were obliged to fulfil one-year labour placements, usually in domestic service in homes and work in hospitals and other institutions. A large number of DP men came through labour contracts in logging, construction, farming, and mining; a smaller number of Jewish DPs, or survivors, went mostly into tailoring and other manufacturing jobs.[7] The DP men would later sponsor their wives and children, who were anxiously waiting back in the camps.

Refugee certificates issued for Czech nationals Jiri (Jiriho) Corna (Corn) and wife Jaroslava Cornova. It was not uncommon to simplify or anglicize names.
(J.G. Corn Photographs, 1938–73, MHSO Photo Collection, F1405 10-2, MSR 0074)

The heaviest concentration of newcomers was in Ontario's southwestern industrial corridor of Toronto-Hamilton-Guelph and the surrounding districts, but rural areas also received an influx of Europeans, including Dutch immigrants who settled the Holland Marsh area near Bradford, north of Toronto. Northern Ontario cities that had long attracted immigrants, such as Port Arthur/Fort William and Sault Ste. Marie, also received significant numbers. But by far the strongest magnet was the metropolis of Toronto, whether newcomers came directly or moved there from elsewhere. By 1965 Toronto was a multi-ethnic city, and by 1971 more than 43 per cent of its population of 713,315 was foreign-born. The corresponding figure of foreign-born for the wider Metropolitan Toronto area of more than two million people was 36 per cent. The British-born topped the list, the Italians coming second and the Germans third.

While they shared certain experiences, the European newcomers were not a homogeneous group. Indeed, some of them were the Dutch, Italian, and other European war brides of Canadian servicemen who had already begun families overseas in wartime, although those brides were greatly outnumbered by their

A Canadian Red Cross worker welcomes a mother and daughter from Italy as they arrive at Union Station, Toronto, en route to their final destination of Windsor, Ont. *Telegram*, undated. (YUA, Toronto Telegram, ASC Image 1281)

British counterparts. Some of them were Balts, Ukrainians, Poles, and others who had experienced the brutality of both Russian and German occupation. Many of them, Catholics and Protestants, had toiled in German-controlled factories or in the private homes of German officers and other privileged Nazis. The Jews had faced a genocide, and the survivors had endured the Nazi slave-labour camps, concentration camps, and the death camps with their gas chambers and mountains of shoes left behind by those who had perished. Some of the newcomers were refugee women, Jews and gentiles, who had lost families to war and formed surrogate families with others. They were among the millions of wartime rape victims, some of whom had claimed the "illegitimate" children born from the violence as blood children and (if their daughters had been raped) grandchildren. Especially in Toronto, wartime enemies would frequently encounter each other in workplaces and ethnic neighbourhoods (which were more ethnically mixed than the labels of Ukrainian or Hungarian Town or Little Italy suggest). They would mingle in social agencies, citizenship ceremonies, and other arenas.

As for class differences, a minority of the East European DPs, both Jews and gentiles, were urban professionals, artists, and intellectuals, setting them apart from the overwhelmingly humble backgrounds of the heavily rural groups from Southern and Eastern Europe. Overall, the refugee streams included a mix of people, from farmers and female technicians to tradesmen and professionals, but the elites among them would attract a disproportionate amount of attention and their political significance was greater than their actual numbers might suggest. Large immigrant populations like the Germans and Italians, as well as smaller groups like the Finns, contained liberals, conservatives, and social democrats; but a majority of the postwar newcomers were unsympathetic or opposed to communism, a pattern reinforced by Canada's political-screening procedures. But there were differences even among the East European DPs. Some of them were only mildly opposed to communism, but a core of right-wing political émigrés were highly aggressive Cold Warriors and more interested in using Canada as a base from which to regroup, defeat communism with the help of the West, and return home to regain political power.

Nor can we forget that anti-Semitism continued to infect the post-Holocaust world; it was fuelled by a number of misplaced allegations, including exaggerated claims about the many Jews who belonged to left, if not Communist, organizations. There were, of course, European Jews in both the Communist and non-Communist left, and some Jews had served in the partisan (Communist) resistance during the war. The numbers of left-wing activists were comparatively small, but that did not keep their opponents from associating Jews with a worldwide communist conspiracy. In the DP camps, exaggerated and misleading rumours had spread about how Communist and Jewish elements had even infiltrated the IRO, which, in truth, was an instrument of the West.[8]

A National Experiment in Citizenship?

A combination of factors – including economic self-interest, labour shortages, international pressures, and pro-refugee lobbies – eventually encouraged and cajoled the Canadian government into prying open its doors to immigrants. Following a slow start, immigration into Canada after the Second World War reached mass proportions – although, in accordance with the country's long-standing "White Canada" policy, almost all of it was from white nations.[9]

Between 1946 and 1962 more than 2.1 million newcomers, the great majority of them white newcomers from Britain and Europe, entered a geographically vast country whose population in 1941 had stood at only 11.5 million people. The postwar Cold War era was a time of almost continuous immigration. During the 1950s the ratio of net migration to total population growth was the largest of any decade in Canadian history, save for the 1901–11 years of mass migration to Western Canada. Between 1951 and 1971 the foreign-born in Canada increased twentyfold, from 100,000 to about two million people. Even the United States, the most paradigmatic immigrant nation, with ten times Canada's population, did not take significantly more immigrants; only Australia and West Germany rivalled Canada as immigrant-receiving nations in these years. Across the country, but especially in the major cities of Montreal, Vancouver, Winnipeg, and Toronto, which drew fully one-quarter of the newcomers as a whole, the European arrivals attracted enormous attention.[10] Toronto itself was the single most popular destination for newcomers.

As this diverse group of newcomers from war-torn Europe and its marginal regions set about to rebuild their shattered or disrupted lives in Canada, they faced many challenges and responded in many ways to the support and biases they found. Many of them encountered a variety of gatekeepers, although the nature of the encounters varied considerably in degree and type. Plenty of Canadians feared or balked at the growing presence of the Europeans, and racial bigots denounced the newcomers as so many traumatized, diseased, and dangerous foreigners who would destroy the country. Indeed, public opinion initially opposed opening the gates and considered certain groups – Jews, Japanese, Germans – as particularly undesirable, though by the early 1950s the Germans were enjoying support. Still, despite the opposition large numbers of Canadians welcomed the new arrivals and saw them as a necessary, vibrant addition to a growing country.

A variety of women and men patrolled the nation's entry points and its newly expanded welfare state. Some of these established Canadians ran the country's many reception campaigns, health and welfare services, and family and community programs. The encounters often consisted of pro-active attempts to guide the adjustment to "Canadian ways" and transform the immigrants into productive, democratic citizens. Projects were designed to "Canadianize" the newcomers and encourage social and cultural mingling between them and the old Canadians. One organization, the Canadian Association for Adult Education, a progressive adult literacy group, identified a key concept behind the reception and citizenship campaigns: "The newcomers can make their full contribution to Canadian life only if they are happy and well-adjusted in their new surroundings."[11]

In response to the European newcomers, Canadians from different social and political backgrounds contemplated the meanings of family, morality, citizenship, and democracy. In the push to have the newcomers conform to "Canadian ways" – which usually reflected Anglo-Canadian middle-class ideals – the accent was on everything from food customs and child-rearing methods, or marriage and family dynamics, to participatory democracy and anti-communist activism. But the established Canadians also fretted about the newcomers' physical, mental, and moral health and their capacity for marriage and parenthood, not least of all because the failure of these people to become good citizens would threaten the values and mores of the Canadian mainstream. The gatekeepers also stressed the superiority and abundance of Western capitalist countries and declared that the newcomers' access to the country's expanded social welfare services and experts would permit their full recovery and put them on the right path towards full integration and citizenship.

All of these activities occurred in a highly charged postwar context, where social optimism and rising expectations based on Canada's strong postwar economy and expanding welfare state were mixed with deep-seated fears of communism and nuclear fallout and rising anxiety about unemployment, poor marriages, fragile families, juvenile delinquency, failing health, spreading mental illness, and an increase in sexual deviance of all kinds, including male sex crimes against women and female promiscuity.

As they faced the prospect of working towards a "return to normalcy" – the phrase that came to represent the efforts to "return" people, especially women who had worked during the war or enjoyed some independence, back into the family fold, and "back" to a supposedly more simple and moral way of life – the gatekeepers not only applauded the European newcomers for choosing democracy over totalitarianism, but also valued their labour power. Still, they worried about the additional burdens that this mass of war-weary (and, later, in the case of immigrant groups such as the Portuguese, impoverished) European women, men, children, and youth posed to the already daunting task of national reconstruction. That task included the conversion of a wartime economy to a peacetime one, as well as the creation of supports for returning veterans, whose integration was also linked to the efforts to push women who had worked in wartime industry back into the home. Government also made efforts in particular to help single women train for certain jobs and to deal with inflation and acute housing shortages.[12]

Among the enthusiastic gatekeepers were sympathetic reporters and magazine journalists who invited everyone to join them in a grand national experiment in citizenship. Even the esteemed cultural institution, the National Film Board of Canada (NFB), proved to be an active gatekeeper of sorts. Within the education system, one English instructor, Toronto school principal J.G. Johnson, wrote that he looked forward not only to teaching the European newcomers a new language but also to introducing them to such enlightened concepts and institutions as the "Canadian democratic family." In invoking this image, Johnson was drawing a contrast between his idealized image of the middle-class Canadian family and a commonly held view among many Canadians that the European family was a more deeply patriarchal and authoritarian institution that was in urgent need of reforming. He also issued the familiar warning that if newcomer parents did not adapt to Canadian standards, they would face the "possibilities of family conflict and heart-ache." Professional social workers, marriage counsellors, and child experts working with European families drew similar conclusions. In Johnson's case, he followed his own advice about the need to sell Canada to the newcomers through an "enthusiasm for things Canadian" to the point that one of his adult students married him.[13] Other gatekeepers would frown on mixed marriages.

Canadian officialdom had its own highly active political gatekeepers. One of them was Vladimir Kaye, a Ukrainian-Canadian academic, an active leader within the nationalist, anti-Communist Ukrainian-Canadian community, a committed Cold Warrior, and the chief liaison officer and head of the foreign press section of the recently established Citizenship Branch within the Department of Citizenship and Immigration. During the war Kaye had been actively involved in the precursor to the Citizenship Branch, the wartime Nationalities Branch, which had engaged in the political surveillance of the ethnic left-wing press, censorship of the press, and other attempts to encourage ethnic Canadians to support the war effort. After the war he continued with many of these activities, though under another guise. In countless reports and addresses, Kaye, the Citizenship official, made much of the newcomers' potential for enriching Canadian culture and called upon Canadians to show them respect and patience as they recovered from their nightmarish experiences and underwent a transition from the old world to the new.

Various ethnic-Canadian organizations of differing political stripes, as well as men's service clubs and women's groups, reached out to professionally trained refugees, homemakers, deserted wives, and needy families. They also liaised with the (mostly male) elites within both the older ethnic-Canadian organizations and the new immigrant mainstream, and with anti-Communist groups and communities, in an effort to combat communism and undermine the left-wing ethnic-Canadian groups and their newspapers. So, too, did Kaye and his Citizenship Branch colleagues. Canadian middle-class women's groups, such as the conservative Imperial Order Daughters of the Empire (IODE), and business organizations, such as the chambers of commerce, funded reception projects, blacklisted Canadians on suspicion of being Communists, and entered into anti-Communist alliances with politically active East European refugee leaders and groups. In effect, all of these groups carried out a strategy that Kaye referred to as "the tactics of close liaison."

Furthermore, these gatekeepers drew clear links between their reception and citizenship work with the newcomers and their battles against communism.

The most active gatekeepers included the army of professional and semi-professional social workers, family and child experts, front-line caseworkers, and volunteers who ran the country's social welfare services, social agencies, and settlement houses. The settlements were often long-standing community-based reform organizations located in inner-city neighbourhoods; they provided recreational, educational, and social services to the low-income residents of the area. The professionally trained social workers who plied their trade in Toronto's downtown settlement organizations included John Haddad, director of St. Christopher House, and Kathleen (Kay) Gorrie, head resident at University Settlement House. At the International Institute of Metropolitan Toronto, Canadian and European social workers, caseworkers, and experienced volunteers ran the social and cultural programs and individualized counselling services. Nutrition experts, food writers, and fashion-makers were also actively involved, in particular working to mount national health and homemaking campaigns aimed at improving children's health and "family living" as well as "spicing up" family meals with novelty or exotic items. They showed a degree of liberal pluralism by, for example, on the one hand encouraging newcomer mothers to adapt to certain Canadian food customs and on the other pressing Canadian mothers to surprise their families by experimenting with (modified) ethnic ingredients or recipes. As with Kaye and the other cultural pluralists who supported ethnic folklore and handicrafts, however, the emphasis was on mining ethnic cultures for the benefit of the Canadian mainstream.

At the other end of the spectrum were the front-line caseworkers, counsellors, and mental health experts who dealt with some of the severest casualties of the war and the most marginal of newcomers: adults suffering from depression and various post-traumatic symptoms, angry and alienated young men, abused wives and young wartime rape victims, and unwed mothers. The work also included families living on welfare who were categorized as highly dysfunctional or as "multiple problem families," a classification that took in a mix of troubling characteristics, such as alcoholism, desertion, criminality, mental illness, severe marital discord, poor school performance, and persistent economic deprivation. The press coverage of the occasional suicide, sexual assault, or murder involving newcomer men and women as victims or perpetrators, or both, elicited sympathy but also served to fuel long-standing stereotypes of Europeans as volatile people who were more prone to crimes of passion or violence than were white Canadians.

This sometimes bewildering display of activity raises a number of important questions. How did the gatekeepers construct the newcomers? How did they interact with them? Did different gatekeepers perceive the different groups of European newcomers in similar or different ways? What were the gender differences?

Similar questions arise concerning the newcomers' responses to the gatekeepers. How did parents view the settlement house workers who recruited their children for social and athletics programs? How did they negotiate with the home visitor who came knocking on their door with clipboard and family budgets in hand? How did they find life-affirming ways of rebuilding their lives in the aftermath of so much loss? How did they try to teach Canadians about the dangers of communism?

As these questions suggest, the social, political, and women's and gender history of early Cold War Canada, and specifically Toronto, was refracted through the prism of immigrant and refugee reception and citizenship work.[14] The conflicts, accommodations, relationships, and ideological alliances that obtained between gatekeepers and various groups of newcomers are a key to this history, as are the encounters between the front-line workers within community-based agencies and government social services and the growing clientele of newcomers.

Toronto in particular was the site of a wide variety of gatekeeper/newcomer encounters. But the range of encounters and wide array of gatekeepers also extended through a variety of contact zones, including the Halifax pier and the trains that brought the newly arrived to Toronto, newspaper advice columns, city settlement houses, newcomers' households, newcomer and ethnic-Canadian newspapers, social agencies, organized political demonstrations, immigration offices, interrogation rooms, and the Kingston Prison for Women, where Canada's two convicted female spies did their time. In these many arenas, specific groups of gatekeepers and newcomers met, collided, and grappled with each other, with the gatekeepers almost always enjoying greater power and resources than the newcomers. Yet the newcomers, even the marginal ones, sought to influence the outcome of these encounters and, as feminist historian Linda Gordon famously put it in her influential study of domestic violence victims, struggled to be the "heroes of their own lives." The records generated at these points of contact are a reflection of the complex relations at play, the product of a dialectic of power between the more powerful gatekeepers, especially experts, caseworkers, and state authorities, and their less powerful but often resourceful clients or citizens in the making.[15]

The Cold War: Origins and Strategies

Canadian immigration historians have demonstrated the important role that the Cold War played in Canada's postwar immigration policy, especially with regards to the admission of the anti-Communist DPs and other refugees. But neither they nor many social and gender historians have fully appreciated, perhaps, the profound impact of Cold War anxieties and ideology on Canadian reception and citizenship efforts and, moreover, on how gatekeeper/newcomer relations and campaigns had an impact on the making of a decidedly more ethnic but Cold War nation. As the Cold War gripped the globe in the years immediately after the war, the growing polarization of the world into two militarized and opposing camps – a pro-Communist Eastern bloc with the Soviet Union at the centre, and a pro-capitalist Western bloc in which the United States held dominance – prompted the Canadian state to join the U.S.-led policy of containing communism abroad and to follow the U.S. lead in seeking to contain and remove any perceived political and other threats to the body politic at home.

The Cold War began in Europe, where even before the end of hostilities the Soviet Union's Joseph Stalin and the Western leaders of the Grand Alliance against Germany had already disagreed over the postwar division of the continent. At war's end the United States and other Allied forces occupied the western part of the continent, and the Red Army held all of Eastern Europe and the Balkans, except for Greece, Albania, and Yugoslavia. The timing of events varied by country, but between 1945 and 1947 pro-Soviet Communist governments were established in Poland, Hungary, Bulgaria, Romania, and East Germany. In Czechoslovakia – which the Western leaders viewed as enjoying stronger democratic institutions and more deserving of their respect – the country's Communists gained control of the government in 1948. Only Yugoslavia, where Tito, or Josip Broz (whose political success was due in part to his leading role with the partisans who fought Hitler), ruled independently of Stalin, and Communist Albania stood outside Moscow's sphere of influence.

While Stalin defended the creation of a buffer zone of compliant states on defensive grounds, declaring that "never again" would Russia's borders be vulnerable to invasion, the West viewed the events as the aggressive actions of an imperialist-minded Moscow. To gain power the Communists had used a number of tactics, such as rigged elections, elimination of opponents, coups, and the creation of one-party governments, but there had also been popular support for communism among those who believed they were voting for a progressive alternative to capitalism. Nevertheless, the West decried that, as British Prime Minister Winston Churchill put it as early as 1946, an Iron Curtain had descended upon Europe, dividing the continent into two ideologically opposed and hostile camps.

The subsequent events occurred in rapid succession, each one creating an arena of potential confrontation between the two superpowers that increasingly held the world's future in their hands. One U.S. diplomat, George Kennan, warned that communism, if left unchecked, would spread like a disease, infecting the free world and eventually destroying it. As a result of that kind of thinking, the U.S. government developed a strategy of containing communism anywhere on the globe. The policy was first articulated during the 1947 civil war in Greece between Communist insurgents (supported by Tito) and a pro-Western government in Athens. U.S.

president Harry S. Truman enunciated the Truman Doctrine, which effectively declared U.S. support for any country claiming to be threatened by Communist expansion. The Marshall Plan (European Recovery Program) followed, pouring billions of dollars into rebuilding war-torn countries and increasing U.S. influence over Western Europe. Stalin denounced the program as U.S. imperialism and tightened his grip on Eastern Europe. His blockade of West Berlin in 1948, a response to U.S. plans to unify the city and Germany under Western influence, intensified hostilities, leading to the division of Germany (and Berlin). After Russia attained nuclear capacity in 1949, the nuclear arms race was truly underway, solidifying tensions on both sides.

A search for security in a nuclear world led to military alliances and the stockpiling of conventional, biochemical, and nuclear weapons. In 1949 the North Atlantic Treaty Organization (NATO) brought together the United States, Canada, Britain, and a string of European nations into a military alliance, with other countries joining in following years. The East bloc states responded in 1955 with the Warsaw Pact, which brought the Soviet Union and its "satellite states" into a formal military alliance. A critical event of the early Cold War was Nikita Khrushchev's public revelations in 1956 of Stalin's anti-Semitic and brutal regime. The acknowledgement that millions of people had been tortured or murdered under Stalin led to a mass exodus out of the international Communist movement, including members in Canada.

The Cold War was cold in that both sides, fearing the horrific consequences, managed to avoid nuclear warfare, but many local, or proxy, wars involving conventional warfare did break out. As the superpowers calculated which moves to make in each conflict, the buildup of military forces and missile sites continued apace. As a result the Cold War also had a direct impact on Asia, Latin America, and Africa. Perhaps the most dramatic episode was Mao Tse-tung's victory in China in 1949 against Chiang Kai-shek's Nationalist government, which had the backing of the United States. The U.S. government now decried the "fall of China" and declared that a Bamboo Curtain had descended upon the East. Wars (hot episodes) followed in Korea and, later, Vietnam. During the four-decade Cold War between 1946 and the collapse of the Soviet Union in 1989, periods of heating up and cooling down did occur, but mutual distrust always remained.[16]

For Canadians, the Cold War first arrived on their doorstep in 1946, when a young Soviet cipher clerk, Igor Gouzenko, defected with a stash of documents proving the existence of a Soviet spy ring in Canada. Initially surprised that Russia wanted to spy on them, and shocked that Canadians – among them research scientists who had worked on the atom bomb, Canadian Communist MP Fred Rose, and two low-level clerks, Doukhobor-Canadian Emma Woikin and Englishwoman Kathleen Willsher of the British High Commission – had supplied secret information

The defection of Soviet cipher clerk Igor Gouzenko in 1945 brought the Cold War to Canada's front door. Always fearful of Soviet reprisals, whenever he appeared in public Gouzenko wore a cloth cover over his face or used other disguises. *The Gazette* (Montreal), undated.
(LAC, PA-129625)

to Russian agents, Canadians quickly supported Ottawa's decision to do like the Americans and make an example of the suspects. The Canadian state armed itself with extraordinary powers to exact a great revenge on the culprits.[17]

While Canadian diplomats like Escott Reid tried to use their country's new middle-rank status to effect a moderating influence on East-West tensions and the United States' penchant for unilateral proclamations, Canada was never a neutral player in the Cold War. William Lyon Mackenzie King's wartime government had joined the U.S.-British collaboration to build an atom bomb and agreed to keep their then-Soviet ally out of the loop. Canada's economy benefited from U.S. policies such as the Marshall Plan as well as from the arms race. Canadian officials enthusiastically supported the North Atlantic Treaty Organization (NATO) – under Louis St. Laurent's Liberal government, they had urged the United States to join the alliance – and they followed the United States into Korea. During the 1950s Canada integrated its air defences with those of the United States and basically accepted U.S. military leadership. Later on Ottawa gave support to U.S. military action in Vietnam. Apart from the early 1960s – when debates raged over whether Canada should adopt nuclear weapons to fulfil its commitment to NATO and NORAD

(North American Air Defence Agreement, 1957), and when the anti-nuclear stance adopted by Conservative prime minister John Diefenbaker annoyed Kennedy and cost Diefenbaker the 1963 election – Ottawa generally went along with Big Brother USA into the 1970s, even though Canadians became more critical of U.S. actions, including CIA-led coups against Latin American countries.[18]

Like the United States, Canada also fought a war on the domestic and immigration front. Always staunch Cold Warriors, the RCMP continued to play a major role in the political screening of immigrant applicants and to push for the rejection of anyone thought to have left-wing views, tarring all of them with the communist brush. They also interrogated newcomers as well as gatekeepers suspected of breaking the country's immigration laws. More broadly, the postwar reception and citizenship campaigns took shape within a domestic Cold War context, in which the national security state was on high alert and poised to do battle against the variously defined threats to the nation's political as well as social and moral order.[19]

Canadians have long believed that Canada fought a less paranoid and damaging Cold War than did their U.S. neighbours and, then as now, they have distinguished their Cold War culture from the excesses of McCarthyism, with its public witch hunts, and the "extra-legal" or illegal methods of the FBI (Federal Bureau of Investigation) under J. Edgar Hoover.[20] Recent histories have revised this image considerably, showing that Canada fought a largely secret but often dirty Cold War, one that trampled on civil rights in the name of protecting liberal rights and democratic freedoms. Canada's domestic Cold War involved the imposition of new domestic restraints on free speech and other civil liberties,[21] the further criminalization of homosexuality and other forms of "immorality," and the denunciation of political dissent as a treasonous act against the nation and sign of loyalty to the evil Soviet empire. While the gatekeepers spoke of liberal democracy, here, too, a fundamentally conservative Cold War consensus had taken hold by the 1950s, one that transformed all forms of criticism and nonconformist behaviour into attacks on democratic decency. The United States did not have a monopoly when it came to the many ironies, hypocrisy, and corrupted democracy of this era. By the same token, in Canada, as in the United States, Britain, and elsewhere, there were cracks in the containment strategy, and some citizens and even newcomers sought to carve out alternative or politically defiant lives.[22]

Certainly, even without a Cold War, mass immigration and a shift from war to peacetime would have spawned reception and Canadianization programs, and debates over the rights and duties of democracy and citizenship; and the RCMP would have continued its hunt for communists. After all, ever since the Bolshevik Revolution of 1917, RCMP security intelligence forces had consistently pursued a hard-line policy against all suspected communists and sympathizers. Still, the Cold War served to reinforce the prevailing gender ideologies and conventional moral and sexual norms of the era and to impart an even greater sense of urgency to reception and citizenship activities.

Indeed, as sexuality and gender historians have argued in recent years, the concept of domestic containment served as a corollary to the U.S.-led foreign-policy strategy of containing communism abroad. According to Cold War historian Geoffrey Smith, "the containment of sexuality to the marriage bed, the sanctification of heterosexual monogamy, and the outlawry of other forms of sexuality – and, as if to accent the rigid distinction between communist enslavement and the Free World – the maintenance of distinct barriers between masculinity and femininity" were part of the arsenal by which mainstream North America sought to bolster and impose "the archetypal white, middle-class family of the 1950s."[23] The surveillance and moral regulation of a wide range of deviants – whether "pinkos," "spies," or "treasonous lesbians" – also offered a means by which the body politic at home could be made to emulate the bourgeois values of obedience, conformity, and belief in capitalism. The state, courts, schools, reform groups, and professional and popular experts all pitched in to contain or eradicate alleged "threats" or "enemies within" who might contaminate the wider society. The mainstream media's sensational or "saturation" coverage of sex crimes and alarmist portrayals of "criminal sexual psychopaths" fed postwar sexual and moral anxieties. At times the buildup of fear and alarmism gave rise to what scholars have called a "moral panic" that, in turn, led to new restrictive legislation – as in 1952, when Canada added homosexuality to the grounds for rejecting immigrant applications.[24]

What is important here, though, is how or to what degree Cold War anxieties and containment techniques influenced the lives of the postwar European refugees and immigrants who settled in North America and elsewhere. How did the pathological portrayals of the postwar newcomers as emotional wrecks, moral and mental misfits, sexual defectives, and casualties of totalitarianism influence the sexual and moral anxieties of these years? How did the gatekeepers deal with newcomer women who came with less-than-conventional sexual histories, and with men and women who transgressed Canadian moral norms and laws? What role did gender play in postwar immigration and its relationship to the moral, sexual, and physical and mental health aspects of nation-building and citizenship? We will return to these questions throughout the following pages.

OFFICERS AND N.C.Os
TO MUSTER WITH THEIR
MEN AT
EMERGENCY STATIONS

British war brides began leaving for Canada before war's end. Here a group is on board a wartime liner taking them to their new homes in time for Christmas 1944. *Telegram*, December 1944. (Canadian Army Photograph, YUA, Toronto Telegram, ASC Image 1297)

Press Narratives of Migration

From Scarcity and Red Slavery to Oranges and Humanity

2

"THE HAPPIEST PEOPLE IN CANADA ARE TRAVELLING WESTWARD TODAY." Thus wrote *Toronto Star* correspondent Norman Phillips from Halifax in August 1947, referring to a group of displaced persons from Europe who had been put on a train headed for Ontario. Two of the passengers, Ericka Rampeal and a "bearded Jakob Niebuhr," were among those who had suffered from Hitler's war on Europe, Phillips reported. Now, in their hearts, was "the feeling they have found their promised land." The reporter's colleague, Marjorie Earl, was equally positive about the arrival of another group of DPs, including Lithuanians and Hungarians, at Union Station in Toronto. Many of the adults had toiled in the Third Reich's wartime factories, and Earl described them as liberated Nazi slave labourers who had traded the "privation and hardship" of the DP camps for "the peace and plenty of Canada." Under photos of smiling children, captions stressed their chance for a new life. A Polish couple remarked that while they hoped in Canada to resume their teaching careers, they first wanted to reunite with a brother and "forget five years of [Nazi] slavery."

In fall 1951 yet another reporter at Union Station covered a crowd of Toronto Poles, the mayor, and others who gathered to give "a rousing welcome" to a group of Polish sailors and pilots who had "fled Red tyranny" by escaping from Communist Poland. The heroes included three young men and a woman (the fiancée of one of the men), who had stolen a single-engine plane from a Warsaw airport where one of the men worked as a pilot instructor. Escaping gunfire, they had flown across the Baltic Sea into a Swedish airfield with little gasoline left in the tank. A photo captured the "Heroine of Escape," the fiancée Stanislawa Nalegowna, planting a kiss on the cheek of a girl dressed in a traditional Polish costume.[1]

These examples are typical of the coverage that such newcomers received in the mainstream Canadian press in the early postwar years. The Europeans who fled difficult or dangerous conditions overseas for Canada received a good deal of sympathy, with journalists actively seeking out their personal stories. Notwithstanding differences in political viewpoints, many popular writers subscribed to an increasingly familiar scenario: Europe in general was a land in ruins; the East, in particular, was enslaved, and its war-wounded and tyrannized labourers were fleeing to Canada, a war-free, rubble-free land of plenty where they could regain their humanity, raise families, and rebuild fruitful lives. The dramatic story of Canada as a land of abundance – in everything from food supplies to consumer goods and political freedom – amid a world of suffering and destruction, and now threatened by spreading Communism, immediately emerged as a major theme in daily newspapers such as *The Toronto Star*, a liberal paper that devoted considerable ink to covering the many newcomers flooding into the city. The story also surfaced in the mass-circulation magazine *Maclean's*, then a monthly, with its emphasis (especially after the Second World War) on presenting engaging and distinctly Canadian perspectives on international affairs and other subjects, and on probing the human dimensions of the major events of the day. (Indeed, *Maclean's* invited people who had lived through dramatic events to share their stories with its staff.) A particularly effective way of carrying out the task was the human interest story, especially when it was penned by talented writers. And what could be more dramatic than stories of men, women, and children fleeing war-devastated and Communist-controlled Europe for Canada?[2] Canada's *Saturday Night* magazine, with its liberal-minded and pro-immigration writers, and the conservative weekly newspaper *Financial Post*, where an intense antipathy to communism led to a pronounced enthusiasm for reception programs, also adopted the human interest approach, though to a lesser degree.[3] So, too, did the press of the mainstream labour movement, which dropped its traditionally anti-immigration stance in favour of a selective immigration approach while waging its own Cold War against Communists in its ranks.[4]

The journalists and popular writers we encounter in these pages wanted to do more than tell dramatic stories set against a global canvas. They also wanted to influence, even mould, public opinion, in this instance in favour of a positive response towards the newcomers. In that regard they donned the cap of sympathetic gatekeeper with a role to play in the postwar rescue mission of Europe's impoverished and oppressed peoples.[5] In recounting the newcomers' narratives of risky and dangerous escapes from Communist or devastated Europe, the writers told romantic tales of courage and redemption and sometimes drew political and moral lessons about the evils and deprivations of life under Communism and the superiority of Western capitalist democracies. They hoped not only to move readers but also to provoke them into reflecting on the heady issues involved. Despite important differences between liberal and conservative journalists, both groups made plain their disdain for communism, and their press coverage, especially of the refugees, reinforced the Cold War consensus of the day.

All of this is not to suggest that the mainstream press did not print disturbing or controversial stories; on the contrary, the press would quickly become an important source of pathetic and pathological images of foreigners as well as of bigoted commentary. Nor do I mean to suggest that the Europeans profiled in the press told their stories to Canadian journalists simply for effect or to garner public adulation. Certainly, for example, the Iron Curtain refugees had suffered greatly under Communism. They had escaped under dangerous conditions and, given the millions of people persecuted or liquidated under Stalinist regimes, were right to fear for families left behind.[6] In relaying the newcomers' stories, the writers – who were always looking for a "hook" to reel in readers – could sometimes get so caught up in the intrigue that they turned people's truly difficult journeys into something approximating melodramatic pulp fiction.

The texts of the time are indeed open to the possibilities of a playful, post-modern, ironic reading – but that would do a disservice to the millions of women and men whose real lives were damaged, endangered, or eliminated by Hitler's and Stalin's ruthless policies.[7] Still, the Cold War era was replete with many ironies, and my discussion of these press narratives highlights some of those quirks, especially in regards to the responses of the RCMP and other authorities to the newcomers, whom the journalists, and others, tended to hail as freedom-lovers.

The Voluntary Immigrants:
British War Brides and Continental Europeans

The first large group of volunteer immigrants consisted of some forty-eight thousand war brides who arrived with their children between 1945 and 1947 to join the Canadian servicemen they had married overseas. The women first came to Halifax by ship before dispersing across the country. Financed by Ottawa, overseen by the army, and carried out by Red Cross workers, the transportation of these British women and children was unofficially dubbed Brides, Babies, Unlimited (BBU). The phrase aptly described the public coverage, which featured numerous photos of young, attractive, white women with chubby fresh-faced babies or toddlers happily drinking Canadian milk or baby formula. (Few images of Dutch, Italian, or other European war brides appeared.)

At the height of operations, as many as twenty trains carrying war brides left daily from Halifax. Journalists interviewed the women and noted the donations of magazines, games, candy, fruit, paper, and postage stamps, and even the music coming from the portable gramophones. Photos of the Red Cross nurseries set up at Halifax and railway stations across the country showed female aides bathing and changing babies, sterilizing bottles, and preparing baby formula while the mothers rested with tea and a smoke. If the smoking imparted an image of the modern woman, the reports reinforced conventional gender norms; the stated purpose of all this activity was to safely hand over a woman to her husband. As with other female migration schemes, the women were watched, chaperoned, and escorted from place to place. There were prohibitions on fraternizing with men, and any bride caught in a compromising situation could be sent back home. The point, of course, was to protect the moral reputations of women who had married Canadian boys, but at least some of the women deeply resented the state's intrusions.

The press covered some of the problems that arose, such as when women were dropped off in a town late at night with no one to meet them or when husbands waited hours for a wife who had been put on a train headed in the wrong direction. Newspapers also reported the occasional story of disgruntled brides who complained about meddling in-laws or, indeed, who chose to return home. One *Toronto Star* headline was blunt about why a pair of twin sisters (very attractive, and terrific dancers) were going home to England without their husbands: "Twin War Brides Give Up, Say Peterborough Too Dull." The papers devoted far more space, however, to the happy arrivals and the standard stories of migration centred on the themes of old world scarcity and new world plenty. Britain had been a battlefield during the war, as German bombs rained from above, and the British too had suffered from postwar shortages and economic woes, making it difficult for women there to care for their families. The conditions had clearly affected the war brides. Aboard the Canadian trains they reportedly filled up on cheap chocolate bars instead of using their meagre government subsidies to buy "a square meal" in the diner car. Convinced that "this wasn't a healthy beginning for the girls," Ottawa "remedied the situation," noted broadcaster Joan Baird, by replacing the subsidy with meal tickets issued on the train. While this policy may have ensured that the women "ate properly," it deprived them of a modest but important source of cash.[8]

As Canada pried open its doors to war-torn Europe, Canadian newspapers published many images of the smiling faces of other early arriving immigrants from Holland, Belgium, Greece, and elsewhere, their youthfulness reflected in the photos of young couples with babies and toddlers. Here, too, journalists noted the many attractive women in the crowds. For groups who faced postwar calamities such as floods (as in the case of the Dutch) and civil war (the Greeks), the texts accompanying the photos of joyful newcomers contained grim details of further destruction, as well as expressions of hope or optimism for their lives in Canada.

The retreating German army had destroyed much in its path, including the dykes of rural Holland, and subsequent floods had submerged the remaining farmland, creating near-starvation conditions. The Dutch, who had a special relationship with the Canadian soldiers who had liberated them from the Nazis, enjoyed public sympathy in Canada, and a Canada-Holland agreement led to almost one hundred thousand Dutch settling in Canada. While urban and middle-class Dutch also came, the early press attention was mostly on the rural flood families. In his coverage of one of the first Dutch families to come to Canada, *Toronto Star* writer Ivan Lavery highlighted the family's rapid transition from ruin to recovery. The Felsbourgs had been sponsored by Dutch-Canadian friends who themselves had lost relatives to the floods. After seeing so much devastation around them and seeing their close friends suffering from "the agony of thirst and chill," the Felsbourgs had decided to leave with their six children. They settled, as did many Dutch immigrants, in southwestern Ontario, where their Canadian friends had found a dairy farmer happy to sponsor "splendid" Dutch workers.

Canadian officials look for a new home for a Dutch family, the Huijs, after the Grimsby, Ont., fruit farmer with whom they were placed could not house such a large family. *Telegram* 20 Sept. 1948. (Canadian Press Photo, Hamilton, Ont., YUA, Toronto Telegram, ASC Image 1280)

Their early successes at farming offered a graphic illustration of how newcomers could contribute to their own recovery and to Canada's prosperity. Touching vignettes and images appeared in the press. A published photograph of a newly arrived Dutch girl showed her planting tulips at the graves of the Canadian soldiers whom her family had befriended in her hometown. A former resistance fighter praised his Canadian liberators and added that after being forced to farm barren land to feed the Nazi occupiers, while practically starving themselves, it was wonderful to be a real farmer again.[9]

The Greek civil war (1946–49) lent a strong Cold War theme to stories of the Greek arrivals. The *Star*'s coverage of the tearful reunion in 1947 of the wives and children of two brothers in Toronto is a case in point. The brothers had been unexpectedly separated from their families during the Second World War and the subsequent civil war. There were grim details of the women's attempts to leave the country – the fear of falling into the clutches of the Communist rebels had nixed several earlier attempts, but finally the Greek air force managed to get them out of a trouble area and to the coast, where they boarded a boat bound for Canada. There were images of the happily reunited husbands with their wives and children. The Canadian Red Cross had located the wives and children for the grateful brothers, who had Anglicized their names, sunk all their savings into a house, and announced that their children would become English-speaking Canadians. The women had almost collapsed on arrival, and when reporters later asked after their health, one of the brothers told them that the women were fine although in a state of shock because "they just can't believe that we are all safe together at last in Canada."[10]

As this example suggests, the mainstream Canadian press saw the Greek civil war in stark Cold War terms – evil Communist rebels out to destroy a democracy – although many opponents of the right-wing regime were not Communists. Eventually victorious, the Athens government later exacted a vicious revenge on its opponents, Communist and non-Communist alike. Whether such distinctions really mattered to Canadian officialdom, including the RCMP officers responsible for the political screening of prospective immigrants, is unclear, but the rebels' own actions worsened the situation. The forcible removal (or kidnapping) of about thirty thousand Greek children, mostly of pro-Communist parents, to Communist Yugoslavia and Bulgaria may have convinced Ottawa to adopt a cautious position on Greece (only fifteen thousand Greeks arrived before the 1960s). It may also have meant keeping out some of the orphaned children who had Canadian relatives willing to sponsor and adopt them.[11]

During the 1950s the press covered the frequent shiploads and trainloads of large crowds of immigrants from almost every European nation. The numerically largest groups were the Italians and Germans, who stole a lot of the spotlight, and the press coverage of their arrival quickly merged with follow-ups on their early days of settling in. The cheerful reports on the many happy arrivals met by excited crowds of relatives and compatriots largely sidestepped the complex subjects of Italy's Fascist and Germany's Nazi past. The emphasis was on the youthful families, jovial ways, ethnic foods, and love of drink – beer for Germans, wine for Italians.

The situation was more complex, of course. As regards Italians, Canadian Immigration, Labour, and External Affairs officials had disagreed over the merits of opening the floodgates to Italy (particularly southern Italy), but self-interested considerations largely won the day. The willingness of Italians to perform brute, low-paying, or risky jobs that Canadians shunned won over concerns about their cultural inferiority. In admitting impoverished Italians desperate to emigrate, Ottawa also claimed credit for removing some of the popular support for the Communists. For the RCMP, the popularity of the Communist Party in Italy made applicants suspicious, with the result that the Mounties' insistence on extensive political screening created huge backlogs in the Rome embassy. Thousands of Italians arrived each year nonetheless.

The German immigrants (who included a number of former East European refugees who had been moved to West Germany) were a more complicated matter, yet government and public hostility towards them was less marked than it was towards the Italians. Amid the praise of Canadian politicians, employers, and journalists, who declared the Germans to be honest toilers and fine people who should not be punished for the sins of their dictators, the Germans flooded into the country during the 1950s. The German immigrants' hatred for the Soviets, who had subjected them to a humiliating defeat, also meant that they could act as a bulwark against communism in Canada. Similarly, the Italians were always questionable democrats, but Italy had ultimately joined the Allies. Still, none of this thinking eliminated the necessity of having to teach both groups about Canadian democratic practices.[12]

The positive coverage of the Germans is suggested by the title of a *Maclean's* article by Ralph Allen: "The Untroublesome Canadians." Allen and others praised German ambition, assimilability, and early successes. In contrast to labouring Italians, the profiles of Germans often included skilled tradesmen and enterprising businessmen. Writer Allan Fenton profiled Henry Wiegmann, a German tool-and-dye worker who had stepped off a boat three weeks earlier with only $30 in his pocket and was now gainfully employed in the Canadian defence industry. Dismissing labour's concerns about immigrants stealing jobs, Fenton declared that skilled men like Wiegmann would help create more jobs in the field.[13]

This positive coverage can be read against the larger issue of Nazi war criminals.[14] In 1946 Canada had declared, by cabinet directive, that no former Nazis and their collaborators (those who had assisted the Nazis, often against their own compatriots, during German occupation) would ever be admitted into the country. But within a few years Ottawa had begun to relax the restrictions, in particular by replacing blanket prohibitions with case-by-case investigations. The growing liberalization of the treatment of former Nazis who had been members of the ss, the ruthless Nazi police force (which included the Gestapo and its combat arm, the Waffen-ss, and other units) reflected in part a recognition that membership in a party in a one-party totalitarian state is at best ambiguous and that after 1942 enlistments in the Waffen ss were increasingly conscripts, not volunteers. For the RCMP, the loosening up of restrictions on former fascists (if not real war criminals) carried the additional bonus that they could help in the war against Communists at home. In response to RCMP claims and the limitations of gaining access to reliable international records on Nazi activities, Ottawa gradually admitted all but the more serious Nazi offenders. In one of the few articles that directly addressed this matter, Peter Newman in the *Financial Post* featured a former East German Nazi party member whom the Berlin court had decided was largely a victim of circumstance and could remain in the West with the hope that he redeem himself. Allen's "Untroublesome Canadians" presented a matter of fact portrait of a young Holocaust denier who boasted that his father was a "real early" Nazi, refused to believe the revelations about the German concentration camps, and claimed to have "encountered no hatred in Canada – except, he said, 'by the Jews.'"[15]

In the Swedish archipelago, a storm-swept Estonian seaman checks his boat, one of dozens of "Viking boats" carrying unauthorized Estonian refugees. Having escaped to Sweden in wartime and fearing Communist expansion afterwards, the refugees risked the high seas in hope of securing asylum in Canada and other Western countries, *circa* 1947.
(MHSO Photo Collection, Estonians, F1405-13-5, MSR 2282, donor Arthur Schonberg)

On the heels of the mainly economic immigrants like Italians and Germans came others, including, by the early 1960s, the Portuguese, who attracted favourable commentary as hard-working people. As the immigrants settled into cities, especially Toronto, feature stories that reported on their progress appeared with growing frequency in the press. The sights, sounds, and growing size of the ethnic neighbourhoods, with their open markets, brightly painted homes, coffee bars, and crowded streets, offered journalists plenty of opportunities for writing colourful stories that at times verged on the voyeuristic.[16] Such stories differed from the suspenseful Cold War tales of refugee arrivals who had refused repatriation to Communist homelands and been placed in the DP camps, or who had escaped from behind the Iron Curtain.

Cold War Refugees: Displaced Persons

Amid the emerging Cold War of the late 1940s, Canadians could follow various dramas of the high seas as journalists covered the voyage of small, overcrowded boats carrying unauthorized or illegal refugees (those without entry visas). Most of them were Estonians who had fled Soviet occupation to Sweden during the war and afterwards refused to return to a homeland more firmly under Soviet rule. Now fearing a Soviet advance into Scandinavia, these Estonians, along with other Balts and East Europeans, risked dangerous crossings and hoped to be taken in as bona fide political refugees. Canadian press coverage once again typically highlighted themes of hunger and plenty in the old and new worlds respectively. In fall 1947 journalists reported that food shortages and a compass failure had forced a battered boat carrying four hundred starving Baltic refugees, many of them women and children, to land at a port in the Irish Republic, where the passengers "tore apart and gulped loaves of bread tossed them from the dock." Originally built to hold about fifty soldiers, the vessel, *Victory*, sported a hole in its bow caused by the warning rockets of the Swedish coast guard, which had tried to prevent its departure. After the boat was repaired and bread, water, and tins of corned beef were crammed into every available space, the Irish authorities, declaring themselves the defenders of all freedom-loving peoples, bid their Russian-hating Baltic friends a safe voyage to Canada.[17]

The plight of three storm-swept ships in danger of capsizing in Canadian waters in August 1949 also grabbed front-page attention. At the end of a stressful day, two of the ships, a former British minesweeper and a Panamanian freighter, were in the Halifax port. The U.S. Coast Guard eventually saved the third ship, its sails torn to shreds, the engine in poor shape, and the passengers out of food and water. The rescued refugees told reporters eager for their stories that the difficult voyage would be worth the hardship if they were allowed to stay in Can-

After sailing from the Swedish port of Göteborg with a group of Eston-ian refugees, the 13-ton yacht *Edith* stops at Penzance, Cornwall, for provisions, 2 July 1947. (MHSO Photo Collection, Eston-ians, F1405-13-5, MSR 2282, donor Arthur Schonberg)

ada (and Toronto in particular). Dressed "in ragged, unwashed clothes, but with smiling faces," were nurses, shipping clerks, fishermen, tradesmen, dentists, and laboratory technicians. There were also children and one Polish orchestra con-ductor. Another group, described as bearing the numbers branded on them in German and Russian concentration camps, huddled together as they waited to disembark.

These illegal Atlantic crossings supplied Canadian reporters with more romantic heroes. In the deep cold of January 1948 the *Star* reported on a boatload of twenty-three smiling Estonian freedom lovers who, rejected at Ellis Island in New York Harbour, had come north to Canada. The coverage featured a smiling Mr. and Mrs. Ernat Lohmus, described as attractive people who could be easily mistaken as Canadians – a revealing racial comment. It also featured the "Blond Seaman," Ludwig Tosine, who had bravely led his countrymen and women to Can-ada via Sweden, Belgium, England, and the United States on a three-month-long "voyage to freedom" over rough Atlantic seas on his own tiny ketch. The photo of the celebrated hero showed a dapper-looking man, dressed in a shirt and tie. He wore a hat cocked slightly at an angle in a rakish way that accentuated his movie-star looks. The arrivals, all Protestants, settled among Lutheran co-religionists in Kitchener.[18]

Canadian journalists agreed with the refugees' compatriots in North Amer-ica who called on Ottawa to give special consideration to the Estonians, who were both anti-Communists and a northern race supposedly well suited for northern nations like Canada. As a *Star* editorial put it, people who risked their lives "in search of freedom" are "the type we need in this country." Reporters also com-mented on a few sobering developments, including the situation of a poor Eston-ian woman, Hilda Mets. A week after arriving in Canada – and having braved the

En route to Canada, a group of refugee men contemplate the vastness of the country. *Telegram* 18 Jan. 1950. (YUA, Toronto Telegram, ASC Image 1278)

perils of a seventy-eight-day trip in a little boat with her husband and son – Mets gave birth to a baby in the back room of a dingy Toronto dwelling, without any medical aid, with her husband still unemployed, and on a bed with no mattress. Such reports served as a reminder of the great deal of work that had to be done on the reception front.[19]

In contrast to the press coverage, Canadian immigration officials initially fretted over the lack of proper procedures for handling these unauthorized refugees. They feared that admitting the earliest arrivals would result in many more Estonians and others following suit. But procedures were quickly put into place, and the feared influx never happened, largely because Estonians were well-treated in Sweden and many stayed put there, especially as their concerns about a Soviet advance into Scandinavia declined. In the end about fifteen hundred Estonians as well as some other "boat people" entered Canada. In subsequent years they were followed by several thousand additional Estonians and other Balts who were judged by Canadian officialdom to be fine immigrants.[20]

The country's generosity towards the Nordic refugees was not extended to Jewish refugees. In February 1948 the Canadian government rejected the appeal of seven desperate Jews who had entered Canadian waters on forged passports. Ottawa ordered them deported back to the dreaded DP camps in Germany on the grounds that if illegal aliens were allowed to remain others would follow suit. As some sympathetic journalists noted in response, a precedent for showing leniency "to unfortunate refugees seeking to rebuild their shattered lives here" had already been established, with the Estonians and with Polish veterans who had entered under farm labour contracts. Some of the Poles, it turned out, had contracted TB, and thus could have been deported on medical grounds. But they were permitted to remain in Canada on compassionate and political grounds: they had fought the Nazis under British command and were considered to be vehement anti-Communists. As an editorial charged, the immigration minister, Walter Harris, was harsher to refugees who were Jews.[21]

The reporters who interviewed and relayed the newcomers' stories also reported on complaints. On one ship, for instance, a couple's aggressive sex had bothered the other passengers, and a child's refusal to drink a glass of proffered milk had deeply embarrassed her mother, who explained that her daughter had never before tasted it and needed it to be mixed into coffee. Such reports also

"No more bars." A group of illegal refugees held in Halifax Immigration quarters for two months are granted admission to Canada. The decision came as a surprise because Ottawa had recently declared a clamping down on illegal arrivals. *Telegram* 11 April 1949.
(Canadian Press Photo, YUA, Toronto Telegram, ASC Image 1203)

underscored the argument that the newcomers were in need of Canadian support and guidance.[22]

But it was in the full-length mass-circulation magazine articles that writers relayed some of the most moving narratives of migration. An excellent example is a 1948 *Maclean's* article penned by Finnish-Canadian journalist Eva-Lis Wuorio, who had followed a group of DP contract workers who had arrived the previous spring on the SS *Marine Falcone* and gone to jobs in Quebec and Ontario. They had included Balts selected as domestic servants, Estonians as miners, and Polish veterans who were part of the first government-sponsored farm-labour contract scheme. Among them several couples, some with children, had been sponsored by close relatives in Canada. And thanks to Jewish-Canadian lobbying, there were some Holocaust survivors (also DPs), including a handful of youths coming under an orphan resettlement plan and contract workers heading for Jewish-owned garment factories.[23]

In the manner of the investigative journalist, Wuorio had met the passengers at the Halifax pier, and her description of their arrival set the article's sombre tone. After waiting hours for fog to clear before their ship was towed into shore, the passengers, wrote Wuorio, had remained eerily silent and still, a "bleak line of reserved faces," until a smiling inspector had waved and shouted a welcome. They had smiled

Journalist Eva-Lis Wuorio offers moving portraits of an early group of DPs whom she accompanied from Halifax to Quebec and Ontario on board a CNR train renamed "DP Special." *Maclean's* 1 June 1948.

back, and the "sudden wave of motion, as though [they] had been brought to life, was literally like light bursting out of a thick cloud bank." She described the immigrant drill, noting the slow line of tired but obliging people, identifying tags pinned to their clothing. They carried children and banged-up luggage down the ship's ramp and upstairs to the immigrant sheds as a loudspeaker shouted instructions in various languages. During the medical examination, which involved a slow walk past a Canadian doctor's mindful eye, a few of them told Wuorio that it was their fifth or sixth screening so far. Others made use of the few amenities, including free smokes at a tobacco company stand, a nursery, and washrooms (with "the world's smallest flush toilet for the infant immigrants").

Wuorio then accompanied the group westward on board a Canadian National Railway train dubbed the "DP Special," which dropped off workers at points along the way. At midnight Wuorio joined the "tall and heavy-set" railway porter, Joseph Podosky, also an immigrant, on his night rounds on the swaying train, as gusts of wind blew in at the rattling passageways between the cars. "In the women's cars," she wrote, "there was a smell of oranges and humanity.... The young girls, some with their hair in curlers, trying to cover themselves with coats, slept in one another's arms, searching reassurance in touch, in closeness to another human being." Everywhere, she added, sleeping adults "sat small, trying to give the kids room to stretch out their legs." A small, blond boy chuckled in his sleep. In "the thick, sweaty air of the miners' car," men too had "sought closeness to another human being, an arm thrown over a friend, or a back to back, firmly." A poetry book lay open on a sleeping man's naked chest; two sleepy-eyed young men played chess in the dull light. Having left many DPs behind "in the bleak camps of Europe," these folks, Wuorio commented, "may hope for Canadian citizenship in five years."[24]

Later that night the last group arrived at the Department of Labour hostel at St.-Paul-l'Ermite, about thirty-two kilometres outside Montreal. Wuorio recounted the scene that transpired at the station: as the train drove away, the group had reacted, not with a shout but a collective sigh, to what they saw beyond the high wire-fence and muddy field – a row of barracks. The sight was a stark reminder of what so many of them had experienced during the war – POW, internment, forced labour, concentration, and extermination camps – and after the war, the euphemistically labelled collection centres or assembly centres that were no more than DP camps hastily constructed out of bombed-out buildings, military barracks, and even former Nazi concentration camps.[25] Wuorio reassured her readers, though, that the Canadian hostel had been a munitions plant and that its handsome modern buildings had housed workers, not prisoners. But she also described an eerie scene in which people filed to the central barracks as an official with dark sunglasses, "incongruous in the lamplight," shouted orders at them. Sharing her first impressions of the DPs, Wuorio stressed their deep desire to forget the past and to start life over again. Even their hatred of both the Germans and Russians was diluted, she added, "in the deep well of tragic experiences" that had left them in need of once again building up "dead reflexes."

Wuorio's moving coverage of the refugees' inauspicious start in Canada was followed by several engaging profiles. George Lukk, twenty-nine, a tall, slender, and sombre-looking Estonian university instructor-turned-miner, said he had enjoyed the "magnificently lonely" Nova Scotian landscape. It had reminded him of home and was just as his father, who had worked in Canada years earlier, had described it: "a fabulous land where 'there is no fear.'"[26] Lukk's story, wrote Wuorio, began with his "happy boyhood in the ancient walled city of Tallin during Estonia's young years of independence" following the First World War. Lukk went to Austria on a scholarship and earned a science doctorate at Vienna Technical University in 1941. Afterwards, leaving his wife and two small children in Vienna, he returned home to a country that had gone from Soviet (1940–41) to German occupation.[27] He quickly returned to Vienna, went into hiding to avoid the Nazi draft, and obtained, through a former professor, a research post at his old university. At war's end, all foreigners of the defeated Reich were instructed to report to the United Nations Relief and Rehabilitation Administration, but the Lukks had refused to live "under the Russians" in what was once again Soviet-occupied Estonia (the Red Army had liberated it from Nazi control in 1944). Instead, they climbed aboard the crowded lorries taking refugees from Austria to Mannheim, Germany, and eventually arrived in Hamburg. Fortunately, Lukk got work at the newly founded Baltic University for Refugees, and the family landed comparatively luxurious living quarters – "a 250 foot square hut, all to themselves."[28]

Before the arrival of the Canadian selection teams dispatched to recruit DP workers, Lukk had made it onto the pre-selected list of candidates approved by the UN officials with UNRRA's successor, the International Refugee Organization, charged with the responsibility of resettling the still remaining one million refugees in the DP camps. As Wuorio recorded it, Lukk had stressed the IRO officials' thoroughness, especially in their political screening of candidates ("you accounted for each move… of the war years") to eliminate former Nazis or collaborators. ("Three factors could eliminate you even though a non-German. If on your arm you wore the blood category scar of the Hitler SS, with which good party members were branded; if you have served in the German armed forces; if you had been a collaborator.") Lukk had also noted the high rejection rates and relayed that the singular interest in young "strong labour" excluded older people who had also suffered a great deal. Selection by the Canadian team meant a move to a transit camp and another round of processing before winning the valued prize, the Temporary Travel Document ("the best thing next to a passport a DP can have").

By then Lukk had also heard news of his family, which like so many others had been split apart; his mother had died and his father was somewhere in Russia. A brother and a sister had reached England; so too had his wife, recruited for work as a children's nurse, and his two young daughters. When Wuorio asked Lukk if he was the leader of his group, he had sternly replied, "No. We have had enough of leadership in Germany." But he added that they all happily understood that in Canada, unlike in the United States, newcomers were not required to change into another person. Lukk's comments about Canada giving him the renewed faith of a child who can look forward to the future prompted Wuorio to ask, "Don't any of you ever want to go home?" She wrote that Lukk stared back "long and blankly," then "slumped back on the seat, leaned forward and said a little harshly, 'Don't you understand? Don't you people here understand at all? We can't go back. Russians would *kill* a man who wanted to think for himself.'"

A reunited Polish couple originally from Warsaw also garnered Wuorio's serious and sympathetic attention. The reporter described Jan Zaramba, a lawyer, as a "lean, aesthetic-looking man with a high-bridged nose, deep-set eyes," and his wife, Alina, as a "pretty, though harassed-looking" woman with "huge brown eyes and a vivacity even exhaustion cannot completely drown." They had a nine-year-old daughter and a seven-year-old son. Their story began with Germany's invasion of Poland in September 1939. A soldier, Jan had been captured and imprisoned in Bavaria, and pregnant Alina and her baby girl had escaped to live with relatives in the mountains. She later gave birth to her son and moved to Cracow for the remainder of the war, all the time, she said, praying for word from Jan. In 1945 the Americans liberated Jan's POW camp, but neither husband nor wife knew what had happened to the other. Then, Jan's sister, now living in Bavaria, discovered that her new Polish neighbours had been the Zarambas's old neighbours, and they told her that Alina was in Cracow. Jan rushed to Cracow. Reunited but keen to flee Soviet-occupied Poland, they headed for West Germany. In the DP camp Alina got a job at a Catholic Welfare office, where she met Ludger Dionne, a controversial Quebec rayon-mill owner and Liberal Member of Parliament who was recruiting workers from the camps. She convinced him to hire Jan as a handyman. They were lucky enough to emigrate together; most contract workers went alone, leaving behind anxious family members hoping to be sponsored.

The Zarambas's friend Tadeusz Piekutowski, an engraver from Cracow who had also been a POW, joined them during one of their conversations with Wuorio and began to share the grim details of his wartime story. He told of the freezing cold morning when he and other Polish soldiers were caught and transported to Auschwitz, of how they had stood for hours outside watching corpse after corpse, blood frozen to faces, an eye hanging out of a socket, the tortured bodies of Poles beaten to death, being whisked away on planks – but Wuorio asked him to stop. In response the group sat silently, until Alina remarked that it was "marvelous to find someone who cannot stand to hear of the horrors [that] have become so common-place to us."

Wuorio's publication of these personal testimonials of loss, escape, and arrival made for compelling reading. Assignments for full-length magazine articles like this one allowed writers to spend more time with their subjects within that contact zone created, albeit temporarily, by the interview. Lengthy or subsequent interviews with the same subjects also increased the possibility of collecting more intimate details and personal insights. Hardly unmediated texts, however, these published stories were selective narratives, the product of the interplay between the journalists (and their editors) and their newcomer subjects. The emphasis in Wuorio's article on the rigorous political screening process and on the sufferings of the Estonian and Polish POWs at the hands of both the Germans and the Soviets is noteworthy, for example, given that Poles, along with Ukrainians, were the two non-German groups most often suspected of including Nazi collaborators. It may have reflected a shared desire by writer and subject to exonerate these newcomers from any suspicion of wrongdoing. Also, the stress on people's optimistic hopes for Canada and Lukk's claim that Canada was superior to the United States in its greater respect for other cultures may have reflected Wuorio's desire to help create a sympathetic climate for the DP newcomers. For most DPs the United States was by far the country of first choice (and, ironically, the last country to admit large numbers from the camps). But given that acceptance into any country greatly boosted a refugee's morale, one need not question the sincerity of comments extolling Canada's virtues.

The newspaper records show a virtual absence of stories of Jewish refugees who had escaped from Nazi ghettos and death camps. No doubt this shortcoming partly reflected the survivors' reluctance to share their experiences (though some later wrote memoirs or consented to interviews),[29] especially when many Canadians, and even Jewish Canadians, did not want to hear their horror stories. The Cold War also mattered; it had shifted attention from the wartime fascist enemies back to the long-standing Red enemy. So, too, did continuing anti-Semitism, which took various forms, including malicious rumours about a spreading Jewish Communist conspiracy, even in the DP camps. (Actually, Communist and non-Communist Jewish leftists were in a distinct minority in the camps and refugee streams.)

The lack of articles on Jewish refugees coincided with a growing liberalization of restrictions on former Nazis – and also occurred after Ottawa's decision in 1948 to admit four pro-Nazi officials and wartime collaborators from Vichy France. One of those men was Jacques de Bernonville, assistant to the "butcher of Lyon," Klaus Barbie. In response to the outraged voices of Canadian Jews, Ottawa considered ordering these men deported back to France, where they had been tried in absentia and convicted of treason, but the government then flip-flopped, declaring that the Vichy officials had been carefully screened and that evidence existed to suggest they might not be guilty of any crime. The Nazis were permitted to settle in Quebec, where the Catholic Church leaders and the Quebec caucus of the Liberal government offered them refuge and support. In a public denunciation of the decision, Toronto rabbi Abraham Feinberg of Holy Blossom Temple noted that the French courts had found them guilty of "moral turpitude in democracy." Canada had deported Jewish DPs for carrying false passports, thereby condemning them "to a living death in Germany," yet gave these men, who had arrived with false identities, a refuge. Feinberg called it a "revolting" case.[30]

Cold War Escape Tales: Iron Curtain Refugees

Following the consolidation of the Eastern Bloc countries by the early 1950s, refugees who had escaped directly from Iron Curtain countries such as Poland, Czechoslovakia, and Hungary, or Tito's Yugoslavia, offered plenty of drama and intrigue. Indeed, one *Globe and Mail* reporter declared that people "who risked their life on a theory that life without freedom is worse than death" had "a story of planning and hoping and daring unequalled in any suspense novel."[31] The excitement generated by the escape plots was tempered by the defectors' accounts of the dangers that their escapes posed to families back home, and the reports of intimidation, imprisonment, and execution behind the Iron Curtain. The ruthlessness with which Stalinists imprisoned or eliminated real and imagined enemies, at times wiping out entire families, haunted many a political defector from Communist Europe.

In recounting the personal testimonies of those who had survived the Gulag's camps, and their estimates of prison populations left behind, the Canadian press gave these refugees an opportunity to speak to Canadians about the evils of communism and thus helped shape the character of the Cold War culture. In October 1981, for instance, *The Toronto Star* covered the arrival in the city of fourteen young "Czech slave labourers" who had escaped from a Soviet uranium mine in Czechoslovakia, tunnelling their way to freedom as Soviet soldiers guarded their barbed-wired camp. Volunteering for overtime work and then slipping into an abandoned shaft, the men had dug for more than three months with small hand tools that could be hidden but made for slow, laborious work. They fled through the forest to the West German border sixty kilometres away and crossed the frontier in two groups, eventually arriving in the U.S. zone still wearing their drab grey prison uniforms. The press coverage highlighted their stories of having survived Soviet-style prisons and the Gulag's forced labour camps, including the men's estimate that their prison camp had held about thirty thousand inmates toiling in five-hundred-foot-deep mines. Such stories reinforced the sense that Canada was doing a truly noble thing in opening its doors to freedom-lovers.[32]

Most escapees were men, and the press coverage underscored their youthfulness and daring. The pilots who had escaped from Poland in the single-engine plane were twenty-two years of age; the one woman, Nalegowna, twenty. Among the daring was a twenty-eight-year-old Serbian physicist, Dusan Kustulich, who jumped from a freighter into the frigid Northern Sea. After he was refused asylum by the British Home Office (a decision that caused a public outcry) he gained entry into Canada when the Serbian National Shield Society of Canada offered to sponsor him. Among the youngest was Edgar Ritter, an eighteen-year-old Estonian orphan and stowaway. By the time he reached Canada in 1950, on a foreign tanker that docked in the port of Montreal, he had spent a few years in a Russian prison camp before escaping. He had walked for miles across the continent and travelled halfway around the world by hiding on ships. According to reporters, when taken into custody he had cried out to officials to please deport him rather than put him in jail again. The Canadian Immigration Board initially rejected the boy's application for entry into Canada, but he won an appeal, prompting reporters to declare proudly that Canada had a heart after all.[33]

The comparatively few women escapees made for particularly romantic Cold War heroes, especially when they were as attractive as Irene Konkova, a twenty-three-year-old doctoral student from Charles University in Prague. Canadian journalists patronizingly described her as a "pretty little Czech" girl, yet also marvelled at how she had outwitted the police and waded through deep mountain snows for three weeks to reach the West.[34] Imprisoned in February 1949 "for not conforming to Communist dictates," Konkova escaped jail a few weeks later with the help of friends (who were probably part of an illegal church group). After going to see her parents, she left with the group and headed towards the Austrian border and West Germany.

The Iron Curtain escape stories usually included gripping moments of terror and critical lucky breaks. For Konkova, the first such incident came early on when the police surrounded the mountain inn where her group had taken temporary refuge. She described how she had sat paralyzed on her bed while the police searched the others' rooms. When they pounded on her door, she "forgot to breathe." Then came the lucky break. "The only reason I got out alive," she explained, "was because the police were too lazy to smash the door of my bedroom down." After the police left, taking the other defectors with them, Konkova jumped out a second-storey window and continued her journey until she reached safety in Germany.

In West Germany Konkova took a job in the U.S. zone as a physical education director with the YWCA/YMCA and gained entry into Canada by accepting a YWCA job in Winnipeg. Once there, she shared her story with reporters and expressed her fears about her parents, with whom she had lost contact since leaving Prague. Even before her escape, she noted, the Communist authorities had been punishing

Irene Konkova, the young Czech escapee who made a perilous trip from Austria to West Germany and, eventually, Winnipeg. The large photo accompanied a front-page story of her dramatic Cold War escape tale under the headline "Outwitted Soviet Police, Waded Mountain Snows, Czech Girl in Winnipeg." *Toronto Star* 23 Sept 1950.
(Toronto Star Archives)

her parents for her defiance, confiscating the family's city and summer homes and most of their belongings, including her mother's jewellery.

The reporters, typically stressing the happy ending, asked an immensely grateful Konkova what most impressed her about Canada. Like many refugees, she said the abundance of food, but also "the lovely looking Canadian girls, their smart clothes and immaculate appearance." That uncommon response fit Konkova's own image, and her obviously middle-class background. The *Star*'s front-page photo, larger than the text itself, showed a beautiful young woman wearing makeup, with a fashionable hairstyle and scarf. Her youthful good looks put her in the same category as the other attractive immigrant women who caught the eye of the journalists and photographers. Moreover, her feminine beauty, like that of Polish hero Nalegowna, could also serve ideological purposes. It provided Canadians with an appealing contrast to the stock image of the frumpy and somewhat masculine-looking woman of the Eastern bloc. North American commentaries on the Communist woman that emphasized their lack of beauty or sexuality offered a means of confirming not only the greater desirability of Western women but also the superiority of a capitalist system that gave women the resources needed to make themselves alluring. Konkova's beauty, and politics, supposedly distinguished her from ugly Marxist ideologues.[35]

The romantic-novel escape tales included a high-profile story of a Czech refugee couple – she a nurse in the United States, he a refugee in Canada – who became known as the "Niagara Falls Lovers." All of the ingredients were there: love, fear, freedom politics, intrigue, and sympathetic Western officials. According to the reporters, Kitty Kleiner and Denny Chrastanku had fallen in love in spring 1946 while they were students at Prague University. Shortly afterwards Kitty won an academic scholarship to study economics at the University of North Carolina in the United States; Denny, a medical student, remained behind in Czechoslovakia. After the Communists came to power in 1948, a lovesick and desperate Denny, carrying only a briefcase, fled the country with his brother at night, crossing the heavily guarded border and eventually reaching Germany. Ineligible for admission to the United States, Denny gained entry into Canada. He had mistakenly assumed that residence in Canada would give him easy access to the United States. When he found out that he could not leave Canada until he became a citizen he tried, unsuccessfully, to secure permission to visit Kitty south of the border.

In the United States Kitty had left school to take up a job in a mental hospital in New Jersey, and she too had become enmeshed in red tape. At Kitty's suggestion, she and Denny both travelled separately to Niagara Falls, where, with the U.S. officials' blessing, they had a brief reunion on the Rainbow Bridge. The immigration laws of both countries made a permanent reunion difficult. As non-citizens, neither of them could cross the 49th parallel without risking deportation back to their now-Red homeland. Finally, in early October 1949, several months after their first encounter, U.S. officials agreed to let Kitty cross the Canadian border again, this time to rendezvous with Denny on the Canadian pleasure craft *Maid of the Mist*. Canadian journalists were there to cover that story.

As a crowd gathered at the Canadian dock in hopes of seeing the Czech lovers aboard the boat, a reporter wrote that the *Maid of the Mist* was "not the world's best place for long parted lovers.... It's like a public show.... They have to spend their time on a spray-swept deck, raincoated and hatted, and try to talk over the roar of Niagara." But that sense of sympathy did not stop the reporters from watching and reporting back with the details: an understanding crew let them make several trips on one fare; they held hands and were "oblivious to everything but each other." Journalists collected information on Denny and his younger brother, also a medical student, an escapee, and a farm worker placed on a farm outside Toronto. All in all this was a story of well-educated and cultured East Europeans forced by war and Communism to lead a drab and dangerous life.

The sense of humour of the pair endeared them to the reporters, as did their graciousness in answering questions and in thanking the U.S. officials for giving them a few private hours to chat. Their story also had a happy ending. In autumn 1950 they were reunited at Toronto's Union Station, where, as *Star* writer Dorothy Howard observed, the "tall, dark and blue-eyed" Denny greeted his "pretty girl friend with a big hug and a bouquet of carnations." They planned to marry at Christmastime provided that Denny, who was still a farm worker, could get a job in Toronto, where he would apply, for the second time, for entry to the medical school at the University of Toronto. (His first application was refused because of quotas on DP applicants to the professional faculties.) Kitty had gained entry into the University of Toronto's School of Social Work with the help of its director, H.M. Cassidy, and university president Sydney Smith. Her words to reporters offered a fitting ending: "It is wonderful to be here… not only because of Dennis. Without my visa into Canada I might have been sent back behind the Iron Curtain, because my U.S. student's visa had expired."[36]

A Family's Story

The complex logistics and extra risks of orchestrating the escape of an entire family from behind the Iron Curtain made those tales especially riveting. This was particularly so when young children were involved; they had to be taught to lie to the authorities and were sometimes drugged to keep them from screaming. In a 1953 feature article in *Maclean's*, the talented June Callwood replayed the story told to her by Peter Keresztes, a Hungarian businessman who had escaped with his wife, Judith, and young daughter, Anne Marie. They first fled from Prague to Vienna, which had entailed several nighttime treks through frontier swamps, thickets, overflowing rivers, and woods while steering clear of the watchtowers' glaring searchlights, barbed-wire fences, snarling dogs, and border patrols. A chilling moment, when Judith had to silence an already sedated child in the woods by saying, "We are escaping from bad men in the forest and if you cry, they will get us," became Callwood's headline. From Vienna the family went to Paris and, later, Toronto.

This fascinating family narrative detailed the many frustrating delays, scary betrayals, and close calls along the way: in Prague itself, where they had to unload an apartment without attracting too much attention; on trains, where they or hired

"We are escaping from bad men in the forest and . . .

IF YOU CRY, THEY WILL GET US"

With these mind-scarring words this Hungarian couple silenced their child as they blundered and bribed their way through the Iron Curtain to freedom in Canada

IN FREEDOM: In Toronto, now six and safe, she has a nursery filled with dolls and crayons. She laughs with her parents and, the ordeal only a memory, they laugh aloud too.

Journalist June Callwood relays a gripping tale of a Hungarian family's circuitous escape from Prague. During a dangerous flight through a frontier region, the parents – shown here with their daughter in Toronto – had to drug the girl, scare her out of crying, and teach her to lie about her identity to Communist authorities. *Maclean's* Nov. 15 1953.

smugglers tried to get documents and money vouchers out of the country; and in the frontier cottages of strangers who took their money but resented their presence and feared getting caught. The story emphasized the prevalence of the black-market economy and the unreliable guides and unsavoury characters who lived off bribes taken from those desperate to escape. One seedy young man snitched on the family after failing to get their apartment for free; a railway porter said he lost the valuables he had been hired to get into Austria; and a female guide took their money and failed to show up at the designated spot to take them to the Hungary-Czech border, sending a message that the child's presence made the trip too risky.

The story was punctuated with moments of terror, including a police arrest in Austria and two weeks in jail under interrogation. They had some critical lucky breaks, including an encounter with a gruff Czech border policeman who did not believe they were Hungarian-speaking Austrians without passports who wanted to return home; he agreed nonetheless to Judith's suggestion that he dump them in an unguarded section of the Czech-Austrian border and let them fend for themselves. A friendly Austrian peasant women gave them shelter on the other side. Relief came when they finally met up with friends in Vienna, and then in Paris, but recovering from a year of planning and the ordeal itself took much longer.

The story of the Keresztes family shared much in common with those of other middle-class refugees from Eastern Europe. It told how Communism had destroyed the lives of productive, well-educated, and cultured people, reducing them to terrified fugitives. How a reign of terror, coupled with scarcity, turned friends into informants and others into alienated hucksters on the make. For Peter and Judith, life before the Communists took control in 1948 had included a large beautiful villa with a grand view of the Danube River and magnificent Prague, valuable art, books, classical music collections, and nights out in lovely outdoor restaurants with lantern-lit trees and violinists. Getting out of the country was expensive and took most of their funds, though, clearly, they could afford it. The journey also involved many indignities, including living in a boat and a friend's utility room. Like other escapees, they arrived in the West with nothing but a few banged-up briefcases, used instead of suitcases to ward off suspicion.

The narrative was also an engrossing political drama. As one guide after another failed them, the Keresztes family even got into the spirit of the intrigue, arranging their own special drop-off points, sending coded messages to friends, and, after selling their apartment and moving into a boarding house, effectively buying their landlady's silence with advance payments of rent while claiming to be heading off on holidays in the off-season. When they lived in the utility room, Judith, who headed out each day in search of yet another guide, became a master of disguise, using a kerchief, glasses, and different hairstyles to keep police at bay. Once in Vienna, they orchestrated their move to Paris, which involved forging documents to get a passport, paying for them with business funds that Peter had arranged to have sent to them. In Paris they promptly threw away their Hungarian passports and declared themselves refugees and requested asylum. Some two years later, they happily took Peter's company transfer to Toronto.[37]

Rather than a Cold War romance, this story was testimony to a devoted husband and wife and loving parents whose grim determination to achieve a better life gets them through the ordeal. Given that Peter was the storyteller, readers got his version of events and his portrait of Judith, as mediated by Callwood. He marvelled at Judith's quick thinking, strength, and ingenuity under ongoing police interrogation, even joking that she was an excellent person with whom to plan an escape. He admitted to having been too weak a man to agree with Judith about fleeing Hungary when the Communists first began to consolidate their power. As their situation worsened, he admitted to a growing sense of self-disgust and shame, even unmanliness, at not having realized that freedom was far more precious than his thriving business. Once settled in Paris, however, where his former company gave him a job, he seemed fully recovered, but Judith suffered so frequently from depression that they decided "to get right away from Europe and to a newer, younger country."

Within a short time they rebuilt a family trade business in Toronto and had even been able to enrol their daughter in a private girl's school, at least for one year. At the story's conclusion, Peter reported that Judith continued to suffer from panic attacks and depression, whereas his health, and masculinity, had been restored. In addition they had been able to send much-needed funds to friends back home and to a sister in England. Plans were underway to bring Judith's elderly mother to Toronto, and they were slowly rebuilding their library and an eclectic art collection that included prints by master artists and a Canadian totem pole.

"Everyone asks us if we like Canada," Peter concluded, "and we are always surprised. "Of course we like it – this is a place of freedom and peace."[38]

Still, in a particularly graphic illustration of Cold War irony, these kinds of Iron Curtain escape narratives made popular heroes out of men, women, and children whom the RCMP saw as potentially grave threats to Canada's national security. Bolstered by an unprecedented expansion of immigration security controls, RCMP intelligence repeatedly warned Ottawa that these refugees of Communism might actually include planted agents of Moscow – highly trained agents sent abroad under the cover of political dissidents to carry out espionage and encourage subversion among Canada's ethnic minorities. The logic was absurd – the East European refugees would have the opposite effect on Canada's ethnic and wider political culture – and can only be understood as part of the RCMP's historic obsession with stamping out Communism. It was also the product of the convergence of European migration with the rise of the Cold War.[39]

Second Wave Refugees:
Hungarian 56ers and the Radnick Returnees

The failed 1956 revolt against Hungary's Communist regime, which the Soviets brutally crushed, produced the largest influx of refugees (sometimes called 56ers) since the end of the war and another spate of Cold War escape tales. The Soviet

Union's brutal crushing of the Hungarian revolt deeply divided the international Communist movement between those who saw it as a genuine revolt by students and workers against Stalinism and those who accepted Moscow's line about it being a bourgeois counter-revolution. Moreover, it again focused attention on a large group of European refugees, many of whom had fled to camps in Austria.

Once again familiar narratives of flight from European scarcity and Red slavery to North American abundance and opportunity appeared in the Canadian mainstream press. Writing from Vienna for the *Financial Post*, Michael Barkway, an early advocate of granting immediate refuge to the Hungarians, described those crowding into the refugee camps as "weary but proud" freedom fighters whose occupations nicely matched Canadian needs. Those who had journeyed from Hungary to Austria included young people, teenagers, and even unaccompanied children. Barkway came across "two urchins" who rushed up to him and breathlessly announced that "we crossed tonight too." One of them, he added, was a dark-haired sixteen-year-old "get-up-and-go sort of youngster whom you could imagine equally well heading up a teenage-age gang or a Scout troupe – depending entirely on how he is treated." Canada, he was suggesting, had a moral obligation towards such children. Barkway's articles drew the obvious political conclusion: the West, having encouraged these people to resist Communism, was now obliged to help them.[40]

Not surprisingly, the Hungarian 56ers were particularly compelling symbols of totalitarian horror and democratic decency, and many onlookers saw them as especially deserving of Canadian sympathy and support. Indeed, this time Immigration Minister J.W. (Jack) Pickersgill effectively dismissed the RCMP's usual worries about planted Communist agents and its call for strict political screening. Instead he established a generous refugee policy, waiving the medical tests, setting up reception programs to settle the refugees, and instructing the RCMP not to let screening procedures create unnecessary delays. Canada fully recognized the ideological and labour gains to be made from opening the floodgates widely and offered refuge to more than thirty-five thousand Hungarian refugees. At the height of the refugee arrivals, the stories of bravery, escape, and arrival dominated.

In yet another instalment of the dominant migration scenario, *The Toronto Star* reported that, according to those involved in "Operation Friendship" – the Hungarian relief program that involved social agencies, churches, and volunteer groups – the refugees were "flabbergasted by the richness and abundance of everything they see." Once rooms and jobs were arranged, reported the Social Planning Council, which had co-ordinated the effort, "the new Canadian usually takes his family by the hand for a Wonderland Tour of downtown Toronto." There the elderly would marvel at the many churches and the free Bibles and rosaries and the men with the many big cars on the traffic-filled streets, while the women and teenaged daughters "could hardly wait till their husbands and fathers are established and earning money again so that they too might try on dresses and hats in department stores to find the one they like best." Then too, "the well-stocked grocery stores and supermarkets in Toronto seem to cast a sort of magic spell over all these people."

Both the gender stereotypes and the refugees' responses were by then familiar features of the media narratives of migration and Cold War escape tales.[41] So, too, were the press profiles of the new refugees and their messages. The first Hungarian refugee student of the University of Toronto's St. Michael's College, for instance, told reporters that he had joined the rebels because "Communism is no good" (his first English words), but that he also feared for his mother back home and for a brother who had been wounded in the revolt. In his profile of the Gallai family, who had dodged police all the way to Austria, writer Douglas Blanchard stressed that "their story is typical of thousands of families who left homes, belongings, and a whole way of life on the spur of the moment" and "sought freedom and happiness in the Western world." Some two years after they had arrived, he added, the Gallai family was doing well. The girls now spoke good English (the mother did not), and Gallai had found work in his trade, carpentry.[42]

The press narratives raise a particularly noteworthy irony: a reverse migration, from Canada to Europe, of the left-wing "Radnick" families. About eighteen hundred naturalized Yugoslav Canadians, mostly Croatians, along with left-wing Slavs from other Western countries, accepted Tito's invitation to come home and help build the workers' paradise. The public spectacle of Slavic Canadians, most of them naturalized citizens, boarding the Yugoslav ship SS *Radnick* (The worker) created concern, and Canadian officials pondered how best to punish them. Yugoslavia was an East European Communist state that had managed to stay out of Soviet control. The Communists had come to power not with Stalin's aid or agents but as the leaders of a popular struggle against the Nazis, and Tito had completely broken with Stalin in 1948. But this made the Radnicks' decision no less palatable to many Canadians. Life in Yugoslavia was difficult, and requests for a return to Canada came almost immediately, prompting the usual security debates in Ottawa. The RCMP, which cared little about distinctions among Communist states, and immigration officials, also wanting to punish the returnees, joined forces against their External Affairs colleagues, who showed some sympathy for these Canadian citizens and also recognized that their re-entry into Canada could deal a damaging blow to the Slavic-Canadian Communist movement (a point that even the RCMP later conceded).

The coverage of the few groups allowed to return to Canada, in spring 1951, four years after they had heeded Tito's call, bears this out. It also features a journalist as a Cold War hero. According to *Toronto Star* correspondent George Bryant, the twenty returnees were lost among the crowds of European immigrants on board the SS *Georgic*, and there were no bands or relatives to greet them. But they, too, had big grins because they were coming home, and their only souvenirs of life in "Tito's Wonderland" were "their haunting memories." Because they still had relatives in Yugoslavia, most of the returnees refused to talk to reporters, but Olga Jocich and her sons eagerly shared their bitter experiences with Bryant. They said they knew the moment they had crossed into Yugoslavia and were told that they were now Yugoslavian citizens and were not allowed to leave that they had made a mistake. Like other Iron Curtain escapees, they emphasized not simply the drab life and scarce resources but the fear and intimidation so central to the regime. The police kept people cowed, and neighbours disappeared in the night. The Jocich brothers were hauled in for questioning and told to spy on their family. The working conditions were oppressive, the so-called additional volunteer work brigades were more like prison terms, and the promised rewards never appeared.

The older son, Stanley, had been serving a prison term for trying to escape. Some sailors had smuggled him onto a ship at a Yugoslav port on the Adriatic coast but he was betrayed by an unknown informant, "a breed which flourishes in that country." He talked about his starvation diet in prison, the months of aggressive interrogation, and his fear that, on a warden's whim, he might be shot. In her slow and halting English, Olga Jocich spoke of the deep pain of a mother whose sons were continually being dragged off by the police. Younger son David noted that his memories of Canada had become vague, adding, "The life I remember now is life in a police state." The family's lucky break came in the form of another *Toronto Star* correspondent, William Stevenson (not to be confused with the spymaster, Intrepid), who found them and, they believed, largely negotiated Stanley's release from prison. Whether that account was accurate or not, their deep gratitude to the man whom the prison guards had described as a "Canadian with the bushy moustache and a pipe" was captured in Olga's claim that it was "better to die in Canada" than live in Yugoslavia.

In the end most of the Radnick families did not return to Canada. Perhaps it was not coincidental that the photos accompanying Bryant's article featured children: two toddlers and a slightly older girl. While their parents' ideology had been thoroughly discredited, their youth and innocence represented a democratic future.[43]

These press narratives of migration, with their dramatic tales of suffering, courage, and redemption, were the result of a series of encounters, however fleeting, between the newcomers and sympathetic journalists who in some way acted as gatekeepers. Whether as short news items or magazine articles, these stories were, again, the product of what newcomers were prepared to tell and what the journalists, and their editors, chose to include. Some newcomers even cast themselves as gatekeepers of their adopted country; for example, the Iron Curtain refugees not only told their stories but also urged Canadians never to falter in their hatred of communism. Overall, the press coverage reinforced the Cold War consensus of these years. Many journalists did not hide their disdain for communism. They also had the upper hand in that they, not their newcomer subjects, penned the final version of each story.

Readers, of course, brought their own understandings, sympathies, allegiances, and prejudices to the media stories that they read, heard, or watched.[44] We cannot determine precisely how ordinary Canadians responded to all the stories of migration that they came across in Canadian papers and magazines – an overview of almost one hundred letters written to newspapers and magazines reveals plenty of both positive and negative responses – and in the highly popular and more powerful U.S. publications or Canadian editions of mass-based U.S. magazines, such as *Time* and *Reader's Digest*. But we do know that large numbers of Canadians, including ethnic Canadians and women, were sufficiently moved by the challenges and possibilities involved to participate in some way in the many reception programs that a range of gatekeepers, from citizenship officials to professional experts and volunteers, established to receive and integrate the newcomers into the Canadian mainstream. At the core of all of this activity was a central question that Wuorio had raised in her *Maclean's* article on the refugees aboard the "DP Special" train in 1948. Could Canada live up to the promise of providing a land of oranges and humanity to impoverished and oppressed people from war-torn Europe?

Teaching English and celebrating
a pro-capitalist democracy often
went hand in hand. Manitoba,
1948.
(Archives of Manitoba, W.J. Sisler
Collection, 229, N7165)

Defining the Agenda

Professional Discourses of
Integration and Citizenship

3

THE NEWLY ARRIVED EUROPEANS – or "new Canadians," as they were also called – differed in their expectations of what life in Canada would be like. While many had an understanding of the difficulties before them, others arrived with false expectations based partly on the reluctance of Canadian overseas immigration officers to tell them the hard cold truth about housing shortages, living costs, unemployment, and language problems. Then, in their early years in Canada, as they began the task of adjusting to the demands of life in their new home, many of the immigrants would encounter a number of Canadian professionals who had their own expectations of how the newcomers should integrate into the society. These professional gatekeepers – including social workers, mental health specialists, Citizenship officials, and community-based activists lobbying for more resources and greater public education – were eager to shape just what kind of citizen these men, women, and children would be.

The various Canadian gatekeepers adopted strategies for guiding the newcomers' physical and psychological recovery as well as the multilayered adjustments to "Canadian ways" and an eventual integration into mainstream society. They differed in their training, expertise, experience, and sensitivity, and in their status and political clout, but generally they agreed on the major aims of reception work. They saw themselves as indispensable problem-solvers and hoped to expand their influence in the country's social welfare services. Their views reflected and reinforced the paradoxical mix of social optimism and deep-seated anxiety, of bold declarations and nagging frustrations common to capitalist welfare democracies in the early Cold War era.

A shared desire for a healthy body politic – in physical and emotional as well as moral and sexual terms – fuelled the participation of the various gatekeepers in postwar reconstruction. Moreover, many of the reform campaigns aimed at the country's newcomers were part of wider nation-building projects to "uplift" (as in improving medical, moral, and homemaking standards) and "contain" (as in regulating sexual behaviour and children's leisure time) the entire Canadian population. Still, these campaigns often served to isolate the Europeans as special problem cases or as having pathologies requiring more heroic remedies. The Cold War itself imparted a political and moral urgency to efforts that would ensure the long-term moral and mental health of Canada's future citizens. Both men and women were targeted, but women, as in the past, were more vulnerable to moral blame.

Many of Canada's postwar gatekeepers operated within a dominant paradigm that normalized conventional ideals of proper gender roles, the family, and sexual behaviour and that sought to cultivate good citizens who would be as cognizant of their civic duties to the state and wider society as of their individual rights and social entitlements or benefits. Paradoxically, the gatekeepers envisioned the ideal citizen as a thinking person, and they warned against the dangers of a complacent citizenry, yet many of them subscribed to the Cold War consensus of the day, which discouraged political criticism. A handful of left and left-liberal colleagues stood against the tide and argued that repressing dissent posed the greatest danger of all to democracy.

In addition to their own interventions with the newcomers, the professional experts, especially social workers and mental health specialists, set the tone for a whole range of front-line workers who interacted with the newcomers, including public health nurses, nutritionists, social agency caseworkers, psycho-therapists, recreation workers, and home visitors. Their debates about Canada's capacity to ensure the physical and psychological recovery of the newcomers, and to remake them into democracy-practising citizens, overlapped with similar debates in the media and other popular arenas. Was Canada a genuine democracy with a humane form of capitalism? Or did it need to get its own house in order before demanding adaptation to Canadian values and standards? What could newcomers fairly ask of their new home and Canadians fairly expect of the newcomers?

Democracy and Citizenship

The concept of modern citizenship has its roots in at least two opposing principles: liberal individualism, with its emphasis on the sanctity of individual rights and autonomy and the state's responsibility to ensure those values; and civic republicanism (or republican citizenship, a concept dating back to classical Greece), which stresses not only the active participation of citizens in the public realm and in the governance of society but also the obligation of those citizens to show loyalty to the state through obedience to its laws and norms.

In advanced capitalist societies such as Britain and Canada, in the period after the Second World War the state adopted an expansive welfare system as a way of cushioning the many inequities produced by capitalism. The list of compensatory rights and social security entitlements was increased in the greater interest of encouraging continuing obedience to the needs and demands of the economic order and its ruling elites. The tensions inherent in a conception of modern citizenship that contained the contradictory pulls of individual rights and social welfare guarantees, as well as a principle of participatory democracy, were much in evidence in early postwar Canada. Discourses of citizenship and the modern welfare state were influenced not only by the gatekeepers' agenda of bringing about a "return to normalcy" after the Second World War but also by the challenge of receiving and incorporating into the body politic huge numbers of foreigners.[1]

Vladimir Kaye (Kysilewsky), one of Canada's most active gatekeepers: a citizenship promoter, academic, and Cold Warrior, 1958. (Newton Photographers, LAC, C-022167)

Canadian reception workers criticized what they portrayed as the misplaced, heavy-handed, and culturally insensitive approaches of the past, which had tried to assimilate immigrants. They praised their own models of integration not only as more culturally enlightened but also as more genuinely liberal and social-scientific. Yet their language of cultural tolerance and liberal pluralism did not entirely eliminate an older vocabulary or imagery of assimilation, as in the oft-cited metaphor of shedding your old skin for an entirely new one. Nor did it displace the presumption that they, as members of the country's dominant majority and as knowledge-based experts, possessed the authority to define, interpret, and enforce the Canadian norms to which newcomers were expected to conform. Using catchwords such as "cultural mosaic" and "unity in diversity," postwar reception and citizenship advocates articulated a modest form of cultural pluralism – in this regard anticipating what would later become an official state policy of multiculturalism. But their definition of cultural pluralism was narrowly restricted to a celebration of individual talents and achievements, and thus of liberal capitalism's opportunities and freedoms, and of cultural forms, such as food, dance, and music, that were considered to be least threatening to the state and its dominant classes.

This pluralism also offered a practical strategy for "consolidating the nation" (as Citizenship official Vladimir Kaye put it), or bolstering the state and its key institutions and value systems, in a context in which mass migration from Europe was seriously altering the makeup of Canadian society. In this and other ways, liberalism, like the expanded welfare state from which even not-yet citizens could benefit, served to undergird capitalism. An ideology of cultural pluralism also guided and contained the pace and manner in which foreigners modified Canada, though the newcomers did find ways, individually and together, of disrupting such efforts.

As reception workers boldly invited all Canadians to join them in the great adventure of transforming war-weary and oppressed Europeans into well-adjusted individuals and families and productive Canadian citizens, they simultaneously warned that the failure to do so could produce individual anomie, dysfunctional families, moral decline, and crime. Indeed, the common portrait of the European in these years was that of a frightened, vulnerable, and potentially explosive or self-destructive "newcomer adrift" who had to be both guided and contained.[2] Nicholas Zay, an immigrant social worker and former lawyer from pre-1956 Hungary, used the sociological term "marginal man" to describe the fragile newcomer and likened the "non-adapted immigrant" to the marginal proletarian.[3]

That the "newcomer adrift" was usually gendered male is not surprising given the superior status accorded to men and their role as family breadwinner. But newcomer women hardly escaped the gatekeepers' gaze, especially as they were producing and raising a generation of new citizens. For example, family and child psychologists observed that mothers' separation anxiety, which could produce personality defects in children, was acute among the new European women, especially Jewish survivors and other female DPs, and the professionals thus called for greater attention to treating this malady. At the International Institute of Metropolitan Toronto (IIMT), staff shared their "newcomer adrift" thesis with their clients. In the Institute's newsletter an English teacher used a biblical metaphor when telling her new Canadian adult students that they must "feel like Jonah being swallowed by the whale" as they make their way to the "great glittering city schools" that "engulf thousands of students each night" and as they "wander down long echoing corridors and sit in big impersonal classrooms with all the others who have been caught in the same kettle of fish.... Two hours of bad digestion and the whale spews you forth again in the impersonal sea of Toronto – home to a lonely room with your dictionary in your pocket."[4]

To suggest that reception workers saw the newcomers as being in need of containment as a means of preventing the spread of illnesses or withdrawal from the mainstream is not to discount their genuine concern. A great deal of that concern informed the urgent pleas of veteran Jewish-Canadian social workers such as Joseph Kage of the Jewish Immigrant Aid Society (JIAS) in Montreal. Kage implored Canadians to show patience and tolerance to the "frightened strangers" and to support war-weary or damaged souls so that they would have a chance to better themselves. Nor did he limit his plea to the Holocaust survivors; he insisted that all Europeans as well as the British deserved sympathy and support. Whether from "war-torn Poland, Austria, Germany, Italy, Hungary, or Czechoslovakia," Kage argued, many a newcomer faced the challenge not only of meeting basic needs, such as housing and jobs, but also of overcoming "the psychological obstacles due to his traumatic experiences overseas." To meet these challenges, immigrants required sympathy and considerable assistance.[5]

As social workers, mental health experts, and Citizenship officials underlined the superiority of liberal capitalist democracy, they also expressed considerable

The first director of the International Institute of Metropolitan Toronto, Nell West (standing, wearing hat and glasses) with colleagues in front of Institute displays in a photo probably taken in the late 1950s.
(IIMT, F884, B-853)

concern that ordinary Canadians, and even caseworkers and clinicians, might not fulfil their responsibilities to help the newcomers in their process of integration. Senior social workers and psychiatrists admitted that their front-line workers often froze when they heard a client speaking a foreign language, or that the workers were indifferent or hostile to newcomer clients.[6] They urged ordinary citizens to join reception projects in their local communities and take every opportunity to interact with the new Canadians. A senior immigration bureaucrat, G.P. Allen, offered folksy if patronizing advice: "Integration demands that each of us have the spirit of the Sioux Indian who prayed 'Great Spirit, help me never to judge another man until I have walked two weeks in his moccasins'.... If we get the spirit of this prayer, we shall have less prejudice, bigotry and intolerance." International Institute director Nell West, another veteran social worker, counselled an over-the-backyard-fence neighbourliness towards the newcomers; family and child experts stressed the positive psychological effects that such warmth and support would have on them.[7]

To this end, Canadian reception workers offered a litany of suggestions for welcoming the new Europeans. Individuals were encouraged to invite a newcomer to tea or dinner or to break the ice with a friendly good morning; become a Big Brother or Big Sister; volunteer at the local settlement house; or give generously to the Community Chest, a forerunner of the United Appeal that funded the many municipally based, semi-private charity agencies. If there was interest in helping European neighbours learn to speak English, the guidebooks were easy to grasp and readily available through provincial education departments. Reception workers profiled the efforts of volunteers in their newsletters, and news stories captured the extent of goodwill from local YWCA swimming programs for newcomers, Rotary Club Christmas parties, Women's Institute lectures, Local Council of Women movie nights, and Citizenship Day ceremonies. Reception workers offered helpful hints about every conceivable act or ritual so that Canadians could avoid unwittingly giving offence to their European neighbours, and vice versa. They explained the differing table manners (Europeans held onto their cutlery and balked at the North American style of constantly picking it up and putting it down) and modes of entertainment (Europeans liked long and leisurely dinner parties, North Americans liked cocktail parties). As for body language, the European shrug was not meant as an offence but was a common way of "expressing neutrality or ignorance of a given subject." Stressing the newcomers' desire to practise conversational English without fear or embarrassment, reception workers encouraged "small house parties at well appointed Canadian homes" to mark special occasions, such as Citizenship Day or the conclusion of an English course. To ensure real mixing, the hosts could arrange chairs and tables for small groups of newcomers and assign one Canadian to each group. Dancing, too, was a "wonderful mixer." Canadians were told that the Europeans enjoyed the same popular dances – the foxtrot, waltz, tango, and samba.[8]

There was also a negative and disturbing corollary to these encouragements: ominous warnings that the failure of Canadians to carry out their duties could endanger their democratic society and way of life. To fail the newcomers was to court moral and social disaster. The experts issued alarmist predictions that resentful and disaffected people who failed to integrate and develop a sense of belonging to their adopted country (one of the necessary ingredients to inculcating patriotism and citizenship), and who remained for too long alienated from the mainstream, would undermine national morale, exhaust welfare resources, and become vulnerable to Communist propaganda (as promulgated, for example, by ethnic-Canadian Communists). According to Canadian social workers and psychiatrists, the alienated newcomer, if let alone, might become truly embittered, anti-social and self-destructive. Alcoholism, severe depression, psychosomatic symptoms (such as cramps and migraines), and suicide were among the common manifestations. In the worst-case scenario painted by psychiatrists, the disaffected men who faced continuing Canadian hostility or rejection (especially by women) could become sexual predators who lashed out at women.[9]

In political terms, alienation due to Canadian indifference or rejection, along with a failure to protect newcomers from the worst excesses of capitalist exploitation, could make the newcomers easy prey to Communists – especially ethnic-Canadian reds who shared a newcomer's culture and language – eager to recruit them or seduce them back into the party of red slavery. Isabel Jordan, a literacy activist with the Canadian Association of Adult Education (CAAE), eloquently expressed the important political issues:

> Adults arriving are thrown upon their own resources, many of them having become accustomed to government supervision in a totalitarian state, nearly all of them having known far more government regulation of their private lives than they find in Canada. Totalitarian governments may have deprived them of intellectual and religious freedom, and may even have used them cruelly, but they did requisition living space and regiment jobs for them and provide them with medical care.... Such people, when confronted with the problem of making new lives for themselves, among Canadians, whose ways and language are unfamiliar, can easily become bitter and fall prey to the influence of fanatical political organizations. If left to flounder here, many might prefer to give back intellectual and political freedom in exchange for government-controlled economic security. Harried by personal problems, haunted by a tortured past, often resented by Canadians, it is not surprising that they fail to understand the Canadian "democracy," about which we talk so much.[10]

Jordan's plea illustrates how postwar experts saw the issues of immigration, citizenship, democracy, and an expanded welfare state as interconnected phenomena.

While many of the gatekeepers feared the dangers of complacency among Canadians and newcomers alike, they differed in their definitions of the problem and in their proposed remedies. For example, Jordan's view that Canadians had to demonstrate to the newcomers the superiority of democracy was congruent with the position of many left-liberals and leftists and with the views of political liberals such as senior mandarin Escott Reid, who said the best antidote to the Soviet Communist threat was a mix of political liberalism (including an end to the exploitation of colonial peoples by rich capitalist countries) and global Keynesianism (a willingness on the part of pro-capitalist democratic states to cover the huge costs involved in managing the economy and providing a larger social safety net for its citizens). The view also overlapped with Kage's call for a more compassionate approach to "interpreting Canada to the newcomer." Too often, Kage noted, "we are too sensitive when the newcomer breaks some unwritten laws, peculiar to our Canadian tradition." We "quickly and impatiently" withdraw our friendship or even conclude, erroneously, "that the immigrant cannot be assimilated and will remain a stranger." Canadians could not expect the immigrant to instantaneously accept "our ways," nor could they force him or her to become a Canadian. They had to demonstrate by "example and education" why a standard of "Canadianism" was such "a worthy concept." "Better food, in greater quantity, mechanized gadgets, lose their importance after a while," he concluded, "unless we show him ethical ideals, better habits and customs, better and saner ways of living, goodwill and willingness to share our country, in a word – democracy."[11] By contrast, some politically conservative gatekeepers, including the chambers of commerce and the

Imperial Order Daughters of the Empire, combined their reception work with anti-Communist lobbying and bristled at the idea of conceding anything to the Communists. For them, a capitalist democracy, warts and all, was always superior to any other political regime.[12]

The pleas issued by Jordan and Kage also touched on the tension between the state's positive promise of a wider social safety net for all – even potential citizens who, like the Europeans, entered the country with a landed-immigrant status that gave them access to some but not all state welfare resources – and the principle of discouraging long-term dependency on the state. This tension lay at the heart of welfare capitalism. For social democrats like Jordan and her CAAE colleagues, including J.R. Kidd, democracy required that citizens be willing to criticize their society's shortcomings and be actively committed to improving it. As citizens of Canada, they were citizens of the globe; they should be informed internationalists in favour of co-operative efforts to ease Cold War tensions and address problems. Furthermore, "the speedier and more satisfactory" the newcomer integrated and became "a useful and producing citizen," the less likely he or she would become "a charge on our welfare and other services." All of this required a well-integrated plan of reception and integration.[13]

This delicate balancing act was made trickier still by the two-tiered gendered welfare system, which particularly subjected women with complex sexual histories or experiences of abuse to be judged by rigid definitions of good moral character, and by the widespread fears among newcomers that taking state handouts made them vulnerable to deportation. A related concern had to do with the newcomers' false expectations about adjusting to the material realities of Canadian life. For liberal reception activists such as Rabbi Feinberg in Toronto, and for radical consumer groups such as the Housewives Consumers Association, this meant addressing the housing shortage and escalating rents. It meant eliminating job exploitation and homelessness. It also meant defending the right of outspoken Communists such as the Black singer Paul Robeson and the "Red Dean of Canterbury," the pro-Communist British archbishop, Rev. Hewlett Johnson, to enter Canada and exercise their freedom of speech.[14]

More conservative moralists, such as Rev. G. Stanley Russell, a United Church minister and religious columnist in *The Toronto Star*, stressed instead the need to eliminate drinking and especially the new women's beverage rooms in taverns. He also railed against sexually candid pulp fiction, the spread of sexual promiscuity, and the Kinsey Report. But he also argued that in so far as the "human misery" resulting from "bad housing, evil labor conditions, unemployment, political ineptitude, or ... dishonesty" created recruits for Communism, these ills were "much more menacing than anything Karl Marx ever wrote or Stalin ever said" and thus had to be eliminated.[15]

The Imperial Order Daughters of the Empire (IODE) advocated more elaborate citizenship ceremonies. Here, flag-bearers raise the Union Jack in front of Christ Church during an annual meeting held in Niagara Falls, Ont. *Maclean's* 15 Aug. 1952.
(Photograph by Paul Rockett; TRL)

From Newcomer Adrift to Integrated Citizen?

The gatekeepers were concerned that the newcomers achieve a deeper, or formal, level of integration – namely, legal and political citizenship. In addition to the five-year residency obligation, citizenship required applicants to pass an examination and take an oath. Patriotic groups such as the IODE called for and designed more elaborate ceremonies to mark the occasion, while Citizenship judges used the occasion to deliver lectures on the superiority of democracy. Still, citizenship was about more than exams, oaths, celebrations, and the numbers of registered citizens. It also involved campaigns to improve – or uplift or modernize – the social, moral, and even mental health of the newcomer population.[16]

The much-heralded postwar model of integration assumed a multilayered process involving a series of adjustments. Canadian citizenship experts insisted that, to be effective, integration had to be free and evolutionary, with newcomers gradually undergoing a transformation in everything from eating habits and style of clothing to work ethic and political practices. They would acquire English-language skills (the French language was rarely mentioned) and practise their civic responsibilities (including applying for citizenship and voting), in essence embracing the dominant majority's ideological value systems. In countless speeches and government materials, Vladimir Kaye of the Citizenship Branch offered many versions of this ideal integration scenario, which also contained a good amount of an old assimilationist impulse.[17] He insisted that each newcomer, regardless of class, cultural, or political background, "must go through a change which affects his body and soul – changes of climate, diet, change of culture, change of… his whole behaviour to the new system of values." Kaye fully admitted that giving up old allegiances and adopting new ones were not easy, and the time required to do so depended on "the type of individual, his age, sex, intelligence, maturity and other factors." Change best took place not by "coaxing or pressure," but by "friendly advice and invitation."[18]

Many agreed, including social worker Nicholas Zay and Claude J. Mulvihill of the Catholic Family Services in Toronto and the International Catholic Migration Congress.[19] Citizenship official Allen explained the state's interests in all this activity: "If [the newcomers] can find an opportunity to settle, grow and develop with security and happiness, Canada will be enriched. If, on the other hand, they receive a poor reception and face prejudice and intolerance, their chances of contributing to the common good will be lessened and the potential growth of Canada will be stunted."[20] In practice, front-line workers were prepared to coax and cajole the newcomers. For example, nutritionists advocated a liberal, pluralist approach to assessing ethnic food ways, yet advocated persuasion à la Mark Twain: "Habit is habit and not to be flung out the window by any man but coaxed downstairs, a step at a time." Still, striving for the ideal of an unimposed integration was considered especially worthwhile in dealing with groups that, as a journalist put it, remembered how "foreign conquerors" had tried "to assimilate them by threat, lash, and imprisonment."[21]

Citizenship as a construct and process does not merely confer political and legal status on individuals who are then permitted to enjoy certain social entitlements. It also operates as ideology. It requires citizens and potential citizens to engage in self-discipline and self-censorship not only out of a fear that transgressing dominant social or moral norms will invite censure or punishment but also out of a desire to belong and to reap the rewards that come with obedience and conformity to the rules. A variety of theorists, including Marxist state theorists, have identified these ideological conditions. Antonio Gramsci, the famous proponent of the theory of hegemony, argued that ruling elites dominate society not solely by the threat of coercive force but by shaping popular consent. French philosopher Michel Foucault, in his notions of how people govern their souls, makes a similar point.[22] And if all social acts were up for interrogation, discussions of modifying the newcomers' social and moral behaviour clearly placed a priority on encouraging a familiarity with and conformity to dominant bourgeois ideals. One of the most important of these was the practice of and dynamics associated with the much vaunted middle-class nuclear family, in which breadwinner fathers, homemaker mothers, and well-adjusted (and rapidly Canadianizing) children performed their assigned duties or appropriate roles.

Dismissing as "only half effective" any efforts to modify only the newcomers' behaviour, postwar reception workers asserted that successful integration involved a two-sided and gradual give-and-take process in which old and new Canadians interacted with each other, actively engaging in meaningful cultural exchanges and developing new and enriched understandings and interrelationships. Out of this active engagement would emerge a stronger and more harmonious society. "It must be assumed," Kage declared at a Canadian welfare conference on immigrants, that the newcomer "not only receives" but also makes "his own distinctive contribution" to the new country, and that the local community in which newcomers were living out their daily lives must also accept its responsibilities in encouraging this mutual adjustment.[23]

Spokespersons for the postwar labour movement also subscribed to the mutual adjustment principle. G.B. Milling of the Toronto Joint Labour Committee to Combat Racial Intolerance explained its value by recounting a story of a Czech refugee machine operator. The man's initial disinterest in the union transformed into active participation as he picked up some English and as his initially frosty Canadian co-workers began to explain the shop's unwritten rules (for example, that no one worked through a rest period because it was a hard-won right) and include him in their lunchroom bull sessions. While admitting that the union's integration efforts were not "altogether altruistic," Milling declared that they were nonetheless necessary for building a stronger labour movement and ensuring wider social order.[24]

A two-sided approach to integration, then, required citizenship training for both newcomers and the general Canadian public. It also assumed, optimistically, that a "better understanding" among all of Canada's groups "will result in better integration which, in turn, will improve the whole social, economic, political and cultural life of Canada."[25] It was silent, however, on how the ethnic groups were to adjust to one another.

Not surprisingly, the leading advocates of integration and cultural pluralism, including the officials in the Citizenship Branch, described their efforts as the enlightened actions of a progressive, tolerant, and civilized citizenry. That they appeared to see little contradiction between these exalted liberal goals and their presumption of superiority vis-à-vis the newcomers, or their complicity in the intrusive surveillance or regulation of people's private lives, was an irony common to democracies. This was certainly true during the Cold War, when passive conformity, with no questions or criticism raised, could become an end in and of itself, at least in certain circles; or when non-conformist political and moral behaviour could be diagnosed as a symptom of mental ill health.

If this situation sat well with many gatekeepers, including the more politically conservative Branch bureaucrats and ardent Cold Warriors, it no doubt troubled more radical social workers. One such was Dora Wilensky, the wife of Communist Party luminary Joe Salsberg and a seasoned Jewish social worker who played a role in the resettlement of child survivors in Canada. Another was the political activist and poet Dorothy Livesay, who was trained as a social worker. Other left-leaning social workers, such as Bessie Touzel of the Toronto Welfare Council and Kay Gorrie of University Settlement House, also criticized the growing influence of psychiatric approaches within postwar social work on the grounds that the methods highlighted personality disorders to the potential neglect of social analyses and a social change agenda. There were, then, dissenting voices among the gatekeepers, even if they did not undermine the profession's central paradigms.[26]

Nevertheless, social work education (then as now) was heavily grounded in middle-class norms, and it aimed at producing graduates who could move smoothly into social service agencies.[27] The overall thrust of postwar reception programs was to encourage conformity to these norms, though some Citizenship officials were prone to far more lofty claims. A senior Citizenship Branch official, R. Alex Sim, explained the superiority of Canadian citizenship campaigns in a manner that effectively portrayed cultural pluralism as the right of the dominant majority to engage in what theorists bell hooks has famously called "eating the other" (the process by which dominant groups co-opt the cultures of racial minorities as a way of strengthening their own power and privilege). According to Sim, the Canadian approach to integration reflected "an ideal in Canadian thinking," namely, solving challenges "by an exercise of moderation and understanding, not from the use of discriminatory practises whether these involve force, legal sanctions, or merely prejudicial treatment." A continuing commitment to the liberal principles of freedom and tolerance made Canada a highly civilized society capable of "highly civilized accomplishments." Like others, Sim argued that whether peoples of diverse cultures were permitted "to flourish and thus through their own inner strength to contribute to the common good" depended mostly on the goodwill of the majority group, which stood to gain or lose in the long run, "depending on the degree of humanitarian treatment it accords a minority." So far, history had offered four ways for minorities and majorities to co-exist: repression, segregation, assimilation, and integration. Sim celebrated Canada's adoption of an integration model, because it "welcomes diversity" and "encourages the smaller group to flourish and grow" in a manner that "does not alter the larger dominant group in a destructive way."[28]

In Sim's definition, the power of the dominant groups is never seriously challenged, while the cultures of the newcomers can be mined (exploited?) for purposes designed by the more powerful groups. In response to the critics who charged that integration was merely a polite word for assimilation or "a melting pot over a slow fire," he argued that integration was a relationship that was not easily understood or practised precisely because "it calls for mutual trust between groups that may be actually or potentially hostile" and demands "the exercise of moderation and understanding and the imaginative acceptance of differences." Discourses of citizenship are prone to generalities. Sim's hazy form of liberalism also included a strong element of the folklorization of immigrants, that is, a process of turning immigrants into folk who carry with them quaint traditions that can be put on display for Canadian consumption. It was an important ingredient in the neatly contained, or packaged, ethnicity that gatekeepers offered Canadians.[29] Sim did ask "majority Canadians" to think through the implications of an integration ideal that respects unique individuals and unique groups and encourages them to grow and flourish. "What will happen to language habits… political likes and dislikes?" he questioned. "Will social habits, dress, food preferences, family life move towards the norms of conformity?" But he also assured Canadians that the liberal approach would "transform good intentions into good citizenship."[30]

A National Film Board adaptation of one of the countless government pamphlets on the subject described the model citizen as a socially responsible and moral person who had core family values and was a politically informed voter. As the camera in *The Citizen as an Individual* scans scenes of everyday life – a woman baking a cake for a wedding anniversary; friends gathered together; a woman reading the newspaper; a man replacing a window accidentally broken by hockey-playing children; a female teacher and male school principal at work; and a church scene – the narrator lists the qualities that make a good citizen who is actively engaged with the whole gamut of society's institutions and values:

> He should be devoted to his family and home and take an active interest in the neighbourhood.… He should be friendly and try to live in harmony with his fellow-citizens… should realize the value of self-control in dealing with members of his family [and] friends and neighbours… should be loyal to his friends and his associates… take pride in his work.… He should know and obey the rules of health [and] realize that art, music, literature and drama are an important part of living… should recognize spiritual values and the importance of religion in everyday life… should know the important problems that face his representatives in Municipal, Provincial and Federal government. He should understand what is being done to solve these problems and use this knowledge when he goes to vote… should be interested in the world around him… [and] make an effort to understand the changes and new developments that are taking place and form some opinions about them.[31]

Canada's gatekeepers acknowledged the important differences between Europe's volunteer immigrants and the refugees. But they also stressed the commonalities, including a shared need to recover from war-inflicted loss or tragedy. They made it clear that, ultimately, all newcomers would be judged by their willingness and capacity to learn and practise the lessons of Canadian democracy and good citizenship. Determined to transform the political values (and scepticism) of men and women who had lived under totalitarian regimes in Fascist Italy, Nazi Germany, and Soviet-occupied and later Communist regimes in Eastern Europe, the gatekeepers placed a strong emphasis on the newcomers' need to overcome what they saw as misplaced and unhealthy suspicions or distrust of Canadian authorities, be they police officers, social workers, home visitors, or medical personnel.

They also differed in their expectations of the ideal citizen. J.R. Kidd, who was director of both the Canadian Citizenship Council and the CAAE, criticized the growing pressure on people "to conform, to be good untroublesome, law-abiding subjects rather than independent-thinking, responsible citizens." He envisioned informed but opinionated, and not passive, citizens.[32] The hardline Cold Warriors, such as Kaye and fellow academic Watson Kirkconnell (later president of Acadia University), and the businessmen on the chambers of commerce and boards of trade, used a vocabulary of democratic citizenship. Their demand for a united front against Communism, however, translated into a repressive call for total obedience and conformity and into denunciations of political dissent of any kind.[33] But then too, social democrats within the labour movement and the CCF (Co-operative Commonwealth Federation) were carrying out their own anti-Communist purges.[34]

Although valued as freedom-loving anti-Communists, the East European DPs and the later Iron Curtain refugees were depicted as most in need of citizenship training. They could be pathologized as victims of Communism who suffered from its ugly symptoms, including paranoia.[35] Among Europe's volunteer immigrants, Italians and Germans were also seen as being in need of democratic training and as highly susceptible to charismatic, authoritarian leaders.

Ethnic Organizations: Agents of Change or Backwardness?

Citizenship officials considered it important to work with Canada's ethnic organizations. By the early 1950s these bodies numbered in the thousands, and older groups boasted national organizations (such as the Canadian Polish Congress, Canadian Jewish Congress, and Ukrainian Canadian Committee) and an array of women's, youth, and cultural affiliations. "Reaching out to the ethnic groups" – this recurring phrase suggests the officials' mainly top-down approach, which usually meant dealing with ethnic elites, such as press editors and society presidents who were expected to influence the rest of their lot. Another guiding principle was what Kaye called the "tactics of close liaison." Most of the Canadian reception workers agreed with the Citizenship Branch's claim that ethnic organizations were useful tools of integration in that they cushioned the shock of migration. By providing newcomers with information in their language, material aid, and social and psychological support, the organizations could ease the acculturation process and encourage feelings of belonging and security, two key ingredients for encouraging patriotism and loyalty to the state, especially during the early difficult years. As Sim put it, they "can contribute in their peculiar way to our national life by serving their people."[36]

In helping to contain the newcomers' fears, the organizations could also provide a critical first line of defence against individual anomie and group disorder. These goals were not solely Cold War elements, but they fit well with the state's national security agenda of ensuring a loyal citizenry. As a newcomer's "teacher, social club and often his sole security," Kaye noted, ethnic organizations could "prolong the period of integration by their perpetuation of European customs, languages [and] interests," but they "diminished the frustration" and alleviated "the feeling of insecurity" brought on by an open or veiled hostility that had to be overcome before full and permanent integration could occur.[37]

Ethnic organizations were sometimes an important third tier of support for newcomers. Whether middle-aged or "semi-adolescent," most newcomers benefited first of all from the presence of relatives, compatriots, and co-religionists who could help them, people they could share their problems with. They could benefit, secondly, from the foreign-language newspapers on which they heavily relied during the early years of adjustment. But if these were not available, they could turn to the ethnic organization. In keeping with the idea of the "newcomer adrift," Kaye saw the ethnic organizations as bridges and buffer zones that could prevent the "sudden disruption" that "would cause serious disintegration, resulting in extreme cases in anti-social behaviour."[38]

Some critics, though, worried that ethnic societies, by meeting their mandate (preserving heritage), would contribute to the problem of creating "national ghettoes" that worked against the Canadianization of the newcomers.[39] Kaye and his colleagues stressed that most of the ethnic societies were "entirely Canadian in outlook" and could thus be effective "change agents" (Allen's phrase). While admitting that newer and smaller postwar groups like the Baltic DPs would be less active on this front until they too were brought into the mainstream, Kaye stressed that "by making them a part of us, we can strengthen their beneficial influence."[40] This strategy would involve providing these groups with pro-Canada and pro-democracy materials that reflected the Canadian anti-Communist position.

The Experts: Social Workers and Psychiatrists

Social work leader H.M. Cassidy declared that his profession was ideally suited to administering the services and institutions of the expanded welfare state, and psychologists stressed their positive role as promoters of healthy and happy persons and families in postwar Canada (as opposed to psychiatry's focus on pathologies).[41] This propensity for claiming to possess a specialized expertise and the skills or techniques to diagnose and treat problems – what Foucault, in describing the rise of the new professions, called knowledge claims – reflected the continuing professionalizing efforts of the semi- or helping professions.[42]

By the 1950s social work and psychology, and the older and more prestigious field of psychiatry, had made some critical gains. Each profession had carved out a substantial niche within various social, penal, educational, and welfare institutions, and now each sought to protect and extend its influence. Canadian social workers, like their U.S. counterparts, had been involved in professionalizing their field for half a century. Distinguishing themselves from nineteenth-century "do-gooders," they promoted themselves as policy experts and social technicians who could fix society's problems. Their professionalizing activities also included efforts to attract men to a predominantly female enterprise.[43] In the postwar decades social work was still not a full-fledged autonomous and prestigious profession, nor had it lost its feminine profile: more men were now entering the field, but most students and fieldworkers (as opposed to a tiny minority of university professors) were women. But postwar Canadian social workers did boast their own professional associations, schools, and journals.

More importantly, social work practice had become institutionalized. As investigators, counsellors, and administrators, social workers had long carried out the mandate of social welfare regimes, approving or rejecting applicants for state supports, and otherwise directly influencing people's lives. Caseworkers, whether fully trained or not, could wield a "localized" power over their individual clients – that is, their decisions could determine whether a client received certain welfare supports, was accepted into a job-training program, got help with a sick child, or was sent for a psychiatric examination. Any of these actions could alter the quality of life for the client and his or her family.[44]

The professionalizing efforts of Canadian psychologists date to the early twentieth century and involved garnering recognition as experts with a definable set of explanatory theories and therapeutic tools. The adoption of child development theories, Intelligence Quotient (IQ) tests, and participation in wartime recruitment programs were some of the strategies that psychologists used to establish their discipline as a relevant social science. Wanting to gain a professional distance from psychiatry and its focus on personal pathology, psychology leaders laid claim to a specialized expertise in promoting healthy personalities through early detection of problems and preventive and remedial treatment. Child psychologists had gained a foothold in Canadian public schools by the 1920s largely on these grounds; by the 1940s they had also joined the ranks of non-legal personnel in the family and juvenile court system. Child and family psychologists compiled detailed inventories of children's behaviour, then touted them as objective means of differentiating and assessing personalities. The analytical categories themselves reflected dominant social and moral codes that served to normalize the bourgeois Anglo-Celtic family ideal. The standards of normalcy were infused by qualities of obedience and conformity, while non-conforming behaviour indicated abnormality or maladjustment. For example, a 1951 study of delinquent girls in Montreal, which concluded that the girls were suffering from feelings of insecurity, inadequacy, and inferiority, put the blame on the parents' failure to raise their children properly. Significantly, the study also noted that several parents were European immigrants evidently unassimilated into Canadian ways.[45]

Since at least the late nineteenth century, Canadian psychiatrists (who had their own theories and models) had made inroads into various institutions, including the criminal justice system, where they acted as expert witnesses assessing defendants on trial. The psychiatric case history was one of the devices by which psychiatrists had gained professional status and an enduring spot in the legal system, though that process had involved serious rifts between medical doctors and psychiatrists, and between court authorities and legal experts. The child psychiatrists had carved out a niche within the family services world as well as the family and juvenile justice system. During the 1940s and 1950s, psychiatrists could be found on the staffs of the country's mental health clinics, including the Toronto Child Psychiatric Centre. They were also involved in immigration services, largely through the referrals of newcomers to their institutional homes in psychiatric wards, clinics, and hospitals.[46] Notwithstanding the competing paradigms of diagnosis and treatment within Canadian postwar psychiatry and the interprofessional conflicts between psychiatrists and both psychologists and medical doctors, the early postwar years saw the growing, albeit uneven, influence of psychiatric categories of behaviour, especially deviant behaviour, within the other professions, including psychology and nursing.[47]

Like their colleagues in social work and other helping professions, Canadian psychiatrists viewed their work with newcomers as part of a broad agenda aimed at addressing what Dr. John D.M. Griffin – executive director of the Canadian Mental Health Association (CMHA) from 1951 to 1971, and nicknamed "Canada's Mr. Mental Health"[48] – described as a widening national mental health problem. His definition of the problem, like his list of the many signifiers of mental illness, was so expansive that virtually any client who came before a therapist (and, for that matter, a front-line social worker or nurse) could be labelled with some kind of mental health problem, be it a personality disorder, severe depression, emotional trauma, or mental disability. Griffin's many indicators of this vexing problem included the high percentage of Canadian soldiers disqualified from military service during the war and the high rates of emotionally disturbed war veterans; the "steady" and "relentless" increase of "psychotic, unstable, ineffective or dull" persons leading "uncomfortable and unhappy" lives and unnecessarily burdening their families; and a virtual epidemic in people suffering from psychosomatic illnesses, those "vague pains and aches and physical disorders" that had their "origin in psychological or emotional disturbances."

While admitting to no general agreement over the definition or assessment of mental "disease" or "disability," Griffin and his colleagues nonetheless declared it to be a virtual epidemic. Their evidence, which included statistics culled from the annual reports of provincial mental hospitals and surveys of communities using sampling techniques, indicated that as much as 1.5 per cent of Canada's population, or more than 150,000 people, suffered from "some disabling form of mental illness." The nation's state of emotional health was equally appalling: one-third to two-thirds of all those using out-patient clinics at Canada's big general hospitals reportedly suffered from "emotional disturbances" as either a primary or contributing cause of their personality disabilities. Drawing on the work of the internationally known Dr. (Helen) Flanders Dunbar and her colleagues, Griffin explained that a high percentage (up to 70 per cent) of patients who suffered from such physical problems as heart or circulatory disease developed serious emotional and psychological disabilities that compounded the problem. Especially worrisome was the rise in "pathological states of mind," which also accounted for the strong increase (by 630 per cent) in indictable criminal offences committed in Canada between 1900 and 1944, despite a mere increase of about 20 per cent in the overall population.

If these sobering statistics were not enough, Griffin also rang the alarm (alarmist?) bells to stress that unless more resources and trained personnel were made available to treat the problem, European immigration would bring in yet more mental or emotional misfits, thereby compounding an already growing epidemic in mental illness in the Canadian population. According to Griffin, the recent rise in "anti-social and criminal behaviour" was due largely to a mix of "a gradual slothing off of the individual sense of responsibility" and "unhealthy indications of aggression, hostility, egocentricity and prejudice." Unless checked, immigration could exacerbate the problem. A similar pathology could occur in groups, transforming crowds into irrational and hysterical mobs prone to impulsive acts of aggression. By way of example, Griffin described a student protest against a brothel in Montreal that had gotten out of control. The students had damaged the house, and Griffin had actually equated their admittedly questionable behaviour with "the pathology of the Nazi storm troopers during the height of their career." The misplaced comparison suggests the experts' tendency towards very broad definitions of the problem.[49]

By pathologizing a range of non-conformist social behaviour, Canada's psyche-based professionals, like their colleagues in social work, equated conformity to middle-class norms, including civil obedience, with mental and moral health. Their treatments similarly encouraged conformity to dominant state-sanctioned authority and ideological value systems. The psyche-based experts could view political dissent, or criticism of state repression, as both a symptom and cause of individual disease and group pathology. By the same token, they saw newcomers from former totalitarian regimes, especially Communist, as political and psychological victims prone to personality problems that required professional mending. Certainly, plenty of newcomers from Communist regimes, or those who had lived under German or Soviet occupation in the war, did exhibit mental or emotional pain, but postwar definitions of mental illness were so expansive that an enormous range of behaviour – from union or Communist Party membership to women's defiance of suffocating sexual codes, and men's sexual assault against women – could be collapsed into a definition of individual abnormality or group pathology.

A graphic example of this process was the considerable degree to which postwar discourses of morality and sexuality became medicalized. While that medicalization was uneven and contested, diagnoses of sexual deviance as a manifestation of personality or psychiatric disorders nonetheless enjoyed much currency in the post-1945 years. Canadian sex and mental health specialists declared an alarming spread of sexual deviance and mental illness across society, including in the immigrant and refugee populations. While the specialists called for public awareness programs and more experts to help deal with the problem on both an individual and national level, the period also witnessed the spread of psychiatric discourses among front-line workers who might have had little psychiatric training but made liberal use of psychiatric labels to categorize their clients.[50]

Canada's various professional problem-solvers joined forces with social planning councils and concerned citizens in an effort to advocate for a specialized stream of immigrant social services and programs. Such programs would train social workers and other helping professionals to better deal with their immigrant clients' emotional and psychological needs and to better appreciate the role that culture played in people's behaviour, including their modes of grieving and coping. Jewish-Canadian social workers, for example, said they had quickly learned that many survivors needed to share their painful experiences and memories, but that the survivors only felt safe in doing so when they believed that the caseworker had some basic understanding of who they were and could be trusted to respect confidentiality. Thus, social work leaders like Kage wanted Jewish Immigrant Aid Society workers, and those employed within the social services sector that dealt with the postwar Europeans, to become more familiar with psychological and psychiatric approaches. This was not a surprising development given that social work had long drawn on perspectives from sociology, psychology, economics, and other disciplines. As in earlier eras, social workers (as well as psychologists and psychiatrists) used a mix of approaches, such as individual counselling, group methods, and community programs, to deal with such problems as intergenerational family conflict, delinquency, unemployment, and the integration of newcomers.[51]

Left to right: Doctors William W. Wigle (president during this era of the Canadian Medical Association and Ontario Medical Association and a director of the Canadian Mental Health Association), Jack Griffin (director general, CMHA), and W. Arthur Blair of Ottawa (also a CMHA director) at a Medical Action for Mental Health conference, Chateau Laurier Hotel, Ottawa, 23-25 March 1964, held in conjunction with the CMHA's landmark publication *More for the Mind*.
(CAMH Archives, CMHA Collection 4-P42)

The Canadian Mental Health Association, composed of medical personnel, social workers, welfare experts, and volunteers from women's and community groups, stressed its multifaceted role not only in curing illness but also in encouraging healthy and happy living. It emphasized its participation in a wide range of programs aimed at "the development of better facilities for treatment of mental illness" and those "more generally designed to develop conditions of a more balanced life in the community." CMHA leaders such as Dr. D. Ewan Cameron, chair of the Department of Psychiatry at the Allan Memorial Institute (and later implicated in the CIA-led brainwashing experiments on patients), called for more mental health experts across the board because they could help to solve a range of problems that emerged during a person's life, from childhood to old age. As well they could help to relieve the tremendous stresses caused by the rapid changes taking place, especially in industrial countries. They could treat drug addicts, sex criminals, and provide psychiatric training to nurses and teachers. (More specifically, CMHA leaders worried about the shortage of psychiatric nurses.)[52] As experts in "dealing with the smooth adjustment of individuals or groups to unusual social conditions," the mental health experts, Cameron argued, were as indispensable to programs to encourage the integration of newcomers as, ironically, they were to programs to integrate Canada's original inhabitants, the "Indians." Interestingly, senior Immigration and Citizenship officials saw the organization's leaders as being overly prone to "negative diagnoses," but to avoid appearing indifferent or callous to those suffering from psychological problems they tried not to antagonize these experts.[53]

Like that of other gatekeepers who liaised with the Department of Citizenship and Immigration, and more specifically the Citizenship Branch, the CMHA's mandate was concerned with the challenges and potential remedies associated with postwar mass migration. At a 1953 CMHA conference, speakers noted that those dealing with refugee and immigrant women, including public health nurses and settlement house staff, needed to be aware of child-rearing theories. One of these was Bowlby's thesis, which linked personality disorders in growing adults, as well as symptoms of neuroses and other mental illnesses in adults and children, to maternal deprivation and early separation between child and mother. Early on, Jewish-Canadian social workers had found high rates of this malady among survivor mothers and other DP women. On a positive note, front-line workers also had to be trained to detect the signs that indicated the newcomers' gradual adjustment to Canadian life. Both professional and lay people had to become better informed about "the mental health implications of migration and dislocation of various peoples," including the high probability that apparently healthy immigrants frequently "broke down" after a short time in Canada, a consequence of the complex factors involved in people being transplanted from one culture to another. Cameron argued that at his institute the broken-down newcomer, whose breakdown usually occurred amid a context of hostility, received a great deal of attention and the "ego strengthening" that was necessary.[54]

Another concern was that newcomers, in addition to their fear or suspicion of authorities of any kind, differed in their familiarity with state-run social services. Benjamin Schlesinger, a professor at the University of Toronto's School of Social Work, summed up the problem as one of "two extremes." That is, newcomers fell largely into two groups. The first group was made up of those who were accustomed to a greater degree of government-funded and supervised health and welfare services and might well be disappointed with the state of Canada's social services. The second included those who came from countries with fewer social services and were thus unschooled in the advantages of the modern welfare state and ignorant of some of its fundamental principles, especially "the community's right to protect children, to regulate family disorganization, and to interfere with difficult family relations." Generally speaking, the East European refugees from Communist homelands fell into the first group, while rural Europeans, particularly from Italy and Portugal, fell into the second. In both cases, problems were exacerbated by the newcomers' need to overcome personal losses and adjust to a different society. In many cases, Canada's social services functioned differently than similar services did in European countries, and this difference also had to be clarified for the newcomers.[55]

In a statement that nicely captured social workers' views and interests, child welfare administrator David Weiss explained that social agencies facilitated immigrant adjustment to "our way of life" and encouraged a "feeling of belonging" by providing "proper reception and information services" and securing jobs and housing. In addition, when necessary, agencies would use their up-to-date casework and counselling procedures to treat individuals suffering from a specific illness or from difficulties that went beyond a lack of job or housing. Weiss also called upon the state to increase hospital and outpatient services, educational facilities, opportunities for religious observance, and recreational venues.[56]

One newlywed couple would have been obliged to travel on to Cuba if a last-minute ruse at Gander hadn't foiled their Red pursuers.

The sketch, by "Rosenthal," accompanied a story about a Canadian nurse who ensured a young couple's defection to the West. Acting quickly at Gander International Airport, Nfld., the nurse helped the two refugees evade the trench-coated Communist agents who were following them. Maclean's Reports, *Maclean's* 7 Aug. 1965.

In their role as problem-solvers, social workers advocated casework as the method by which neutral assessments and appropriate treatments could be made. As an individualized procedure, casework took up the scientific methods of intensive interviews, observation, and data-collecting, followed up by diagnostic analysis and appropriate treatment. Depending on the situation, more than one data collector and diagnostician could be present in the case file. For example, there might be reports from social workers with social agencies such as the Big Sisters or Big Brothers associations or the city welfare department, as well as child psychologists based at mental health clinics. But the basic principles applied. The case file could contain different pieces of expert knowledge that included notes on the intake interview, a medical examination and social summary reports compiled by a home investigator dispatched by a settlement house, an immigrant aid agency, the Children's Aid Society, or the local Immigration office to observe the home and conduct interviews with family members. If the client was referred to a psychiatrist or psychologist, that professional might conduct IQ tests and interviews with the client before making final diagnoses and recommendations.

Canadian social workers had adopted the principles of the casework method well before the postwar era, borrowing largely from U.S. casework leaders such as Mary Richmond, the acknowledged matriarch of the method. By the 1940s and 1950s, these principles had permeated all aspects of social work training and practice in Canada, including at the University of Toronto's Social Work school, whose students had exposure to immigrant clients through, for example, placements with a social agency or settlement house.[57] A key principle was impartiality, so much so that social work schools assessed their own students for appropriate personality types, counselling or weeding out those diagnosed as suffering from such disorders as "severe neurotic symptoms," "hostility," or "inadequate" social skills. In the interests of purging moral bias and facilitating non-judgmental analysis, students were encouraged to write self-critical journals and undergo counselling or psychiatric self-diagnosis.[58]

Within social work, the growing number of immigrants who turned to social welfare agencies prompted what Schlesinger described as sporadic efforts to develop socio-cultural approaches that recognized the significant influence of group-defined culture and custom in people's behaviour and attitudes. Charles Fine, a University of Toronto graduate who wrote his master's thesis on the subject, similarly argued that a more progressive social work practice could not develop until Canadian caseworkers acknowledged that they were as much a child of their culture as their clients and abandoned the notion that any one culture was a priori superior. The best way that a social worker could develop "some detachment from the value of one's own culture" and thus avoid judgmental assessments was to understand the basic premise that every individual is born into a world already defined by existing cultural patterns and then to develop a specific knowledge of the client's different socio-cultural background, whether or not the client had picked up North American standards and values.[59]

Canadian social workers often drew upon British models in the area of social welfare policy, but they turned to U.S. social workers for help in developing socio-cultural approaches. Despite the United States' "melting pot" ideology – an official discourse that contrasted markedly with Canada's emerging "cultural mosaic" ideology – U.S. social scientists and social workers had been experimenting with culturally pluralist approaches since at least the 1920s, and by the 1940s a literature on the subject was available. Canadians took their definition of culture from such anthropological classics as E.B. Taylor's *Primitive Culture* (1895), which defined it as "that complex whole which includes knowledge, belief, art, law, morals, customs, and any other capabilities and habits acquired by man as a member of society." In her *Patterns of Culture* (1946) Ruth Benedict wrote, "No man can thoroughly participate in any culture unless he has been brought up and has lived according to its forms, but he can grant to other cultures the same significance to their participants which he recognizes in his own."[60] Canadians drew on U.S. "psycho-cultural approaches" emphasizing how the individual, beginning with the parent-child relationship, is "culturalized" along "the persistent traditional patterns of the group." Advocates of the model argued that an understanding of the significant role that cultural stresses played in an individual's "social pathology" – which ranged from "improper diets" and "avoidance to seek help" to "persistence in destructive behaviour" – would enable social workers to be better caseworkers with ethnic clients and even to predict behaviour.[61]

Without dismissing the value of psychological approaches, cultural pluralists within social work argued that "social-science knowledge" (the study of social phenomena such as class, religion, and ethnicity) had to be added to the medical and psychological forms of knowledge informing social work methods. Schlesinger noted that too often front-line caseworkers diagnosed the behaviour of new Canadians as "psychological problems, when in reality it is culturally determined behaviour, which is quite normal in the milieu of the client." A volatile, outgoing, and emotional Greek client, for example, may not always be "hostile and aggressive towards the social worker" but may be expressing his feelings in an acceptable "Greek manner." Schlesinger pointed out that most newcomer clients "cling to old beliefs and customs" because these are often the only familiar things left after they emigrate, and they view change with "fear and suspicion." Thus the social worker had to be "very careful in interpreting the services of the agency" and "the new patterns of living prevalent in the Canadian setting" to the newcomer. Acknowledging that it would be impossible for social workers in multi-ethnic cities like Toronto to learn all of their clients' languages, Schlesinger noted that it would be helpful to learn a bit of the key languages, because it could put immigrant clients at ease. He encouraged social work schools to introduce courses on the subject and caseworkers to attend lectures and seminars on the socio-cultural patterns of major ethnic groups in their city. To be helpful to the new Canadians, social workers did not have to become cultural anthropologists, but they did need to "recognize the existence of cultural differences, and not impose [their] own cultural background."[62]

Not surprisingly, Canadian social workers tried to make the claim for distinctive Canadian circumstances and a distinctly Canadian socio-cultural approach. According to Fine, the social work profession in Canada and the United States reflected the widely shared values associated with a democratic society, such as the worth of the individual, the inherent dignity of human beings, society's responsibility for individual welfare, and the individual's duty to contribute to the common good. Notwithstanding the American "melting pot" ideology, which implied the necessity of melting in order to become Americanized and that "ethnic differences are undesirable and efforts to maintain them un-American," U.S. social work, with its training in cultural pluralist models, showed a respect for ethnic groups and their customs. This respect had mediated the emphasis on the need for conformity to and acceptance of the American way of life. The "Canadian viewpoint," however, had taken the theory and practice of cultural pluralism (or integration) one step further, argued Fine, and developed a model that assumed that national unity was achieved by what one advocate (Arthur Lermer) called a "crossfertilization of heterogenous cultures" and that stressed "the harmonizing of host and immigrant cultures." While dissenting voices existed,[63] Canadian discussions of newcomers "focussed on the unique contributions to be made to Canadian life by the diverse cultural heritages of ethnic groups."

Fine did acknowledge the limitations of the practice. He explained that there were two dimensions to the cultural life of ethnic groups: the visible one, with features such as songs, dress, and folklore, and the invisible or intangible one, such as status structure, child-rearing practices, moral standards, and husband-wife relationships. He admitted that it was easier for the pluralist-minded social worker to welcome the outward manifestations of cultural life in concerts or festivals, or when visiting a client's home, or to appreciate the comfort and security arising from one's "attachment to traditional foods." But it was difficult to deal with the "deeply rooted ethnic features such as a too-dominant (by Canadian standards) father, or the dogmatic (by Canadian standards) adherence to the idea of marriage within one's class, etc." Noting that it was one thing for the social worker "to generalize about self-determination and individualization" and another thing "to guide the client through the psychocultural shoals," Fine suggested that in view of the different cultural milieus presented by the United States and Canada, Canadian social workers might appropriately guide their clients in one direction, and their U.S. counterparts might guide theirs in another.

Fine, again following U.S. writers, did address a central paradox: social workers who embraced a culturally pluralist approach – one that supposedly avoided cultural chauvinism and instead treated everyone as bearers of certain cultural values, customs, and goals – still had to set standards of behaviour and "goals of treatment" for the client, which were themselves "based on a judgment of value which is culturally determined." Given this situation, the caseworker's job was not to help clients "rush headlong towards assimilation" or to remain "within their cultural ghetto," but instead to see the cultural dimension within the casework process as " a process." In setting treatment goals, caseworkers should help clients make the most comfortable cultural adaptation, depending upon such key factors as cultural milieu, stage of acculturation, and the psycho-cultural dynamics of their families. In other words, Fine acknowledged that social work itself took its values from the society of which it was a part. He also admitted that in the face of conflicting values and standards, the profession, like other segments of society, selected certain choices over others.[64]

While social work leaders and senior citizenship bureaucrats defined an agenda, it remained to be seen how the wide array of front-line gatekeepers who worked with European newcomers would deal with high-level abstractions, models, and ideals. What did a social-cultural approach mean in practice? Invariably there would be a gap between the theory and method and the actual implementation, but the range of encounters or relationships that emerged on the front lines was not entirely predictable, nor were the encounters or relationships identical to one another.[65]

Canada's expert gatekeepers tended to see their much-celebrated postwar democratic social welfare state as offering a strong antidote to Communism. But apart from the more hard-core Cold Warriors, who said it was blasphemous to make any accusations of corrupted democracy, many of the country's knowledge-based professionals agreed that the challenge of delivering the promised oranges and humanity to the many European refugees and immigrants rebuilding lives in Canada would require great, perhaps even heroic, efforts.

Institutional Gatekeepers

Democratic Pluralism or Ethnic Containment?

4

IN HIS COMMENTS ON A NATIONAL FILM BOARD SCRIPT for a documentary on immigration being made with the Canadian Citizenship Branch in 1958, branch director Jean Boucher complained about the many errors and statistics, the use of the term assimilation instead of integration, and the overdrawn cultural contrasts between ethnic groups. He advised the film's scriptwriter, Gordon Burwash, to try to make a more interesting film with "more visual emphasis on cultural contributions, like soccer teams, attendance at concerts, visits to galleries and museums, touring the countryside" and "European restaurants, food stores and bakeries." The scenes should show how the newcomers' "complete freedom" brings all of them to the same goal of integration.

Burwash evidently complied. The revised script called for camera shots of soccer players, busy ethnic shops and neighbourhoods, the ballet, and other colourful scenes of Toronto's "growing cosmopolitanism." A voiceover stated, "The newcomers have brought with them a vast array of tastes, traditions, habits, manners, ideas, all different from those of the old Queen City."[1]

In her positive report on the international night held at the International Institute of Metropolitan Toronto in fall 1959, Mrs. Thomas Roberts of the Toronto Local Council of Women described how the lively event had brought Europeans and Canadians together in a celebration of the newcomers' cultures and Canadian citizenship. Against a backdrop of the flags of fifty nations, talented new Canadians had performed. A high-school student, Anne from Poland, played the piano and accordion, and Macedonian-born Joseph, now a public-school teacher, "showed folk dancing of his native country in colourful costume." People shared their "harrowing" experiences in Europe and expressed satisfaction with life in "the freedom of

Opposite: "To dance is to integrate," declared the International Institute of Metropolitan Toronto, which organized dance classes and regular dances in hopes of bringing new and old Canadians together.
(IIMT, F884, B-853)

a democratic country." A Canadian-born schoolgirl and winner of an essay contest spoke on the "World We Want," and another sang a toast to Canada. Surprisingly, given that in the 1950s few survivors spoke publicly about their experiences, the speakers included a young Jewish woman, Rose. As Roberts offensively put it, she "gave a thrilling account of life in the concentration camp." The unfortunate phrase had the effect of trivializing the woman's story, but was also in keeping with the tendency among some of the gatekeepers to repackage the newcomers' complex and traumatic lives into a form of ethnic entertainment.[2]

In the decades after the Second World War international music nights, parades and pageants, craft shows, and folk societies were among the popular strategies used by Canada's institutional gatekeepers to bring about what the chief liaison officer of the Citizenship Branch, Vladimir Kaye, called "the consolidation of the nation." For Kaye and his colleagues, the challenge of moving ahead on this front involved several related tasks. One was to educate all Canadians in the principles of Canadian democracy and develop in all "the pride of belonging to a country built by the common efforts of many peoples." A second was to assist the newcomers' integration into Canadian life by interpreting Canadian culture to them and by ensuring that established or native-born Canadians would accept them – which also meant convincing old Canadians of the valuable contributions that immigrants (and ethnic Canadians) were making to their society and culture.[3] One way of doing this was to facilitate cultural exchanges between new and old Canadians by, for example, inviting both groups to put on pleasing cultural events that would encourage mutual respect and an appreciation of how the lively ethnic cultures could enrich Canada's cultural life.

The officials of the Citizenship Branch saw cultural events and programs as excellent tools for building national unity out of the country's growing ethnic diversity. The term "unity in diversity," which became popular in these years, suggested an appreciative nod to the newcomers' European cultures, although these cultures were valued mainly for their capacity to enrich Canadian society, and not to change it in any substantive way.[4]

The social and cultural programs of the International Institute of Metropolitan Toronto, one of the many social agencies that liaised with the Citizenship Branch, provide a prime example of these complex themes.[5] The Institute's promotion of cultural pluralism involved cleansing the newcomers' threatening elements and reducing intricate traditions into so much entertainment for Canadian consumption. It was a strategy of both cultural appropriation and ethnic containment that can be seen alongside other efforts to contain other perceived threats in early Cold War Canada. Still, there were cracks in this containment approach, as revealed by the newcomers' ability to use cultural platforms to deliver hard-hitting political messages. In the end, ethnicity, far from being an entirely personal identity or objective category, is socially constructed; it is the cultural product of dynamic encounters between unequal groups with both similar and different agendas.[6]

Cultural Interpreters: Origins and Agendas

When the International Institute of Metropolitan Toronto officially opened its doors in October 1956 amid public fanfare, it initiated an important, if flawed, cultural experiment in a rapidly changing city. Assuming the role of cultural interpreter, the Institute proudly declared that it would "build a bridge whose traffic is the interpretation of the newcomer to the Canadian, and of Canadian society to the newcomer."[7]

According to Nell West, its first director, the Institute was not just another social service agency but aimed to bring about a fundamental "readjustment" in the newcomers' social, psychological, and cultural makeup, something that would turn them into model Canadian citizens. Moreover, the Institute aspired to become a meeting place where social mingling between Canadians and newcomers would facilitate mutual respect and appreciation for each other's cultures.[8] Indeed, West and the other founding board members envisioned the Institute as a lively international community, or a local United Nations, where new and old Canadians would work together to build a harmonious, democratic, and multi-ethnic Canada. As the ambassadors of this community, the board and staff would help the two groups "to pursue together common purposes on a basis of mutual respect, equality and non-discrimination in regard to race, nationality, and religion."[9]

These goals of promoting citizenship and democratic values, facilitating the newcomers' integration, and encouraging Canadians to appreciate the newcomers' diverse cultures fit well with the mandate of the Citizenship Branch. Although presented as a new department in 1945, the Citizenship Branch had evolved out of the wartime Nationalities Branch of the Department of War Services. In 1942 the government, in an effort to spy on and rally ethnic Canadians to the war effort, had created the Nationalities Branch as well as the Committee on Co-operation in Canadian Citizenship (CCCC), which advised Ottawa on how to encourage a united war effort among the "other" ethnic groups who had come to represent a sizeable minority (between one-sixth and one-fifth by 1941) of the Canadian population. Many of these "other" Canadians were from Europe, or they were the children of immigrants from Europe, including enemy nations with whom Canada was at war. While other government directives banned foreign-language groups and publications deemed a danger to the Canadian war effort, and interned "enemy aliens" associated with both pro-Communist organizations (mostly progressive Ukrainians) and pro-Nazi and Fascist sympathies (mostly Germans and Italians), the Nationalities Branch, as the administrative arm of the CCCC, was to play a more positive role in encouraging ethnic loyalty to the war by, for example, interpreting the war in Canadian and not merely European terms. It also sought to temper Anglo- and French-Canadian prejudice by reporting on the war work carried out by various ethnic groups.

Both the CCCC and the Nationalities Branch were composed largely of academics with expertise on the European groups. They included G.W. Simpson, a historian and Ukrainian expert at the University of Saskatchewan; Judge W.L. Lindall, an Icelandic specialist in Winnipeg; Tracy Phillips, a British-born academic and senior civil servant who advised on European Affairs; social scientist Robert England; and Watson Kirkconnell, a linguist newly moved to McMaster University and a self-proclaimed defender of Canada's European groups as well as a militant red-baiter. At the Nationalities Branch, Kaye was put in charge of liaison and editorial relations, a job that required him to nurture contacts with Canadian and foreign-language newspaper editors, track the ethnic press for its views on the war, and provide newspapers with war-related press releases and pro-Canadian materials.

The Nationalities Branch, which led a largely precarious existence, was reorganized in 1944 as a Citizenship Division within the Department of War Services. At war's end the CCCC and Department of War Services were dismantled, but the Citizenship Division survived, in 1945 becoming the new Citizenship Branch within the Secretary of State.[10] Later, in 1950, it became part of the new Department of Citizenship and Immigration.[11] During the postwar years Kaye and the staff at the Citizenship Branch continued many of the same activities that they had engaged in during wartime, such as liaising with ethnic press editors (including the new DP refugee editors) and supplying them with pro-democracy materials, and carrying out the political surveillance of the ethnic left and its press, even expanding its operations.[12]

The Citizenship Branch was particularly to address the problems faced by the newcomers as they tried to adapt to a Canadian "national life," which included encouraging their acceptance by "native" Canadians. Frank Foulds, the first director, later admitted in an article that during the war the Nationalities Branch mandate had never been carried out because of the urgency of securing the largest war effort possible; and that Ottawa had established the Citizenship Branch because improving ethnic relations in Canada became more of a priority with renewed immigration in peacetime. Ottawa had also arranged for provincial departments of education to fund local English and citizenship classes held at schools, city settlement houses, and various social agencies. The Citizenship Branch officials promoted basic English (or French) – that is, teaching the language within vocational or other practical contexts – and checked on the progress being made in countless locales. In addition to conducting research on ethnic groups, the Citizenship Branch's Research Division produced the "tools of citizenship training," such as educational materials on Canada's history and government, guides for the citizenship exam, and an array of pamphlets, films, and radio broadcasts. These tools were used to tell newcomers that Canada was a democratic country "where you have the right to life, liberty, security of person, enjoyment of property, protection of the law without discrimination... where you have freedom of speech, freedom of press, of assembly and association and... worship."[13]

The Citizenship Branch officers emphasized that integration was a two-way street; it required the commitment of both established and new Canadians. Furthermore, they were committed to "the enrichment of our Canadian way of life" and fostering national unity. "In a country as vast as Canada, with as many different ethnic groups," explained Foulds,

A teacher at Dewson Public School in heavily immigrant west-end Toronto lets his Polish student bring her two-year-old daughter, born in a German DP camp, to English classes. *Telegram* 17 Sept. 1948.
(YUA, Toronto Telegram, ASC Image 1298)

"it is imperative in the interests of national unity, that the various peoples understand one another, and maintain a sympathetic interest in the problems affecting different groups." Indeed, the Branch articulated an ideology of cultural pluralism within a bilingual, two-founding-nations context that became a central feature of the postwar gatekeepers' liberal discourse. It acknowledged that there were "very large numbers" of "other Canadians" who had made and were continuing to make "important contributions to our society." But it also confirmed the receiving nation's right to mine these cultures for greater national ends. Noting that "Canadian culture had borrowed much from older civilizations," Foulds asserted that Canadians had to recognize that today's newcomers were also bringing in new skills, techniques, and even customs that could greatly benefit the country. While Canadians had a right to ask the newcomers "to adapt to our Canadian way of doing things as quickly as possible in their own interests," there was "no attempt" being made, he claimed, "to mold them into any preconceived form." Instead, they were to appreciate that "while we are offering them opportunity to start life anew, we may benefit from their arrival." (Little was said about the distinctions or tensions between English- and French-Canadian cultures.)

Citizenship Branch officials also depicted the newcomers in a positive light, describing them as eager and anxious to take advantage of the opportunities. Foulds argued that many of them did not even need encouragement to take citizenship classes, but signed up for them wherever they were offered – on the ship, in the city, or in a remote resource town. While there was plenty of interest in many locales, the claim was exaggerated. It also ignored a gender gap: more men than women completed language and citizenship classes in these years, and the gap was greater among lesser-educated Europeans.[14]

Kaye was a fitting choice as the Branch's chief liaison officer. A Ukrainian Canadian with a successful career as a professional academic and government bureaucrat, he met the Canadian state's notion of a model ethnic Canadian. Later on, in 1971, he would receive an Order of Canada. Born Vladimir Kysilewsky, Kaye had fought in the First World War and later studied history at Vienna University, earning his Ph.D. in 1924. He emigrated a year later, at age twenty-nine, to Canada, where he became editor of a Ukrainian newspaper in Edmonton. A few years later he travelled to Chicago and once again worked as a newspaper editor. After returning to Europe in the early 1930s he worked as director of the Ukrainian Press Bureau in London while competing a doctorate at the School of Slavonic and East European Studies, an accomplishment of which he was very proud. He was also very proud of the English woman he married in London. They returned to Canada in 1940, and Kaye accepted the liaison post at the Nationalities Branch. Kaye quickly helped to form the Ukrainian Canadian Committee (UCC), a coalition of conservative, nationalist Ukrainian Canadians, many of them active in the Catholic and Orthodox churches, who wanted to display their public support for the Canadian war effort. In large part this government initiative was meant to secure the loyalty of the nationalist, anti-Communist Ukrainian Canadians. The UCC supported integration into Canadian society, retention of language and culture, and an independent Ukrainian state in Eastern Europe (by the 1920s, ethnic Ukrainians were divided among Poland, Romania, Czechoslovakia, and the Soviet Union). It also actively opposed the left-wing Ukrainian Canadian community, in an ideological war that persisted into the Cold War years.

Kaye continued his career as a civil servant in the postwar Citizenship Branch where, both as a bureaucrat and a Ukrainian-Canadian nationalist, he continued to put plenty of energy into fighting the Ukrainian-Canadian left and seeking ways of undermining it. He also worried lest the obsession of the highly politicized DPs with the liberation of the Ukrainian territories now under Soviet control, to be followed by the creation of an independent Ukraine, would retard the process of transforming Ukrainian newcomers into Ukrainian Canadians. Kaye also taught at the University of Ottawa and wrote a great deal on Ukrainian-Canadian history. A Cold Warrior and crusader for liberal democracy and British traditions in Canada, Kaye saw no contradiction between espousing his liberal and pluralist values while being involved in the political manipulation of the ethnic left.[15]

Kaye's upbeat speeches stressed the Citizenship Branch's contributions to consolidating the nation. In an address to Ukrainian Canadians in Winnipeg in 1951, he typically advised his audience to be patient, to understand that the efforts to integrate newcomers would not produce instantaneous results but, rather, would take time, effort, and even a bit of luck. Kaye likened himself and his Branch staff to the farmer who "ploughs in the spring, sows the seed but has to wait anxious months until autumn arrives… to reap the results of his toil, provided, of course, providence was gracious and sent him rain and sunshine at the right time and hail or frost did not kill or spoil his investment." If all goes well, the farmer can "produce the grain that will be made into bread for your table or sold abroad to help to build a favourable trade balance for our country." Conversely, without precautions and patience, disaster could occur. Kaye concluded that his staff of "modest toilers" similarly hoped that the results of their toil would bring "dividends for individuals [and] the country as a whole" in the form of "growing happiness in your own home, in your community, in harmonious co-operation of its citizens, in diminution of prejudices and intolerance."[16]

In articulating an early version of the unity-in-diversity theme that would later become the basis for a state-defined multiculturalism policy, Kaye used a variety of images and metaphors. In some cases he spoke of how the newcomers were to become members of a colourful Canadian orchestra, with the state as the powerful but culturally sensitive conductor. Another metaphor was the salad: in contrast to the melted-down soup of the United States, for example, Kaye depicted Canada as a delicious salad, with the newcomers providing many of the tasty ingredients. He often used food examples to argue that immigration was saving Canada from standardization and blandness. In at least one speech, Kaye rhetorically asked his audience to imagine a menu that consisted solely of canned tomato soup.

To carry out the Branch's role as the link between the federal government and the many groups concerned with the citizenship and integration of immigrants, Kaye supervised a staff of front-line liaison officers who, like him, travelled extensively to gather information and dispense advice or materials. Initially a small group of liaison officers based at national headquarters in Ottawa visited locales across the country. By 1950 a level of regional officers was added, beginning with Toronto. By 1956 regional officers were based in Montreal, Vancouver, Winnipeg, Edmonton, Saskatoon, Hamilton, Sackville, and Toronto. Besides civil servants, the officers included a lawyer, a survivor, and university graduates with some social work training.

With respect to the cultural mandate, the officers worked with countless volunteer groups, citizenship committees and councils, folk societies, interfaith groups, and ethnic Canadian organizations. They helped to organize folk festivals, art exhibitions, and choirs. They brought groups together to mount cultural events. For example, if a citizenship committee connected to a women's, veteran's, or service group wanted to organize a cultural event but had no "cultural contacts," the liaison officers put them in touch with a folk society or a refugee artist or folk-dancing troupe. The officers distributed citizenship materials, delivered addresses, and attended conferences and meetings. At times they provided personal counselling, almost entirely with professionally trained and intellectual refugees whose integration, Kaye argued, enhanced the department's prestige. The officers ran workshops on citizenship training (with titles such as "Freedom of Expression" and "The State and the Individual") and leadership training camps. They stayed in touch with ethnic-Canadian societies because, as Kaye put it, the societies had a "special contribution to make to the integration of newcomers" and to "general citizenship," provided they had acceptable politics. Indeed, Kaye boasted that his staff had the most "specialized knowledge" of the ethnic groups and "carried out a constant exchange of information" with them. Special liaison officers for women (Constance Hayward) and youth (W.M. Haughan) performed similar duties. For example, Hayward advised women's groups on the choice of educational materials (such as Margaret McWilliams's *This Is Canada*, Vincent Massey's *On Being Canadian*, and Robert England's *Contemporary Canada*) and helped develop "dialogue material" for group discussions. Haughan liaised with Canadian youth groups such as the Boys Scouts and Girl Guides, and encouraged European youth to join these groups rather than European-based groups, some of which were thought to have questionable politics.[17]

The Citizenship Branch especially encouraged activities that facilitated social mingling and cultural exchange between new and old Canadians. Once the newcomers had acquired some knowledge of either official language, argued Kaye, they could "best learn about Canada at lectures, conferences and social gatherings where newcomers and Canadians participate together and by which their integration is completed." The local and regional liaison officers were to assist the various groups interested in encouraging this cultural and social exchange. One of the most active organizations in this regard was the International Institute of Metropolitan Toronto.[18]

Towards a Local United Nations in Toronto?

The origins of the International Institute of Metropolitan Toronto date to 1952, when a group of concerned citizens, supported by the Imperial Order Daughters of the Empire, established the New Canadians Service Agency (NCSA), a counselling service for newcomers that operated out of one, and then two, small rooms in downtown Toronto. In 1954, when the Junior League of Toronto adopted the Agency as a charitable project, it moved to larger quarters and as its director of services hired Nell West, who had been the assistant deputy minister of Public Welfare in Ontario during the Depression of the 1930s and had worked as an administrator for UNRRA after the war.

The NCSA was mainly concerned with job placement but also participated in citizenship receptions. In October 1956 it amalgamated with St. Andrew's Memorial House, a friendship house for newcomers that had also been providing job placement and counselling services as well as running cultural activities, particularly for refugees who were academics, and for other professionals. The new agency, operating out of the St Andrew's building at 415 Jarvis Street, joined the American Federation of International Institutes, becoming the International Institute of Metropolitan Toronto. The Toronto Institute, the Federation's only Canadian affiliate, also became a member agency of the United Appeal and thus received charitable funds from several levels of government.[19]

The first American International Institute, created in New York City in 1910, had grown out of the YWCA movement, which had focused on serving the needs of working women, including immigrant women and girls, in the city. By 1956 more than sixty U.S. immigrant social agencies were affiliated with the Federation, whose mandate was to provide practical assistance to newcomers while also working to preserve immigrant cultures through, for example, cultural clubs and children's language classes. The Institutes had developed a philosophy of integration that encouraged the different "nationality groups" to retain a good part of their cultural heritage and to continue to participate in their ethnic community life while also accepting and incorporating American culture and becoming loyal Americans. They invited "ethnic representatives" to join their staffs and local "ethnic communities" to contribute programs, and even talked of wanting to build "multi-ethnic community centres."[20]

The Toronto Institute's first board did not entirely agree with the Federation's pluralist philosophy of integration, emphasizing instead the need to help newcomers move out of their own ethnic groups as quickly as possible. Indeed, they had a policy of discouraging newcomers from using their own languages and from clustering in their "nationality groups," and this approach created resentment on the part of the newcomers.[21] But they did share other aspects of the Federation's mandate, including that of wanting the various "ethnic groups" to eventually join in the democratic running of the Institute's social and cultural programs. Still, the International Institute of Metropolitan Toronto did not clearly define what it meant by ethnic groups and cultures, or whether a recognition of ethnic groups fit with its principle of speedy integration and fostering a renewed Canadian culture enriched by the Europeans. Nor did it ever invite more than a few "ethnic representatives," mostly men, to join its board, which was always dominated by well-heeled Toronto citizens, politicians, and social welfare personnel. The first board, for example, included David Croll, the pro-immigration Liberal MP and later a Senator; Father Mulvihill of Catholic Immigrant Services; William Archer, a Toronto city councilman and later an MP; Peggy Jennings of the IODE; and citizenship official Stephen Davidovich.[22]

Nell West, a founding board member of the Toronto Institute, was its first executive director. A University of Chicago-trained social worker, veteran welfare bureaucrat, and a childless war widow, she was nicknamed "Mrs. International Institute" and remained devoted to the organization even after her demotion, in 1962,

Nell West hosts a Christmas dinner for members at the International Institute, *circa* 1958.
(IIMT, F884, B-853)

from executive director to director of group services in charge of social and cultural programs – a demotion that seems to smack of male chauvinism.[23] Her immediate successors, all men, did not match her credentials for the job. They included two retired military officers: H.C. Forbell, who had supervised a multinational NATO squadron; and wealthy British immigrant John Montfort, who had learned Italian at a private school and done public relations work for the Royal Family. The staff included middle-class Canadian professionals and volunteers and some newcomers who were mainly East Europeans from middle-class backgrounds. A few of the staff members, including Estonian-born Robert Kreem, had social work training. Kreem had worked in the refugee camps, studied social work in Canada and the United States, and became director of group services after West's retirement in 1965.[24]

The Toronto Institute performed three roles: community relations and advocacy work; group services (running in-house programs such as English classes, table tennis games, and dance nights), and individual services (counselling and referral). The community relations and advocacy work involved various efforts to create a local United Nations with a mix of people enjoying cultural programs and lessons in Canadian freedom, citizenship, and democratic decision-making. Initially, things looked promising. The Institute quickly became Toronto's largest immigrant agency. Its projects and events gained plenty of attention, and tens of thousands of newcomers and many "old Canadians" entered its doors during the late 1950s and the 1960s. But by 1974, amid charges of irrelevance and financial mismanagement, it had closed its doors.[25]

Reaching out to "the Ethnic Groups"

Most of Canada's gatekeepers tried in some way to reach out to various immigrant and ethnic constituencies, and, like Kaye and other Citizenship Branch officers, they saw ethnic-Canadian organizations (except for left-wing ones) not only as cushions against initial shock but also as Canadianization agents in their own right. The International Institute of Metropolitan Toronto was hostile to the idea of ethnic organizations serving as agents of Canadianization. While it is not entirely clear why, the hostility does help to explain some of the Institute's curious behaviour and perhaps why, ultimately, it was perceived to be so out of touch with Toronto's newcomers.

As part of its community outreach, the group services staff encouraged newcomers to take out House memberships for a small fee, which allowed them to participate in the Institute's various clubs and programs. The group services staff also organized events to attract and encourage social mingling of new and old Canadians. Most of the members were white Europeans,[26] and most of those were men, particularly young single men who joined specific groups, such as the chess or outdoor clubs, or attended the weekly dances hoping to meet young single women. (On this score, they were sorely disappointed because the few women who did attend were mostly Canadian volunteers.)

As a way of attracting more people, the Institute also invited ethnic-Canadian organizations to take on group memberships and to help mount events that would attract other prospective members. The Institute created a Community Relations Branch to establish positive relations with individuals of influence within ethnic communities – again, largely in the hope of recruiting more members. With little regard to who actually composed these different immigrant and ethnic societies, however, the board and staff simply collapsed them into an abstract category, "the ethnic groups," or, alternatively, the Scandinavians, Bulgarians, and so on. Hence the board spoke of planning "an entertainment night" by "the ethnic groups" to celebrate the winning of a large grant. Similarly, a staff member suggested that the organization give "inter-ethnic relations" a boost by organizing a "colourful and memorable event," namely, "an all-out parade of our ethnic groups."[27]

This cultural streamlining reflected the Toronto Institute's philosophy that the best way of speeding up the newcomers' full integration into the mainstream was to replace, indeed, usurp, the role of immigrant or ethnic organizations as quickly as possible. Ethnic organizations might help to preserve cultural heritages, which was fine, but they also encouraged that disagreeable pattern of ethnic "huddling" and retarded Canadianization. By contrast, the Institute was serving to produce "a mix of groups, of newcomer and old-timers and natives," argued Czech-Canadian John

Gellner, a retired air force officer who served on the organization's board of directors. Thus it was "comparably more beneficial than any ethnic organization."[28]

The Institute's leaders argued that they could bring about "a closer and more cooperative relationship between the various ethnic groups" and thus ease the "various inter-ethnic tensions... carried over from Europe." For West and her colleagues, a key prerequisite for easing tensions was to stamp out "old country prejudices" and misplaced feuds from Europe and to urge all immigrants to disperse into the wider population. They highly approved of the Scandinavians and Hungarians who, in contrast to the Italians, did not form "strong" nationality groups by sticking together.[29] At the same time they invited all of the immigrant and ethnic-Canadian groups and organizations to make their needs and interests known, and to participate fully in the programs. But with no structures in place for facilitating concrete input, many newcomers did not do much more than attend a few meetings or help organize a number of events.[30]

The Toronto Institute's approach to ethnic organizations revealed a degree of cultural chauvinism and insensitivity, not to mention political naïveté . In a manner akin to that familiar imperialist policy of ruling through the collaboration of elites, the staff and board assumed that ordinary immigrants and ethnic Canadians could be most efficiently mobilized through well-placed ethnic elites. Reasoning that ethnic leaders wielded considerable influence over their own groups, they sought out those whom they believed could effectively deliver them the members and publicity. These people included ethnic-press editors, and, like Kaye and his liaison staff, West and her colleagues tried to cultivate their support. At one point West invited a group of editors to her cottage. Afterwards she happily reported that all of them had agreed on the importance of "creating good public relations and understanding between the ethnic groups and the Institute" and that the editors had promised to give "marvelous publicity" to the Institute for an upcoming membership drive.[31] Her successor as director of services, Kreem, continued along the same lines by throwing cocktail parties (something that Citizenship Branch officials also did for ethnic-press editors) and by creating a Nationality Council of ethnic leaders who were invited to help the Institute better define the newcomers' needs. These efforts garnered media coverage for the Institute, but produced no long-term results.[32]

Given that ethnic organizations do not usually represent more than a small percentage of people in a given immigrant or ethnic group, the Institute's strategy of recruiting newcomers through ethnic elites or organizations was familiar but flawed. More importantly, the Toronto Institute and the ethnic organizations were pursuing antithetical goals. The Institute wanted to bring as many newcomers as possible under its Canadianizing bosom with the ultimate aim of moving immigrants out of their so-called nationality groups as quickly and fully as possible. The Institute's ethnic organizations obviously supported the principle of integration, but they did not want to make themselves redundant; they were not interested in being temporary "shock absorbers" that would simply wear themselves out and be discarded after the newcomers' "absorption" into the mainstream. Whether mainly immigrant or ethnic Canadian in origin, many of the organizations planned to stick around, and, like Kaye, some of them espoused an early form of hyphenated-Canadian identity.

The Toronto Institute's position suggests a lack of understanding of the era's complex ethnic-community politics. After the war many older ethnic-Canadian organizations needed new immigrant members if they were to make up for the war-time loss of members. Greater numbers would ensure their continuing existence and, depending upon their success, expand their base and increase their political clout both within the particular ethnic community and the Canadian political arena. This need helps to explain, for example, why older ethnic-Canadian organizations such as the Canadian Polish Congress became involved in immigrant aid work. Their handbooks did not simply replicate government publications but stressed their role as an ethnic intermediary whose members shared the newcomers' language and culture and could provide them with the support that no outsider could. Among Ukrainian Canadians and other groups, the women's organizations reached out particularly to female newcomers, offering them advice, information, and English classes.[33]

However, many of the pre-war groups ultimately failed to rebuild organizations that had been crushed during the war or to create larger new ones with many postwar newcomers. Tensions generally characterized the relations between pre-war and postwar members in many ethnic communities, and in many cases the postwar immigrants eventually created their own organizations. A significant exception was the Ukrainian Canadian Committee. Here, too, tensions existed between the pre-war nationalist Ukrainian Canadians and postwar nationalist Ukrainian DP members. The most important tension was triggered by the militantly nationalist politics of the highly politicized DP arrivals, but class and educational differences also played a role: the postwar refugees included more urban and professional people, whereas the earlier immigrants were largely of peasant stock. But in the long run the anti-Communist new arrivals and the anti-Communist Canadian-born Ukrainians expanded the base of the Ukrainian Canadian Committee, which called itself the official voice of the nationalist community (that is, those groups that denounced communism and lobbied vigorously for the liberation of Ukraine from the Soviet Union). Numerically small refugee groups, such as the Latvians or Lithuanians, whose pre-war migration had also been small, were almost entirely composed of newcomers.[34]

Kaye and his Citizenship Branch officers better respected the (non-Communist) ethnic organizations as agents of Canadianization and defenders of Canadian democracy in the Cold War, but they too focused on elites and collaboration. They routinely met to draw up lists of well-placed people, usually male ethnic-press editors, presidents of ethnic organizations, judges, politicians, professors, and industrialists. Kaye advised his staff to maintain "close contacts with prominent persons of the new immigrants, former University professors, members of European parliaments, publishers and journalists." Conversely, he and his officers complained about heavily rural and formally uneducated immigrants such as the Italians, because they did not appear to have "natural leaders" among them. The officials also worked through the Canadian elites who dealt with the newcomers, and especially through churches. For example, liaison reports on Quebec show an ongoing reliance on Catholic priests and organizations. Also, notwithstanding claims to the contrary, Kaye and his colleagues regularly summed up an ethnic group by reference to one or another set of characteristics, thereby collapsing a host of internal differences. At times this tendency could be positive, as when the liaison officers were told to bear in mind that the Mennonite group "never enters into a written contract but prefers to be dealt with on a basis of understanding and confidence." The officers also briefed each other about tensions and rivalries within the ethnic groups. Of the Germans, it was reported that the postwar newcomers felt superior to the older German Canadians and also resented them for not having helped Germany during the war.[35]

It is not that individual Institute leaders did not have good personal relations with Toronto's ethnic leaders – West and the press editors seemed to be on good terms – but Kaye's faith in the capacity of ethnic-Canadian organizations to act as integration agents, and the Citizenship Branch's acceptance that the groups would remain a permanent feature of a consolidated Canadian nation, made for more positive relations with ethnic leaders and societies than was the case at the Institute. Still, this approach did not necessarily translate into different kinds of activities. As one of his first tasks in the Citizenship Branch Kaye helped to organize celebrations marking the sixtieth anniversary of the arrival of Ukrainians in Canada. For this event, held at the National Museum and National Gallery in Ottawa, Kaye, too, went with colourful pageantry.

Promoting Democracy, Cultivating Citizenship

One of the major goals of the gatekeepers was to encourage and prepare the newcomers to apply for Canadian citizenship. The various officials involved advocated vivid ceremonies to mark the occasion in every local court, as well as sponsoring school essay competitions and other citizenship activities throughout the year. To bring publicity to the new Canadian Citizenship Act, which became law in January 1947, and to demonstrate to newcomers the great value of becoming citizens, the

Citizenship Branch organized an elaborate National Citizenship Ceremony in the Supreme Court of Canada. In front of a large crowd, the country's top judges handed out special symbolic certificates to a distinguished group of Canadians – from photographer Yousuf Karsh to the elderly Ukrainian pioneer settler Wasyl Elyniak – who were meant to represent the whole spectrum of Canada's citizenry.[36] For most citizenship celebrations, however, volunteers organized local citizenship ceremonies, which often involved "a social hour with refreshments" following the swearing-in ceremony at the local court. While not nearly as extravagant, these events, too, were meant to be colourful affairs that would "make the new Canadian feel that he has become an important member of the community, and impress him with the responsibilities and privileges of Canadian citizenship."[37]

The National Citizenship Ceremony to celebrate Canada's first Citizenship Act. Here, Nestor Roakowitza, a Romanian-born farmer, takes the oath of allegiance before Chief Justice Thibaudeau Rinfret of the Supreme Court of Canada, Ottawa, 3 Jan. 1947. (Photograph by Chris Lund; LAC, National Film Board, PA-189258)

A particularly enthusiastic group was the IODE. It pushed for more elaborate citizenship celebrations (so as to better underscore the importance of the moment) while lobbying Ottawa for more demanding exams that would require greater study and commitment on the applicants' part. Ottawa repeatedly rejected the proposal about the tests on the reasonable grounds that overly difficult exams would mean many failures and discourage others from taking the exam.[38] When judges complained about a lack of guidelines for assessing candidates, they were told to simply exercise good judgment, or in other words to be generous. As they faced people who had lived in war-torn or Communist Europe, some judges and candidates used the occasion to stress that the people had made the right choice in coming to a free and democratic Canada.[39]

Canadian citizenship advocates, including those at the Toronto Institute, were also particularly concerned that the European newcomers, especially people who had lived under totalitarian regimes of the right or left, learn (or relearn) their civic duties in a liberal democracy and gain practical experience at exercising those duties, beginning at the local or community level. To develop the appropriate skills the Institute's group services staff used a mix of what they called serious or intellectual techniques of integration, such as lectures and study groups, and lighter social techniques, such as card games, sports, and dances. To be most effective, however, all of these activities required a mix of new, ethnic, and old Canadians. Indeed, the presence of old Canadians was paramount to the Institute's self-perception as a meeting place in which the newcomers could make the shift, through supervised conditions, from their insular ethnic worlds to the broader society and its

Staff members of the International Institute of Metropolitan Toronto pose with new citizens at a city hall citizenship reception, Toronto, 19 May 1959.
(IIMT, F884, B-853)

various duties. At the Institute, publicity flyers declared, "The established Canadian meets the 'new' Canadian and gets to know him and social contacts are made that eventually provide the opportunity for the new immigrant to take part in social and cultural activity in the broader community and enable him to assume the responsibility of citizenship."[40] Thus the Canadian also gained something important from the process. As Kreem explained it, the Institute's social programs were vehicles that prepared the newcomers to step into the wider community. As they learned more about themselves, Canadians, and Canada through discussions, films, field trips, dances, and other joint activities, their self-worth would grow and their usefulness to Canadian society would increase.[41]

Educational materials, many of them produced by the Citizenship Branch, also provided lessons in the moral superiority of Western democracies like Canada. In addition to a small library, the Institute ran lecture series and workshops (with sessions on topics such as "What Makes a Good Citizen?") that were intended not only to teach Canadian civics or democracy but also to encourage the newcomers to reflect upon their own integration into Canadian society. In 1959 this technique reportedly worked well with recently formed practical psychology and discussion groups.[42] By the early 1960s the Institute's Individual Services Department was attracting far more immigrants from low-income groups, including Italians, Greeks, and Portuguese, but the group services staff stuck largely to the intellectual techniques that evidently had more appeal among middle-class refugees.[43]

The lighter techniques of bridge, chess, or dancing were recognized to be more of an equalizer, though their influence was exaggerated. According to the Institute, when a mix of newcomers and old Canadians played cards or took dance lessons, they were "learning tolerance, understanding of one another and truly, the concept of integration."[44] Glowing reports of these social events abound, especially as recorded by the Institute staff, who stressed the positive atmosphere that resulted when the members enjoyed appealing music or fun dances, or acted in good fellowship – and when they avoided the expression of prejudice created by historical conflicts and showed mutual respect.

But by far the best way that the newcomers could learn the organizational and leadership skills so necessary to doing their civic duty in a liberal democracy was to be given the opportunity to run their own clubs and events and to join in the running of the sports leagues, ethnic weeks, and other events. As a staff supervisor observed, when they were well organized, these group activities could ensure that the newcomer was being "rechanneled into the mainstream of the life of his new social environment."[45] Once again, however, a key condition of success was that they do so as part of a mixed group of old Canadians and newcomers from different homelands. Conversely, the staff frowned on those who evidently used the Institute merely as a social club or, worse, for just lounging or

As part of the organized recreational program for members, most of them men, an Institute female staff member plays table tennis with a new Canadian male partner. (IIMT, F884, B-853)

hanging out. If alienation led to dangerous possibilities (such as a seduction to communism) so too did just hanging out. It attracted "the least stable elements" and discouraged "the more conservative and stable person" – an untenable situation given that "a substantial number" of the stable sort were considered necessary if the "least stable" were to be "absorbed."[46] Here, the danger was clearly gendered as male. "Unstable element" was a code for groups of idle young men, who were seen as being more prone than women to destructive or pathological behaviour.

Participatory Democracy within Limits

Whatever its limitations, the Toronto Institute's approach to encouraging participatory democracy, building civic-mindedness, and developing leadership skills paralleled those of most other institutional gatekeepers, including the YWCA and the settlement houses of Toronto. Indeed, imparting such values and skills had long been a central purpose of modern urban social and recreational movements in North America and elsewhere. When the YWCA in Toronto agreed to the government's request to help settle a group of DP domestic worker recruits, it offered each woman a gift – a new dress and pair of heels – that combined practicality with a touch of modern fashion. It also took on the role of cultural interpreter for the women and their employers, explaining the wages and workload expectations and, on occasion, intervening in disputes. Moreover, it gave out free Y memberships to the women in hopes that they would become full-fledged members and eventually participate in the democratic running of their own and other Y programs and thus develop civic skills. Seeing itself as a democratically run organization with many groups that led their own programs, the Y clearly hoped that young female refugees of totalitarianism would learn first-hand the responsibilities and rewards of democracy. The Toronto Institute also believed that club memberships and "inter-ethnic" events would allow the newcomers to learn the new habits and behaviour of participatory democracy.[47]

Many of the institutional gatekeepers agreed that these activities had to be well structured and adequately supervised, but, once again, the Institute appears to have been more strict or elitist, or perceived as such by the newcomers, than were other, community-based agencies such as the settlement houses. At the Institute the board and staff insisted on maintaining firm control over all the groups and activities and delivered the impression that they would never entirely trust the newcomers to run activities on their own. Thus, for all of the Institute's talk about encouraging grassroots democracy, community leadership skills, and civic-mindedness, the staff carried out a top-down policy of ethnic containment. When newcomers did organize a club or group, a staff member had to attend every meeting to ensure conformity to all the rules. The staff even inspected the correspondence of each group, thus, ironically, engaging in the surveillance of newcomers while extolling the virtues of democratic openness and trying to stamp out the problems inherited from Europe, including totalitarian-induced fears of Big Brother-type authorities. At least a few of the newcomers deeply resented the staff's intrusion into their activities. But once again no structures were introduced that would have allowed for a respectable degree of group autonomy. The principle of cultural pluralism, however modest, again faltered on the elitism and even distrust of these gatekeepers towards their clientele.[48]

The protesters would have been mostly men given that the Institute drew comparatively small numbers of women, Canadian or newcomer, to its clubs and social programs. Although the Individual Services Department had a large female immigrant clientele, who sought practical help to get jobs and solve a range of personal and family problems, comparatively few of them attended the social, cultural, or recreational programs. In response the staff tried to develop programs specifically to draw in more women. These programs were highly predictable: "We think in terms of crafts from other countries, practical skills, and subjects of interest to hostesses and others," read a 1960 report.[49] But the staff also created film and study groups and educational programs aimed specifically at the newcomer woman, who, it was argued, was either too isolated in her home and community to be sufficiently exposed to Canadian ways or too busy juggling the double day of paid and unpaid work to become involved with community programs aimed at Canadianization.

As an inducement to women, especially homemakers, the Institute ran programs relating to home and children. For instance, staff brought in speakers "to talk about Canadian food, Home and School Association, how to buy clothes, etc." Whatever the program, one rule remained the same: "At all times, English should be encouraged."[50] These activities drew some occasional and paid-up members, but in general attendance remained low and intermittent. By contrast, industrial-power sewing classes introduced in the early 1960s attracted a regular flow of working-class women, especially Italian and Portuguese, seeking jobs or hoping to land better jobs in the city's garment shops. These less-educated women made pragmatic use of the Institute's practical services, such as job training, but few of them joined its cultural programs.[51]

In contrast to community-based agencies, such as the settlement houses, which ran sports programs for both genders, the Institute's sports clubs and leagues appeared to focus mainly on men's sports teams. Still, the Institute was serving its main constituency, young single men who could participate in summer baseball leagues and play "that great Canadian game, hockey" (on roads and on ice). In recognition of the popularity of soccer (or European football) among European newcomers, the staff also arranged competitions in that game, but, like their counterparts elsewhere, they were disturbed by the rowdiness that came with the sport. Complaints about flare-ups at parks were common, especially in large cities like Toronto, and came to the attention of the Citizenship Branch officials on more than one occasion. Like West of the Institute, many Canadian gatekeepers blamed the importation of old prejudices and rivalries between European groups and nations, but badly trained referees and umpires were also singled out as a problem. A bad call often insulted people on one or the other side and prompted the shouting matches that sometimes led to fistfights and even veritable riots.

Given the Institute's view that the main cause of the problem was that "local soccer is organized on a strongly nationalist and ethnic basis" and thus "European wars are being fought" in city parks, its board and staff would have preferred mixed or inter-ethnic teams, but no such league appears to have gotten off the ground in these years. Still, the Citizenship Branch officers made a few modest but positive interventions. In 1957, for example, the Toronto Ukrainian Soccer Team had been suspended from the National Football League after its fans, angry over various referee calls, had totally disrupted several games. The Toronto regional officer John Sharp had dealt with the "hard feelings" resulting from the suspension by negotiating with the league to have the club reinstated and the newcomer referees sent to a referee school in winter months to learn Canadian rules. The move appeared to improve the situation. One other explanation for the soccer problem was considered – namely, that ethnic Canadian Communists were deliberately trying to create mayhem in the city parks – but this argument was discarded.[52]

Many of Canada's institutional gatekeepers agreed with the principle of social mingling among new and old Canadians, but perhaps none were as adamant as the

Toronto Institute, which saw the presence of large numbers of old Canadians as absolutely necessary to ensuring that "old world prejudices" were not permanently transplanted to Canadian soil. This position reflected the board and staff's view of integration as a cleansing process that removed or at least contained the contaminations of an old and festering Europe, with its ravished war zones, hunger and suffering, age-old ethnic conflicts, and spreading communism.[53] The newcomers were pathologized as the products of a corrupt and embattled Europe, and it was up to Canadians – lots of Canadians – to transform them into Canadian citizens who could "enter all the rooms of our House and live as true Canadians under the Union Jack, symbol of freedom and equality."[54]

Given the fundamental role that Canadian-born Torontonians were expected to play in the Institute's integration program and cultural mandate, the Institute's failure to attract a large and permanent group of Canadian volunteers ultimately undermined its project. This lack of support was a perennial problem, which partly explains why the Institute was so fulsome in its praise of the volunteer (a great democratic "catalyzer"). At times the Institute was virtually forced to beg ordinary Torontonians to act as "truly democratic, considerate citizens" and befriend the newcomers.[55]

Although no precise figures exist on the numbers of old Torontonians who joined the Institute, there are plenty of references to their insufficient numbers by the staff and board as well as an external assessor, the Toronto Welfare Council (precursor to the Social Planning Council), which reviewed city agencies that received United Appeal funds. Most of the Canadian volunteer members appear to have been single, educated, middle-class women, who included nurses, teachers, and social workers. The social workers probably included University of Toronto social work students, male and female, doing placements or field work – that is, they had a professional interest in being at the Institute. The other female helping professionals may well have been there for similar reasons – encountering newcomers in their own workplaces, they may have wanted to get a better "fix" on them or simply wanted to help. These were not exactly "ordinary" Canadians freely joining the Institute's important cultural experiment.[56]

Newcomers on Display

Although the organization failed to attract as many old Canadians as desired, the Toronto Institute's social and cultural events did attract audiences, including Institute members and those connected to the schools and women's groups that helped to organize these events. Organizers were well aware that many Torontonians harboured fears about the growing numbers of foreigners in their city, and that many newcomers distrusted Canadians. One way to break through this wall of mutual fear and hostility, they believed, was to mount lively, interesting, and fun events that presented the newcomers in the best possible light by showcasing their cultural talents and demonstrating their appreciation for having been given the opportunity to live in Canada.

The Toronto Institute was not alone in seeking to counteract negative images of the Europeans by providing Canadians with pleasant portraits of them as friendly folk wearing lavish costumes, following quaint traditions, and filling the room with their moving music. The newcomers were invited by one Canadian group after another to perform their ethnicity – and to do so in ways that displayed their desire to become Canadian citizens as well as demonstrate the pleasing cultural forms that they were offering as a contribution to society. Canadians were thus being provided with a form of contained ethnicity by which strange and even potentially dangerous foreigners were rendered into fascinating ethnic folk. West's comments about the value of an annual "folk ball" were to the point: it "gives New Canadians an opportunity to identify themselves through their colourful costumes and their lively nationality dances, as well as to meet people from outside their groups."[57]

Both the ethnic and mainstream media featured plenty of images of European newcomers in "traditional" costumes. The most common image was that of young women, like this Dutch woman celebrating Christmas, decked out in full ethnic regalia. (MHSO, A-388 12-16, MSR 00876, no.17)

Alternatively, there were the performers of high culture – violinists, pianists, ballet dancers, opera singers – who could also be brought into the Canadian bosom and used to enrich the quality of Canadian culture. In return the Canadian audiences could be gracious in their appreciation of the newcomers' talents and efforts. On occasion they could do more than that. For example, one twelve-year-old Polish school girl clearly outperformed everyone else in a violin contest at the Canadian National Exhibition, but could not take home the $500 prize because she was not yet a citizen. In response the director of the competition promised to raise the equivalent of the scholarship, which was meant to cover piano lessons, even

Many organized ethnic events, such as this Ontario Human Rights Commission dinner, *circa* 1959, had attractive young immigrant and ethnic women in full ethnic regalia serving tea or food or performing.
(IIMT, F884, B-853)

if he had to give up smoking to come up with some of the money himself. He then upped the ante by stressing that the girl was an especially fitting recipient. Her brave family had walked many miles "to get away from Communist control." They lived in a one-room flat in Toronto, where the girl had to practise her violin in a cold, musty basement.[58]

This same complicated process of both celebrating and appropriating the newcomers' European cultural forms for Canada's greater benefit was at work in the Institute's ethnic weeks. West had initiated the program, which again involved the collaboration of new and old Canadian groups. Each ethnic week featured a different group but followed a set pattern: Sunday tea with music, songs, and dances; a cultural lecture on Wednesday; a nationality dinner on Thursday; and folk dancing on Friday night. Throughout the week the appropriate crafts and handicrafts were on display at the Institute for everyone to enjoy.[59] People from other ethnic groups as well as old Canadians were to be there too. Indeed, success depended on the established Canadians' enjoyment and approval. For their part, the newcomers were expected to perform their role as pleasing, decorative symbols of Canadian tolerance and pluralism, and to perform an ethnicity that was a carefully contained presentation of music, costumes, dances, handicrafts, and food.[60]

Over the last thirty years, historians of immigrant and ethnic cultures in North America and elsewhere have come to better appreciate immigrant folk culture as a flexible and evolving phenomenon. They have highlighted the adaptive role that transplanted cultures can play as newcomers remake their lives in new contexts. Far from being merely a means of clinging to the past, the newcomers' folk culture – which includes their values, rituals, and customs as well as traditional dances, music, and craft work – can provide them with an alternative source of knowledge, meaning, and understanding. For example, immigrant and radical ethnic workers such as the left-wing Ukrainians and Finns, whose cultural world was heavily rooted in the ethnic cultural halls and labour temples, not only used familiar music, songs, plays, and poetry to promote solidarity, but also altered the music or words as they were exposed to North American sounds and rhythms. Similarly, many new and ethnic Canadians continued to celebrate ancient holiday rituals in Canada while modifying their routines and customs to integrate "Canadian" holiday rituals and foods into their lives.[61] These newer understandings of ethnicity challenged earlier social science models that treated the traditions as being more or less the result of a natural collective identity that emerges among like groups or as a static snapshot of culture.[62]

The gatekeepers, however, could reduce the complex and always evolving folk cultures into simple set pieces. A portrait of a Ukrainian woodcarver that appeared in the Institute newsletter presented the man more as a colourful trinket-maker than as a proud and virile craftsman.[63] At the Institute and elsewhere, young immigrant women were dressed up as ornaments to bring colour to various cultural events. They might act as "pretty attendants" at a handicraft or food fair exhibit or as "pretty servers" helping with tea or food at a citizenship party or charity fundraiser. Decked out in full ethnic regalia, these pretty women – among them Bulgarians, Lithuanians, Estonians, Hungarians, and Greeks – were the cute come-on expected to draw in more people.[64] Some ethnic men appeared in similar contexts. In a *Toronto Star* feature headlined "Macedonian, Serbian and Ukrainian Communities Celebrate New Year in Gay and Colorful Costumes," a photograph depicted both pretty smiling women and the fun and harmless customs involving young men. The article noted, "In the tradition of their country, Ukrainian boys roved from house to house bringing good wishes to all." The men were in essence being packaged as non-threatening ethnics who, contrary to common stereotypes of them as louts or dangerous men, were pleasant and entertaining folk.[65]

In their coverage of the social events of ethnic societies, especially dances and balls, Toronto's newspapers printed eye-catching photos of glamorous ethnic women wearing revealing gowns and shimmering jewellery. The image of a German-born, Marilyn Monroe look-alike dominated the local coverage of the founding by immigrants of the German Aero Club Harmonie in Toronto. Similarly, media coverage of the debutante parties of ethnic Canadian women, such as one held by the Canadian Polish Congress, featured glamour shots of young, pretty ethnic girls. The ethnic organizations ran their own beauty contests, and in 1950 the *Star* featured a captivating photograph of the winner of the "Miss Holland Marsh" beauty pageant. Sixteen-year-old Gertrude Kanyo was wearing a bathing suit and banner, and proudly displayed "a beautiful stalk of celery" as a corsage. Like the media narratives of escape that featured attractive East European women, these slim and colourfully or elegantly dressed women challenged the prevailing North American images of both the masculine East European woman and the plump Ukrainian baba or Italian, German, or Portuguese mama.[66]

Many newcomer artists – dancers, painters, and musicians – were aghast at the state of Canadian culture and complained about Canada being a cultural backwater. But some of them would play key roles in enlarging the Canadian high-culture scene. They took on positions as dancers and choreographers in the ballet companies, which had long been open to Russian and other European influences.

Ludmilla Chiriaeff, a Latvian-born prima ballerina who immigrated to Canada after first settling in Switzerland, founded Les Grands Ballets Canadiens de Montréal. Many elite refugee artists and musicians considered Canada a cultural backwater, but some, like Chiriaeff, vowed to improve the nation's cultural scene – and did so.
(Collection de la Bibliothéque de la danse de l'école superieure de ballet contemporain)

They joined orchestras and symphonies. Perhaps no one took to this role as quickly as the ballet dancer and choreographer Ludmilla Chiriaeff. Born in Riga, Latvia, of a Russian family who had fled the Bolshevik Revolution in 1917, she spent several years of the Second World War performing in Berlin before being imprisoned in a German work camp. Escaping from the camp, to avoid capture by the liberating Russian Army, which, she had heard, was punishing Russians or former Russians who had supported Germany, she sought refuge in Hanover, Germany. A speaker of many languages, Chiriaeff worked with Allied personnel during the resettlement of the refugees and then emigrated to Switzerland, where she lived, unhappily, for several years. She gained admission to Canada in 1952 and settled in Montreal, accepting a job with CBC-Television to produce short ballet pieces. The ballet troupe she organized eventually became Les Grands Ballets Canadiens de Montréal.[67]

While the packaged portrait of pleasant ethnic folk applied to both men and women, it was in some significant respects most commonly gendered female. If the threatening "newcomer adrift" portrait was usually gendered male, even though it also applied to women, the folk image of newcomers as colourfully dressed musicians or bearers of quaint customs usually featured women. If not exactly a symbol of an emasculated or feminine male, the traditionally dressed folk dancer or, alternatively, the classically trained violinist or male ballet dancer represented two types of very different and sharp contrasts to the more common images of the highly excitable and violence-prone foreign European male – a threatening image that would in turn prove to be key to another widely used technique of containment.

Arts and Crafts as Political Commentary

As representatives of a self-declared non-partisan agency, the Toronto Institute's board and staff expressly prohibited the members from using the Institute to engage in overt political activity. They were not allowed to import divisive political struggles from their homelands to infect relations between ethnic groups in Canada. At times this position, which effectively reduced deeply felt politics to ancient prejudices in need of elimination or containment, was used to justify insensitive or arrogant dismissals of the newcomers' serious political concerns. When, for example, some Hungarian members complained about a Czech guest speaker who, in their view, had misrepresented the tragic plight of the Hungarian minority in his country, the board issued a condescending reply, penned by IODE veteran Peggy Jennings. She wrote that since the Institute's main aim was "to induce new Canadians to start afresh, accepting the spirit of tolerant unity in which this new nation is being built," it would not intervene in the "disputes and feuds that have caused such tragedy and distress in Europe." If they wanted to report on the injustices afflicted upon European minorities, she added, they could contact a more appropriate organization, such as the UN. The Institute may have aspired to be a local UN, but here the main aim was to contain the spread of Europe's nasty battles and cleanse the newcomers of disagreeable political disputes.[68]

But, supposedly like all God-fearing and law-abiding Canadians, the board and staff members were anti-Communists and thus not opposed to events that highlighted Communist sins. Indeed, these events could be seen as pro-democracy affairs that also celebrated Canadian freedoms. The minority of highly committed anti-Communist European refugees who saw themselves more as political émigrés exiled from their Communist homelands than as permanent newcomers in Canada took advantage of this situation not simply to cast aspersions on communism but to promote their own political campaigns against the Communist regimes in their home countries. And since those who belonged to governments-in-exile hoped that after defeating Communism at home they would return there, they often showed a greater interest in raising awareness about Communist horrors abroad than in resettling fully into the Canadian mainstream.[69]

At the Toronto Institute, as in other arenas, to promote their political goals through cultural forums these refugees were able to use their position as welcomed newcomers in whom Canada had invested a great deal. In this way they subverted the Institute's non-sectarian, or apolitical, objectives without exactly challenging or transgressing its generally anti-Communist ideology. Their actions suggest that there could be cracks in the cultural containment policy even as those actions reinforced the Institute's anti-Communist mandate. Or, to put it another way, they "negotiated with the Institute another allowable construction of ethnicity,"[70] a politicized approach that matched the Institute's preoccupation with gate-keeping democracy.

This is not to say that the Institute leaders were always clear about the politics involved or sensitive to them. They passed judgment without explanation, as when director Forbell rejected an application for group membership from the United Croats of Canada Dance Group, on the grounds that he had been advised that theirs was "a political organization."[71] Alternatively, they accepted invitations from highly politicized groups that organized events to commemorate their homelands' glorious histories before Communist control. In this way, these groups continued homeland battles while also exhibiting a commitment to Canada. The Institute also permitted highly political messages to be conveyed during its own non-partisan cultural events. During Latvian week, for instance, the Latvian Federation distributed a pamphlet on Latvian Arts and Crafts that linked the persistence of Latvian crafts in Canada with the ongoing political struggle against the Communist regime in their homeland. In contrast to the Institute's folklorization of the newcomers' cultural customs, this group of refugees imbued their folk craft with deep political meaning.[72]

The link between political commentary and craft, including female crafts, was common among various groups of new and ethnic Canadians, including the Ukrainians. The pro-Communist women of the pre-1945 generation had embroidered the hammer and sickle into their linens. Now the anti-Communist newcomers and their ethnic Canadian counterparts publicized the fate of women behind the Iron Curtain at craft exhibits, and they distributed gifts, such as embroidered bookmarks, to help spread the message. DP female activists also politicized images of the ideal Ukrainian mother, with her embroidery, cooking, and decorated Easter eggs (an image linked to the pre-war peasant immigrants with whom the urban DPs had little in common), fashioning her into an anti-Communist hero.[73]

Although a non-denominational as well as non-sectarian agency, the Institute particularly welcomed stories of how people had kept the faith under atheist regimes. This was the message delivered by a young Polish woman, the valedictorian of her 1964 Institute citizenship class. She linked her religious beliefs with her defiance of Marxism and thanked Canada for the freedom of religious practice. She noted her people's historical role in helping to build this "free and rich country," remarking that Canada's humane laws were "exceptionally precious to those who have been exposed so long to all the cruel injustice and immorality of atheistic materialism.... The sunshine is brightest to those who know the dungeons of darkness."[74]

On occasion the Institute effectively endorsed the nationalist, anti-Communist tracts, even rants, of highly politicized groups by publishing them in its newsletter,

The Intercom. In 1963 the Byelorussian Alliance of Canada (established in 1948) issued a typically impassioned attack against Russian tyranny and "a systematic policy of genocide" against ethnic minorities like themselves. It, too, noted the historical contributions of earlier compatriots (who, it added, had been mislabelled as Russians or White Russians) and expressed pride in and support for their freedom-loving compatriots and their "heartfelt hope" that "someday Byelorussia will be free." Like other anti-Communist speeches and tracts that East Europeans delivered and produced, this article linked citizenship, democracy, and Cold War work by stressing the need to undermine the legitimacy of communism both abroad and in Canada, a nation that, to many refugees' confusion, had not permanently outlawed Communist organizations. Portraying Byelorussian Canadians as the world's most vigorous freedom lovers and democrats, it described their politics as essentially Canadian in that they were working for democracy in Canada through their Alliance. The group was also laying claim to a hyphenated-Canadian identity, one that was political to the core, but it would have been naïve of the Institute workers to assume that such claims meant that the newcomers were completely shedding their cultures, politics, and identities for entirely new Canadian versions.[75]

Ethnic identity, then, proves not to be merely the product of the newcomers' adaptation to the dominant mores and rules of their new society, but, rather, a dynamic process, an evolving phenomenon that emerged out of the many interactions, conflicts, and accommodations – over rituals, politics, folk culture, and more – that took place between the newcomers and gatekeepers. Certainly, cultural customs, arts, crafts, dance, and musical performances played an important role in sustaining the often difficult lives of the newcomers and ethnic Canadians. These facets of life would continue to carry significant cultural and symbolic value in the future. In the specific context of European-Canadian encounters during the early Cold War decades, the various cultural rituals, performances, food, and artifacts that became identified as "ethnic," however vaguely or abstractly, not only influenced the Canadian cultural landscape but were also suffused with political intent and content.[76] In this and other ways, the newcomers, especially the political émigrés, helped to shape Canada's Cold War democratic discourse and culture.

This IODE cartoon graphically depicted the ordinary Canadian housewife as active Cold Warrior capable of scrubbing communism clean out of her country. *Echoes* (IODE) Autumn 1948.

Tactics of Close Liaison

Political Gatekeepers, the Ethnic Press,
and Anti-Communist Citizens

5

AT A CONFIDENTIAL MEETING HELD IN TORONTO in March 1954, the Citizenship Branch's chief liaison officer spoke about how the country might keep its newcomers from coming under the influence of the Communists, in particular ethnic-Canadian Communists. Vladimir Kaye began with a familiar denunciation of Communism as "a Godless religion... with all the violent attributes of a militant religion" and the Communists as dangerous zealots bent on world domination, people who used a variety of insidious propaganda tactics to "arouse mass psychoses" and encourage conversion to the creed. Speaking of Communist "infiltration techniques," Kaye described the strategy of boring from within, noting that the Communists were "firmly convinced that gradual penetration of strategic positions by a small, well disciplined and centrally directed force can gain control of the ruling machinery in all non-communist countries... without employing direct military force."

These Marxist cells, he added, existed in Asia, Central America, and other parts of the globe, including Canada. A popular strategy in this country was to infiltrate "the ethnic groups," especially the large Slavic groups such as Ukrainians, Poles, and Yugoslavs (which included Croatians, Serbs, and Slovenes), in an effort to create confusion and encourage disloyalty. These groups were targeted, he explained, because they made up the bulk of Canada's unskilled workers and included "the greatest enemies of communism," and thus had to be converted to communism, neutralized, or paralyzed into inactivity.[1]

The political gatekeepers and their citizen allies, including not only the Imperial Order Daughters of the Empire and the chambers of commerce but also the anti-Communist ethnic Canadian organizations and DPs, were keen to educate Canadians about Communist front groups that operated under the cover of neutral-sounding names. In his address Kaye highlighted the nefarious role played by the Communist-led All-Slav Committee, which issued directives to affiliates like the Canadian Slav Committee and supplied the Slav Communist press in Canada with a steady stream of articles depicting "the happy life" of Slavs behind the Iron Curtain. Another Soviet tactic, he noted, was to invite the editors and correspondents of Canada's pro-Communist ethnic newspapers to visit the Soviet Union, where they were put up in nice hotels, entertained, and taken to places that were "hermetically sealed off and inaccessible to any other visitors from abroad." The resulting newspaper accounts of the visits, he added with obvious sarcasm, invariably referred to some mysterious companion who travelled with them (as in "we visited Kirov collective farm at Zastavna") and repeatedly praised the regime for having transformed once backward, ignorant villages into modern, beautiful places. The stories included photographs of villagers and greetings from relatives who invited their Canadian kin to come home and "share our happy life."

Apart from increasing circulation, the point of these visits, Kaye explained, was to strengthen the faith of Canadian followers by offering assurances that all was well abroad and to entice non-Communists, especially newcomers, to read the Communist press. The Communists, he concluded, "calculate that if somebody reads a paper for a considerable length of time he will absorb at least something of the offered propaganda and if he does not become a convert to Communist [sic], he may cease to remain a supporter of the non-Communist press and its organizations." After all, "Soviet psychologists believe that if a lie is repeated often enough it will be accepted (at least by some) as truth."[2]

Kaye could have added that the Canadian security state, and its civilian allies, agreed that newspapers can influence opinion and that a constant exposure to the Communist press might make newcomers vulnerable to its ideology. If the anti-Communist DPs were to carry out their expected political role of discrediting the ethnic Canadian left, they needed to be protected from potentially countervailing ideological forces. As a result, Citizenship Branch officials and other anti-Communist groups actively worked to undermine the old pro-Communist ethnic press and other left-wing ethnic newspapers and to enhance the status and public presence of the anti-Communist newcomers.

Highly active citizen Cold Warriors lent a hand to the various endeavours, helping to run the Communist "alert" services that churned out flyers and pamphlets informing ordinary Canadians about the Communists and their front organizations. W.J. Sheridan, a senior official with the Canadian Chamber of Commerce, wrote some of the alerts and supported the multiple approaches to disarming Communists in Canada. As he put it in an address to the IODE, "In order to combat Communism, it is necessary for us to study it, to know what it means, and thus provide ourselves with the weapons to defeat it."[3] The political gatekeepers saw the alerts and other anti-Communist activities as tools of citizenship.

Cold War Encounters and Ethnic Battles

The Canadian state's efforts in monitoring and influencing the ethnic press, or the foreign-language press, as it was also called, long predated the Cold War. So, too, did its censorship and repression of the left-wing ethnic press, which occurred during earlier red scares and both world wars.[4] But the context of Cold War politics and mass migration, with its closely intertwined reception and political agendas, led to a renewed interest in the postwar ethnic press. Even before many European newcomers arrived, the Cold War had heightened the long-standing ideological splits within the older, polarized ethnic groups. During 1946 hearings held by the Senate Committee on Immigration and Labour, for instance, the pro-Communist Ukrainians and Poles pushed the Soviet position in favour of repatriating all of the East European refugees to their homelands and supported Stalin's allegation that many of the DPs were war criminals and Nazi collaborators; their anti-Soviet rivals opposed repatriation and urged Ottawa to embrace their democracy-loving co-nationals.[5]

The anti-Communist DPs, besides providing the country with necessary labour, could clearly be put to good political use in fighting Canada's Cold War, but the political émigrés within the East European refugee groups, though welcomed as staunch anti-Communists, were considered a challenge. They were more interested in mobilizing support for their militant, indeed violent and revolutionary, liberation movements against the Communist regimes in Eastern Europe than they were in settling in Canada and adapting to Canadian ways. The possibility of disgruntled newcomers represented another challenge: they might be vulnerable to Communist propaganda, especially when delivered in their own languages. Those concerns were reinforced by stories to the effect that ethnic Communists, under orders from Moscow and specially trained in the art of misinformation, were trying to stir up confusion and discontent among newcomers by telling them that they had been sent to Canada as slave labourers and were doomed to miserable lives unless they returned home. The Soviet Union and Eastern bloc states had initiated "come-home drives" to induce refugees living in Western Europe into returning to their now-Communist homelands with promises of support and no retribution. A similar drive occurred in Canada, and it received coverage in the mainstream as well as ethnic press. There were reports of Communists intercepting DP workers on the trains and in workplaces and pressuring them to return home or join the Communist Party of Canada (or Labour Progressive Party, as it was known at the time). Using a "wage slavery" discourse, some sources issued confusing promises about raising the ransom money required to rescue the displaced persons from being forced into slave labour. A Lithuanian priest reported that Lithuanian domestics working as cleaners in various Montreal hospitals complained that the Communists "bring the girls sweets and other gifts and try to tell them they will be slaves in Canada," and some hospital workers in Winnipeg reportedly asked for protection against "red" harassment.[6]

Similar reports came from Toronto front-line social workers who were helping to secure housing for DP recruits (a mix of Jews and Ukrainians, Poles and Balts) selected to work in the city's needle trades. When a group of 160 recruits plus their wives and children arrived in January 1953, the staff at University Settlement House worked with the mainstream ethnic Canadian organizations, especially the Canadian Jewish Congress (CJC), as well as the Ukrainian Canadian Committee and the Canadian Polish Congress, to settle the families. A social worker reported that conflicts had broken out when several agitators showed up at the place where the recruits were being temporarily held – Spadina Avenue's Labour Lyceum, long the centre of Toronto labour activity. The intruders included a Communist Ukrainian who "approached the Ukrainian group [and] asked them why they had come to Canada to starve when they could have gone to Russia. He said there was not true freedom in Canada, that they would be exploited as workers… and discriminated against on racial and religious grounds, and ended by suggesting they must all be Nazis, fleeing punishment for crimes committed in Europe." He and the others rushed off when the Ukrainian Canadian Committee people intervened.[7] News reports also told of violence breaking out between pre-war left-wing Ukrainians and postwar anti-Communist Ukrainians in Toronto, Winnipeg, Sudbury, and Vancouver, among other places.

For the gatekeepers, the upside was that the newcomers rejected the Communist co-nationals who approached them. The Lithuanian priest said of the Montreal situation: "They aren't getting very far with these Lithuanians, who left Europe precisely to escape the Communists." The highly active Cold War journalist Ronald Williams (who also wrote some of the anti-Communist alerts) made the same point in a *Financial Post* piece on the refugee reception program led by the Board of Trade in Thorold, Ontario, where some Communists had reportedly been chased out of town. Thorold (and neighbouring Welland) had a history of ethnic militancy, and left-wing political candidates enjoyed strong local support. Williams reassured his readers that new refugees like Ukrainian Eustacly Dumyn (renamed Stanley) and his wife Daria had come to Canada because they hated Communism, which had robbed them of their livelihood and sentenced family members to imprisonment in Siberia. Like many refugees, Stanley expressed his mystification as to why anyone would be a Communist in plentiful Canada, and thanked the Board of Trade for helping him establish a grocery business. He also declared that newcomers like himself could perform a great democratic service by telling Canadians the ugly truth about Communism. Indeed, when some Ukrainian-Canadian Communists had tried to recruit him, he had done just that, told them about the grim conditions of life under Communism. The news, he said, had disturbed them.[8]

In the long run the anti-Communist DPs would indeed help to undermine the old ethnic left, but at this point the gatekeepers worried about the newcomers' capacity to withstand the constant bombardment. As the priest also said of the Montreal domestic workers, "They brush them off, but the 'commies' keep hammering away."[9] Others noted that most Canadian Communists (and other leftists), now as in the past, were foreign-born and of non-Anglo-Saxon or non-French origin, and that the population of that type was on the increase, which meant that the well-organized "reds" might succeed in recruiting some of the newcomers. A number of critics identified the pro-Communist Association of United Ukrainian Canadians (AUUC) as the single biggest threat to Canadian political peace.[10]

News of the case of two young Polish DP domestic workers also raised alarms. The women had entered Canada under the auspices of Ludger Dionne, the Quebec industrialist and Liberal MP who had been allowed to recruit one hundred Polish women, mainly Roman Catholics, from the DP camps. He had offered them two-year labour contracts to work at his spinning mill in Quebec. At the time Dionne was facing mounting criticism for being an exploitative employer and petty patriarch. Government officials were also concerned that the Polish women were not integrating more quickly, socially as well as linguistically.[11] Dionne's attempts to dismiss the criticisms as Communist hogwash failed, and most of the contracted women were allowed to leave their jobs within one year.[12] The two Polish girls in question, Zula Loira and Maria Palucha, had both left the Dionne mill for jobs in Ottawa, where they were approached by the secretary of the Polish Legation, also a woman, and through her accepted jobs on the staff of *Kronika* (Chronicle), a Polish Communist newspaper in Toronto. One of them had been a maid in the house of the senior federal civil servant who broke the story. The incident sparked fears that other foreign legations of Communist states were recruiting young refugee girls for subversive purposes. The Polish Legation retorted by asking, do workers in Canada not have the right to improve their working conditions?[13] No one noted that the women might have been Communists in the first place. At any rate, the come-home campaigns continued, creating tensions within other groups as well.[14]

The Ethnic Press: Friends and Enemies

The gatekeepers attached much importance to the ethnic press as "a powerful opinion moulding body," to use journalist Peter Newman's words. The Citizenship Branch officials who advocated a strategy of integration "in co-operation with the ethnic groups" took the ethnic newspapers very seriously, especially because the papers had a much larger following among old and new immigrants than did the ethnic organizations. In the first few years, the officials explained, many newcomers were virtually dependent upon ethnic newspapers for most of the information they got – everything from practical advice about Canadian laws and culture to home-land news and international affairs. If properly guided, then, the ethnic press could be an effective tool of integration; it could be a shock absorber for the bewildered newcomer and a bridge between the old and new societies. From the gatekeepers' perspective, the ethnic press could fulfil a critical role as cultural interpreter of Canadian ways and thus facilitate the newcomers' contribution to the enrichment of their new country.[15]

To encourage and influence the non-Communist and anti-Communist ethnic press, Kaye advocated "the tactics of close liaison" with the editors of these ethnic newspapers. Then too, although the world of this ethnic press and of ethnic anti-Communism in general was dominated by men, women were not entirely left by the wayside. Newcomer and ethnic Canadian women were on the staffs of many newspapers and, whatever their political persuasion, most ethnic papers had materials that were directed at women partly because they were seen as critical to shaping children's perspectives. As the gatekeepers readily acknowledged, the ethnic newspapers were the single most important source of information the gate-keepers had on the different newcomer and ethnic groups and constituencies and the opinions of those constituencies about Canadians and Canadian institutions. In a country where, by the mid-1950s, almost 30 per cent of the Canadian population was of non-English and non-French origin, including more than one million people born abroad and still more arriving, a knowledge of the ethnic leaders, organiza-tions, and activities was, as a Branch official put it, "of considerable value to the Canadian government."[16] The newspaper industry was volatile, and the number of newspapers constantly fluctuated, but both before and after the Second World War most foreign-language papers in Canada served European-based communities.[17]

Kaye and his colleagues in the Citizenship Branch, monitoring the ethnic press just as they had done in the wartime Nationalities Branch, saw the publica-tions generally as falling into a number of not necessarily mutually exclusive cat-egories. So, too, did the RCMP, whose own staff tracked about forty Canadian and ethnic papers "with Communist leanings." One category of publication was made up of the many small papers serving particular religious communities. These were seen as effective integration tools that helped to create obedient newcomers by tending to their spiritual needs and moral standards. A bonus was that religious papers such as the Ukrainian Catholic *Nasha Meta* (Our goal) were also staunchly anti-Communist. The majority of ethnic newspapers were secular in orientation, including those read for largely "sentimental reasons." Often written partly in

English, they included a mix of literary, social, and homeland news and appealed to many ethnic Canadians who had long read the English-language or French-Canadian press but still felt an attachment to their homelands and ethnic groups.[18] The Citizenship Branch tended to view these publications as being mainly Canadian in outlook.

The largest number of newspapers belonged to what the gatekeepers categorized as "the democratic press," which included liberal and conservative papers read by the foreign-born and, to a lesser extent, the first Canadian-born generation. The "democratic press" included older newspapers, many of which dated to the interwar decades, that were seen as being almost entirely Canadian in outlook while retaining an acceptable interest in homeland affairs. It also included the rapidly increasing newcomer newspapers, which were virulently anti-Communist and showed what Branch officials unfavourably described as "a near obsession" with "international politics, especially those aspects of the 'cold war' which bear on the eventual liberation of their homelands." Indeed, within many of the larger East Euro-

A woman holds up a copy of the Dutch-Canadian newspaper *De nederlandse courant* (Dutch Canadian weekly), which fell into the democratic foreign-language press category.
(MHSO, Dutch, F1405, Acc. no. 21210, 12-16, MSR 0087, no.48)

pean groups tensions arose because the pre-war old timers, though they shared the newcomers' interest in the homelands, did not share the same political experiences. They were years removed from their homelands and thus could "not bring themselves to the same crusading pitch." A concern for the Canadian government would be how to defuse, or contain, the "extreme anti-Communism" or right-wing nationalist politics of these "ultra patriotic" refugees, or political émigrés, whose goal was to "dismember" the Soviet Union and the Eastern bloc into independent nations.[19]

After the war, as before and during it, the political gatekeepers were especially concerned about tracking and undermining the newspapers that belonged to the category of the left-wing or pro-Communist ethnic press. Many of the left-wing papers had been established in the early twentieth century by immigrants, and in the postwar years they were run by aging radicals or the Canadian-born. In his March 1954 speech Kaye identified leading Slavic-Canadian Communists such as Ukrainians John Weir (Ivan Wywiursky) and Matthew Shatulsky, and noted that the most active Communist agitators included the editors of Communist ethnic newspapers, including Maxim Bielich (Serbian), George Matesich (Slovenian), and Andrew Christoff (Bulgarian).

The left-wing ethnic newspapers and the groups they served showed some important political differences, but, with certain exceptions, the gatekeepers generally described them as pro-Soviet or pro-Communist and "very vocal." They considered the most moderate paper to be the Finnish *Vapaus* (Liberty), which, they noted, occasionally criticized the Soviet Union. In the 1950s a few dozen such newspapers were being published, with a total circulation of between 50,000 and 60,000. Most if not all of these papers, or their predecessors, had been in existence before the Second World War, when the Canadian state banned them. Before Hitler defied the non-aggression pact that he had negotiated with Stalin, and invaded the Soviet Union in June 1941, the anti-war position of these newspapers, which denounced the war as a capitalist-imperialist venture, led to their banning. When the Soviet Union responded by declaring war against Germany and joining the Allied forces, many of these pro-Communist newspapers (like the ethnic organizations that supported them) quickly reappeared, usually with a new name but often with many of the same staff. As the Citizenship Branch officials put it, they resumed their practice of toeing the Communist line. After the war that line was decided upon by the Cominform, a successor (but equally dictatorial, they quickly added) to the Comintern (or Communist International), which Stalin had dissolved in 1943. As Russia quickly morphed from wartime ally to Cold War enemy, the Communist or pro-Communist ethnic press became the target of an intensive state-directed campaign of surveillance and manipulation.

Tracking the Ethnic Press: Democratic and Cold War Agendas

Among his other duties Kaye was head of the Citizenship Branch's editorial section, where he worked with a staff of readers who tracked the foreign-language press. In the Branch's predecessor, the wartime Nationalities Branch, a handful of readers had worked at reviewing the ethnic newspapers. By the late 1950s the Citizenship Branch had about a dozen readers, multilingual men and women who read more than 130 newspapers written in more than twenty-five languages. In addition a few staff members, including Kaye, edited the readers' translated summaries. Most of the material was informative and was filed in the Branch's documentation section; it was used to field questions and to help the liaison officers develop ethnic contacts in the field. (By the end of the decade, the Branch reported that it had gathered information on more than 2,600 ethnic organizations.) Other material went to the Research Division and was used to produce Branch publications such as *Citizen* and *Notes on the Canadian Family Tree*, which glowingly praised Canadian democracy, detailed the rights and duties of citizenship, and promoted the gatekeepers' model of cultural pluralism.[20] The material judged to be of general interest to those involved in reception work was sent to the relevant government departments, social agencies, and voluntary organizations.[21] A smaller amount of sensitive material gleaned from both the Communist and non-Communist press was classified as restricted and sent to senior officials in key government departments, including the RCMP, though it sometimes ended up in other hands.[22] The Branch also issued special releases, which mostly reported on criticisms of government policies, sending them out to relevant posts, though there were frequent delays in getting them there in time for prompt replies.[23]

Citizenship Branch officials tracked the ethnic press in order to monitor political trends and ethnic opinion on various issues and, when necessary, to try to contain or influence that opinion. They praised the "democratic press" but also saw the need for improvement. By 1953 they were praising non-Communist newspapers for what they called their fair coverage of the different party platforms during that year's federal election, although they were also delighted that many of these papers had celebrated "the utter defeat of the Labour Progressive Party." Given that so many of their readers could not yet vote, the editors were particularly commended for their commitment to developing an informed future electorate and for respecting the fine traditions of an independent democratic press. By this time the papers also reflected the growing interest in federal politics among certain ethnic elites and an articulation of ethnic voters as a third force in Canadian politics, a concept central to the rise of multicultural politics.[24]

An incident dubbed the "baby talk" scandal suggests the range of ethnic opinion that the Branch's press readers could catch. In spring 1955 Jack Pickersgill, minister of immigration in the Liberal government of Louis St. Laurent, delivered a speech to a group of his party faithfuls in Victoria, B.C., during which he said, in reference to why Canada continued to encourage immigration, that because Canadians were not producing enough large families, the government had to import babies who could eventually become valuable citizens. He then added that he did not believe that "any immigrant – no matter where he comes from, or how good he is" – was "as good as another Canadian baby." The comments prompted much criticism in the English- and French-language press and ethnic press. The editorials in major dailies such as the Montreal *Gazette* condemned the speech for sanctioning a "pernicious" two-tiered racial system of citizenship. Indeed, an editorial cartoon depicted an Aboriginal man inviting Pickersgill "to the tribe" of the only really true Native Canadians. The Toronto *Telegram* and other dailies printed angry letters from immigrants and the Canadian children of immigrants.

The Branch press readers surveyed about two dozen ethnic papers, including pro-Liberal Party Italian, anti-Communist Ukrainian, and Communist Jewish papers, and the results showed that opinion was largely but not overwhelmingly negative regarding Pickersgill's statement. Most of the anti-Communist papers called the comments insulting, unfortunate, chauvinist, or immature. The most critical of the Ukrainian anti-Communist papers, *Novy Shliakh* (New pathway), wrote that Pickersgill had touched "a sore spot" that had "almost healed" after the blood that both Canadians and ethnic Canadians had shed in two world wars defending Canada, and that the harmful ranking of citizens threatened the fragile social unity only recently achieved. The Communist papers used the incident to denounce the country's leaders. An editorial in the Communist *Vochenblatt* (Canadian Jewish weekly) declared that Pickersgill's speech "symbolizes the rottenness and the reactionary character of the St Laurent regime, the anti-Semite regime in Quebec and the Tory regime in Ontario." The Communist *Ukraineske Zhyttia* (Ukrainian life) drew a connection between Pickersgill's "stupid" baby talk and the recent decision of a Winnipeg school board to reject a Slav name for one of its schools. It contrasted both incidents to the insidious way in which the capitalist media was always quick to emphasize the ethnicity of the odd Slav who committed a crime.

The different responses also reflected political divisions within ethnic groups. For example, *Vochenblatt* attacked the anti-Communist *Der Yiddisher Journal* for defending Pickersgill as "a very liberal and intelligent man" who had simply acknowledged a truth (that Canadian-born babies are preferable to imports who have to become Canadians) when, they argued, he was nothing but a "sly politician who felt free to show his true colour in [Wasp] Victoria." With few exceptions, including the Italian-Canadian paper *Corriere Canadese*, the liberal press generally criticized this argument on the grounds that it ignored how all children, no matter their places of birth, had to be educated and socialized into becoming citizens, and that immigrants contributed much to the building of Canada. In response Pickersgill claimed that he had been misunderstood, and though his critics remained unhappy he weathered the storm.[25]

The political gatekeepers were especially preoccupied with exposing to the public what they saw as the dangerously sensationalist reporting and nefarious activities of the pro-Communist press and, ultimately, with undermining its legitimacy. They repeatedly told Canadians that because these papers' international coverage came from the Soviet Union and its satellite states, the content could not be believed. Nor should Canadians believe the many denunciations of the free world's supposedly imperialist policies, or the arguments for recognizing Communist China and encouraging trade with the so-called people's democracies, namely, other Communist countries. They noted the many items in the pro-Communist newspapers that dealt with Canada–U.S. relations and explained that the emphasis on Canada as a mere satellite of the United States was part of a smear campaign meant to instil fear and resentment towards a key ally. Similarly, the gatekeepers reported, the Canadian coverage exaggerated the incidents of discrimination and exploitation, tried to discredit the refugees, and deliberately conveyed the inaccurate impression of a continuing class struggle as well as an impending economic crisis that was sure to trigger massive unrest. Instead of being dedicated to the ideals of Canadian unity and a democratic society, the pro-Communist press, the gatekeepers declared, was determined to undermine and even destroy it.[26]

Although they insisted that only a small portion of the newcomers regularly read these left-wing ethnic newspapers, the gatekeepers nonetheless worried, as Kaye noted in his speech in Toronto in March 1954, that the papers were attracting many non-Communist readers by publishing news from their former homelands that was not otherwise available to them. In addition, popular journalists helped to create a public climate of fear with alarmist magazine articles that reflected the position of the national security state. Peter Newman, for instance, advised Canadian employers to spy on their workers and figure out which ethnic papers they were reading during their breaks and lunch hours, on the grounds that with one of seven papers being "as communist as the Kremlin's own '*Pravda*'" (Truth), this kind of activity could seriously harm their businesses and the nation. Drawing on the sort of material provided by the Citizenship Branch, Newman described how the Moscow-backed left-wing ethnic newspapers falsely depicted life in Communist countries in glowing terms and tried "to breed dissatisfaction" among Canada's ethnic groups by encouraging factional divisions and opposing camps as a means of weakening the free, or democratic, ethnic press. Everything in the pro-Communist papers adhered strictly to Cominform philosophy, he noted, even the crossword puzzles and kiddies corners. (Not surprisingly, the DP newspapers similarly tried to have something for everyone, including the children being raised in a Cold War culture.)

With their combined circulation, the pro-Communist papers, Newman continued, blanketed nearly every ethnic group. The editors were "smooth operators," well versed in "twisting domestic issues into the party-line pattern." Many of them were also key men in local or national Communist front groups and had some Moscow editorial training. They were knowledgeable about Canada's libel laws, and their tirades against the capitalists were always "subtle enough not to overstep the line of legal action." When necessary, Moscow also provided funds to keep a paper going. It also cabled, in every tongue imaginable, a slew of international bulletins, pictures, and special articles, mostly written by Moscow's Foreign Commission of the Union of Soviet Writers, to newspapers around the globe. In describing Communist techniques, Newman noted, by way of example, that the Bulgarian *Novo Vreme* (New times) had recently claimed that Canada's rulers were mistreating their Slavic workers and that working conditions were "steadily deteriorating due to economic militarization, increased spending on war preparations, and the rupture of trade with the Soviet Union, China and the European People's Democracies." Indeed, the head of the USSR's All Slav Committee, Lt.-Gen. A. Gundorov, he added, had gone so far as to issue the bald-faced lie that there were many thousands of

Baby Killers Are NOT Welcome Here!

The letter we reproduce below speaks for itself. Here a Yugoslav woman, a collaborationist, boasts of the fact that she has been killing innocent children "like chickens", and promises to do so again if given an opportunity.

Is this the type of immigrant Canada needs? Is this why sons of Canada went to lay down their lives to defeat our enemy only to win the war and open our doors to our enemies and their collaborators? We, together with all democratic Canadians say emphatically no!

We urge upon the Canadian government to immediately institute an enquiry into the case of Vera Potkonjak and to rid Canada of a war criminal. We appeal to all liberty-loving Canadians to join with us in urging action by the Canadian authorities in the case of Vera Potkonjak.

Front page of the flyer "Baby Killers Are NOT Welcome Here!" produced by the League of Canadian Croatians, Serbs, and Slovenes, and the Croatian Republic Peasant Party, 1947.
(TFRBL, University of Toronto, Robert S. Kenny Collection, MS 179, Box 57)

graves of unknown Ukrainian workers who had perished while "toiling to build up Canada's wealth"[27]

Staying on top of these political battles was important for many reasons. For one thing, the warring parties usually lobbied the government to intervene on their behalf. For example, in 1947 a young Serbian widow, and Chetnik rebel, who boasted that during the war she had "slaughtered Croatian children as if they were little chickens," triggered a political war among Yugoslavs in Canada. In April 1940 the Yugoslav royal army had formed a Serbian guerrilla nationalist group to resist the German invaders and Croatian collaborators in their midst. However, they were quickly forced to surrender to Germany and from 1941 onward the Chetniks, or nationalist guerrillas, mainly fought a civil war against the Yugoslav Communist guerrillas, the partisans. The partisans earned kudos for their role in the resistance and, under Tito's leadership, established a Communist state independent of Stalin.[28] The Canadian episode was triggered by a letter that the Serbian widow had sent to *Novosti* (News), a pro-Communist Croatian newspaper,[29] in which she explained her actions in terms of avenging the wartime massacre of Serbs, including her family, by the "Bloodthirsty Croatians."

The woman's letter, which gave a Windsor, Ontario, address, provoked an immediate reaction from the anti-Communist Yugoslav groups. The Windsor branches of the League of Canadian Croatians, Serbs, and Slovenes came together with the Croatian Republic Peasant Party, which published the anti-Tito and pro-Liberal Party *Hrvtski Glas* (Croatian voice),[30] and called themselves the "All Slav Alliance." They discovered the woman's identity (her name was Vera Potkonjak, and she was working at her aunt and uncle's hotel) and plastered it on flyers that declared "Baby Killers Are NOT Welcome Here!" They distributed English-language copies of the letter, picketed the hotel, and demanded an immediate government inquiry into the case of "this self-confessed war criminal and child murderess," with a view to deporting her. Canada's Yugoslavs, they argued, had a right to make such demands for they, together with all Canadians, had given unstintingly to the Canadian war effort, and some of them had lost sons in the conflict.[31]

As it did in similar cases, the Immigration Department investigated the situation, no doubt enlisting the RCMP's help, in part, it seems, because Ottawa already had expressed concern about the extreme degree of anti-Croatian sentiment expressed by militantly nationalist Serb organizations, such as the Serbian National Shield Society of Canada and the Serbian National League, and their newspapers. Much to the disappointment of the All Slav Alliance, Ottawa reported that its records showed the woman had entered Canada legally six months earlier. She had been sponsored by her aunt and uncle, and would be permitted to stay.[32]

The Citizenship Branch officials hoped to contain the bitter ideological battles that occurred within polarized ethnic groups. The highly sensitive issues of collaboration with the Germans during the Nazi occupation, and involvement in war crimes – participation in anti-Jewish atrocities, including the rounding up and transporting of Jews to death camps and filling command posts in concentration camps – always threatened to explode into a political crisis that would require heroic remedies to defuse. Failure to contain the problem might jeopardize the task of transforming Europeans into happy and democracy-practising Canadian citizens and thus of achieving national unity. Such fights were thus worth keeping tabs on.

Their historians tell us that one of the DPs' greatest fears was being accused of collaboration or, worse, war crimes, and that when they were accused, for most of them it was a wrongful accusation. Certainly, a number of collaborators and war criminals did enter Canada, and most did so as part of the streams of displaced persons.[33] But within polarized groups such as the Ukrainians and Poles, the charges of collaboration were also ideologically motivated. The charges also emerged early on. In these cases the Citizenship Branch press translations helped Ottawa to monitor the situation at a time when it was facing considerable pressure from Britain and pro-refugee groups to admit more DPs.

One such conflict broke out among the Ukrainians in July 1947, when a Soviet embassy official, I.O. Shcherbatyuk, delivered a speech at a left-wing Ukrainian fundraising picnic to help war orphans in Ukraine (the event raised $200,000). In his talk Shcherbatyuk referred to the criminal acts of Ukrainian nationalists who had collaborated in the Ukrainian territories during the Nazi occupation and afterwards ran off with the Germans. These traitors, and their defenders, he added, were now seeking to exonerate themselves before the world's democracies, including Canada, where anyone looking could find yet more of these Ukrainian Canadians – "black in the face from their terrible hate of Ukraine" – who "embraced the traitors and bewailed their grievous fate." Both the traitors and their defenders insulted the "heroic" Ukrainian people, "who in friendship with all the other peoples of the Soviet Union [had] created [a] real basis for the exuberant development of Ukraine." Shcherbatyuk added that anyone who believed the stories of the displaced people had "made their beds on lies, sleep on lies and cover themselves up with lies."[34]

Predictably, the nationalist Ukrainian Canadians expressed their outrage with the allegations as well as the suggestion that Ukraine enjoyed sovereign status with the USSR. While Canadians in general followed the debate in the mainstream press, the Branch and RCMP readers followed the pro-Communist and anti-Communist Ukrainian newspapers for new developments or additional information. The Branch translations of various reports capture something of the European style of debate, with its provocative proverbs, rhetorical flourishes, and dripping sarcasm. Various Ukrainian-Canadian organizations (and their affiliated women's and youth groups), including the nationalist Ukrainian National Federation (UNF) and the Ukrainian Canadian Committee, denounced the speech as abusive filth that insulted all Canadians. UCC leaders such as Canadian-born John Hladun, a former Communist who had renounced his "bolshevism," demanded that Ottawa recall the embassy official. He declared, "I and 90% of my friends, Canadians of Ukrainian origin, sympathize with displaced persons," adding that Shcherbatyuk's cynical ploy "to create disunion among Canadians" would not work. Monsignor Wasyl Kushnir, chancellor of Winnipeg's Greek Catholic diocese and UCC president, issued similar statements, while others accused the *Winnipeg Free Press*, which had covered the event, of biased reporting.

The Branch readers tracked the Communist response through pro-Communist papers such as *Ukrainian Life* (Ukrainske zhyttia).[35] With a mix of proverbs ("if fools went not to market, bad wares would not be sold") and biting criticism, its editor, Matthew Shatulsky, wrote that Shcherbatyuk's speech would provide "an annihilating answer" to those who tried to slander (Soviet) Ukraine and Ukrainian Canadians. He stressed that Shcherbatyuk's speech had not meant to offend the honourable Ukrainian Canadians who were "honest toilers of their new fatherland" but to inform them of the destruction that Ukraine had suffered under German occupation (and that brave Ukrainians were now trying to rebuild). It meant to expose those Ukrainians who had "betrayed their people and country by their voluntary service to German fascists." Shcherbatyuk, he added, had even acknowledged that many Ukrainians had been forced to serve the Nazis rather than act as their willing accomplices.[36]

No doubt the Soviet embassy official's charges were part of a strategy to undermine the efforts of the established nationalist Ukrainian-Canadian groups such as the UCC to sponsor Ukrainian DPs to Canada – thus aiming at instead facilitating their repatriation to the Soviet Union and its satellite states. In 1947 the UCC and others were indeed lobbying Ottawa to admit the refugees, whom they publicly described as fine and honourable Nazi-hating and Communist-hating people. At the same time, in the DP camps in Europe, the refugees were also being encouraged to go to Canada by the militantly anti-Soviet Ukrainian nationalist leaders who, like other highly committed East European political émigrés, had come to see Canada as a place to regroup and recoup strength for the protracted anti-Communist struggle for a national homeland of the future. In truth a number of the established Ukrainian-Canadian leaders, including Kaye, were concerned about the extremism of the political émigrés, who supported a violent, revolutionary nationalist movement, and their obvious disinterest in settling permanently in Canada or in adjusting to Canadian ways. But, for obvious reasons, Kaye and his ilk did not say so publicly. Some of them also hoped to eventually Canadianize some of the right-wing nationalists. Still, in 1947 and for the next three years Ottawa rejected their pleas to admit certain DPs on the grounds that men who had belonged to the German armed forces fell under one of the "inadmissible" categories in the Immigration Act.[37]

The picnic speech controversy had occurred, then, within this larger political context. The Communists hoped to undermine the nationalist Ukrainian-Canadian lobbyists by trying to discredit them along with the refugees, and thus undermining their political clout in Ottawa. An editorial in *Ukrainian Life* remarked that Hladun and other UCC leaders must be suffering from "pathological illusions" if they thought that they represented the majority of Ukrainian Canadians who were sympathetic to the DPs. A biting proverb provided the title of another editorial tirade against the UCC: "Tis only the truth can give offense" (or, literally translated, "the truth pricks in the eyes"), which implied that the vocal critics had outed themselves as supporters of "Nazi henchmen" and "local Hitlerites" and thus were fair game for attack. They were no better, the editorial concluded, than the hard-core Nazis in the DP camps who "attack their political opponents [with] telephone cables [and] iron rods… torture young boys in cellars, pass death sentences, on whole families."[38]

The allegations of collaboration may well have delayed Ottawa's decision about admitting Ukrainians who had been recruits, whether volunteers or conscripts, in the armed forces of the occupying Nazis, but in the end the UCC got what it wanted. In spring 1950, following a decision to expand the category of "admissibles" and lift the prohibitions against non-German citizens of ethnic German origin who had served in the German armed forces either as conscripts or volunteers, the Liberal cabinet also decided to permit a modest number of the young Ukrainian men (now in Britain) who had served, mostly as volunteers, with the SS Halychyna, or Galician Division, the Ukrainian sharpshooter unit that the Nazis had created in spring 1943, after suffering a major defeat at Stalingrad and a critical loss of manpower. No Ukrainian group came under more suspicion of war crimes than this one, and the decision provoked more heated debate.

Indeed, it was not only the pro-Communist Ukrainian Canadians and the nationalist Ukrainian Canadians who did battle over the Galician Division. So, too, did Jews and nationalist Ukrainians, and again, for Ottawa, the debates were worth watching. The Canadian Jewish Congress and other mainstream Jewish-Canadian leaders expressed outrage over Ottawa's decision, especially because the Galician Division had been not only an active Nazi military unit but an SS unit, and the men had seen active duty. From the Jewish left, the pro-Soviet *Vochenblatt* declared, "Keep out Nazi Thugs, Admit Their Victims!" The pro-Communist Ukrainian Canadians were happy to join this attack on the Galician Division and to denounce the anti-Soviet Ukrainian supporters in Canada and the Canadian government as being soft on fascists, charging that the men had been willing volunteers, not unwilling conscripts. The Canadian Jewish Congress, however, did not get the hard evidence it wanted of wrongdoing, and its efforts also became embroiled in an ideological quagmire. Loathe to get dragged into the left-right fights among the Ukrainians, especially when those tussles did not deal solely with the Galician Division, the Canadian Jewish Congress dropped the matter.

In the context of the Cold War, the issue of collaboration had encouraged a tentative but uneasy alliance between the mainstream Canadian Jewish Congress and pro-Communist Ukrainian groups such as the Association of United Ukrainian Canadians, but in the end the anti-Communist CJC, which had purged from its own ranks the left-wing United Jewish People's Order, rejected the AUUC's offer to work together. Ottawa probably issued a sigh of relief. The tensions resurfaced when the Galician Division members began arriving in 1952, and over the following decades they would be sustained by a deep-seated sense of mutual distrust. Many Ukrainian nationalists would always see Communists and Jews as being in league with each other to destroy their movement, while many Jewish Canadians long remained suspicious of the Galician recruits.[39]

Pointing the Press Editors in the "Right Direction"

The political gatekeepers called on Canadians to give their support to the small and financially weak but determined "free opposition press" so valiantly "fighting the propaganda of the left." They sang the praises of these anti-Communist newspapers and their editors, many of them intellectuals and professionals who, unable to transplant their professional or artistic careers to Canada, turned to newspaper work. The literary quality of the new papers surpassed those of the past, the gatekeepers claimed, though they were more expensive to run and cut off from their traditional European news sources. Moreover, many of the postwar editors, having experienced and fled Soviet oppression, deeply appreciated Canadian freedoms and were eager to combat subversive elements among their own people. Kaye and his colleagues were delighted when the new DP newspapers quickly began to outnumber the old pro-Communist ethnic papers. In 1950 Kaye reported that Toronto, which had become home to "practically the whole Communist Foreign Language press" after the war, was witnessing the rapid increase of anti-Communist papers. He noted that the once-strong Communist papers, thirteen in all, were outnumbered by twenty-five new, mostly anti-Communist papers, and he attributed this shift to the concentration of postwar newcomers in the province.[40]

Still, the gatekeepers were convinced about the need to bolster these ethnic papers and make them more effective tools of integration and democratic citizenship. For one thing, the newspapers were always highly vulnerable to business failure. Many of the editors were fine writers – they were well educated and had culturally sophisticated backgrounds – but they were inexperienced at journalism and had limited access to Canadian news.[41] The factionalism within many of the ethnic groups also reduced the impact of their work. In addition many of the papers were short in length (from four to twelve pages), and the necessary inches devoted to advertising, which brought in the much-needed funds, left insufficient space for covering a range of news. Forced to keep overhead costs to a minimum, the editors of all but the largest papers usually worked as proofreader, compositor, reporter, business manager, publisher, publicity person, and advertising solicitor. Because many of the editors earned a low salary, they had to find other work to stay afloat and so took on commercial jobs, usually within their ethnic constituencies, on the side. Moreover, these ethnic editors, the Branch officials noted, were expected to carry out the important task of linking "the new world way of life with former traditions" and introducing Canada to their readers, yet they did not have access to a press service outside the Communist world and could not afford to pay for translators "to extract Canadian news." All the while they were being bombarded with "Commie news" from their homeland embassies or Central Communist Committee, with the troubling result that the new "democratic" ethnic press (non-Communist and anti-Communist) carried far too little pro-Canadian and pro-democracy material.

In response the Citizenship Branch began to ply these ethnic papers with suitable Canadian material, including items on Canadian history and politics, biographies of Canadian figures, and stories of immigrant successes. Indeed, the Branch also sent this material to the pro-Communist press in the hope that the editors' need to provide readers with information about Canada would lead them to publish at least some of the material, which they did. Various problems hampered these early efforts, though. At first the Branch had not translated the items into the different languages, and the ethnic editors, who could not afford the translation costs, had simply ignored them. Later, when the items were translated, the editors complained that the items were too long and boring, prompting Kaye to instruct his staff on the necessity of knowing their audience and writing short and interesting pieces pitched at the appropriate intellectual level. The Branch also made continuing efforts to provide more materials for women, especially items relating to child-rearing and job opportunities, as well as pieces on political issues. At one point Branch staff reported on a meeting with the Lithuanian paper *Briva Balss* (Free voice), an unusual enterprise because it had a female editor and a mostly female staff. At first the paper's staff had felt uneasy about meeting a government official, but they had warmed to the idea of receiving the materials. Kaye recommended items indicating that women's occupational opportunities in Canada were better than those in Britain and the United States, as well as in Russia. He also suggested pieces that informed readers about women's right to vote and their growing influence in all of "the main fields of Canadian life."[42]

These efforts at promoting the "democratic" ethnic press and propaganda materials celebrating Canadian virtues were enhanced in 1952, when a group of

National president Mrs. H.H. Chipman opens an annual meeting of the IODE at General Brock Hotel, Niagara Falls, 1952. The executive gave "unanimous approval to Mrs. B.B. Osler, of the anti-Communist committee," for the work of her group. McKenzie Porter, "The Empire's Dutiful Daughters," *Maclean's* 15 Aug. 1952
(Photograph by Paul Rockett; TRL)

wealthy and energetic anti-Communist citizens in Toronto decided, at the suggestion of John Gellner, to support an independent news translation service for the papers. The service produced "Canadian Scene," a weekly news report printed in more than two dozen languages and distributed free of charge to about seventy papers (circulation about 500,000 readers). The service had an editor and more than a dozen translators whose job it was to produce the "general Canadianizing material" and items on "timely topics" in "an interesting fashion," and to "editorialize and interpret" the materials in a way that would influence the press in the "right direction." The IODE actively supported the project, which was funded by donations from oil and paper companies, banks, and insurance companies. All involved boasted that the donors had no say over editorial policy, but given a shared anti-Communism they could be confident that the service was in the "right hands." They even hired a Toronto publicity firm to give the Canadian material the best possible spin. Within a year the amount of Canadian content in the papers had reportedly increased substantially (from 1 to 11 per cent in 1951 to about 40 per cent). The Branch largely credited "Canadian Scene," and a key supporter, the IODE, for this success.[43]

Kaye and his liaison officers were more directly involved in another strategy for increasing the Canadian pro-democracy content in the ethnic press, namely, constant liaising with the mostly male ethnic editors themselves. Kaye emphasized the importance of giving these editors constant counsel on the grounds that "if left without attention... some of the newly arrived editors may interpret the Canadian democratic freedom in the wrong direction thus causing embarrassment to themselves and their readers."[44] While he had in mind a whole range of ethnic newspapers, he was talking primarily about the Polish, Estonian, Slovenian, Czech, Ukrainian, and other anti-Soviet newspapers that advocated a nationalist line in support of the governments in exile. A number of these ethnic papers, including *Homin Ukrainy* (Ukrainian echo),[45] represented what the Citizenship Branch called the "most extreme" wing of these nationalist movements and would thus involve more work to "Canadianize." Still, Kaye's reports indicate that the editor of *Homin Ukrainy* was keen to publish material on Canada, and many of the other papers were seen as being less militant and more open to democratic guidance from the Canadian state.[46]

When asked to describe his duties and accomplishments as a government citizenship bureaucrat, Kaye often highlighted his work with the anti-Communist ethnic press and its editors. In 1952 he boasted that his Branch was the only federal government department to follow every single ethnic publication, that he and his liaison officers had the "full confidence" of some 120 editors and were working hard to increase that number.[47] In many respects the ethnic editors, many of them intellectuals like himself, were Kaye's natural allies. During his many liaison trips across the country he nurtured these contacts and, by many accounts, established a good rapport with editors. Of course, his success was based in part on the ethnic editors' own interest in pursuing the tactics of close liaison with the Canadian state. According to his superiors, Kaye's strengths were also his weaknesses: he was a bit of a "lone wolf," a quiet and energetic man who darted from place to place, talking to everyone but often too busy to actually file the massive amounts of information he had accumulated for Branch use, thereby limiting the potential value of the information.[48]

The mutual interest of both groups was also evident in the founding of the Toronto Ethnic Press Club in 1952. Based in the city that now had the largest number of ethnic newspapers, the club was primarily interested in co-ordinating efforts to counteract communism through the press and to present a united democratic front. This tactic had been adopted in wartime, when the state had created the Winnipeg Press Club – Winnipeg then being the site of most of Canada's ethnic newspapers, including left-wing organs. Although the postwar gatekeepers now referred to the Winnipeg organization as being largely a cultural club, during the war it had pursued the political goals defined by a wartime state and supported state-imposed censorship in the left press.[49] The new club in Toronto helped to reinforce the already established pattern of increasing Canadian content in the ethnic papers. It lobbied successfully for the placement of government advertisements in ethnic papers and, in the early 1960s, succeeded in establishing a national ethnic press club.[50]

Tools of Citizenship: Anti-Communist Alerts and Alliances

The political gatekeepers and their citizen (and would-be citizen) allies also made use of fact sheets detailing Communist vices and atrocities – including titles such as "Teaching the Young for Stalin," "Forced Labour in the USSR," and "Some Facts about Communists and Freedom of the Press." Canadian citizenship officials and active anti-Communist volunteer groups such as the IODE and Catholic Women's League had access to U.S. State Department materials – "How to Spot a Communist" was one of them – as well as to the published testimonials of refugee newcomers who delivered heart-wrenching stories of living conditions in Communist regimes. Moreover, these various Canadian Cold Warriors were connected to active anti-Communist newcomer groups through the Communist Alert Services – that is, the various outfits that printed and distributed flyers and pamphlets that told ordinary citizens about Communist activities at home and abroad.

In this way a wide range of gatekeepers, including government and volunteer reception and citizenship workers, the churches, and other keen Cold Warriors, forged alliances with the politically sophisticated anti-Communist refugees and members of nationalist governments in exile. Through these networks the

East European anti-Communist activists took every opportunity to remind Canadians that they knew from first-hand experience, or from loved ones who had been imprisoned or murdered back home, the evil that was communism. They impressed upon Canadians the necessity of quashing any views and activities that even remotely resembled communist tendencies. They offered a mix of compelling stories of Communist oppression and right-wing critiques of freedom of speech.

One of the anti-Communist networks was La Ligue Anti-Communiste Canadienne, a Montreal-based organization whose members included Catholic priests, the IODE, academics and intellectuals, and refugee organizations such as the Toronto-based Latvian Information Centre of Canada, which distributed Ligue material. The secretary of the Latvian group, M.N. Timiras, was one of the many refugees who emphasized the links between Canada's citizenship campaigns and anti-Communism. A Catholic Romanian lawyer and diplomat who had fled to the West, Timiras taught at the Institute of East European Studies at the University of Ottawa (one of Kaye's academic homes). He networked with other Balkan academics in Canada and gave lectures about communism. As an alert organization with a strong Catholic bent, the Ligue helped organize lecture circuits for the "religious survivors of Communism" in both Europe and China[51] and distributed fact sheets, newsletters, and flyers that reported on Communist activities. One of the flyers it distributed, and one that went to Kaye's Branch office, was "Soviet Version of Religious Freedom," a mimeographed copy of an Italian newspaper story about an Italian priest who had served a ten-year prison term in Soviet Union forced-labour camps for refusing to stop carrying out his religious work. He had told the reporter about the inhumane conditions of the Siberian labour camps, where tens of thousands of Ukrainian, Balt, and other prisoners, charged with the ambiguous crime of "political machinations against the State," toiled in freezing weather and suffered from inadequate food and shelter. When the prisoners rioted, Soviet machine guns had mowed hundreds of them down. Like some of the Iron Curtain refugees who escaped to the West, the priest also offered words of hope, declaring that "the Russian people had preserved their religious faith" despite the risks.[52]

A fact sheet distributed by anti-Communist groups, "The Real Conditions in Soviet Russia: Some Facts," emphasized (as most fact sheets did) the huge gaps between Soviet propaganda and reality. The aim was not only to expose Communist myths but also to equip ordinary people with the information necessary to counteract the false claims and to enable them to sniff out any Communists lurking among their co-workers and neighbours. The materials were written in plain language and often took the form of a carefully argued short essay with a central thesis developed point by point. They singled out key individuals and organizations and provided statistics and quotations from Communist and anti-Communist sources to make their case. They used a heavy dose of irony and sarcasm when contrasting Soviet claims of the workers' paradise against the grim realities for the masses. "The Real Conditions in Soviet Russia" asserted that in the Soviet Union, freedom of speech really meant freedom of "the compliant only," and freedom of the press meant the choiceless choice of voting for "Kremlin appointees." Freedom of assembly meant the freedom to attend state-organized demonstrations. The workers' low wages as well as the fines, speed-ups, high cost of living, relentless taxes, and inadequate social welfare supports for the injured, sick, and elderly exposed the lie that Soviet workers enjoyed a better standard of living than did Canadian workers. Added to all of this was the inadequate food, crowded housing, lack of fuel and plumbing, and the corrupt housing inspectors who fed off the common folk and tossed them out if they used more than their paltry quota of electricity.

Like many others, this fact sheet used the strategy of comparing Stalin's measures (for example, with regard to censorship) to Nazi Germany, concluding that Stalin's dictatorial practices went even further than Hitler's. The writing made references to the secret police and their arbitrary arrests as well as the extensive forced-labour camp system; both conditions, the analysis pointed out, made a mockery of Stalin's declarations about political freedoms behind the Iron Curtain. Every Soviet citizen was fully aware that at any time of day or night, "he may be torn from his family and home and be sentenced to as much as 25 years forced labour in the remotest parts of Siberia, from which he has little chance of returning alive." As with published broadsheets that were devoted entirely to the subject of the forced-labour camps of the Gulag, this fact sheet stressed how the Soviets had built up a "vast army of slave labour" that they used to carry out their mining, railway, and development projects, and, moreover, that the USSR had become so dependent upon this source of cheap workers for its projects that it had institutionalized the system by creating a seemingly infinite variety of crimes that could be punished in this way. The number of slave labourers being "worked to death," the document noted, was in the "twenty millions" (or one in ten of the whole population). The inhumane system had become so important to the Soviet economy that the rulers had a vested interest in keeping the number of prisoners as high as possible.

With a rhetorical flourish the fact sheet concluded, "The socialist tenet of equality has been grossly perverted in the Soviet Union." At one end of the scale were the many millions of workers who led difficult lives and earned paltry wages and, at the other, "the bureaucrats, factory and trust directors, party leaders, military and police elite, party authors and academics who earn many thousands more, live in considerable luxury, own several houses, a car, and a summer residence in the Caucasus." Some thirty years of Bolshevist socialism had "produced greater class privileges than modern western democracies know," and the material benefits enjoyed by the Soviet citizen are as much of a myth as his "democratic liberties."[53]

The authors or sources of the anti-Communist newsletters and fact sheets are not always known, but we do know that, in Canada as elsewhere, there were writers, ranging from conservative journalists (such as *Financial Post* writer Ronald Williams), to "freelance crusaders" (such as a former CBC manager, Gladstone Murray), who published serial exposés or ran news services and printed newsletters devoted to exposing Communist activities at home and abroad. Canadian women also played a key role in this anti-Communist activism, as did politically well-organized refugees who could use their own international networks to find reports of Communist abuses and atrocities and bring them into Canada.[54]

Indeed, the Cold War context created important opportunities for politicized refugee groups, from leaders to ordinary members, to influence Canada's political culture. Some groups turned their traditional celebrations into vigils for those killed. People wrote letters to the major dailies reinforcing the ugly news about Soviet "barbarity" and expressing gratitude for Canadian democracy. In this way, too, citizenship and Cold War agendas converged. At citizenship ceremonies the judges frequently noted that the refugees of Communism best appreciated the rights and freedoms they now enjoyed. Certainly, as we've seen (chapter 4), some refugee émigrés were able to successfully transform cultural events into political engagements.

A dramatic example of how they tried to recruit support for their militant national struggles back home and at the same time influence discussions in Canada was a mass rally, "No Peace without Freedom for All Nations and Individuals," held at Toronto's Massey Hall in November 1950. The event was organized by a group calling itself the Canadian members of the Anti-Bolshevik Bloc of Nations (ABN), which represented people from a number of "Russian oppressed nations." Organized in 1943 by Ukrainian nationalists in the western Ukrainian territories under Soviet control, the ABN, which soon included delegates from other "captive nations," was affiliated with one of the two factions of the extreme Ukrainian nationalist movement, some of whose members had entered Canada as part of the DP population. The ABN was committed to the violent dismantling of the Soviet Union (and Eastern bloc) into national states but also took on the task of warning Canadians about the dangers of Communism.[55]

The Ukrainian, Byelorussian, Hungarian, Slovak, Croatian, Latvian, and other speakers who took the stage at Massey Hall were activists. All but one of them were men, and they all spoke in English. Their speeches shared major themes as well as a similar rhetorical style. They emphasized that "Bolshevist Communism," that is, the Soviet extension into Eastern Europe and parts of Asia, was congruent with the earlier imperialism of Tsarist Russia. The speakers all spoke of a golden age, when their peoples had developed thriving independent republics and democratic practices only to be eclipsed by Russia. Nevertheless, the people had managed to resist the attempts to stamp out all of their values and customs and their dream of a free state. That dream had borne fruit after the First World War when new nation-states, such as Latvia and Poland, were carved out of the defeated empires. Yet they had quickly lost their freedom again, this time to Bolshevik imperialism, by coercion or with the help of traitorous collaborators. The Ukrainian speaker, for example, explained that after a three-year military campaign, the invading Bolshevik army had occupied the whole country, forcing the Ukrainian government into exile and the independence movement to go underground, from which it had been fighting ever since. The Byelorussian speaker described the Bolsheviks' rule over his people as a long reign of terror during which the Soviets exterminated some twenty thousand scientists, poets, intellectuals, and students (that is, those most likely to lead resistance and independence movements) and three million peasants and working-class people.

The speakers praised the anti-Communist partisans who bravely led the resistance movement in their countries, then and now, as well as the martyrs. Not surprisingly, they avoided the issue of collaboration in Byelorussia, Slovakia, and other territories already under Soviet domination before the war, where the invading and occupying German army had received support from local populations who detested the Russians even more than they did the Germans, and who hoped to cut a political deal with the soon-to-be-victorious Nazis. Instead, the speakers stressed their people's anti-Nazi as well as anti-Communist credentials. They noted, for instance, how "Communist vandals" had hanged their young, raped their women, and destroyed their homes. In speaking of the underground resistance that their compatriots continued to wage against the Communists, they spoke of annihilating the Russian master race and liquidating every Bolshevik who got in their way.

Another major (and familiar) theme was that the Western nations should assist without compromise the enslaved but brave peoples of Eastern Europe in defeating Soviet Communism. Bolshevism was such "a universal peril" that it could not be defeated without the full material and moral support of the West. The speakers were critical of what they saw as Canada's lax attitude to defeating Canadian Communists who, they argued, were fifth columnists working from within to help world Communism take over everywhere. Allowing Communist organizations like the Labour Progressive Party to operate was a sign not of democratic virtue, they argued, but of the Western powers' passive and defensive policy towards the Communists. It was nothing more than a continuation of the lame appeasement policy that had let Hitler and Mussolini get away with their conquests. It was time for Western governments to promote a more aggressive policy against continuing Soviet aggression and to give their full support to the enslaved nations of Eastern Europe.[56]

The one woman who spoke was a Latvian identified only as Miss Francis, and her speech was both similar to and different from the men's speeches. In contrast to the men, she referred to women's experiences under Communism, perhaps in an effort to connect with the women in the audience. She began with a personal anecdote about Christmas and how "this bright festival has for many years not been the wonderful time of joy, when the heart is warmer and the eyes are sparkling by the candle-light, the time when everybody is longing for a silent moment, when the child rests on his mother's knees and when father's hands – rough from work – seem so mild and gentle." It had become, for Latvians, and so many others, "a time of tears, dreary and even cynical thoughts" that "real peace will never come," especially when world organizations such as the United Nations were doing so little to address the situation. Like the men, she criticized Canada's relative passivity in the face of world Communism. But unlike them, she singled out the Canadian women who had joined "the Communist-led world peace campaign" and told these silly women to stop helping the Communist cause. "Believe me," she said, "that in Stalin's famous 5-years' plan, there is also marked the date when he intends to let his armies invade the cathedrals of this country, to insert Judas and Cain in the place of Christ, and the sickle and hammer instead of the cross." It was thus "ridiculous to see Canadian mothers gathering signatures for 'the appeal for peace,' which is organized by the Kremlin as a lullaby, for the western powers, so that the East can fully prepare themselves for the final push!" Indeed, the brutality behind the Iron Curtain was so great, she added, that the hundreds of thousands of her people starving and struggling in the Siberian slave camps were "expecting the 'A-Bomb' as the dearest gift."[57]

Collectively, and in hindsight, these kinds of activities can be seen as part of the political strategy for mobilizing anti-Communist support and influencing reception and citizenship work. The evidence suggests that these militant political speeches, or writings, were not always entirely accurate in their information, though we now know that the spokespersons were not wrong to refer to the many millions whose lives had been destroyed or eliminated by the ruthlessness with which Stalin, Tito, and other Communist leaders had dealt with real and perceived enemies – or of how these leaders had institutionalized massive prison labour systems by criminalizing even the most innocuous behaviour and sentencing so many, from workers to scientists, to the camps of the gulag and elsewhere.[58] At the same time, however, the refugees' extremely conservative, or right-wing, politics, and their tendency to equate all forms of political disagreement or protest as evil Bolshevism, clearly contributed to the Cold War consensus that equated all forms of political dissent as un-Canadian and un-democratic and that supported a repressive security state that trampled on people's civil liberties in the name of protecting individual rights and freedoms. Their words and activities also contributed to a climate of paranoia.

The deeply conspiratorial approach that the politicized refugees took on most matters, including any public criticism of government, may well have worried at least a few of the more moderate or liberal Canadians who attended events like the Massey Hall demonstration. By the same token, the Cold War alliances forged between gatekeepers and newcomers could make for strange bed-partners, but bed-partners nonetheless. Many Canadians distinguished their anti-Communism from McCarthyism, but their anti-Communist networks, including groups like the right-wing refugee and ethnic organizations, and their use of some of the U.S. alert services and the U.S. State Department materials, from cartoons (including comic books aimed at youth) to newsletters and fact sheets, did bring them into contact with McCarthy-style propaganda.[59] The Branch's files of La Ligue Anti-Communiste Canadienne, for instance, included a broadsheet entitled "The Ugly Truth about the NAACP." The ugly truth was the oft-cited claim, issued by white Southern bigots trying to undermine the civil rights movement, that the National Association for the Advancement of Colored People was a Communist front. This supposedly "Negro civil rights organization" was, apparently, nothing more than an organization founded and led by Jewish Communists, the descendants of "rabble-rousing" white abolitionists keen to foment civil strife, and a few Black Communists or fellow travellers and "Commie sympathizers" such as W.E.B. Du Bois, the honorary chairman. The document offered a mix of truth and distortion, named names (including the founder, William E. Walling, described as "a Southern scalawag journalist and Russian-trained revolutionary"), and criticized the duped do-gooders and other misguided folk who were taken in by the civil rights language. In doing this it displayed the guilt by association technique central to the McCarthy witch hunts. According to the Citizenship Branch's file, the broadsheet was in the possession of the Latvian Information Centre, which may have distributed it to others.[60] Similarly, the militantly pro-British and patriotic Canadian women of the IODE appeared willing to be in networks with right-wing anti-Communists, including racial bigots.[61]

New Battles in the "War of Ideologies"

In their anti-Communist activism, the gatekeepers and newcomers did share an exaggerated sense of alarm, and they put this element to use in an effort to scare or jolt ordinary people into action. They were fighting an ideological war, and to win they needed to mobilize citizens and would-be citizens to assist in the protection of the national security state, not only by educating themselves about communism but also by actively spying on co-workers, neighbours, and communities. From the pulpit to the school, in the English-, French-, and foreign-language press, ordinary Canadians, new and old, were encouraged to become informed and involved.

Newspaper columns and published alerts alike explained the differences between communism and democracy in deceptively simple terms.

The Catholic newspaper *Canadian Register* used a series of simple, brief statements to highlight the contrast between a Christian and atheistic ideology: "The Catholic believes there is God; The Communist denies His existence.... The Catholic practices the teachings of Our Lord Jesus Christ; The Communist follows the teachings of Marx, Engels, Lenin and Stalin.... The Catholic desires social justice. The Communist fans class struggle." The exercise concluded with a defence of capitalism, but not of its excesses, and a denunciation of communist atheism and totalitarianism. In deeply sinister tones, it also suggested what life might be like in a Communist Canada.

> In a Communist Canada every surviving citizen would be subjected to a rigidly tyrannical control of every detail of his existence. He could not choose his job or change it. For grousing he could be ejected from his home. For lateness he could be sent to a slave-camp in the Yukon. His radio programmes would be controlled as would the literature he read. Even his leisure would be confiscated for 'voluntary' work on Communist projects. He could not leave Canada – an attempt at this would mean that he would be shot and his family given five years of penal service. In fact, every phase of his daily life would be pried into by political police and his freedom would be taken. Our Canadian way of life is perhaps the freest in human history and our scale of living second only to that of the United States. Communism would solve nothing; for to shoot one's citizens or oppress them by the millions in concentration camps is no real solution for a country's economic ills. Therefore, it is our duty as citizens to further study the aims and methods of the Communists so that we may draw the attention of all the citizens.[62]

The Canadians who wrote and printed anti-Communist alerts and pamphlets included the Canadian Chamber of Commerce's W.J. Sheridan, author of the pamphlet "The Communist Threat to Canada," and the IODE's Marjorie Lamb. The IODE began running a Communist alert service in 1950, and it hired Lamb to write the alerts out of a Toronto office. An interior decorator, Lamb was educated in Canada, England, and France and became interested in the anti-Communist movement while a student at the Sorbonne in the 1920s. She was described as a nationally and internationally qualified expert on "Communist above-ground activity and the methods of countering it."[63] In explaining the need for such a service, alert writers like Sheridan and Lamb often invoked the name of Hitler in the great cautionary tale of the dangers of complacency. The world had mistakenly dismissed Hitler's *Mein Kampf* as the egotistical rants of a power-obsessed mind, but it now knew just how close he had come to making his horrid dream a reality. In the "war of ideologies," all democracy-loving people had to show constant vigilance in the face of communism and act diligently to strengthen their way of life.

While the focus and details differed, the character and tone of the short alerts and related materials were similar. Many of them included definitions of communism ("an extreme form of socialism") that, as in Sheridan's pamphlet, contrasted Marx's utopian dream of a classless society with Marx and Engels' militant call for the dictatorship of the proletariat – and especially with Stalin's practice of holding "the reins of supreme power backed by a powerful army, a controlled press, ruthless police, spies, informers, and the perpetual terror which such power induces." They stressed that it was naïve to believe anything other than that communism in practice meant the total destruction of personal liberty and parliamentary democracy and a one-party state that controlled all of its subjects from the cradle to the grave. Like the fact sheets, the alerts highlighted as well the gap between communist claims and realities.

The Canadian alerts also identified local Canadian Communists and fellow-travellers and reported on their subversive activities. They spoke of how the Labour Progressive Party had a well-trained legion of more than twenty-three thousand party members, led by Moscow-trained men like Tim Buck and Stewart Smith, female comrades such as party organizer Annie Buller, and ethnic comrades such as Wilbert Doneleyko, a Manitoba MLA (expelled from the CCF for his Communist politics) and the editor of *Jedinstvo* (Unity), a pro-Communist Yugoslav weekly published in Toronto by the Federation of Yugoslav Canadians. This force was making inroads into the Canadian political system, assisted by men and women who insisted they were not Communists but were doing Communism's work nonetheless.[64] The alerts identified the front organizations, including the Canadian Congress of Women, the National Federation of Labor Youth, and the Canadian Peace Congress, and noted that although Canadian unions had done their "house-cleaning" (purging their organizations of Communist members), two large unions were still under Communist control: the International Union of Mine, Mill and Smelter Workers (Mine-Mill) and the United Electrical, Radio and Machine Workers of America (UE). Finally, the alerts and pamphlets provided concrete suggestions for how Canadians might expose the Communists in their midst. Usually this approach consisted of how to ask well-placed questions about current events and then assessing whether the response indicated an anti-government or left-wing position.[65]

The IODE was especially keen on rallying Canadian women, old and new alike, to the anti-Communist cause, which included teaching their children about the British and Canadian traditions of democracy and the rights and responsibilities of participatory citizenship. As a politically conservative but reform-oriented middle-class women's group, the IODE upheld the family-values ideology and heightened

A Manitoba MLA, 1946–49, and editor of the pro-Communist Yugoslav weekly *Jedinstvo* (Unity), Wilbert Doneleyko was expelled from the CCF for his Communist politics. The Communist alert writers identified him as an influential ethnic leader within the party and its front organizations. (AM, W. Doneleyko, 1946–49, MLA St. Clements)

domesticity of the era while calling on all women, including housewives, to become involved in a range of charitable and citizenship campaigns. Its anti-Communist activism was also aimed at creating a more informed and active female citizenry. The group urged women to use their franchise to engage in strategic voting against Communist candidates or, indeed, any perceived left-winger, in every election. Its magazine, *Echoes*, offered striking female images, including that of a Canadian housewife (depicted as white, slim, and attractive) with a scrub brush purging not just her kitchen but the entire country of communism. Like the Latvian speaker in the "No Peace without Freedom" rally, the IODE from the start targeted the peace movement. In 1948 it had lobbied unsuccessfully to prevent "the Red Dean," Rev. Hewlett Johnson, from entering Canada to promote peace. Lamb's 1958 pamphlet, "The Canadian Peace Congress and the World Peace Movement," published by the Alert Service in Toronto in spring 1958, summarized the IODE's position: the call for peace was part of the Soviet Union's plot to mobilize world opinion behind policies favourable to itself and to sabotage the West's industrial and military defence efforts while its guard was down. It echoed the Latvian speaker's charges of Canadian naïveté and duplicity in a Communist conspiracy.[66]

"The Canadian Peace Congress and the World Peace Movement" offered the standard explanation that, in times of hot war, as in Korea, Stalin emphasized disruption and sabotage whereas in periods of comparative quiet, as at present, the aim was to convince the West that there was nothing to fear from Communism because it supported "economic competitive co-existence but all the while working hard to surpass the west economically by stepping up industrial production and trying to gain control of its world markets and thereby bring about its industrial collapse."

Similarly, from Lamb's point of view, the Soviets' creation in 1948 of the World Peace Council was supposed to convince the West that the Communists were a "benign, peace-loving, paternal system." The West would thus let down its guard and the Communists could make progress towards attaining world domination. To manipulate the West, the Communists had to make it appear as though a grassroots movement for peace was sprouting up everywhere, including in Canada, where, as elsewhere, Communist front groups were directed to launch a peace movement in such a way as to make it appear that it was a grassroots movement rather than what it really was, a campaign managed from above. Overnight, peace became the main preoccupation of the Labour Progressive Party and its various branch affiliates, including the National Federation of Labour Youth (now called the Socialist Youth League of Canada), the Congress of Canadian Women, the Communist-led unions UE and Mine-Mill, as well as front groups such as the National Council of Canadian Soviet Friendship (later, the Canadian Soviet Friendship Council).

Lamb named key strategists, including men such as Stanley Ryerson, a Marxist scholar, and Joe Salsberg, a union organizer, and women such as Buller and Mrs. Rae Luckock (identified as the member of two "Communist fronts," the Housewives Consumers Association and the Canadian Soviet Friendship Council), who did the work necessary in locales across the country to create the illusion of a "spontaneous development of local 'Peace Councils' throughout Canada." The women had been very active, distributing leaflets, forming the Women's Committee for Peace Action, and helping with the youth groups, including the Beaver Brigade (in 1958, just returned from a "youth-friendship" tour of Iron Curtain countries). Of course, the fear was that the efforts of Canadian Communists, including ethnic Canadian Communists, helped to attracted naïve Canadians, including women and mothers, into joining them.

Lamb also exposed the people who had founded the first Peace Council in Toronto, in October 1948, in a United Church. Among them were Rev. I.G. Perkins, Rev. James Endicott (who was often singled out in the alerts for his support for Communist China and his charges that the U.S. military forces were using germ warfare against their Communists foes), Mary Jennison of the Canadian Soviet Friendship Council, Margaret Gould, an editorial writer with *The Toronto Star* and organizer for the Soviet Friendship group and the Canadian Aid to Russia campaign, and UE union leaders Ross Russell and Sam Walsh. She also identified some of the ethnic Communists, including Doneleyko. She noted that some non-Communists were involved in the peace movement but that enough Communists were also there to ensure that "the Party line is toed."

Lamb also set out to discredit the Communists' launching of the Stockholm Peace Appeal, or the ban-the-bomb petition, in 1950. She explained that the campaign was intended not to outlaw war but to outlaw the one weapon (the atomic bomb) that the Communists believed gave military superiority to the West. But in Canada, as elsewhere, she noted, many well-intentioned people "fell for the campaign" despite warnings about its real nature from various groups in the know, including the (anti-Communist) Toronto Labour Council (CIO-CLC) and United Steelworkers of America. Fortunately, the alert groups had exposed the fifth columnists who in recent years had stepped up the intensity of a peace offensive designed to cripple the West's defences. In response, previously duped Canadians, such as Dr. A.J. Wilson, editor of *The United Church Observer*, had repudiated their signatures on the peace petition. The World Council of Churches, supporting the UN action in Korea, had also declared that, while outlawing atomic weapons was a desirable goal, the Stockholm Appeal was a Soviet "strategy of propaganda rather than a genuine peace proposal." All of this, Lamb charged, made a liar out of Canadian Communists like Endicott, who had claimed that there was nothing Communist about the peace petition. Fortunately, from her point of view, the "good sense of Canadians" gradually "overcame the illusion of the moment " and the peace petition campaign petered out.[67]

In addition to targeting the peace movement, the IODE also turned its attention to the importance of educating youth because, as many fact sheets and newsletters declared, the Communists relentlessly targeted the youth and, through lavish praise and recruitment into front organizations, indoctrinated them. As the caregivers of their families, or as teachers of young pupils, women were especially morally obliged to do this work. In combating communism, they faced the challenge of debunking an ideology that seemed to offer not only a simple and direct answer to what was wrong with the world but also deceptively simple answers for changing that world, whereas democracy was a process that evolved across the generations. It was therefore important, the IODE argued, to find ways of presenting democracy to the young in an exciting form. It hence gave its support for using comic books and cartoons. Women had also to encourage their family members to love and co-operate with each other, to learn discipline, tolerance, and self-restraint. Mothers had to teach their children everything from the basic tenets of democracy to ways of participating in the country's civil defence. For girls those activities included some nurse's training; for boys, it was target practice. Some militants worried about flabby children and urged Canadians to beat the Russians in physical fitness as well as in education.[68]

The IODE and other groups compared the freedom-loving DPs and Hungarian 56ers to Canadians who took their democratic freedoms for granted, and they used the newcomers' stories to inspire greater reaction in Canadians. Their umbrella organizations included ethnic Canadian women's groups with similar agendas. The Provincial Council of Women of Ontario, for example, linked many Canadian as well as ethnic groups, including the conservative Ukrainian Women's Association of Canada. The UWAC was composed of the Canadian daughters and granddaughters of the older immigrants and combined a strong anti-Communist stance with a middle-class, pro-Canadian perspective. Its members hoped to attract recently arrived DP compatriots and encourage them to subscribe to their maternalist ideology, and to play out their roles as wives and mothers in a Canadianized fashion. As its Ontario president explained, the organization aimed "to help the Ukrainian women to become ideal homemakers and encourage them to take an active interest in [Canadian] community affairs." That goal included fighting communism and educating children about democracy.[69] The Citizenship Branch liaison officers, who included a women's officer, also drew on networks of Canadian and ethnic Canadian women's groups and encouraged them in their citizenship and anti-Communist projects.[70]

The political gatekeepers, then, wanted not only to make Canadians more vigilant but also to transform the newcomers into vigilant citizens. One of their first concerns in doing this was to address the newcomers' fears and confusion about why Communists were allowed to operate in Canada. In answering this question, the gatekeepers could wax eloquent about Canada's morally superior commitment to protecting the democratic freedoms even of those who hoped to destroy them, and they could explain that the best way of defeating communism was through public opinion and the vote. As people who had seen "the Communists back home seize power and take over schools, industry, churches, in fact, control everything," the newcomers, they noted, were justifiably

Pro-Communist Jews in the United Jewish People's Order, which was expelled from the Canadian Jewish Congress in 1950, formed an obvious target for anti-Communist crusaders. Both old and new Canadian anti-Communist women expressed considerable disdain for radical Canadian women, including the members of the National Delegation of Working Women, seen here, who visited the USSR in 1955.

(Becky Lapedes Photos; MHSO, Jewish Canadians, F1405, 2120 23-60, MSR 6674)

confused and fearful about Communists in Canada being allowed "to form organizations, hold free meetings, distribute literature, run for civic, provincial, and federal office, and to generally go about their job of trying to make Canada Communist."

It was thus essential that Canadians be sensitive to the newcomers' situation and to help them understand the superior Canadian democratic way of life. Indeed, the gatekeepers lied in the pursuit of this argument, wittingly or otherwise, claiming, for instance, that the RCMP kept a watch on but did not actually "take action against Communists who are attempting to infiltrate into trade unions, churches or voluntary organizations or who run for government office." They invited ordinary Canadians, old and new alike, to report any suspected communists (which, of course, included those who might be considered pinkos or fellow-travellers rather than card-carrying members of the Communist Party) to their alert service or directly to the RCMP. They drew up lists for how the new Canadians could counteract communism, beginning with the advice that they "cooperate in every way with our law enforcement officers" and "avoid giving the Communists a handle for publicity by any form of public demonstration likely to create trouble." They should also take their adjustment to Canadian ways very seriously and carefully develop a useful game plan and then work quietly and obediently to become integrated.

Every new Canadian, they stressed, should "shoulder his or her responsibility to be informed of the fallacies of Communist propaganda and be aware of their current 'tricks and traps.'" They should work diligently to become citizens and then to use their democratic right of the franchise to "guard against the appointment of Communists to positions of influence" as well as "pray that Communists may be converted from their way of thinking and accept a true Christian and democratic way of life."[71]

These political networks – the interconnections between immigrant reception, integration, citizenship, and Cold War work, and the formal and informal anti-Communist alliances between gatekeepers and newcomers – thus worked to shape the postwar project of transforming European newcomers into democratic citizens. Still, in their efforts not only to influence the new "democratic" ethnic press and undermine the old left-wing ethnic press, but also to use the ethnic press as a political tool, Kaye and his colleagues at the Citizenship Branch could not have done their jobs without the willingness and active participation of the editors and the other anti-Communist newcomers involved.

In the end the state's success in undermining the old ethnic left owed much to the new and large presence of the anti-Communist East Europeans. By the late 1950s the Citizenship Branch officials were reporting that the amount of material on the Communist press that they were passing on to key officials had dropped substantially compared with the beginning of the decade. Although the Branch officials do not discuss it in their correspondence and reports, Nikita Khrushchev's revelations in 1956 about Stalin's murderous policies had decimated the Communist ranks. In Canada Joe Salsberg led most of the remaining ethnic members out of the Labour Progressive Party. The revelations also gave greater legitimacy to anti-Communists everywhere, including East European refugees in Canada. The newcomers themselves, from the sophisticated political émigrés to the ordinary newcomers who attended the rallies and shared their stories, both women and men, played an active, in some cases highly public, role in shaping Canada's Cold War democratic discourse and culture.

The original caption: "British immigrants arriving in Toronto are amazed at the abundance of fresh fruit. Here Mrs. Reginald Patricia Gordon of London shares a banana (pronounced with a long 'a') with her husband." *Telegram* 11 Aug. 1947.

Culinary Containment?

Cooking for the Family,
Democracy, and Nation

6

IN THOSE POSTWAR YEARS the struggle to win the hearts and minds of the newcomers was also contested on another less immediately apparent terrain: the culinary front. As the gatekeepers well understood, the culture of food – the newcomers' kitchens and family meals, and women's shopping and cooking methods – was no less political than were the workings of the ethnic organizations and press. People's foodways were shaped not simply by choice but by a constellation of forces: material circumstances, educational and cultural backgrounds, the mass media, including the saturation advertising of food corporations and appliance manufacturers, and even government campaigns. As a result, Canada's postwar food and nutritional gatekeepers – a group including professional dietitians, public health nurses, social workers, food writers, and fashion-makers as well as Citizenship Branch officials – were at the ready to assess and shape the newcomers' nutritional profiles and food practices – and thereby to promote a pro-capitalist and pro-democracy ideal of family and kitchen consumerism.

Just as they were concerned about Canadianizing and democratizing – and also containing – the ethnic press, the gatekeepers' approach to the newcomers' food customs reflected a mix of democratic ideals, Cold War politics, and cultural pluralism. In this case the pro-capitalist democratic discourse stressed the paradoxical ideal of the democratic but patriarchal family. It also played with notions of affordable abundance tempered by Cold War anxieties and the challenge of helping harried and financially strapped mothers feed their families properly on limited family incomes.

The greater emphasis on cultural pluralism as opposed to Cold War politics largely reflected the gatekeepers' view that ethnic foodways could be more easily contained and were less threatening to the Canadian state or mainstream culture than were the subversive activities of either the ethnic left or far right. As they did with ethnic craft shows and international music nights, the gatekeepers endorsed, mined, and appropriated ethnic foodways as part of their nation-building strategy of promoting national unity through an embrace of cultural diversity. There was also a significant gender difference: whereas the state's dealings with the ethnic press occurred within a largely male world, the food gatekeepers included large numbers of women, and they primarily targeted their own sex on the grounds that a better informed and Canadianized wife and mother would have a positive influence over the rest of her family.

Working within this complex realm of foodways – and its class, gender, and cultural dynamics – the postwar health and food campaigns would become the site of conflicts and accommodations between, on one side, the experts who promoted good health and modern cooking and family lifestyles and, on the other, the new-comer mothers from war-torn or impoverished regions of Europe. These mothers, having had little access to convenience foods or the latest kitchen technology, were now told to abandon their folkways for "modern" shopping and homemaking tech-niques. Canada's postwar food gatekeepers would also make pronounced efforts to bring certain ethnic foods into the mainstream, and even celebrate multi-ethnic foodways as a nation-making device.

Historically, in receiving societies, immigrant and ethnic foods were rel-egated to the margins, dismissed as unhealthy or inappropriate. Or they were mined by mainstream food writers and fashion-makers in search of novelty arti-cles and to help Canadian mothers add variety to family meals – in the process often producing bland versions of the "exotic" dishes that were supposed to pick up the palates of bored eaters. The popularity of certain ethnic foods in a given locale has not necessarily been contingent upon large-scale immigration. But for a major receiving city like Toronto, which had long been home to a variety of ethnic enclaves, shops, and cuisines based on earlier waves of immigration, the postwar migration intensified this trend. The growing presence of immigrant and ethnic consumers, ethnic food shops and markets, and cafés and restaurants helped to modify the city's mainstream cuisine even as the newcomers' own food customs were also modified. Speaking on this subject in 1957, the Citizenship Branch's Kaye told a Toronto audience that on a recent trip to the city he had "encountered on the menus of one of your leading restaurants, gulash – which actually tasted like real Hungarian gulash." He added, a bit wistfully, "And so, be not surprised when one nice day the chef of the Royal York Hotel will surprise you with Kned-licky [dumplings]." Still, as both new and old Canadians began to experiment with a wider array of foods, a modest degree of culinary pluralism also occurred from the bottom up.

The postwar discourses of the ideal Canadian homemaker played a large part in these developments, as did the gatekeepers' promises to new Canadian mothers that a middle-class standard of homemaking and family living was within their grasp. Once again, too, these trends were influenced by the Cold War and related notions of North American abundance, capitalist superiority, democratic modernity, and "kitchen consumerism."[1] In this sphere the Canadian government and Canadian manufacturers as well as a host of professional and volunteer gatekeepers encouraged the newcomers, even those with modest incomes, to become modern consumers, and in the end they were delighted when the newcomers' purchasing incomes did increase. Later on, for example, a 1961 article in the *Canadian Register* stressed just how much immigrants were needed, not only as builders and small businesses people, but also as consumers. It reported that the immigration minister, Ellen Fairclough, "reckoned that since the 1951 census, the 1,365,000 newcomers to Canada have furnished 248,000 households. That's a lot of tables, beds, chairs and curtains. They have bought 173,000 stoves, 105,000 refrigerators, 207,000 radios and 81,000 cars. It has been estimated that the newcomers spend 500 million dollars a year on food alone." In the past decade or so immigrants had established 2,500 small businesses employing over 9,000 people. "Apparently," the report noted, "these facts are unknown to the occasional complainer, 'that immigrants take away jobs.'"[2]

From Famine to Well-Stocked Kitchens and Shops

When the gatekeepers articulated the dominant family values and heightened domesticity of the early postwar era, they frequently invoked images of "wholesome" and "modern" family living. These images were premised upon a dominant and highly influential bourgeois model of a breadwinner husband and homemaker wife and mother – though this model was far from universal, even within Canada. Indeed, the model privileged middle-class ideals that had never entirely reflected most people's lives.[3]

This ideal, whose celebration also reflected a conservative reaction again women's increased freedoms and economic gains in wartime, focused attention on women's primary responsibility for feeding and nurturing healthy families, managing modern, efficient, and well-equipped households, and raising well-adjusted children.[4] It was also the ubiquitous subject of contemporary debates over women's roles engendered by the growing presence of working mothers, day-care lobbies, increasing divorce rates, and other signs of women's changing status in post-1945 society.[5]

The dominant homemaker ideology called for the "domestic containment" of women – which necessarily included the many European women who would enter the Canadian workforce, in very large numbers, in Toronto. At the same time, as the IODE illustrated in its image of the woman sweeping out communism (chapter 5), both old and new Canadian women could practise democracy and fight communism from their kitchens.

The Canadian postwar discussions of the ideal homemaker often made much of the differing economic situations prevailing in postwar Europe and Canada. For example, even in the late 1940s, when Canadians faced continued rationing, spiralling inflation (after the lifting of wartime price controls), and an acute housing crisis, various gatekeepers drew comparisons between a Europe of scarcity and a Canada of abundance. Canadian relief workers posted overseas emphasized that Canadian homemakers, though struggling, were still better off than those in Britain and Europe. In 1948 a Canadian nutritionist posted in England with the United Emergency Fund for Britain noted the particularly horrid plight of the British housewife, who was still lining up for long hours to get her paltry weekly family rations (lamb chop, egg, bits of bacon, cheese, some milk) and perhaps a bit of unrationed meat (heart, kidney, tripe). By comparison, she said, Canadian women lived "in a land of plenty," and should donate to the British fund.

Within Canada, liberal and conservative social critics expressed alarm about inflation. They combined the concepts of democratic capitalism and economic citizenship to argue that responsible citizen consumers were entitled to a decent level of purchasing power and that the state was obliged to ensure its citizens a reasonable cost of living. Moreover, the failure to do so would provide fodder for the Communists. In Toronto, liberals like Rabbi Abraham Feinberg and conservatives like the *Star*'s religious columnist Rev. Stanley Russell agreed that the soaring food and milk prices, rising rents, deteriorating accommodation, and corporate profiteering could discredit capitalism and benefit communism. In making these arguments, they too invoked the Canadian homemaker. As Feinberg put it, families forced to limit their children's nourishment in "one of the world's best stocked countries" would soon question "a system which seemingly permits profiteers... to exploit a fiscal emergency for their own enrichment." Calling for an end to government complacency, he declared that over the next few years the average housewife's food budget would be an index of Canada's economic health or sickness. If the prices of essential foodstuffs continued to go up, he said, the ultimate beneficiary would not be the consumer, or even the producer, but communism.[6]

Canadian homemakers also became consumer activists. In cities across the country, women from a broad section of the population took to the streets, joined consumer organizations, and called for government protections against inflation and for the right to purchase household necessities at reasonable prices. These female consumer activists included liberals, social democrats, and radicals; francophone and allophone Montrealers; labour activists and workers' wives; and middle-class women. Their consumer activism was premised on the principle that as the family's household manager, the price-watching housewife was a responsible consumer and had a right to make economic as well as social welfare demands of the government. (In Quebec, issues of nationalism and anti-federal politics were added to the mix.) Not all consumer lobbyists were treated equally, however. The radical Housewives Consumers Association, for instance, suffered from the red-baiting tactics of critics who denounced them as Communists. In the end the inflation crisis was short-lived, and consumption increased over the next two decades, especially among an expanding middle class and better-paid unionized workers. Even then, many old and new Canadians, including middle-class housewives, could not immediately meet their pent-up demand for such high-ticket items as a new stove or fridge (or a suburban bungalow) and thus become the consumerist homemaker so widely advertised in the early postwar years.[7]

The ideal Canadian homemaker typically appeared in Canadian magazines and propaganda materials as a slim, attractive, middle-class, white Wasp woman with a well-stocked grocery cart, pantry, or freezer. Here mother and daughter shop together, and the daughter begins to learn the skill. *Chatelaine*, front cover, October 1956.

The impact of the Cold War does not in and of itself explain the renewed popularity of the nuclear family and the homemaker ideal as postwar ideology. But insofar as the homemaker ideal also symbolized the stability and superiority of Western democratic families, the Cold War did have an important effect. Just as the Communist alerts and fact sheets of the time tended to emphasize the contrast between claims about the quality of life under Communism and the difficult realities of workers' lives in the Soviet Union, the Cold War versions of the homemaker ideology stressed the huge gap in the quality of life between North America and the Soviet Union. In Canada, as in the United States (and Canadians were regularly exposed to U.S. propaganda), mothers were portrayed as the beneficiaries of an economic system that ensured them a decent standard of living, good health, the resources to raise children properly, and opportunities for personal and cultural fulfilment. By contrast, Soviet women were depicted as beasts of burden brutalized by heavy work and acute scarcity, as people denied the opportunity to ensure "a wholesome family life."

The U.S. State Department produced pamphlets on the "typical" "Mrs. America" and "Mrs. Soviet Union." The U.S. mother was a woman of modest affluence who "cooks the meals, cleans the house, washes, irons, and mends the clothes, cares for the children, and works in her flower garden." She goes to church, does "useful volunteer work," and "enjoys beautifying her home." The Soviet mother faced acute food shortages and the indignity of poorly paid, degrading work and long periods away from her children. Forced to rise at 4 A.M. to go to market before work, she waited in long lineups simply to purchase "milk for her children, a sliver of cheese, a few wilted vegetables (cabbage or potatoes), a loaf of black bread, and a little tea."[8] Similarly, following a group tour in the Soviet Union, Rev. James F. Drane wrote a scathing report in the *Canadian Register*, describing the shocking presence everywhere of white-kerchiefed peasant women who, far removed from their families, performed heavy, filthy, and dangerous (male) jobs on railway work crews, in construction and farm work, and factories producing heavy machinery. With wages that were inadequate to meet their families' needs, their masculinized bodies, "with muscles hardened," were a fitting "tribute" to the harsh "doctrine of Bebel, Engels, Marx and Lenin."[9]

Far from being merely rhetorical devices or cultural by-products of the Cold War, these propaganda materials were carefully constructed, gendered ideological weapons meant to promote Western capitalism's superiority and to cultivate loyalty and conformity to North American ideals. Once again, however, some social critics, including liberal Cold Warriors, warned that rampant consumerism and the planned obsolescence (including of appliances) that was becoming a hallmark of capitalism might produce entirely materialistic citizens.[10] Then too, women, including those who could purchase and furnish suburban homes in these years, were not necessarily the dupes of industrial designers, corporate manufacturers, and food advertising.[11]

When Canadian gatekeepers introduced European women to "Canadian ways," including Canadian food customs and households, they promoted a Canada of middle-class affluence and modernity, promising the women that they too could have the resources required to meet all of their family's needs. They used teaching tools that, whether produced by government departments or corporate capital, featured consumer images of the ideal homemaker and the many modern conveniences that supposedly defined the Canadian way of life. For example, some of the Canadian overseas relief workers and social workers in Canada ran orientation and English classes in the refugee camps, on the ships, and in Canada using Eaton's department store catalogues. The massive publications contained enticing pictures of those big-ticket kitchen and other consumer items that wives normally purchased with their husbands – fridges, stoves, and furniture. Of course, Canadian manufacturers and department stores alike were keen to tap the new and growing "foreign market" in their midst, and to sell their goods in huge quantities.

Front-line social workers and nutritionists also made use of commercial magazines, newspapers, and government publications, as well as NFB films produced with the Citizenship Branch for the purpose of educating the staff of social service agencies working with new Canadians. These materials presented the usual image of the Canadian homemaker as a white, slim, attractive, well-dressed and nicely coifed middle-class woman pushing an overflowing grocery cart down store aisles between well-stocked shelves. At home she was at work in a well-appointed modern kitchen using canned, frozen, and other items from her well-stocked shelves, fridge, and freezer. She might whip up a family snack or impromptu cocktail party using the latest tabletop appliances, such as blenders and bun warmers. She could use the brightly coloured plastic Tupperware containers to store leftovers or for packing a child's school lunch.[12]

The primarily educational NFB films – such as *Mystery in the Kitchen* (1958) – that told all women in Canada how to shop and cook for their families also offered ideological celebrations of Canada's abundance and modernity. This was especially so of films produced for the benefit both of reception workers and newcomers, especially women. For example, *Arrival* (1957) tells the story of Luisa, an Italian woman who is rejoining her husband, Mario, in Toronto. In a series of vignettes, Mario meets Luisa at Union Station after a two-year separation and takes her home to an apartment that is "neither shabby nor fancy." Although uncertain of her surroundings, Luisa is pleased with the new fridge and stove that Mario had saved up to buy for her – already acculturated, Mario understands the value of these modern appliances. In one segment, "Supermarket Day," the script directions call for a scene in "the biggest splashiest supermarket we can find." Luisa and son Silvio "look in awe" at the "mountainous displays of food" but are also frightened by the seeming "cool impersonality of people brushing past them." Back in the apartment, Luisa lovingly unwraps her coffee pot and dishes, brought from overseas, and chats with her husband. Along with friendly Canadian neighbours, he will help Luisa make the transition from the old world to her new, modern life.[13]

In co-operation with the Citizenship Branch, the NFB produced several films featuring this domestic ideology. In *Canadian Notebook* (1953), a film about immigrant jobs in Canada, several European families are shown in their different rural, urban, and resource-industry settings. The men are family breadwinners, the women homemakers (though the film does recognize farm women's work). The film emphasizes that Canadian wages allow male workers to buy modern appliances for the new Canadian homemakers. In a Maritime farm scene a narrator reports that the mail-order catalogue has brought the "big-city shopping centre" to the rural homemaker's fingertips, so that she can shop with almost the same ease as a homemaker in the city. The urban department store is celebrated as a "meeting place" for "fine imports and local products." Its greatest asset is "the wide range of items and variety of styles." Indeed, the narrator exclaims, "Sometimes it may seem that there is too much to choose from" what with "buttons for father's overcoat, a purse for mother, clocks, perfume, fishing tackle, chocolates, safety pins, crowbars, novels." With everything on display, the prices clearly marked, the shopper can "walk for miles and buy everything he needs without ever leaving the store."[14]

The ubiquitous Mrs. Canada (she is called "Mrs. Sparks" in the film) appears in a supermarket scene that also stresses convenience, abundance, and quality. The meat is cut and cellophane-wrapped with the grade, weight, and price in clear view. The wide array of foods allows for efficient weekly shopping. Mrs. Sparks can also buy magazines, cigarettes, and other articles. When she reaches the cash register aisle, the cashier totals her bill and gives her an itemized receipt. Canadians, the narrator reports, "find the self-service store well-suited to the faster pace of city

The famous 1959 "kitchen debate" suggested how the struggle over the superiority of Soviet-style communism or capitalism could shift from a debate over the relative merits of missiles, bombs, and political systems to women's roles, well-stocked grocery stores, modern appliances, and (rampant) consumerism. Against a backdrop of U.S.-made washing machines, model kitchens, and "a model dream home" at a U.S. exhibition in Moscow, U.S. vice-president Richard Nixon celebrated the items of modernity that were supposedly within the reach of the average homemaker – including well-appointed kitchens and well-furnished bungalows in a Communist-free suburbia. He equated kitchen consumerism with democracy by celebrating a free-market system in which appliance manufactures freed the housewife from drudgery and gave her plenty of consumer choice. Soviet Premier Nikita Khrushchev and the Soviet media countered that the exhibition was a vulgar display of bourgeois materialism, that instead of "U.S. Sputniks," they got a tour of a department store. (Canadian Press Images, ID 8649501)

life, where a busy housewife has to buy the week's groceries, go to the bank and the hairdresser's and still get home in time to prepare supper."[15] Yet another film dealing with job opportunities for women praised the "spectacular" modern supermarket and the "newest" emerging trend in merchandising, the suburban shopping centre, with its one-stop buying, many stores, and ample parking space for cars.[16] This tendency to kitchen consumerism in the Cold War era would find its most famous political moment in the 1959 "kitchen debate" between U.S. vice-president Richard Nixon and Soviet premier Nikita Khrushchev at a U.S. trade exhibition in Moscow.

The heightened domesticity of the Cold War era, and the dominant homemaker ideology, did not mean that Canadian (or U.S.) gatekeepers ignored working women. NFB films also dealt with professional, white-collar, and pink-collar jobs for newcomer women. A range of experts, from educational psychologists at the Department of Labour to liaison officers of the Citizenship Branch, effectively argued that capitalism offered a fair range of opportunities and decent wages or salaries to both single women seeking jobs or careers and less fortunate wives and mothers needing to bolster family incomes. While working mothers were criticized, the discourses of employability and domesticity co-existed in the postwar era, even if uncomfortably. The argument was made that job opportunities always existed, and that all a woman had to do was prepare for the job or career that was most right for her. That argument sidestepped the harsh realities of capitalist economies and the plight of low-skilled newcomers who toiled in low-waged jobs.[17]

Dietetic Gatekeepers: Fattening up the Body Politic

Health lobbyists, nutritionists, and social workers drew links between ensuring a healthy body politic and a healthy nation and Western democracy in the Cold War. Even the act of fattening up thin and malnourished newcomers was celebrated as a moral and political victory. When writer Ronald Williams praised Thorold, Ontario, businessmen for fighting Communism through an aggressive refugee reception program, he used a Ukrainian DP woman's body as one indicator of success: "When Daria left the camp, she was a skinny 86 pounds. Today she's a plump 150 pounds." He was referring, perhaps too flippantly, to how hearty portions of Ukrainian dishes such as borscht and dumplings (served with thick gravy or sour cream) and high-fat sausages could do the trick.[18] In the reception programs the medical screenings and the containment of infected newcomers also provided a defence against imported diseases.[19]

Given that a healthy body politic meant ensuring the health of the entire population, the newcomers' health was not discussed in isolation. With declarations that Canada, like the United States, was falling behind the Soviet Union in promoting health, Canadian health advocates lobbied for more public funding to teach everyone, especially mothers, the importance of stringent health standards, healthy food habits, and "modern" eating regimes. Professional dietitians, social workers, and public health nurses used the flexible *Canada Food Guide* to raise awareness about nutrition, illness prevention, and the importance of early diagnosis and treatment.[20] A good diet, they stressed, improved children's growth rates and physiques, built up resistance to diseases, and meant longer lives. A faulty diet from early in life might not show immediate results, but could produce far greater damage than a vice such as adult drinking. It was essential, argued child welfare specialist David Weiss, that women who came from regions "where austerity prevails," or who lacked adequate knowledge about nutrition, learn "how to purchase and prepare food."[21]

In keeping with the era's sense of liberal pluralism, in evaluating immigrant food customs Canadian nutritionists counselled flexibility (not assimilation). They cast themselves both as the experts with the scientific authority to assess foods and as the cultural interpreters who could "coax" newcomers into adapting their food habits to Canadian conditions. Both themes are captured in a postwar guidebook, *Food Customs of New Canadians*, produced by the Toronto Nutrition Committee.

Aimed at health workers dealing with newcomer clients across Canada, the book reflected the basic principles of the postwar food and health campaigns: it emphasized efficient and economical food shopping and preparation, with a focus on nutrition (and variety).[22]

Chatelaine magazine also proved to be a valuable source in the postwar food campaigns. A team of professional home economists staffed the magazine's Institute Kitchen, where they created recipes and meal plans and tested their readers' recipes, all in the service, once again, of promoting healthy, efficient, and economical food shopping and cooking. A common piece of advice for consumers was to avoid expensive out-of-season fruit and vegetable imports in winter, and instead purchase tinned foods or, if they could afford it and had the freezer space, the slightly more expensive frozen foods. Predictably, given the magazine's dependence on advertising, it sometimes gave its seal of approval to the products of corporate sponsors – as no doubt suggested by the business department. This practice illustrates one of the ways in which food corporations fashioned taste, that is, by saturating the popular media with their products.[23] But the *Chatelaine* experts did enjoy a degree of autonomy and sometimes refused to promote the advertisers' products (many of them processed convenience goods) on the grounds that they were too expensive. Their food features highlighted affordable and healthy meals based on economical cuts of meat, including hamburger. They might suggest a quick potato or rice side dish and vegetables, or the ubiquitous casserole, which stretched modest amounts of meat mixed with potatoes, rice, or other starches. A popular feature with readers, including the admittedly small number of immigrant and ethnic Canadian women who wrote in to say so, was "Meals of the Month," a month-long table of daily menu plans that provided the new, busy, or unimaginative cook with ideas for making a variety of nutritious meals on a modest budget. Some front-line health workers used this and other *Chatelaine* guides, as well as supplementary publications such as *A Bride's Guide to Cooking*, in their work with female and family clients, who would have included the European newcomers.[24]

Canadian food experts thus promoted a scaled-down version of affluence, one that recognized the modest incomes of many new and old Canadian mothers, though they certainly celebrated democratic living by extolling the virtues of affordable abundance and capitalist modernity. In England, Canadian Red Cross dietitians had told the British war brides that the greater array of foods in Canada meant they could produce the all-Canadian well-balanced diet, which included fresh salads and homemade fruit pies – and in the process save them from doctor and dentist bills.[25] In the widely read *Chatelaine* the popular recipe competitions – featuring the proud contest winners photographed alongside their prizewinning Jell-O mould salads, carrot medleys, casseroles, or dessert parfaits – promised women readers ease of preparation and family fun. In their come-on ads, brand-name manufacturers of prepared products, such as canned soups and vegetables, promised convenience and maximum return for minimal preparation, while baking-supply companies told mothers to show their love by making real homemade bread and pies.[26]

The Toronto Nutrition Committee argued that new Canadian mothers from war-torn or impoverished regions would need to be told about nutritious and affordable foods available in Canada that they might otherwise not know about, especially the many raw and processed fruits and vegetables that were available all year round. Newcomers needed instruction in how to prepare and cook these items to preserve their food value, which often meant advising against overcooking vegetables. While many Europeans could find their "familiar breads" in a city like Toronto, they also needed to know that "Canadian bread" (commercially baked white bread with enriched flour) was an excellent source of nutrients, and they needed to be encouraged to eat it or at least serve it to their children. Noting that many rural Europeans had laboured with primitive and time-consuming cooking facilities, the nutritionists stressed the need to teach new Canadian mothers how to use modern kitchen technologies and equipment so that these women could "adjust more easily, produce better meals, and prevent costly waste." In short, they encouraged kitchen consumerism.

In dispensing advice about the well-balanced meal, efficient shopping, planned menus, and modern household regimes, Canada's various food experts prioritized middle-class ideals about preparation and consumption that were derived from capitalist time-management principles. They operated with notions of a modern household with clean and uncluttered rooms, well-appointed kitchen, formal dining room or kitchen dinette set, and family gatherings. The *Chatelaine* image of the family meal, especially dinner, privileged a white nuclear family. Its well-groomed members were ideally seated around a nicely set table. They shared proper table manners and engaged in polite conversation as they ate mother's well-presented and healthy meal – the perfect image of civilized dining and democratic family living amid respectable affluence.

These kinds of efforts to improve and modernize women's culinary skills also nicely served the interests of Canadian capitalists, who were well aware that the establishment of tens of thousands of new Canadian households would involve the purchase of countless kitchen and other appliances as well as furniture and other household items. (An irony of the latest "labour-saving" devices was that the constantly escalating standards of homemaking meant that few women ever enjoyed the promised leisure that was to come with the purchase of a new stove, fridge, washing machine, or vacuum cleaner.) Similarly, Canadian dietitians used definitions of Canadian ways and standards that were as much about class and capitalist notions of efficiency, budgeting, and time management as about nutrition

Refugee fare: Latvian intellectual and DP Rüdolfs Eksteins, at a distribution point for CARE parcels, receives food supplies for his family.
(Courtesy of Modris Eksteins)

and food. They held that the North American pattern of three square meals per day was sacrosanct, for example, on the grounds that it perfectly suited the normal school and working hours.[27]

From Countering Hunger to Encountering Abundance

Not surprisingly, European newcomer wives and mothers also viewed their primary role as that of family food provider, and their abilities to fulfil this task, no matter the obstacles, profoundly influenced their sense of self-worth and even their status and power within their households. Then too, any discussion of how they responded to Canada's postwar food campaigns must take account of their pre-arrival experiences. As the narratives of Mennonites, Poles, Ukrainians, Latvians, and other postwar refugee women so movingly illustrate, mothers had gone to heroic lengths to keep their children alive during the war. When the bread or buns they baked (and carefully parcelled out) ran out, they had cooked and fed their children sawdust and thistles. They had raided farmers' fields and homes, enlisting their children's help. They had turned the bits of grain swept off a granary floor into porridge. When necessary, some had bartered with the one thing they had left, their bodies. German and Italian women in dire straits adopted similar strategies.

The women's stories also speak to the long-term scars of embattled mothers who had not been able to "counter hunger in their families."[28] Even after understanding the full might of the Nazi killing machine, many Jewish mothers could not fully forgive themselves for not having saved their children from death. The reality of living for years in a culture of physical deprivation helps to explain why so many memoirs are full of heart-wrenching stories of trying to get food to feed the hungry or starving. When English soldiers liberated the Bergen-Belsen death camp, a young woman joined the flood of people who rushed out to the plots to dig beetroots and potatoes with their hands. She and others suffering from typhus were sent to a quarantined hospital in Sweden, where Red Cross personnel nursed them back to health. A gentile Polish resistance fighter arrested during the Warsaw uprising of 1944 stressed the lack of food and poor sanitary conditions in her German POW camp and the maddening isolation. Doing, and later recalling, basic things like cooking and eating could also bring relief, even humour, to the litany of tragic events.[29]

After the war the food, though in greater supply, had remained scarce. In the DP camps the amount of food, like medical supplies, varied from camp to camp. But everywhere monotonous diets prevailed. The camp meals were heavy on starch (bread, potatoes, and, in the Italian zone, pasta). The vegetables served were mainly turnips, onions, and spinach. The Latvians called the ubiquitous split pea soup *salas briesmas*, or green horror.[30] In some of the DP camps, female relief workers cooked up batches of mashed potatoes and spinach, or watery soup, over an open fire, in huge soup containers taken from the Nazi labour camps. In others, refugee mothers prepared food for their own families. In the cramped quarters of converted schools, warehouses, and other buildings, where family members might sleep and eat in one room and share one outdoor water tap with everyone else, they cooked on an electric plate or

heater-stove. They fried tinned sardines and Spam, North America's famous tinned luncheon meat, courtesy of their food parcels. They cooked potatoes, made stew. Because there was never enough food, they bartered with local farmers, trading their weekly ration of cigarettes (a hot item in the underground economy) for a sack of potatoes or for bread, butter, a bit of bacon. Everyone participated in the black market, including the Allied soldiers, who according to one writer "were supposed to reeducate Europeans in democracy and decency."[31] Like men, some women stole from the camp store or used forged ration cards. If they could, they hoarded. The penalties for getting caught were hardly a deterrent for mothers trying to feed hungry mouths (in the Baltic camp at Wurzburg, a convicted "thief" had to clean toilets for a month).[32]

Some women had once cooked in the relative comfort of their middle-class homes, in urban kitchens with modern amenities, in Riga, Budapest, or Prague. But now they coped with a different situation, just as they had done during the war. So too did German city women, who, outside the camps, struggled with even fewer supplies. But most of the female DPs came from rural villages and towns where women had worked with "primitive" cooking facilities (as Canadian experts put it) as a matter of course. They had carried out the "time-consuming preparation" required, such as constantly stoking outdoor ovens with wood or charcoal. So too had the Greek, Italian, Yugoslavian, and Portugese women who had fed the hungry in the marginal rural and fishing regions of Southern Europe.[33]

For many of the young European wives and mothers who went to Canada, or elsewhere, the war, lack of fuel and food, and dislocation had disrupted the normal routine by which daughters traditionally learned to cook from mothers, aunts, and grandmothers. They had not learned to bake, in the company of other women

Two Hungarian women (described as housewives), who refused to give their names for fear of retaliation against relatives still living in Budapest in the aftermath of the 1956 revolt, make soup in large vats in the kitchen at Wiener Neudstadt refugee camp, a former Russian barracks in Austria, December 1956. (YUA, Toronto Telegram, ASC Image 1311)

The original caption: "Smiles light the faces of these immigrants as they sample fruit while waiting to go through Canadian customs." *Telegram* 11 Aug. 1947. (YUA, Toronto Telegram, ASC Image 1275)

(sisters, cousins, female elders), the familiar festive foods that marked a happy occasion. Instead, they had endured bombing, military occupation, slave labour in the Nazi factories, the death camps – though some of them had cooked for the enemy when, following the Nazi occupation, they had become domestic workers in German homes. The young Lithuanian women recruited as domestics for Canada, for example, had eaten in camp cafeterias or had pooled their rations with kin and older women and cooked stews or soups eaten along with bread.[34]

It is no wonder, then, that the newly arrived would take such notice of the abundance of food, as well as of the shiny new appliances and furniture, that they saw in Canadian stores.[35] Or that, years later, they would vividly recall the moment of joy that came from biting into a piece of fruit that for so long had been unavailable: a tasty strawberry, a juicy orange, or a delicious apple that, as a German immigrant woman would always remember, tasted "just like heaven." Many others would vividly remember their first thin slice of "Canadian bread." But whether they liked it ("it tasted like light cake") or not ("it tasted like cloth"), they usually preferred their own – be it a dark, dense rye (enjoyed by Germans, Austrians, Poles), a sourdough rye (the Dutch), or a white and crusty loaf (Italians, Greeks, Portuguese).

Being surrounded by abundance did not necessarily mean being able to enjoy it, at least initially. Most of the newcomers arrived with little cash or capital, and they initially endured a spartan diet. Some would also be offended by the waste: imagine, a restaurant's leftovers were enough to feed several refugees for a few weeks in a camp.[36]

Negotiating and Resisting Homemaker Training

In handling the pressures placed on them by the gatekeepers' food and homemaking campaigns and by their husbands and children, newcomer women took on their responsibilities with alacrity. Their activities reveal general patterns, and the many anecdotes highlight the importance of choice and circumstance.

While their capacity for exercising individual choice or resistance to outsiders could differ greatly, they generally responded in selective and pragmatic ways to Canadian health experts and to the homemaking campaigns, even if they could not entirely control the terms of these encounters. Some of them also found particular ways of negotiating family culinary conflicts, especially between husband and children. Many women were able to reproduce old world family dishes and diets fairly soon after their arrival, and they also gradually integrated Canadian foods, though the timing and degree differed across households. The many different hybrid family cuisines that emerged as a result reveal a variety of patterns that defy easy categorization. Alongside the many immigrant mothers who steadfastly stuck to "traditional" meals were some mothers who deliberately experimented with certain Canadian recipes or convenience foods. Canadian nutritionists would have happily applauded Dagmar Z., a Czech woman who said she had maintained a "traditional Czechoslovakian kitchen" but "altered it" to be "more nutritious and healthy," as she had "learned" to do in Canada.[37]

The differing patterns exhibited by two Jewish mothers who were Polish survivors (as recalled by their daughters) also suggest the importance of individual choice. One woman insisted on cooking her familiar Jewish food (which in this case meant lots of eggs and cheese, gefilte fish and chicken, hearty soups, and cheese blintz desserts) as a way of continuing to defy Hitler's final solution. As soon as she could afford it, the other woman embraced the cake and pudding mixes, tinned soups, and other commercially packaged North American products because they helped to put the past behind her. But even she did not entirely eliminate Jewish food.[38]

Newcomer women were exposed to Canadian foodways in different contexts. The British war brides, for instance, were encouraged to attend nutrition and cooking lectures in Britain before sailing for Canada. In Canada, Red Cross personnel and others taught them how to make muffins, tea biscuits, cream sauces, salads, and cakes, and showed them canning techniques, while public health workers ran nutrition classes and made home visits to advise them about "meal planning and budgeting." In their positive reports, Red Cross workers noted that the British "girls" learned to use Canadian equipment and measurements, got practical cooking experience, enjoyed the chance to socialize with other women, and liked their "Canadian" gift of a set of plastic measuring spoons. Some British women were encouraged by their husbands (and in-laws) to make Canadian meals, while others complained that Canadians failed to appreciate the differences between British and Canadian foodways.[39] The Dutch war brides had a reputation as healthy and hearty eaters. Their favourite meals included beef or pork pot roasts and stews (which could be made with cheaper cuts of meat), smoked sausages, or herring, served with potatoes, vegetables, and gravy.[40]

A number of the government-recruited domestic workers from the DP camps had picked up home economics lessons in the camps or on the ships (through films), but most of them learned to cook on the job, whether in Canadian hospital kitchens or private homes. Private maids had to learn to cook "Canadian-style" while also doing the cleaning and laundry or watching the children. In doing their household labour, some of them had to wrestle with unfamiliar modern technology, such as washing machines or vacuum cleaners. The heavy work and an often-demanding schedule took its toll on still-malnourished women, who felt "run down" and easily got sick. The Canadian women's groups who had agreed to Ottawa's request to help the DP "girls" with any problems sometimes intervened on a domestic's behalf. In Toronto, the YWCA (which looked out for the Protestant domestic workers) and the Catholic Women's League (which dealt with the Catholics) visited the employers of domestics who had collapsed on the job or been ill, asking them to reduce the women's workloads until their health improved. But in the absence of government controls or unions, these interventions lacked force. The Y donated parcels of canned food for the women to use or send to folks in Europe. Many domestics did as expected, completing their contracts, marrying, and raising families, though many did so as working mothers juggling the double day.[41]

The frequency and intensity of the European women's encounters with Canadian nutritionists, dietitians, or nurses varied greatly, but generally these occasions were not of lengthy duration. In Toronto some women discussed their children's health needs in a new Canadian mother's club or local nursery school. Others used the baby clinics staffed by public health nurses. After giving birth, a mother might be visited by a nurse, at the hospital or at home, who tried to counsel her about meal planning, nutrition, and family budgets. Some settlement houses arranged field trips to stores and supermarkets. In this and other ways, the women picked up information or advice and could choose how and when to use it.[42]

The women's encounters with the "experts" cannot be separated from their material conditions upon arrival or from their family dynamics. Wherever they settled, their household conditions were often far from ideal. In contrast to the boosterish and consumer images of "typical" Canadian dining rooms, modern kitchens, and suburban houses, many of Toronto's newly arrived Europeans lived in crowded, even substandard flats, or in equally unappealing rooming houses. A woman and her family might share a bathroom or kitchen with other families, or boarders, and perhaps make do with makeshift sleeping arrangements. A Greek woman's description of her first family home in the west end of Toronto applied to many of the newcomers' first rental flats. Since it had "no kitchen," her mother cooked on an electric hot plate in a room that also did for a bedroom. She washed the dishes in the bathroom sink. A lack of hot water meant a lot of boiling, and the absence of a refrigerator meant daily shopping to purchase fresh milk and other perishables. In another little flat a German couple slept on the living-room couch, with their children using the one tiny bedroom. In the multiple-family households of Italians and others, women hung bedsheets to create several bedrooms, for adults and children, out of one room. Many families lived with landladies who complained about the children or threatened to boot them out. Those who rented cottages or tiny dwellings on the outskirts of Toronto coped without any running water or electricity (just as many Canadian farm women were doing at this time).[43]

For many of the newly arrived, then, kitchen consumerism did not mean visiting Eaton's or Simpsons to order a shiny new stove or fridge, even less a washing machine or, least of all, a dishwasher. Eaton's did make efforts to draw European women into its stores, partly by hiring Baltic, Hungarian, and other European women as saleswomen, but the large crowds of better-off European women did not materialize. Nor did consumerism mean a car trip to a new suburban shopping mall such as Toronto's Golden Mile, an outdoor strip mall, or, later, Yorkdale, the first of the large indoor shopping malls. For many newly arrived women, it more likely meant shopping for pots and other basic kitchen equipment at bargain-basement stores such as Toronto's Honest Ed's, and a few cheap pieces of furniture from a second-hand store or an ethnic store that extended credit to newcomers. It is not that the women did not want that stove or fridge; on the contrary, they were delighted once they could make these purchases. When they could first afford it, the appliance was not usually part of a brand new kitchen but tucked into a corner of a tight space. Purchasing a house did not immediately resolve the problem.

The Pilli family, a couple and two boys, were typical of the many Italians who had bought a house by the early 1960s. To make the mortgage payments, they lived on the main floor and rented out various rooms. As noted by Edna Staebler, a food writer who interviewed them for *Chatelaine*, they lived in "a narrow, white-walled kitchen with a small refrigerator, a gas stove, and a stainless-steel sink" and a "Formica-topped table and six padded chrome chairs." The small bedroom had second-hand furniture and a television that could be viewed from the kitchen. A toilet, shower, and laundry tubs were in the basement.[44]

Ethnic Approaches to Feeding Families

Despite their less than ideal early households, many European women in Toronto needed either to learn new cooking skills or, when necessary, modify existing skills in order to feed their families and reproduce traditional meals. They could do so largely because of the presence of ethnic food shops and markets established by the members of earlier migrations. Whatever their class background, many European women shopped for food not in the splashy new supermarkets, but in the many ma and pa ethnic shops, with their pungent smells, lopsided aisles, unwrapped foods, and old-fashioned cash registers. These stores had what they wanted. In west-end Toronto, Italians and Portuguese flocked to the tiny shops and outdoor stands of Kensington Market just off Spadina Avenue, where they could find everything from bread and oil-drenched olives (much preferred to the "tasteless" tinned black or bottled green varieties) to rabbits and pigeons. Or they went to the shops in the quickly expanding Little Italy and Portuguese areas roughly west of Bathurst between Dundas Street in the south and Bloor Street West in the north. Further west, in the High Park area, the growing number of Germans, Poles, and Ukrainians moving into the area in the 1950s (and also propelling the middle-class Canadians to move out) supported not only a range of neighbourhood European-style cafés serving strong and aromatic coffee but also a number of delicatessens, whose spicy salamis, cheeses, and hanging pork had their own smells and ambiance. With increased migration, new shops, as well as restaurants, were established.[45]

For a man who had preceded his wife to Canada, her arrival usually ended a "bachelor" period of "perpetual hunger" or of stomach aches from too many greasy fried sausages and eggs. When wives saw their husbands after a separation of a year or two, they were often shocked by the men's serious weight loss. "So skinny, I barely recognized him," was how they put it. An Italian woman who came in 1953 said she spent the first few months in Toronto preoccupied with feeding her husband so that he would again look like the handsome man she had married.

When a Portuguese women encountered her "too thin" husband after a few years apart, she was particularly mortified. She had detested the "Canadian" food in the hotel she and her daughter had stayed in, and the restaurant food they had been served, during a circuitous flight from Portugal to Toronto via a wrong stop in Winnipeg. On the trip she had stuck to some homemade pound cake and figs brought from home, but had fed her daughter eggs and milk. Relief came in Toronto when she was invited to an Italian-Canadian home for dinner. "The salami, tomato, cucumbers, bread," she recalled, "I was so happy." The next morning she was also pleased to find "Portugese foods" (fresh fish and olives) in her west-end Toronto neighbourhood.

By contrast, those who first lived on the outskirts of Toronto, and in places with few ethnic shops, recalled the challenge of shopping in "English" stores. They had to make do with what they could find. Some stuck to familiar items. Others, having failed to explain what they wanted, went with what the shopkeeper or clerk gave them, and hoped for the best. The situation also impelled women to quickly learn at least a smattering of English so that they could ask for specific foods.[46]

Spartan diets, based on budget food items, were not necessarily outrageously unhealthy, as suggested by a couple who lived for a few years on bread, coffee, bean soup, and hocks (stewed pig's feet) while saving to start up a small family bakery.[47] Many Baltic, Ukrainian, Polish, German, Italian, and Portuguese mothers could reproduce a significant portion of their family's pre-migration diet because they relied on low-budget food items, such as potatoes or pasta, flour, and bread, and inexpensive fish or cuts of meat. Often, what distinguished a European dish from a Canadian (or North American) one came down to a specific ingredient (for example, Lithuanians liked caraway seeds, the Hungarians, paprika) or to the amount of seasoning used. In Toronto, as in some other cities where earlier immigrants had set up shops, these ingredients were available in the specialty ethnic stores as well as in supermarkets. In the case of paprika, for example, a Canadian mother, following her favourite cookbook, might use a dash of paprika powder bought in a supermarket to add a touch of colour to devilled eggs to be served at a family picnic or as a party treat. A Hungarian mother might use generous amounts of this ancient Turkish import for a goulash, which she would make with pieces of pork or lamb, potatoes, onions, and tomatoes. It was all the better if the paprika was a high-quality, hence more pungent, variety purchased at a Hungarian or other European butcher shop or delicatessen. In Greek families, where lamb was a favourite meat, women could make dishes that involved rolling minced lamb meat and rice in grape or vine leaves (dolmades), partly because they could buy the prepared leaves in one of the specialty Greek shops, especially in the city's east end on the Danforth. Besides fresh fish, European preferences of smoked, pickled, or tinned fish (herring, sardines) could also be found in specialty shops and even in some supermarkets.

Certain ethnic foods, including Italian pasta dishes, had long been enjoyed as mainstream dishes in North America. Many Italian women in postwar Toronto quickly turned to commercially produced dry pasta for their daily meals because it was convenient (so many of them worked outside the home), cheap, and tasty (because pasta absorbs whatever is put on it – olive oil and garlic, tomato sauce, a white sauce). Making homemade pasta was usually limited to weekends and special occasions. For holidays European women baked festive foods, often with other women, or bought fruit breads, strudels, or custards from an ethnic shop. They could order a special pastry, such as the particular tarts favoured by Hungarians, in an ethnic café.[48]

When European women said they found Canadian meat "unappetizing," they largely meant that they preferred their own well-seasoned dishes, which, again, could be made on a budget. For example, German, Czech, and Polish women frequently cooked pork or beef along with seasoned potatoes and vegetables. They might cook everything in a one-pot, stovetop stew. If they could afford it, they would top the dish off with a cream sauce, or sour cream, or a gravy made from the meat juices. The same vegetables, cooked in a variety of ways, produced a range of European dishes. For example, women used cabbage in homemade sauerkraut, a common German, Austrian, Dutch, Polish, and Ukrainian dish. Or they made cabbage rolls stuffed with rice or meat, a favourite dish among Latvians, Estonians, and Lithuanians. Soups and vegetables cooked with roasted flour produced a flavour characteristic of meals made in parts of Hungary and surrounding regions.

Apart from Italians, who relied heavily on pasta, European women cooked potatoes in an endless variety of ways. They sliced and fried them, baked and roasted them, or boiled them in a pot with vegetables and fish. If the cook was Portuguese, the fish was commonly inexpensive salt cod, which required soaking in water before cooking. The women served potato dishes with oil and vinegar, or sour cream, or gravy. Flour-based dumplings that came in different sizes, with a variety of fillings (potato and cheese, meat, vegetables, fruit), were another favourite with many East Europeans, who referred to them by different names, including pierogi (or perogy), pyrohy, and vareniki.

Canadian Approaches to Feeding Families

Significantly, Canadian food experts, including the Toronto nutritionists who designed the postwar food guide *Food Customs of New Canadians*, acknowledged the capacity of European newcomer women to manage, in their new environment, to cook traditional or familiar meals that were relatively inexpensive and reasonably nutritious. But they also found plenty to criticize, especially with respect to ensuring children's health. In keeping with its liberal slant, the guide did not give any one group an entirely negative or positive evaluation.

On the positive side, the guide reported that in their family diets most of the European groups had a good mix of vegetables, including lettuce, cabbage, carrots, spinach, kale, turnips, beets, cauliflower, tomatoes, peas, leeks, parsnips, and mushrooms. The guide also noted particular vegetable preferences. Greeks and Italians, for instance, ate more eggplant than did the other groups, and they liked dandelion and other bitter-tasting greens. (The guide did not note that Canadians often ridiculed the strange foreigners whom they saw picking dandelions by the railway tracks or in a field.) The guide recognized that many European women from modest rural backgrounds, and even urban ones, knew about stretching economical cuts of meat with starches and vegetables and producing one-dish meals using meat alternatives such as fish. Comments made about the Polish homemaker, that she could make "a small amount of inexpensive meat" go "a long way in soups and stews" and that she often substituted meat for "legumes, eggs and fish in all forms," were echoed in the assessments of the other European groups. The guide also observed that many of the women had adapted easily to the availability of certain foods, such as citrus fruits, that had been prohibitively expensive back home.

On the negative side, the nutritionists made specific criticisms and recommendations for each group. Some of their advice applied as much to old Canadian as to new Canadian mothers, as in the case of teaching the value of canned or frozen fruits, vegetables, and fruit juices as substitutes for fresh but expensive and out-of-season imports. The call to cook more hearty breakfasts was another common piece of advice. In this case, European women who cooked milk-based mushes with bread or oatmeal-type breakfasts (such as the Portuguese) or pancakes with fruit (such as the Dutch) scored well in comparison to many Canadian mothers. But those who stuck to their "continental-style" breakfast of crusty bun, or toast, and coffee had to be reformed. As newcomers' children quickly became too fond of candy, sweet carbonated pop, and sugared cereals, the guide also instructed front-line workers to discourage the mothers from purchasing these items. Again, Canadian mothers, especially working mothers who did not have the time to make cooked cereals or other dishes, faced similar criticism. In other cases the advice was specific to a group. For example, the guide stated that Polish women had to learn to cook their vegetables for less time in order to preserve the nutrients.

Furthermore, the guide established a hierarchy of ethnic groups based on the principle of who could most easily make the transition to Canadian food customs. The hierarchy bore a strong resemblance to Canada's traditional ethnic preference ladder, with the biggest winners being the Germans and Dutch. The "similarity of foods in the home countries and Canada," the guide observed of Germans and Austrians, "makes adjustment relatively easy." The most positive evaluation of all went to the "Dutch housewife," who "prizes culinary skill combined with economy and these abilities enable her to make a smooth transition in any adjustment of foods and food customs necessitated by changed environment." Her generous use of cheese and milk, fruits, and a wide variety of vegetables, and her limited use of candy and soft drinks, were "particularly commendable." A typical meal pattern, as described by the guide, was a breakfast of fruit juice and ready to eat cereal or cooked oatmeal; a lunch of soup, sandwich, and pudding or fruit dessert; and the main meal, dinner, of meat, potatoes, and a vegetable, no bread, and a dessert of pudding, ice cream, canned fruit, or gelatin (which surely, in some cases, would mean Jell-O). But even the Dutch homemaker could improve her skills: the guide advised a greater use of liver and organ meats. It also made specific recommendations for other highly rated groups. The Czechs adapted comparatively easily to Canadian foodways and used a healthy array of food groups, but they had a propensity to be overweight because of their love of dumplings – which they often ate together with potatoes – as well as sweetened beverages and high-fat meats. The adults needed to drink more milk and eat more cheese. The Austrians ate too many sweets.

The Southern Europeans (as well as the few non-European groups profiled), particularly the Portuguese and Italians, came in for more critical comments and recommendations, but the guide praised Greek mothers for producing "a happy combination of both Greek and typically Canadian dishes." The guide approved of dishes such as moussaka, described as "a casserole with ground beef and potatoes," as well as of bean and lentil soups and tomato and cucumber salads. As the supposedly most humble rural newcomers, Portuguese and Italian women were portrayed as the furthest removed from modern Canadian foodways. Not only did they need to be introduced to the necessary tools of a modern household (a gas or electric stove, refrigerator, and storage space), but they had to reform their food-shopping regimes. According to the experts, these women foolishly spent too much of their meagre family budgets on expensive imported goods, such as olive oil, meats, and cheeses for the Italians and fresh fish for the Portuguese. These were particular food no-nos given the availability of cheaper Canadian alternatives, such as corn oil and frozen fish, respectively. Front-line workers were instructed to encourage these women to forgo familiar items, now dubbed expensive luxury foods, in favour of more affordable Canadian products. The experts' family-budget focus trumped their respect for the newcomers' cultural preferences even though the items in question were healthy. For no group was alcoholism identified as a problem, though all of them, save Jews, were described as regular consumers of beer or wine. But Italian mothers were scolded for permitting children to drink a bit of wine (with water or pop) with meals. The *Food Customs* guide recommended carbonated soft drinks as the lesser evil.

Certain class and cultural biases also emerge in the nutritionists' negative evaluations of European women's frequent food-shopping habits, attributing them entirely to poverty (lack of storage or refrigeration) or rural underdevelopment, while ignoring the cultural and social significance. In the bakeries, butcher and fish shops, and other specialty stores of old world towns and villages, women had developed important lines of trust and credit with shopkeepers and critical networks of information and support. For Canadian nutritionists, however, North American middle-class notions of efficiency and cleanliness predominated (access to clean, well-stocked, modern stores meant shopping less frequently and more efficiently), and indeed were equated with modernity. But in the postwar years the celebrated modern supermarket that was being promoted – large chain stores such as Dominion, Loblaws, and Power – were hardly places in which immigrant women well versed in marketplace "haggling" could practise their craft. For these women the ethnic shops and open markets made better economic sense: the frequency of contact helped low-income women to forge bonds of trust with local shopkeepers, who often extended credit to families in financial straits. Even for the middle-class Europeans who had lived in the world's most historic cities, the assumption that daily shopping was "backward" revealed an ignorance of food and shopping customs that involved daily or frequent trips to local bakeries, coffee bars, butcher shops, or greengrocers.

The nutritional gatekeepers issued harsher professional judgments of nursing mothers and child-feeding regimes. Again, they evaluated newcomer mothers in terms of their conformity to "modern" health regimes, which involved an assessment of the child-feeding practices (breastfeeding or artificial), availability of specialty foods for children, level of public instruction for mothers, and the state of prenatal health services in their homeland countries. In Canada many school children were served milk at school, and the state-subsidized school lunches helped poorer children meet "minimal nutritional requirements."

As in the past, the nutrition experts showed little respect for women's folk traditions and mothering remedies, reserving their praise for European women whose routines more closely resembled Canadian or North American methods. Thus they made positive assessments of women in Germany and Austria: "Infants are mostly breastfed up to 3 or 4 months of age; other foods introduced as in Canada. Nutrition education good; deficiency diseases in children practically non-existent." Again, the highest praise went to (the once almost starving) Dutch women whose child-feeding patterns – which followed a progression from formula feeding to the gradual introduction of solid foods – were decidedly "modern." In Holland, "formula feeding is generally accepted" and "a variety of evaporated milk formulae and canned infant foods," as well as vitamin supplements, were widely used. Hungarian women were praised for improving their habits upon arrival in Toronto, where, it was said, they "visit the doctor regularly and follow his instructions closely, adding solid foods as directed in the first year." Italian and Portuguese mothers came in for the strongest criticisms.[49]

Resisting Conformity

Generally speaking, European mothers were both preserving and, in some cases, modifying their food habits in Canada. In certain cases they clearly resisted the pressures to adopt Canadian foodways. When the medical health of a child was not at stake, some women tried to draw boundaries around what they, as mothers and food providers, were prepared to "give up" to the gatekeepers. To the frustration of the public health nurses who staffed the baby clinics in Toronto neighbourhoods, for example, immigrant mothers willingly brought their children in for their vaccination shots, weigh-ins, and free milk, but comparatively few of them stuck around for the lectures on nutrition and child-rearing, which at any rate were in English. Women from a variety of European countries responded in this pragmatic way, although the Italian mothers were singled out as the worst offenders.[50]

European mothers also protested social workers and summer camp counsellors who challenged their authority as family food providers. In the early 1950s, Toronto's settlement houses wanted to attract immigrant children, including very young children and their mothers, to their summer camps. The point was to give all of them a chance to enjoy the beautiful Canadian outdoors and "Canadian-style" camp cookouts, with hamburgers, hot dogs, and marshmallows. The plan was also to introduce them to yet more routines and encourage them to speak English.[51] At

Camp St. Christopher on Lake Scugog, in the mid-1950s, about one-third of the nursery-school mothers were Europeans, most of them East Europeans, including a few Jewish women. There were some Italian women, a few of them acting as guardians because the mothers were at work, and a few African-Canadian mothers. Evidently the mornings went well, with the young children at nursery school, and the mothers hiking, doing crafts, or playing croquet. (Sunday visiting was another matter, however, as the immigrant families evidently made too much noise and overstayed their welcome.) However, the European mothers objected to the idea that their young children were to be separated from them at feeding times and fed by the staff. They insisted on bringing their own food and feeding their own children. The mothers of infants also clashed with the camp nurse over routines for babies on bottles. The disruption prompted the St. Christopher director to insist that, in future, his staff should better prepare the women for camp routines, and to enlist a nurse to help them. Notwithstanding this patronizing response, the conflict suggests the importance that new Canadian women attached to their mothering skills.[52]

Like all mothers, European women had to negotiate the daily pressures that emerged within their own families, and their responses influenced the various family dynamics and cuisines that developed. While most European couples generally preferred familiar foods, various intriguing patterns, as well as some divergent patterns, did emerge. When husbands insisted that, at home, the family was "to eat Estonian" or Greek or German, they usually did so as a bold, even manly, declaration of their pride in their culture. This gender and cultural dynamic could also overlap with class politics, as in the case of left-wing Ukrainian Canadians. The men believed as strongly as the women that "eating Ukrainian" was critical to their twinned cultural and political identity as progressive Ukrainian Canadians, but they left the women to make the meals. The women's willingness to shop and prepare such favourite dishes as *holubtsi* (cabbage rolls) and *pyrohy* reflected their own commitment and emotional attachment to those foods. Their labour also saved costs at their various community events, so that it was also a form of kitchen activism.[53] By the same token, the husband who encouraged his wife to incorporate Canadian foods into their family rituals usually constructed himself as the family's representative in the outside world, the one who would guide his own family's accommodation to Canadian ways. At times this feature also related directly to the man having obtained Canadian citizenship, an act that many men linked to their role as the family head.[54]

By far the greatest pressures on women to experiment with Canadian foods came from their children, especially those who were exposed to the vastly different lunches of their Canadian schoolmates. At school, many a European child quickly became embarrassed by the spicy salami or sausage sandwiches that mother made with crusty or dark bread. They dreaded opening up their bags lest the smells offend the other children and prompt insulting remarks. They looked with envy at the neat "Canadian" sandwiches of white bread with peanut butter and jam, or at the bright orange slices of cheese that had little or no odour. Along with sugar-coated cereals, immigrant children's favourites were hot dogs, hamburgers, and the airy buns served with them. Many a Polish, German, Hungarian, Greek, and Portugese mother first experimented with store-bought hot dogs (as opposed to "real sausages"), tinned soups, Kraft singles, hamburgers and hamburg buns, mayonnaise, Spam, Jell-O, and sugared cereals because of her children's persistent requests. Getting this food sometimes required going to a Loblaws or Dominion store, so that both changes occurred in tandem. The issue of food could also cause mothers embarrassment or emotional hurt. During her *Chatelaine* interview with Edna Staebler, Alda Pilli was visibly embarrassed when her son Luigi declared his love of "Canadian" food – "hamburgers, hot dogs, potato chips," and Coke. His brother Paul added "chewie gum." It was only when her husband said, "I still like best how my wife cook – spaghetti, pizza, radicchio, lasagne," that she smiled in relief. But many newcomer mothers agreed to include "Canadian" foods because many of them were convenient (an important facet for the many working mothers), inexpensive, and reasonably healthy as well as being a hit with the kids.[55]

Hybrid Ethnic-Canadian Meals

These modest efforts at experimentation led to a variety of hybrid family diets, though the timing and degree differed across households. A common early pattern in many families was one in which the mother cooked a "Canadian meal" for her children while she and her husband stuck to familiar old world fare. She could thus placate the children without totally upsetting her husband, and she could also exercise a measure of control over the process of change. A mother's shopping budget could influence her decision to indulge her children's desire for the more expensive convenience items, such as sugar-coated cereal. Furthermore, a concession to a "Canadian breakfast" for the children (even one that the experts disliked), or lunch, was not a serious threat to cultural traditions when the evening and weekend meals included traditional fare.

In some cases the changes happened in such an incremental fashion that even mothers claimed to have barely noticed it. One German woman said she had not consciously tried to raise her children "in a German way," yet emphasized that she had initially cooked primarily German food and spoken German in her home. But over the years more Canadian foods had crept into her meal plans. Like many others, she saw no contradiction between a continuing commitment to homeland food customs and her strong identity as a Canadian. In any case hybrid meals had emerged earlier in Canada, among the pre-1945 immigrant and ethnic Canadian families and communities, and the postwar newcomers' encounter with these compatriots further encouraged this experimentation.[56]

These dynamics could give rise to family conflicts, however, especially when newcomer husbands objected to their wives' willingness to accommodate their children's desire for hot dogs and such. Another German woman (a former refugee from East Germany) who enjoyed supplementing her "mostly German" diet with Canadian and other ethnic foods recalled the "tensions" that emerged between her and her children over her husband's domineering approach to maintaining "strict" German standards. Still, in the end, her family developed a hybrid diet.

Families that were the result of mixed ethnic marriages between newcomers from different European countries also produced hybrid diets. An Austrian woman who married an Italian man in Toronto in the 1950s said that they had developed "international" tastes and outlook. She also stressed that her daughter, also a cosmopolitan eater, identified entirely as a Canadian.[57] At holiday times the tendency among mothers to mix the old with the new became more pronounced. For instance, the Canadian wife of a Budapest man made his favourite chicken paprika dish for the holidays, but instead of the traditional Hungarian Christmas fish dinner (eaten on Christmas eve), she prepared "the good old English turkey." A Canadian woman married to a Greek man learned to make baklava (a sticky pastry with chopped walnuts, honey, and cinnamon) using ready-made phyllo pastry bought at a store. Such stories can be seen as a form of culinary pluralism from the bottom up. By the 1960s some European families had begun to incorporate "ethnic foods" from other origins, with common examples being takeout Chinese meals and (among non-Italians) lasagne and pizza.[58]

The class and occupational status of the newcomers, or their upward mobility, could also influence the willingness of different newcomers to experiment with Canadian foods and recipes, though we cannot always predict their responses based simply on their class profiles. For example, in postwar Toronto, generally speaking the Germans were better off economically than the Italians and tended to disperse into the wider population, while the Italians clustered among their own and in poorer neighbourhoods. Yet both groups showed a strong attachment to cooking and eating their homeland or, indeed, regional foods. A family's move into a "better" neighbourhood with easy access to Canadian supermarkets could also make a difference. Some of the professionally trained refugees who had successfully retooled or updated their fields of work, or families in which both partners had found a reasonably well-paying alternative, did move into more heavily Canadian neighbourhoods, such as the new Toronto suburb of Don Mills. These women probably shopped in the supermarkets and incorporated Canadian foods sooner or to a greater degree than did the less-well-off Italians and Portugese who stayed in the old immigrant neighbourhoods downtown.[59]

Poor Mothers Feeding Families Poorly

When it came to what was being fed to families, the Italian and Portuguese mothers of the inner-city neighbourhoods came under continuing criticism. Indeed, by the early 1960s front-line social workers and health-care workers based in the inner-city "ghettos" of west-end Toronto had become profoundly concerned, even alarmist, in their view that the mothers of the low-income and uneducated Italian and Portuguese families who now dominated these areas could not afford to meet their families' nutritional needs. Their efforts to promote Canadian nutrition standards and menus plans, however genuine, served to pathologize these mothers as being too isolated, stubborn, and suspicious of well-intentioned professionals to improve their homemaking skills.

The experts worried about the ill effects of prolonged living in crowded, substandard housing with poor cooking facilities, and about the special burdens that low wages imposed on women who, whether housewives or working mothers, had to stretch inadequate funds to cover rent, food, drugs, clothing, furniture, and other necessities. If families had purchased large-ticket household items on credit, which in the 1960s became more available to low-income people, they would also be carrying debt and having collection agencies hounding them to demand payment. If a family was "fleeced" by ethnic salesmen or "gouging landlords," it went further into debt. Since food was one of the more "flexible" items on the budget, the fear was that, to pay the bill, the mother would rely on increasingly cheap, starch-heavy foods and cut out comparatively more expensive and healthy alternatives.[60]

One result was childhood malnutrition, which could produce long-term physical, mental, and emotional problems. In response the experts basically applied the old remedies to the current context – home visits, family budgets, and austere meal plans.[61] Some modest successes were recorded, including a hot-lunch program that in conjunction with various charitable and service agencies was launched in a public school within the St. Christopher House neighbourhood – roughly the area bounded by Spadina Avenue in the east, Markham Street in the west, College Street in the north, and Queen Street West in the south. A useful program, it nevertheless used the carrot-and-stick approach so common to welfare measures. A dozen "undernourished" children were given money subsidies to purchase nutritious hot meals from the school cafeteria, provided their mothers agreed to attend fortnightly classes at St. Christopher for "help in nutrition and meal planning." Within two years the teachers reported on the children's improved academic performance but expressed concern that, while many of the mothers had enjoyed the nutrition classes, some of them had spent their child's subsidy on other items.[62]

Women in Ukrainian costume at the Foreign Food Show, Calgary, January 1955.
(GMA, NA-5600-7110d)

Popularizing and Containing Ethnic Food Cultures

As with other cultural activities, the gatekeepers used food as a social device and ethnic dinners as an integration device that could encourage cultural exchange and thus contribute to nation-building and national unity. Food did break the ice with some malnourished children like Abbie, a "very sad" European boy at the St. Christopher nursery school. Abbie, fortunately, brightened up at the sight of milk and biscuits. While eating remained his favourite part of the nursery program, he learned to speak some English and enjoyed singing the children's songs and doing gymnastics.[63]

Ethnic banquets were used as social icebreakers or catalysts for cultural exchange. At St. Christopher House the staff invited ethnic groups to host dinners featuring some of their popular food, with other ethnic group members to attend. While the staff probably exaggerated the success of these events and their role in promoting "integration," the participating European women and their families clearly enjoyed them. In 1954 the "New Canadian party" was the biggest event of the year at St. Christopher, attracting more than 150 people. Indeed, the crowd was far too big for the space provided because the members had all brought friends along. "International dancers" added "a colourful touch to the party." The women cooked a variety of "European dishes." The staff were amused when some of the folks mistakenly added sugar and milk to the first course of bouillon with "pirokad" (piroshki) because they thought the broth was some sort of tea or coffee. But when some of the newcomers stayed seated during the singing of "O Canada," the organizers were not amused. Rather, they lectured the group on the necessity of standing up. They then used the incident as an example of just how helpful they could be "in showing our Canadian way of life and customs to these people and preparing them towards integration."[64]

On other occasions the St. Christopher staff acknowledged the independent capacity of peoples from different homelands to co-exist peacefully. In 1955, at the first in a series of ethnic dinners initiated by a St. Christopher female social worker, the Italian House members prepared a Calabrian-style spaghetti dinner for the Portuguese members. The two groups by then made up most of St. Christopher's 150 members, because many of the other Europeans had already moved out of the area. The social worker described the dinner as "a very great success." Everyone enjoyed the meal and the dancing afterwards, she noted, and the Portuguese members jumped right in and helped with all of the cleaning up. They also agreed to host the next dinner, which would feature their "national food" – probably an islander's cod fish stovetop dish or casserole, with potatoes and vegetables. For the social worker the event showed that "friendship and understanding" had developed between the two groups, and she hoped to see more of this. Dinners like this one took place in service clubs and community halls across the country, representing a form of culinary exchange and encouraging cultural pluralism.[65]

Women at work at the Ethnic Food Fair, Al Azhar Temple, Calgary, April 1956.
(GMA, NA-5600-7976a)

With similar motives in mind the Citizenship Branch, the International Institute of Metropolitan Toronto, and other gatekeepers promoted ethnic foodways, especially European ones, by hosting ethnic banquets and sponsoring cookbook projects. While many newcomers enjoyed these events, and helped to organize them, the showcasing of ethnic cuisine, like the celebration of ethnic crafts and folk dancing, was also part of a strategy by which the gatekeepers mined ethnic culture to serve the larger goal of consolidating the postwar Canadian nation. The promotion of ethnic foods provided a way of stripping the immigrants of their more threatening features, or reducing ethnicity to entertainment and novelty. A form of ethnic containment, the approach created a safe and confined context in which cultural diversity could be endorsed.[66]

In keeping with these cultural politics, the Citizenship Branch gave its backing to cookbook projects featuring ethnic recipes. In 1950 Kaye complimented the Canadian National Unity Council of Hamilton for publishing "an excellent cookbook containing recipes of some 30 nations, Albanian, Armenian, Austrian, Belgian, etc." Besides being "artistically executed," he explained, it was "an excellent medium to further the idea of Canadian unity."[67] Holidays were an obvious opportunity for generating cookbooks as well as food columns encouraging people to spruce up their festivities by, perhaps, trying a Dutch recipe for "love letters" (an almond-paste-filled pastry shaped in the letter of a person's sweetheart's name). A 1963 Christmas recipe booklet typically declared that as "each nationality in the Canadian mosaic celebrates the Christmas season in the tradition of its forefathers," the melding of these customs brought "a richness to the festive season" and to the mutual desire for peace and freedom. It contained descriptions of colourful Christmas customs of various ethnic groups, such as the Czech St. Nicholas and the Italian Befana (fairy), and festive ethnic recipes, including Lithuanian red beet

Gregory Bruskin at the Samovar Restaurant, serving up blinis. (Photograph by Steve Russell; Toronto Star Archives, Image no. fg3kkoz2)

salad with herring and poppyseed roll; Czech fish soup with fried carp and bread crumbs; Portuguese turkey dinner with pudding, fish fillets, and pumpkin croquettes; Hungarian hazelnut cake, and spareribs goulash; and Danish cookies and cabbage rolls. These cookbooks, whether state-funded or commercially produced, helped to create a safe cultural terrain on which the "hosts" could be encouraged to accept "difference."[68]

When Kaye praised the culinary value of the European newcomers, he, like other figures, spoke about how they were helping to fight blandness in an age of mechanism and standardization. In a speech on citizenship delivered at the Masaryk Hall in Toronto in 1957, he quoted Governor General Vincent Massey, who had remarked on "how colorless it would be if the world was inhabited by people who had the same tastes, talked the same language, and more frightening still – thought the same way." According to Kaye, such standardization "was threatening to make of us automatons served the same cream of tomato soup, and the same hamburger with ketchup from Halifax to Vancouver." Canadians did not succumb to this evil, however, "thanks mostly to the one million new immigrants who not only revived the culinary art threatened with extinction but also taught Canadians to enjoy meals like they do in Paris… or Prague… or Vienna or Dublin…. We are building a Canadian Nation," Kaye added, giving the official line, "not by boiling the ingredients in a melting pot but by blending them together harmoniously and deriving strength in diversity." By adding the many valuable cultural heritages to the "young Canadian treasure chest," Kaye declared, we add "beauty, charm and strength" to the Canadian way of life.[69]

At this time European women and more "ethnic" recipes began appearing in *Chatelaine*, along with more stories on working wives and mothers. One of the first feature-length articles on the newcomers, Janine Locke's 1957 piece on a Hungarian couple, Katey and Frank Myer, was a classic Cold War escape narrative that ended in a modern Canadian paradise. The caption accompanying a photo of a slim and smiling Katey described her as having the "inconspicuously attractive" good looks typical of the average Canadian housewife. Katey's domestication is telling, given that she had a professional background and had just landed a bank-teller job. The article offers a lighthearted story of how this couple, having lost so much in Communist Hungary, could truly appreciate Canada's abundance and North American middle-class standards.

In Budapest the couple had shared a three-room apartment with three other family members; they had no electrical household appliances and had endured a "perpetual chill" due to the scarcity and high cost of fuel. In Toronto, their patrons, a doctor and his family, had given them commodious accommodations: a suite of two rooms, a new refrigerator and stove, and their own bathroom. During her first trip to a Canadian supermarket, Katey happily loaded up with many "newly discovered delicacies" (sardines, instant coffee, canned soups, ham, chicken legs) and with so much ice cream that "they used it in great scoops even in their coffee." She enthused, "There is everything you could want… in the supermarket… not like the little shops at home where there was little to buy and what we wanted we could never afford." As a treat to celebrate her husband's acceptance to the University of Toronto and her new job, Katey had gone to a department store to buy a practical item, a slip. But once there she could not resist some high-heeled red leather pumps (at $35 they cost about a week's salary for Frank). She "limped, painfully but persistently" in them until she could wear them proudly in public. The Myers were planning to save for a car and a suburban home.

The Myers' enthusiasm for all things Canadian was tempered by wistful memories of Hungarian food and music. They were delighted to find a Hungarian restaurant, the Csarda, in downtown Toronto and felt "transported home by the smells and sounds." When they "eat goulash and cheese strudel," they "believe they are back in their favourite restaurant" at their favourite lakeside holiday resort back home. Although the couple never enjoyed "gypsy" music back home (a sign of their class status), it now pleases them very much. So do the slightly tart desserts that remind Katey of her mother's cooking.

One way of reading this piece is to say that the tension between the newcomers' adaptation to Canadian ways and the gatekeepers' liberal nod to European customs is not completely resolved. Another is to say that it fits with the often ambiguous, even contradictory, assumptions that informed the gatekeepers' cultural pluralism.[70] By comparison Staebler's 1965 piece on Italian Alda Pilli (also slim and attractive) and her family was a sadder tale of struggle. Yet Staebler's evocative descriptions introduced readers to various Italian specialties still foreign to most Canadians, such as radicchio ("a bitter tasting" salad green that is reportedly "very good for the blood"). In discussing Alda's preference for the ethnic stores in her neighbourhood (in the newer Little Italy further north on St. Clair Avenue West), Staebler presents daily food shopping as a viable alternative to the weekly Canadian supermarket model (this way, "everything is fresh"). Staebler evocatively describes the shops ("Italian butcher shops have gutted kids and fleecy black lambs hanging in their windows, with salami and mortadella sausages") and features Alda's simple specialties: spaghetti, thin slices of veal, green salad dressed with lemon and olive oil, cauliflower or eggplant or broccoli "dipped in a batter and fried golden brown." In describing the meat servings ("usually thin slices of fried veal or boiled chicken"), Staebler explains that in Toronto Alda can afford to serve more beef than she had been able to do in Italy, where it was tough and expensive. On Sundays they had homemade pizza, made from dough and dotted with anchovies, olives, and sauce. As for dinner, Staebler noted that they all drank the husband's homemade wine, even the boys, who took some wine in their glasses of water.[71] Staebler's approach to the Pillis' foodways was typical of the magazine in the 1960s, when the *Chatelaine* Institute staff and a variety of food writers were featuring more ethnic recipes and more strongly encouraging Canadian mothers to try them out.

Una Abrahamson's January 1965 article on the double day profiled an ethnic woman, Susan Stastny, who juggled her day between work at home and outside. Stastny shared her helpful hints about food shopping and preparation and getting her husband, Milan, and children to help with the domestic chores. The article included photographs and recipes of her specialties, including Caraway Beef Goulash, and her time-saving "triple-duty menus." A pork loin served as spiced pork roast for a weekend dinner, for example, could be used to make "a hurry up meal as Pungent Pork with Oranges," and the rest of the leftovers were used in lunch-time sandwiches.[72]

In Toronto the 1960s also began to see a decline in the city's typically British fish and chip shops and a corresponding increase in pizza parlours.[73] The growing attention given to ethnic or exotic recipes (or Canadian versions of them) also reflected other factors, including the saturation-advertising techniques of U.S. food corporations, such as Dole's pineapple campaign, which promoted "exotic" meals with pineapples and other fruits extracted from the toil of exploited workers in Southern countries. Another was the increased affluence of the decade, which encouraged at least some better-off Canadians to experiment with the gourmet cuisine promoted by highly successful food writers such as Julia Child, whose books sparked an interest in French cooking. An interest in the alternative tastes of organic and "global" foods also enticed some middle-class baby boomers who, having reached young adulthood, saw their rebellion against a "meat-mashed-potatoes-and-peas" background as part of a larger interest in cultural, political, and sexual experimentation. Moreover, the change suggests a growing appreciation of the different "sensualities" of foods.[74] According to the author of an encyclopedia on Canadian foodways, Canadian food fashion-makers in the 1970s were catching up with, and in part "cashing in" on, trends of multi-ethnic eating that were already developing from the bottom up, among ordinary people from working-class and modestly middle-class households.[75]

We should not exaggerate this important nod to cultural pluralism, however, or exaggerate the impact of ethnic foods or multicultural eating in the early postwar decades. As with other cases of the increasingly mainstream ethnic foods in North America and elsewhere, the ethnic recipes meant to add "spice" to the family meals were hardly "authentic." The homogenizing process is apparent in a 1960 recipe for "Easy-to-Make Pizza Pin Wheels" (small individual pizzas), which had substituted Canadian for Italian ingredients. The recipe called for biscuit mix, tomato soup and ketchup, pressed meat, cheese wafers, and cheddar cheese, and for "modest" amounts of (dry) oregano, green pepper, and onion. Even by end of the 1960s

Chatelaine was promoting Canadian foods by invoking the budget-conscious Canadian homemaker who cooked updated classics such as "hamburgers with class" or "ten ways with a pound of hamburg."[76] Indeed, a Canadian centennial cookbook project called *Discovering Canadian Cuisine* was dominated by "Canadian" recipes for flapjacks, seafood salad, biscuit cheese squares, pies, turkey, French-Canadian pea soup, and venison. For those Torontonians who could afford it, "dining out" still meant patronizing high-end Wasp restaurants like the dining room of the Royal York Hotel, which, Kaye's optimistic 1957 comments aside, would have appealed to a clientele that preferred a Canadian steak and potato dinner to "real Hungarian gulash" or, if they ever carried it, knedlicky.[77] When devising their weekly or monthly family meals, or preparing for family picnics and holidays, many mothers turned to their tried and trusted recipes. For Canadian mothers, that meant the clipped pages of *Chatelaine* or the glossy-coloured *Joys of Jell-O* recipe books put out by the General Foods Corporation. For European mothers, it meant old world favourites, especially in the case of holiday specialties. In some cases mothers indulged their children by adding some of their favourite "other" foods.[78]

All in all, the cookbook projects involved acts of cultural appropriation meant to benefit the Canadian nation, whose prerogative it was to mine ethnic customs in ways that would enrich mainstream culture without its power being diminished. Insofar as the gatekeepers reduced ethnic foodways into non-threatening forms of entertainment and novelty, their strategy was one of culinary containment.[79] And, lest we forget, the people who bore the greatest brunt of the nutritionists' and social workers' harshest health judgments in these years were the low-income Portuguese and Italian mothers of the families who remained in the poor inner-city neighbourhoods – though, with the benefit of hindsight, we can say that they too eventually helped to transform Toronto's culinary landscape.

Indeed, the relationship between the nutritional and food gatekeepers and newcomer mothers is perhaps best understand as a series of negotiations and encounters that transformed both food cultures, though not equally. The gatekeepers had the power and position to define "ethnic" food as un-Canadian, while the *Food Customs* guidebook and similar projects suggest that nutrition experts and food fashion-makers, like other gatekeepers, sought to modify, not obliterate the food (and other) cultures of emigrating groups, even though their liberal intentions did not eliminate a rampant cultural chauvinism. If the recent allure of multicultural and conspicuous dining has brought immigrant food cultures into the forefront of North American standards of "taste," the 1950s and 1960s were a much more tentative, contested terrain – and, of course, class and cultural conflicts over food continue. But we are still left with a final conundrum, namely that culinary pluralism, even when practised in positive and affirming ways, always involves a degree of cultural appropriation, an act of "eating the other."[80]

Shaping the Democratic Family

Popular Advice Experts and Settlement House Workers

7

JUST AS CANADIAN FOOD EXPERTS tried to bring the newcomers' culinary experiences more into line with middle-class models, another set of gatekeepers, including popular advice columnists and social workers staffing city settlement houses, sought to reshape the newcomers' sense of marriage and family so that those institutions would better emulate Canadian bourgeois ideals. These gatekeepers' efforts to "modernize" newcomer families and teach their youth the merits of organized play and participatory democracy were part of wider campaigns to strengthen families across the whole population. They were also part of the reception activities specifically directed at integrating the newcomers into the Canadian mainstream and preparing them for citizenship in a capitalist democracy. A key concern in this regard was to Canadianize, hence democratize, what was seen as the more deeply patriarchal and authoritarian European family.

When postwar social workers spoke about Canadian family ideals or Canadian ways of parenting and growing up, they invariably invoked the image of a modern, democratic Canadian home – an image assuming, ironically, that a wife could enjoy an egalitarian relationship with her husband within a patriarchal institution. Although they viewed themselves as quite willing to accept certain cultural differences, they nonetheless promoted conservative and contradictory family values that privileged a white (which in English Canada meant Anglo-Celtic), middle-class, and heterosexual nuclear household. In doing this they ignored or downplayed the reality that gender inequities, not to mention domestic violence, occurred in families of all kinds, including Canadian middle-class homes. At the same time the gatekeepers considered the postwar nuclear family to be fragile and under attack and thus in need of shoring up, especially in the face of threats that ranged from rising

Opposite: The stereotype of European men as unbending patriarchs left little room for appreciating touching displays of fatherhood. Here a Baltic refugee holds up his baby upon arrival in Halifax, as if to say: I came to Canada to make a better life for my child. *Telegram* 14 Aug. 1950. (Studio Roger Bedard; YUA, Toronto Telegram, ASC Image 1330)

An emotional father greets his children at Union Station, Toronto, as his wife, with a pensive look, watches. The original caption describes them as "Italian DPs," so they may be Italo-Slovenians. (Photograph by Whyte; YUA, Toronto Telegram, ASC Image 1291)

divorce rates and juvenile delinquency to the nuclear bomb. The task was seen as critical because as a basic social institution the family could serve the nation by raising well-adjusted democratic citizens and acting as a bulwark against communism.

Among the most active players in these efforts were settlement houses, which had long promoted democratic family values and relationships in major cities such as Winnipeg, Vancouver, and Toronto. Already by the early 1950s, St. Christopher House in west-end Toronto was asking the city for additional funds to hire more staff to deal with the growing number of European newcomer families in the neighbourhood. The newcomers included Ukrainian, Jewish, and Polish DPs as well as Italian and Portuguese immigrants, although the DPs of middle-class origin were beginning to move out of the district, along with better-off Canadians. In making the request, the board stressed that if St. Christopher was to continue to carry out its historically important role of serving disadvantaged and immigrant families in the inner city, it needed more front-line social workers to meet the challenges involved.

Many of the families were living in crowded and substandard housing, the board reported, and the parents were overly strict with their children and neglecting their needs out of ignorance of the available social services. The need for organized educational and recreational programs was "very great for all ages." St. Christopher needed more teachers to help run the nursery school, parent study groups, and "Kitchen English" classes for women. It needed more group workers to handle its clubs for girls and boys and its craft classes, athletics program, field trips, music group, and teen dances. It especially wanted more adult workers to make door to door visits in the neighbourhood and identify different needs. "Intensive" home visiting was one of the most effective methods of "stabilizing family life" and preventing or containing juvenile delinquency.

In addition, the staff would be fulfilling their conventional role of immersing the newcomers, parents and children alike, in Canadian practices and demonstrating the everyday ways of living in a democracy. This encouragement was all the more necessary because board members suspected that certain families in the area had "Communistic leanings." Furthermore, a failure to achieve the organization's goals could produce whole families and communities with "no sense of loyalty to the Canadian way of life."

The St. Christopher board was ringing the alarm bells with a familiar message: newcomer families that went "adrift" might produce dysfunctional members of society, perhaps alcoholic fathers, depressed mothers, or delinquent children. Even if these families did not become vulnerable to communism, they might instead become multiproblem households that would overburden the social welfare state.[1]

As women and men who had lost so many loved ones, the European newcomers also cared a great deal about families. Many of them were keen to make or remake families, raise children, and in other ways rebuild their lives. They had their own views of what made for a decent marriage, proper children, and good family. Some thousands of women who entered Canada as single women would eventually marry and raise families.

A Canadian father reunites with his family at Union Station, Toronto, in 1953 after serving in the U.S.-led United Nations "police action" against Communist North Korea. The war, which began after North Korea invaded pro-Western South Korea in June 1950, ended in 1953 with Korea still divided. Of the approximately 25,000 Canadians who participated, 300 were killed.
(Photograph by Gordon W. Powley; AO, Digital Image no. 10002815, C 5-1-0-180-5)

The desire "to have families again," as a Jewish DP camp resident put it, was evident in the high rates of marriage and birth in the refugee camps, both Jewish and mixed, and in the large presence of youthful families among the volunteer immigrants from different European countries. Driven by a fear of being left completely on their own, many of the refugees entered into short courtships, quick marriages, and early families. In the DP camps, malnourished women, Jewish and gentile, had risked their health, even lives, to give birth. Certain concerns, first of being infertile and later of suffering from complications due to pregnancy or birth, were strongest among the Jewish women, especially among those whose bodies had been mutilated by the Nazi experiments. Across the European continent there were new mothers who did not have access to a mother or female elders to advise them. After seeing so much death, many of them understandably suffered from serious maternal anxieties. They took on the extra duties of motherhood amid conditions of uncertainty, scarcity, and poor health.

The difficult conditions that reigned across postwar Europe tended to reinforce traditional gender roles, particularly for mothers who had to keep their husbands and children fed and clothed. In the DP camps the women's time-consuming labours released the men to get involved in public activities. In the rural and fishing households of Southern Europe the women's capacity to maintain families had released men to migrate to earn wages, a strategy that often led to family migration and settlement abroad.[2] The practical, if not ideological, family had become more fluid during the war, and different types of "family living units" had emerged, including "surrogate" or "grab-bag families" composed of kin and non-kin who had come together in survival mode to share housing, food, and other resources. Both men and women had entered into these arrangements, but it was the women who usually initiated and sustained these "war families."

Once they were in Canada, the situation as a whole held many ironies: war widows who had performed heroic roles for their families, such as orchestrating risky escapes, were now viewed as weak and in need of support; women who had been family decision-makers and protectors now reverted to conventional family forms, with their husbands as the acknowledged patriarch. Still, in these seemingly conventional marriages, with traditional gender norms reinstated, the women hardly became shrinking violets.

Promoting an Ideal: The Canadian Democratic Family

In the rapidly proliferating histories of the Cold War's domestic side in North America, studies of the alarmist discourses of dysfunctional families, the moral regulation of juvenile delinquents, and the vilification of neglectful mothers producing misfit children have shown how the state, courts, schools, and professional and popular experts sought to contain and eradicate all alleged deviants or threats to the body politic. As a corollary to the U.S. (and NATO) strategy of containing Communism abroad, domestic containment became both a defensive strategy aimed at all defined threats to acceptable norms and a proactive strategy through which the body politic could be made to emulate the values of obedience, conformity, and belief in capitalism.

In Cold War capitalist democracies, the experts' efforts to limit sex to marriage, to contain and socialize youth in controlled sites, to maintain clear gender hierarchies and distinctions, and to promote the nuclear family were part of a highly charged turf on which moral victories against Communism were fought. The gatekeepers' efforts to contain perceived threats from within – whether from ethnic Canadian Communists or alienated newcomers – were linked to the resurgence of conservative family and gender ideologies and Cold War anxieties.[3]

Even without the Cold War, though, mass immigration and a shift from war to peacetime would have spawned pro-family, democracy, and Canadianization programs. Canadian family and child experts agreed that, along with gaining decent family incomes, building happy families was essential to the newcomers' successful integration into the mainstream; and that family conflicts would hamper the achievement of these goals. As problem-fixers they expected to intervene in families that they saw as dysfunctional or otherwise in need of support. This is not surprising given that social experts had long promoted a bourgeois family ideal as the key to good living and citizenship and had long railed against the many threats to the family, from urban overcrowding to working mothers. But they insisted (as experts in our own time do) that never before was the family more under siege and in more danger of falling apart.

Canada's postwar social workers, psychologists, and social commentators expressed strongly felt anxieties that after the long upheavals in economic and social relations occasioned by the Depression and the Second World War, Canadians did not know what a "normal" family life was. The 1930s had destroyed many role models, they argued. Many children had grown up in families in which unemployed fathers had lost their self-respect and were reduced to weeping emotional wrecks – a crisis in masculinity. Mothers had not only resorted to nagging, a great female sin, but had also undermined their own well-being in order to feed the others. The war had flung many young couples apart, and their reunions were not always happy affairs. In the experts' view, many women had become too headstrong and independent because of the jobs and greater social and sexual freedom they had enjoyed in wartime; they now had to be brought back into the family fold.

The Cold War and nuclear bomb reinforced the need for emotional security for everyone. As the experts invariably argued, the satisfaction of this need could be best achieved within the confines of the nuclear family, which, like the family that hunkered down in the safety of the backyard bomb shelter, had to protect itself from outside dangers and from succumbing to contaminating influences. On top of all this, Canada was becoming home to thousands of Europeans whose families had taken an even greater beating. There were parents still frantic about children left behind in war zones or, worse, behind the Iron Curtain. The severe housing shortage of the early postwar years forced many couples to "double up," adding to the collective angst. The housing situation both endangered healthy family living and resembled the cramped living conditions that prevailed in the Soviet Union.

The postwar family faced other identified threats, including the rising divorce rate, "sex perverts," juvenile delinquents, and the spread of "obscene" literature. Canadian child experts declared that children were growing up in "an anxious age, where there is a threat of war," where "homes are broken or both parents work," and where "modern life stresses" and "scientific advancement" had "outrun comprehension."[4] The child orphans brought into Canada for adoption presented far more challenges than the social workers had assumed, in part because they included teenagers still living in survivor mode. A range of social critics, family court judges, and other gatekeepers (even when they sympathized with women who had to work to support their families) particularly blamed mothers for the period's social ills, real and perceived, whether those ills were "latch-key children," juvenile delinquents, purveyors of obscene literature, or homosexuals. Given that the nation's security forces viewed gays and lesbians in the civil service as weak links in the fight against Communism because of their susceptibility to the blackmail-induced leaking of government secrets, the homophobic discourses, especially about homosexual sons, had a clear Cold War component. Other social critics, including women's groups, decried the "invasion" of U.S. mass-circulation confession novels and magazines and their popularity among impressionable girls. With plots that mixed sexual scandal and morality tale, the dime-store pulp fiction gained notoriety in the United States and Canada, where women's groups lobbied against them and family court officials and caseworkers blamed them for contributing to more delinquency.[5]

In response to a perceived need to strengthen the weakened family in a rapidly changing world, the experts promoted a family model that included a bread-winning husband, homemaking wife (or, depending upon circumstances, a working wife), and well-reared children. In addition to her household skills, the ideal wife was an engaging conversationalist who deferred to her husband but felt free to share her opinions with him and never became a complete slave to domestic drudgery. She had a good sense of humour and treated her children with affection and love. For his part, the ideal father was a good provider whose earnings allowed for a carefully managed household that would eventually purchase the much-desired home in the Communist-free and delinquency-free suburbs. He was a firm but kind authority figure who took an interest in the children's homework and hobbies, and took the family on picnics and vacations, but never hesitated to discipline his children when required. A greater emphasis on the need to secure the emotional and psychological needs of children also raised the standards of good parenting.

Although fathers never drew as much attention as mothers did, there were Cold War versions of Mr. America and Mr. Canada. In the pro-capitalist propaganda and anti-Communist materials, Soviet fathers, like mothers, emerged as victims of a regime that forced them to toil for long periods away from their children, who, in turn, were subjected to Communist indoctrination by an array of state-directed educational ideologues. Communism prevented fathers from becoming family bread-winners. In the portraits of the morally degraded families of Communist regimes, we can, by extension, see husbands and fathers as cold and unhappy figures who drink vodka and worry lest their children one day betray them to the authorities. The stories of the Radnick family, the Jociches (chapter 2), who told Canadian reporters about their life in Tito's Yugoslavia, stressed how the state indoctrinated the youth and used them to intimidate and keep their parents in line.

At the other end of the spectrum, some of the most romantic portraits of the pro-capitalist democratic father could be found in the slew of popular U.S. family TV sitcoms of the 1950s and early 1960s, such as *Father Knows Best*, *Leave It to Beaver*, and *The Adventures of Ozzie & Harriet*, which portrayed the nuclear family as a site of domestic bliss and social harmony. A program about growing up in the suburbs, *Leave It to Beaver* followed the cute adventures of Beaver and his brother, Wally, and the interventions of their two loving and selfless parents, Ward and June Cleaver. These programs depicted a self-enclosed suburban world of white picket fences, malt shops, and corner drugstores, ignoring the "other America" of racism and poverty. Their sappy nostalgia and simple morality tales were at odds with the scary realities and distress of the era. As regards masculinity, the fathers conformed to the era's dominant model of domesticated men and family consumers: in contrast to the past, they were more likely to make their wives (and children) and not their male "buddies" their regular companions on evenings out and on weekends. Canadian-made films echoed this portrait, though a few filmmakers managed to produce ironic formulations of this postwar male ideal.[6]

Canada's family boosters also endorsed a nostalgic family that not only harkened back to a supposedly less morally ambiguous time but was also dressed up with modern, democratic features. On one level, the gatekeepers saw the democratic family as the logical outcome of the companionate marriage ideal that family experts had been promoting since the turn of the twentieth century. A husband and wife enjoyed the benefits of a relatively egalitarian marriage, with each playing separate but complementary roles, and they raised their children within a wholesome family environment in which everyone was encouraged to participate. On another level this type of family, in which children were accorded a certain respect and encouraged to converse with adults, was expected to produce well-adjusted citizens who could take their place in the wider world. The democratic family was juxtaposed with both the "traditional" European family, said to be strict and father-dominated, and the Communist family, which, as the anti-Communist propaganda explained, separated parents from children and brainwashed the children into becoming slaves to Stalin. A fundamental paradox, again, was that men remained at the head of these supposedly more companionate and egalitarian arrangements.[7]

When dispensing advice about marriage and family, Canada's popular experts, like their U.S. counterparts, largely adhered to these dominant paradigms. The emphasis on guiding Canadian men and women back into a normative family disrupted by the war pervaded the advice that, for instance, a retired army (RCAF) psychologist, Squadron Leader J.D. Parks, gave to Canadian ex-servicemen and their wives in his *Toronto Star* column, "Let's Talk It Over." In response to letters from ex-soldiers who were having trouble readjusting to married life and from "liberated wives" who were unhappy with the return of a demanding or emotionally troubled husband, Parks offered a degree of sympathy laced with a strong dose of family-values ideology. A pro-family approach also informed the counsel given in two other advice columns in the *Star*, Dorothy Lash's "New Horizons" and Mary Starr's "If You Take My Advice." Lash's "New Horizons" was meant for newcomers, although some long-time Canadians, mostly women, also sent letters.

Like Lash's, Starr's column attracted a largely female audience, but the people who wrote to her were mainly Anglo-Canadians, with a smattering of letters from European and British newcomers. A handful of men also wrote letters to these columns.[8]

The advice that Lash and Starr meted out was aimed at both old and new Canadian readers. They singled out "companionability" in both wife and husband as the "outstanding trait" of a successful marriage. A good marriage, though similar to a good friendship or business relationship, Lash wrote, was distinguished by a strong bond of affection. Using a phrase that invoked the image of the bomb shelter family, Lash defined that bond as "a 'oneness' that is impregnable to outside influence or interference." These columnists largely upheld the homemaker ideal, although they supported the idea of a working wife, even a working mother, when the couple needed the money or the husband approved of her going out to a job. At the same time they held men to high standards, at least theoretically. According to Lash, the truly companionate husband treated his wife as an equal. He did not baby her, nor did he expect her to mother him. He talked, joked, and discussed both business and social matters with his wife. He respected her opinions, though he might not always agree with those opinions any more than he would always agree with a business associate or male friend. When choosing a husband, women were to look for a man who was adult and altruistic in outlook, not infantile (selfish, an egoist). He should have intelligence, character, and integrity as well as good health. Sympathy, understanding, kindness, and dependability were also musts. Above all, he should be "a good provider." Lash advised avoiding men with such traits as a lack of understanding, uncleanliness, alcoholism, disinterest in home and kids, a lack of culture, stinginess, and too much interest in the "almighty dollar." In this last point Lash was echoing the view of liberal Cold Warriors who warned against excessive materialism. Also to be avoided were men who were irresponsible, petty, and moody, who had unstable work records and a tendency to crude language. Finally, women should shun men who had a "roving eye" and liked the company of other women.[9]

Starr and Lash encouraged and admonished women to mind their wifely and motherly duties, to nurture, not suffocate, their children, and to avoid being door mats to their husbands. A woman should make her opinions clear to her husband, but when she did not get her way she should never nag or adopt "a petulant or martyred tone." When trying to convince a stubborn or lazy husband to help out at home, for example, she should be "cheerful and reasonable" and "try a little coaxing." Like other experts, Lash and Starr talked about the need for newlyweds to live on their own, apart from parents, and adjust to each other's needs. When conflicts emerged, however, they invariably counselled the woman to defer to her husband, whether it was about controlling the household budget, who should make his breakfast on a workday morning, a wife's less than fashionable wardrobe, or a husband's opposition to a wife returning to work. Women who embarrassed their husbands by talking to strange men in public or humiliated them by keeping a secret friendship with an old boyfriend were raked over the coals. They were told to do everything possible to win back their husbands' love and trust.[10]

Starr and Lash generally asked the women to make whatever sacrifice was necessary to avoid or defuse family conflict. They occasionally told a cloying husband to grow up and respect his wife's need for female companionship, but it was usually the other way around. They told bored housewives who wanted to work against their husbands' wishes to become volunteers instead of finding paid jobs. When her husband ignored her or went out a lot, a wife should spruce up her look, put on some makeup, get some up-to-date clothes, and act perky. When one young wife complained that her husband, though a good provider, was thoughtless when it came to anniversaries because he never gave her gifts, Lash scolded her for being silly and selfish. To have "a nice home and two fine children," and "a husband [who] loves you," she chided, was "about the greatest treasure you could ever possess and far more important than trifling gifts on anniversaries."[11] Both columnists showered sympathy on the neglected husband because it was a wife's duty to make him feel appreciated, respected, loved, and admired. A wife should never become so wrapped up in her home or children that she took her husband for granted.[12]

Significantly, Starr and Lash expressed sympathy for the unhappy and mistreated wife, but invariably they asked whether she might be partly to blame. In responding to women who lived with alcoholic and emotionally or physically abusive men, for example, they were adamant that, as Starr put it, "no woman should have to suffer such abuse and humiliation." Yet they usually asked if the wife had "inadvertently disappointed" her husband in any way. They asked if he "had reason" to mistrust her, or "feel jealous of his child."[13] They would also refer her to a family or social agency for counselling, with assurances that Canada had lots of well-trained experts and experienced staff who would have their best interests at heart. Finally, both Starr and Lash counselled against mixed marriages, including those between old and new Canadians, on the grounds that marriage already had enough pressures without adding the extra difficulties of a mixed-ethnic or, worse, mixed-race family.[14]

When Lash and Starr responded to new Canadian women who asked for help with family problems, they took every opportunity to sing the praises of Canadian institutions and democratic capitalism. Of course, the letters as printed do not provide us with the women's unmediated voices; some were written by others on a woman's behalf, and translators and press editors might have revised and edited them. But they do permit us to see both how popular experts counselled newcomer women and how the newcomers assessed their own situations before a wider Canadian reading public. Taken together, the letters and responses arguably constitute a site of gatekeeper-newcomer encounter, with the newspaper as contact zone. Indeed, some readers intervened in these exchanges. By criticizing the advice expert for an overly glib or insensitive comment, or sharing their own stories, the readers, including new Canadian readers, could also shape the dynamics of these interchanges.[15]

What is particularly noteworthy is that these non-citizen women, who were socially marginalized in so many ways – through the effects of material scarcity, statelessness, and language, for example – went public with their family woes and asked outsiders for help. In response, Lash and Starr usually combined personal bits of wisdom with referrals to government offices, social welfare agencies, family and child services, settlement houses, and the International Institute of Metropolitan Toronto. They saw themselves as enlightened experts offering up-to-date advice, though what they dished out ranged from the practical to the insulting. Their claims to cultural sensitivity were undercut by their commitment to a bourgeois morality that, for example, required female chastity before marriage and then, after a wedding, complete marital fidelity, especially on the woman's part. They also revealed a tendency to resort to a "stiff-upper-lip" and "it's-for-the-best" approach to people's disappointments and tragedies.

Given the focus of her "New Horizons" column, Lash was actively involved in responding to questions raised by Europeans. She received letters from parents trying to locate their children or families still in Europe, or perhaps trying to adopt an orphaned child. The letters, some of them from fathers, spoke loudly to the newcomers' desire to building meaningful family lives. In response Lash offered sympathy and referrals to a Canadian organization such as the Red Cross or maybe the International Red Cross and other organizations involved in tracking children and reuniting families.

The letters to Lash often came from women dealing with husbands who had turned out to be difficult, unfaithful, or, in few cases, abusive. In response Lash usually offered practical advice and sympathy along with a "silver-lining-in-the-black-cloud" admonition. Emblematic was her advice to a refugee woman who had been deserted by a newcomer man she had met and married shortly after coming to Canada. After arriving as a domestic worker, the woman had later got an office job, where she met and married "a nice good-looking newcomer of another nationality." Like many other employed refugee women, she agreed to support her husband, who had at first been unhappily stuck in a manual job, so that he could resume his university studies. After three years during which the couple lived on a very tight budget, he became a teacher and they moved into a decent apartment and bought some furniture. The woman's story to that point was a typical Cold War narrative: after first being victimized by Communism, she had, by working hard in a capitalist democracy and saving, begun to attain a better life in a family setting. But then disaster struck. Just as "life began to be pleasant for us," she wrote, he "met another girl, fell in love with her and... walked out on me." She was now unable to afford the apartment and forced to sell the furniture. "After six years hard work I am back where I was at the beginning, living in a rooming house." She was angry about Canada's weak divorce laws (a lawyer had warned her that even if she won an alimony case, collecting any decent money would be another issue). Yet she was still left wondering whether her case was hopeless.

In response Lash told her to look at life as a challenge. "Sometimes it's a mixed blessing showing the world how capable you are!" she wrote, adding that so often it is the helpless women who get aid they don't deserve. She noted that the lawyer was right (the amount would be "pitifully small" and the court order hard to enforce) but offered the patronizing advice that "in this country, just because we've caught a man doesn't mean the privilege of living off him until the end of time." She told the young woman to "carry on" and "to see people who are cheerful and will help you get out of yourself." She held out the possibility that "he might change his mind about the other woman" but that, regardless, she had to go on with her life without so much bitterness.[16]

For another female letter-writer, "Broken Hearted," Lash offered some stiff-upper-lip advice that bordered on victim-blaming. The woman wanted to leave a cruel husband who both refused to offer her any child support and threatened that if she hired a lawyer to get a court order, he would "leave his work, draw out all his money and Insurance and roam the world so that I will either starve or have to work to bring my children up." Efforts to talk it over with her priest had failed, she said, because her husband had fed the priest, and others, "a lot of lies" about her being "a useless gad-about," when, in fact, he was a bully whose quarrelling had gotten them thrown out of apartment after apartment. Aware that Canadian law did not permit divorce on cruelty grounds alone, she wanted to know "how to get a separation and make him pay so much a month," because she had small children and could not go out to work.

In response Lash stressed the difficulties of single motherhood, gave the husband the benefit of the doubt, and celebrated the nuclear family. "A separated wife," she advised, "usually has a very hard and unsatisfactory life." Lash noted that even with a court order for child support the woman's husband "may refuse to pay and carry out his threat to quit his job just out of spite." Eventually, she claimed, as though determined to say something positive about Canadian institutions, "the law catches up with him," but the uncertainty would be distracting and demand constant vigilance. She then switched gears, saying that the husband was unlikely to "throw up a good job just out of spite.... He must want you around if he makes threats about your leaving." She added, "You can't have your cake and eat it too." Lash advised the woman to either face the struggle of raising her children alone or make "the best of the situation."[17]

Starr's advice to writers similarly combined sympathy for unhappy or neglected wives with an endorsement of the ideals of companionate marriage and a dutiful wife. Starr, too, tended to blame the unhappy wife for a husband's lack of attention, though, also like Lash – and like the social workers who staffed the city's social agencies – she occasionally condoned a woman's decision to leave a husband whom she thought was beyond reforming.[18] When that happened, she too drew positive portraits of Canada's legal institutions and assured the writer that the experts would do what was best for all involved. For example, a Dutch mother wrote saying that she was worried about the situation of her daughter, whose Dutch husband had cheated on her, beat her, and then left her but refused to divorce her. The mother was afraid that her daughter would be legally obliged to nurse the husband when he became old and ill. Lash advised that Canadian law contained no such obligation. When another woman wrote in saying that she was writing for a Slovenian friend who spoke no English but desperately needed family counselling, Lash referred her to the International Institute. The Slovenian woman had married a widower in Canada, and had a little girl, but he was now beating her and trying to drive her away so that she would forfeit a right to a share of their property or his income. Lash said that at the Institute she would find a sympathetic and skilled person to help her out.[19]

A few European women made personal testimonials in the hopes of helping other women, especially mothers in danger of losing their children. An East European refugee and mother of two young children, dubbed "Friendly Mother," told Lash that soon after the family had settled in Canada her husband, an engineer, landed a job in a "far-away town" and effectively deserted them. She attributed his actions to the stresses of displacement, but also noted that it had put her in an extremely difficult situation. With two babies to watch over, she could not go out to work and so had applied for "public help." But she had found it "impossible" to manage on the welfare payments alone, and eventually her children had been taken away from her.

In what was yet another typical Cold War tale, this woman presented her middle-class background as a handicap. A woman who knew how to "economize" and find "the cheapest places for shopping," she noted, might have made do with such modest funds. But she had been "fairly well-to-do in [her] home country behind the Iron Curtain" before the Communists had destroyed her life, and thus lacked such skills. She and her children ended up friendless and hungry, and her lack of English meant that she "could not even speak to the welfare worker." The woman explained how she had lost her children to the authorities. "As I am young and good looking," she explained, "men got interested in me and came to visit me.... They helped me out now and again and in my longing for human relationship, I became friendly with them. Somebody reported me to the Children's Aid that I am prostitute and they have taken my children." She insisted that she was "not a bad mother," but "just a desperate woman" who wanted her children back. Without them, she said, "Nothing remains for me in a new country among strangers."[20]

Once again Lash's response, though sympathetic, showed a liberal's faith in bourgeois standards of morality and in the child experts and offered a large dose of paternalism. She lectured the woman, telling her that "the Children's Aid Society always wants to return children to their parents if it's humanly possible" and "don't want to punish you," but that the only chance of getting the children back was to "convince [the Society] you'll be a good mother in the future." Given that, especially in those days, child experts were as likely to remove children from their family as reunite them, such assurances ring false. Lash also told the woman to "make a fresh start" and get work even if it is "a dreary job." She could then learn "how to manage with a small amount of money" so that "if you get the children back and have to live on relief again, you'll know how to stretch the dollars and get along somehow." Like the social workers who delivered family-budget lectures, Lash advised this woman that she would have to sacrifice a lot: "You won't have much fun and no pretty clothes," but "just think of having those children, and all being together again. It's worth everything."

Lash's response annoyed some of her female readers, including a Canadian woman ("Another Friend") who noted that the "plea for help" of "Friendly Mother" was not for money but for "understanding and friendship" and "help in regaining her beloved children." She wrote that Lash had ignored the special problems faced by a lone refugee woman "greatly handicapped in a strange country, and a stranger to our ways.... Many Canadian wives deserted by their husbands wring their hands in despair and grief," but at least they have "relatives and friends to help to overcome the shock and difficulties." This woman had neither. Furthermore, Lash's tighten-the-belt advice was not very helpful, perhaps even insulting, given that welfare budgets were drawn up by experts who never had to live on them. "Another Friend" urged Lash to do better, but her own suggestions (see a minister, a women's church group) and tone ("there are many warm-hearted people willing to help her") echoed the ones dispensed by Lash. Still, Lash praised her critic for not standing in judgment of "Friendly Mother" and said that her situation was "looking brighter."[21]

Lash showed considerable sympathy towards the few deserted newcomer husbands who shared their stories about their wives' infidelities and bad mothering. One Hungarian DP, for instance, wrote to complain about his dismal marriage to a refugee of the 1956 revolt. The woman's previous husband had disappeared in the Hungarian uprising, and she had a baby from that union. Now his wife was deeply disappointed in him, he said, because he was "only a working man" with no "special education or trade." He wasn't as financially "well set as she expected." One day, after they had been together for five months, she had left, taking her child and most of the furnishings. She insulted him by saying that she was better off being a maid to a strange family than being his wife. She would not divorce him unless he gave her "a certain sum of money." He had discussed the problem with a lawyer, the family court, and a minister, and learned that he could not force her hand. Lash confirmed the bad news: he could get a divorce only by "producing the grounds" (adultery), but she might not give him the chance. As with her advice to the women, she held out some hope that the erring partner might return, but warned against "waiting and hoping for years." She advised him: "Make as much of a life for yourself as you can and enjoy your friends… try not to be alone too much and see cheery people whenever you can."[22]

Front-Line Encounters: Parents, Children, and Settlement Houses

To achieve their goal of transforming the supposedly more deeply patriarchal European marriage and family – or, to use their term, the "father-dominated" family – into a more modern and egalitarian Canadian-style household, Canadian social workers advocated curtailing immigrant mothers' old world influences over their children as well as breaking down the wall of isolation between the stay-at-home immigrant mother and the wider society.

Ironically, the women who most conformed to the homemaker ideology were pathologized for being too cut off from the outside mainstream world. The family and child experts had a near-obsession with the issue of generational conflict or family pathology occasioned by the differing pace at which parents and children acculturated to Canadian norms. Indeed, damaging images of brutal European fathers and obedient wives but culturally unbending mothers were invoked as explanations for family conflict, juvenile delinquency, and other problems among immigrants. In a graphic example of mother-blaming, one school of thought posited that family disorganization resulting from generational conflicts created by the immigrant mother's inability to catch up with her modernizing children led to criminal activity among second-generation immigrants.[23] But there was also a big gap between social work theories and the messier encounters and relationships that took place on the front lines of social service agencies such as the local welfare departments, immigrant aid organizations, family service agencies, and the settlement houses.

With origins dating back to the turn of the twentieth century, the settlement house movement had a mandate to give aid to families and children combined with a tradition of intervening or intruding into working-class, immigrant, and poor families. Since the early twentieth century Toronto had been home to several settlement establishments, including St. Christopher House, University Settlement, and Central Neighbourhood House.[24] Postwar settlements sought "to help parents in the district" improve parenting skills and "bring up happy, healthy, well adjusted children." They "put the service spotlight upon the children and teen-agers of our families," as the Central Neighbourhood House staff put it. In their view, so many of the youngsters were "troubled today with serious family problems." The staff warned that "children from broken homes, homes lacking in guidance, security, affection, or homes where discipline is too severe, may be rebellious, destructive, or withdrawn."[25]

The settlement houses and other community-based agencies were keen to attract newcomer children and their families to their social, cultural, and educational programs. Here two Polish brothers, age six and four, try out their new Canadian gift, a toy xylophone. *Telegram*, undated. (Photograph by Towers; YUA, Toronto Telegram, ASC Image 1326)

Settlement house staffs relied on several familiar social-work approaches, including an "intensive group work" approach, focusing on organized play, including athletics, crafts, drama, and clubs, and home visits with the families. When a problem with a child arose, staff visited the parents on the grounds that most problems began at home. One of the popular theories of the day, which some called the good-apple-from-the-well-tended-orchard theory, argued that the parents and family environment were most responsible for producing good or bad children.[26] The settlements also carried out counselling services. At St. Christopher, for instance, the head of the New Canadian Department carried out home visits as well as conducting family counselling sessions at the House a few afternoons each week, often with the help of other staff or volunteers who could act as interpreters. Many of the settlement workers were not fully trained social workers, psychologists, or psychiatrists, and they also referred people to a family or child service or mental health facility, where specialists using casework methods and various forms of testing were expected to identify illnesses and recommend treatments.[27]

The settlement staffs included a mix of professional social workers, social work graduate students on placement, and a variety of mostly volunteers, including women, high-school students, and university undergraduate students.[28] The social workers, most of them Anglo-Canadians, filled the house director and head worker posts. In addition to their workloads, the directors and head workers helped students and field workers identify and resolve problems and assessed their performance. The volunteers were also mostly Anglo-Canadian women and men, although some ethnic Canadians and a few immigrants acted as interpreters. The volunteers' importance to a settlement's ability to run a range of clubs, sports, and other activities probably at least partly explains the glowing reports they received.[29] At St. Christopher, the young and enthusiastic women volunteers, including those teaching English, were applauded for the consideration and respect they showed the newcomers, whose cultures were so different from their own and who were still trying to recover from their losses and rebuild lives. The newcomers responded

The original caption: "A 4-year-old child with probing hands and puzzled eyes gets sticky introduction to the Canadian donut." His family was one of the "TB Families" sponsored by the Canadian government in connection with World Refugee Year, 1960. The goal of the year was to clear out the last of the remaining residents in the DP camps.
(Photograph by Frank Grant; YUA, Toronto Telegram, ASC Image 1332)

in kind, thereby reinforcing the volunteers' growing social conscience. The interaction was what a democratic family or community was all about. At times, however, the volunteers faced discipline problems, and a constant turnover meant that the staff were always recruiting new candidates.[30]

Clearly, a gap existed between the theories and methods as developed by social work leaders such as Benjamin Schlesinger, the advocate of the sociocultural approach, and the mix of front-line workers, many of whom did not have a master of social work degree or many theoretical readings under their belt. Many social work methods, and not only casework, assumed a continuing relationship with the "clients," but on the front lines fleeting or much-interrupted encounters were often the norm. The group workers tried to apply the different social-work methods, often under the professional supervision of a settlement house director or head, but most of them, as part-time workers or volunteers, were not a constant presence. The younger children, already living in a transient district where no sooner did they make a friend than the friend left, reportedly found it difficult to feel connected to group workers who were there only some of the time. The settlement workers faced the challenge of carrying out the classic social welfare balancing act – on the one hand educating parents about the superiority of welfare capitalism and how to gain access to the social services that would help them better tend to their family's needs and, on the other, discouraging an unhealthy dependency on the state's social services.[31]

In describing their role the settlement staffs often used family metaphors. They likened their house (or set of buildings) to a welcoming home that was always open, from morning until night, year round. The children with "indifferent parents" or otherwise deprived of positive "home surroundings" could find a friendly and interested adult and make use of the house's many rooms and facilities. At St. Christopher these features included a "shiny modern kitchen," library, gym, fenced-in backyard, craft room, and an assembly room with a stage and curtain for plays. In reference to its teen dances, St. Christopher compared itself to "the successful mother who stocks up Cokes, cake and swing records so that her children will have their parties at home, and who provides the kind of understanding friendship that makes her children bring all their problems to her for help."[32] The group workers, drama and swim coaches, and music directors were expected to teach and provide good role models for the girls and boys, and to befriend the children. A young male worker who discovered that a Greek boy had stolen a pair of running shoes from St. Christopher's gym earned praise for his willingness to act as a big brother to the boy. A home visit revealed that the young – and remorseful – thief was one of seven children whose unemployed parents could not afford to buy them shoes, even for school. The worker thrilled the boy by giving him a pair of new sturdy shoes.[33]

Boys and girls at the Reliable Toy exhibit at Simpsons, 1957. (Photograph by Alex Gray; CTA, Central Neighbourhood House, 1005, Item 81)

During winter employment layoffs the settlement workers tried to create a friendly family atmosphere for the worried, jobless young men who were without families, but they also reported with approval that many of the men "accepted the situation philosophically." As the social workers pointed out, the men told them that "Everyone suffers – even the Canadians, that we have to manage and wait for Springtime," and "Canada offers us far more than money can buy – real democracy."[34] When they felt it necessary, the staff took on adopted children for the whole day. At one point St. Christopher workers took in three young Yugoslavian sisters who had been sneaking into the house each night, looking cold and worried, after discovering that the mother worked nights and the unemployed father was never around. The house, they reported, quickly became "a second home" to the girls, who overcame their shyness. The settlements attracted far fewer single adult women than men, but when staff helped out a woman – for example, by getting her away from a sexually aggressive landlord – they invited her to join their home and learn the virtues of good democratic living.[35]

Containing and Training Youth

The postwar settlements drew on a familiar repertoire of diagnoses and remedies regarding family ills, including juvenile delinquency, but also stressed that the situation was much more grave than in earlier periods. Their views were part of a wider alarmist discourse about rapidly spreading juvenile delinquency in the postwar years, a subject that garnered much coverage in the mainstream press, professional journals, sex education classes, and films.

The Toronto media conveyed the melodramatic narratives and dire warnings that infused this postwar panic. Countless articles reported on the growing tendency of boys and girls to defy curfews, drink liquor, and have sex; of "young punks" who assaulted police officers, harassed innocent bystanders, and engaged in petty theft on the road to a criminal life. Articles reported on boys using knives in schoolyard fights and the rising "hooliganism" aimed at "DP" and immigrant schoolchildren.[36] Certain "notorious" inner-city neighbourhoods were demonized as inherently deviant spaces that corrupted their residents. Even suburban youth, it appeared, were not immune to city contaminants. With girls the main fear was about spreading sexual promiscuity, even when the sins committed were petty crimes, not sexual acts. The experts worried about the boys' sexuality but the discussions more often focused on their anti-social behaviour. As in the past, the prevailing gender norms seriously restricted the options by which girls could "act up" without being morally branded.[37]

Toronto's downtown settlements were located in some of the "notorious" neighbourhoods, which were also said to be home to racial and ethnic tensions and gang wars involving poor white Canadian, African-Canadian, and recently arrived European youth. The settlement staff accounted for the delinquency problem by referring to a familiar mix of psychological, social, and environmental factors, such as poor parenting skills, unstable and transient families, and poor neighbourhood relationships. In response they advocated a range of familiar remedies – parent education programs and organized games, sports, and dances that could provide outlets for youthful energy and sexuality: in effect, the containment of youth through structured and supervised activity that would largely reproduce gender hierarchies. Having group workers in charge of organized social groups was the favoured strategy. Like other family and child experts, the settlement staff declared that never before were children and teens more volatile or the corrupting influences more pronounced. In an otherwise upbeat history of St. Christopher House, the chair of the board, H.W. Crossin, prioritized the need to confront spreading "juvenile delinquency, the young's irresponsibility, disregard of authority, lack of loyalty to our best traditions." Since a key cause was the "bad habits" developed "in spare time improperly used," social workers had to "provide guidance in the use of spare time and point the way to pleasant and profitable occupation." In doing this they could help people to be better Canadians.[38]

The professional staff at University Settlement similarly argued that twenty years earlier its neighbourhood had been poorer and less Canadianized but the children lived in more stable homes. Now the high cost of living was tempting or compelling mothers, new and old Canadians alike, to go out to work. The result, as one social worker suggested, was: "Home life is disintegrating, children are bombarded by sensational radio programs and comics. Parents are bewildered by their children's destructive, excitable and uncontrolled behaviour and lack of respect, and often react in unwise ways." Drawing on the common social work argument that a primary cause of ill-adjusted children was unhealthy home conditions, the staff stressed the need to target and help the most "troublesome" children by investigating their parents and home lives. For head resident Kay Gorrie (who, interestingly, opposed day-care centres but supported nursery schools) it was critically important that University Settlement reach out to the European newcomers in their neighbourhood and that, in addition to identifying problem children and visiting their families, the staff also recruit the parents and children into their recreational and educational programs.[39]

The social work approach enjoyed great popularity in the early postwar years, but settlement staff also used a psychological approach. They attributed a "discipline problem" to the growing number of children and youth who were "overwhelmed by their feelings of hostility and frustration."[40] Such feelings were intensified, they argued, in the case of newcomer children, who, as a worker said of an early group of DP children who joined a nursery program, had the extra challenge of learning a new language and dealing with family conflicts generated by their parents' authoritarianism and opposition to Canadian ways. While Canadian parents were too permissive, European parents, especially fathers, were too strict. In these father-dominated households, the children and wife deferred to the demands of an intimidating patriarch who used corporeal punishment to keep children (and, in some cases, a wife) in line. If such behaviour was acceptable in Europe, including Communist Europe, it was not acceptable here.[41]

The view that generational conflicts within immigrant families contributed to delinquency made a good fit with social work models, including the modestly liberal socio-cultural approach that warned against easy diagnoses of psychological problems and suggested that attention should instead be paid to "culturally determined" behaviours and attitudes. But sensitivity to cultural differences did not preclude the larger goal of eventually reshaping what social-work instructors like Schlesinger called "the European traditional family roles" along the lines of "the American family roles of the 'equalitarian' type of family constellation." Rather, the social worker who understood the "patrocentric" immigrant family, to use Schlesinger's term, could better determine who needed help in adjusting to Canadian norms. This adjustment was counselled even though it might involve a certain degree of exaggeration or hypocrisy. Hence, for example, a European man who was threatened by his wife's working could be advised that in Canada it was acceptable behaviour for women to work – even though women who worked in certain occupations were fired when they got married. The father who beat his children could be sternly told that this was utterly unacceptable behaviour in Canada (thereby conveying the impression that child abuse did not occur in Canadian families) and that if he persisted in it, the child authorities would take away his children. The experts expected that the "parent-child conflicts" would be most intense where teenaged children were involved, and that the resulting "clash of cultures" would lead anxious parents to turn to social agencies for help with rebellious children who had suddenly become "just like" Canadian children. It was not that social workers completely denied the reality of child neglect or abuse in Canadian families, but they assumed that it was more likely to occur within immigrant, working-class, and poor families. They also tended to attribute the problem within newcomer homes to the "cultural backwardness" of those families.[42]

In the mainstream media journalists interviewed family and child experts and popularized their arguments. When speaking of the generational conflicts that arose between the more quickly assimilated children and the parents who resisted or lagged behind, the normally sympathetic Sidney Katz, writing in *Maclean's*, came close to blaming immigrant parents for producing mentally and emotionally unbalanced children who might be the future's misfits. When newcomer parents resented their children for acquiring the "language, values and interests" of their school chums, Katz concluded, they can cause real harm. He cited a U.S. sociologist who used an example of a boy whose father had not let him watch boxing on TV because he considered it vulgar and barbaric. The boy had responded with, "Down with foreigners! Foreigners are anti-American!" The lesson was clear: if newcomer parents refused to permit their children to become Canadians, and the "cultural gulf" between them widened, "the children could become increasingly defiant." Or, as the Citizenship Branch's Kaye put it to Katz, "The child torn between two cultures may grow up to be hypersensitive, anxious, and hostile."[43]

In addition to the group approach – that is, implementing a range of well-structured, age-specific, usually gender-specific group activity meant to funnel youthful energy into healthy outlets – the settlement workers noted the importance of giving children "a feeling of affectionate acceptance of themselves, an opportunity to release their suppressed energies, while imposing definite limits on their behaviour." At University Settlement, Gorrie reported that a new penalty system for bad behaviour had resulted in less vandalism, though the workers had found it difficult to be consistent. But they would keep trying because the children's "desperate craving for attention and affection is so deep that we cannot help but respond."[44]

Many European parents were aware of how they were portrayed by established Canadians. Some of them deeply resented how others caricatured the difficult situation in which they found themselves. As their letters to newspaper editors and columnists show, a good number of them publicly criticized the arrogance of Canadians on this score, especially when, in their view, Canadian children were spoiled and disrespectful of their elders. Some two years after they had been interviewed by Eva-Lis Wuorio for *Maclean's* in 1948, the Polish DP couple Alina and Jan Zaramba, now living in Toronto, told Wuorio in a follow-up interview that Canadian children were noisy and rude. Social work instructors noted similar cases in their teaching-oriented publications.

One such case, reported by Schlesinger, involved a young German mother whose neighbours had criticized her for being too harsh with her seven-year-old daughter. The woman "indignantly replied" that her daughter had been a perfectly fine and popular girl in Germany but that since coming to Canada, "the Canadian approach to Child Rearing" had "spoiled and pampered her" and made her "undisciplined." In Germany, she said, children were taught to be polite, quiet, and to respect their elders, and no one interfered with the parents; in Canada parents seemed to have little say over their children. She could not understand why an agency should interfere. In response Schlesinger noted that while we cannot "blame all the troubles on cultural elements," the matter of child-rearing was indeed a site where "difficulties frequently appear." Social workers had the job, he said, of "interpreting the new community standards to the 'New Canadian.'"[45]

A powerful example of "talking back" to Canadians came from Alina and Jan Zaramba, in the follow-up *Maclean's* article of 1950. The couple had rented a small flat in the west end of Toronto. It was a cramped but immaculate and freshly painted home with a kitchen, a bathroom, and a bedroom that also functioned as a sitting room. Jan, a lawyer, worked in an electrical appliances plant and Alina had a job in the adjustments department at Simpsons. Although Catholic, the children attended the local public school, Dewson Street.

The Zarambas had lost a comfortable life in Warsaw, where they had a modern apartment and maid and took holidays in mountain villas; but they said that, finally, they had begun to hope to eventually acquire some of the accoutrements of that former life. They had suburban dreams: they had bought a used car for family picnics and holidays, and Alina hoped for "a home of my own – with no boarders." They joked about their "two little Canadians," their children Bashia and Maciej, now Barbara and Mark. The children were thriving, Wuorio reported. They enjoyed their school, which was full of immigrant and Anglo children who got along most of the time, though Mark mentioned the ugly schoolyard fights. He loved playing marbles and hockey. Barbara dreamt of ballerinas and other girlish things. On the subject of parenting, the Zarambas said they let their children "do most things," but, interestingly, drew the line at comic books because they "breed lazy reading." (The child experts and lobbyists would have been delighted.)

Moreover, Alina was openly critical of Canadian parents for producing spoiled children who were often "noisy, rude, and indolent." She made clear her disappointment. "We had hoped," she said, "that after so much moving about and insecurity our children, who were getting a bit out of hand, would have as good examples the happy Canadian children." Instead, she found, "Children are spoiled here. They get everything they ask for and they don't seem to have any sort of a sense of responsibility toward anyone else or their family." She added, "Even in this small home of ours, Mark and Barbara have their own duties. They must make their beds before they go to school, keep their clothes tidy, their shoes polished. It's good discipline and we feel, too, it gives them a sense of belonging and being part of the family."

As if in support, Wuorio observed that the children were "quiet but not backward." They never interrupted the adults but, when asked, they loved telling stories, and they laughed easily and often. Their immediate goal was to get a collie dog.[46]

Parents, Programs, and Problems

When it came to young children, many newcomer parents were not opposed to the Canadianizing influence of school and community programs, games, and sports but, rather, tried to judge the relative merits of the old and new influences in their children's lives. This was a delicate juggling act. Just as in the case of mothers and what food they were prepared to put on the table, these parents drew boundaries around what they were prepared to "give up," what they believed was acceptable change, or, indeed, what they saw as new opportunities for their children. This tendency probably explains why the sites of least contestation between newcomer parents and gatekeepers were nursery school programs and programs for young children. Many parents did not balk at the idea that their young children learn English early or have a safe place to play or learn new games, though they often had an anxiety about the unknown.

The workers did not wait for parents to come and register their young children in their house programs but actively sought them out by visiting door to door or by approaching preschool children playing in the streets and then contacting their parents. More often than not, the fathers earned low wages and were not steadily employed, or they were on relief and could barely afford winter clothing for their children. Some of them, though, were better-educated refugees who had landed better-paying jobs and planned to leave the area as soon as possible. Especially during the 1950s, when the districts were more ethnically and occupationally mixed than later, plenty of parents, as one worker noted, were friendly and interested in the settlement house programs for their children; some of them were keen, anxious even, to put their kids in the nursery school.[47]

Even allowing for a professional interest in promoting "positive interventions," the settlement house reports indicate that many children enjoyed the programs and that many parents appreciated the services, which also saved them babysitting costs. According to the staff, the nursery kids, regardless of background, picked up English quickly, which benefited them later in school. The mothers' clubs helped with certain events, such as Christmas carolling, and the parent groups occasionally pitched in to buy a piece of furniture or toys for the nursery or to raise funds for a field trip. The mother of a shy little German girl thanked her English teachers for helping her daughter open up and play "in a much happier way." A little Ukrainian girl in an arts and craft class showed "great ingenuity and imagination in all her handwork" and stimulated "the other children in their creative activities." An eleven-year-old Jewish boy who took advanced English wowed the St. Christopher workers with his intelligence. "He speaks of Marco Polo and Beethoven like an old professor," they said.

Some of the parents enjoyed bringing their children to the reading and play-time programs, where volunteers read fairy tales in English and provided crayons and Plasticine to play with. The music programs were small but successful. The children's concerts, which brought together a mix of children, including Jewish, Ukrainian, German, Italian, and African Canadian, were usually a hit with the parents, who came to the events that featured their children. The "most co-operative" parents, to use the gatekeepers' term, signed up their kids for kindergarten, music, ballet, and some clubs.[48]

Revealing a certain class and ethnic prejudice, the settlement workers were happily surprised that even the children of the poorly educated rural Italian families learned English as quickly as did the East European and Baltic children, and did as well at the music and creative programs. Many reports included amusing anecdotes, but they were often made at a parent's, usually a mother's, expense. A St. Christopher worker reported that Argentine, a little Italian girl, "shocked us all one morning when she arrived with her curls all shaved off, her mother having the odd idea that her hair would come in thickly if she did this. It doesn't bother Argentine, but the other children all think she is a boy."[49] The workers also complained about problem parents, such as anxious or meddling mothers, some of whom they described as being "very nervous" or suffering from "a nervous condition." While they probably too easily applied these labels, they appeared to be describing mostly women who suffered from maternal separation anxiety, the malady that afflicted many Holocaust survivors and other European women who, having watched so many babies and young children die, became very anxious about leaving a child even at a neighbourhood nursery or playground. As one survivor recalled, she always felt frightened for her daughter and wanted her always at home and safe. In the late 1950s various nurseries reported on high rates of maternal anxiety among the most recently arrived Hungarian refugee women, no doubt a result of the stresses occasioned by the events of 1956.[50]

There was also some parent-blaming when children appeared to suffer from ongoing separation anxiety, with the workers sometimes attributing this condition to an attachment to an overly protective or possessive mother. On occasion, the fathers were blamed. A St. Christopher worker reported that some of the new Portuguese boys were having "a rather difficult time learning to be away from their parents" and that their out-of-work fathers were compounding the problem by hanging around all morning because they had "nothing to do anyway." Evidently, the staff convinced the fathers of the importance of leaving their children to play with the Canadian and other immigrant kids. In another case the St. Christopher staff enrolled a boy in both the morning and afternoon nursery programs because of "a serious disturbance at home, emotional tension and conflict between the parents and the other members of the family." A worker judged the boy's mother, who was clearly being abused, harshly. The report read: "The mother is confused and bitter about her unhappy life – one morning she arrived at Nursery School with her face all disfigured, her husband having pushed her downstairs." His real concern was that "these highly emotional scenes are having a bad effect on her little boy," who needed to be "in an atmosphere of interesting activities removed from family tension." Staff efforts to refer the mother to a social agency for help were "unsuccessful."[51]

Since "problem children" also had a negative impact on staff morale, it was important to get to the bottom of things quickly and provide the workers with a learning experience. A case in point was Lena, a "slight," "pale," and "serious" eight-year-old Italian girl with "enormous" eyes who was in St. Christopher's Saturday house program for beginners. The staff, including two high-school volunteers, got to know her well because she was always there. At first they felt sorry for the poor thing, "hovering in the hall often without stockings, soiled skimpy clothes and usually without a coat," and paid her a lot of attention. But as Lena began to "monopolize" their attention, the volunteers, "both warm-hearted, enthusiastic girls," tried to stop her from clutching hold of them all of the time. Failing that, they began to ignore Lena, who became noticeably upset. The professional staff blamed the parents for Lena's behavioural problems. When the family had first arrived in the area, the parents had "lavished all their attention on Lena" and ignored her older sister. But then came "a baby brother" and they turned their affections on him, forcing Lena "to seek it elsewhere." All of this was discussed at a training session with the volunteers, with the result that, as the head worker claimed, the leaders re-established a positive relationship with Lena.[52] In effect the volunteers were taught some social work principles, including empathy. The classic casework method (which group workers also tried to apply when dealing with a problem individual) held that the worker had to come to "know" and "understand" clients in order to help them "grapple with and solve a difficulty." The caseworker should also empathize with the client while remaining detached and objective (an ever-elusive goal).[53]

When they believed that a child's problem with discipline had more serious psychological roots, the staff tried to convince the parents to see a child specialist, but they were not always successful in this. The parents' resistence was due not only to fear or denial but also to an uneasiness with this far more dramatic intervention and its potential consequences, such as forced hospitalization in a mental institution. In the case of an immigrant boy whom the University Settlement staff nicknamed "Walter, the Moody Bully," the parents were trying to beat him out of his behaviour. A thin, pale, unhappy boy who never joined in the games but went into "blind fits of rage" and hit the younger children and yelled obscenities, Walter, they reported, was emotionally disturbed and "in urgent need of psychiatric service with trained workers who have time to spend with people like Walter and his parents." But, alas, his old-country parents would not co-operate and were compounding the problem "by the use of severe corporeal punishment." As they tried to control him, the staff wondered whether Walter would finally end up in a mental hospital.[54]

Moulding Personalities: Sports, Field Trips, and Culture Clash

With or without a "moral panic"[55] about juvenile delinquency, the settlements would have provided organized athletics and other group activities, especially for teens, because this was standard practice that fit with the dominant models of encouraging healthy child development. The child-development theories associated with Jean Piaget, John Hall, and, with greater focus on psycho-sexual characteristics, Freud, posited that adolescence was a critical but turbulent stage of life, and that a "normal" personality developed as an individual successfully completed various stages of life. Parents who knew what to expect at each age level could thus monitor their children, checking for personal pathologies (irresponsibility, self-centredness) and guiding their children's evolution into emotionally secure, well-adjusted citizens. Those who could not do so risked producing anti-social misfits whose deviant behaviours could range from temper tantrums to cruelty, and who would seek out "bad company," steal, and engage in "precocious sex activities." The settlements could play a surrogate parental role with disadvantaged urban youth by getting them involved in organized team sports and other wholesome activities. They could give them the opportunity to plan their own club programs and thus practise democratic citizenship, all with the help of a caring supervisor. But the sense of moral panic about spreading delinquency in these years did bring greater attention to the issue of developing more effective programs for improving the bodies and minds of new as well as old Canadian youth.[56]

In an effort to compete with the popular amusements of the day, including movies, television, and, for older youth, nightclubs, settlement house workers

Boys playing floor hockey at a settlement house, *circa* 1960. (Photograph by Alex Gray; CTA, Central Neighbourhood House, 1005, Item 86)

organized "fun" field trips, which produced their own amusing anecdotes. A "big hit" with the St. Christopher kids was a tour of the Bell Telephone Company building, where "one of Mrs. Moore's Italian boys" put St. Chris on the map with his rendering of "Davy Crockett," which was tape-recorded and played over the loudspeaker. The group leaders reported that the trips were great for the teenagers, who were developing better manners all around. In restaurants, for instance, they collected for a tip and chipped in for those without enough money, without any coaxing from the group leader.[57]

Still, sports provided the most popular activity, especially with the older boys, whose favourite sport was soccer. The child experts saw competitive athletics as important to "character development," to the moulding of good personalities, and to the training of citizen adults. Like the ethnic dinners and international nights, the sports events were also meant to encourage mingling between old and new Canadian children, and improve relations among the different newcomer and racial groups in the neighbourhood. There were also regular house competitions in basketball, broomball, and other sports, with certain groups, such as the Lithuanians, earning reputations as stellar athletes. Special events included tournaments with outside groups. One year St. Christopher's Athletics Department celebrated Brotherhood Week by arranging a hockey tournament with teams from University Settlement and a basketball tournament with a "Chinese basketball team" from St. Albans Boys Club (another west-end community centre). The girls also played basketball, but their games didn't get the same attention.

When the Portuguese boys participated in an Ontario-based volleyball tournament, the workers commented, "This should help to make better understanding between the members of different ethnic origins." The theory was borne out when the Portuguese boys handled themselves well in a competition that they lost to a Latvian team and "accepted their defeat graciously." Without any prompting from their coach, they shook hands with their opponents. Such behaviour, the staff concluded, confirmed the view "that competitive Athletics handled properly is a destroyer of racial prejudice and social barriers." It also led to "the development of small friendship groups," which further encouraged the integration process.[58]

It was better to prevent delinquency than to have to handle problem teens, of course, but the settlements did try to save delinquents. When some young Italian boys got into trouble with the police in June 1955 "for hanging around the streets late at night and waiting around for a dime" (begging), which was illegal, the police reported the boys to the Big Brother organization. But one of the St. Christopher volunteers heard about them and got them enrolled at St. Christopher instead. The head of the Boys Department, Ken Stewart, set up an Italian boys club and, shortly afterwards, the youngsters were reportedly "having a wonderful time." They were "energetic and eager to try everything" and "fairly busting to do as much as they can." They learned to play softball and other games, and made kites and puppets.[59]

The settlement workers used sports, as well as mediation skills, to mitigate racial-ethnic tensions among teenaged boys. As a University Settlement worker put it, team sports encouraged "a comfortable sense of 'belonging,'" and "race prejudice can't exist in that atmosphere." In a pickup baseball team, where a mix of boys – white, Black, Asian, old and new Canadian – played together, "all sorts of personality problems disappear."[60] But racial tensions between the teenagers also came to the surface, some of them due to the "resistance" of white, including white ethnic, members "to accepting the Negroes as members." The group workers themselves admitted to having difficulties dealing with the Black teens, who they said did not readily obey them. Still, despite their own prejudices they tried to deal with the racism issue. One strategy was to respect the wishes of the Black boys and girls to have separate clubs, even though the staff preferred mixed groups. Whenever Black clubs invited European youths to join, the workers were full of praise.[61]

As the Toronto papers reported, the neighbourhoods in question had some boy gangs, including Black and Italian groups, with some girl members. Although they expressed concern about the situation, the settlement workers nonetheless rejected the alarmist depictions of their district as a crime-ridden ghetto. In 1951 the staff at St. Christopher described their area as containing "numerous public halls, one for practically every nationality, where amusements and mass programmes – education and culture are carried on." There were "groups of young men" who organized "their own clubs" on a "social" or "nationality basis," and while the clubs did display "some anti-social behaviour," the area had a low crime rate and the police had "very little trouble with gangs in the district." Still, they were anxious about the gangs and hoped that the local churches would have more influence on newcomer youth. They were also worried about some local families having "communistic tendencies."[62]

When gang trouble involving "their boys" did arise, they responded, and in at least one case, in 1954, they did so in a compassionate, even creative, manner. The incident involved an Italian boy, Nick, who was attacked at night by a Black youth who belonged to the teenage dance group. Nick was hit on the head with a broken bottle and required ten stitches. One of the group workers, John Braithwaite, the first Black staff person hired at a Toronto settlement, met with the Black boys. Braithwaite, who would later become a social worker, said the boys "were nervous and upset but would not admit who was responsible." The boys, he said, "did not want people to think all colored boys were like the one who actually attacked Nick," and so they decided to raise money at their next dance and give it to Nick as "a group apology." Braithwaite persisted, however, because he felt "the guilty boy was getting off very easy, hiding behind the group apology" and that "the personal responsibility of the assailant was the important thing." In the meantime the Italian boys had "rallied around Nick" and wanted to press charges. But it never came to that because the guilty boy agreed to meet with Nick and apologize: "They shook hands after the boy admitted he had been very wrong and said he was sorry." The dance group honoured their promise, upped their admission fee, and raised $10 for Nick. John Haddad was clearly proud of his staff's successful resolution of a conflict that might have created continuing "bad feeling" between Italians and Blacks in the area. But the outcome was also due to the Black boys' willingness to resolve the problem.[63]

When, in 1950, three teenage girls at St. Christopher became involved in "a prostitution case," the workers became, as one of them put it, "more than ever anxious to provide extra help and activities" for the teen girls. They tried to encourage a sense of belonging, as well as social and citizenship skills, by letting the girls decide, albeit under supervision, on what they wanted – within reason. When some of the older girls got bored with a craft club, for example, they were asked what they wanted – dance classes – and given them. In response, "group interest and spirit" reportedly "picked up considerably."[64] Staff tried to contain the older girls' sexually aggressive behaviour by, for example, running a six-month charm school class, taught by a modelling school graduate. As in U.S. cities, Black and Italian girls were considered to be among the more brash and sexually aggressive, and thus in greatest need of containment. At the other end, the (mixed-gender) dramatics group helped shy girls with "vivid imaginations" to "overcome self-consciousness." The girls' athletics programs did reasonably well, but as coach Bert Mezo observed, the older girls' participation was always cut short "because their parents expect them to do more work at home than the boys." That helps to explain why the weekly teen dances became monthly ones, though, much to the boys' chagrin, there were still never "enough girls."[65]

The continuing attempts to contain rowdy girls claimed some modest successes, such as convincing a group of noisy girls who reached any decision "by who could shout the loudest" to engage in a collective decision-making, hence democratic, process. Another strategy was to put these girls in touch with "good Canadian girls." For example, St. Christopher House invited in a group of majorettes, who performed and gave each girl a baton and twirling lesson.[66] The staff were also pleased when the Italian Girls Club, considered to be the most clannish group after the "Negro girls," and the most resistant to speaking English, began to mingle with the other girls. The staff considered Southern European girls to be stuck in the most authoritarian families, with the worse off being the Italian girls. At least one of them had showed up with bruises, thanks to a beating at the hands of her father, who had punished her for withholding her paycheque from him. According to a group worker, the girl's mother had simply said that her daughter was "too much Canadian. She is not a good Italian."[67]

The situation of these girls was distressing because the child and delinquency experts believed that overly strict families were more likely to produce rebels and delinquents. Some of them also assumed that child abuse was more likely to occur within father-dominated families; and, according to the theories, the victims of incest or domestic abuse were the most likely to go astray and become unwed mothers or prostitutes. This "clash of cultures" and the task of getting parents and children to bridge the cultural gap would remain one of the most challenging problems of all.[68]

Blaming "Backward" Parents: The Early 1960s

By the early 1960s the earlier stream of DPs had long ended while that of economic migrants from peripheral Southern European regions continued to be significant. The west-end districts in Toronto, including those that lay within the boundaries of St. Christopher House and University Settlement, became increasingly dominated by the most poor and poorly educated immigrants, especially rural peasants from Southern Italy and fisher families from the Azores in Portugal. At the same time the district became less transient, which was reflected in the settlement house programs, where more of the children continued their participation as they got older.[69]

The main problem, it was said, was the parents, who had particularly "backward" marriages and parenting methods. In their efforts to modernize these parents, the settlement workers recorded modest successes. When, for example, St. Christopher's staff learned that the Portuguese men did not like their wives attending the mixed-gender English classes at night, they set up all-women classes and the female enrolment increased. When the women attended an evening banquet or play without the men, they declared that they had helped to liberate them at least a little bit.[70]

Nevertheless, the settlement staff identified the Italians and Portuguese as particularly evasive parents who were the most resistant to social work interventions. They declared that these parents' ignorance of Canada's social services and distrust of outsiders was hurting their children.[71] They complained about the working mothers who left their babies and toddlers in the care of relatives and other makeshift sitters who were incapable of providing proper supervision, recreation, or moral guidance. The result, declared John Haddad of St. Christopher, was an epidemic of inadequate child-care arrangements in downtown areas. The home visitors had found many inappropriate sitters, including an old-age pensioner who lived next door and a six-year-old child in charge of a two-year-old.[72] The parents' distrust of outsiders, they added, was keeping their children from enjoying play and exercise in healthy and supervised environments. When these parents did enrol their children for nursery school, and the children exhibited emotional or behavioural problems, they resisted home visits and referrals. Their "loose" sense of time meant that they were often very late in picking up their children. According to Haddad, the Italians was the most "scapegoated group." The brightest students were Ukrainians and Poles; the Italians and Portuguese did "not do well academically."[73]

In response to these problems, the settlements recruited some Italian- and Portuguese-speaking workers and volunteers in the 1960s, and some of the group workers, like the city's public health nurses, took language classes in Italian – a strategy advocated by Schlesinger.[74] Workers accompanied families to hospitals and clinics for eye tests, vaccinations, and surgery. When they got inside an Italian or Portuguese home, in an effort to build up trust they tried to be as helpful as possible to every family member – helping with a father's job applications, a mother's difficult pregnancy, a daughter's schooling. They also tried to "raise" the "standard of child care in the community" by, for example, starting up small day-care programs "in specially selected family settings."

Again, they had modest successes. St. Christopher used the carrot-and-stick approach so that the day-care service was free, provided that the selected mothers attended the child-care classes.[75] Its staff also launched a more ambitious two-year "family life" project meant to address the whole "complex of problems of family living" in the modern city by giving rural women "a very basic adult education," from shopping to "citizenship." The main target was the growing number of Portuguese families in the Kensington Market area, though Italian as well as newly arrived Chinese and Caribbean families were also targeted. St. Christopher hired a full-time "family life" worker who spoke Portuguese. This project, too, produced modest results. It also prompted more commentary on these rural immigrants, a response that combined sympathy, insight, and paternalism. Above all, the workers stressed that the parents had to be educated about the simple basics – the value of social, health, and recreational services – before they could appreciate their importance. To reach that goal, one had to break through the wall of suspicion and distrust. Getting back to basics, however, basically meant more of the same – more home visits, lectures, and referrals to other helping agencies.[76]

The strategies that the settlement house social workers adopted towards the later arrivals did not differ all that much from the kind of advice that Lash and Starr had given to the earlier-arriving Dutch, DP, and other new Canadians who had contacted them. With the Cold War continuing into the 1960s, Canada's family and child experts continued to speak of the need to protect and bolster the family from internal and external threats. They continued to talk about the need to modernize and improve parenting skills, and to transform both new and old Canadians into democratic citizens who would join the war against communism, juvenile delinquency, and other insidious threats to wholesome family living. But at the same time the settlement house workers' analysis of the Southern Europeans differed from the analysis of the DPs in a significant respect: they attributed these peoples' anxieties not to Communist-induced anxieties but to a culture of rural poverty. They did this even though, like the DP and other Europeans who had come before them, these poorer parents also tried to exercise some control over their encounters with intrusive Canadians who poured over their medical forms or treated them as misfits in the examination room.

The evasiveness did not simply reflect old world suspicions. Rather, it was based on a mix of factors: for example, a lack of time or energy to deal with intruding experts at the end of very long working days; a discomfort at sharing intimate concerns with total strangers; the need to rely on one's child as an interpreter who had to report on a mother's miscarriage, an unemployed father's mental health, or the family's escalating debts; and open hostility towards aggressive outsiders who were trying to dictate rules and routines to them.

In the end, the gatekeepers' objective proved to be the same: the newcomers had to be integrated into the mainstream and learn to become democracy-practising citizens of the nation. From the gatekeepers' vantage point, the struggle to reshape the Canadian democratic family continued. But cracks did appear in the domestic containment strategy. While both gatekeepers and newcomers valued families, European parents did resist pressures to conform to Canadian ways or drew boundaries around what they would tolerate from well-intentioned but meddling outsiders, even when they appreciated the free or inexpensive recreational programs for their children or the timely professional interventions into a family crisis. Others talked back and complained about Canadian parents and their children. Thus, even in a context in which both old and new Canadians clearly cared about those closest to them, the family was contested terrain.

The original caption: "Immigrant
Nicholas Sakellariou, a 28 year-
old Greek, walks Toronto streets,
his face reflecting the loneliness
felt by New Canadians adjusting
to an alien world." Sidney Katz's
Maclean's article on mental illness
among newcomers focused on
men and featured the opinions
of Canadian psychiatrists, therapists, and immigrant men. Katz,
"How Mental Illness Is Attacking Our Immigrants," *Maclean's*
4 Jan. 1958.
(Photograph by Paul Rockett; TRL)

From Newcomers to Dangerous Foreigners

Containing Deviant and Violent Men

8

THE TWIN FORCES OF MASS MIGRATION AND COLD WAR may have raised great concern about the need to produce well-adjusted citizens and protect pro-capitalist liberal democracies against all enemies, but they did more as well. They heightened the sense of moral panic about spreading immorality, dysfunctional families, Communist agitators, and how spreading mental illness would endanger the Canadian nation and its moral and social fibre. They justified the greater media exposure, state surveillance, and professional experts' admonitions of people thought to be contaminants invading and infecting the body politic. Both in the public realm and behind the scenes, a number of gatekeepers – including the police, mental health specialists, popular journalists, and front-line social workers – portrayed emotionally troubled, psychologically disturbed, and violent newcomer men from Europe as constituting a particularly grave threat to women and the Canadian way of life.

The very same press that provided the extensive sympathetic and positive coverage of the arrival of newcomers from war-torn and Communist Europe – especially the "freedom-loving" anti-Communist refugees – was also a key source of negative, indeed threatening, images of another kind of newcomer: men who had acted violently towards women, families, and Canadian authorities. During the 1950s Toronto newspapers carried sensational stories about "mad" Baltic men who killed their landlords and held family members hostage. They told of "crazed" Italian men who assaulted their wives and Canadian women, and "insane" DPs who killed their neighbours and themselves. The coverage of these ethnic crimes served to reinforce age-old stereotypes of European men, especially Southern Europeans, as being prone to emotional outbursts, psychological ills, and violent, including sexually violent, behaviour. They prompted renewed attacks by racial bigots who railed against the "swarthy" knife-wielding European and prompted calls for the government to cut back on the immigrant flow and for police to get tough with the criminals, who were also more likely to be called foreigners than newcomers or new Canadians.

The treatment of this subject in the English-Canadian mainstream press also reflected the growing popularity of psychiatric categories to explain anti-social and especially sexually delinquent behaviour. According to Canada's medical gatekeepers, including "Mr. Mental Health" himself, Dr. John Griffin, a rapidly growing number of men in the Canadian population matched the profile of the "criminal sexual psychopath" – a man who appeared to be normal but could not control his sexually violent impulses. Drawing on loose definitions of the "sex pervert," concerned parents, women's groups, and journalists lobbied for the medical treatment rather than simply the incarceration of sex offenders. The sexual and moral anxieties of the Cold War period, a time when perceived threats to the citizenry took on enormous ideological importance, also reinforced the tendency among many gatekeepers to view alienated or mentally unstable newcomer men as threats to Canadian standards of democratic decency.[1]

As North American historians of sexuality have documented, the postwar moral panics were fed not only by various experts, police, and lobby groups but also by the lurid media coverage of sex crimes and other "epidemics" that were represented in ways that suggested an increase in the number of "criminal sexual psychopaths." The deep anxieties of the era manifested themselves in the national "insecurity" state to the point that, in Canada, the RCMP experimented with a "fruit machine" that quantified reactions to magazine pictures – all in the hopes of ferreting out homosexuals from government posts.[2] Certainly, a large part of the anxieties emanated from the press coverage of violent ethnic crimes, including sex crimes, and from the public discourses of journalists, politicians, psychiatrists, social workers, and ordinary Canadians who debated the causes and ways of dealing with mentally unstable and violent European men. But more private discourses are also highly revealing. The confidential case files of the counsellors who staffed the International Institute of Metropolitan Toronto's Department of Individual Services, for instance, provide a record of how a particular group of front-line gatekeepers – professionally trained social workers and volunteer caseworkers – dealt with the violent husbands they encountered, especially in light of their commitment to a pro-family approach and to the women who turned to them for help.

Together the popular and professional and the public and confidential discussions of emotionally troubled, mentally anguished, and violent European men capture themes central to the gender and sexual history of Cold War Canada and its twinned understandings of moral decency and mental health – or what I call, with deliberate irony, democratic decency, because such notions also served to bolster state surveillance and gatekeeper intrusions.[3] Still, once again, there could be cracks in the containment strategy, as when supposed "sex deviants" gained entry into the country and the newcomers resisted or defied the moralizing pressures of Canadian authorities. Within this highly charged terrain, although certain discourses could falsely brand all foreign men as brutes, and thus their wives as the archetypal victims of an imported patriarchy or male disorder, abused women adopted their own strategies to fight back, in part by enlisting the gatekeepers' help.

Sex Deviates or Mental Misfits?
The Mainstream Press and Violent Newcomer Men

The mainstream reporting or saturation coverage of grisly crimes, including sex crimes, can help to manufacture a "social problem" at a given time and place by conveying the impression that such crimes are on the rapid increase and thus require a strong and immediate response. The reports can heighten societal anxieties to the point that a good portion of the public comes to agree with the authorities and professional experts who are advocating tough measures to capture the culprits and contain the problem before it gets completely out of control. In such situations, the reporters and journalists may claim just to be delivering a news story to their readers, but their repeated coverage of the gruesome details and experts' dire warnings and worse-case scenarios actually makes them participants in the creation of a moral panic that, as the term implies, is out of all proportion to the actual events being described.[4] In a period already shaped by a heightened concern about the supposed fragility of Canadian families, moral standards, and democracy itself – as well as by the challenges of integrating large numbers of newcomers plagued by their own problems – the news of ethnic crimes, including violent attacks by European men on women, especially Canadian women, was bound to reinforce the sense that Canadians and their society were under siege by foreign threats.

In an immigrant-receiving nation with a history of explaining ethnic crimes in racial or cultural terms, the postwar press coverage was bound to stir up familiar arguments about "foreign" men being culturally or genetically more prone to criminal violence, including crimes of passion. In earlier eras a whole range of newspaper reporters and editors, police officers, court judges, experts, and ordinary Canadians had explained the crimes committed by men who belonged to supposedly undesirable and much-maligned "races" and ethnic groups – the East European "bohunks," Italian "dagos," Asian "heathens," and African-Canadian "negroes." They portrayed the crimes as the actions of these highly excitable and/or mentally inferior men who were all too quick to use a knife, stiletto, or gun to settle disputes, including domestic ones, and to attack, defile, or abduct the forbidden white Canadian women. In the early postwar period the press coverage of ethnic crimes of violence perpetrated by seemingly mad or evil European men engendered anti-immigrant and anti-refugee feelings that made it easy for many people to exaggerate the degree to which European men were responsible for a rise in sexual and violent attacks on women.

The Cold War itself also complicated matters. When the perpetrator was one of the much-celebrated anti-Communist refugees, some onlookers took it as a sober reminder of the need for more Canadianization campaigns; but others saw it as a sign that Canada was becoming overrun by degenerate and diseased DPs. If, on the other hand, the criminal was a Communist, especially an ethnic Canadian Communist, the story underscored the demonized image that most Canadians held of these people. If a male Italian or German lashed out, he might be seen as the alienated product of a totalitarian regime. If he was a Nazi collaborator, why not a rapist or wife beater? What better indicator that communism brutalized men than to read about a 56er who abused his wife and children? The European newcomer men could easily become the "folk devils" whose dangerous ways threatened postwar Canada's moral and social fabric.

Toronto's mainstream newspapers published plenty of frightening and tragic stories involving evidently troubled or mentally anguished European men. Not all of them were the alleged perpetrators of sexual or violent crimes. Some were the victims of exploitative landlords and employers, of hostile or indifferent police, and of tragic circumstances – a wife's suicide, a house fire that killed family members. Ironically, though, even the sympathetic coverage of men obviously overcome by their feelings could feed stereotypes of European men as being easily prone to emotional overreaction, especially uncontrollable weeping. Similarly, news of a suicide, viewed by many as the ultimate act of despair, could evoke in readers a mix of sympathy, curiosity, pity, fear, and even revulsion.[5] The Cold War could also turn suicide into a political morality tale. In 1952, for instance, a member of the Association of United Ukrainian Canadians – the left-wing organization considered to be the biggest and most dangerous pro-Communist group – hanged himself in Toronto. The *Star* focused on the discovery by "anti-subversive squad detectives" of a boxful of communist documents in his home. His mental anguish thus became a product of his contamination by a foreign political disease, communism. A lieutenant, probably Ukrainian Canadian, told reporters that the AUUC was "100 per cent Red" and that the documents contained valuable information on the organization's activities.[6]

The demon image of the wild or evil European patriarch received a boost whenever a mainstream newspaper or magazine covered a violent ethnic crime. That several gruesome cases of "ethnic" murder and domestic violence occurred in the early 1950s, just as the streams of DPs and immigrants were reaching significant levels, helped to set off alarm bells about the dangers of mass migration, especially when the influx included troubled DPs who, as several critics warned, might have the right anti-Communist politics but were mentally and emotionally scarred by the war and its aftermath and by the fear, even paranoia, unleashed by the events occurring within their now-Communist homelands. One such case was a double murder and suicide committed by a thirty-three-year-old Polish DP in Crowland, Ontario, a multi-ethnic, working-class town near Welland.

In Crowland, as in Welland, the local chamber of commerce was organizing a refugee reception program in an effort to integrate the newcomers and undermine the town's radical ethnic traditions. To the horror of the residents, one of the freedom-loving DPs killed his neighbours and then himself. The neighbours, a wife and husband, had, like the killer, spent time in Polish concentration and refugee camps. The killer's wife found the three bodies in the main room of her house – a converted chicken coop that her husband had been turning into a larger house using pieces of board, tile, asphalt roofing, cement blocks, and planks – when she returned home at night from her job in a cotton mill. She ran screaming through the town's heavily ethnic district, then became partially paralyzed from the shock and grief. The male neighbour's skull was shattered by hatchet blows. His wife's throat was slashed with a razor. The murderer had cut his own throat. Both murder weapons, a hatchet and razor blade, were there. The children of both couples were also there, soaked in blood but alive.

The reporters interviewed the neighbours to piece together a profile of the man they called the "insane DP," "dark DP," and the "butcher." A Toronto *Telegram* reporter featured a neighbour who said that he had been expecting "something like this" because the killer, who suffered from stomach ulcers, had become distraught over being unemployed and obsessed with returning to Communist Poland despite having barely escaped death there after the war. His wife had apparently wanted to remain in Canada. The neighbour, also unemployed, had said, in his friend's defence, that the man had been a "nice" and "honest" person who had become a victim, first of the horrible events of the war, and then of chronic unemployment in Canada. The site (and photo) of the murders, the converted chicken coop, enhanced the "mad" character of the case. It was also a reminder that not everyone shared in the benefits of Canadian abundance. The "ramshackle" structure, the *Telegram* reporter wrote, resembled a "bomb-battered European shack," not a Canadian home.[7]

Another story told of a "moody" Estonian miner in Sudbury who "went bezerk" and stabbed his landlady and then her husband when he returned home one day with his children. The miner fit the "madman" label perfectly. He reportedly killed the couple over an argument about membership fees at their funeral home. According to police reports, both victims were knifed to death in the kitchen, and the woman's badly slashed body indicated that she had put up a fight. Although barely able to walk, the husband had alerted a neighbour. When she saw the children screaming and trying to prop up their staggering father, the neighbour contacted the police. It took about six policemen to finally subdue the Estonian, who, they said, had charged at them like "a mad bull" with a German-made hunting knife. If the Estonian first appeared to be impulsively violent, the police testimony at the subsequent trial turned him into a military-trained "psycho" who had used the knife so expertly that he must have had "commando training." He too had been acting strangely before the murders, even smashing his car into a rock wall. Also noteworthy was that the female victim was a homemaker, a respectable French-Canadian woman who had raised good girls (the eldest, thirteen, was studying at a convent). It sent out the message that even a good mother in a small town was not safe from a mad, knife-wielding foreigner.[8]

Other reports were issued of sexual assault cases involving newcomer men attacking white women. In 1955 an Italian man assaulted a married Canadian woman on a downtown street in Toronto, an incident that bolstered the image of European men as "crazy" and dangerous and fed the fear that the number of "criminal sexual psychopaths" (the sort who pounced on a total stranger) was on the rise. While homosexual men were seen as being the most prone to this sexual disease – even though most abusers were identified as heterosexual men – heterosexual foreigners were also considered highly suspect. This Italian man was a textbook case of the irrational "perp." According to the police officers who came to the screaming woman's aid, he had displayed a dramatic mood swing, going from an impulsive attacker (who had grabbed the woman's leg and tried to force her down and rape her) to a broken-down mess who cried and begged for mercy. Still, notwithstanding the alarm surrounding the "criminal sexual psychopath," most women were abused or killed by men they knew, often their intimate partners or ex-partners.

The damaging stereotypes of brutish Mediterranean husbands were reinforced by men who viciously attacked their wives in public – which is what another Italian man in Toronto did after getting into a shouting match with his wife as they walked home with the groceries. He stabbed her fourteen times in the abdomen with a butcher knife. When a good Samaritan tried to intervene, the "wild-looking man with his hair standing up on end" chased him away. The police charged him with attempted murder. Some readers no doubt asked, who brings a butcher knife to go grocery shopping? The weapon suited the typical portrait of the stiletto-wielding Italian.[9]

Other gruesome tales of newcomer wife abusers garnered front-page attention, and, like the coverage of a "crazed" Russian railway worker in Northern Ontario, the main characters were usually depicted as mentally unstable patriarchs. The railway worker had held his new young wife hostage for two days and had a spectacular shootout with the police from inside his "tear-gas-filled-shack." Later he ran out to a desolate stretch of railway line, hauling his terrified, pregnant wife on a sleigh, before the police eventually caught up with him. Once again the local folks told inquiring reporters that the killer had been acting strangely for a while before the event. At one point he had terrified his co-workers by brandishing a rifle. The man's motive for hurting his wife was unclear, but one hint was that she was no virginal bride; she had done time in a Kenora jail for vagrancy, often a code for prostitution. Still, the husband who flies into a rage at the news of an unfaithful wife matched the stereotype of the overly jealous and vengeful ethnic patriarch.[10]

At least one newcomer, an Italian, did carry out this ultimate revenge, in St. Catharines, Ontario, in 1952, when he strangled his supposedly unfaithful wife. He fit the bill of a mad foreigner perfectly, right down to his emotional outbursts in the courtroom. The man's defence put forward an insanity plea, arguing that the sight of the wife, who had just joined her husband with their two children, had triggered a jealous rage, during which the accused did not know what he was doing. When photographs of the wife and children were entered into evidence, the defendant "snatched them, hugged them and burst into tears" and said that they were pictures of his "dearest wife." The Crown then showed the jury that he had cut his wife's image out of each photo. The jury convicted him.[11]

One of the most high-profile cases covered by Toronto reporters – a 1954 double murder involving European refugees as both victims and perpetrator – occurred in their own backyard. It shared enough similarities with the Jack the Ripper murders in Victorian London that some dubbed it the "DP Strangler case." Both victims, Maria Lypoweckyj and Olga Zacharko, were living with their families in the immigrant neighbourhoods of west-end Toronto.

Maria Lypoweckyj was a Ukrainian refugee who had been in a Nazi slave-labour camp in Ukraine before entering Canada in 1952 with her husband and teenage son. Her body had been dumped in an alley near her uncle's home. No witnesses came forward, but police found her purse in a nearby garbage can and some other personal items in the vicinity. A few weeks later Olga Zacharko, a Russian-born cleaning lady employed by the University of Toronto, was murdered while returning to her rooming house after grocery shopping. Together the two events raised fears that a serial killer was on the loose. Married to a man she had met in a German DP camp, Zacharko had a daughter and was pregnant. Her body was in a laneway near her front door. She was not raped, but the semen on her clothing indicated that her murderer had been sexually violent.

Local journalists reporting on the police investigation noted early on that Lypoweckyj had not been raped or mutilated, though a safety pin had been pushed into her upper body. They also drew some independent conclusions – for instance, that her crushed throat indicated her murderer's "abnormal strength." Both Maria Lypoweckyj and her husband John worked the night shift at the posh King Edward Hotel and usually took the streetcar home together, but when John worked a later shift Maria went home alone. Apparently Maria had been accosted before on her way home from work and would have liked to get a day job. According to acquaintances, she was nervous travelling alone and often ran the distance between streetcar and home.

Almost immediately after the discovery of the crime, the press offered more elaborate plots of political intrigue. In a Communist-bogeyman meets Jack the Ripper narrative, the *Star* coverage highlighted the police theories that Maria Lypoweckyj's murder was revenge for her husband's "campaign against communism." He belonged to the Ukrainian government in exile, the National Republicans, and produced what was described as "violent anti-communist propaganda" for the organization's magazine. The husband, dismissing the theory, insisted that his wife had never been involved in his political activities. Other Cold War plots surfaced when police discovered a portrait of a Russian woman known for her anti-Communist views hanging in Maria's bedroom. But the woman turned out to be Lieutenant Lyudmila Pavlichenko, whose killing of German soldiers during the Russian offensive against Hitler's invading army had endeared her to the Allied forces. The discovery soon afterwards of a snapshot of a smiling Maria posing with a German storm trooper triggered a lovers' triangle theory, according to which Maria, now cast as a femme fatale who had ended an affair with a Nazi, had been killed by the vengeful ex-lover.

The news coverage helped give a human face to the victims and expose the vulnerability of immigrant working women toiling at low-paying and risky jobs and heading home alone late at night. But it also fed into stereotypes of European women as exploited and mistreated by their men. In interviews with reporters, Maria Lypoweckyj's friends wove a compelling Cold War morality tale. Lypoweckyj, it seemed, had been doubly victimized, first by Communism and then by a crazy man. Once an educated and cultured woman who travelled in the best circles and thrilled audiences with a fine soprano voice trained at the Warsaw Conservatory of Music, she had been transformed by Communism into a refugee and exploited salad-maker. Others insisted that plots of foreign intrigue were diverting police from the obvious explanation: Lypoweckyj had been killed by a criminal known the world over, "the man who walks dark streets by night and preys on solitary women." The women's husbands also came under the media gaze. Maria Lypoweckyj's husband won the media's sympathy as a man whose own vulnerable position as an exploited worker had rendered him incapable of being by his wife's side as she travelled the streets. But this explanation had a double edge: it also exposed him as a weak man who could not protect his wife.

By contrast, Olga Zacharko's husband was criticized as a selfish man. He had first told reporters that he had gone out to play pool that evening despite his wife's protest that a married man and father should not be out at night. Later he switched his story, telling reporters that this time Olga, though normally opposed to his pool playing, had encouraged him to join his friends at the billiards hall because he deserved a reward for having worked so hard.[12]

The DP strangler case raised the spectre of the criminal sexual psychopath. The journalists sought out the opinion of psychiatrists and sex experts, who warned of the growing number of sadistic sex fiends who might commit such a crime. The case gave further credence to psychiatric categories of sexual deviance while bolstering a link between sex fiend and foreigner. The police reinforced the sex-pervert theory by promising to round up the city's known sex offenders. They combed the immigrant wards in search of sexual harassers, and they told women not to go out at night, except with an escort. They offered a $700 award for any tips leading to the arrest of the strangler, whom they racialized as a man likely to be a European with a dark complexion. After conferring with the police and the sex experts, the journalists declared that, as a *Star* reporter put it, the many "acts of immorality" committed in recent years indicated that more and more of these difficult-to-diagnose perverts were on the loose.

The strangler case brought more attention to psychiatric definitions of sex crimes that, in turn, challenged traditional policing and judicial concepts. Despite continuing tensions between the legal system and psychiatric experts,[13] the police and psyche-based experts agreed that the strangler had to be mentally deranged. Their views gave credence to the theory that sex criminals could seem perfectly normal in status and appearance and could thus resist detection. Far from being merely a DP problem, the case also became one about sexual danger in the Cold War city. As the Radnick families had told Canadians after returning from Tito's Yugoslavia, everywhere in the city where they had lived the people were afraid, and the fear of being robbed by thugs and abducted by police fuelled the paranoia.

The immigrant-refugee dimensions of the case were critical, serving to bolster both professional and popular notions of the Europeans as being more susceptible to mental instability and crimes of passion. No doubt in an effort to get "to the bottom" of the story, and not out of malicious intent, the journalists indulged in all sorts of speculation about categorizing the crime by racial-ethnic group. They reported that the police had infiltrated the immigrant quarters to find out which European group(s) favoured strangulation as a mode of murder, and whether the safety pin stuck in Maria Lypoweckyj had a specific cultural meaning. For their part, Anglo-Celtic bigots who were vocal critics of immigration linked the strangler murders to other recent crimes involving newcomer men and angrily declared that there was a virtual epidemic of degenerate and diseased European men lashing out. In his *Globe and Mail* column, J.V. McAree featured the opinions of a number of angry and partisan Canadians who decried the arrival of so many mentally inferior and threatening foreigners. A self-described "Tory Loyalist" blamed the "shocking increase of murders, rapes and robberies by DP's" on the Liberal government's "arrogant" and "dictatorial" plot to "flood Canada with German, Italian, Ukrainian, Polish, Slavic and other non-British immigrants." In a manner befitting an atmosphere of anti-immigrant and Cold War moral panic, he grouped together violent and non-violent crimes and Europeans from all regions and regimes, to denounce the dumping of "tens of thousands of illiterate, diseased and mentally unfit" newcomers into Canada at a time when the embattled country was facing many threats, including recession and serious unemployment.[14]

Within the ethnic Canadian organizations and communities, the strangler case prompted embarrassment, annoyance, and efforts at damage control. It is not that the ethnic elites and newspapers denied that a problem existed. But when they addressed the topic of men's mental problems within their communities, they typically emphasized the very small numbers involved. For example, when the German-Canadian paper *Torontoer Zeit'g* (Toronto news) reported on the German ambassador's criticism of Ottawa for its apparent indifference to immigrants suffering from emotional or psychological hardships, it typically stressed that while a handful of mentally ill folks did indeed need professional help (and a few had committed suicide), most cases of severe depression were linked to adjustment difficulties that could be "easily rectified with suitable work and living conditions." It also stressed the greater vulnerability of non-English-speaking newcomers "to be put in asylums and left there."[15]

In response to the strangler case, various ethnic spokesmen tried to alleviate the embarrassment by openly declaring that, like the experts said, the culprit was terrorizing all women, not only newcomers, and thus was a menace to all Canadians. They also offered to set up "vigilante committees" to help catch him.[16] Others protested the unfair way in which, once again, a single criminal case was encouraging a criminalized image of all immigrant men. *The Globe and Mail* reprinted a petition written by Ukrainian-Canadian lawyers that had appeared in the recently created Ukrainian-Canadian Catholic newspaper *Nasha Meta* (Our goal). The petitioners declared that as freedom- and justice-loving people who had chosen freedom over slavery, and who respected "the mutual responsibility which underlies the principles of the society of civilized nations," they objected strenuously to the idea that anyone would "judge over a million immigrants in Canada by mentioning a few confused criminal cases," especially since the immigrant criminality rate was lower than the national average. They asserted that the "true picture of the DP's" lay in the hard work, "excellent records," and "good character" of the "thousands of new Canadians who got their citizenship papers recently" and in the many contributions that the scientists, artists, and intellectuals among them had made to Canada. The rapidity with which so many adults and children had mastered English (it "amazes even their teachers"), they added, also reflected their commitment to Canada and their desire "to create a strong Canadian nation despite not having had the opportunity to be born as Anglo-Saxons." The petitioners also denounced as false the charges that they were "illiterate, diseased and mentally unfit" newcomers. They declared (in a bit of overstatement) that "no diseased person" of Ukrainian origin had ever entered Canada.[17]

Some sympathetic gatekeepers, including *Globe* columnist McAree, defended the newcomers (and called them just that, and not foreigners) with the strange-sounding names. McAree advised Canadians to accept that the "English Toronto" of the 1880s was gone and that the more multi-ethnic Toronto of today would eventually "be indistinguishable from a city like Cleveland or Warsaw." Moreover, this was no cause for alarm because the official statistics showed that the newcomers were mostly law-abiding. A University of Toronto professor of social work, Stuart Jaffray, similarly argued that "the incidence of crime by New Canadians is so very, very small as to be almost negligible." He also explained how the media helped to create the wrong impression about who committed most crimes. Still, Jaffray placed most of the blame for the exaggerated fears of foreign men on impressionable Canadian readers who made too much of the occasional criminal who carried a foreign, difficult-to-pronounce name:

> Old prejudices survive. Among them is the very widely spread belief that these newcomers with the odd names are contributing heavily to our criminal statistics. This is not so. The impression is created in the mind of the newspaper reader when he strikes an odd name, and finds that it belongs to a man accused of a crime. The name sticks in his mind because it is odd, and then next time he sees a foreign name connected with a crime, it, too, will stick, and so on until he has noted perhaps a dozen such names associated with as many crimes. He forgets that for half a dozen such names there have been a couple hundred names like O'Brien, Smith, and McGregor. Because they are familiar to him he passes them over. They make no impression on him and he is convinced that the New Canadians are the natural born criminals.[18]

In the end the public was not informed of the final outcome of the case. After investigating several psychiatric institutions, the police quietly determined that a Ukrainian, a former patient at the Ontario Psychiatric Hospital in Whitby, near Toronto, had committed the murders but was mentally unfit to stand trial; and they closed the case.[19] Ironically, the strangler turned out to be an East European refugee, yet neither the police nor government officials revealed this identity to the Canadian public. Perhaps the state, in trying to contain dangerous threats to the body politic, was equally concerned about preventing further spreading of fears about threatening foreign men. Authorities were prepared to deny women information of critical importance to their safety. In this regard, the DP strangler case, though much publicized, shares much in common with similar decisions made by social agency staff who tried to avoid pandering to racism by suppressing information about sexual assault cases involving newcomer men.[20] Given their role in opening the doors to Europe, it is also not surprising that Liberal government officials (and perhaps their high-ranking civil servants) would want to downplay anti-immigrant fears unleashed by this or other violent crimes.

Criminal acts of violence often evoke passionate and moral responses not only from the general public but also from journalists, political pundits, and professional experts who, according to writers Richard Erickson, Patricia Baranek, and Janet Chan, can act as "a kind of 'deviance-defining elite,' using the news media to provide a continuing articulation of the proper bounds of behaviour in all spheres of life."[21] The media coverage of violence can serve to bring different events together in a way that might suggest a collective discussion of the event(s) and thus shape collective responses in the wider public. In other words, the media's "perpetual public conversation about morality, deviance, and control" helps to shape "the moral boundaries of society," which in turn, involves "an on-going articulation of who and what are in and out of bounds."[22]

Taken together, the violent criminal cases described here provoked debate about the merits of Canada's immigration policy and reinforced alarmist predictions about the spreading threat of foreign sexual psychopaths and other violent criminals. They also reinforced alarmist and protectionist views of Cold Warriors who declared that above all Canadians had to protect their society against all foreign threats to the body politic, including moral and sexual threats. If the DP strangler case contributed towards the further stigmatizing of the inner-city neighbourhoods as dangerous foreign ghettoes, the other Ontario-based crimes suggested that the foreign threats to women and children were everywhere. The perpetrators' foreignness gave at least some Canadian critics a convenient scapegoat, or "folk devil," something that absolved themselves, and their society, of any responsibility for these men's rage, psychological ills, or sexism.[23]

The inflammatory statements of government officials fed these anxieties and further embarrassed or enraged newcomers and ethnic Canadians. In the fall of 1955, on the heels of a number of violent ethnic crimes against women, the deputy attorney general of Ontario, Clifford Magnone, declared in a meeting with probation officers that new Canadian men had committed fully 90 per cent of the recent murders in the province. Various ethnic leaders and press editors, including the head of the Canadian Polish Congress and the editor of *Corriere Canadese*, were outraged. They protested what they saw as efforts to link certain violent crimes to certain groups (what today we might call racial or ethnic profiling).[24] They noted that Magnone had gotten the figures reversed: Canadians exhibited higher crime rates than did immigrants. The Canadian Citizenship Council suggested that it was Magnone who had been "carried away by his emotions." Magnone's boss, Ontario attorney general Kelso Roberts, avoided immediate judgment but ordered a breakdown of the statistics. In yet another ironic instance of how the gatekeepers "othered" the Europeans as products of a backward, hence less civil, culture, Roberts also promised that he would try to determine whether the convicted men had received a "training in the Canadian way of life." The implications of this – that European societies tolerated violence and murder but that Canada did not – were hypocritical and insulting both to Europeans and to the victims of Canadian criminals. The federal deputy minister of citizenship and immigration, Laval Fortier, did publicly refute Magnone's claim, and noted that all of the statistics, including those for Ontario (where only five of the twenty-two men convicted for murder during the period 1951–54 were born outside Canada), showed that "immigrants are less crime-prone than native Canadians."

In response Magnone apologized, declaring that "the vast majority" of the many newcomers in the province "are law-abiding citizens and a welcome addition to our population." The probation officers, he reassured people, were equally aware that newcomers made up "an infinitely small percentage" of recently convicted murderers in Ontario. (Less than 3 per cent of men admitted to Canadian penitentiaries for 1952–54 were European-born, while the European-born made up about 5 per cent of the nation's population.) Some of the newspaper editors gave Magnone a somewhat reserved praise for the apology, but the warden of Kingston Penitentiary was more blunt: "The notion that foreigners cause most of the crime is just one of those myths. Unhappily, it's our Canadian-born who are committing the crimes, and getting into the penitentiaries." Toronto journalist Ross Harkness made the sobering point that the next time a newcomer committed a violent crime, many Canadians would again jump to the wrong conclusion.[25]

Assessing Alarmist Discourses and Modern Psychologies

Against this backdrop, journalist Brian Cahill reported in *Saturday Night* that Canadian doctors, social workers, and other "responsible" people were stressing the "urgent need" for "sound" programs to treat the newcomers' mental health. Noting that he was entering "an area highly charged with emotion," Cahill conveyed the gatekeepers' message that unless they were properly treated, the newcomers who had survived such "terrible experiences," or were having difficult adjustment problems, might well form "a pool of mental ill-health," thereby compounding an already "impressive total problem" of mental illness in Canada. Meanwhile, Griffin and his colleagues were continuing to use wide definitions of mental health and speaking of a virtual epidemic in mental illness. They were also identifying mental illness as an underlying cause of male violence.[26]

An investigative journalist, Sidney Katz wrote many *Maclean's* articles on provocative and important topics.
(Photograph by Paul Rockett; *Maclean's*)

A number of journalists helped to popularize the medical models that viewed male violence against women as a manifestation of mental illness. When the prolific Sidney Katz of *Maclean's* wrote about the subject in 1958, he focused on the problem of young, single European men who had been psychologically weakened by war or displacement or had endured mental and physical abuse as the inmates of hospitals or prisons in Communist regimes. They were now, he said, displaying certain symptoms, such as paranoia, and had psychosomatic illnesses such as chronic fatigue and asthma. He highlighted the sexual consequences that could occur given a growing number of young, single European men who were deeply frustrated or angry over their lack of "social contact with women." The psychologists, psychiatrists, and lawyers, ministers, and citizenship officials he had consulted warned that such deprivation could lead to "serious sex conflicts" with women. A number of possible scenarios could develop. Some men would resort to prostitutes, an unfortunate sexual delinquency. Others would become overly aggressive in their efforts to meet or seduce women. This situation, especially when Canadian women were involved, could land them in legal troubles. But the most frightening of all were the men who, unable to control their anger or impulses, would lash out violently against women.[27]

At the same time greater media attention was being given to the topics of "sex deviates," "sex criminals," and sex crimes, including assaults on children. High-profile liberal journalists such as June Callwood and Katz, as well as the prominent psychologists who reached out to lay audiences, helped to popularize the newer psychiatric theories of sex perversion. News stories appeared about the growing number of sex crimes against children, the growing frequency of "sex abnormality," and the need for better sex education (including sex education for mothers, whose own sexual hang-ups, it was argued, could produce a pervert). The experts noted the failure of penal institutions to treat sex offenders (indeed, the prisons had become training grounds for "sex perversion," they argued) and called for more psychiatric resources for treating sex deviates. Lobby groups such as the Parents' Action League, formed in 1955 following the death of a strangled Toronto girl, called for tighter child protections and compulsory medical treatment for convicted sex criminals.[28]

In his 1958 *Maclean's* piece on mental illness and the newcomers, Katz dismissed all the arguments about the men's propensity to criminal acts and stressed instead what he called the alarmingly high rates of mental illness among foreign-born men, especially when compared to Canadian men. He described several types of sufferers (such as the depressed professional refugees who had been reduced to being manual labourers), but was most interested in lonely and disturbed young men. Drawing on a mix of professional and lay opinion and statistical studies, Katz emphasized that both the experts (social workers, psychiatrists, therapists) and government officials argued that unless identified, contained, and treated, this growing army of frustrated, alienated or psychotic European men could become serious sexual threats to women. The studies documenting that new immigrants registered a higher first-time admission rate to mental hospitals than did the general Canadian population, he noted, also showed that the people most susceptible to mental illness were men between fifteen and forty-four years of age who had been in Canada for five years or less. The studies also showed that an overt, acute reaction to deeply distressing events might take years to surface, which meant that constant vigilance was required.[29] Moreover, the actual "immigrant breakdown rate" was much higher than the statistics suggested because fear of deportation or ignorance kept many newcomers from approaching doctors, psychiatrists, or state-funded mental health clinics.

The mental health specialists whom Katz consulted delivered disturbing news. One psychiatrist, Dr. Libuse Tyhurst of Montreal, was one of the many medical personnel who liaised with the Canadian Citizenship Branch in an advisory capacity. He told Katz about a recent study of forty-eight mental patients that had revealed "several" instances of paranoia, including some involving refugee men "who believed that Canadian state authorities and employers had it in for them; that they were being spied on." Others warned that Canada's decision to give quick refuge to the anti-Communist Hungarians, and thus waive the usual medical screening tests, was bound to increase "appreciably" the immigrant crime and mental illness rate. The observation might have partly reflected exaggerated reports that when the rebels opened the prison gates to liberate political prisoners, ordinary criminals and even the criminally insane had thereby gained freedom and later joined the refugee stream to Canada.[30] A prominent McGill University psychiatrist, Dr. Alastair MacLeod, claimed to have spotted "several psychotics" among a group of Hungarian 56ers, including two or three people who "showed the scars of brain operations" and a man haunted by the voice of a former vicious female factory boss.[31]

In trying to explain the problem of the sexually frustrated and alienated European male, Katz placed some blame on Canadians, including frosty Canadian "girls," whose indifference to or rejection of these lonely young men posed a "mental health hazard." He discussed the changed contexts in which single European men and women were now negotiating relationships, in the process offering yet another version of the gatekeepers' romanticized portrayal of Canada as an abundant and modern society in which egalitarian relationships were the norm. Thus, he wrote, single European women figure out that by dating and marrying a Canadian man – and thus rejecting their own more domineering men – they have the chance to enjoy a modern and companionate relationship. But the poor European bachelor who "aspires to court a Canadian girl runs the risk of being cold-shouldered." A young Pole articulated a common complaint: "Canadian girls talk and dance with us at an affair sponsored by an organization or a club," but "won't date with us privately." A blond Italian said that whenever women discover he is Italian, they dump him.

For their part, at least some Canadian women resented being portrayed as frosty. One self-declared "Queen of Sheba" defended her free and democratic right to choose her own dance partners. She argued that the issue was not "Who do the Canadian girls think they are?" but instead "Just who do the fellows going to stag dances in Toronto think they are?" She even invoked a discourse of European dictatorship and Canadian democratic decency – not to mention a Hollywood leading hunk, Rock Hudson (ironically, a closeted gay man) and the urban African-American-influenced "zoot suit" phenomenon – to defend Canada's single women. "Canada is a land of many freedoms," she noted.

> Some fellows are under the impression this is a dictatorship, they being the dictators. Why should we Queens of Sheba dance with every Tom, Dick and Harry that asks us? Must we because of our sex be denied the privilege of free will? I usually attend a stag dance on a Friday night. Twenty-five per cent of the fellows stand in groups of three or four, study the available females, look them up and down, debate among themselves, and then ask the best of the stag girls to dance. Not being any Rock Hudsons themselves they seem quite put out that they are refused. Another 25 per cent have been out drinking with the boys before coming to the dance. We Canadian girls certainly do not like our liquor second hand. Fifteen per cent are smart alec zoot-suiters and 10 per cent give you the impression they are doing you a favor by asking you to dance. You choose your partners, let us choose ours.[32]

Katz also identified related factors, including the cultural differences in "wooing habits." The European "pickup" was an acceptable way of meeting women back home, but it was far too direct and aggressive for Canadian women. Above all, however, Katz and his professional experts stressed that the young European men's failure to resolve their heterosexual needs, and to contain and channel their sexual drive into appropriate codes of courtship and marriage, could turn them into moral and mental misfits or, indeed, sexually aggressive and even violent men. He did not refer explicitly to homosexuality, which had been added to the "unsuitability" clause in the Immigration Act in 1952, nor did he note that Canadians reacted with disapproval, even taunts, to the sight of European men kissing each other on the cheeks, a social act that carried no negative connotations in their own culture.[33]

Finally, Katz let the mental health specialists have the final word. They declared that even with the government's expanded financial commitment to treating mental health, Canada was still failing to keep in step with the spreading problem, one made worse by the mass influx of newcomers. Once again, the experts stressed their indispensability to treating problems and called for more resources. Again, the European newcomers were discussed both as part of a growing trend and as isolated people with a specific problem requiring specialized remedies.

In response to Katz's sympathetic but alarmist article, Laval Fortier of Citizenship and Immigration had a senior researcher in the Research Division of the Citizenship Branch assess his claims. Nancy Elgie concluded that while the statement held an element of truth, Katz had grossly exaggerated his findings and ignored any findings that challenged his argument. He had neglected to note, for instance, that in certain years the Canadian rate of registration in mental hospitals exceeded the immigrant rate. Or that immigrants who had lived in Canada for more than ten years exhibited lower first-admission rates (by 6 per cent) than did native-born Canadians. He had avoided reporting that the researchers who had detected "mental illness" among the DPs had not considered it to be "a particular problem *quantitatively*." Katz had also ignored age- and sex-related distinctions; for example, that for most age groups, Canadian women had a higher hospital admission rate than did foreign-born women. Elgie also criticized Katz for attributing the underreporting of immigrant mental illness to a deportation chill. With only about one immigrant deported on mental illness grounds·for every five hundred admitted to a mental hospital, Elgie doubted that the newcomers were as terrified as Katz presumed.

While she was far too dismissive of the deportation issue, Elgie clearly challenged Katz's claim that the newcomers posed a major mental health problem. In her view the problems had been largely confined to the early arriving DPs, whose traumatic history and "absolutely devastating wartime memories," along with the special adjustment problems created by their poverty, unfamiliarity with English, and absence of kin networks of support, had increased their chances of suffering from "despair, depression and extreme mental anguish." The volunteer immigrants who began arriving in large numbers after 1950 had also suffered in the war, and had faced similar barriers, but most of them had re-established "a considerable degree of security" before emigrating. Many of them had migrated in "family groups" and had benefited from the many organizations in place to provide economic and emotional support. Elgie concluded that the recent newcomers raised no serious mental illness problems, and that the same could be expected of future immigrants, who would benefit from still better social services. A partial exception was the Hungarian 56ers: Elgie agreed that there might be a higher rate of psychological illness among people who had lived under a totalitarian regime, especially those whose anti-Communism had landed them in prison or even mental hospitals, but that, like the DPs, their "difficulties" would be "transient," that is, confined to the adjustment years.[34] Although Elgie's confidential assessments cannot be treated as a parallel public discourse or rebuttal to Katz, her political superiors used them in public ways, to allay, or contain, public anxieties at home, and to demonstrate to the international community that Canada was looking out for the newcomers' mental as well as physical health. To do otherwise would be to risk appearing indifferent or callous.[35]

Despite its exaggerations and alarmism, Katz's article prompted a muted but generally positive response from *Maclean's* readers, though most of the letter writers were British men who agreed that they needed sympathy and companionship. A few Canadians urged him also to write about newcomers who were adjusting well to Canada. The most critical response was from an Albertan booster who quipped: "Who in hell needs a psychiatrist west of Winnipeg? Why not give the New Canadian a break and start him away from these boiling vats of humanity."[36]

Treatment Regimes: The "Psychiatric Turn"

By the late 1950s and early 1960s, psychological or psychiatric profiles of the newcomers had become more common. So too had the kind of advice that Katz's psychiatrists and therapists dispensed. In explaining the need for patience in face of persistent complaining, one psychiatrist told people to think of the newcomers as adopted children who had been mistreated and thus could not be expected to always be reasonable. But with long-term support, they would eventually adjust, stop complaining, and learn to appreciate their adopted country. Many gatekeepers, even those without professional medical training, including Citizenship Branch officials like Kaye, liaised with mental health specialists and sometimes used their vocabulary or paradigms. Similarly, front-line workers in the social services drew explicit links between mental stresses and psychosomatic illness (chronic fatigue, insomnia, asthma, stomach pain, palpitations), and warned that those who refused professional help risked having a total mental breakdown.

Although postwar Canadians were becoming more accustomed to psychiatric analyses of deviant behaviour, most of them probably knew little about the state of Canadian postwar psychiatry or the treatment regimes for men diagnosed with mental illness or incarcerated for sex crimes.[37] The field was characterized by competing paradigms of diagnosis and treatment. The presence of multidisciplinary lobby groups such as the Canadian Mental Health Association had not eliminated the long-standing interprofessional conflicts and tensions between psychiatrists and both psychologists and medical doctors. In Canada's postwar mental hospitals, the newer approaches – which were associated with more psychologically oriented and Freudian-influenced psychiatry and psychoanalysis, and therapeutic models that combined psychotherapy with efforts to resocialize the patient – did not replace older, organic-based theories of mental illness to nearly the same extent as occurred in Europe and the United States. If popular writers tended to highlight the newer paradigms, including talk therapy, perhaps because they appeared to be more enlightened, in practice in Canada (and most particularly at the Toronto Psychiatric Hospital), doctors still commonly applied the traditional treatments, namely shock therapies (including ECT, electro-convulsive therapy) and lobotomies. With growing frequency they also used drugs, especially the breakthrough psychoactive drug of the 1950s, chlorpromazine. To some psychiatrists' dismay, medical doctors could now prescribe the drug to clients. (The 1970s to 1990s would see a return to organic and biochemical paradigms, in which heredity and brain biology are considered key factors, particularly in neurological diagnoses.)

In addition, the social welfare field was undergoing something of "a psychiatric turn." As part of their training, Canadian psychologists, social workers, and nurses were exposed to a range of paradigms, including the psychological and psychiatric, and many of them also took part in psychiatric clinic therapy teams in hospitals, mental health clinics, and mental hospitals. Even so, the degree to which the "semi-professional" social workers actually adopted psychiatric paradigms varied considerably, and probably never to the extent desired by leading psychiatrists, especially in light of what they claimed to be a virtual epidemic in mental illness.

Still, the postwar psychiatric turn was significant. According to Griffin, thousands of young medical doctors had learned from their war experiences the "necessity of understanding the psychological and emotional significance of illness." As they returned to civilian work, many of them were now scrambling for intensive training courses in psychosomatic medicine and even taking the additional training required to become mental health specialists. All of this was necessary, Griffin said, because of the rapidly growing number of people with personality disorders and psychological or emotional "disturbances" that might not be serious enough to warrant a clinic but were still causing much individual suffering and "disorganized family life." A growing use of psychiatric approaches was similarly taking place within social work, much to the chagrin of radical social workers who feared the loss of social reform programs in favour of an exclusively individual program of counselling and drug or other psychiatric therapies.

At the same time some psychiatrists, psychotherapists, and psychologists admitted to a less than impressive track record when it came to treating their mentally ill-adjusted newcomer patients. Of course, insufficient staff and resources were common complaints. So too was the unwillingness of many newcomers to undergo psychiatric treatment or therapy, including occupational and talk therapy – a reluctance that some front-line gatekeepers attributed partly to the fear that the immigrants, particularly refugees and DPs, held of authorities and institutions of any kind, primarily because they had been mistreated in the past. By the same token, the implied corollary, that Canadian doctors could be trusted completely, crumbles in the face of what we now know about the CIA-funded experiments conducted on psychiatric patients in Canada.

Certain psychiatrists, including Dr. Anthony Meszaros of Montreal, publicly discussed the linguistic barriers to effective treatment with Katz, noting that even when non-English-speaking newcomers could be convinced to visit a therapist or psychiatric clinic, they usually came with a companion and said very little. The language difficulties further undermined the quality of treatment. Since most therapists could not speak the necessary languages, they relied on medically untrained interpreters, such as technicians or relatives. Some of the therapists resorted to telephone interviews with other doctors. All of these conditions produced poor results. Indeed, a Quebec psychiatrist admitted to Katz that most of the doctors who worked in regular and even in mental hospitals were "so handicapped by language" that they sometimes could not tell whether a patient was "mildly or seriously ill." Given this situation, "foreign-speaking" clients, even those agitated by "normal" problems such as unemployment or bad news from home, were no doubt vulnerable to being wrongly diagnosed, unnecessarily or overly medicated, and institutionalized.

If the language divide made newer talk therapies impractical, except perhaps when European psychiatrists were available, the newcomer patients were probably more likely than Canadian patients to be prescribed various drugs or shock therapies. It might also have reinforced their inferior status in relation to their more biologically and biochemically oriented Canadian colleagues. A few administrators of mental hospitals admitted to Katz that psychiatrists were often hostile towards new Canadians, especially when the patient constantly criticized the Canadian way of life. Such hostility could further damage the newcomer already suffering from feelings of inferiority.

Caseworkers: Containing Violent Men in the Private Sphere

In the professional periodicals, the psychiatric social worker emerged as the quintessential female helpmate to senior male specialists, who diagnosed and treated patients, and as the front-line liaison person who continued to work both with clients as outpatients and with their families and communities. There were psychiatric male nurses who had the physical strength to deal with difficult or out of control psychiatric patients, but lacked the same status as the overwhelming number of female registered nurses.

Still, the reality was far more messy.[38] It was often the front-line caseworker in the social service field, and not a psychiatrist or a psychiatric nurse in a mental health facility, who encountered a violent man who might be suffering from mental illness, whether in a social welfare office, family court, or immigrant aid agency.

At the International Institute of Metropolitan Toronto, the counsellors included a few professional social workers, both Canadian and newcomers, some social work students, and experienced volunteers, including newcomers and ethnic Canadians. While every caseworker got at least some on-the-job training, the records reveal a mix of social work and psychiatric vocabulary and subjective opinion as well as differing degrees of sensitivity and empathy towards the client. Overworked, and with mounting caseloads, they often made difficult on the spot decisions, including referral to a psychiatric clinic.

The confidential case files detailing the situations of wives who turned to the International Institute for help in dealing with their husbands' sexual and violent rages offer a valuable glimpse into how the gatekeepers – in this case, a mix of professional social workers and volunteers – tried to contain the problem, largely by trying to get the men professional psychiatric help while also holding out the hope that, in the end, the men could be rehabilitated and the families would be reunited and strengthened.[39] These goals did not always match what the wives wanted, however, especially after years of enduring abuse. Moreover, the files show how some female victims responded to their nasty predicaments; a few wives were able to convince the Institute counsellors to forgo their pro-family approach and help them to get rid of cruel and brutal men. In essence these particular gatekeepers played a critical role in referrals to mental health clinics or institutions and thus wielded tremendous power over the men's lives.

For example, two bulky files follow the cases of two violent refugee men, both Hungarians – one from a middle-class background, the other working-class – who abused their wives and threatened or mistreated their children. In the first case, that of Mr. A. and his wife (Mrs. A.), a couple who lived, with their baby, in a small flat in a rooming house, the Institute caseworkers identified almost immediately that they had a "wife abuse problem" on their hands.[40] Mrs. A.'s caseworker, Mr. N., a multilingual social worker who spoke several East European languages, recorded that the woman called her husband "a good-for-nothing." Apparently he drank a lot, never worked, beat her often, and mistreated the baby. He spent her mother's allowance on wine and, interestingly, theatre tickets. He ate up all of the food and sold her (donated) clothing to treat himself, and their Ukrainian landlord, with drink. Moreover, as the caseworker noted, a Hungarian friend, Mrs. W., a married woman who lived one floor up in the same rooming house, corroborated the wife's accusations. Mrs. W. reported a few times that the husband was threatening his wife again, or bothering the child, or ransacking the room for things to sell. Another witness, a local Immigration Branch officer, reported that the husband was "crazy" and needed some serious talking to. The caseworker agreed. Typically, however, he and the other caseworkers who became involved with Mrs. A. wanted the family to stay together, and they initially advised her to get her husband some psychiatric help. Even as they became more concerned for her welfare, they still hoped he might be rehabilitated and the family kept together.

For the Institute staff, given their own reports of what they witnessed, keeping the family together was a tall order indeed. An experienced female caseworker who conducted many of the Institute's home visits with clients was dispatched to Mr. and Mrs. A's home. She described Mr. A. as "tall, very handsome and well dressed," but said their rooming house flat was substandard. It had a tiny kitchen, a broken window, and a few furnishings – a bed, table and chairs, and an old dirty chesterfield. Mr. A., who had insisted on speaking to the home visitor first, told her stories that the wife and her friend later contradicted. The home visitor concluded that Mr. A. was unemployed because he refused to take on any job that he considered beneath him. She noted with horror that he told her the baby slept soundly because of gas fumes coming from the charcoal heating in the house.

The home visitor also spoke with the wife's friend upstairs. Mrs. W. reported that, once again, the father had spent the mothers' allowance and emergency welfare on "wine and girls," and that, while wielding a knife in front of others, he had threatened to kill the wife. He had also said he would commit her to a psychiatric institution. Mrs. W. said that he had given the baby sleeping pills in order to keep it quiet. Another time, she added, he had spiked his wife's coffee with a drug given to animals to arouse sexual instincts (she did not know the name or explain how she knew what it was), and when the wife became "very nervous and upset and hysterical," he declared that she was "not normal" and must be put into "a mental hospital." After Mr. A. left the flat that day, Mrs. A. begged the home visitor "to get her some place else to stay with her baby as she was afraid of her husband."

In response to the report, the Institute counsellors asked the Catholic Children's Aid Society to investigate the situation. The wife's caseworker, Mr. N., managed to convince the husband to come in for an interview, and later reported that Mr. A. had undergone several mood swings, suggesting mental ill health. At first Mr. A was "cheerful" and "very sure of himself," but when he realized that the staff were on to him, he became "aggressive and resentful" and "gave the impression of being very confused." As he ranted about his wife's many sins, he contradicted himself, and alternated between "shouting" and "break[ing] into tears."

On the day after the interview Mr. A. returned to the Institute offices and demanded to see "the lady" who had visited his flat because his wife was now in the hospital and he wanted help. He ended up with a different staff caseworker, a woman, who also recorded his mood shifts. At first, he was "perfectly charming – good manners, polite, not wishing to inconvenience us," and agreed to wait patiently in the waiting room until she was ready for him. After he was ushered into her office, along with his wife's caseworker and a Hungarian interpreter, the new caseworker demanded to know about the drugs he had been giving the baby.

"The change in his manner was instantaneous," she noted. "The suave charm disappeared – he glared at us, eyes strained and intense." He aggressively denied having drugged the child or beaten his wife. He accused his wife of lying, and her friend of having stolen their furniture and china.[41]

These and other entries indicate that the man had serious emotional or psychological problems, as the caseworkers surmised. What is also significant, and a pattern common to many wife abuse cases, is that he tried to justify his violence by defending his male honour and blaming his wife's failings. Like many abusers, he portrayed himself as a good man and husband unfairly undermined or provoked by a bad wife who failed to meet her domestic duties.[42] He said that his wife "was no good," that she "didn't look after him properly," was a bad mother, and he was going to divorce her. He was glad that the Children's Aid was involved, he said, adding that he would "pay any amount of money to have the child taken away." As he spoke, "His eyes were fierce and threatening, while the pulse in his cheek throbbed quite visibly and with increasing rapidity."

Interwoven into this ugly tale of violence was an anti-Communist morality tale of middle-class persecution. The Institute caseworkers determined that the man was "completely out of balance," that he was "mentally confused and needed psychiatric help." Their theories as to the possible underlying or contributing causes had a definite Cold War spin, one that fit well with the common view that Communist regimes, and their Big Brother intrusions, produced a persecution complex in their citizens. Class also mattered. Mr. N. noted that a key piece of information was that Mr. A. had come from "a fairly good and old Hungarian family which probably suffered much persecution during the communist regime in Hungary," whereas Mrs. A. was of "peasant origin."

But they did not use their Cold War theory to excuse Mr. A., perhaps because they had witnessed his disturbing behaviour more than once. A critical episode involved the family court. Again, at Mrs. A.'s initiative, she and her caseworker were discussing the procedure for requesting that the court submit her husband to a psychiatric assessment. Again, the man had charged into the Institute offices. When the staff told him that they were going to escort his wife to city hall (which housed the family court), he insisted on coming along, and they let him, in the hopes of preventing another uproar. As the group (two caseworkers, an interpreter, the couple, and their baby) walked to court, he was amiable, not nervous, and teased them.

Once charges were filed the process moved along very quickly, perhaps because of the corroborating witnesses, and later that day the group came before the magistrate. He called upon Mrs. A.'s caseworker as a witness. As Mr. N. later recorded it, "I explained our experiences and our general impression that Mr. A. was mentally disturbed, convinced of his own rightness and projected all his own deeds onto others." In response the magistrate immediately remanded Mr. A. to a psychiatric hospital for observation. Mr. A. was escorted out of the courtroom by police. He was evidently unaware of what was happening until he realized he was being led off to the cells, at which point he screamed and tried to fight his way back into the courtroom. The wife showed no emotion. The Institute staff took her home.

In this case Mrs. A. benefited from her encounter with the gatekeepers, even if the Institute caseworkers never did fully abandon the possibility that psychiatric rehabilitation might "fix" her husband and reunite the family. Mrs. A. had clearly reached the point of no return. When, shortly after the court case, she returned to the Institute for a visit, she was "relaxed and friendly" and firmly declared that she never again wanted to see her husband. When her caseworker suggested, "If the hospital was able to do anything for him, he might not be the same person," she did not reply. Instead, she noted that she and her friend (and friend's husband) were looking for a place together just in case their landlord (a drinking buddy of her husband's) decided to make things unpleasant for them. When the staff told her that the hospital had called to say that her husband was refusing to speak to any interpreter except his wife, she was unmoved. Ironically, earlier the caseworker Mr. N. and the hospital intake worker had expressed the hope that "if the hospital was to make a new man out of him," the wife might be willing to see him and perhaps even ultimately reconcile with him. As the case file reaches its conclusion, the husband has begun writing love letters to his wife, but, it appears, to no avail.

The case file on a second wife abuser, Mr. B., a former police officer in Hungary, shares much in common with the case of Mr. A., including the caseworkers' pro-family paradigm of treatment (which was common to many Institute files). The differing responses of the varied social welfare personnel involved in this second case remind us that front-line workers themselves differed with respect to training, sensitivity, and insight. The materials in the file, especially a set of letters, also shed light on the wife's experience of marital cruelty and her valiant efforts to defend herself and her family, which included two young boys. If there is a difference between the cases, it is in the even greater degree of contempt and violence displayed by this husband towards his wife.

The husband, Mr. B., first became an Institute client in 1957 as an unemployed newcomer who was registered with the local National Employment Service and was thus required to be seeking work. He was collecting emergency welfare support (mostly food vouchers) from the Immigration Department (which paid his rent) and Catholic Family Services. His caseworker, again the multilingual social worker Mr. N., found Mr. B. a dishwashing job. But a sordid family situation involving charges of mental illness, sexual perversions, and violence quickly presented itself. The man told his caseworker that his wife, Mrs. B., was having "intercourse" with her brother, recently released from the Queen Street Mental Hospital. Given that Mr. B. was already caught in the web of welfare agencies, Mr. N. contacted his colleagues at Catholic Family Services and the local Immigration office for more details about him. He learned that a belligerent Mr. B. had refused to hold down a job, and had taken his sons away from his wife, and that Mrs. B had tried earlier to leave Mr. B. after he had "threatened her with a knife." Also, the brother's mental illness made it very "unlikely" that he would have sex with anyone.

Mr. N. also assumed, correctly, that the Catholic Children's Aid Society would try to take the boys away from their negligent father. But Mr. B. had evidently eluded or defied the child authorities because almost a year later, when he returned to the Institute, he still had the boys and wanted help in placing them in foster care while he looked for a job. He then changed his tune and said that he would take them out of school and let them earn their keep at his place by doing odd jobs. Shortly afterwards, Mr. N. saw the boys and noted that they were underfed and that the father spoke harshly to them. He learned (no doubt from his colleagues at the Catholic Children's Aid Society) that in the past year Mr. B. had raped his wife and impregnated her, and that after the baby's birth she had given it up to Children's Aid and left her husband.

Mrs. B. then came to the Institute, and Mr. N. became her caseworker as well. She brought letters that captured the taunts and torments she had endured at the hands of a man whom she and her caseworkers at the Institute and Catholic Family Services were now convinced was mentally ill. Her efforts to handle the situation also provide a graphic illustration of the "weapons of the weak," of how a woman disadvantaged by class, poverty, and language tapped into the state institutions in an effort to help her family and herself. On the legal front, Mrs. B. first took the advice of her Catholic Family Service caseworker and filed a complaint against her husband at Toronto family court. When the caseworker could not join her in court, she went alone. The court hearing proved disastrous because no witnesses showed up. The judge dispensed the most common advice given to women in her predicament: try working things out with your husband. Mrs. B. refused to do so. In preparing for the court action, her Institute caseworker learned even more grim details about the man's history of abuse: there had been beatings and knife threats in Hungary; he had served a prison term (fourteen months) for a rape conviction, and another one (four months) for threatening to kill a teenaged boy; and he had forced the wife, at knifepoint and following a beating, to "confess" that she had slept with her brother, and then raped her. "All this was too much for her," wrote Mr. N., "and she left him again." Clearly, Mr. N. believed her and, unlike the family court, he now supported her desire to be rid of the brute, although he never explicitly advocated divorce.

Following the first court hearing, Mrs. B. courageously defied her husband again and met with her boys. She ignored a letter from her husband's lawyer

The information on this ward's notice board, on the wall, extreme left, was updated daily to help orient clients as to time and place: "Queen Street / Mental Health / Centre / The year is 1972 / Today is Thursday / March 5 / Ward 1B."

Ward 1B was located on the first floor above the ground-level basement in the East Tully Wing, built 1868–70 and demolished a year or two after this shot was taken. An earlier shot, *circa* 1910, also shows this corridor or perhaps a similar one in another wing (CAMH Archives, glass negative [c]). Ward 1B was probably a psycho-geriatric unit because a nurse is shown in uniform, whereas by 1972 most nurses in Queen Street's active treatment units wore civilian dress.

(CAMH Archives, Queen Street Mental Health Centre, 1972)

"requesting" that she "return to him" and to the "responsibilities of wife and mother." The husband then tried to kill her, but a male tenant in her rooming house intervened. In response to the attack, she again took her husband to court. This time he was convicted of assault, ordered to stay away from his wife, and jailed, albeit briefly. Upon release, he continued to taunt her and to keep her sons away. Yet again the family court advised immediate "reconciliation with her husband" while deferring a decision for the children. A month later, when Mrs. B. went to the courthouse asking about her children, she was told (perhaps by sympathetic staff) that her best bet might be simply to steal them back.

Not all of Mrs. B.'s caseworkers were equally sympathetic, but she enlisted the aid of more supportive ones to pressure those seemingly less so. She told Mr. N. that her Children's Aid worker had failed to appear for a scheduled appointment even though she waited for hours. She kept the Institute staff up to date about the Children's Aid matters and about secret meetings with her sons. Alas, the paper trail ends without noting what happened to her and the boys, save for the information that in summer 1959, when her husband again returned to the Institute looking for work, she was still alive.

Mrs. B. did, however, wield a second weapon of the weak – she contacted medical staff at the Queen Street Mental Hospital. She sent a lengthy letter to her brother's doctor, enclosing as well a letter that her husband had sent her, in which he threatened to kill her, their sons, and the "others" who had helped her. He boasted about having "kidnapped" the sons and having convinced the "stupid" doctors to put her brother in a mental hospital. It ends with misogynist attacks: "I will cut your neck anyway... everybody will know what you are before I hang you... you dirty person... you mattress for all the judges and police... you garbage can [and] prostitute."

Although it is not clear whether Mrs. B. wrote, dictated, or approved her letter to the Queen Street psychiatrist, the communication nonetheless graphically conveyed her predicament and her determination to get out of a horrendous situation.[43] The letter explained the court fiascos and said that the police and others agreed that her husband was "not normal" and "require[d] treatment." It reported that he had once beaten up a Hungarian neighbour who had helped her. Ironically, he accused the neighbour of being "a spy." She wrote that her husband had

Occupationalist therapist Julie Turylo, with two of her clients in the ceramics studio at Lakeshore Psychiatric Hospital, 1959. (CMHA Archives, Lakeshore Psychiatric Hospital)

admitted to feeling "not normal," adding, cryptically, that he had "a paper" from a mental hospital that "lawfully protects him from all responsibility."

Noting the irony that "such a bad and foolish man can be free from all responsibilities," she begged the doctor to "please take my husband and examine him to see if he is a mental case." In Hungary, she said, he had been sadistic and "he has continued this cruelty with me." Her letter explained that she was well beyond reconciliation, noting the futility of earlier promises to "make peace" or "take him back." Moreover, Mrs. B. concluded with her own Cold War morality tale. Asking the doctor to "save us" from a "confused and foolish" man, she expressed the hope that "in a free country we can have a life with my little family."

The two files contain all the ingredients of the gatekeepers' worst-case scenario: both men had lived under a Communist regime – one had been a prisoner and the other, ironically, a police officer – and both exhibited a mix of deep-seated envy, paranoia, and brutishness.[44] It may well have crossed the minds of the caseworkers that, in the first instance, the man had been mistreated in prison and now suffered from mental health problems, and, in the second, that the brutality of the regime could corrupt or mentally infect those required to enforce it. The two men also had far from ideal therapeutic relationships with the experts. Ultimately, the different class backgrounds of the women – the first, the wife of a doctor (though herself of peasant background), the second, of a policeman – meant less than their shared vulnerability as refugee women. Indeed, the cases speak to the commonalities among the female victims of male abusers, no matter the class, racial-ethnic, or social background. Moreover, these abused women valiantly sought to wield the limited "weapons" available to them, such as enlisting the help of caseworkers, to deal with a seemingly impossible situation, and be "heroes of their own lives." They even demanded that the gatekeepers live up to their own rhetoric of Canada as a land of compassion.[45]

At the same time the painful details contained in the Institute files on these two men (and on the other cases involving violent husbands) help to explain why a handful of confidential case files on evidently deranged and cruel men had such a powerful impact on front-line gatekeepers. But just as the news reporting of ethnic crimes could encourage racial profiling among police and Canadian readers alike, these cases could reinforce the gatekeepers' tendency to pathologize the European male as backward and brutish, even uncivilized. By extension, they could essentialize European women as victims of domineering patriarchs. Here, too, ironies abound. With few exceptions, the caseworkers who intervened in these cases advised the women to return to their violent husbands, to get their husbands psychiatric help, and to work towards improving, or modernizing, their marital and family dynamics. The assumption was that, first, the husband could be contained and treated, and then put back into the home, where the wife had to work as hard as the husband at improving their relationship. Thus the caseworkers revealed their faith in the capacity of experts to reshape European patriarchs and their father-dominated families along more egalitarian Canadian lines. Indeed, they revealed their very belief in the ideal of the "Canadian democratic family," despite evidence that, as their counterparts in social agencies, clinics, and hospitals could confirm, domestic violence also occurred in the households of Canadians across the class and racial-ethnic spectrum. Only after persistent torment did some of the Institute's front-line caseworkers come to make the woman's escape from a demented and brutal man the priority. At that point they clearly took sides, becoming allies in the woman's struggle against a brutal husband. For the husband they remained unwelcome intruders of the state and its social welfare system.[46]

The alarmist and damaging Cold War discourses that demonized European men as potential paranoids, psychotics, and sexual predators underscored the centrality of questions of morality, sexuality, and mental health in an immigrant-receiving nation. They also raised the already high stakes involved not only in excluding those considered to be morally or mentally unsuitable from entering the country but also in the gatekeeping task of containing (or regulating), treating, and eventually integrating male newcomers – people who were valued for their labour or politics but seen as vulnerable to immoral, even deranged, acts of violence against women, even Canadian women. Given the popularity of psychiatric approaches in the postwar era – a trend reinforced by the Cold War – the gatekeepers' discourses of sexual morality in both the public and private arenas were not surprisingly intertwined with complex questions about mental health and psychiatric interventions. What remains is the thorny question of whether the medicalization of male violence and other sexual transgressions was necessarily more progressive than criminalization.

The gatekeepers' tendency to assess European male violence as though it were primarily a symptom of an individual man's mental illness, personality disorder, or cultural and sexual perversion meant that to some extent they could sidestep the larger problem of patriarchal privileges and structures that make all women vulnerable to male sexual aggression and violence. By never publicly acknowledging that domestic violence occurs across all classes and races, the gatekeepers may have made it easier for people to "other" sexual and domestic violence as a foreign crime.[47] By displacing the problem of patriarchy and male violence onto the male "other," some Canadian gatekeepers found their "folk devil" and sidestepped the damage done to women everywhere in the name of male privilege, moral order, and the family.

A woman resistance fighter, Paris. The original caption for this photo illustrates how even women who took on heroic roles were subject to patronizing portrayals: "Mademoiselle Hunts Nazis with Submachine Gun. Clad in an outfit designed for action, this young French girl of the resistance movement is a member of the patrol to rout out the remaining German snipers in Paris." *Telegram* 28 Aug. 1944. (Signal Corps Radiotelephoto, New York Bureau; YUA, Toronto Telegram, ASC Image 1263)

The Sexual Politics of
Survival and Citizenship

Social Workers, Damaged Women,
and Canada's Moral Democracy

9

IMMIGRATION POLICIES AND CITIZENSHIP AGENDAS were not just shaped by the prevailing bourgeois and heterosexual norms within the receiving nation; they were also sexualized. Canadian Immigration officials could exercise their wide discretionary powers to reject applicants dubbed morally unsuitable – but in addition, if suspect immigrants did manage to get into the country Immigration officials could recommend their deportation, often without having to admit to moral prejudices or facing public scrutiny.[1] Whether the rates of deportations were high or not, the gatekeepers could use the very threat of deportation to coax or cajole newcomers into reforming what was seen as sexually deviant behaviour. In the case of women, dominant notions of them as "good" or "bad" influenced the judging and regulation of even those newcomers who were considered racially and politically preferable.[2]

The politics of the Cold War underpinned the gatekeepers' efforts to contain "sexual delinquencies" and mould behaviour. It shaped their responses to and reception efforts among European women who had transgressed conventional moral codes. Once again, in keeping with the Cold War concept of domestic containment, the popular press and front-line caseworkers exerted themselves to assess, regulate, and treat deviant newcomer women, in the process revealing important gender differences. While the gatekeepers generally depicted deeply troubled European men as potential sexual predators or wife abusers, in contrast they tended to view European women who had less than conventional sexual histories, or who transgressed sexual norms in Canada, as morally damaged people – and these women, before fully qualifying for citizenship, would have to undergo psychological and emotional rehabilitation.

In contrast to the treatment of men, whose sexual or violent crimes garnered plenty of media attention, discussions of women's transgressions were more confined to the confidential arena of "experts" and case records. But the need to reshape women's sexual morality was seen as being no less significant or urgent. Indeed, the age-old standard of women as the protectors of family morality meant that their cases were in some respects seen as being more important. The experts hoped to transform morally tenuous women into responsible wives and mothers capable of making a good partnership with a responsible man and raising a future generation of healthy and well-adjusted Canadian children.

The interventions were linked to wider efforts of inculcating and policing the norms that regulated good girls, proper wives, and decent mothers across the population, and to the national reconstruction plans and Cold War initiatives carried out in the name of democratic decency. The efforts dovetailed nicely with the gendered principles of the modern social welfare state, where the concept of female citizenship and entitlement was embedded in a moralizing discourse demanding that women recipients meet dominant notions of proper female behaviour. Then too, in this realm of the moral politics of citizenship, a prevailing double sexual standard meant that women were held to a higher moral standard than were men. Unless they committed cruel or violent crimes, men – especially if they were single men – were more easily forgiven any number of sexual indiscretions. The gatekeepers (like many Canadians) also never did fully understand the enormous sense of sexual vulnerability that had become a deep part of the lives of European women during the war and stayed with them long after. Despite the usual declarations of cultural sensitivity or liberal pluralism, the various gatekeepers thus could not entirely stop themselves from taking what amounted to moralizing positions when they encountered these women.[3]

Surviving Europe's War Zones

During the Second World War and its aftermath, women's experiences of violence and the difficult moral and sexual choices that many of them had to make would have an enduring impact, not just on themselves and their families but also on the communities in which they later settled.[4] Even those who had willingly defied sexual codes by having extramarital affairs, experiencing a mix of emancipation and guilt, faced the challenge afterwards of renegotiating relations with fiancés and husbands who came back from war amid loud public calls for a return to conventional morality. For many of Europe's displaced women, and those who survived the war zones, the challenge of renewing or forging new relationships with men was further complicated by their sexual histories, their fertility, and their desire, or not, to have children.

These newcomer women seeking to adjust to life in Canada tended, then, to be sexually vulnerable. They had faced difficult moral dilemmas and reacted in different ways to the opportunities and contradictions created by the war, and to their liberation or defeat by the Allied forces. Although not all women had directly experienced sexual violence or adopted a "situational morality" that, for instance, allowed them to exchange sex for food, the moral dilemmas and sexual realities of wartime had an impact on all gender relations during and after the war.[5] The experiences that newcomer women had previous to their emigration would influence their choices and responses in Canada, and their actions in the new country would be circumscribed by their material conditions, the availability of social services and treatment regimes, and the quality of their encounters with front-line gatekeepers – some of whom sought to regulate (or contain) and rehabilitate any women they saw as being morally, sexually, or psychologically damaged by experiences in war-torn or Communist Europe.

Rape is one of the most direct ways in which women experience the violence of war. The reality is that rape in military conflicts has long been used as a strategy of violating the male enemy's "property," in particular women and children. It is a particularly gendered form of military violence that is perpetrated against civilians – whether they are mothers and daughters in occupation zones, "comfort women" forced to sexually serve enemy soldiers, or concentration camp inmates. Rape also serves as a means by which men can reassert their male power over women in situations in which male dominance has been disrupted – a common occurrence in wartime, when women often assume non-traditional roles.[6] Although the estimates vary – exact numbers for women raped during the Second World War are difficult to determine, in part because many women were reluctant to report rape – it does appear that in Europe alone several million women had this experience. Whether rapes were carried out at a commanding officer's encouragement or as the sporadic acts of vengeful soldiers or collaborating elites, sexual predators could be found everywhere. In the European arenas of conflict, soldier rapists were among the Soviets troops who occupied the Baltic countries of Latvia, Estonia, and Lithuania. They were with the German troops who annexed much of the European continent, the Soviet troops who later forced the German army out of Eastern Europe, and the Allied troops who ultimately defeated the Axis forces.[7]

Many women's deepest fear was of falling into the hands of enemy soldiers because of the very real prospect of being raped and murdered. For instance, one middle-class Dutch woman, engaged to be married, effectively became a soldier by joining the underground resistance. Later, in a prisoner of war camp, she was raped repeatedly by Nazi guards. Like many female victims of sexual violence who are revictimized by their male partners and families, who treat them like "damaged

Mennonite women on the forced trek eastward from what had been Nazi-occupied Ukraine gather sticks for fuel. Women such as these tried to avoid falling into the hands of the Soviet soldiers pushing German troops out of Eastern Europe. German soldiers also posed a threat.
(CMBS, Archives, Winnipeg, NP 10-1-14)

goods," she found that her Dutch fiancé could not accept what had happened, and he left her.[8]

Among civilian women, mothers in particular agonized over the rape of their daughters, sometimes very young daughters, and often unfairly blamed themselves for having let it happen. These themes run through the recollections and memoirs of women who recalled the widespread raping by Soviet soldiers of Baltic women under the occupation. They run through the experiences of Romanian, Croatian, Hungarian, Mennonite, and German women as the Soviets pushed the Nazi army back towards the German borders, and in the war's aftermath. Much of this violence was attributed to the spontaneous desire to gain revenge for German atrocities during Hitler's invasion of the Soviet Union, but there also appears to have been some "systematic incitement" of Soviet soldiers to rape women as they occupied the territory, if not a policy directive. At any rate Stalin justified and condoned the mass rapes.[9]

In their recollections the European women spoke about wartime rape in ways that suggested their need to protect their fragile memories of such horrific events. Some women described the events in such detailed ways that it is hard to imagine that they were not among the victims being described, yet they depersonalized the story by switching to the third person or by otherwise indicating that they were a witness to the horrid crime and not the victim. (Of course, the witnesses too were psychologically hurt by what happened.) Other women referred to the events obliquely, as events too horrid to fathom; or they referred to the consequences of rape rather than to the act, as in references to having seen so many "young girls with babies, older women with babies in the war time. Horrible."[10]

The recollections of Holocaust survivors reveal Jewish women's sexual vulnerability to German soldiers, Nazi camp guards, and other men they met along the way. Polish-born Gerda Frieberg was only fifteen years old when she, her mother, and older sister were rounded up and dumped into the Warsaw ghetto, where she witnessed Nazi brutality on a daily basis. She lived with the constant fear of being raped even though she barely understood the sexual facts of life. She first "inherited" the fear from the older women, who knew enough to be afraid. They told Frieberg how the SS officers were known to spot a beautiful girl, go to her home and rape her, then shoot her and have her body carted away in a horse-drawn hearse. As vulnerable as they were, some tried to reduce the threat. One strategy was to try to make oneself as inconspicuous as possible. Frieberg's mother and sister made a paste from flour and water and applied it to the girls' faces in an attempt to make them less pretty and thus less vulnerable to sexual assault. Another strategy was to hide from the soldiers when possible. Frieberg and some of the other girls assigned to harvest potatoes and other vegetables in the fields just outside the ghetto borders discovered barns and snuck out at night to sleep there in hope of avoiding nighttime attacks.

At one point, amid frightening but misplaced rumours that the camps were full and the Nazis no longer needed Jewish labour, Frieberg gave in to her mother's plea to stay at home. She spent the night awake and terrified each time she heard banging on the doors and women's screams. "They" eventually came for her, but she was not raped. Instead she, her sister, and the other young women in the area were taken to a women's labour camp run by SS guards in Czechoslovakia. Now sixteen and developing a woman's body, she felt more vulnerable than ever, and joined in the conversations of the older girls who talked nervously about their fears of being raped. It was not until many years later that Frieberg realized that the SS commander who had beaten and threatened the women, even if they were model factory workers, had done so partly as a way of fighting "a certain sexual attraction" that he experienced in the presence of so many young women.

The journals and testimonies of other women, Jewish and gentile alike, also reveal their vulnerability at the hands of certain men who were not even enemies, including other POWs, men who were hiding in the woods, and partisan comrades.[11]

For many Canadians and others far removed from the war and occupation zones, perhaps the most difficult concept to grasp or accept was the situational morality that some women were forced to adopt in life-threatening circumstances. The women might, for instance, consent to be raped by one soldier in order to avoid repetitive rapes by others. They might agree to perform sexual acts for soldiers in order to protect their children or get help in crossing the guarded borders into the Western zone. Once flight was no longer an option, Mennonite women in the Soviet zones, who were ethnically German, devised their own survival strategies: many of them hid at night from potential attackers; others cross-dressed in order to pass as boys or older men. Displaced women might barter sex for food, fuel, or transportation, doing so because their bodies were one of the few items they could use for trade.

The "voluntary" or "consensual rapes" provide an extreme example of how women exercised agency in a context that threatened to dehumanize and destroy them. Consensual rape, although a "grotesque" choice, was a significant aspect of the experiences of women on the defeated side. For example, German women resorted to this strategy in the aftermath of the war when they faced repeated rapes, especially but not exclusively by Soviet soldiers. In the life-threatening situation created by the Allies' military occupation (when women were forced into sexual relations with released POWs and even returning German soldiers), the difference between rape and prostitution became highly blurred.[12] After experiencing successive rapes or threats of rape, some women sought out a protector, usually a Soviet officer, and agreed to be "voluntarily raped" by him as a means of escaping repeated attacks from numerous soldiers.

To avoid repatriation to the Soviet Union, some women agreed to marry their German boyfriends and settle in Western Germany. Even after the threat of repatriation declined in the Allied occupation zones by late 1945, Russian-born and anti-Soviet refugees, or DPs, in the Russian zones feared detection and focused their energies on getting to the West. When they didn't have alcohol or cigarettes to exchange, some women offered sex for "freedom" or for a safe passage for their children.

The fear of rape, and its consequences, led to further morally difficult decisions, including abortion and suicide. Some women, including Mennonites, armed themselves with cyanide capsules to avoid rape. If they were impregnated by their rapists, women had to decide whether to have abortions, and if they turned to "back-alley butchers" they put their health and lives at risk. A refugee nurse and midwife who performed abortions on German women raped by Soviet soldiers said her hospital was filled with rape victims, some as young as eight years old. But as common as abortions were, many children were born in the aftermath of rape.[13]

Women liberated by the Allied forces, including Jewish survivors, faced similar threats. Gerda Frieberg's story about the Red Army's liberation of her women's camp in May 1945 offers a chilling reminder that liberation did not bring an end to sexual threats or violence. "We ran out to welcome our liberators," she recounted. "We pulled the flowers out of the garden of the factory owners and the German people … and threw it at the Soviet soldiers, jumped on the tanks and rolled on the tanks – until suddenly one of the Commanders stopped the whole column that was occupying the town." Realizing that these were young women greeting them, the commander asked them where their camp was. Then, Frieberg remembered, he "drove his armoured tank into the camp and addressed us in Yiddish, and said: 'Don't tell the soldiers where your camp is. We've been pushing now for months, they haven't had a woman. I can't guarantee your safety.'"[14] Frieberg and the other women, heeding the Soviet commander's warning, hid for weeks in their camp until they decided that the situation had "stabilized." She recalled how Jewish women in the camps had kept themselves and each other alive, despite starvation and overwork, largely through hope and in the grim determination to survive "so we could tell the world what happened." Yet, in the end, they forestalled their own liberation to hide from potential sexual predators. They pushed their sheet-metal beds in front of the barrack's door, and when soldiers tried to push it open, the women screamed until they went away. To keep the men at bay they also drew up a flyer with the words "Typhoid Fever" and posted it on the door. After all the Soviet soldiers had departed the area, the women left the camp, travelling in groups for protection.[15]

The displaced women, both Jewish and gentile, who travelled alone or in couples or small groups were "easy prey" not only for Soviet troops but also for Allied military personnel "seeking sexual adventure or reward" or, on occasion, for their own liberated male counterparts.[16] While liberation improved their chances, Jewish women still needed to take steps to protect themselves, and they justified their actions – whether theft, eating non-kosher food, prostitution, or consensual rape – as the necessary tactics of survival. Women directly affected by the war in Italy, Greece, and elsewhere had similar experiences as they hid or fled from rival forces, rebuilt bombed-out homes and towns, and negotiated wartime and postwar scarcity – all the while raising their children.[17]

Not surprisingly, many women came to see that the morality of the "normal" or "civilized" world mattered little to their survival. Not until they had attained a modicum of shelter and a means of sustenance could they regain control over their bodies and begin thinking again in terms of making what they saw as genuinely moral choices.[18] In the end, women who had been enemies in war arrived in Canada with similar as well as different fears, and their shared fears often involved sexual dangers.

Not all of the sexual conflicts that occurred in those years were matters of force or even instances of consensual rape. Some conflicts emerged when soldiers mistakenly saw sexual intercourse as a reward being offered in exchange for helping women reach safety. Often unaware of the experiences of the young women they encountered, and themselves starved of intimacy and affection, some soldiers wrongly interpreted women's friendly reception as a sexual invitation. Many young female survivors, robbed of their adolescence and of the rituals of courtship, were not aware of or ready for the sexual interest they aroused in men. They could only react with fear and confusion to liberation encounters that quickly turned into sexualized encounters.[19] With their emaciated bodies, short hair, ragged clothing, and years of brutality and dehumanization etched onto their bodies and into their psyches, many of these young women did not see themselves as sexual subjects or objects of desire, and they neither anticipated nor understood the men's sexual advances or demands. One survivor recalled how she and her two sisters and others had blown kisses to the U.S. soldiers who had liberated them, without any understanding that the elated soldiers might become sexually aroused. "Odd-looking as we may have been," she said, "we were still five young girls." That night, she said, two of the men "came for us." The women managed to turn them away.[20]

Generally speaking, Dutch women's experiences of liberation were positive, and relationships between young Dutch women and Canadian soldiers developed quickly amid the victory parties, drinking fetes, and public spectacles that marked

Whether they were young or old women – here an elderly Hungarian refugee woman, the oldest of 230 DP arrivals at Union Station, and wearing her dog tags – the head scarf invariably marked them as hailing from poor or backward rural or peripheral Europe. *Telegram* 9 Aug. 1949. (Photograph by Jack Judges; YUA, Toronto Telegram, ASC Image 1305)

these glory days. Some of these relationships ended in marriage and pregnancy, though not always in that order. But like their British counterparts, Dutch war brides endured rumours about being "good time girls" who had gotten their "hooks" into good Canadian boys, although their own recollections better capture the complexity, and even spontaneity, of the situation. As one of them, Caterina A., remembered it, when young Dutch women happily welcomed – with large smiles, kisses, embraces, and long warm hugs – their young Canadian "liberators," freshly tanned from the Italian campaigns, the show of appreciation could become very physical indeed. She might have agreed with the Dutch journalist who complained that his countrymen had lost their women to the Allied soldiers. She recalled that while some Dutch people "frowned" on the women dating or becoming engaged to Canadian men, most of them did not really care.

Still, distinctions were drawn between relationships that ended in marriage and those that did not. In Caterina A.'s case, she did get married, and, like other war brides, she stressed the men's respectable reputation and thereby her own. The Canadian soldiers, she said, were "very polite." They were more like Dutch men than the loud and flamboyant U.S. soldiers. She had initially dated a Quebec man because her French was better than her English, but later she met an English-Canadian officer at a house party. At age twenty-one, she accepted his marriage proposal and left her family for Canada, hoping to put behind bitter memories of war and German occupation. Caterina said that her mother did not interfere with the engagement, though her relatives and neighbours, their ears attuned to gossip about bigamist soldiers, asked whether there was any chance the fiancé was already married. Caterina was pregnant before her marriage and wanted "to leave quickly" and give birth in Canada so that the child would be a Canadian.[21]

Both in the DP camps and in regions across Europe, many young people quickly courted, married, and produced children. International refugee relief workers, religious leaders, and social experts were alarmed by what they saw as sexual female promiscuity and its harmful effect on a single woman's chances for a proper marriage and stable future. They declared that too many young women continued to participate in a survival culture. To be sure, especially when it came to occupation soldiers, some women did find the temptation for lustful if dangerous

Mothers went to extraordinary lengths to feed and protect their children in the war and its aftermath and unfairly blamed themselves for any misfortune that befell their loved ones, creating emotional and psychological scars. Women's memories also speak powerfully to the emotionally intense relationship between mothers and daughters. In this tearful reunion in Toronto in 1956, an elderly Mrs. Josephine Zvanyki is reunited with her daughters following an almost ten-year separation during which the mother had struggled to get out of Communist Romania.
(Photograph by Don Grant; YUA, Toronto Telegram, ASC Image 1277)

pleasures simply too compelling. The U.S. troops, who offered food, cigarettes, and nylon stockings as well as "a dream of plenty" across the ocean, were particularly popular.[22] The soldiers easily found "girlfriends," especially among the defeated and displaced women who crowded into war-devastated Germany. A 1946 military inquiry reported that well over half of the U.S. occupation troops "fraternized" with German women, and the *Ami-Liebchen* (Yankee sweetheart) earned the scorn of her compatriots.[23]

The presence of many young women seemingly "adrift" in Europe's cities, apparently indifferent to anything but securing some advantage, prompted moralizing journalists to cast aspersions on their characters. Writing from Salzburg, Austria, in late summer 1946, after visiting several major European cities, U.S. reporter Leland Stowe told his North American readers that postwar Europe was a terribly confusing place, even for those who, like him, had lived there for years. For one thing, it was teeming with political exiles or stateless refugees – all part of the "flotsam legion of the uprooted" who had been "scattered across western Europe like shingles after a typhoon." Furthermore, all of them, especially the women, many of whom attached themselves to soldiers, had a heartbreaking story, but one never knew "how much to believe." He described a typical evening in a big and crowded Salzburg beer hall serving as a G.I. club, where he sat at a table next to "several

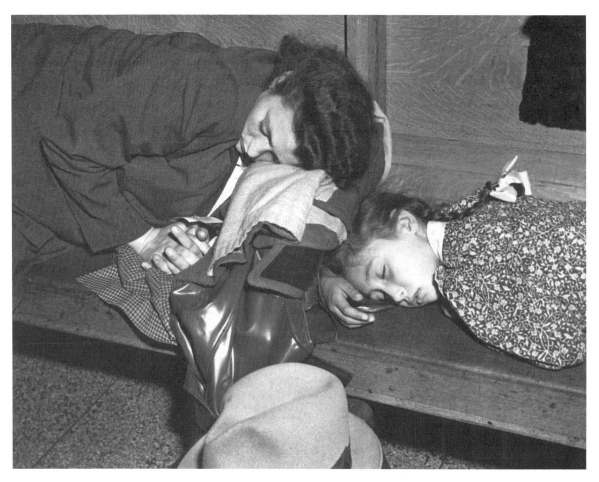

Waiting for a train to take them to their new home and job on a farm in Delhi, Ont., a Hungarian mother and daughter get some sleep on a bench.
(Photograph by Evans; YUA, Toronto Telegram, ASC Image 1307)

Yanks" (soldiers) and their young dates, two Hungarians and a Pole. When he mentioned Budapest, one of them, "a little blue-eyed Hungarian," brushed back tears and said she had been "without a country" for two and a half years and knew nothing about what had happened to her parents or sisters. But she then hastily added that she was now "almost engaged" to her sergeant escort and dreamed of "America."

Stowe showed sympathy for these "homeless" women, but he believed that most of them had "something to sell," especially the DP women who had "told their stories over and over to countless Americans, British and others... work[ing] their personal dramas over into a pattern which puts them in the most appealing light." The ones who frequented the officers' clubs were the most "sophisticated" at the game, he noted, and "doing very well indeed by the [Allied] occupation." But, he said, you could find women on the make everywhere. In an ironic twist to the usual tale of sexual danger, Stowe concluded that the scores of "reasonably young or reasonably attractive" women who had learned how to wield their sexual "weapons" had made postwar Europe "a dangerous place for the naive male."[24]

Sexual cross-currents and contradictions also shaped life inside the refugee camps, where sexual activity was frequent and, given the crowded quarters, far from private. Relations among the refugees and between the displaced women and Allied soldiers were common aspects of daily life. Sexual liaisons, like romance, often led to marriage, which in turn created a range of "mixed marriages" among refugees from different countries. Not surprisingly, though, the DP camp regimes, and their crowded and dilapidated if not squalid conditions, largely precluded a customary courtship – or, in the words of experts and authorities on both sides of the ocean, "normal" and "healthy" romance without sex and leading to marriage.[25] One young survivor told a friend that because their desires had been "tied up in knots" for too long, many couples found or created opportunities for sex. Relief workers commented on the frequency of sex in the camps. One camp resident said sex was the number-one activity among the young. Another said it made the young folk cheerful at last. Some women, too, experienced sex as "an exhilarating emotional high" and a confirmation of their humanity.[26]

In part, sex flourished in the refugee camps because, as Margaret Finestein observes, both women and men felt a sense of greater safety and security there, particularly as they encountered kin, friends, and co-nationals.[27] Even so, many women survivors still found the ritual of courtship awkward in the refugee camps, although, understandably, for Jewish women in particular the fear of unwelcome sexual advances decreased as they moved from mixed to all-Jewish DP camps. In contrast, Jewish men's narratives, like those of gentile DP men, focused more on their public activities than on personal or emotional issues, and devoted little attention to camp courtships or sexual relations. But those who did talk about it revealed a range of experiences. Some of these men were self-conscious about their appearances – they too were physically ravaged – and felt awkward about initiating sexual encounters. Others were thrilled to be alive and were eager for sex, but they were uneasy about imposing on Jewish women. They thus turned elsewhere, sometimes using provisions from their U.S. Joint Distribution packages to buy sex from prostitutes or other women. Ovaltine was a popular exchange item. One refugee told a camp interviewer that finally having sex again had returned his masculinity to him and made him feel "safe at last" – speaking loudly to the positive and restorative power that sex had for some men. For some of the men who "used" German women for their first sexual encounters after the war, sex was a tool of revenge.

Given that fewer women than men survived the Holocaust, the resulting sex imbalance among the survivors meant that men invariably had to go outside the community for (paid or unpaid) sex and companionship, much to the chagrin of rabbis and others.[28] In general, though, most Jewish DPs sought partners among other Jews, and many of these couples married just months after meeting each other. At one point the UNRRA officials became so anxious about the soaring birth rates in the Jewish DP camps that they actually contemplated sterilization, but quickly dropped the offensive idea.[29]

A shortage of rubber gloves in the camps meant that medical personnel checking for venereal disease reused them in their vaginal inspections of women – an important procedure that nonetheless stigmatized the women while laying less blame for venereal disease on the men, civilian and military alike. North American selection teams in search of women with strong backs and moral virtue complained that many did not meet their exacting (and hypocritical) moral standards. In screening out the morally suspect, Canadian teams recruiting domestic servants watched carefully for any clues of sinful living, such as the woman's use of U.S. slang (picked up from American boyfriends), good cotton underwear, and that highly prized luxury item, nylon stockings (thanks to U.S. money and army supply stores).[30]

Some of the more sexually gregarious women in the camps met with sharp disapproval at the hands of the international officials – a disapproval that would be matched when they fell among Canadian gatekeepers at the end of the road in Canada.

Carrying Baggage into Canada

Matters of sexual morality were part of the complex emotional and psychological baggage that many European women carried with them to Canada, where many struggled to adjust to life in a new country in which few citizens really understood the sexual or emotional trauma they had experienced. For some female "war casualties" (depending upon the context, a code word for rape victim), Canada offered new opportunities but not necessarily personally satisfying or happy lives. That was what happened to the middle-class Dutch partisan who was jilted when her fiancé was not able to accept her "past." Soon after that she became involved with a working-class Ukrainian-Canadian soldier, who proposed to her. At first she turned him down, thinking he wasn't the one for her. But then, after she became pregnant and found it too difficult to remain in Holland, she changed her mind and accepted. In Canada the marriage eventually ended in divorce. Too many years, she said, had been lost to quiet suffering and loneliness, to family squabbles, and other conflicts.[31]

By contrast, an older Ukrainian refugee woman in a loveless marriage did what many such women did and remained in the situation, largely because after experiencing so much loss and death she could not bear to break up her marriage or family. It was only after she had what her Canadian psychiatrists called a "nervous breakdown" that she was actually encouraged to leave her husband. For many other women, however, a marriage even with a lack of love or sex was preferable to a life of loneliness. Indeed, loneliness would lead many women to seek out marriage even to virtual strangers, sometimes with positive and other times with disastrous consequences.[32]

In Canada gatekeepers would prove to be preoccupied with the morality of newcomer women, a preoccupation reinforced by further cases of rape that occurred in "hot spots" across the Cold War globe. In response to international requests, Canadian women's groups such as the National Council of Women of Canada, the Imperial Order Daughters of the Empire, and the Catholic Women's League lobbied Ottawa to denounce sexual assault and to send aid to the victims. In June 1946 the IODE passed a strongly worded motion protesting "the treatment of women in Russian-occupied Europe" and urging the prime minister to support a United Nations investigation into the alleged abuses. In response to a statement from the Athens-based Association of Greek University Women to "All Free Women the World Over," the IODE passed another strongly worded motion in March 1948 citing the Greek Communist rebels for their "barbarous acts committed against the Greek people" and "the inhuman system of kidnapping and violation of women." Declaring that "the people of Greece fought bravely and suffered grievously in the recent war in defence of democracy," and that these "barbaric actions" are "common knowledge throughout the world," the motion called upon Ottawa to denounce "these outrages" at the United Nations Council "in the name of universal motherhood." The interplay between these kinds of appropriate protests against wartime sexual assault and Cold War battles is also suggested by the imbalance in the Canadian response to the Greek civil war; no one appears to have asked whether Greek government troops had assaulted women belonging to the Communist and non-Communist opponents of the regime.[33]

Sexual anxieties were also kept alive by events within Canada, including the allegations about ethnic Canadian Communists trying to woo DP women workers to communism with stories of capitalist exploitation and flowers and chocolates.[34] Women's psychological problems were not always viewed as necessarily leading to sexual immorality – and even less so than with men – but they fed the generalized Cold War concerns about the need to contain and redress spreading immorality and, by extension, the falling standards of motherhood and family life and increasing rates of social deviance and mental illness. With some exceptions, such as suspected female spies, the mainstream English-language press coverage of European women in connection with moral, sexual, or mental health issues highlighted them as victims (poor widows, deserted wives, suicides).

As with men, the newspaper coverage of tragic incidents such as female suicides or attempted suicides could evoke sympathy and feed fears about the deeper psychological problems of European women. One dramatic example took place in 1949 at the National Employment Service in downtown Toronto, when a twenty-two-year-old Jewish survivor visiting the office climbed out of the building and onto a narrow metal pole about forty feet above the ground. Inside the building the staff in the employment office offered reporters an on the spot diagnosis: "The years she spent in a Nazi concentration camp had affected her mental health." According to the *Star*'s front-page coverage, the "young D.P. girl" had remained "immovable, "like a pigeon on a perch," while a horrified noon-hour crowd of business people, pedestrians, and drivers stuck in a huge traffic jam urged her to crawl back in. When firefighters first reached her, she slipped from her half-sitting position and swayed dangerously from her arms until they grabbed her. She put up a fight and "screamed hysterically," but the firefighters managed to restrain her, carried her down, and hustled her off to the Toronto Psychiatric Hospital.

National Employment officers attributed her suicide attempt to an inability to hold down a job (in domestic service) since coming to Canada a year earlier.[35] The incident provoked alarm in some quarters and raised calls for stiffer screening tests and more psychiatric resources for newcomers. The Toronto YWCA Committee on Newcomers, for example, expressed regret over the negative publicity generated by "mentally unsuited" DPs like "the girl who swung from a pipe," adding that such incidents showed a "need for greater facilities for observation and treatment" of newcomers.[36]

The plight of women stuck in relationships with abusive men was usually hidden from the public purview, but when it resulted in death the news media were on the case. In the winter of 1947 a twenty-four-year-old Polish woman grabbed headlines in Toronto when she was accused of killing her much older and abusive Canadian lover. When the manslaughter charge was read in police court, the woman cried and collapsed in tears. The court showed her sympathy. The Crown counsel recommended a lenient bail ($500) because the evidence indicated that the man had "beat her, then dropped dead." The judge agreed and told the crying woman, "Pull yourself together… the court is trying to help you." The murder charge was dropped because the autopsy showed "no external marks of violence."

However brief, this news item offers a glimpse into the life of a sexually deviant, and abused, refugee woman. Living on the margins of both the mainstream and her own ethnic community, she was surviving as best she could. Her mother was dead and her father had abandoned her. She had been living in a filthy apartment with a sixty-five-year-old man who often refused to work (he blamed his inactivity on his arthritis). While poor women were often accused of "shacking up" with men for material security, this woman, like others in similar circumstances, was the couple's primary breadwinner, though she barely made enough for them to survive on. The fight had been triggered by her refusal to hand over her hard-earned money to him. He had started beating her and throwing things at her, before suddenly collapsing. Ironically, his death left her in even more desperate circumstances. She had to give up the apartment for a dingy space in a rooming house. At the court's request, she became a ward of the Salvation Army, which helped her with rent and food.[37]

As the advice columns of the day demonstrate, some mistreated newcomer women were prepared to make their complaints public, and the Toronto press did cover a few stories of women who fought back against abusive partners through the courts and called upon the legal gatekeepers to live up to the rhetoric of Canada as a fair and democratic country. For example, two young German women took legal steps after getting into a brouhaha that involved both an ex-boyfriend of one of them and the Metro police. The two women had arrived home at their apartment one day only to find the former boyfriend and two other men (who turned out to be police officers) removing a TV set that the boyfriend had given his girlfriend and her roommate. The women told the men to leave, but the men refused to do so. According to the later testimony, the women had lunged at the men and the ex-boyfriend had kicked them. The police officers, the women said, had physically restrained and rough-handled the women. As a result the two women took both the ex-boyfriend and the police to court. In the hearing the women complained about having been locked up overnight in a "filthy and smelly" jail and explained that the ex-boyfriend had been dropped because he had been physically and verbally abusive towards his girlfriend. They also declared that the experience had shattered their image of Canada as a moral and fair democracy where such things were not supposed to happen.[38]

Counsellors, Clients, and Contexts

Some European women struggling to overcome difficult or complicated sexual histories and adjust to Canadian society turned to social workers and counsellors for advice and support. Sometimes they were referred to them by Immigration, National Employment Service, family court, or social agency staff who, at times, pressured them into visiting counsellors under threat of losing state subsidies or even of deportation. These front-line gatekeepers took very seriously the task of transforming newcomer women with unconventional sexual histories into fit and proper women and mothers deserving of Canadian citizenship. Indeed, the double sexual standard of the day, reinforced by a Cold War ideology that equated good women with moral democracy and bad women with Communist perversity, among other evils, meant that the gatekeepers, while concerned with men's moral character, more directly equated women's morality with the capacity for female citizenship in Canada.

In drawing such a clear link between sexual morality and female citizenship, the gatekeepers in turn reinforced a double sexual and moral standard that also operated within the ethnic Canadian communities, where elites and groups who worked with newly arrived female compatriots also stigmatized those with unconventional sexual histories, even when it was through no fault of their own. As Marlene Epp's research has powerfully demonstrated, Mennonite-Canadian refugee workers, church leaders, and congregations morally branded the refugee women whose arrival they had sponsored. The treatment could also extend to the women's "illegitimate" daughters, who might well have been the product of wartime rape (in whatever guise). While individual brethren could be sympathetic, the general community saw these women as adding "a dimension of immorality" to the postwar migration. Those who wanted to remain in the church and remarry – whether out of deep loneliness, desire for physical intimacy, or a need for greater economic stability – came up against the church fathers' rigid enforcement of restrictions on remarriage (which could only happen after a seven-year separation period). In response some women were openly defiant and moved to more sympathetic denominations to marry, or they entered into common-law marriages or left the church altogether.

Significantly, the increase in the number of transgressive relationships prompted the Mennonite leadership to modify the penalties involved – for example, moving from excommunication to a refusal to administer communion to the offending couple. At the local congregation level the reaction was more varied, with some congregations (or their male committees) showing greater tolerance than others. A willingness to permit remarriage suggests some sensitivity to those involved, but it also reflected the Canadian Mennonite church's affirmation of a conventional family form. It also served to reduce the size of a troubling, and potentially burdensome, group of women whose presence was a painful reminder of the Mennonites' tragic history in the Soviet Union.

Just as the Citizenship Branch officials and other gatekeepers saw the Canadianized ethnic groups and ethnic newspapers as potential tools of Canadian citizenship, so too did they see ethnic Canadian churches as contributing to the integration of the newcomers into the Canadian mainstream. They would have approved of the Mennonite church's efforts to reassert conventional marital and family models. For the remarrying widow, the outcomes varied, but there were some truly sad failures: women who married men who, it turned out, merely wanted a farmhand or a housekeeper or a nanny for children from a previous marriage.[39]

The fears within the organized ethnic communities that unmarried mothers and illegitimate children, especially daughters, posed a threat to their community's moral fibre largely mirrored the moralizing discourses within the Canadian mainstream. When Canadian gatekeepers like the social workers who staffed the counselling services of the International Institute of Metropolitan Toronto encountered newcomer women with sexually deviant pasts or who transgressed Canadian moral codes, they responded in a number of ways. They were more quick to judge sexually transgressive women than they were to judge men with similar tendencies, but also better able to develop more positive relationships with these women than with the sexually violent men – even though therapeutic relationships often ended abruptly. In their efforts to apply the principles of the socio-cultural approach, which aimed to understand and not stigmatize their clients' cultural codes and practices, the Institute's social workers clearly tried to curb their moralizing; but they could not fully do so, partly because they were operating within a social welfare system (and wider society) that harshly judged, and penalized, women who led supposedly morally compromising lives.

Women were also more likely than men to be deported on moral grounds. Even if we accept the argument made by Nancy Elgie, the Citizenship Branch researcher who determined that the deportation rates for the postwar newcomers were low, there was plenty of pressure on newcomer women to become morally virtuous wives and mothers or otherwise risk moral branding and disqualification of social welfare supports. As they did with all women, the gatekeepers assessed the women's capacity to become good and moral mothers who could raise morally adjusted children, especially daughters, and thereby help in the strengthening of Canada's moral democracy. By the same token, the women's failure to become fit and proper mothers could threaten Canada's moral fibre. They might, for example, raise illegitimate children, wayward daughters, and sexually perverse sons who would go on to corrupt the behaviour of others they came into contact with, thereby perpetuating the problem. At times the caseworkers were willing to invoke the deportation bogeyman in order to convince a single newcomer woman or sexually delinquent wife to clean up her act.

While the caseworkers of the International Institute did occasionally attribute a woman's paranoia or other "behavioural problems" to having lived under a totalitarian regime – in much the same way as they did with men – they were more likely to attribute female ills to sexual victimization or delinquency and the damage done to the women's psyches and sense of self-worth.

All of these patterns appear in the Institute's confidential case files, which include about three dozen clients viewed as sexually deviant or morally damaged women – cases that the professional and student social workers and experienced volunteers deemed to be in need of psychological counselling, emotional support, and psychiatric treatment.

One file, for instance, tells the story of Mrs. C., a working-class German divorcee wracked with guilt about having destroyed her marriage. In contrast to most of the Institute's clients, who were recent arrivals, Mrs. C. came to the Institute a few years after she entered Canada.[40] She had gone through an extramarital affair in wartime Germany with a man she met at her job in a canteen while her husband was at the front. The affair had ended her marriage. Indeed, her story offered the professional experts a textbook case of how the wartime removal of men from their homes could lead to female promiscuity and destroy marriages. Now, at age forty-five, Mrs. C. appeared to be doomed to a marginal life as a lonely and guilt-ridden newcomer woman unhappily resettled in Toronto. She had lost a series of domestic and factory jobs, and jobs as a waitress and saleswoman, each time blaming it on her employer or co-workers.

Both of her social workers – one of them with the local Immigration office and the other, Mr. N., the multilingual Institute social worker – agreed that Mrs. C. had psychological and emotional problems, including paranoia as well as an exaggerated sense of the power of government officials. They saw these conditions as resulting both from her life under Nazism and from the years spent with guilt about her sexual "delinquency." They also believed that her distrust of well-intentioned experts and officials like themselves was preventing her full recovery. They took as further evidence of her troubled personality a letter she had sent to Ottawa in which she blamed her prolonged unemployment on certain people who had conspired to hurt her. They noted her "refusal" to be personally forthcoming with her caseworkers. Mr. N. found that she was "defensive" about her lacklustre job record, and he tried to reassure her that the situation was common among newcomers. When he promised to try to find her a job that she wanted as a hospital cleaner, she finally opened up and "provided information" about herself.

Mr. N.'s long-term strategy was to encourage Mrs. C. to enter into a counselling or therapeutic relationship with him – in other words, to apply the casework method with the sensitivity demanded of a socio-cultural approach. Indeed, the local Immigration Department worker had referred her to the Institute on the grounds that its staff might better understand her European background and thus get her to open up. Mr. N. did make headway with her. She eventually told him her sad tale, speaking well of her husband and blaming herself for the divorce. The social worker reached the obvious conclusion: she had come to Canada "to escape" her broken marriage and the ensuing scandal, and she was still racked with guilt. But he also learned that her marital experience was not the only source of her guilt. Mrs. C. had convinced her sister, who had lost her family in the war, to join her in Canada and felt "added guilt" when the sister, after coming, developed a tumour. For the past few years Mrs. C. had not slept well, and various pills had not helped. When Mr. N. advised her to consult a specialist, she refused at first, insisting that once she got a job her other problems would disappear. Later she agreed to consider the referral. Mr. N. also learned that her sister had not returned to the hospital despite worsening pain because they could not afford the cost and didn't know that immigrants had access to a hospital plan. The social worker told Mrs. C. about the plan.

Mr. N.'s subsequent assessments were in a similar vein: she had "all the appearance of one who has suffered for a long time," "does not relate well," and "is quite suspicious and lacks spontaneity in her discussion." He analyzed her forthright manner ("I felt that in her past she had been quite outspoken, but due to frequent failure in adjustment, had become hostile to people to protect herself") and attributed her poor job record partly to this personality defect. All of this led Mr. N. to conclude that she required "psychiatric treatment." Convinced that she would refuse to see a psychiatrist, he decided to continue building her confidence, and strengthening their therapeutic relationship, until she would be ready to discuss a "referral to psychiatry."

In the meantime he focused on getting Mrs. C. some work, using his personal contacts at a local Toronto hospital to land her a cleaner's job. When she did not rush off for an arranged interview, he put it down to her continuing psychological problems (she was "quite hostile" and insisted that "it is up to her whether she goes to work or not"). Interestingly, she had invoked her right in a democracy to choose not to go to the interview, but she may have thought that right was constrained by her marginal status, and perhaps by the possibility that her disobedience might be used as grounds for deportation, because she quickly apologized and went to the hospital.

She got the job, and her case file ends – making it thus appear that while Mr. N. had developed a positive expert-client relationship, he had ultimately failed to convince Mrs. C. to undergo psychiatric treatment, which he believed she needed in order to fully recover from her past delinquency and psychological problems and thus become a fit and proper new female citizen. For her part, Mrs. C., though clearly struggling hard to adjust to life in Canada, appeared to be sticking to her own theory – that getting a job would help to solve her other problems. Although the file does not tell us whether she ever saw a psychiatrist, its contents do capture the gatekeepers' tendency to see the moral and sexual "uplift" of newcomer women with complex pasts as being inextricably mingled with their integration into the Canadian mainstream.

This theme of the moral politics of female citizenship emerges even more clearly in a case involving a young single Hungarian refugee mother who had three "illegitimate" children by different male lovers. Miss D. became a client shortly after arriving in Toronto. Like Mrs. C., Miss D. was from the working class and had held waitress and domestic jobs. Unlike Mrs. C., Miss D.'s caseworkers labelled her as a hard-core "clinging vine" – a term that Canadian social workers, including the Institute counsellors, frequently used in their assessments. Indeed, the majority of "sexually delinquent" women in the Institute files are described as "clinging vines" – women who attached themselves to men, usually of the wrong sort, out of loneliness, desperation, poverty, or self-interest. In this case they saw Miss D. as a woman who had grown dependent upon men and, moreover, used sex with men as a survival tool. Ironically, her relationships also resulted in the added burdens of pregnancies and of raising children without a reliable partner.

In the case of newcomer women, the Institute caseworkers often saw the origins of a problem as relating to events or behaviour associated with the war, displacement, or, to paraphrase the journalist Leland Stowe, a sex-poisoned postwar Europe full of sad or amoral women on the make. While not on a par with such psychiatric diagnostic categories as paranoia or persecution complex, the label "clinging vine" nonetheless marked a woman with a set of dysfunctional personality traits, and it could just as effectively become the basis for highly intrusive gatekeeper interventions in her life.

The caseworkers depicted these women in one of several and overlapping ways: as gullible girls (especially those who moved in with married men, some who had families still in Europe, who promised to marry them); poor judges of men; amoral women unschooled in the proper mores of courtship and marriage; and easy prey of manipulative men. In a few cases the caseworkers suspected that the woman was protecting an abusive man in her life out of fear of his leaving her and of being left alone. And since lone women who became public charges could be deported, fears of loneliness could be compounded by fears of being sent back to war-torn or Communist European homelands.

According to the Institute caseworkers, Miss D. had become pregnant by a fellow East European refugee on the voyage over, finding out only too late that he had a wife and child in his now-Communist home country. When that man abandoned her, she filed and won a family court case for child support, but he disappeared before making any payments. She then landed work as a cleaning woman, met another male refugee, and again became pregnant. During her first Institute interview she claimed to be married to this second man, but was not legally so. She was also unemployed, poor, and a major user of the city's social services – her list of community referrals included the National Employment Service, welfare, Immigration, a Catholic family agency, and the family court – prompting her female Institute caseworker, Mrs. S., to predict doom for the misguided girl unless they could get her on the right track.

Miss D. explained that she had come to the Institute because she needed a job (she held a few of them over the following year) as well as "food for the children" because "her husband spent the money on the race track and drinking with friends." While her caseworker obliged, she also wanted to deal with the woman's "sexual delinquencies" and emotional problems and advised Miss D. to make return visits and send her partner to the office. Why Mrs. S. thought an obviously irresponsible man would come to the Institute for counselling is not fully clear (and indeed, he didn't come), but it certainly reflected the agency's pro-family approach, which focused on first trying to keep a family together.

Exhausted from work and from caring for her children with little help from her partner, Miss D. became ill, and resulting complications with the pregnancy required her to have an emergency birth. The Institute placed her children in a foster home for the duration. Shortly before being released from hospital, Miss D. contacted Mrs. S. and asked for some clothing, saying that any "old dress and a coat" would do. She was given some items from the agency's used-clothing depot.

For the next year her file deals mainly with jobs, until she phoned one day to say she was "pennyless and ill," that "the welfare is paying just for the rent [not] groceries," and her "husband is not willing to work and lives most of the time on Welfare." When a woman friend tried to help Miss D. by telling the caseworker that Miss D.'s husband was "beating her and the children" and "taking every penny from them for liker [liquor]," an annoyed Mrs. S. told the friend that Miss D. "knows all the sources – and she can get help if she wanted" – a reference to her being a manipulator of the social welfare system.

It was, of course, not a stretch for the caseworker to assume that what she saw as a sexually delinquent women would also abuse Canada's generous welfare state. Indeed, the caseworker reported that because Miss D. was clearly "protecting her husband," and allowing him to live with her, the social agencies could "not do anything." That is, they could not provide her with additional funds, such as mother's allowance, because she did not fit the category of abandoned wife or single mother deserving of welfare supports. These moral judgments reflected not merely the caseworkers' personal view but were fundamental to the practices of the welfare state, which expected women to meet unrealistic standards of the morally fit and proper mother.[41] Having a man in the house disqualified her from collecting mother's allowance. Mrs. S.'s comments also suggest that the Institute staff had long known about the domestic abuse, yet had not directly intervened.

Mrs. S. admonished Miss D. for not doing more to contain her husband, but her various suggestions – send him to see me, tell the Catholic Family Service that he is squandering the money – were not terribly helpful. In response to Miss D.'s repeated requests for food and grocery money, Mrs. S. decided to check out the woman's other sources of help. She concluded that Miss D. and her children had become a "multiple problem family" too dependent on the social welfare system. The caseworker considered Miss D. – like other clinging vines who ended up with abusive partners – as being partly responsible for her own misfortune.

In the file's final entry, Mrs. S. reports that she and a welfare department worker had inspected Miss D.'s home several times, and each time it was in slovenly shape and the unemployed partner was asleep on the couch. In their view Miss D. fit the depressing profile of the needy delinquent mother who, having grown into adulthood in the abnormal conditions of war and displacement, and being inexperienced in the craft of choosing a proper husband, attached herself to men of dubious character and cared little about her moral reputation. The diagnosis thus included an element of victim-blaming.[42]

Two young Hungarian refugees get lunch at the Sanitarium in Weston, Ont., 1956. The waiving of usual medical requirements for admission for the 56ers meant that TB-infected newcomers like these young women could gain entry into Canada and receive attention upon arrival. *Telegram* 3 Dec. 1947.
(Photograph by Don Grant; YUA, Toronto Telegram, ASC Image 1279)

Both of these cases illustrate the complex class, gender, and ethnic dynamics of the newcomer-gatekeeper encounter. They also illustrate that similar scenarios did not necessarily play out in identical ways. Another outstanding case file involved a Cold War tale of a young woman's escape from sexual violence in Communist Europe. Far from having a quick and happy ending in a moral, democratic Canada, this story produced yet another "clinging vine" whose sexual delinquencies presented a major challenge to her Canadian gatekeepers.

At nineteen years of age, Miss E., a Yugoslavian refugee of mixed Italian and Croatian ethnicity (in other words, Italian Slovenian), was the youngest clinging vine that the Institute caseworkers encountered in those years. Her file captures the sordid sexual tale of a young woman who escaped sexual abuse in Europe and reached the West only to find herself living on the margins of poverty in Toronto. There she was forced to make decisions that further tainted her moral character. Questions of situational morality were not confined to war-ravaged Europe. Miss E. also became labelled as a hard-core "welfare case" or habitual user of social services. She also resorted to a supposedly familiar strategy of impoverished women – "shacking up" with men – though it bears noting that her men usually found her a job. She was frank about her sexual history and proved to be a demanding client who made it clear that she felt entitled to support in a rich nation that claimed superiority to Eastern bloc countries like her own. She was also an unashamed anti-Semite who ridiculed the Canadian Jewish family that had employed her as a domestic; she insisted on being placed in a German or Italian household. Yet she was also worried that her various caseworkers might recommend her deportation on grounds of moral unsuitability.[43]

A senior social worker with the Social Planning Council of Toronto referred Miss E. to the Institute. He reported that she was a troublesome woman. So, too, did her male caseworker at the local Immigration office, who had placed her with the Jewish-Canadian family. He saw her sexual delinquency and hostility towards everything as a manifestation of "a personality problem," compounded by her poverty. It did not take long for Miss E.'s Institute caseworker, Mr. N., to decide that the "short, dark, overweight young girl with an untidy appearance" was a difficult case.

At this point Miss E. admitted that she had moved in with a man she had just met. She also thought she had contracted VD, which potentially made her a foreign contaminant in need of containment. After consulting her other caseworkers, Mr. N. reported that Miss E., who refused medical treatment, had probably contracted the disease from her current lover. Apparently the lover had "lost interest in her" and wanted her to leave, but she was refusing to do so because she had just lost a job and could not afford to support herself. Although hostile to her, the man had agreed to let her stay until she found work, provided she visited a medical clinic. Mr. N. cajoled her into doing so.[44]

Mr. N. also began to question Miss E. about her sexual history. Aware that her answers did not place her in a good light, she insisted that her unfortunate circumstances had required her to use sex in exchange for a modicum of material security. Her current lover only had a room in a rooming house, but she had moved in with him – even though "she did not feel any attachment towards him" and knew that he had "a wife and family in Yugoslavia" as well as "a child with a married woman in Toronto" – because she could not support herself. After all, she was still a penniless refugee. Interestingly, she defended her lover's decision to kick her out, saying that if she did have VD he would not have been able to afford to take care of her. She also admitted that she had avoided being tested because she was afraid that she would test positive and be deported, and she really wanted to become a Canadian citizen.

Mr. N. took this as an opportunity to lecture her about the need to become a morally upstanding female citizen. In a clear effort to intimidate the woman into cleaning up her act, Mr. N. recorded that he "explained that citizenship would depend a great deal on how she conducted herself in future and explained the great importance of having the medical treatment." She obliged and tested negative. The clinic advised that since she was experiencing recurring abdominal pain she should keep coming until they diagnosed her problem.

Although pleased with the medical news, Miss E. was once again out on the street. Still, she refused to see her Immigration caseworker because, according to her, he was a horrible gossip who was forever lecturing her about being a bad Catholic. It appears that he was also threatening her with the deportation bogey-man. Mr. N. agreed to help her with rent and in finding a job, but he was also keen to establish a therapeutic relationship with her in order to understand why she "fell in" so easily with men. This would be a critical first step towards curing her of her "amoral" approach to sex. He used their appointments to ask about her life in Communist Europe, and he soon got some of the gritty details. She had fled Yugoslavia illegally, in order to escape her father and the threat of incest, and also hinted that she had used sex with men to get her to the West. As Mr. N. recorded it, the war had also destroyed the woman's family. After her parents' marriage and family business failed, the father began drinking excessively. Her mother became emo-tionally unstable, and two younger siblings were placed in an institution while she went to live with her father. She saw him cavorting with women and lost all hope that her parents would reunite. After he tried to rape her, she left home. Shortly afterwards she fled Yugoslavia with some "friends," making it across the border into Austria and a refugee camp.

In surmising that this sexual crisis lay at the root of Miss E.'s psychological problems and continuing sexual delinquencies, Mr. N. was drawing on accepted social work theories that assumed that sex delinquents, like unwed mothers and prostitutes, probably came from abusive or dysfunctional families and may well have been sexually molested as youth. Likewise, his diagnosis that Miss E.'s deep resentment of her parents was compounding her emotional problems also drew from accepted social work theories.[45] Miss E. was also clearly not as tough as she seemed. When Mr. N. suggested a referral to a Catholic agency for welfare support, she "burst into tears" and said she feared that any Catholic agency would report her to Immigration and she would be deported. Mr. N. promised to help her find a place to live and, although this intervention was "not professional," he gave her a bit of his own money because the Institute had no relief funds and she was desperate. His motives seem genuine enough and reflected his growing concern that she was too unstable to take care of herself. "I was concerned," Mr. N. wrote, "because she was so depressed that she might get into difficulties." But he also insisted she visit the Catholic family agency that she was trying to avoid.

Mr. N.'s fear that Miss S. might harm herself was soon proven correct. When he learned that she had not shown up for another scheduled visit at the VD clinic, he tracked down the former lover, who said that she had "attempted to cut her wrist" and then disappeared. According to Mr. N., the man also "expressed considerable concern about her, saying that he would help her, if he were in a better financial position," which suggested that this former lover was not an entirely indifferent or callous man.

Mr. N. was caught off guard when Miss E. "showed up" at the Institute a few days later, appearing "quite cheerful." She said she had moved in with "a girl from her country," and had been given some money to live on, but the situation "was only temporary" because the "girl friend" was getting married in a few days. She also said that she had to find work. Though reluctant to take a domestic job, she agreed to pursue Mr. N.'s suggestions provided she did not have to see the Immigration caseworker, who spoke her language but "did not understand her problems." Mr. N. called the local Immigration staff and (indulging her anti-Semitism?) requested that Miss E. be placed with an Italian or German family. Since she also needed "a great deal of help in adjustment," he asked them to find a job conveniently located to the Institute so that he could continue to counsel her. They agreed.

Miss E. did not settle easily into domestic service, prompting a series of exchanges between her, Mr. N., and the Immigration office staff. But Mr. N. was more concerned about Miss E.'s emotional problems and her recurring physical pain, which the doctors could not explain despite repeated tests. Over the next while Mr. N. stayed involved, visiting her when she had her appointments at the hospital. According to his notes, she was always "quite happy" to see him and shared her anxieties about her continuing pain and her fears that "some other illness had developed." It thus appears that caseworker and client had developed a reasonably good therapeutic relationship, helped in large part, it appears, by Miss E.'s obvious desire to avoid any more dealings with the ethnic Canadian Immigration caseworker, whom she denounced as a moralizer and a gossip.

Yet the bonds of trust that Mr. N. believed he had built with Miss E. over the course of a few years ended abruptly. A close to final entry reported that Miss E. had met another "countryman" who was going to try to find her a factory job. No doubt Mr. N. wondered whether she would have to sleep with the man to get the job. The final entry noted only that Mr. N. had urged his client to keep visiting the hospital until they discovered the source of her recurring pain.

Remaking Lives, Becoming Female Citizens

The public and confidential discourses surrounding the predicaments of "damaged" European newcomer women typically reveal a mix of professional and subjective commentary. They also show a tendency, even among gatekeepers who probably did not have a full training in psychiatry or psychology, to attach psychiatric labels to clients who they suspected suffered from somatic illnesses or who seemed overly wrought by worry or guilt or, alternatively, showed little or no remorse for their questionable sexual morals.

The experts feared that "loneliness" and "strangeness" in a new land could, if not contained and treated but instead left unchecked, seriously compound these women's already problematic histories and by extension pose an immoral threat to their adopted country. This situation could result in permanently damaged women who would become dependent upon the Canadian social welfare state, or in contaminated mothers incapable of raising healthy and moral children – a vital feature of healthy female citizenship. Unless contained and cured, amoral or immoral women could doom their children to leading similarly immoral lives, and the tendency could also lead to them corrupting or damaging those with whom they established relationships. In this way, bad mothers could threaten Canada's moral democracy.

Yet these broad generalizations do not fully capture or explain these frontline encounters. The same caseworker could respond differently to different clients; the response depended in part on whether the caseworker believed in or empathized with his or her client. Some women were treated as both ideal victim and client; others – the hard-core "clinging vines" – were seen as requiring more persistent, even heroic, treatment. Some women earned sympathy or pity as the unfortunate but curable products of women's greater liberation in wartime; others were dismissed as utter "disappointments." When a newcomer woman's questionable moral behaviour or troubled past was attributed largely or partly to emotional or psychological problems, the social workers despaired of being able to reform their behaviour or morals without resorting to long-term psychiatric treatment, which meant referral to a mental hospital or clinic. If some women were partly forgiven their past transgressions because they had clearly paid a high price for them, such as divorce or a disabling guilt, others were seen as the unfortunate but permanent products of Europe's war-poisoned society, with its perverted moral codes and young wily refugee women on the make. These women also usually paid a high price for their transgressions, such as raising children as single mothers, supporting selfish or alcoholic men who avoided work, and losing out of wedlock children to the child protection authorities.

Still, a focus on relatively rare confidential case files should not lead us to exaggerate the extent or degree of damage done to the psychological, emotional, or sexual identity of European newcomer women who underwent painful wartime and immigrant experiences. In many respects the files deal with the most marginal women, people who had little choice but to turn to, or be referred to, the gatekeepers for material or professional help. But the majority of newcomer women who had to struggle to deal with sexually violent or delinquent pasts and adjust to life in Canada did not seek out or were not referred to the family gatekeepers or mental health specialists. Just as many poor and uneducated European women remade their lives for themselves and their families in postwar Canada, so, too, did many women who, by force or "grotesque choice" had transgressed conventional sexual codes. Whatever the degree of guilt or damage to their self-identities and psyches, many European women – whether they had spent the war years in almost mortal fear of being raped by the Nazis or other enemy soldiers, been wartime rape victims, transgressed the moral codes by sleeping with the liberating soldiers or having extramarital affairs, or attached themselves to U.S. soldiers after the war – did remake their lives in new contexts. Countless undocumented women courageously remade sexual lives that were self-affirming, even if they did not conform entirely to North American (or European) bourgeois ideals.

Indeed, many women reaffirmed their lives through motherhood; they took advantage of the city settlement houses and other social agencies that provided them and their children with opportunities and resources for rebuilding solid family lives. Recovering from the ravages of war and genocide could take many long years, and when we look forward in time, and consider, for instance, the memoirs that women refugees and survivors wrote years later, or the interviews and testimonials they eventually offered, we can see that many, perhaps most, of the women remade their lives while carrying deep emotional scars that could never fully be wiped away.[46]

One such woman was Gerda Frieberg, who in 1991 told an audience of historians her powerful stories about the sexual vulnerability that young Jewish survivors like herself had experienced at the hands of both the Nazis and the liberating Red Army soldiers. She told about how, in the concentration camps, she had stood up to the camp guards and insisted upon being moved to the women's labour camp where her mother and sister had been sent. But for all of that courage, she said, her wartime experiences had made her forever fearful of the authorities, especially of men in uniform (she recalled her complete horror at being pulled over by a traffic constable in Toronto), and indeed all men. Such fears, she observed in retrospect, may have helped to destroy her marriage to a man whose authority she had never questioned. By her own admission, during her first years in Toronto in the 1950s she had harboured an abnormal fear of men.

With time she not only recovered from her emotional difficulties but also triumphed, as evidenced by her long-standing activist profile as a Holocaust education worker, which dates from the 1960s, and her decision, following her divorce, to fulfil a childhood dream and get her pilot's licence. In the late 1960s she became the first woman in Toronto with an instrument-rated licence. Ironically, even that dream had links to the war and her vivid memory of the "German bombers" over Warsaw: "I stood in the background fascinated with planes."[47] She also raised a daughter.

At the same time, as Holocaust historian Paula Draper observes, and as her important oral history project documents, survivors like Frieberg continue to "survive their survival" every day. So, too, do the many other women with their stories of sexual innocence and violation, of risking their lives to get pregnant, of being fearful of raising children in a post-Holocaust world but doing so nonetheless. Or those who coped with the ugly reality that their bodies, mangled by the Nazi doctors' barbaric experiments, could not produce children, and so they either remained childless or adopted a child in Canada.[48] Or the thousands of gentile DP women and immigrant women who had to deal with the sexual threat of enemy or liberating soldiers and, in some cases, even of their own neighbours – partisan comrades or fellow refugee-camp residents – or make the "grotesque" sexual choices that Mennonite, German, and other women in regions of occupation had to make.

Although the women who had these experiences might well differ in the degree and extent of their healing and recovery, their narratives provide graphic examples of how storytelling, memoirs, and new beginnings can help women who have survived war and once-unspeakable crimes to rebuild their lives, both emotionally and sexually.[49]

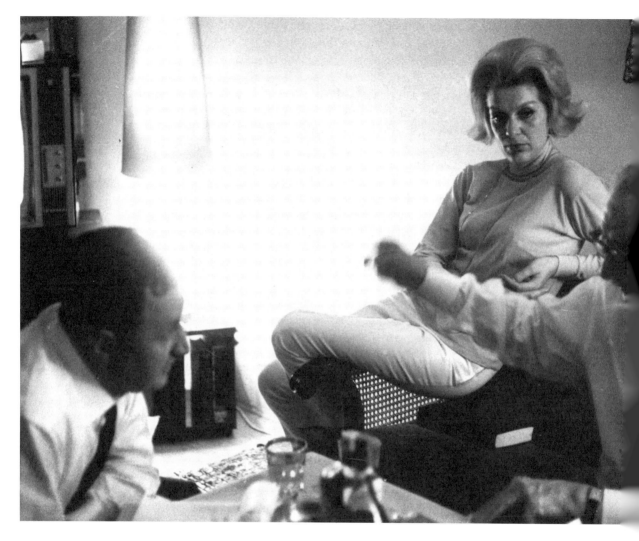

The original caption: "Arguing over rights, Gerda, wearing slinky slacks, talks with her interpreter, Baron von Redwitz. Now 37 and beyond her prime, Mrs. Munsinger is still an attractive woman. She wears her hair off her forehead and puts on just enough eye shadow and deep red lipstick to make her blue eyes and full lips stand out." *Toronto Star* 14 March 1966.
(Toronto Star Archives)

Guarding the Nation's Security

On the Lookout for Femmes Fatales, Scam Artists, and Spies

10

COLD WAR ANXIETIES, MASS MIGRATION, SEXUAL MISCONDUCT, and dominant gender ideologies: these forces also reached out into the arena of national security. The Canadian security state, the most powerful of gatekeepers, and, more particularly, the RCMP, a formidable front-line security force, patrolled the nation's borders against illegal arrivals and immigration scams and sought to protect the nation from all internal and external threats. RCMP officers aggressively pursued a strategy of interrogating, detaining, and, if they were foreigners, deporting anyone who they thought might pose a potential threat to the nation's security and immigration laws.

The origins of the Canadian national security state stretch back to well before the world's second major red scare after 1945. In fact, a first red scare, calling for increased security measures, had been triggered by the Russian Revolution of 1917 and an upsurge in labour militancy and workers' internationalism during and just after the First World War. The practice of stretching the law or violating civil liberties in order to catch the politically suspect was equally well established. But the renewed climate of fear and distrust, indeed the paranoia, unleashed by the Cold War once again prompted the RCMP to cast its surveillance net widely. In the early postwar decades RCMP officers became zealots who created security files on an ever widening circle of people, even high-school students. They blacklisted suspected Communists and "sympathizers" or "fellow travellers" on the flimsiest of evidence, and persecuted homosexuals in the civil service.

The paranoia of the time permitted the state to justify its suspension of legal rights and to commit countless civil liberty violations, in the process destroying reputations, costing people their jobs and isolating them from family, friends, co-workers, and neighbours. Cold War Canada's national security state – like security states elsewhere – might, then, best be understood as an insecurity state that lashed out at perceived and real enemies. Indeed, both Canadian and newcomer Cold Warriors helped to shape a Canadian brand of McCarthyism, with its guilt by association tactics – challenging the conventional view that Canada fought a largely benign Cold War. Some of the most flagrant civil liberty violations in Canadian history occurred in the aftermath of the 1945 political defection of Igor Gouzenko, a Soviet embassy employee in Ottawa who exposed the existence of a spy ring of research scientists, Communist Party members, and civil servants who had allegedly passed on secret scientific and strategic information to the Soviets. The security state launched a full frontal assault against the men and two women involved, arresting and detaining them without informing them of the charges or of their right to an attorney, subjecting them to persistent interrogation that bordered on mental torture. Incriminating information was released to the public before any of the arrested got their day in court, and a number of them were convicted in the subsequent spy trials.[1]

The RCMP's security work also featured the less well-known task of routing out women seen as a threat to the nation's security and its immigration apparatus. In addition to investigations of a handful of women suspected of having supplied the Soviet enemy with government secrets, the nation's police force was also regularly called upon to investigate allegations that the unscrupulous activities of certain women were compromising the country's immigration and criminal laws. These activities included efforts to detain or deport European and ethnic Canadian women whose sexual delinquencies, encouragement of sexual illegalities, or related infractions were deemed dangerous to the nation and the integrity of its immigration apparatus. Clearly, the security gatekeepers feared the consequences of permitting wily women to move freely within society at large, sponsoring immigrants for nefarious ends and running scams that bilked ethnic Canadians desperate to bring in their relatives. As often happens when minorities commit a crime, the gatekeepers treated suspicious ethnic Canadian women – whether Canadian-born or foreign-born but Canadian-raised – as foreign outsiders who had failed to respect or absorb "Canadian" values or morals.

The few women accused of being spies, including Doukhobor-Canadian Emma Woikin – who with Englishwoman Kathleen Willsher was convicted of espionage in spy trials in 1946 – and especially the German Gerda Munsinger – whose sexual escapades triggered a security scandal in the 1960s – dramatically brought security concerns into focus. But other newcomer and ethnic Canadian women were also suspected of being dangerous women who had seduced men into divulging state secrets or committing other illegal acts. The RCMP's investigation of immigration irregularities and potential illegalities, and its interrogation of the suspects, provide a number of portrayals of women who came under the force's stern legal and moral gaze – engaging with types such as the femme fatale, decoy, brothel-keeper, and corrupt petty bureaucrat – and, as it turned out, many of the women who fell under this gaze were rather ordinary people trying to improve their circumstances. In other words, they were not the usual political militants of the right or left. To improve their lives they appeared to be willing to circumvent the immigration regulations, and to grease the palms of middle-men or middle-women. Some low-level but conniving officials in the Canadian immigration bureaucracy also came into play, making attempts to benefit from the great desire of many Canadians and newcomers to bring family members into Canada.

Significantly, too, in the almost twenty years between the 1946 spy trials and the Munsinger affair of the early 1960s, a marked shift occurred in Canadian public opinion about how the state and its security gatekeepers should handle sex and security scandals.

The Popular Press and Suspicious Femmes Fatales

The mainstream press covered a number of scandals involving foreign or ethnic femmes fatales evidently capable of seducing men into performing illegal acts. In 1952, for example, *Maclean's* writer Blair Fraser blew the whistle on illegal immigration schemes from Italy and the "unscrupulous travel agents" and "corrupt Canadian government officials" involved. Among the Canadian officials was a bureaucrat in Rome, George G. Wilson, who for a fee had issued false visas to Italian applicants. Fraser relayed Wilson's "curious" story of having been seduced by a "gorgeous blonde" Italian who had approached him shortly after he took up his post a few years earlier. Desiring to secure a visa for a brother whose application for one had been recently rejected, the woman had "offered as compensation her virtue." "The brother," Fraser wrote with a nudge to his readers, "got his visa a few days later." From that point on, Wilson said, "unsavoury characters" kept turning up, demanding visas and threatening to expose him if he did not comply. The RCMP dismissed Wilson's blackmail story as being "mostly poppycock," but concluded that the Italian seductress was probably not a figment of his imagination. Like other bureaucrats caught cheating, Wilson lost his job but was not charged with a crime. After a failed attempt to run a private travel agency in Rome, he applied for repatriation as a destitute Canadian and was shipped home at state expense.[2]

More standard, perhaps, were the cases of Communist and other left-wing women, who were highly vulnerable to the critique that they were not just sexually amoral or promiscuous but also politically dangerous elements who could use their charms to seduce unsuspecting men into the party. In this regard the pulp fiction images of the Communist tart or seductress stood alongside the masculine and frumpy images of Communist women that appeared in popular U.S. magazines.

Canadian magazines such as *Chatelaine* did not entirely follow the U.S. lead in demonizing or caricaturing the Soviet woman, but some parallels occurred when it came to comparing slim and attractive North American female bodies with stocky or overly muscular Communist features.

In the U.S. magazines of the early Cold War, beauty experts, fashion-makers and other cultural Cold Warriors opined that "real Soviet women," as opposed to the brainwashed ideologues, wanted to get rid of their severe faces, grimy hands, and squat bodies. They wanted to become what all women naturally wanted, to be more feminine and attractive. But, the story went, the Communist economic system had failed to produce the necessary goods and services that could help women achieve this goal. Brassieres, girdles, cosmetics, fashionable clothes, and decent hair salons were in short supply, unlike the filthy grunt jobs that wrecked women's bodies and the perverse ideology that denounced feminine beauty as bourgeois nonsense and that glorified defeminized women. Although Canadian magazines did not entirely replicate this pattern, some Canadian critics did, including Rev. James F. Drane, who toured Russia in the 1950s. Drane reported that one of the saddest scenes he had ever witnessed was that of an "extraordinarily attractive" young Russian girl (with hair so light and features so classical that she looked like "one of Botticelli's angels") who was operating a smelly tar machine to repair a black-topped square in Kiev. Before too long, he warned, the job would destroy her body and charm. As for the few female leaders within the Eastern bloc, such as Ann Pauker, who became Romanian foreign minister in 1947, commentators applied masculine words such as "large" and "forceful."[3]

By the same token, in 1959, North American fashion writers were positively giddy over the popularity of the Christian Dior fashion show that went to Moscow. Both U.S. and Canadian newspapers reported on the standing-room-only crowds, the women's mad rush for tickets, and the presence afterwards of imitation Paris fashions on Gorky Street. There was also the story of how Tanya, a carpenter who had built the runway for the U.S. fashion show in Moscow, was given a beauty makeover and cried tears of happiness over her dazzling new look.[4] Such stories ignored the irony that women supposedly had to use artificial products, dieting, tight-fitting undergarments, and high heels to achieve a "natural" beauty. But they also served to celebrate capitalism – which the slim and packaged woman embodied – and to normalize the reassertion of a conventional gender order after the war.[5]

The twinned themes of sexual and political Communist deviant emerged, albeit in muted form, in a number of Canadian deportation cases that drew close public attention. In one case the press reported that German-born Ursula Schmidt was said to "qualify in every respect as the popular idea of an alluring 'Mata Hari' " – a reference to the First World War spy with an unsurpassed reputation as an alluring but doomed femme fatale.[6] In 1954 Schmidt left her typist job in Montreal to return home to West Germany and face trial as a Communist spy. Wearing a black gown and "speaking perfect English in a husky voice," the young divorcee told Toronto reporters that she was dropping her appeal against her deportation in order to clear her name of charges that she had helped to recruit spies for Moscow while employed at the U.S. air force base at Frankfurt. No doubt the RCMP had investigated the case at the request of U.S. officials, who would have frowned on the idea of Canada harbouring a Communist mole, though Schmidt blamed the accusations on a jealous jilted lover.

Another deportation case that prompted public controversy involved a U.S. citizen, Shirley Taylor Brent, an "attractive young brunette" who had legally entered Canada from her home in Buffalo on a visitor's permit, and then had met and married a Toronto man. When she later applied for landed immigrant status in spring 1954, the Immigration authorities decided to deport her instead. The case was heard by an Immigration Board inquiry, and the confidential correspondence indicates that the officials saw Brent as a sexual and political subversive. The Immigration staff reported that she was "unsuitable from a moral standpoint" and was "a security risk" – a reference, it appears, to her possibly being a Communist.[7] But she was never informed of this view. A central feature of the policies and practices of the immigration security system as it concerned applicants for admission and citizenship was its secrecy. The process was deliberately concealed from the Canadian public, the press, elected Members of Parliament, and government bureaucrats who, according to the RCMP, fit the "no need to know" designation. In the logic of the RCMP, staunch defenders of the secrecy principle, to inform applicants that they were suspected of being security threats would compromise the nation's security. So would telling them that they were being rejected on grounds other than security ones, for that, too, might give too much away.[8]

Thus, at her deportation hearing, when Brent asked why she was being deported, the Immigration Board replied that she had failed to meet certain requirements of the Immigration Act. When she persisted, they simply directed her to the relevant clause, which read in part that admission into Canada could be denied to any person based on "unsuitability" (whether it was for economic, social, industrial, educational, labour, health, moral, or other reasons) or for their "probable inability to become readily assimilated or to assume the duties and responsibilities of Canadian citizenship within a reasonable time after [their] admission." The case underscored the highly discretionary powers of the Immigration officials, who could reject applicants or deport foreigners by reference to a highly elastic term that covered everything from so-called climatic (that is, racial) issues to moral and political unsuitability. The critics emphasized the arbitrariness of the regulations and the lack of due process. "We bar some people from Canada and won't tell them why. We bar others because of their race. We refuse to listen to appeals," was how journalist C.F. Bosworth summed up the problem in *Maclean's*. He added that this approach was damaging Canada's reputation among governments and trade commissions abroad.[9]

The Brent case became a *cause célèbre* when it went to the courts, and Brent won the first round. The judge ruled that the Immigration Board's assumption – that Canadian immigration laws empowered it to deny Brent entry into the country without properly informing her of its grounds for doing so – did not comply with "the essential elements of justice." Ottawa won the case on appeal, but the Supreme Court later quashed the deportation order, permitting Brent to remain in the country. In a unanimous decision, the judges declared that individuals had a right to know why they were being rejected for admission or being deported.

Although temporarily embarrassed by this case, the immigration and security establishment in Ottawa quickly repackaged the regulations in more acceptable language without effectively removing any of the offending prohibitions.[10]

Sexual Illegalities

A variety of suspicious East European and ethnic Canadian women emerge in the RCMP's investigations into immigration-related illegalities such as smuggling rings and prostitution.[11] When Immigration officials suspected an Estonian refugee woman, Rita, of having wooed an Estonian merchant sailor based in England into jumping ship and entering Canada illegally, they followed normal procedure and requested an RCMP investigation.

This case was unusual because the woman appeared to be the mastermind; most marriage scams were orchestrated by dubious travel agents based in Europe and Canada, and they commonly involved young men who posed as foreign sailors and young women in Canada who posed as fiancées and signed fake marriage certificates.[12] The RCMP's investigation of Rita ("on suspicion of the illegal sheltering of a foreign seaman deserter") occurred at the request of the chief of operations in the Immigration Department, and was headed by Special Investigator L.V. Turner.

Several things had triggered the investigation: the ship master reported the Estonian sailor missing to the Montreal Port Authorities when he did not return to work following a short holiday, and a letter was discovered in the sailor's possessions written by a "Rita" of Toronto urging him to desert and join her. Rita's letter also claimed that an Estonian minister in Toronto who had helped other compatriots to desert ship and "disappear" into Canada would extend the same help to them. Clearly part of an ongoing correspondence between the couple, Rita's letter was suggestive on several levels. She was both self-deprecating and anxious, willing to break the law to bring her lover into Canada. Evidently he had planned to ask his captain for permission to go ashore, head to the local Immigration office in Montreal, ask for refugee status and the help of an Estonian pastor in the city, and then wait until the minister could free him. Rita countered that without proof of marriage to a Canadian or landed immigrant, he would be sent back immediately. She told him not to trust the Montreal pastor, saying that she had been in a refugee camp with him and heard "only bad talk about him, he is selfish, takes bribes… makes a lot of words." She also injected an anti-Communist note, saying "he might be pink or red."

Rita insisted that they follow the advice of her Toronto pastor – a "wonderful" man who "has helped all the Estonians who have knocked at his door," even those who, like her, did not regularly attend church. She also used the pastor as a source of justification for the illegalities in which she was involving her lover. She wrote that the minister had told her that while he agreed with God's laws, he felt differently about manmade laws that created false "border lines" and kept loved ones apart. She said he had already helped other seamen "who disappeared by skipping the ship to reach the shore, and later on married, bought houses, and had their children." This was the only way to get in, Rita concluded. It would entail no trouble with police, and they would be able to "live a whole life in peace" in a democratic Canada. Despite the steely determination and clever, even manipulative, mind revealed by her letter, Rita ended in the same apologetic and self-effacing way in which she had begun, asking her lover to "excuse my bad writing and scribbling." She assured him that while she was "not as good as you think," she did care for him.[13]

Special Investigator Turner first interviewed the Toronto pastor, whom he quickly eliminated as a suspect, describing him as "a conscientious man" who was "helping his countrymen to settle in Canada and become useful citizens." He then turned to Rita, and under interrogation she admitted that she had lied about the Toronto pastor in order to encourage her friend to come. Yet she proved to be less a foreign seductress than a lonely refugee woman wanting to rekindle an old childhood friendship. It turned out that Rita was a divorcee and a widow. She explained that her second husband had died in a Russian slave-labour camp and that she had lost other loved ones during the war. Her desire for companionship was so acute that she had been willing to break the law to marry the Estonian sailor, who was hardly innocent himself. Rita had not known his whereabouts until she read about him in an Estonian-language newspaper. He had been part of a group of Estonian refugee sailors deported back to England after an earlier attempt to smuggle themselves into Canada had been foiled.[14]

The RCMP also investigated alleged prostitution rings, including a case involving domestic workers recruited from Greece. The case focused on a clever and brash Greek-Canadian woman in Montreal, probably a pre-war immigrant, who

An RCMP officer poses in front of his car, 1948.
(Photograph by A.E. Cross; GMA, NA 5327-747)

with her husband was also suspected of running a gaming house and blind pig (bootleg joint). As one officer put it, they were "bad news." The staff at the local National Employment Service office had placed the young Greek women in various domestic posts, but had become suspicious when, only a few months later, some of them returned to terminate their one-year labour contracts. They said they had taken a job with a Mrs. Z., a Greek immigrant who owned a couple of downtown "greasy spoon-style" restaurants. Mrs. Z. had also barged into the Employment office on several occasions and recruited a few of the women. The staff alerted their superiors to the possibility that she was "harbouring" them for "immoral purposes." Shortly afterwards, Mrs. Z. was arrested on a morals charge, specifically of inciting one of the Greek women, now a waitress in her waterfront restaurant, into prostitution. The waitress was hauled in on "vagrancy charges" (in other words, prostitution).

A disappointed Turner soon reported, however, that neither woman had been convicted at trial, largely because local police officers had botched the sting operation that had led to the women's arrest. The RCMP corporal overseeing the undercover stakeout had used a couple of local officers from the Montreal police morality squad. Dressed as stevedores, the officers had acted as patrons at Mrs. Z.'s restaurant. They testified that Mrs. Z. had solicited them individually, asking them whether they might be interested in her young waitress, and they agreed on an amount ($8 and $10). A taxi then took them to a rooming house, where the three of them stayed for a short time before returning to the café.

The undercover officers also testified to having witnessed Mrs. Z. taking money in the restaurant from other men, who then left with the same girl in a taxi. But they couldn't provide proof of direct sexual contact without admitting that one of them had actually had sex with the waitress. Telling the truth "would have jeopardized his position with the Department," wrote Turner in his dry prose, and so the "inexperienced" officer was told to be quiet.[15]

Although hampered by various problems, Turner gathered additional evidence in the hopes of prosecuting Mrs. Z., who, in his opinion, fit "the type who might conceivably incite girls to prostitution" and indeed "resort to any practice for the purpose of making money." It turned out that some of the domestic workers she recruited hailed from the woman's original hometown in Greece. Also, some of the women who had terminated their labour contracts early on were not only working for Mrs. Z. but had also already sponsored, or submitted applications to sponsor, their brothers. In this regard they resembled the many postwar European domestics who arrived in Canada (with landed immigrant status) through government labour schemes and then sponsored family members as soon as they could prove a sufficient capacity to support them.[16] Turner also learned that at least three of Mrs. Z.'s "girls" were pregnant. Given their efforts to screen for moral suitability –

female recruits often required a letter from a priest or local official attesting to their good character – and the requisite medical tests, Canadian selection officials would have bristled at this news. But it shows how humble folk, even single young women, could circumvent the admission requirements.

Mrs. Z. proved very able at withstanding the pressures of an RCMP interrogation. During questioning, she was, as Turner put it, at times "evasive." At other times she "resorted to blustering and foul language." She always denied everything. She defended the moral reputation of all of her girls (one of whom, she said, was her niece) by saying that they had turned to her for help and she had found them legitimate jobs. She claimed "complete innocence" with respect to the procuring charges, calling it an RCMP frame-up and insisting that she was not legally responsible for her employees' "immoral manner." Taking on the persona of a kind auntie, she said that she had even given shelter and comfort to a girl who had left home pregnant, assuring Turner that the father was the girl's fiancé and she planned to sponsor him. She had been similarly generous, she added, to two girls who had gotten pregnant during the voyage over. One of them had put the baby up for adoption; the other had kept the baby and returned to work. This, too, was troubling news because it meant that Ottawa had failed to meet its promise to the Greek government, and by extension, the women's families, to chaperone and protect the moral reputation of the domestic recruits.

However fragmentary, the slim profiles of the Greek domestic workers, particularly those who came from Mrs. Z.'s hometown, suggest that they were not entirely innocent girls vulnerable to predators. But even if one or two of them had agreed to prostitute themselves in order to make better money, they still did not completely fit the profile of wily European girls on the make. In any event, since Turner did not gather enough evidence to proceed with a legal case, the pregnant girls evidently got away with their sexual transgressions, even though pregnant single women could be deported on moral grounds. As for Mrs. Z., she was a clever and conniving woman who evidently enjoyed her status as a female padrone (middle agent, boss), at least among the women from her old hometown. But like most ethnic agents, she might well have been despised by the same clients who made use of her services.

The same observations apply to the few other ethnic Canadian women who emerged as low-level operators within the murky world of immigration scams. They included another Rita, in this case a twenty-five-year-old Greek Canadian who worked as a typist and interpreter in a downtown Immigration office in Montreal. Rita apparently extorted money from elderly Greek Canadians who came to submit applications to sponsor relatives to Canada. Speaking in Greek, she would strike up a conversation with someone in the waiting room and convey the impression that she could get their application approved provided they paid a fee (usually about

$100) and dealt strictly with her. She then handed them the appropriate forms and, following them out of the room into the hallway or elevator, asked them for part of the cash in advance. Most of them paid in modest instalments (ranging from $5 to $25) at pickups that took place in nearby coffee shops or the office elevator. If they did not show up, she would phone and cajole them into making small payments. In truth, Rita could not have run the scam without help from the office's Immigration inspector, who was implicated along with her. He was very likely also her lover. It is not entirely clear whether he could actually fix most of the applications, but the people who filed complaints, and spoke with RCMP agent Turner, had had their applications rejected.[17]

Turner quickly fingered Rita as the brains behind the extortion scam. He also reported, with frustration, that she played the interrogation game beautifully by admitting to certain banal acts or minor sins while claiming to know nothing about more serious wrongdoing or illegal behaviour. Her partner, the Immigration inspector, was also very careful, though after he resigned from his job he effectively named Rita as the ringleader in order to protect himself. Significantly, what had triggered the RCMP investigation in the first place was a formal complaint launched by a seemingly gullible Italian butcher who had entered Canada as a visitor via the United States. For a time he was perfectly willing to go along with Rita's suggestions that he cover the tab for cocktails in her favourite nightclubs and for various house dinners and parties. Soon, though, he decided that she and her partner were not getting him what he wanted, which was an approval to remain in Canada as a landed immigrant, which would also allow him to sponsor his family.

Turner failed to gather sufficient evidence to prosecute either Rita or the inspector for any of the alleged crimes, but both of them did quit their jobs, no doubt in hopes of avoiding further investigation or arrest. After investigating Rita on several more occasions, and again failing to prosecute her (this time on charges of running an illegal travel agency), Turner finally concluded that she had run out of scam ideas, and he consoled himself with the thought that the RCMP might finally have put her out of business for good.

Trading Secrets: Woikin, Willsher, and the 1946 Spy Trials

The misdemeanours committed by low-level clerks like Rita or brothel-keepers like Mrs Z. were no match for national security scandals. Indeed, few women were more notorious than those implicated in the explosive spy scandals of 1946, which occurred amid the rapidly escalating Cold War, when paranoia about Communist spies infiltrating every sector of society reached a fever pitch. One of them, Emma Woikin, a twenty-five-year-old Canadian of Doukhobor origin, worked as a cipher clerk in the Department of External Affairs. Another, Kathleen Willsher, a forty-year-old English woman, worked as a deputy registrar in the High Commissioner's office in Ottawa. Both were convicted of espionage. Neither of them fit the usual portrait of the cool, professional female spy, though they did break the law and pass on secrets to the Soviet Union. As far as the spy game went, they were definitely "small fry," especially compared with the impressive list of research scientists and Communist Party luminaries, all men, who were convicted along with them. Still, their treasonous acts contributed to the climate of paranoia that allowed the state to justify its violation of their legal rights. In sharp contrast to their U.S. counterparts, Ethel and Julius Rosenberg, who paid the highest price for their commitment to the Soviet Union, neither they nor any of the convicted Canadian spies ever faced the possibility of a state execution.[18]

The 1946 spy trials involving Woikin and Willsher were triggered by the fall 1945 defection of Igor Gouzenko, the young Soviet cipher clerk who had stolen documents from the Soviet embassy in Ottawa. The material revealed that during the war a number of Canadians had been supplying Soviet intelligence with confidential information about non-nuclear weapons, political strategies, and atomic research. The news of a "Soviet spy network" in hot pursuit of the West's secret atom bomb shocked Canadians when they first heard about it in February 1946. The news made headlines around the world. By then, Gouzenko, his wife Svetlana[19] – who had encouraged her husband to defect and to take with him documents as proof of a spy network – and their baby had been granted asylum in Canada and begun their life of seclusion. In subsequent interviews with reporters and TV journalists, Gouzenko, himself paranoid about being pursued by Soviet agents, wore a cloth bag over his head.

After an initial hesitation, Prime Minister Mackenzie King acted decisively against the Canadian suspects. He authorized the RCMP to seize, isolate, and interrogate a dozen Canadian civil servants on suspicion of espionage. Canada had played a junior but significant role in the atom bomb's research and development during the war. The Western Allies, led by the United States, had deliberately excluded Russia from the project and from knowledge of all subsequent plans. In response Stalin had enlisted agents to recruit Canadian moles from among the progressive scientists and party faithful who had believed that world peace would be better served by sharing the knowledge about various Second World War weapons, including the ultimate killing machine. But the shock and outrage provoked by the news of traitorous Canadians who gave secrets to the enemy, even low-level secrets, trumped more complex political or academic arguments about the merits of sharing scientific knowledge. King appointed a Royal Commission on Espionage, headed by two Supreme Court judges, Roy Lindsay Kellock and Robert Taschereau, which grilled the thirteen detainees for six months and

The Supreme Court judges who conducted the Royal Commission on Espionage: Roy Lindsay Kellock (left) and Robert Taschereau (right).
(Unknown photographers; Supreme Court of Canada)

named some additional suspects, including the Communist MP Fred Rose and party organizer Sam Carr. The commissioners published interim reports replete with graphic details of the cloak and dagger activities of Soviet intelligence officers in Canada, including top gun Colonel Nikolai Zabotin, and the Canadian sympathizers who helped them.[20]

In contrast to the United States, where the state's efforts to destroy communism, including the guilt by association tactics adopted by Senator Joseph McCarthy and the inquisitorial investigators of the House Committee on Un-American Activities and the Senate Internal Security Subcommittee, were highly public, the Canadian state largely kept its anti-Communist activities hidden from public purview. But while avoiding some of the public excesses of McCarthyism, the Canadian "national insecurity state" committed many of its own civil-liberty abuses in the cause of battling communism. The blacklisting of men and women on suspicion of being Communists, even when there was no evidence to support it, caused havoc with people's lives and further fuelled the climate of mutual fear and hate. J. Edgar Hoover and the FBI may have become the most expert at adopting quasi-illegal and illegal methods, such as wiretaps and entrapment techniques, in their efforts to get at the enemy, but their allies north of the border also deployed such techniques. Some of Canada's most active volunteer gatekeepers, including the IODE, were willing to help out too, as were other civilian allies who encouraged ordinary Canadians to blacklist friends, family, and neighbours who expressed suspicious political viewpoints. Moreover, on occasion, as in 1946, the Canadian security forces and political authorities were quite public about how, for them, defeating communism took priority over protecting civil liberties, especially in regards to foreigners and ethnic Canadians (whether Canadian or foreign-born) whose (alleged) actions earned them the label of "unCanadians" who had failed to become "proper" Canadian subjects. As Gregory Kealey observes, "Since its inception, the RCMP has equated dissent with the foreign-born."[21]

To apply the full force of the state to expose, prosecute, and convict the suspects, the key players in the Prime Minister's Office, the Justice Department, and the RCMP adopted measures that made a mockery of the legal justice system. Most of the charges involved violations of the Official Secrets Act (OSA) and criminal conspiracy to violate the OSA, a separate offence under the Criminal Code. The key actors knew that Gouzenko's evidence alone might not secure a court conviction of the suspects because judges and juries did not like to convict on the basis of the uncorroborated evidence of co-conspirators. To demonstrate a violation of the OSA, or to link an accused to a conspiracy to violate the OSA, they had to find a way of extracting additional evidence from the suspects before they went to trial, and confessions were one means of doing this. But even with this additional evidence, the RCMP and government prosecutors still believed that they might, at best, convict only a few of the suspects. The solution was a royal commission precisely because its looser rules of evidence allowed for "witnesses" to be summoned and questioned "in the widest way possible," all without a lawyer present. The commissioners could publish evidence, even if uncorroborated, as well as their own unsubstantiated theories, which would not have been admissible in court proceedings. They were also armed with the extraordinary powers granted by various pieces of legislation. Under the War Measures Act (which was still in effect in 1946), the state could seize and interrogate suspects and detain them incommunicado for an indefinite period without charging them with a crime. The Inquiries Act permitted the commissioners to force the testimony of the suspects and to punish them with charges of contempt if they refused. The commissioners interpreted the Official Secrets Act as allowing them to presume that all suspects were guilty until proven innocent. The Commission was also given the authority to make its own interpretations of these laws and make up its own rules for the secret hearings. Moreover, the Commission's willingness to use arbitrary and ruthless methods to build a case against "the moles" met with the acceptance, even approval, of many Canadians.[22]

The suspects were rounded up in early morning raids and taken to the emptied military barracks in Rockcliffe, an Ottawa suburb. They were isolated in individual rooms that had rows of empty single cots, overhead lights burning all night, and windows nailed shut. Cut off from family, attorneys, and the public, each person was interrogated, first by the RCMP officers in the barracks and then by the commissioners, in a secret hearing held in the Justice Department. Although charges still had not been laid, at the hearing the suspects were told to testify or be punished for refusing. Most of the detainees were unaware of the Canada Evidence Act, a Canadian law that (like the better-known U.S. Fifth Amendment) protected witnesses from self-incrimination. The commissioners did not inform them of this law and managed to prevent most of them from consulting legal counsel. Once the suspects had offered useful evidence, through self-incrimination or by incriminating others, they were released from custody. But as they left the barracks they were arrested, charged with espionage, and jailed. Charges were issued against all of the detainees, and several others, including Rose and Carr.[23]

In the courts, with their stricter rules of evidence, only eleven of the twenty suspects ultimately named by Commissioners Kellock and Taschereau (and only seven of the original thirteen detainees) were convicted. Apart from the Communist Party faithful, the "spies" had been recruited from among well-placed, left-wing intellectuals and research scientists who themselves had been dismayed by the West's

Part of Emma Woikin's $1,500 bail was put up by her brother John, shown here with Emma after her 1946 court appearance. *Toronto Star* 5 March 1946. (Toronto Star Archives)

decision to exclude the Soviet Union from all discussions and experiments involving nuclear weapons and other weapons technology.[24] The suspects included Dr. Raymond Boyer, a chemist at McGill University and an explosives expert with the National Research Council (NRC), and a political analyst, Gordon Lunan. Also convicted was Edward Mazerall, an electrical engineer and radar specialist with the NRC, and Israel Halperin, a Queen's University mathematician.

In becoming "Soviet moles," most of the men and two women at the centre of the controversy had not seen themselves as betraying their country but rather as preparing for what they hoped would be a postwar world of co-operation and sharing of scientific knowledge, especially regarding nuclear armaments.[25] The party faithful, of course, believed deeply in the promise of communism, and their commitment to the Soviet Union, at least until 1956, had led them to pass on secrets to the enemy.

Some of the other spies had been recruited by Soviet embassy officials in Canada during that critical interlude of 1943–44, when Russian soldiers were repelling the German forces and the Allied countries were celebrating the Red Army as well as Russian culture and history. In Canada, as elsewhere, movie-house reels and newspapers praised the brave Russians soldiers; interned Communists were released (a move that nonetheless worried the RCMP). Moscow opened up an embassy in Ottawa and staffed it with handsome officers who "made dashing figures around town."[26] Canadian-Soviet friendship groups sprang up, and Russian choirs and orchestras got receptive audiences. Left and left-liberal groups debated Marxism at study groups.

Many of the "spies" arrested and interrogated in 1946 had been part of these loose networks of progressives in Ottawa rather than any tight-knit Soviet spy network. In addition they had handed over mostly unimportant scientific material or information that was or would soon be published in newspapers and journals, though, of course, they had broken their oath of secrecy to Canada and had passed on secret documents to Soviet intelligence. As Canada's wartime honeymoon with Russia quickly turned cold at war's end, the suspects faced enormous public hostility. There was plenty of outrage, and Canadians largely supported the state's aggressive prosecution of the suspects even when it meant violating the suspects' legal rights. The prison terms for the convicted spies ranged from two and one-half years for Woikin and three for Willsher to six for Rose and Carr.[27]

Woikin and Willsher, along with Mazerall and Lunan (the more outspoken of the detainees), were listed in the royal commissioners' first interim report, published in March 1946, announcing the first of the traitors to be exposed by the secret hearings.[28] The rumours that both women were devastated and hysterical in the barracks were exaggerated (Woikin cried a lot, but Willsher remained composed). But they were the first "spies" to confess under interrogation. Neither of them had tried to use "evasive" or "blustering" tactics in hope of avoiding arrest. In court, on advice of counsel, they changed their pleas, but both were quickly convicted. It was thus two women who became the first Soviet spies in Canada to be convicted. Willsher would be called upon time and again to implicate other suspects.

Kathleen Willsher (but identified as Mary), lawyer R.K. Laishley, and a friend leave the Ottawa police station after posting bail of $1,500. *Toronto Star* 5 March 1946.
(Toronto Star Archives)

The reporters who jammed the press tables in the packed courtroom reported on everything, from the women's outfits to their comportment in court. In the suspects' first court appearance, at their bail hearing, the reporters noted that they wore no makeup and were dressed almost identically, "in Hudson seal coats, silk stockings and short rubber boots." (Willsher also wore a small fur hat.) The reporters described the auburn-haired Willsher as "small, plain and frightened looking," "studious and of quiet habit," and "a meek-looking little woman" who "showed the effects of the strain." They wrote that Woikin "stepped timidly forward" to take the stand "with eyes downcast," and "looked almost tearful as she resumed her seat on the hard worn bench in the Victorian courtroom." There was a difference of opinion over Woikin's physical attributes. For some she was "small and mousey," for others, attractive and youthful.[29]

After the suspects made bail, the reporters swooped down on Emma Woikin. "A little woman in blue" and "all dressed up in her Easter best," she came out of the jail and "blinked in the sunshine of a warm spring-like day." Woikin was accompanied by her brother, John, a Prairie farmer and the first family member that Emma had seen since her arrest. She was polite with the reporters, even showing a sense of humour. When asked how she felt, she replied, "If I had another pair of strong feet to stand on, I would feel perfectly fine." She posed for the cameras, but did not oblige a request to smile. Beyond noting that his sister had been living under grim conditions, John would not discuss her ordeal with the reporters. Instead, he told them that he had to get Emma some oranges. "She hasn't had oranges in a month," he explained. "She wants an orange." Oranges and humanity, he might have said.[30]

At trial, each woman's lawyer offered a similar defence, namely that their client's spying had been of such a low order that she deserved to have the charges dropped. Willsher's lawyer, Rowell Laishley, argued that his client was charged with "a technical breach of the OSA but without much substance behind it," by which he meant that the secret information passed on had been of such little consequence that her crime was even "less serious" than forgery, shoplifting, or theft. He elicited responses from Willsher that were meant to emphasize the innocuous nature of many of the secret documents in her office. They included memos about battle boards (a waterproof device for maps that her lawyer referred to as "baffle boards") and a speedy calculator.[31] Nevertheless, as the reporters duly reported, Willsher was convicted on grounds of having taken advantage of her sensitive position as assistant registrar in the High Commissioner's office, which gave her access to secret documents, to provide Russia with a "direct pipeline" to secret discussions among the Allies from which Stalin had been deliberately excluded.

Attorney J.P. Erickson-Brown faced the same difficulty with Woikin, who, the court ruled, had exploited her sensitive position as a cipher clerk in the code room of the Department of External Affairs. Woikin deciphered the secret telegrams received from the offices of the Secretary of State for Dominion Affairs in London and was accused of passing on their contents to Soviet officials, in particular to Major Vsevolod Sokolov, the commercial attaché at the Soviet embassy. Many Ottawa insiders believed that Sokolov had seduced her into working for the Russians.

The Making of a Spy

Thanks to journalist June Callwood's popular biography, far more is known about Emma Woikin than about Willsher, but enough information exists on both to draw a few comparisons. In addition to the significant difference in their ages, the two had serious class and educational differences. Willsher was a graduate of the London School of Economics – and evidently spoke with a crisp upper-class English accent – while Woikin was a Doukhobor farm girl from Blaine Lake, Saskatchewan, who had gone to high school and later completed a secretarial program. The two of them may never have crossed paths in Ottawa. Woikin did not know any of the other "spies," whereas Willsher was a part of Ottawa's left-wing and left-liberal circles. A resident of Ottawa since 1938, she had been secretary of the Ottawa branch of the Fellowship for a Christian Social Order, which was connected with leading CCF intellectuals and Christian pacifists (it broke up, in 1942, after links with Communists were exposed).

She was associated with Agatha Chapman (also named by Gouzenko), an organizer of study group meetings that drew left and left-of-centre types, and she knew Mazerall and Halperin.[32]

June Callwood, Emma Woikin's biographer, as a young journalist. (Photograph by Walter Curtin; Toronto Star Archives)

Woikin also held leftist ideals, and supported the Soviet Union, but her politics were more rooted in her Russian culture and painful personal history. During the Depression she had lost a child and, later, a husband. The spy scandal revealed her deep infatuation with a dashing Soviet officer who apparently never had similar feelings towards her. The mix of tragedy and sexual intrigue, as well as her ethnic marker as a Russian-speaking Doukhobor from a remote and desolate prairie town, might also explain why Woikin captured the public attention in a way that Willsher did not. Woikin's short trial contained various highlights, including her admission that she had been flattered by the handsome Major Sokolov's attention; indeed, the mere mention of his name brought a smile to her lips. When asked to elaborate on her attitude towards the Soviet Union, she waited a moment and softly replied: "I have a love for that country. We may be wrong or we may be right, but there is hope for the poor there."

Woikin also took the opportunity to provide the court, and Canadians, with an account of her life.[33] A third-generation Canadian Doukhobor whose grandparents had fled persecution in Russia and settled on remote land on the North Saskatchewan River, she had inherited a culture that not only was sympathetic to socialist ideals of collectivism and pacifism but also valued private ownership. The brightest of five children, she grew up in a struggling but warm Russian-speaking farm family and in a sectarian community. Indeed, for many, perhaps most, Canadians, the Doukhobors were still foreigners in their midst. At age sixteen, Woikin fell in love with and married Peter Perversoff, whose Doukhobor family was much worse off than her own. As newlyweds they survived the worst years of the Depression, with drought and a grasshopper infestation following on the heels of crop failure. They lived on bread and potatoes – and the occasional orange, Emma's favourite. In the second year of marriage, she endured a difficult pregnancy and was hospitalized in Saskatoon. The baby, which had been breeched, was born dead, the umbilical cord wrapped around its throat. It was the single most tragic event of Emma Woikin's life, and one she always linked to her poverty. A few years later came another blow: her husband's suicide, in 1942. She would always attribute her child's death to poverty and believe that the poor received better health care in Russia.

Widowed and childless, and always considered too thin for farm work, Woikin went to secretarial school and upon graduation, with a lack of jobs in her area, wrote the federal civil service exams in Saskatoon. She did very well and accepted a typist job with the Department of External Affairs. Arriving in Ottawa in the fall of 1943, she lived frugally, renting rooms and bargain-shopping for office clothes, and eventually settled in with a couple and their children (in the place where the RCMP would later arrest her). As her letters home reveal, she often felt like a Russian outsider in the nation's capital, though she made a few friends. She was critical of the government for its lack of support for farmers. The letters also show that her poverty and personal losses influenced her eventual decision to spy for Russia.

Equally important was the timing of her arrival in Ottawa in the fall of 1943 – a time when the Russians were Canada's great friends. Woikin suddenly found herself invited to parties with Russian guests. She attended a Russian church and went to hear the USSR army choir. A poorly paid clerk who delighted in Soviet military victories, she found herself being encouraged to praise communism. She was very taken with her new Russian émigré friends and impressed by the high-ranking civil servants she met, most of all the Soviet military attaché and handsome war hero, Colonel Zabotin. Along with the NKVD (Soviet secret police) chief, Zabotin was assigned the task of obtaining information about secrets that the Western powers were concealing from their temporary ally – with Stalin never expecting the friendship with the West to last. The task required recruiting Canadians within key government offices and laboratories.

The Soviet embassy first made contact with Woikin through Sokolov and his wife, Lida, also on the embassy staff. When Sokolov told his superiors that he had befriended a Canadian cipher clerk, whom he described as a young and impressionable romantic who saw the Soviet Union as a promised land, he was instructed to cultivate a relationship and gain her trust. The couple brought Woikin into their circle of friends and comrades, spent time with her, and discussed her painful past. Woikin became infatuated with the charming Sokolov, who spent hours with her discussing music, literature, and politics. He graciously accepted her gift of one of her own landscape paintings, representing a hobby she had picked up to fill the lonely hours. Lida Sokolov also nurtured the friendship, and after Woikin agreed to spy for them Lida became her main contact. Once Woikin crossed the line, she even got caught up in the cloak and dagger intrigue of being a spy. A woman with a remarkable memory, she would memorize the contents of the documents she decoded and then write them out for Sokolov. Secret hand-offs with Lida Sokolov took place in various locales, including theatre lineups and the bathroom of a dentist's office, where Woikin attached her envelope to the toilet tank.[34]

Emma Woikin's biographer argued, and most others agree, that she was emotionally and not sexually seduced into becoming a Soviet spy. She was, they say, a plain, lonely, and impressionable young woman who had become completely infatuated with the Sokolovs, but she was also an utterly conventional woman who would have balked at the idea of a backroom affair with a friend's husband. Certainly she appears to have loved being in the company of both of the Sokolovs. Amid the news of Gouzenko's defection, she applied to the Soviet embassy for Soviet citizenship in hope of accompanying the Sokolovs and other diplomats returning home. Her arrest shortly afterwards put an end to those plans.

Yet it also seems clear that there was more to this woman than the descriptors of plain, lonely, and impressionable can fully convey. For one thing, Woikin fed Sokolov material that was useful enough to keep him interested but that would not compromise her loyalty to Canada. It suggests a shrewder mind than the one implied by the image of the pathetic, deviant ethnic Canadian woman. Nor does it help to draw distinct lines between emotional and sexual seduction. It might well be wrong to assume that Sokolov never embraced Emma or danced closely with her, or that he never held her hand, stroked her hair, or perhaps even kissed her. After she left prison, Woikin picked up boyfriends fairly easily, though she quickly settled down with one man. Still later there were rumours of an affair with a partner in the law firm that employed her. These examples may come from later years, but they are nonetheless suggestive.[35]

Prison and Release

Woikin's ability to endure prison suggests a great inner strength and further undermines the portrait of her as a pathetic woman. Indeed, in her first letter home she announced, "Right, now it is a hard cold fact.... Yet even now, I can see that this time spent here will not be a waste of time but should be a great school of character." She did her time with Kathleen Willsher in the Kingston Penitentiary for Women. They coped with lice and cockroaches. Willsher was such an effective teacher to the other inmates that the prison matron despaired that they would never be able to replace her. Woikin returned to her hobby of painting, and spent hours on scenes she could see from the upstairs window, including the Rockwood Asylum for the Insane. She took correspondence courses and basically got a university education. At one point she caused a bit of a public stir when the press learned that she, a traitor, had aced a Latin course offered by the Department of Veteran Affairs.[36]

She wrote many letters home, asking for family news and snapshots, exercise books, oil paints, and a Bible. She cited Dostoevsky and Shakespeare. She was not connected to the militant Doukhobors, the Sons of Freedom, but reported, with delight, that among the Freedomite women doing time in Kingston, for arson and other charges, were two old friends. She also spoke of her loneliness and sadness

("Mine eyes, my brain, my heart are sad – sad to the very core").[37] She complained that the Hamilton socialite Evelyn Dick, a notorious woman who had just been convicted of killing her baby and husband in a high-profile case, was constantly "bothering her." On this front, she was conventional. Woikin was disgusted by the lesbian sex she witnessed, at one point reporting on two women who were having sex in a cell. Shortly afterwards someone attacked her, but if she knew who it was, she never said.[38]

Woikin and Willsher were both released on the same day in August 1948, having received a maximum time off their sentence for exemplary behaviour. Willsher returned to England and was largely forgotten, although various theories floated around about the identity of the Soviet spies in Britain with whom she had communicated in the 1940s.[39] Woikin's arrival back in Blaine Lake was covered by the press. The Saskatoon *Star-Phoenix* treated her as a celebrity. The daily featured a few of her paintings (including the one of the Rockwood Asylum) and, in a folksy tone, told readers that she was still youthful and pretty but "prefers not to discuss her adventures with anyone."[40] Shortly afterwards, she settled in Saskatoon.

Emma Woikin faced the prospect of rebuilding her life after prison while the Cold War raged on, and she did so partly through a second marriage to an affable man, Louie Sawula, and a career as a well-regarded legal secretary. In Saskatoon she earned the respect and fondness of family and friends as well as of her employers – she worked for the large Hnatyshyn family law firm until the early 1960s and then for a firm headed by R.C. Cuelenaere until her death in 1974. In their recollections the lawyers who did find out about her past said they had not been overly concerned about it and preferred not to talk about it. She was, they did say, a terrific employee, and they did not think she could do any real legal damage to them. In 1969 she finally visited the Soviet Union, where, according to local gossip, she was "treated like royalty." People at home did not think the trip was especially strange, because many Russian-speaking Canadians lived in or near Saskatoon and travel to the Soviet Union was not uncommon. It also appears that Woikin enjoyed her role as a loving wife, generous hostess, avid gardener, and proud homeowner of a modest bungalow. She was fashion-conscious and loved her brown mink coat. She remained childless, but was an indulgent auntie who baked cookies for the children.[41]

Yet, again, her story is more complex and ambiguous than this synopsis suggests. She did not remain completely silent about her past or politics. A former co-worker, also a legal secretary, recalled that the local folks knew that Emma Woikin was a "Communist." Emma, she said, had once scolded her for criticizing Russia. On occasion Woikin raised her past in conversation at home and work. When the diplomat E. Herbert Norman, a true victim of the Canadian red scare hysteria, committed suicide in 1957, she wanted to talk about her Ottawa days but found few willing to listen. Then there was her heavy drinking. Apart from her husband, who was also a big drinker but twice her size, the one-hundred-pound woman kept her drinking habit hidden from people, at least until the last year of her life. She finally became seriously ill, suffering from a severe case of cirrhosis compounded by chronic depression, anorexia, and heart troubles. In May 1974 she died of acute alcoholism.

In the almost thirty years since her disgrace, Emma Woikin had remade her life and even found some happiness in work, family, and friends. But her alcoholism and other ills somehow offer a frustrating yet fitting ending – replete with ambiguity and contradictions – to her Cold War story.

The Munsinger Affair

In the later Cold War period an even bigger sex and security scandal broke. The Gerda Munsinger case, which broke in 1966, was considered on a par with the high-profile Profumo affair that had rocked British politics in 1963. In the British scandal, Secretary of State John Profumo had resigned amid public revelations that he had carried on an affair with a call girl, Christine Keeler, while she was also having sexual relations with a Russian naval attaché. The key issue was whether Keeler had seduced Profumo into divulging sensitive government information and then traded it to the Soviets.[42]

The Munsinger affair also followed on the heels of the hottest episode of the early Cold War, the Cuban Missile Crisis of 1962, which in turn had occurred after the erection of the Berlin Wall (another "hot" episode) a year previously. The Cuban crisis occurred against the backdrop of Fidel Castro's 1959 Communist revolution against the pro-U.S. dictator Fulgencio Batista and Washington's failed attempt to overthrow the Soviet-supported regime in 1961 (in the Bay of Pigs fiasco). A year later U.S. president John F. Kennedy responded to the Soviet plans to place nuclear missiles in Cuba by imposing a blockade on the Soviet fleet transporting the missiles. With the world watching in horror, Soviet leader Nikita Khrushchev agreed to turn the fleet back, and onlookers sighed in relief.[43]

The Canadian sex scandal involving the German-born Munsinger began as an RCMP investigation conducted at the request of the Department of Citizenship and Immigration. The officials were alerted to Munsinger's June 1960 application for citizenship, on which she had listed as references two cabinet ministers in Prime Minister John Diefenbaker's Conservative government: Pierre Sévigny, associate minister of national defence, and George Hees, minister of transport and, later, minister of trade and commerce. In an interview with the RCMP, Munsinger raised the stakes by intimating that she was Sévigny's mistress and Hees's friend. The investigation pointed to certain curious circumstances surrounding her admission into Canada and her landed immigrant status. She had first tried to enter Canada in 1952, using her maiden name, Heseler, but was rejected. A year later Munsinger tried, unsuccessfully, to enter the United States to join a recently returned U.S. serviceman she had married in Germany. She finally gained admission to Canada under the name Munsinger. The RCMP investigators also determined that both the Canadian and U.S. rejections were linked to reports received from "counterintelligence services" in Europe that in West Germany she had been involved in criminal activity, including prostitution, and had done minor espionage work, such as stealing transit passes, for Soviet intelligence.

The RCMP placed Munsinger under surveillance for several months. Her turf was the Montreal nightclub scene, where she worked as a cocktail hostess. The undercover cops also watched her apartment, where she regularly received visits from men known and unknown to the RCMP. The agents recorded various meetings between Munsinger and Sévigny's executive assistant. They argued that her prostitution activity brought her in touch with underworld crime figures in Montreal. In their final report to Diefenbaker in December 1960, the RCMP brass concluded that Munsinger's possible links with Soviet intelligence and her tainted lifestyle made those with whom she associated potentially vulnerable to blackmail, including, of course, Sévigny and Hees, who, by virtue of their high-level government positions, would possess information that the Soviets might want. If they had not been seduced into divulging sensitive material, they could potentially be blackmailed into doing so. In response, an annoyed Diefenbaker did not demand Sévigny's resignation but ordered him to immediately cease all relations with the woman. Shortly afterwards Munsinger was arrested for passing bad cheques in a shopping spree. The charges were quietly dropped and she was released from jail. In 1961 she left for West Germany or, perhaps more accurately, was whisked away so that she could cause no further embarrassment to the government.

With no leaks to the press or public, the Munsinger affair appeared to be dead and buried. Then, in March 1966, with the Liberals back in power, the case went public during a parliamentary debate. Amid Tory attacks that the Liberals had soft-pedalled a recent security case involving a postal clerk who had done some minor spying for the Soviets, the Liberal justice minister, Lucien Cardin, retaliated by invoking Munsinger's name. After some initial confusion over the details, the news quickly created a media frenzy.[44] The newspapers and radio and TV stations competed for the rights to Munsinger's story. *Toronto Star* reporter Robert Reguly tracked her down in Munich, and the international press camped outside her apartment. At first Munsinger refused the offer for an exclusive story, saying she was suffering from "acute nervous meltdown," but later she agreed to an interview with CBC reporter Norman DePoe. She flatly denied any links to the CIA or KGB. (DePoe commented on her blue eyes, makeup, and false eyelashes.) As the parliamentary debate grew vicious, curious onlookers packed the House of Commons hoping to hear about the sexual escapades of randy ministers.[45]

In response, Prime Minister Lester Pearson ordered a Royal Commission of Inquiry into the Munsinger affair, and its open and closed sessions were completed by May 1966. In the final report the chair, Justice Wishart Spence, was highly critical of Sévigny's indiscretions and Diefenbaker's handling of the matter, especially his failure to remove the defence minister from his post. He thought that Munsinger's relationship with Hees was casual but unfortunate. He concluded that there had been no security breach, though even the threat of one had prompted plenty of anxiety. Munsinger, publicly rebuking the Spence inquiry, which had referred to her as a prostitute and petty thief, called herself a victim of mudslinging.

The Cold War sexual politics of this case deserve close attention, especially since most political treatments of the scandal focus on the politicians involved. As Deborah Van Seters observes, an analysis of the gendered language and images used to depict Gerda Munsinger during the 1966 Royal Commission highlights how the various groups constructed her in different and contradictory ways.[46] These portraits also echo the Cold War discourses of morally damaged women who, having become accustomed to using both sex and deceit as strategies for surviving the chaos of war-poisoned Europe, went on to entrap or corrupt the reputation of fine men. In this case, the stakes were higher because Munsinger had allegedly seduced high-ranking cabinet ministers who may have divulged top-level secrets to her and thus compromised the nation's security; or they had made themselves vulnerable to blackmail by Munsinger's criminal contacts; or any other alternative version.

A fundamental conflict was in how the RCMP portrayed Munsinger – as a devious prostitute who simply could not be trusted and would not hesitate to pass on secret information to the Russians or her criminal friends – and how the former cabinet ministers and a female friend portrayed her – as a cultured, worldly, and well-connected European woman who would never compromise anyone's reputation. For Sévigny and Hees, the strategy was, in a sense, to depoliticize her, that is, to remove any suggestion that she might have blackmailed or spied for anyone. At the inquiry Sévigny stressed that he had first met Munsinger at a formal dinner with people of the "highest respectability," and that he and others had always considered her to be "a lady of distinction" and "a good conversationalist" who enjoyed the respect and popularity of many of the "prominent people" who visited Montreal's "finest clubs, finest restaurants." He expressly denied any knowledge that Gerda Munsinger was a call girl or that she had ever committed any indiscretions that would have left him vulnerable to blackmail. Hees also said that he had naturally become friends with this "attractive," "outgoing," "reserved," and sophisticated European woman. He said that she did not smoke and was a "light drinker"

The iconic female spy, Mata Hari, in her earlier career as an exotic dancer.
(Toronto Star Archives)

(some would later say the opposite) and might even have aristocratic origins. A friend of Munsinger's, Jacqueline Delorme, also denied the allegations that Gerda had been a prostitute or sexually involved with Sévigny, and said that Gerda's nickname, princess, spoke for itself.[47]

Munsinger's supporters faced a tough opposition in the RCMP's Commission counsel and the counsel for Liberal justice minister Cardin. Drawing on its earlier 1960 investigation and almost two hundred pages of transcripts from wiretaps on Munsinger's phone, the RCMP took as its strategy the goal of convincing the Commission that the woman was a prostitute with a past of spying, and that she had links to the criminal underworld and thus posed a security risk to any government personnel with whom she had relations. By mere association with her, Sévigny and Hees had opened themselves up to blackmail.

The RCMP presented various versions of its main thesis, that Munsinger was a serious security threat. One version was to argue that the theory that Munsinger had been a spy in Canada was entirely plausible despite a lack of evidence, particularly given the intelligence information about her earlier record in Germany in the 1940s. Another was to insist that Munsinger's infiltration of high-ranking political circles within the Canadian government so perfectly fit the classic spy scenario that it just could not be ignored. As RCMP commissioner George McClellan put it, the "circumstances" of her change of last names to gain entry into Canada, her earlier work for Soviet intelligence, and the mere fact of her having developed an "association" with a cabinet minister of so "vital" a department as national defence offered a "textbook" case of how to conduct espionage. Conveniently ignoring the details that did not easily fit with their theory – for instance, that Munsinger had been indiscreet about her relationships with Canadian politicians – the RCMP worked hard to present her as a sophisticated female spy in the style of Mata Hari.

The Commission counsels, John O'Brien and J.J. Urie, and Cardin's lawyer, A.J. Campbell, also pursued this line of reasoning. As their sarcastic and even cruel caricatures of Munsinger as a common whore suggest, they also intended to fully discredit her moral character. Thus Campbell pressed Sévigny about his late-night visits to Munsinger's place and presented RCMP evidence that in at least one instance Sévigny had been her fourth male visitor in the same night. During closing arguments, as a means of undermining the "cultured European lady" argument, all three lawyers used the wiretap transcripts that implicated Munsinger in prostitution activity. "The hard unpleasant truth," declared O'Brien, was that "Mrs. Munsinger had the deportment and language of a common harlot." They argued that when they combined the evidence indicating Munsinger's prostitution activity and her association with criminal figures with the reports of her Soviet intelligence work in Germany, the only logical conclusion was that the woman's association with cabinet ministers created an opportunity for her Montreal criminal associates or Soviet agents to blackmail the government. Like the RCMP, the lawyers dismissed the suggestion that Munsinger herself might have been a pawn of Soviet forces who had used her shady past to force her into spying for them – even though they apparently agreed with the RCMP evaluation that the German woman had not actually carried out espionage activity while in Canada. Instead, they relied on innuendo and circumstantial evidence to evoke an image of the foreign female agent. They insisted that a woman in Munsinger's position could have used her feminine wiles to draw out sensitive information from men like Hees or Sévigny, much as Christine Keeler had done in the Profumo case in England.

In the end many Canadian journalists and readers were not convinced that Munsinger was a spy, and as Deborah Van Scters' study of responses to the Royal Commission in the Anglo-Canadian press suggests, many ordinary Canadians evidently believed that the extramarital affairs of politicians and public figures should not be a matter of public scrutiny.[48] At least initially, though, some Canadian journalists embraced the lurid political and sexual possibilities raised by the story. Newspaper headlines hinted at Munsinger's alleged espionage activities and relations with East German intelligence officers, and the CBC-Television news show *This Hour Has Seven Days* brought back Igor Gouzenko and his cloth bag. But the flirtation with femme fatale theories was short-lived. As the reporters "encountered" Gerda Munsinger and interviewed former "friends" and "associates," they offered an alternative portrayal of her, one that leaned heavily towards that of a "party girl" with a loose tongue.[49]

In rejecting the argument that Munsinger could be both a professional foreign agent and a "common whore," the journalists often used sarcastic humour and invoked popular culture icons. Expressing bemusement over the "extraordinary fuss" being made "over a very ordinary woman," a columnist for a northern Ontario paper quipped, "Not that we're trying to take anything away from Munsinger's obvious charms, mind you, it's that our idea of sexy foreign spies runs more to Brigitte Bardot or Sophia Loren types." He asked, rhetorically, hadn't Canada reached enough of a worldly stature that "our cabinet ministers should be able to demand the very best?" The Calgary *Albertan* featured an interview with a supposedly professional spy from the United States, a "Mrs. Rita Gonzales," who explained

An unmasked Igor Gouzenko and his wife, Svetlana, leaving a Toronto courtroom, 1982, several years before his death. The original caption: "His own children didn't recognize him on TV." (Photograph by Bob Olsen; Toronto Star Archives)

that her country's female spies were "really beautiful and talented" college grads who spoke at least five languages. They differed from the "the typical German barmaid type" like Gerda Munsinger. Overall, these images – "blonde playgirl," "cheap tramp," "trollop" – and not professional seductress spy – dominated media coverage of the scandal. The "tramp" images, like the image of the worldly European, also contrasted sharply with another major German female stereotype – the homely but intelligent girl with her hair in braids – suggesting, perhaps, that many North Americans could not fathom the possibility that a German woman could be both sexy and smart.

As to whether the sexual delinquencies of the country's politicians should come under public scrutiny, onlookers tended to disagree. Some journalists and readers believed that a politician's personal life "belongs to the country," as a Saskatchewan newspaper put it. But the most vocal contingent took a "boys will be boys" line, stressing that the matter had been blown out of proportion. Some writers expressed dismay that Sévigny's privacy had been violated, while others asserted that sexual affairs by government men should not become a matter of public debate. Given the homophobia of the era, author Austin Clarke's version of the argument is particularly noteworthy. He said that a politician's adultery, whether homosexual or heterosexual in nature, should not be used to "compromise his parliamentary or public capabilities" because private acts by themselves did not "tarnish" the government's "public image." Munsinger herself spent the rest of her life in relative obscurity, although in a rare CBC interview with journalist Barbara Frum in 1974 she said the whole affair "wasn't scandal, it was life," nothing else.

Beyond the matter of deciding whether or not Munsinger was a spy, the testimonies and press stories indicate that, as Van Seters notes, there was a shared understanding, based largely on popular culture images, about what went into the making of a foreign female spy. The key ingredients were beauty, brains, and cunning, and the ability to infiltrate the social world of a nation's political elite; in other words, a Mata Hari. This understanding was clearly behind how the reporters and others viewed Woikin and Willsher and how the RCMP sized up its surveillance targets. Yet many Canadians disagreed with the argument put forth by the RCMP and Spence Commission counsels, that the Munsinger affair offered a classic Cold War case of how sexual misconduct can raise a national security threat. This disagreement suggests that a shift in public opinion about spies had occurred from the heady days of the 1946 spy trials, when many ordinary Canadians appeared willing to accept without question the RCMP's most "wide-ranging notions" of what constituted a legitimate security threat and its strategies for dealing with that threat.[50] A poll taken at the height of the detentions in the 1940s suggested that 93 per cent of Canadians had heard of the Gouzenko spy affair and, moreover, that 61 per cent of them believed that the government had "acted wisely."[51] Some two decades later, as the Cold War dragged on, Canadian popular opinion had evidently softened its position on the matter of the state pulling out all of its political guns to go after alleged sexual misconduct and security cases. While Canadians were happy to ridicule women like Gerda Munsinger, they were apparently less interested in embarrassing, interrogating, and prosecuting the political men involved.

Peace and Freedom in Their Steps

11

A YOUNG GIRL D.P.

How nice she looks in her new
    dress,
Her fair hair in a shiny braid,
Tripping along on stilted heels,
Half in the sunshine, half in shade.
She walks as to the manner born,
Her garments clean and proudly
    worn.

Behind her quiet eyes there lurks
A world of sorrow and despair,
As if the terror she has seen
Had left a brand forever there,
An image graven on her heart,
Like the deep markings on a chart.

And yet she walks with happy feet,
With peace and freedom in her step,
Companioned by the young and gay,
As if by unseen forces kept.
Hate had no power to destroy
The wellspring of her love and joy.

God grant she finds among us here
Ways that are beautiful and good,
A home and love and happiness
To crown her lonely womanhood.
She asks so little for her share
From us who have so much to spare.

Perhaps the long years will erase,
That haunted look upon her face.

—Edna Jaques, Toronto

IN A GRAPHIC ILLUSTRATION of how many Canadians, including ordinary women and men, assumed the role of sympathetic gatekeepers in early Cold War Canada, a Toronto resident penned this ode to the young, East European refugee women rebuilding lives in postwar Canada, and to the Canadians who sought to lead and assist them. It appeared in *The Toronto Star* on September 27, 1952. The location is fitting given that the English-language mainstream press, including newspapers and magazines, were devoting so much ink to covering the newcomers' arrival and early experiences and to the debates and activities engendered by their presence.

The poem presents a highly romantic but not untypical version of how many of Canada's well-intentioned gatekeepers, from professional social workers and Citizenship officials to popular writers, women's groups, and volunteers, portrayed the European newcomers: as fragile or damaged women, men, and children in need of sympathy, patience, support, guidance, and psychological or moral rehabilitation as well as training in participatory democracy and citizenship. It expresses how many of those Canadians understood their involvement in the various campaigns intended to guide the newcomers' adjustment to middle-class Canadian social, cultural, moral, and political norms. In joining what some gatekeepers described as a national experiment in citizenship, these Canadians took efforts to contain or remove the newcomers' more threatening or undesirable ways and reshape their behaviour according to "Canadian standards." They worked hard to push for their eventual integration into the Canadian mainstream.

Like other gatekeepers, our poet expressed a Christian sentiment that linked the efforts to rehabilitate young women from war-torn, war-poisoned Europe with a heroic battle against the godless communist religion and the kinds of amoral and immoral behaviour that communism supposedly allowed or condoned. Indeed, the "young girl DP" offered Canada a powerful symbol of freedom and democracy, which is why so many gatekeepers, even those who recognized the limits or faults of their own society, saw her successful integration as evidence of the superiority of pro-capitalist Western democracies. The poem also reflects women's significant role in postwar immigrant and reception campaigns, both as gatekeepers and newcomers. Gender, after all, was of key importance in shaping the gatekeepers' campaigns and the interactions between different groups of male and female gatekeepers and newcomers.

In carrying out their multilayered and sometimes contradictory agendas, the gatekeepers, especially state officials and experts, willingly intruded into people's lives and regulated or punished those who transgressed dominant norms. Some gatekeepers were concerned and compassionate; some of them came to appreciate the sacrifices and the struggles of the newcomers even if they also drew distinctions between those whom they considered to be more – or less – deserving of their time, effort, expertise, and respect. Some were intrusive and insensitive. Sometimes their Cold War alliances reinforced a political culture that denounced all forms of dissent. In the process Canada was remade, both into a more culturally pluralist society and into a Cold War "corrupted democracy" or national "insecurity" state.

Was Canada a land of oranges and humanity? For many, perhaps most, newcomers, the answer was a qualified yes. In Canada they could feed their families, rebuild their lives, and regain a sense of self-worth and dignity. For those who had experienced disappointment, prejudice, or, worse, disabling illness or tragic losses, the declarations of Canadian abundance and opportunity could leave a bitter taste in their mouths. For many immigrants, even the successful ones, integration and citizenship came at a price, namely, a willingness to defer to the gatekeepers' agendas or suffer the consequences of indifference, defiance, or disobedience. This was a terrain that upheld bourgeois norms, trampled on civil rights in the name of protecting them, and sought to contain immigrant families, sexualities, cultures, and communities. Both liberals and social democrats were implicated in these less than flattering conservative agendas.

The gatekeepers were of primary importance in these developments, but the newcomers also made their presence known. In their relationships with spouses and children, and in their encounters with Canadian social workers, cultural promoters, and food and family experts, the European refugees and immigrants influenced the contours of postwar Canada in cultural, social, and political directions, even as their own customs were modified. They helped to transform major immigrant cities. In the various contact zones of Toronto, for example, the gatekeepers clearly enjoyed greater power and resources, but the newcomers were also active agents. While the most enthusiastic and politically sophisticated Cold Warriors among the anti-Communist DPs and Iron Curtain refugees worked to reinforce and strengthen the Cold War consensus, thereby contributing to the mutual distrust and paranoia of the era, other newcomers were more interested in rebuilding meaningful personal, sexual, and family lives in often challenging contexts.

The gatekeepers carried out their campaigns and interactions with the newcomers in a highly charged context. A sense of social optimism and cultural superiority was mixed with fears of communism and an anxiety about fragile families and spreading sexual deviance and mental ill health. As a result, the encounters had sharp consequences for both groups. Today, given our greater knowledge of the Soviet Union's despicable human rights record, we can no longer characterize the testimonials of the anti-Communist East European refugees regarding human rights violations and atrocities in the Soviet Union and other Eastern bloc states as being entirely ideologically motivated exaggerations emerging from right-wing fanaticism. Still, at the time those attitudes did help to sustain a repressive culture within the Canadian Cold War state; they enhanced the legitimacy of reactionary forces. Given the ideological alliances forged between gatekeeper and newcomer

Cold Warriors, the East Europeans played a large role in shaping Canada's Cold War democratic culture.

Indeed, a key feature of the Cold War – and of today's so-called "war on terror" – is the complicity of liberals in maintaining the consensus despite their self-proclaimed commitment to liberal-democratic values, including freedom of speech. Significantly, the new century's war on terror has displayed other similar and disturbing elements, such as the equating of certain family values and uncritical acceptance of the national security state with respectability, loyalty, and democracy. Then too, as in the Cold War, the Canadian national security state is a junior but enthusiastic player taking its cue from the United States and the hawks in its military-industrial complex. The great enemy has shifted from communism to Muslim terrorism – though that is not to say that communists or leftists are not targeted, especially when they criticize the repression – but what remains in place is how the politicians, security forces, and their civilian allies and supporters demonize the enemy.

The communist had his or her godless religion; the terrorist has his or her Islamic fundamentalism. Both enemies were and are constructed as fanatics and ideologues who brainwash the naïve and encourage a mass psychosis in the population. Just as the communist, like the homosexual sex pervert, was thought to be everywhere – a sentiment that permitted civil liberty violations, aggressive state surveillance and infiltration, and the insidious guilt by association tactics practised by the FBI, CIA, and RCMP – so, too, is the Muslim terrorist said to be everywhere, in your neighbourhood, schools, and workplaces. Thus, in the name of constant vigilance the targeting of all suspicious "Arabs" is largely tolerated and justified.

After the fall of communism, the United States became the globe's sole superpower, and as yet no state has emerged to replace the great evil Soviet empire. But in the post-9/11 war being waged against "the axis of evil" and so-called rogue states, such as Iran, Iraq, and Afghanistan, defeating the enemy forces has again taken precedence over protecting individual rights in a democracy. The insidious nature of the war on terror also reminds us of the Cold War – of the time when the conservative consensus and family ideology created a context in which all non-conformists, and not just real or suspected communists, were viewed as threats that had to be contained, neutralized, or, failing that, imprisoned or deported. Today we see, too, the use of psychiatric theories and labels, in this case of the Islamic fundamentalists' brainwashing techniques and of the brainwashed themselves, who, like the convicted Canadian spies of 1946, are seen as being duped by evil, malignant forces.

In Canada this theme emerged strongly in response to the "Toronto 17," a group of young Canadian Islamic men from Mississauga accused in early June 2006 of plotting to blow up key sites in Southern Ontario and assassinate the prime minster. The angry and alarmist response to the "Toronto 17," whom the news media and legal authorities effectively portrayed as guilty even before the case went to court, recalls similar scenarios of earlier repressive eras, including the red scares of both world wars. The declarations about multiculturalism having fostered zealotry and disloyalty to Canada have their parallels in the Cold War.

Once again, when the suspected or convicted terrorists (or criminals) turn out to be "homegrown" products, in this case Canadians by birth or choice, Canadian authorities and social commentators alike depict them as foreigners who have failed to respect or absorb Canadian values, or what I call "democratic decency."[1]

Another prime example, of course, is the case of Maher Arar, the Canadian citizen who was picked up in September 2002 by authorities in a New York City airport on suspicion of being linked to the al-Qaeda terrorist network. Arar was quickly deported from the United States to Syria – where he was imprisoned in a cell barely larger than a coffin and beaten, whipped, and threatened with electrocution. He was finally released 374 days after his deportation. It turned out that the RCMP had handed U.S. and Canadian authorities faulty information that linked Arar to the terrorists, which had led to his detention and the subsequent ordeal, and that the RCMP had later deliberately leaked false information to damage his reputation. At first the Canadian government denied that it had anything to do with sending Arar to Syria. On September 28, 2006, after the results of a full-scale public inquiry were issued – the report exonerated Arar and was sharply critical of the RCMP and Canadian government departments – the RCMP Commissioner issued an apology to Arar. The only honorable figure in the chilling story of McCarthy-like persecution of an innocent man was Arar himself, who graciously accepted the apology and called for safeguards to be set in place to prevent such an ordeal happening to someone else.

These issues have repercussions for how Canada deals with its immigration and refugee laws, although globalization and continuing refugee crises are also important factors. The war on terror has led to the greater policing of borders, though the process began earlier, and Canada is again taking its lead from the United States, with its contradictory calls for free trade and greater protection of borders. The forces of globalization have compelled more and more people (and increasingly they are women) to move from the poor countries of the South to the rich countries of the North. At the same time rich nations, including Canada, implement greater controls over where and for how long the newcomers or migrants can stay. As "ethnic" wars and refugee crises persist, the rape and forced impregnation of women and girls continue, as does the neglect of children's basic rights of schooling and decent food. As substandard refugee camps proliferate, the world seems to just sit and watch.

In contrast to the post-1945 immigration, in which the Europeans who arrived, including the DP labour recruits, were landed immigrants with certain rights and social entitlements, Canada's increasing reliance on temporary guest workers or seasonal workers has created specific pools of unfree labour, including Mexican migrant workers and Asian garment workers. This phenomenon comes during a time when liberals proudly declare that Canada has become a multicultural nation that respects and protects racial-ethnic diversity (within a bilingual framework). Indeed, a fundamental flaw in Canada's official multiculturalism is the erroneous claim that people can be both different and equal, for this is so often not the case.[2] The gatekeepers' efforts to articulate a model of cultural pluralism in the early post-war decades faltered precisely because they believed it possible and desirable both to celebrate and exploit the colourful and quaint aspects of the newcomers' cultural customs and to contain, censor, and reshape the evidently more threatening or less appealing features. Like those who had come before them, the postwar Europeans brought with them considerable cultural baggage, and their willingness or capacity to adapt to "Canadian ways" rarely meant a willingness to eradicate their customary ways or homeland politics.

In the end, too, there is another major difference between the immigrants of the past few decades and the earlier-arriving Europeans who, with the exception of Jews, represented more racially preferred groups. Today people of colour figure prominently among the world's refugee and migration streams. In significant respects, when all is said and done, the European newcomers of the early postwar era held a status that the immigrants and migrants from non-white Third World locales, such as South Asia, the Caribbean, and Africa, would not – and still do not – enjoy.

Abbreviations Used in the Photo Captions

AM	Archives of Manitoba
AO	Archives of Ontario
CAMH	Centre for Addiction and Mental Health Archives
CMBS	Centre for Mennonite Brethren Studies
CMHA	Canadian Mental Health Association
CRC	Canadian Red Cross
CTA	City of Toronto Archives
GMA	Glenbow Museum Archives
IIMT	International Institute of Metropolitan Toronto Collection
LAC	Library and Archives Canada
MHSO	Multicultural History Society of Ontario Photo Collection, AO
TFRBL	Thomas Fisher Rare Books Library
TRL	Toronto Reference Library
YUA	York University Archives

Notes

1 Mass Immigration and the Making of the Postwar Nation

1. The best book on postwar Europe is Tony Judt's majestic *Postwar: A History of Europe Since 1945* (New York 2005). My brief discussion here incorporates Canadian primary sources such as *The Toronto Star*, news magazines such as *Maclean's, Saturday Night*, and *Financial Post*; news footage compiled on video; professional journals such as *The Social Worker*; and secondary sources: Modris Eksteins, *Walking Since Daybreak: A Story of Eastern Europe, World War II, and the Heart of Our Century* (New York 1989); Donald Avery, *Reluctant Host: Canada's Response to Immigrant Workers 1896–1994* (Toronto 1995); Gerald Tulchinsky, *Branching Out: The Transformation of the Canadian Jewish Community* (Toronto 1998); Marlene Epp, *Women without Men: Mennonite Refugees of the Second World War* (Toronto 2000); Fraidie Martz, *Open Your Hearts: The Story of the Jewish War Orphans in Canada* (Don Mills, Ont. 1996); Irving Abella and Harold Troper, *None Is Too Many: Canada and the Jews of Europe* (Toronto 1986); Howard Margolian, *Unauthorized Entry: The Truth about Nazi War Criminals in Canada, 1946–1956* (Toronto 2000); Michael Marrus, *The Unwanted: European Refugees in the Twentieth Century* (New York 1985); and Mark Wyman, *DP: Europe's Displaced Persons* (Ithaca, N.Y. 1989). See also Vicki Goldberg, *The Autobiography of Margaret Bourke White* (New York 1986).

2. Ethel Ostry Genkind, "Children from Europe," *Canadian Welfare* 25,1-2 (April-June 1949). As executive director of the Jewish Children's and Home Aid Society of Western Canada in Winnipeg, Ostry served as the Canadian Jewish Congress representative on the Canadian immigration teams to select child orphans for resettlement in Canada.

3. Edith Ferguson, "Large Source of Labour in Europe's D.P.'s," *Saturday Night* 13 Dec. 1947. On the reports of Jewish-Canadian relief workers sent out by the Canadian Jewish Congress, such as Hananiah Meir Caiserman, see Tulchinsky, *Branching Out*, ch. 10.

4. United Church Archives (UCA), Toronto, Women's Missionary Society (WMS), United Church of Canada Yearbook, *Annual Report*, 1950–51, Board of Home Missions, Jeanie King, Community Missions East, 37–38; UCA, WMS, Excerpt of Helen Day, "The Woman Missionary Society, *The Observer* (1950), 13, from WMS, Minutes of Executive Committee of Toronto Branch, 1950–54, Box 156, Record Book; UCA, WMS, Dominion Board, Correspondence with Workers, 1954–55, Box 208, File 2/6B, Re: Immigration Work, Montreal, Louiza Mayova, Report on Immigration Work. I thank Enrico Cumbo for this research.

5. Ninette Kelley and Michael Trebilcock, *The Making of the Mosaic: A History of Canadian Immigration Policy* (Toronto 1998), 313; Avery, *Reluctant Host*, ch. 7; David Higgs, ed., *Portuguese Migration in Global Perspective* (Toronto 1990).

6. Calculations from the Dominion Bureau of Statistics, 1961, unpublished tables.

7. In 1947 Ottawa had adopted a contract-labour scheme aimed at filling acute labour shortages in certain industries. The initial contracts, involving some 4,527 Polish veterans, were for two years, but the term was later reduced to one year.

8. This section draws on Freda Hawkins, *Canada and Immigration: Public Policy and Public*

Concern, 2nd ed. (Montreal and Kingston 1988), table, 54; Kelley and Trebilcock, *Making of the Mosaic*, ch. 8; James Lemon, *Toronto Since 1918: An Illustrated History* (Toronto 1985), table vii, 196; Reg Whitaker, *Double Standard: The Secret History of Canadian Immigration* (Toronto 1987), 7–9. For more detailed statistical breakdowns of the census material, see, for arrivals, Franca Iacovetta, "Remaking Their Lives: Women Immigrants, Survivors, and Refugees," in Joy Parr, ed., *A Diversity of Women: Ontario 1945–1980* (Toronto 1995); and, for European women in the postwar Toronto labour force, Iacovetta, *Such Hardworking People: Italians in Postwar Toronto* (Montreal and Kingston 1992), especially appendix 22.

9. Not until 1967 did Canada eliminate most of its racist restrictions on immigration, and although officials found new ways of restricting immigration from Third World nations, the 1967 changes (which had begun in 1962) did result in a significant alteration in Canada's racial makeup.

10. *Historical Atlas* (Edmonton 1988), l720; Whitaker, *Double Standard*, 12–13.

11. Introduction, Special Issue, "Newcomers to Canada," *Food for Thought* (Canadian Association for Adult Education, Toronto) 13,4 (January 1953).

12. Alvin Finkel, *Our Lives: Canada after 1945* (Toronto 1997); Ruth Pierson, *"They're Still Women After All": The Second World War and Canadian Womanhood* (Toronto 1986); Magda Fahrni, *Household Politics: Montreal Families and Postwar Construction* (Toronto 2005); Jennifer Stephen, *Pick One Intelligent Girl: Employability, Domesticity and the Gendering of Canada's Welfare State, 1940s–1950s* (Toronto forthcoming).

13. J.G. Johnson, "Immigrant Meets Teacher," in Special Issue, "Newcomers to Canada," *Food for Thought* 13,4 (January 1953).

14. In this study I am adopting a broad definition of citizenship, one that considers the bodily, moral, sexual, psychological, and cultural as well as political and ideological features involved. Recent Canadian efforts to expand definitions of citizenship include Himani Bannerji, *The Dark Side of the Nation: Essays on Multiculturalism, Nationalism, and Gender* (Toronto 2000); Veronica Strong-Boag et al., eds., *Painting the Maple: Essays on Race, Gender and the Construction of Canada* (Vancouver 1998); and Robert Adamoski, Dorothy E. Chunn, and Robert Menzies, eds., *Contesting Citizenship: Historical Readings* (Toronto 2002). On moral regulation and nation-building, see, for example, Mariana Valverde, *The Age of Light, Soap and Water: Moral Reform in English Canada* (Toronto 1993); and essays by Nandita Sharma, Cynthia Wright, and others in Special Issue, "Whose Canada Is It?" *Atlantis* 24,2 (Spring 2000).

15. My discussion of contact zones and points of contact draws on the different but related approaches in these immigration, feminist, and post-colonial works: John Bodnar, *The Transplanted: A History of Immigrants in Urban America* (Bloomington, Ill. 1987); Linda Gordon, *Heroes of Their Own Lives: The Politics and History of Family Violence* (New York 1989); Mary Louise Pratt, *Imperial Eyes: Travel Writing and Transculturation* (New York 1992).

16. William J. Duiker, *Twentieth-Century World History*, 2nd ed. (Belmont, Cal. 2002), ch. 9; Reg Whitaker and Gary Marcuse, *Cold War Canada: The Making of a National Insecurity State, 1945–1957* (Toronto 1994), Pt. 1–2; Finkel, *Our Lives*, chs.1, 4.

17. Whitaker and Marcuse, *Cold War Canada*; Frank K. Clarke, "Debilitating Divisions: The Civil Liberties Movement in Early Cold War Canada, 1946–48," in Gary Kinsman, Dieter K. Buse, and Mercedes Steedman, eds., *Whose National Security? Canadian State Security and the Creation of Enemies* (Toronto 2000). On the subject of spies, newcomers, and women, see chapter 10 here.

18. The joint projects included constructing Arctic lines for monitoring the North, including the Distant Early Warning or Dew Line, created to screen incoming Soviet bombers, and, in 1957, NORAD, the North American Aerospace Defence Command.

19. Whitaker and Marcuse, *Cold War Canada*, Pt. 1–2; Whitaker, *Double Standard*; Finkel, *Our Lives*, chs.1, 4.

20. McCarthyism is "the paranoid identification of individuals as Communists and Soviet spies on the basis of irrelevant or unreliable information, and the creation of mass hysteria about Soviet infiltration." Finkel, *Our Lives*, 37.

21. On the United States, see, for example, Elaine Schrecker, *Many Are the Crimes: McCarthyism in America* (Boston 1998), chs.6 (Hoover) and 7 (McCarthy). On the Gouzenko affair, and the Royal Commission and spy trials that followed in its wake, see chapter 10 here, which deals with the draconian War Measures Act and civil rights abuses as well as the situation of the convicted women spies, Emma Woikin and Kathleen Willsher.

22. Whitaker and Marcuse, *Cold War Canada*; Len Scher, *The Un-Canadians: True Stories of the Blacklist Era* (Toronto 1992); Kinsman, Buse, and Steedman, eds., *Whose National Security?*; Irving Abella, *Nationalism, Communism and Canadian Labour: The CIO, the Communist Party and the Canadian Congress of Labour, 1935–1956* (Toronto 1973); Mercedes Steedman, Peter Suschnigg, and Dieter K. Buse, eds., *Hard Lessons: The Mine Mill Union in Canadian Labour* (Toronto 1995).

23. Geoffrey Smith, "Containments, 'Disease,' and Cold War Popular Culture," in Brian J.C. McKercher and Michael Hennessy, eds., *War in the Twentieth Century* (Westport, Conn. 2003), with thanks for the manuscript; and Geoffrey Smith, "National Security and Personal Isolation: Sex, Gender and Disease in the Cold-War United States," *International History Review* 14,2 (May 1992); and articles in Kinsman, Buse, and Steedman, eds., *Whose National Security?*

24. Gary Kinsman, "'Character Weaknesses' and 'Fruit Machines': Towards an Analysis of the Anti-Homosexual Security Campaign in the Canadian Civil Service," *Labour/Le Travail* 35 (Spring 1995); Gary Kinsman, *The Regulation of Desire: Homo and Hetero Sexualities*, 2nd ed. (Montreal 1996); David Kimmel and Daniel J. Robinson "The Queer Career of Homosexual

Security Vetting in Cold War Canada," *Canadian Historical Review* 75,3 (September 1994). For the flip side to such concerns, see Patrizia Gentile's humorous and illuminating treatment of civil service beauty contests in her "'Government Girls' and 'Ottawa Men': Cold War Management of Gender Relations in the Civil Service," in Kinsman, Buse, and Steedman, eds., *Whose National Security?*

Discussion of the disease metaphor, which became closely associated with U.S. policy-makers such as George Kennan and FBI Director J. Edgar Hoover, and became part of Western popular culture, appears in numerous studies, but for a few examples see all of the above, plus: Schrecker, *Many Are the Crimes*; Paul A. Chilton, *Security Metaphors: Cold War Discourse from Containment to Common House* (New York 1996); Whitaker and Marcuse, *Cold War Canada*; Kinsman, *Regulation of Desire*; Deborah Van Seters, "The Munsinger Affair: Images of Espionage and Security in 1960s Canada," *Intelligence and National Security* 13:2 (Summer 1998); Jennifer Terry, *An American Obsession: Science, Medicine and Homosexuality in Modern Society* (Chicago 1999) (on treasonous lesbians); Elaine Tyler May, *Homeward Bound: American Families in the Cold War Era* (New York 1988).

On "moral panic," see, for example, Sam Cohen, *Folk Devils and Moral Panics* (London 1972; Stuart Hall et al., *Policing the Crisis: Mugging, the State, and Law and Order* (London 1978); Jeffrey Weeks, *Sex, Politics and Society: The Regulation of Sexuality Since 1800* (London and New York 1981); Simon Watney, *Policing Desire: Pornography, Aids, and the Media* (Minneapolis 1989) (who uses the term media "excess"). As Kinsman observes in *Regulation of Desire*, the term moral panic "tends to get so over-used in the literature that it almost seems to be self-generating," and like him, I have tried to avoid using moral panic as "an explanation of a social process" and instead see it as "pointing towards an investigation of social relations," such as that between the media, the police, the courts, citizens' groups, professional experts, and state agencies, that need to be interrogated in a specific time and place because such relations "combine in different ways in different 'panics.'" See also chapter 7, note 55 here.

2   Press Narratives of Migration: From Scarcity and Red Slavery to Oranges and Humanity

1. Norman Phillips, *Toronto Star* 23 Aug. 1947; Marjorie Earl, "D.P. Baby Won't Drink Milk Had Not Tasted It Before," *Toronto Star* 18 Oct. 1947, 1; *Toronto Star* 18 Oct. 1947; "Toronto Poles Give Rousing Welcome to Fliers and Sailors Who Fled Red Tyranny," *Toronto Star* 15 Sept. 1951.

2. This discussion draws on several sources, including David Mackenzie, *Arthur Irwin: A Biography* (Toronto 1993); Fraser Sutherland, *The Monthly Epic: A History of Canadian Magazines 1789–1989* (Toronto 1989). On *Chatelaine*, see Valerie Korinek, "'It's a Tough Time to Be in Love': The Darker Side of *Chatelaine* during the Cold War," in Richard Cavell, ed., *Love, Hate, and Fear in Canada's Cold War* (Toronto 2004).

3. Regarding *Saturday Night*, see, for example, B.K. Sandwell, "It's Easy for Officials," 26 April 1952; Pauline Shapiro, "The Better Sort of Emigrants and Refugees,"17 May 1941; W.G. Friedmann, "Our Growing Immigration Is Everyone's Business," 16 Feb. 1952. Regarding the *Financial Post*, see Peter C. Newman, "Are We Doing Enough? 2 Aug. 1952; Ronald Williams, "How to Keep Red Hands off Our New Canadians: Commie Hucksters Haven't a Chance with DP's in Town's Crusade for Democracy," 3 Dec.1949.

4. See, for example, in *The Canadian Unionist*: Donald MacDonald, "Canadian Labour and Immigration," December 1953; MacDonald. "Congress Policy on Immigration," July-August 1955; G.J. Goedhart van Heuven, "Refugee Problem Concerns Everybody," October 1955. Also "No Need for the Displaced to Displace Canadians," *Trades and Labour Congress Journal*, March 1948; and G.B. Milling, "Immigrant Meets the Union," *Food for Thought* 13,4

(January 1953). On labour's Cold War, see Whitaker and Marcuse, *Cold War Canada*, chs.14, 15; Steedman, Suschnigg, and Buse, eds., *Hard Lessons*.

5. This was the case of those whom *Maclean's* editor Arthur Irwin helped to train, including Eva-Lis Wuorio, June Callwood, Ralph Allen, Sidney Katz, and others whose articles appear in this and later chapters. Mackenzie, *Arthur Irwin*.

6. See, for example, Galina Mikhailovna Ivanova, *Labor Camp Socialism: The Gulag in the Soviet Totalitarian System* (Armonk, N.Y. and London 2000). Thanks to Lynne Viola for directing me to several sources, including this one, which can be read against Alexander Solzhenitsyn, *The Gulag Archipelago 1918–1956* (London 1973). See also Helene Celmins, *Women in Soviet Prisons* (New York 1985).

7. That is, we need to be careful not to assume that these journalist writings are completely unmediated texts that provide the one truth, an entirely objective and wholly accurate version of everything and everyone they describe, and to be attentive to what is said and not said, what is emphasized and what is underplayed. In a number of my other writings, for instance, I discuss the simplistic materialist vs. postmodern debates and the trap of assuming that all gender-minded historians are a homogeneous group of postmodernists when they are not. I also suggest ways in which, in particular, socialist feminists (who have long been sensitive to matters, such as language, that are seemingly less rooted in the material) can integrate useful poststructuralist insights about the discursive nature of historical evidence into material feminist frameworks. See Iacovetta, "Postmodern Ethnography, Historical Materialism, and Decentring the (Male) Authorial Voice: A Feminist Conversation, *Histoire Sociale/Social History* 32,64 (November 1999), 275–93; Iacovetta, "Gossip, Contest, and Power in the Making of Suburban Bad Girls: Toronto, 1945–60," *Canadian Historical Review* 80,4 (December 1999); Iacovetta, "Gendering Trans/National Historiographies: Feminists Rewriting Canadian History," *Journal of Women's History* 18,1

(Spring 2006); and Iacovetta, "The Personal, Political, and Intellectual in Left Feminist History," *Left History* 11,1 (Spring 2006).

8. "Happy in Canada, War Bride Wins Beauty Prize," and "Twin War Brides Give Up, Say Peterborough Too Dull," *Toronto Star* 19 Oct. 1946. See the oral histories and stories collected in Estella Spergel (herself a former war bride), "British War Brides, World War II: A Unique Experiment for Unique Immigrants – The Process That Brought Them to Canada," M.A. research paper, Department of History, University of Toronto, 1997; Joan Baird, "British War Brides," script of a Canadian Broadcasting Corporation broadcast, Halifax, 25 Oct. 1944 (Canadian Red Cross Publications); "Blighty Brides Are Overjoyed by Shoes, Food," *Toronto Star* 20 Nov. 1944; CRC, Ontario Division, *News Bulletin*, special issue on British war brides, September 1946. See also "Salute to Canadian Women," *Globe and Mail*, editorial page, 19 Aug. 1944; Joyce Hibbert, ed., *The War Brides* (Toronto 1978); Cherly A. Butler, "Janey Canuck: The Experiences of World War II British War Brides Who Emigrated to Canada," M.A. thesis, OISE, University of Toronto, 1995. Thanks to Frances Swyripa for sharing the CRC materials with me.

9. Ivan Lavery, "Left Homeless by Floods, First Dutch on Way Here," *Toronto Star* 28 Feb. 1953; "Good Land, Say Dutchmen 'But Toil Too Much Sunday,'" *Toronto Star* 17 July 1948. See also "Immigrant Train Brings 600 More Dutch Folk to Till Our Land," *Toronto Star* 28 May 1951; "Dutch Immigrants Arrive to Begin New Life in Canada," *Toronto Star* 15 April 1950. See also Avery, *Reluctant Host*.

10. "Separated 11 and 14 Years, 2 Greek Families Reunited," *Toronto Star*, 5 July 1947.

11. See Whitaker, *Double Standard*, 69–73.

12. Avery, *Reluctant Host*, ch. 7 (which also discusses German scientists); Whitaker, *Double Standard*, 69–73.

13. Ralph Allen, "The Untroublesome Canadians," *Maclean's* 7 March 1964; Allan Fenton, "Immigrants Ease Tradesmen Shortage," *Toronto Star*, 9 Feb. 1952.

14. See also chapter 5, p. 115, and note 33.

15. Allen, "Untroublesome Canadians."

16. See, for examples, Dorothy Fraser, "Immigration" (Portuguese), *Saturday Night* 7 Jan. 1964; Iacovetta, *Such Hardworking People*.

17. "Won't Hinder Them – Eire 402 Load Irish Food for Trip to Canada," *Toronto Star* 1 Oct. 1947. See also "Baltic Refugees Drink St. Lawrence River Valley Like Pop," *Toronto Star* 12 Aug. 1950.

18. "Rescue Vessels Speed to 81 in Battered Ships," *Globe and Mail* 20 Aug. 1949; "Refugees Rush Swamps, Halifax Increases Staff," *Toronto Star* 20 Aug. 1949, 1; "Refugee Vessel Taken in Tow by Coast Guard," *Globe and Mail* 22 Aug. 1949; "Happy Estonians Welcomed to Kitchener after Hazardous Atlantic Crossing in Tiny Crowded Boat," *Toronto Star* 17 Jan. 1948; "Home in Canada Last Hope of Estonians U.S. Barred," *Toronto Star* 4 Dec. 1948.

19. "Refugee Immigrants, editorial, *Toronto Star* 7 Aug. 1948; "Alone, Penniless, Wife of Estonian Refugee Has Baby without Aid," *Toronto Star* 8 Jan. 1949, 3. See also *Toronto Star* 4 Dec. 1948, 31 Jan. 1949.

20. Whitaker, *Double Standard*, 78–79; Margolian, *Unauthorized Entry*, ch. 6.

21. Editorial, "Could It Be Prejudice?" *Toronto Star* 7 Feb. 1948; "Aliens Seized in Toronto on Illegal Count Lose Deportation Plea," *Globe and Mail* 5 Feb. 1948 See also Whitaker, *Double Standard*; Abella and Troper, *None Is Too Many*, 201–44.

22. Earl, "D.P. Baby Won't Drink Milk," *Toronto Star* 18 Oct. 1947.

23. Given the restrictions that Immigration officials imposed on recruiting Jews – for instance, issuing quiet bureaucratic orders to selection teams to keep Jewish recruits to a minimum and requiring Jewish-sponsored programs providing jobs for Jews in the Canadian clothing industry to a 50 per cent Jewish/non-Jewish quota – these workers most likely included both Jewish and gentile Europeans. Abella and Troper, *None Is Too Many*, 244.

24. Eva-Lis Wuorio, "We Can't Go Back," *Maclean's* 1 June 1948.

25. Eksteins, *Walking Since Daybreak*, 154–56; Wyman, DP, 41–46.

26. Wuorio, "We Can't Go Back."

27. Following the First World War the victorious Allies carved out new nation-states, including Estonia, Latvia and Lithuania, and Poland. In 1940–41 the Russians swept into the Baltic region and other parts of Eastern Europe to claim their part of the territorial reward of the Nazi-Soviet non-aggression pact (according to which each side agreed not to act as an aggressor against the other). In 1941 Hitler defied the pact and invaded the region. For more details, see, for example, Eksteins, *Walking Since Daybreak*; Peter Gay and R.K. Webb, *History of Modern Europe* (New York 1973); and, with reference to refugees who came to Canada, Abella and Troper, *None Is Too Many*; Avery, *Reluctant Host*; Whitaker, *Double Standard*; and Milda Danys, DP: *Lithuanian Immigration to Canada after the Second World War* (Toronto 1986).

28. On the Baltic DPs and establishing the university, which UNRRA officials later demoted to a "DP University Study Centre," see Wyman, DP, 125–27.

29. Tulchinsky, *Branching Out*, especially ch. 10. It would be years before many survivors could tell even their own children their stories, but some of them, upon reaching an elderly age, agreed to taped and videotaped interviews not only to assist historians but also to create a living document to pass on to following generations. See, for example, Paula Draper, "Surviving Their Survival: Women, Memory and the Holocaust," in Marlene Epp, Franca Iacovetta, and Frances Swyripa, eds., *Sisters or Strangers? Immigrant, Ethnic and Racialized Women in Canadian History* (Toronto 2003).

30. "Oust D.P.'s, Admit Vichy Men 'Revolting,' Declares Rabbi," *Toronto Star* 16 Oct. 1948, 3; Robert Taylor, "Decision to Admit 4 Men Said Purely Political One," *Toronto Star* 16 Oct. 1948, 41; A.O.C. Cole, "Canada Haven Like U.K. for Political Refugees, Gardiner Tells House," *Toronto Star* 10 Dec. 1949, 3. For one of the very few articles dealing with Nazi escapes, see Samuel Campbell, "Dug Grave, Faced Guns, Now Toronto Resident," *Toronto Star* 19 April 1955; "Saw Polish Blood Flow in Streets, Refugee Here," *Toronto Star* 11 Sept. 1948.

31. "Civic Reception for 22 Escapers from Red Control," *Globe and Mail* 13 Sept. 1951.

32. "Tunnelled 3 ½ Months Escaping Soviet Mine to Make Canada Home," *Toronto Star* 6 Oct. 1951, 3.

33. "Risked Sea to Flee Tito, Finds Refuge in Canada," *Toronto Star* 17 Aug. 1957, 2; "Kin Slain, Fled Russians, 18, Refused Canada Entry," *Toronto Star* 27 May 1950; "Roams Sea without Home, Canada Has a Heart," *Toronto Star* 3 June 1950.

34. "Outwitted Soviet Police, Waded Mountain Snows, Czech Girl in Winnipeg," *Toronto Star* 23 Sept. 1950, 1.

35. Robert L. Griswold, "Russian Blonde in Space: Americans View the Soviet Woman in the Early Cold War." My thanks to the author for the paper.

36. "Report US Relenting to Let Lovers on Boat Meet Briefly Ashore," and "Spend Yule by Fire, Is Hope of Lovers on Maid of Mist," *Toronto Star* 1 Oct. 1949; Dorothy Howarth, "Maid of Mist Lovers Conquer Border Ban," *Toronto Telegram* 22 Sept. 1950, 1 (with photo of the couple). See also Robert Taylor, "Canada Can Do Nothing to Unite Niagara Lovers," *Toronto Star* 1 Oct. 1949. On other Czechs, specifically diplomats, see Austin Cross, "They Chose Canada!" *Canadian Business* 21 (July 1950).

37. By that time they would have met Canadian criteria that required former citizens of Communist states to spend two years living in an acceptable Western country before being eligible for entry into Canada.

38. June Callwood, as told by Peter Keresztes, "We Are Hiding from Bad Men in the Forest," *Maclean's* 15 Nov. 1957.

39. Whitaker, *Double Standard*, ch. 4. See also "Berlin Refugees Need Screening, Harris Warns, *Toronto Star* 7 March 1953, 21; C.F. Bosworth, "What's Behind the Immigration Wrangle?" *Maclean's* 14 May 1955.

40. Michael Barkway, "We Can Still 'Save Face' with Our Refugee Policy," and "The Human

Side," *Financial Post* 29 Dec. 1956; Barkway, "Is Canada Botching the Refugee Job? *Financial Post*, 22 Dec. 1956; Barkway, "Are We Botching Biggest Immigration?" *Financial Post* 30 March 1957. See also Leslie Wilson, "Universities Step Up First with Refugee Help Offers," *Financial Post* 29 Dec. 1956; Peter C. Newman, "The Hungarians" (part of "a special *Maclean's* album: What They Mean to Canada"), *Maclean's* 16 Feb. 1957.

41. " 'Operation Friendship' Aids New Arrivals," *Toronto Star* 15 June 1957.

42. "First Hungarian Student Enrols at St. Michael's," *Canadian Register* 16 Feb. 1957; Douglas Blanchard, "Hungarians Find Canada Offers Freedom, Happiness – and Work," *Toronto Star* 3 Jan. 1959.

43. George Bryant, "From Tito Jail by Star Writer's Visit, Returning Family Sure," *Toronto Star* 31 March 1957; Whitaker, *Double Standard*, ch. 4.

44. Drawing on such scholars as Roland Barthes, Pierre Bourdieu, John Fiske, and Michel Foucault, cultural and feminist historians have explored the "polysemic" nature of popular texts such as women's magazines and stressed the readers' active role in creating the "multiple meanings" produced in such texts. See, for example, Lawrence Grossberg, Cary Nelson, and Paula Treichler, eds., *Cultural Studies* (London 1992); Valerie Korinek, *Roughing It in the Suburbs: Reading Chatelaine Magazine in the Fifties and Sixties* (Toronto 2000); and Joanne Meyerowitz, "Beyond the Feminine Mystique: A Reassessment of Postwar Mass Culture," in Meyerowitz, ed., *Not June Cleaver: Women and Gender in Postwar America, 1945–1960* (Philadelphia 1994).

3   Defining the Agenda: Professional Discourses of Integration and Citizenship

1. A small sample of the theoretical and empirical studies of citizenship, especially regarding cultural pluralism, gender and the welfare state, and moral regulation, includes Adamoski, Chunn, and Menzies, eds., *Contesting Canadian Citizenship* (Toronto 2002); Bannerji, *Dark Side of the Nation*; Shirley Tillotson, *The Public at Play: Gender and the Politics of Recreation in Post-War Ontario* (Toronto 2000); Will Kymlicka, *Multicultural Citizenship: A Liberal Theory of Minority Rights* (Oxford 2001); Charles Taylor, *Reconciling the Solitudes: Essays on Canadian Federalism and Nationalism* (Montreal and Kingston 1993); Nancy Fraser and Linda Gordon, "Civil Citizenship against Social Citizenship," in Bart von Steenbergen, ed., *The Condition of Citizenship* (Thousand Oaks, Cal. 1993); Linda Gordon, *Pitied but Not Entitled: Single Mothers and the History of Welfare, 1890–1935* (New York 1994); Jane Jenson and Susan Phillips, "Regime Shift: New Citizenship Practices in Canada," *International Journal of Canadian Studies* 14 (Fall 1996); William Kaplan, ed., *Belonging: The Meaning and Future of Citizenship* (Montreal and Kingston, 1993).

2. The term is a play on the phrase "women adrift," which reformers applied to single working women considered to be highly vulnerable to the industrial city's many dangers. See, for example, Joanne J. Meyerowitz, *Women Adrift: Independent Wage Earners in Chicago, 1880–1930* (Chicago 1988); and Carolyn Strange, *Toronto's Girl Problem: The Perils and Pleasures of the City, 1880–1930* (Toronto 1995). My thanks to former graduate student Martha Ophir, who coined the term "immigrant adrift" in a research paper on postwar immigration.

3. Nicholas Zay, "Adaptation of the Immigrant," address to the Canadian Association of Social Workers, *Canadian Welfare* 28 (2 Jan. 1953), 25–29. Hungarian-born Zay studied in Paris and Budapest, obtaining his doctorate in law in 1947. He came to Canada in 1951, worked as an interpreter for an agency in Montreal, and, at the time of this article, was completing a master's degree in social work at the University of Montreal.

4. Archives of Ontario (AO), International Institute of Metropolitan Toronto (IIMT), MU6442, Kay Alderson, "Report on English Classes at the Institute," *The Intercom* September 1963, 3–4; Library and Archives Canada (LAC), RG26, Vol. 12, File: The New Canadians, Joseph Kage,

JIAS [Jewish Immigrant Aid Society], "Social Service for New Immigrants," 20 Aug. 1948.

5. Joseph Kage, "Immigration and Social Service," *Canadian Welfare* 24,3 (January 1949), 3–8.

6. Cited in Sidney Katz, "How Mental Health Is Attacking Our Immigrants," *Maclean's* 4 Jan. 1958.

7. G.P. Allen, "Helping Immigrants Belong," *Canadian Welfare* 15 May 1961, 112; AO, IIMT, Records, MU6326, personnel files, file on Nell West, newspaper clippings; West cited in Ralph Hyman, "They Oil the Hinges of Integration's Door," *Globe Magazine* 20 Feb. 1960.

8. For example, see Samuel Edwards, "Insights of Domesticity," Kapos, "Newcomer and the Community," and Frazer Earl, "The Making of Citizens," all in *Food For Thought*, special issue, "Newcomers to Canada," January 1953; Mary Starr, "If You Take My Advice" columns in *Toronto Star* (for example, 22 May 1954); Dorothy Lash, "New Horizons" columns in *Toronto Star* (for example, 14 June 1958); Anne L. Fitzpatrick, "Volunteers, A Source of Strength," *Canadian Welfare* 30,3–4 (September 1954); Frieda Held, "Social Workers and Volunteers as Partners," *Canadian Welfare* 15,1 (September 1946); "Parish Will Have 'Charity Week' to Aid Immigrants through Difficult Days," *Canadian Register* 26 Jan. 1952; "Chest Campaign Opens October 21," *Canadian Register* 12 Oct. 1946; "Red Feather Funds," *Toronto Star* 21 Oct. 1950; Peter Newman, "Are We Doing Enough? *Financial Post* 2 Aug. 1952; J.E. Parsons, "Christmas with My New Canadians," *Saturday Night* 24 Dec. 1960; City of Toronto Archives (CTA), Social Planning Council (SPC), Vol. 40, Box 6, File 17, I, M, E, G – Conference on Services for Immigrants, 1952–53.

9. Cited in Katz, "How Mental Health Is Attacking Our Immigrants."

10. Isabel M. Jordan (Canadian Association for Adult Education), "Canada – Land of Promises?" *Food for Thought* January 1953. Some scholars have described these tensions in terms of the dilemmas of "social citizenship," which straddles older notions of individual rights and responsibilities to the state and expanded citizen social entitlements in post-1945 welfare capitalist societies. See Adamoski, Chunn, and Menzies, eds., "Introduction," *Contesting Canadian Citizenship*, and the references on citizenship here, chapter 3, note 1.

11. Kage, "Immigration and Social Service," 3–8.

12. For example, LAC, MG 31 D69, Vol. 11, 1954, "Methods of Marxist Propaganda among Ethnic Groups in Canada," confidential meeting, 30 March 1954, Toronto; LAC, MG 28, I 17, File: IODE, "A Primer on Democracy" (nd); File: Anti-Communist Activities, 1949; Marjorie Lamb, "Communism in Canada," February 1957. See also Whitaker and Marcuse, *Cold War Canada*, 121–23.

13. LAC, RG26, Vol. 140, File 3-38-19, J. R. [Roby] Kidd, Executive Director, Canadian Citizenship Council, address on "Assimilation of New Canadians and What the Municipalities Can Do," 15th Annual Conference, Canadian Federation of Mayors and Municipalities, 2 July 1952, Calgary, Alta.

14. Rabbi Abraham Feinberg, "Soaring Food Prices Menace to Democracy's Prestige," *Toronto Star* January 1948; "Women Protest Lack of Subsidized Houses" (on National Council of Women), *Toronto Star* 24 Dec. 1948; *Toronto Star* editorials, 11 June 1949, 28 June 1950; Charles Herbert Huestis: "The World Is Very Sick," *Toronto Star* 16 April 49, 6; Whitaker, *Double Standard*, 150–98; Julie Guard, "Women Worth Watching: Radical Housewives in Cold War Canada," in Kinsman, Buse, and Steedman, eds., *Whose National Security?*; "Canadian Citizens or Dangerous Foreign Women? Canada's Radical Consumer Movement, 1947–1950," in Epp, Iacovetta, and Swyripa, eds., *Sisters or Strangers?*; and Joy Parr, *Domestic Goods: The Material, the Moral, and the Economic in the Postwar Years* (Toronto 1999). For the United States: Deborah A. Gerson, "Is Family Devotion Now Subversive? Familialism against McCarthyism," in Meyerowitz, ed., *Not June Cleaver*, and other essays in that collection.

15. Rev. Stanley Russell, "A Clergyman Looks at the World" columns, *Toronto Star*: "Must Offer Better World to Stop Communism Trend,"

9 April 1949; "Unemployment Helps Communism," 11 March 1950; "Claims 'Murky' Beer Rooms Cause Immorality," 6 Nov. 1948; "Describes Kinsey Report 'Portentously Ridiculous,'" 3 July 1948; "Society Is Badly Diseased, Cure It or Nation Is Lost," 28 Feb. 1948. See also Rabbi Feinberg, "Rabbi Mourns Dr. Russell, Sees Community Poorer," *Toronto Star* 21 June 1957. The article "Dr. G. Stanley Russell Preacher, Writer, 74 Dies," *Toronto Star* 21 June 1957, praises Russell's fight against anti-Semitism and other forms of racism. Russell argued that while organizations such as NATO could provide a military defence against spreading Communism, the only effective way to disarm a Communist was to place the person in the midst of a contented, united, and progressive people, and to eliminate all sources for grievance. A conservative moralist, Russel was old-fashioned but not anachronistic.

16. For example, LAC, MG 28 I 17, Vol. 26, File 1-24-1, Pt.1, includes reports on the Immigration and Citizenship Committee, proposals for raising standards of citizenship and for certificates, 1940s and 1950s. On moral "uplift," immigration and/or nation-building, see, for example, Valverde, *Age of Light, Soap and Water*; Nira Yuval-Davis, *Gender and Nation* (London 1987); Ruth Roach Pierson and Nupur Chaudhuri, eds., *Nation, Empire, Colony: Historicizing Gender and Race* (Bloomington, Ill. 1998); Adele Perry, *On the Edge of Empire: Gender, Race and the Making of British Columbia* (Toronto 2001); and essays in Epp, Iacovetta, and Swyripa, *Sisters or Strangers?*

17. For example, see LAC, MG 31 D69, Vol. 11, File: Kaye, Department of Citizenship and Immigration, Liaison Officer, Report of Liaison Work (1952), 4 July 1952, Report.

18. V.J. Kaye, "Like Seeks Like," *Food for Thought* January 1953, 23–25.

19. In an address to the International Catholic Migration Congress, Mulvihill declared that church-based reception activity should never use "coercion to unduly hasten this process of integration" but "morally and psychologically sound programming." Zay asserted that "the sympathetic atmosphere" increased the rate of adaptation to Canadian life. *Canadian Register* 10 Sept. 1960; Zay, "Adaptation of the Immigrant."

20. Allen, "Helping Immigrants Belong."

21. Twain quotation cited in Toronto Nutrition Committee, *Food Customs of New Canadians*, booklet, AO, IIMT, MU6410, File: Cookbook Project; Katz, "How Mental Health Is Attacking Our Immigrants."

22. Antonio Gramsci, *Letters from Prison* (New York 1973); Michel Foucault, *Discipline and Punishment: The Birth of the Prison* (London 1977); Foucault, *History of Sexuality*, Vol. 1 (New York 1978); Philip Corrigan and Derek Sayer, *The Great Arch: English State Formation as Cultural Revolution* (Oxford 1985); Nicholas Rose, *Governing the Soul*; Mariana Valverde, ed., *Studies in Moral Regulation* (Toronto 1994).

23. LAC, RG26, Vol. 84, File 1-24-107, Pt.2, report on the Minaki Conference, "Social and Cultural Integration of Newcomers," sponsored by the CWC, address by Joseph Kage, Executive Director of JIAS, to the Committee on the Welfare of Immigrants, *Canadian Welfare* Council, 15 Oct. 1958.

24. Eventually, the newcomer bought tickets for the union's Christmas party, and then began attending union meetings. Gilbert concluded his story by reiterating the labour movement's position on postwar immigration, that it be planned and regulated. G.B. Milling, "Immigrant Meets the Union," *Food for Thought* January 1953.

25. Allen, "Helping Immigrants Belong," 112.

26. The literature on left-wing social workers is slim, but for useful information on Wilensky, Livesay, Tousel, and Gorrie, see Gale Wills, *A Marriage of Convenience: Business and Social Work in Toronto, 1918–1957* (Toronto 1995); James Struthers, *The Limits of Affluence: Welfare in Ontario, 1920–1970* (Toronto 1994); Ken Moffatt, *A Poetics of Social Work: Personal Agency and Social Transformation in Canada, 1920–1939* (Toronto 2001); Allan Irving, Harriet Parsons, and Donald Bellamy, eds., *Neighbours: Three Social Settlements in Downtown Toronto* (Toronto 1995), ch. 13;

Gerald Tulchinsky, "Joe Salsberg: Towards a Biography," paper presented to the Canadian Historical Association, Winnipeg, 2004.

27. Ben Carniol, *Case Critical: Challenging Social Services in Canada*, 5th ed. (Toronto 2005).

28. LAC, RG26, Vol. 84, File 1-24-107, Pt.2, R. Alex Sim, "The Concept of Integration in Canada's Treatment of Ethnic Groups," National Citizenship Seminar, Minaki, Ont., 24–28 Aug. 1958. One of his more curious points was that policies of segregation and brutal repression, such as practised by the Nazi regime, created unfortunate heroes and artists like Anne Frank, who produced great literature under duress, as well as religious zealots whose "genuine need for spiritual fervour" took on "exaggerated forms" thereby "spill[ing] over into high emotionalism with a rapid budding of radical sects."

29. Immigration historians see folklorization as one of several processes involved in the social construction of ethnicity. See Kathleen Neils Conzen et al., "The Invention of Ethnicity: A Perspective from the USA," *Journal of American Ethnic History* 12 (Fall 1992).

30. Sim, "Concept of Integration."

31. National Film Board (NFB) Archives, Montreal, Production Files, Canadian Notebook, File 51–214, "The Citizen as an Individual," text of a film adaption of the pamphlet. For other examples, see AO, YWCA Collection, MU3527, Box 11, Annual Reports, Toronto Branch, 1874–1955 (especially on teaching DP domestics about democracy); CTA, SCP, Vol. 5D, Box 1.

32. LAC, RG26, Vol. 140, File 3-38-19, J.R. Kidd, Executive Director, Canadian Citizenship Council, "Assimilation of New Canadians and What the Municipalities Can Do."

33. Franca Iacovetta, "Making Model Citizens: Gender, Corrupted Democracy, and Immigrant Reception Work in Cold War Canada," in Buse, Kinsman, and Steedman, eds., *Whose National Security?* 154–67; Cavell, ed., *Love, Hate and Fear in Canada's Cold War*; Whitaker and Marcuse, *Cold War Canada*.

34. See, for example, Whitaker and Marcuse's discussion of labour's cold war in *Cold War Canada*, chs.14–15.

35. Few gatekeepers recognized their own paranoia. Kirkconnell, for example, warned, "Fluoridation is a Communist plot to make Canadian brains susceptible to domination." Quoted in Whitaker and Marcuse, *Cold War Canada*, 279. See also Cavell, "Introduction," *Love, Hate and Fear in Canada's Cold War*.

36. Sim, "Concept of Integration"; Allen, "Helping Immigrants Belong."

37. LAC, MG31D69, Vol. 11, File: Kaye, Dept of Citizenship, Liaison Office, Report of Liaison Work (1952), 4 July 1952.

38. Ibid.

39. AO, MU6390, J. Gellner to C. Bourquet, 19 Oct. 1973, File: Board of Directors, Executive Minutes.

40. LAC, MG31D69, Vol. 11, File: Kaye, Dept of Citizenship, Liaison Office, Report of Liaison Work (1952), 4 July 1952.

41. John Graham, "A History of the Toronto School of Social Work," Ph.D. thesis, University of Toronto 1995; Struthers, *Limits of Affluence*; Mona Gleason, *Normalizing the Ideal: Psychology, Schooling, and the Family in Postwar Canada* (Toronto 1999).

42. Michel Foucault, *Knowledge/Power* (London 1980). See also Amitai Etzioni, ed., *The Semi-Professions and Their Organizations: Teachers, Nurses, Social Workers* (New York 1969). For just a small sample of the now extensive historical literature on professions and professionalization, see the essays in Franca Iacovetta and Wendy Mitchinson, eds., *On the Case: Explorations in Social History* (Toronto 1998).

43. The literature on social welfare and professionalization of social work in North America is vast, but valuable works include Regina Kunzel, *Fallen Women, Problem Girls: The Unmarried Mothers and the Professionalization of Social Work* (New Haven, Conn. 1993); Kunzel, "Pulp Fictions and Problem Girls: Reading and Rewriting Single Pregnancy in the Postwar United States," *American Historical Review* 100 (December 1995); Struthers, *Limits of Affluence*; Graham, "History of the Toronto School of Social Work"; James Leiby, *A History of Social Welfare and Social Work in the United*

States (New York 1987); and Linda Gordon, ed., *Women, the State, and Welfare* (Madison, Wis. 1990).

44. Graham "History of the Toronto School of Social Work." Many of Toronto's social workers were Anglo-Celtic Canadians, a feature reflecting the Protestant origins of English-Canadian social reform work, but the topic of Catholic and Jewish social welfare work deserves more attention. The notion of localized power is usually attributed to Foucault, but the principle is also congruent with Marxist, socialist, and feminist theories of the dynamics of power.

45. The study, led by social worker Roberta M. Bruce at the Montreal Mental Hygiene Institute, is cited in various studies, including Gleason, *Normalizing the Ideal*, ch. 4, and Mary Louise Adams, *The Trouble with Normal: Postwar Youth and the Making of Heterosexuality* (Toronto 1997).

46. Steven Maynard, "On the Case of the Case: The Emergence of the Homosexual as a Case History in Early-Twentieth-Century Ontario," and Carolyn Strange, "Stories of Their Lives: The Historian and the Capital Case Files," both in Iacovetta and Mitchinson, eds., *On the Case*; Jennifer Stephen, "The 'Incorrigible,' the 'Bad,' and the 'Immoral': Toronto's 'Factory Girls' and the Work of the Toronto Psychiatric Clinic," in Louis A. Knafla and Susan W.S. Binnie, eds., *Law, Society, and the State: Essays in Modern Legal History* (Toronto 1995); Elizabeth Muir White, "Expert Witness Discourse: C.K. Clarke, and the Rise of the Psychiatric 'Expert' in Canada, 1880–1920," M.A. research paper, Centre of Criminology, University of Toronto, 1996; Mariana Valverde, "Social Facticity and the Law: A Social Expert's Eyewitness Account of Law," *Social and Legal Studies* 5,2 (1996); Stephen, *Pick One Intelligent Girl*.

47. The 1970s to 1990s have seen a return to organic and biochemical paradigms, in which heredity and brain biology are considered key factors, particularly in neurological diagnoses. ECT is electro-convulsive therapy. Post-1945 Canadian psychiatry is sorely in need of historians, but if one reads past the editor's swipes at

Marxist historians, Edward Shorter, ed., *TPH History and Memories of the Toronto Psychiatry Hospital, 1925–1966* (Toronto 1996), is a useful starting point. See also the postwar studies, including on CIA brainwashing experiments at the Memorial Institute, in Geoffrey Reaume, *A Classified Bibliography on the History of Psychiatry and Mental Health Services in Canada* (Toronto 1998). My thanks to Alison Kirk-Montgomery for helping to clarify the postwar psychiatric scene, and Mona Gleason for her references to the large number of lobotomies performed on women.

48. On the nickname and other biographical details, see "John Griffin Gave Human Face to Psychiatry," Obituaries, *Globe and Mail*, 25 July 2001. My thanks to Cynthia Wright for the reference. See also Gleason, *Normalizing the Ideal*.

49. J.D. Griffin, M.D., "The Problem of Mental Health in Canada," *Social Worker* 15,1 (September 1946), 3–10. The description reflects the more psychologically and socially oriented approach; he also stressed the growing number of mentally disabled people who escape detection. See also Terry Copp and Bill McAndrew, *Battle Exhaustion: Soldiers and Psychiatrists in the Canadian Army, 1939–1945* (Montreal and Kingston 1990); Gleason, *Normalizing the Ideal*; and Iacovetta, "Gossip, Contest and Power."

50. Contemporary examples include: Griffin, "Problem of Mental Health in Canada"; Margaret M. Burns, M.S., "The Allan Memorial Institute of Psychiatry," *Social Worker* 15,2 (December 1946); Dr. R.R. Prosser, "The Community Psychiatric Clinic and the Social Worker," *Social Worker* 19,4 (April 1951); LAC, RG26, Vol. 80, File 1-19-5, Pt.2 (Psychiatry) Director, Citizenship Branch to Deputy Minister of Immigration and Citizenship, Re World Conference on Mental Health, Uprooting and Resettlement, 16 June 1958; File 1-19-5, Pt.1, Dr Ewen Cameron, MD, to Chairman of Department of Psychiatry, Allan Memorial Institute, McGill University, to Mr. Laval Fortier, OBE, QC, Deputy Minister of Immigration, Ottawa, 16 Jan. 1953. The secondary literature includes Dorothy Chunn, *From Punishment to Doing*

Good: Family Courts and Socialized Justice in Ontario, 1880–1940 (Toronto 1992); Iacovetta, "Gossip, Contest and Power"; Gleason, *Normalizing the Ideal*; Terry, *American Obsession*; Shorter, ed., *TPH*.

51. Joseph Kage, "The Jewish Immigrant Aid Society of Canada," *Social Worker* 18 (3 Feb. 1950). In light of the large numbers involved, Kage, like others, called for more centralized supervision of all of this casework, so that front-line workers as well as agency administrators could co-ordinate efforts, exchange knowledge and experience, and thus increase the efficiency and efficacy of casework methods for producing "a more wholesome and smoother adjustment of the immigrant" while at the same time preventing an unnecessary reproduction of services and thus financial strain on existing agencies and community funds.

52. Dr. Cameron's opening remarks, as chair of the Canadian Mental Health Association, and other discussion, cited in LAC, RG26, Vol. 80, File 1-19-5, Pt.1 (Psychiatry), Minutes, Meeting of Scientific Planning Committee of CMHA, Toronto, 14–15 Feb. 1953. The discussion of the shortage of psychiatric nurses noted that fully qualified registered nurses were reluctant to accept posts in mental hospitals, and discussed the success of a pilot project involving teachers with Dr. Griffin as chief CMHA liaison officer. With a small grant from the Carnegie Corporation, a group of teachers took a training course in a Toronto school and were later assessed by another CMHA liaison officer, whose barometer of success included how none of the thirty-five teachers involved had set themselves up as "a specialist, a psychologist, or a mental hygienist," but rather continued to be front-line teachers, and how all of the teachers surveyed reported that they had been "greatly stimulated" by the course and wanted "greater amplification in all subjects," and how other teachers were expressing an interest in these training sessions. On CIA brainwashing experiments, see Anne Collins, *In the Sleep Room: The Story of the CIA Brainwashing Experiments in Canada* (Toronto 1988).

53. LAC, RG26, Vol. 80, File 1-19-5, Pt. 2, Director of Citizenship Branch to Deputy Minister of Immigration and Citizenship, Re World Conference on Mental Health, 4 June 1958, 16 June 1958; and Minutes of Meeting of Scientific Planning Committee, CMHA, Toronto, 14-15 Feb. 1953, plus attached reports and appendices.

54. LAC, RG26, Vol. 80, File 1-19, Pt.1 (Psychiatry), Minutes of Meeting, SPC, CMHA, 14-15 Feb. 1953, especially attached reports: Dinner Speeches, Pratt, Hendry (who also showed films on preventive mental health care in the schools) York Club, Toronto. See also "The Waves of Immigration," editorial, *Toronto Star* 7 May 1949, which discusses how the newcomers' "emotional and mental upset" have "strained employers' patience."

55. Benjamin Schlesinger, "Socio-Cultural Elements in Casework – The Canadian Scene," *Social Worker* 30 (1 Jan. 1962). The sources cited, in order of appearance, included: Katherine Newkirk Handley, "Social Casework and Intercultural Problems," in Family Service Association of America, *New Emphasis on Cultural Factors*, papers reprinted from *Journal of Social Casework*, 1946–48; Council on Social Work Education, *Socio-Cultural Elements in Casework: A Case Book of Seven Ethnic Case Studies* (New York 1955); E.B. Taylor, *Primitive Culture* (London 1885); Frank, "Psycho-Cultural Approach," *Intercultural Education News* June 1946.

56. David Weiss, Executive Director, Montreal Jewish Child Bureau, "Immigrant Meets the Agency," *Social Casework* December 1952.

57. Graham, "History of the Toronto School of Social Work," ch. 4; Struthers, *Limits of Affluence*, ch. 5; Margaret Avison, *The Research Compendium 1942–1962: Review and Abstracts of Graduate Research* (University of Toronto Social Work, 1964). On casework, see also Iacovetta and Mitchinson, eds., *On the Case*; Kunzel, *Fallen Women, Problem Girls*.

58. Graham, "History of the Toronto School of Social Work," 236–38; Kunzel, *Fallen Women, Problem Girls*.

59. Schlesinger, "Socio-Cultural Elements"; Charles Fine, "Canadian and American Ethnic

Viewpoints: A Study in Contrast," *Social Worker* 29 (4 Oct. 1961). Fine had a B.A. in political science and economics and had worked for six years with children in a variety of capacities from club leader to camp director before he returned to the School of Social Work at the University of Toronto in 1957, taking group work sequence. He graduated with a M.S.W. in 1959, and at the time this article appeared he was employed with a treatment and research group therapy program with children at the Toronto Psychiatric Hospital. His article cited U.S. colleagues such as Hertha Kraus, "The Newcomer's Orientation to the American Community," in *New Emphasis on Cultural Factors* (New York, Family Service Association of America), and William Gioseffi, "The Relations of Culture to the Principles of Casework," *Social Casework* 34 (July 1953).

60. Studies cited in Schlesinger, "Socio-Cultural Elements."

61. Fine, "Canadian and American Ethnic Viewpoints," cites Lawrence K. Frank's 1946 definition of "psycho-cultural approaches" and casework expert Morton I. Teicher's discussion of social pathology.

62. Schlesinger, "Socio-Cultural Elements."

63. The dissenting voices included historian and immigration critic Arthur Lower, who dismissed the mosaic versus melting pot argument as soft thinking, arguing that Canadians did not want "a dozen little racial enclaves separated from the general community" and that while there was this vague national sense that Canadians did not want to force conformity, "in ordinary private life there would seem to be just as much pressure for conformity as there is in the United States." Cited in Fine, "Canadian and American Ethnic Viewpoints."

64. Fine, "Canadian and American Ethnic Viewpoints." See also Kage, "From Bohunk to New Canadian," *Social Worker* 29,4 (October 1961), who similarly defends a "constructive program of immigrant integration," but draws a stronger contrast between the U.S. melting pot assimilation model and the Canadian integration model by which newcomers gradually become active participants in the economic, social, civil, cultural, and spiritual affairs of the new homeland. He also called it a dynamic process in which values are enriched through mutual acquaintance, accommodation, and understanding, a process in which both old and new Canadians participate.

65. As Ben Carniol and other critics (including feminists) within social work have observed, a great gap continues to exist between the principles of social work and the practice and experiences of both front-line social workers and clients. See Carniol, *Case Critical*; Nan Van Den Bergh and Lynn B. Cooper, eds., *Feminist Visions for Social Work* (New York 1986); Debra M. McPhee, "The Child Protection System: Organizational Responses to Child Sexual Abuse and the Social Construction of Social Problems," Ph.D. thesis, University of Toronto, 1998.

4 Institutional Gatekeepers: Democratic Pluralism or Ethnic Containment?

1. NFB Archives, File 58-606, Frontier Series, *A Million and a Half of Us: European Integration* (1958), Gordon Burwash, director; Jean Boucher to David Bairstow, NFB executive producer, 13 Aug. 1958.

2. AO, Local Council of Women (LCW) Toronto Collection, Reports, report by Mrs. Thomas Roberts, "International Night" at International Institute of Metropolitan Toronto, 15 Nov. 1959.

3. LAC, Canadian Citizenship Branch (CB), MG31, D69, Vol. 11, 1951, Kaye Speeches, address prepared for Conference on Executive Committee of Ukrainian Canadian Committee, Winnipeg, 7 Nov. 1951.

4. This discussion draws on numerous sources, including: LAC, CB, MG31, D69, Vol. 11, File: Citizenship Branch, V.J Kaye, "Historical Material on the Establishment of the Canadian Citizenship Branch," February 1961; Vol. 11, File: Citizenship Branch, W.H. Agnew, Chief, Publications and Information Division, "Historical Review of the Canadian Citizenship Branch," December 1967; Vol. 12, File 54-56-26.

5. A fine preliminary look at the Institute is Martha Ophir, "Defining Ethnicity in Postwar

Canada: The International Institute of Metropolitan Toronto," major research paper, Graduate History, University of Toronto,1993. I am
indebted to Ophir, a former graduate student
and research assistant who undertook several
major chunks of research on the Institute records and other sources. I have incorporated
some of her excellent insights throughout this
chapter.

6. Conzen et al., "Invention of Ethnicity"; Ohpir,
"Defining Ethnicity." See also Stuart Hall, who
notes that many people use the term race, and
racial identity, when they actually mean culture
(as in Jamaican immigrant cultural customs):
David Morley and Kuan-Hsing Chen, *Stuart
Hall: Critical Dialogues in Cultural Studies*
(London 1997).

7. AO, IIMT, MU6444, File: Group Services, David
A. Stewart, Annual Report, 1958–59.

8. Nell West, cited in Hyman, "They Oil the Hinges of Integration's Door," 10.

9. AO, IIMT, MU6381, Constitution of the International Institute, "Statement of Purpose, Program and Needs for Expansion," File: memos,
notices, promotion, etc.

10. Fred N. Dreiziger, "The Rise of a Bureaucracy
for Multiculturalism: The Origins of the Nationalities Branch," in Normal Hillmer, Bohdan
Kordan, and Lubomyr Luciuk, eds., *On Guard
for Thee: Ethnicity and the Canadian State,
1939–1945* (Ottawa 1985); Franca Iacovetta,
Roberto Perin, and Angelo Principe, eds.,
*Enemies Within: Italian and Other Wartime
Internees in Canada and Beyond* (Toronto
1998); Bohdan Kordan, *Canada and the Ukrainian Question, 1939–45: A Study in Statecraft*
(Montreal 2001), ch. 4.

11. In 1950 Prime Minister Mackenzie King established the new Department of Citizenship
and Immigration by combining the Citizenship Branch with the Citizenship Registration
Branch, and with the Immigration Branch and
the Indian Affairs Branch (both formerly in
the Department of Mines and Resources). The
rationale behind the restructuring was that
all of the branches involved were designed
"to bring human beings to the status of full
citizenship as rapidly as possible." The Citizenship Branch itself had been established in
recognition of the growing numbers of "other"
Canadians in the population (that is, non-British
and non-French newcomers and ethnic Canadians, most of whom were of European origin)
and in anticipation of passing the first Canadian
Citizenship Act, which became law in 1947.

12. LAC, MG 31 D69, Vol. 11, File 1951, Kaye
Speeches, address prepared for conference of
Executive Committee of Ukrainian Canadian
Committee in Winnipeg, 7 Nov. 1951; LAC, MG
31 D69, Vol. 11, File 1957, Kaye Summary of
Work, prepared for then Acting Director (later
Director) Jean Boucher, 1957.

13. Frank Foulds, "The Canadian Citizenship
Branch," *Canadian Welfare* 25,1-2 (April/June
1950), 30–33. For the citizenship pamphlet
(nd) and other CB publications and educational materials, see LAC, CB, MG28, 117, Vol.
26, Publications of the Canadian Citizenship
Branch.

14. Foulds, "Canadian Citizenship Branch"; Agnew,
"Historical Review of the Citizenship Branch";
LAC, MG31, D69, Vol. 111, File: Historical
Material on the Establishment of the Citizen-
ship Branch, 1961, 1967; "Historical Facts Lead-
ing up to the Establishment of the Citizenship
Branch"; V.J. Kaye to Jean Boucher, Acting
Director, 18 July 1957; RG26, Vol. 13A, Robert
England, "Report on the Reorganization of the
Nationalities Branch," Department of War Ser-
vices, 12 June 1944. On basic English (French),
see, for example, CB reports contained in
LAC, MG31 D69, Vol. 17 (1957), Information
Department, File (1957), 27, on the "Learning
in English Language Series" in Saskatchewan,
June 1951; File (1952–58), report on Frontier
College; reports on Montreal, Victoria, Vancou-
ver, and elsewhere; RG26, Vol. 140, File 3-38-19,
Eugene Bussiere, Director, CB, to G.W. Lynds,
Supervisor, Division of Vocational Education,
Department of Education, Halifax, N.S., 19 July
1954.

15. Frances Swyripa, "Ukrainian Canadians," in
Gerald Hallowell, ed., *The Oxford Companion
to Canadian History* (Don Mills, Ont. 2004);

Frances Swyripa and John Herd Thompson, *Loyalties in Conflict: Ukrainian Canadians*; essays by Fred N. Dreiziger, Bohdan S. Kordan, and Lubomyr Y. Luciuk in Hillmer, Kordan, and Luciuk, *On Guard for Thee*; Watson Kirkconnell (also an expert academic), *Canadians All: A Primer of National Unity* (Ottawa 1941); Kordan, *Canada and the Ukrainian Question*; Lubomyr Luciuk, *Searching for Place: Ukrainian Displaced Persons, Canada, and the Migration of Memory* (Toronto 2000).

16. LAC, MG 31, D69, Vol. 11, 1951, Kaye Speeches, address prepared for the conference of the Executive Council of the Ukrainian Canadian Committee, Winnipeg, 7 Nov. 1951. On the biography, see Dmytro M. Shtohryn, ed., *Ukrainians in North America: A Biographical Directory of Noteworthy Men and Women of Ukrainian Origin in the United States and Canada* (Champaign, Ill. 1975). My thanks to Frances Swyripa for this and other Ukrainian-Canadian sources. See also Bohdan S. Kordan and Lubomyr Y. Luciuk, "A Prescription for Nation-Building: Ukrainian Canadians and the Canadian State, 1939–1945," in Hillmer, Kordan, and Luciuk, *On Guard for Thee*.

17. The examples are from the CB Staff Minutes and reports by Kaye and various regional officers contained in: LAC, MG 31, D69, Vol. 11, File: Kaye, Department of Citizenship, Kaye reports, 1945–1949; MG 31 D69, Vol. 12, File 1952–58; MG 31 D69, Vol. 17, File (1957), 27 (CB Reports, August-September 1951).

18. LAC, MG 31, D69, Vol. 12, File 54-56-26 (1957).

19. AO, IIMT, MU6381, File: St. Andrew's House Study, Toronto Welfare Council report of St. Andrew's House; File Governing Committee Minutes 1952–56, minutes for meeting 15 Dec. 1955. In 1959 they moved into larger quarters at 709 College Street and also acquired a former synagogue nearby, at 903 College St., which they used for dances and other adult activities. In 1967 they moved to 321 Davenport Rd.

20. Nicholas V. Montalto, "The International Institute Movement: A Guide to Records of Immigrant Service Agencies in the United States," St. Paul, Minn., Immigration Research Center, 1978; Elsie D. Harper, *The Past Is Prelude: Fifty Years of Social Action in the YWCA* (New York 1963). See also Donna Gabaccia, *Immigration and American Diversity* (Malden, Mass. 2002).

21. Montalto, "International Institute Movement"; Harper, *Past Is Prelude*; AO, IIMT, MU6381, File: St. Andrew's House Study, Toronto Welfare Council report of St. Andrew's House; File: Governing Committee Minutes 1952–56, minutes 6 Oct. 1956; minutes 14 Dec. 1955, Appendix, Jack Thomas, Report on the International Institute of Detroit; File: memos, notices, promotion, etc., Statement of Purpose, Programme and Needs for Expansion.

22. AO, MU6382, File: Board Minutes 1956–57, minutes of meeting 26 Sept. 1956.

23. AO, MU6474, File: Immigrant Assistance 1957–61, memorandum, "History of the Institute"; File: Individual Services Department 1961–64, Report on the First Year 1956–57; MU6326, Personnel Files, file on Nell West, includes newspaper clippings her activities, on her retirement in 1965; MU6426, Nell West File, Kathleen Walters to the Board, March 1973, on the occasion of West's death.

24. AO, MU6425, Personnel Files, on H.C. Forbell, John DeMonfort, Robert Kreem. In the 1960s a few women held senior positions such as president; in the early 1970s there were some Caribbean and South Asian staff.

25. AO, MU6389, File: Programme Committee, 1970–71.

26. It was not until the late 1960s and the early 1970s that many Caribbean and South Asian newcomers came to the Institute, prompting the board to hire a counsellor from each group. The experiment in reaching beyond Europeans did not last for long, given that the Institute shut down in 1972. AO, MU6426, Personnel Files, files on Murali Nair and Roy Johnston.

27. AO, MU6382, File: Board Minutes 1961–62, minutes of Board of Directors, 11 June 1962; MU6442, "The Community Groups and the Institute," *The Intercom* July 1961.

28. AO, MU6390, File: Board of Directors, executive minutes, J. Gellner to C. Bourquet, 19 Oct. 1973. West used the term "huddling," for

example, in Hyman, "They Oil the Hinges of Integration's Door." See also MU6419, File: Immigration (General) 1957–66, address by Robert Kreem, Director of Services, to St. George Chapter, IODE, 28 March 1966.

29. AO, MU6426, File: Institute Programs and Policies, Report of the Social Planning Council, 1959; MU6399, File on Scandinavians; MU6442, *The Intercom* [on the Hungarians], February 1964. *The Intercom* noted that the Hungarians "have melded into our life and contributed to Canadian development to an extent few newcomers could surpass," and offered the following questionable explanation for it: "Because of their strong family ties which discourage uniting on a larger ethnic basis, and the differences in their class origins, Hungarians haven't formed into strong national groups. The Finno-Ugrian nature of their language has discouraged cohesiveness with other European elements."

30. AO, MU6442, Robert Kreen, "Our Services," *The Intercom* December 1965; Ophir, "Defining Ethnicity."

31. AO, MU6382, File: Board Minutes 1959–60, minutes of meeting of Board of Directors, 3 Oct. 1963.

32. AO, MU6382, File: Board of Directors, board minutes 21 Sept. 1959; MU6430, File: Staff Meetings, July 9, 1965, minutes of staff meeting 21 Sept. 1959; MU6442, Robert Kreem's Report, *The Intercom* October 1965.

33. Krzsztof Gebhard, "Handbooks for Postwar Polish Immigrants," *Polyphony* 3 (Winter 1981); Ophir, "Defining Ethnicity"; Frances Swyripa, *Wedded to the Cause: Ukrainian-Canadian Women and Ethnic Identity 1891–1991* (Toronto 1993), ch. 5.

34. AO, MU6381, Toronto Welfare Council Report, "Member Groups." For a range of examples of political and organizational divisions among different ethnic groups, see Swyripa, "Ukrainian Canadians"; Swyripa, *Wedded to the Cause*; Luciuk, *Searching for Place*; Danys, *DP*; N.F. Dreisziger, *Struggle and Hope: The Hungarian-Canadian Experience* (Toronto 1982); Iacovetta, *Such Hardworking People*; Karl Aun, *The Polit-*

ical Refugees: A History of the Estonians in Canada (Toronto 1985); Anthony Rasporich, *For a Better Life: A History of Croatians in Canada* (Toronto 1982); and Susan Papp, "Hungarian Immigration after 1945," *Polyphony* 2 (1979–80).

35. CB Staff Minutes and reports by Kaye and various Regional Officers: LAC, MG 31, D69, Vol. 11, File: Kaye, Department of Citizenship, Kaye reports, 1945–1949; MG 31 D69, Vol. 12, File 1952–58; MG 31 D69, Vol. 17, File (1957), 27 (CB Reports, August-September 1951).

36. For example, see Agnew, "Historical Review"; Foulds, "Canadian Citizenship Branch. " With the Canadian Citizenship Act of 1947, Canada became the first Commonwealth nation to create its own class of citizenship separate from that of Britain. Non-Canadian residents who had lived in Canada for five years and could pass the citizenship test (which involved answering questions about Canadian politics, geography, and history during a citizenship hearing over which a Citizenship judge presided) could attain Canadian citizenship. A major citizenship right was the franchise.

37. Foulds, "Canadian Citizenship Branch. " See also MG31 D69, Vol. 12, File (1955) 25, CB staff minutes on citizenship ceremonies, February 1949, June 1951, August-September 1951, File: 1952–58. See also the Branch publications: *How to Become a Canadian Citizen* (62 pages); the booklet Citizenship Series: *Our Land, Our History, Our History of Government*; and *The Citizen as Parent, The Citizen as Community Member, The Citizen as a Member of the World Community*.

38. See, for example, LAC, MG 28 (IODE) I17, Vol. 26, "The 17 Headings... Principle Activities of the IODE Immigration and Citizenship Work; LAC, MG 28 (IODE), File (10), M. Harris to Mrs. J.G. Spragge, Past National Secretary, IODE, Junior Branch, Toronto, 14 July 1952; LAC, RG26, Vol. 80, File 1-24-1, Pt. 1, J.W. Pickersgill, Department of Immigration and Citizenship, to Mrs. W.B. Sovery, Assistant National Secretary, IODE, Toronto, 22 Jan. 1957.

39. Foulds, "Canadian Citizenship Branch. "

40. AO, MU6389, File: Publicity and Public

Relations Committee 1958–1966, flyer, January 1959.

41. AO, MU6419, File: Immigration (General) 1957–66, address by Robert Kreem, Director of Services, to St. George Chapter, IODE, 28 March 1966.

42. AO, MU6444, File: Group Services – Annual Report, 1958–59, Annual Report, January 1958–59; MU6382, File: Board of Directors, 1960, Group Services – Monthly Report, January 1960; MU6442, File: Board and Committee Minutes 1958, Groups Services Report, April, 1958.

43. Both assessors and a few staff members gave the Institute's failure to attract larger numbers of these groups, especially Greeks, Italians, and Portuguese, into its House's social and cultural programs as the prime explanation for the agency's growing irrelevance to the city's immigrant scene by the late 1960s and early 1970s. During a survey in the mid-1960s, one anonymous board member suggested that the agency had to rethink its entire theory of integration. AO, MU6403, "Future Plans for the International Institute: Survey Analysis"; MU6389, Group Services Report – Programme Evaluation, May 1969, File: Programme Committee, 1970–71; MU6381, File: St. Andrew's House Study. See also David Stewart, Supervisor of Group Services, reports.

44. AO, MU6442, "To Dance Is to Integrate," *The Intercom* March 1962.

45. AO, MU6442, Richard Kolm, "Purpose through Program," *International Institute News*, June 5, 1957.

46. AO, MU6382, File: Board and Committee Minutes 1958, Group Services: Evaluation of the Department's Work from October 1956 to Date.

47. AO, YWCA Collection, MU3527, Box 11, Annual Reports, Toronto Branch, 1874–1955.

48. AO, MU6406, File: Programme Committee Reports, 1959–61, Programme Committee – Group Work Section, minutes of meeting 31 March 1960.

49. AO, MU6463, File: Individual/Group Services – Reports, 1959–61, Group Services Report, January 1960–December 1960.

50. AO, MU6444, File: Group Services, General 1956–64, Group Services Report, 1967.

51. Franca Iacovetta, "Making New Canadians: Social Workers, Women, and the Reshaping of Immigrant Families," in Franca Iacovetta and Mariana Valverde, eds., *Gender Conflicts: New Essays in Women's History* (Toronto 1992).

52. AO, MU6381, File: Board Minutes 1956–57, Programme Committee minutes 13 March 1957; LAC, MG31, D69, File: 1957 [Citizenship Branch Reports], 27, Toronto Regional Officer, John Sharp's report on his intervention regarding the expelled Ukrainian team. On fear of communists, LAC, MG31, D69, Vol. 11, File: Kaye, Department of Citizenship and Immigration, Gilbert E. Jackson to Kaye, 8 Sept. 1950.

53. West cited in Hyman, "They Oil the Hinges of Integration's Door"; Ophir, "Defining Ethnicity."

54. AO, MU6415, File: "Ethnic Press 1959–60," press release, Anne Davison, no title.

55. AO, MU6442, Richard Kolm, "Purpose through Program," *International Institute News* June 5, 1957; MU6415, File: Ethnic Press, 1959–60, press release, Anne Davison.

56. AO, MU6381, File: St. Andrew's House Study, 1954–55, Toronto Welfare Council Report; MU6389, File: Programme Committee, 1970–71, Groups Services Report – Programme Evaluation, May 1969; Graham, "History of the Toronto School of Social Work."

57. AO, MU6413, File: Ethnic Occasions, 1957, Nell West to Institute staff, memorandum on folk ball, 10 Jan. 1956. This observation applies to other gatekeepers, including, for example, the University Settlement House's international folk-dancing events. The organizers explained the popularity of the dances partly by saying they did not require anyone to speak English. *Toronto Star* 2 Feb. 1959, 34, with photos. The Citizenship Branch liaison reports also contain numerous references to folk dancing and folk balls.

58. "Will Even Give up Smoking to Aid DP, Violinist Says," *Toronto Star* 11 Sept. 1948. The girl, Halina Biloshysky, won the contest again in the following year and, under the revised rules, was allowed to keep the $500 scholarship prize.

"Won, But Lost Last Year, New Canadian Wins Now," *Toronto Star* 3 Sept. 1949.

59. AO, MU6411, File: Cultural Festival (Member Organizations), Institute Director, Harry Forbell, notes from an organizing meeting. See also MU6415, File: Latvian Federation, 1957.

60. AO, MU6397, File: Director of Services 1965, Public Relations and Publicity Committee, Robert Kreem to Central Organization of Ethnic Groups in Toronto, 1956; MU6413, File: Ethnic Occasions, Nell West to President, Forest Hill Rotary Club, 31 Jan. 1957; MU6415, File: Latvian Federation, 1957; Orphir, "Defining Ethnicity."

61. Bodnar, *Transplanted*; Ophir, "Defining Ethnicity"; Varpu Lindstrom, *Defiant Sisters: A Social History of Finnish Women in Canada, 1880–1930* (Toronto 1988); Swyripa, *Wedded to the Cause.*

62. See, for example, earlier studies such as Wsevelod Isajiw, *Definitions of Ethnicity* (Toronto 1979); essays in Jorgen Dahlie and Tissa Fernando, eds., *Ethnicity, Power and Politics in Canada* (Toronto 1981); and, for a critique of static models and other problems in the volumes of the Canadian government's "Generation" series of books on ethnic groups, see Roberto Perin, "Clio as an Ethnic: The Third Force in Canadian Historiography," *Canadian Historical Review* 64 (1983), and Franca Iacovetta, "Manly Militants, Cohesive Communities, and Defiant Domestics: Writing about Immigrants in Canadian Historical Scholarship," *Labour/Le Travail* 36 (Fall 1995).

63. See, for example, AO, MU6419, File: Human Interest Stories, "A Ukrainian Woodcarving Family."

64. See, for examples, AO, MU6427, File: Publicity Scrapbook Clippings from *Globe and Mail, Toronto Star, Toronto Telegram*; MU6389, File: Immigration (General) 1957–66; MU6413, File, "Ethnic Groups – Clippings, 1971–74; MU6398, File: Croatian Organizations, File: Bulgarian 1961–64; MU6411, File: Mrs. Stewart's Log; MU6413, File: Ethnic Organization Lists; Godfrey Barrass to Nell West, 27 June 1960.

65. "Macedonian, Serbian and Ukrainian Communities Celebrate New Year [according to the Julian calendar] in Gay and Colorful Costumes," *Toronto Star*, 14 Jan. 1956.

66. *Toronto Star*, 9 July 1955, 1, 16 April 1955, 1, 5 Aug. 1950, 3. On the plump "ethnic mama," see, for example, Iacovetta, *Such Hardworking People*, ch. 5.

67. Cheryl Smith, "Stepping Out: The Emergence of Professional Ballet in Canada, 1938–1963," Ph.D. thesis, University of Toronto, 1998, especially ch. 3.

68. AO, MU6398, File: Czechoslovakian Society, correspondence between National Committee of Hungarians of Czechoslovakia and Mrs. Peggy Jennings, February 1953.

69. Danys, *DP*; Aun, *Political Refugees*; Luciuk, "Trouble All Around," and his *Searching for Place.*

70. Ophir, "Defining Ethnicity."

71. AO, MU6398, File: United Croats of Canada Dance Group, Forbell to Dance Group, 15 May 1964. It is possible that the Citizenship Branch liaison officers would have supplied information about groups with suspicious politics.

72. AO, MU6415, File: Latvian Federation, "Latvian Arts and Crafts," by Latvian Federation.

73. Swyripa argues that ultimately a less politicized version won out. Swyripa, *Wedded to the Cause*, ch. 5; Rhonda Hinther, "'Sincerest Revolutionary Greetings': Progressive Ukrainians in Twentieth Century Canada," Ph.D. thesis, McMaster University, Hamilton, Ont., 2005, ch. 4.

74. AO, MU6442, *The Intercom* June 1964.

75. AO, MU6442, "Our Byelorussian Canadians," *The Intercom* October 1963. My point is not to assess the accuracy of the claims but to highlight the politicized cultural strategy being used. See also Swyripa, *Wedded to the Cause*, ch. 5.

76. Conzen et al., "Invention of Ethnicity"; Bodnar, *Transplanted.*

5   Tactics of Close Liaison: Political Gatekeepers, the Ethnic Press, and Anti-Communist Citizens

1. LAC, MG31 D69, Vol. 11, File: 1954, Vladimir Kaye, "Methods of Marxist Propaganda among Ethnic Groups in Canada," paper read at a confidential meeting, March 30, 1954, Toronto.

2. Ibid.

3. LAC, MG28 I17 (IODE Collection), Vol. 24, File: Anti-Communist Activities, copy of address on "Communism" delivered by W.J. Sheridan, manager of the Department of Economic Development, Chamber of Commerce, Montreal, to members of IODE, Annual Meeting, New Brunswick Provincial Chapter, 22 April 1948. The members were instructed "to devote special attention and study to this address." See also W.J. Sheridan, *The Communist Threat to Canada*, pamphlet, June 1947, in the same file.

4. For a sampling of work dealing with both world wars and red scares, see: Donald Avery, *"Dangerous Foreigners": European Immigrant Workers and Labour Radicalism in Canada, 1896–1932* (Toronto 1979); Avery, *Reluctant Host*; Gregory S. Kealey, "State Repression of Labour and the Left in Canada, 1914–1920: The Impact of the First World War," *Canadian Historical Review* 73,3 (1992); Hillmer, Kordan, and Luciuk, eds., *On Guard for Thee*; and Iacovetta, Perin, and Principe, eds., *Enemies Within*.

5. This battle had been prompted in part by Ottawa's decision at the time to admit the four thousand Polish veterans on farm labour contracts, provided they passed the security screening tests. Depending upon the political perspective of the onlooker, the vets were either fascists or heroes. Earlier studies, such as Whitaker, *Double Standard*, 27–28, pointed out that screening procedures were used for anti-Semitic purposes, namely to restrict the numbers of Jews (only one Jew was recruited among the first 1,700 veterans admitted, for instance). More recently, Margolian, in *Unauthorized Entry*, has suggested that the Polish veterans, who did include some collaborators and war criminals, underwent rigorous political screening and that even with the easing of certain restrictions, very few collaborators and criminals got into Canada.

6. "Charge Widely Endorsed That Immigrants Wooed by Communist Agents," *Canadian Register*, 3 Jan.1948; "Canada Faces Test in DP Immigration: Communist Agents Reported Very Active but Girls Eager to Become Canadians,"
Canadian Register, 29 Nov. 1947; "Pressure by Communists on DP's in Canada, Ottawa Is Suspicious," *Canadian Register*, Nov. 1, 1947. For the behind the scenes discussions, see, for example, MG31 D69, Vol. 11, File: Kaye Correspondence, Tracy Phillips (formerly of Nationalities Branch), copy of report on Communist Committee for Return Home, prepared for the Home Office, entitled "Emigrés, Return! Come Home," copy and letter from Berlin, to Vladimir Kaye, 1 Aug.1955.

7. CTA, University Settlement (US), SPC 24 W, Box 1, File 2, Immigration 1952–53, Appendix A, Report on Displaced Persons. The scheme had come about as a result of a Jewish-Canadian lobby, which included manufacturers and Jewish-led unions, to bring survivors to Canada. Ottawa had agreed to the scheme, but in another display of continuing anti-Semitism it imposed a quota on the number of Jews recruited, to 50 per cent. Abella and Troper, *None Is Too Many*; Luciuk, *Searching for Place*, ch. 9.

8. Williams, "How to Keep Red Hands off Our New Canadians"; Luciuk and others argue that this impact was widespread: see Luciuk, *Searching for Place*.

9. The priest added that the women "can usually recognize the Communists who call them 'comrade,' while we usually address them as 'Miss.'" Cited in "Canada Faces Test in DP Immigration," *Canadian Register*, 29 Nov. 1947.

10. The changeover in names made such errors fairly common. During the Second World War the pro-Communist Ukrainian Labour–Farmer Temple Association (ULFTA), which in 1924 had replaced the original Ukrainian Labour Temple Association (1918), was banned. In 1942 the pro-Communists resurfaced as the Association of Canadian Ukrainians, which in 1946 became the Association of United Ukrainian Canadians (AUUC). See also Williams, "How to Keep Red Hands off Our New Canadians."

11. The women were all Polish and Catholic except for a few Yugoslavs, two Russians, and a Lithuanian.

12. Dionne reportedly paid the minimum hourly wage (twenty-five cents) for a forty-eight-hour week, but the many deductions (for rent as well as instalments of the money owed him for the transatlantic flight) reduced their weekly wages to paltry levels ($3.60). The women could leave their residence only two evenings each week, with a 10:00 P.M. curfew. Dionne also required them to call him "Tatus" (father), to have their shopping lists approved by him, and even to report on any marriage proposals. In response he portrayed himself as a humanitarian businessman and a true son of Quebec – "the rampart against agitators and advocates of socialism, communism and atheism" – who was a victim of a Communist smear campaign. Although the debate over the degree of exploitation continued for several years afterwards, the plan was so heavily criticized that nearly all of the women were allowed to leave within one year. See "Dionne Blames Communists for Criticism of 100 Girls," *Toronto Star* 14 June 1947; "Dionne Learning Polish but 100 Girls Slow on French," *Toronto Star* 2 Aug. 1947; Peter Newman, "Are New Canadians Hurting Canada?" *Maclean's* 18 July 1959.

13. It was Armande Sylvestre, deputy chief commissioner of the Board of Transport Commissioners for Canada. "Pressure by Communists on DP's in Canada, Ottawa Is 'Suspicious,'" *Canadian Register* 1 Nov. 1947; "Polish Legation Charges 'Distrust' Campaign Exists," *Toronto Star* 1 Nov. 1947.

14. LAC, RG26, Vol. 75, File: 1-5-11, Pt. 1, memo, Laval Fortier, Deputy Minister, memorandum for Mr. Smith, Ottawa, 6 July 1950; "Pastor Says Consul Spies for Yugoslavs," *Toronto Star* 17 Sept. 1955; Eric Geiger, "New Canadians" columns, "Reds Write of Prison for Migrants in Toronto" and "Lithuanians New Targets of Red Come-Home Drive," *Toronto Star* 16 June 1956, 2 Feb. 1957; "Lonely Hungarians Going Home," *Toronto Star* 20 April 1957; "Tried to Lure Migrants Back, Pole Expelled" (referring to the attaché with the Polish Legation), *Toronto Star* 22 March 1958.

15. Peter C. Newman, "The Big Battle for Our New Citizens' Minds," *Financial Post* 1 Nov. 1952; LAC, RG26, Vol. 11, File: 1945–1961, "A Review of the Press Other Than English or French," *Press Review* 2,9 (1 May 1954). See also MG 31 D19, Vol. 11, File: "Historical Review of the Canadian Citizenship Branch," prepared by W.H. Agnew, Chief, Publications and Information Division, December 1967.

16. MG 31 D69, Vol. 11, File: Dr. Kaye, Liaison Officer, correspondence, 1953–55, W.H Agnew, Chief, Programmes and Materials Division, CB, memorandum, to Mr. E. Bussiere Re: Foreign-Language Press, Ottawa, 15 Sept. 1955, 43. See also the documents in MG 31 D69, Vol. 11, File: Kaye: Historical Materials, Establishment of Canadian Citizenship Branch, 1961–67.

17. In addition some important U.S. ethnic newspapers had a Canadian section and enjoyed a fairly large Canadian circulation. Most papers were not dailies; about one-third were weeklies and the rest monthlies or bimonthlies. LAC, RG26, Vol. 11, File: 1945–1961, Fortier, "Review of the Press in Canada," and *The Ethnic Press and the Foreign Language Press Review Service* (nd); RG26, Vol. 75, File 1-5-11, Pt. 1, Director of CB, Eugene Bussiere, memorandum to Deputy Minister of Citizenship and Immigration, 9 Sept. 1953; RG26, Vol. 11, File: 1945–1961.

18. We should also remember that a number of pro-Nazi and pro-Fascist ethnic newspapers had also emerged during the interwar decades, following Mussolini's and Hitler's rise to power in Italy and Germany respectively. Before the changing situation in Europe had led Ottawa to imprison some of the editors on the eve of the Second World War, these right-wing papers had toed a right-wing and staunchly anti-Communist line. Iacovetta , Perin, and Principe, eds., *Enemies Within*.

19. "Dismember" is from Luciuk, *Searching for Place*. See also Fortier, "Review of the Press in Canada." See also LAC, RG26, Vol. 76, File:1-5-11, "On Editorial Policies of the Ethnic Press," CB, Ottawa, March 1958; RG26, Vol. 11, File: 1945–1961, "Cross Section of the Foreign Language Press of Canada," November 1945 and 1946;

"The Ethnic Press in Canada," March 1955; "List of Ethnic Group Communist Publications," November 1956, and other lists and descriptions. On the readers, and instructions to readers, see, for example: RG26, Vol. 11, File: 1945–1961, *The Ethnic Press and the Foreign Language Press Review Service* (nd); RG26, Vol. 75, File: 1-5-11, Pt. 1, Frank Foulds, Director, to WJF Pratt, May 8, 1950; MG 31 D69, Vol. 11, File: Kaye, Department of Citizenship, correspondence, 1953–1955, "W.H. Agnew, Chief, Programmes and Materials Division, memo to E. Bussiere re foreign language press, Sept. 15, 1955.

20. For a typical propaganda pamphlet (nd) about Canada, see, for example, LAC, RG26, Vol. 11, File: 1945–1961, Research Division (staff), CCB, Research Division, memo to HN Lockead, (copy to F. Foulds),1946; LAC, MG 28 I17, Vol. 26, Files: Publications of the Canadian Citizenship Branch.

21. Of the government departments, External Affairs received the largest number of ethnic press summaries. The other recipients included the departments of Labour and National Health and Welfare, the NFB, and the Prime Minister's Office. The summaries also went to various churches, the Austrian Legation, departments of education and university education programs, Canadian Congress of Labour, Canadian Jewish Congress (CJC), Supervisor of Indian Agencies, North Bay, J.R. Kidd, CBC Radio-Canada, Chinese Benevolent Society, president of the Latvian Society (Major V.E.K. Weldie, Vancouver), Provincial Mennonite Relief Ontario, Jewish Labour Committee, Neighbourhood Workers Association, Toronto, YWCA and YMCA branches, Dr. Albert Rose (University of Toronto School of Social Work), Catholic Women's League, IODE, and the Ukrainian Canadian Committee. For the list and descriptions see LAC, RG26, Vol. 75, File 1-5-11, Pt. 1, Director of CB, Eugene Bussiere, Memorandum to Deputy Minister of Citizenship and Immigration, Re: Progress Report on Foreign-Language Press Review and Press Digest, 9 Sept. 1953. By 1953 the Branch was publishing its summary material as the *Press Review*.

22. Since the RCMP's own press review focused on Canadian and ethnic papers "with Communist leanings," it welcomed information from the other newspapers that the CB tracked. LAC, MG 31 D69, Vol. 11, File: Dr. Kaye, Liaison Officer, Correspondence, 1953–55, W.H Agnew, Chief, Programmes and Materials Division, CB, Memorandum to Mr. E. Bussiere RE: Foreign-Language Press, Ottawa, 15 Sept. 1955; LAC, RG26, Vol. 75, File 1-5-11, Pt. 2, Director, CCB to Deputy Minister, Subject: The Foreign Language Press Digest, Oct. 31, 1958; LAC, RG26, Vol. 75, File 1-5-11, Pt.1, Director of CB, Eugene Bussiere, Memorandum to Deputy Minister of Citizenship and Immigration, 9 Sept. 1953. The list includes the RCMP, Health and Welfare, Labour, CBC, National Library, High Commissioner for U.K. Office, Stephen Davidovich, Community Programs, Toronto, and the U.S. Embassy. On the Canadian scene, see Fortier, "A Review of the Press in Canada"; RG26, Vol. 11, File: 1945–1961, *The Ethnic Press and the Foreign Language Press Review Service* (nd). From 1953 onward the sensitive material was published as the *Press Digest*.

23. MG 31 D69, Vol. 11, File: Dr. Kaye, Liaison Officer, Correspondence, 1953–55, W.H Agnew, Chief, Programmes and Materials Division, CB, memorandum to Mr. E. Bussiere Re: Foreign-Language Press, Ottawa, 15 Sept. 1955.

24. They also claimed not to be troubled by the few exceptions, which included a pair of Finnish- and German-language newspapers, that supported the CCF platform, because that position was consistent with the declared policy of those papers. LAC, RG26, Vol. 11, File: 1945–1961, Fortier, "A Review of the Press in Canada."

25. This discussion draws on the translations of the ethnic press in LAC, RG26, Vol. 75, File: 1-1-8, Pt. 1, which contains the summaries of about twenty foreign-language papers as well as samples of press translations. Regarding *Yiddisher Journal*, the direct translation is "Yiddish" but I understand that this Toronto paper was called *Hebrew Journal* in English. Thanks to Ruth Frager.

26. Williams, "How to Keep Red Hands off Our New Canadians; "Many New Canadians Ask

Why Is Communism Allowed Here?" *Canadian Register*, 5 Jan. 1957; LAC, MG 28 I17, IODE Collection, File: Anti-Communist Activities, copy of address on Communism delivered by W.J. Sheridan, 22 April 1948; LAC, RG26, Vol. 76, File:1-5-11, "On Editorial Policies of the Ethnic Press," CB, Ottawa, March 1958, Descriptions of Communist Press; RG26, Vol. 11, File: 1945–1961, "List of Ethnic Group Communist Publications," November 1956.

27. Newman's figures were 19 Communist papers out of a total of 156 foreign-language newspapers. Newman, "Big Battle for Our New Citizens' Minds"; LAC, RG26, Vol. 11, File 1945–1961, "A Review of the Press in Canada other than English and French," *Press Review* 2,9 (1 May 1954). See also reports on the activities of their respective ethnic organizations in Canada: LAC, RG26, Vol. 11, File: 1945–1961, Appendix, The Communist Ethic Press, "Editorial Policies," nd.

28. Daniel R. Brower, *The World in the Twentieth Century: The Age of Global War and Revolution* (New York 1996),167–85.

29. LAC, RG26, Vol. 11, File:1945–1961, CB, Editorial Section, Cross-section of the Foreign Language Press of Canada (1946). Published in Toronto, *Novosti* called itself "the only Croatian Democratic Newspaper in Canada," and the CB profiled it as "Communist. Supports LPP in Canada and Marshal Tito in Yugoslavia. Follows strictly the official communist line." The CB minds believed that *Novosti*, founded in 1941, was probably the successor of the banned Communist paper *Slobodna Misao* (Free thought), partly because both papers had the same editor, Marijan Krusic. The 1941 census did not break down the Yugoslav group into Croatians, Serbs, and Slovenes, but of the total figure of 21,214 Yugoslavs, the majority were Croatian.

30. *Hrvtski Glas*, published in Winnipeg, was also the first Croatian paper in Canada. According to the CB, its "Yugoslav affairs" material had a "definite 'slant,'" taken from the U.S. press, or supplied by Croatian writers in exile, refuting Tito's dictatorship and advocating Western-style democracy. The CB supplied most of its Canadian material. LAC, RG26, Vol. 11, File:1945–1961, CB, Editorial Section, Cross-section of the Foreign Language Press of Canada (1946).

31. University of Toronto Archives (UTA), Robert S. Kenny Collection, MS 179, Box 57, Flyer: "Baby Killers Are NOT Welcome Here!" Resolution by League of Canadian Croatians, Serbs, Slovenes, and the Croatian Peasant Republic Party (with letter and explanation). For a more detailed treatment of the European context, see Judt, *Postwar*.

32. "Claim Girl Boasted of Killing Children," *Toronto Star* 5 July 1947; LAC, RG26, Vol. 11, File:1945–1961, CB, Editorial Section, Cross-section of Foreign Language Press of Canada.

33. The debate over how many collaborators and war criminals entered Canada continues, though a recent study argues that Canada was tougher in the political screening of refugees, and the numbers of collaborators or criminals who slipped through the gate was lower, than many have previously argued or assumed. Margolian, in *Unauthorized Entry*, posits that Canada had a strong record on keeping out war criminals and collaborators. Employing a narrow interpretation of war criminal and collaborator, he estimates that 2,000 of the nearly 1.5 million newcomers who were admitted to Canada between 1946 and 1951, or just over one-eighth of 1 per cent of the total number of new Canadians, fell into this category. Margolian maintains that the evidence shows that the RCMP made a valiant attempt to keep out real war criminals but that their efforts were sometimes undermined by clever criminals and lack of documentation. For the debate, see Whitaker, *Double Standard*, and Margolian, *Unauthorized Entry*. In my view Margolian's carefully researched study, while offering a helpful corrective, does not ultimately refute the major claim made by Whitaker and others, namely that for the security forces, the greater and greatest enemy was Communism and Communists. The historians who have staunchly defended the wartime record of the

various East European groups include Danys, *DP*, and Luciuk, *Searching for Place*.

34. The press translations of articles and editorials and other correspondence regarding the picnic speech controversy are contained in LAC, CB MG31 D69, Vol. 11, File: Kaye, Editorial Section, correspondence, 1945–47.

35. A Toronto weekly established in 1941 with a circulation of about 16,000, *Ukrainian Life* had several predecessors before the war. LAC, RG26, Vol. 76, File:1-5-11, "On Editorial Policies of the Ethnic Press," CB, Ottawa, March 1958, Descriptions of Communist Press. On Ukrainian collaboration and war crimes, see Margolian, *Unauthorized Entry*; Whitaker, *Double Standard*; Harold Troper and Morton Weinfield, *Old Wounds: Jews, Ukrainians and the Hunt for Nazi War Criminals in Canada* (Markham, Ont.1989); and Luciuk, *Searching for Place*.

36. LAC, CB MG31 D69, Vol. 11, File: Kaye, Editorial Section, correspondence, 1945–47.

37. Margolian, *Unauthorized Entry*, ch. 6; Troper and Weinfield, *Old Wounds*.

38. LAC, CB MG31 D69, Vol. 11, File: Kaye, Editorial Section, correspondence, 1945–47.

39. Troper and Weinfield, *Old Wounds*, ch. 7. Even when, many years later, the much-anticipated 1986 Deschenes Commission on Nazi War Criminals ultimately determined that the members of the Galicia Division living in Canada were not war criminals, the suspicions continued.

40. LAC, MG31 D69, Vol. 12, CB, File: 1950, V.J. Kaye, Liaison Officer, Report of Trip to Toronto and Hamilton, Sept. 27–2 Oct. 1950.

41. Newman drew up list of "red" and "democratic" ethnic presses, with details regarding publication, circulation, editors, and mandate. Again, these probably came from the CB, whose descriptions are interesting for at least two reasons: the large number of new refugee papers that are described as democratic but sensationalist in their depiction of the Soviet Union or satellite states; and the concern expressed about a handful of papers considered to be too right-wing and sensationalist.

42. LAC, RG26, Vol. 11, File: 1945–1961, "A Review of the Press in Canada Other Than English or French"; LAC, MG 31 D69, Vol. 11, File: Kaye, Editorial Section, Kaye, "Observations: The Editorial Department of the Citizenship Division," 21 May 1945; RG26, Vol. 11, File 1945–1961, M.J. Diakowsky, Liaison Officer, Report of Trip to the Foreign-Language Press, Toronto, Jan. 9, 1951 to Jan. 20, 1951. See also LAC, MG 31 D69, Vol. 11, File: Kaye, Editorial Section, Kaye, Kaye's "Observations on Press Releases," 26 April 1945; F. Foulds, Research Division, to H.N. Lockhead, Editor of Press Releases, 24 Aug. 1946.

43. Newman, "Big Battle for Our Citizens' Minds."

44. LAC, MG 31 D69, Vol. 12, File 1950, V.J. Kaye, Liaison Officer, Report of Trip to Toronto and Hamilton, Sept. 27–2 Oct. 1950.

45. *Homin Ukrainy* (Ukrainian echo) was described as the organ of the "extreme nationalist wing" of the League for the Liberation of the Ukraine. LAC, RG26, Vol. 76, File: 1-5-11, Editorial Policies of the Ethnic Press, CB, Ottawa, March 1958. For similar reasons, the CB also investigated certain ethnic organizations, including the Union of Victims of Communist and Russian Terror (SUZERO), which appeared in the late 1950s. The liaison officer, Diakowsky, met with the vice-president, Petro Volyniak, in Toronto, and reported that "the membership is several hundred former inmates of Soviet concentration camps," and while the small group appeared to be "very aggressive," he felt that they were motivated largely by "a desire to warn Canadians of dangers presented to the Canadian way of life by the Soviets." LAC, MG 31 D69, File (1957), CB Reports, August-September 1951.

46. For example, see LAC, MG31 D69, Vol. 12, File 1950, V.J. Kaye, Liaison Officer, Report of Trip to Toronto and Hamilton, March 24–25, 1950; Report of Day's Activity in Toronto, Jan. 24, 1955; RG26, Vol. 11, File 1945–1961, M.J. Diakowsky, Liaison Officer, Report of Trip to the Foreign-Language Press, Toronto, Jan. 9, 1951 to Jan. 20, 1951.

47. LAC, MG31D69, Vol. 11, Dr. Vladimir Kaye, Department of Citizenship (and Immigration),

Liaison Office, File: Dr. V.J. Kaye, Report on Liaison Work, 4 July 1952. Other examples include a report for January 1957.

48. "Lone wolf" is from a memo from Laval Fortier, personal and confidential memorandum for the acting minister, 20 Nov. 1957, in LAC, RG26, Vol. 75, File 1-5-11, Pt. 1. As Fortier's reports show, Kaye also met with academics developing Slavic studies university programs, and with local unemployment and immigration officers who updated him on local matters. He helped to set up language classes for immigrant mothers, and then urged the ethnic priests to drag them to class, and personally counselled professionally trained refugee men. He obliged friends and colleagues, including those who received the restricted *Press Digest*, when they asked for materials to help them defeat local left-wing candidates. One such request came from Gilbert Jackson, the Toronto academic and banking consultant who had worried about possible Communist tampering at Ukrainian soccer games in Toronto. He asked for some anti-Communist materials that could be distributed to Toronto voters in the forthcoming municipal election, especially in Wards 4 and 5, where "the commies cut quite a lot of ice," and for the names of well-known ethnics, preferably Italians and Ukrainians, who lived in the area (as defined by Yonge, Dufferin, Bloor, and Bay streets) and could use their "conscientious opposition to communism" to defeat the reds. LAC, RG26, Vol. 75, File: 1-1-8, Pt. 1, and other files; MG31 D69, Vol. 11, File: Kaye, Department of Citizenship, Liaison Officer, Gilbert E. Jackson to Dr. V. Kaye, Ottawa, 8 Sept. 1950. On Kaye's liaison reports and meetings with other liaison officers, see also files in LAC, MG31D69, Vol. 12, File 54-56-26; File 1951 (for example, Report of CB for months of June 1951, January 1952, February 1952).

49. LAC, RG26, Vol. 11, File: 1945–1961, "A Review of the Press in Canada Other Than English or French"; MG 31 D69 Vol. 11 File: 1945, "Judge Lindall, Citizenship Division, Speech to Press Club," report, 29 March 1945.

50. The Toronto Press Club's first president was Bruno Tenhumin, editor of *Vapaa Sana* (Free press), a Finnish-Canadian paper, established in 1931, that supported the CCF party and whose readers were primarily old-timers. Interestingly, the Branch described it as one of the oldest democratic ethnic newspapers in Canada and applauded its stated aim "to furnish Canadians with information about the true situation in the countries now under communist rule." That they also recognized it as being "mildly socialist" suggests how the anti-Communism of social-democratic groups made them important allies in the state's fight against Communists, be they unions, ethnic groups, or the press. LAC, RG26 Vol. 11 File: 1945–1961, "A Review of the Press in Canada Other Than English or French. "

51. LAC, RG26, Vol. 12, File: La Ligue Anti-Communiste Canadienne, one-page document "Monsieiur le Docteur JEAN HO Fang Ly," in which a theme is that he is a devoted Catholic leader.

52. MG31 D69, File: Kaye, Department of Liaison Office, CB, Soviet Version of Religious Freedom (mimeographed), account of Father Pietro Leoni, S.J., forty-six, as published by the Rome newspaper *Il Essaggero*, 18, 21, 22 May 1956.

53. This fact sheet was in the Citizenship Branch files on the New Canadians Service Bureau, the precursor of the International Institute of Metropolitan Toronto. LAC, RG26, Vol. 11, File: New Canadians Service Bureau, January 1949. On other alerts, see, for example, Vol. 12, File: La Ligue Anti-Communiste Canadienne, Alert to Organizations, Some Meetings of International Front Organizations – A New Communist Front Organization (Stockholm Peace Plan), 12 pages, distributed by Latvian Information Centre; RG26, Vol. 11, File: New Canadians Service Bureau, January 1949, Some Facts about Communists and the Freedom of the Press; Forced Labour in the USSR; Christianity in the Soviet Union: The Anti-Religious State and the Churches.

54. Whitaker and Marcuse, *Cold War Canada*, 275–79.

55. The ABN was affiliated with the Banderivtsi, or Bandera faction, of the Organization of Ukrainian Nationalists (OUBb), which was also linked with the League for the Liberation of Ukraine and its organ *Ukrainian Echo* and organized the Massey Hall rally. RG26, Vol. 12, File: No Peace Without Freedom for All Nations and Individuals, Anticommunist Demonstration at Massey Hall, Toronto, Nov. 26, 1950, Speeches and Conclusions (14 pages). Other examples include "Czechs Forsake Dances to Pray for Countrymen," *Toronto Star* 12 Sept. 1955; Letter to Editor, "Was Day of Joy," signed, A. Latvian, *Toronto Star* 9 July 1955; Letter to Editor, "Proud of Canada," D. Pinkus, *Toronto Star* 1 May 1948; "Ethnic Groups Condemn Softness toward Reds," *Toronto Star* 21 Oct. 1958 (reporting on a meeting of two groups, the Canadian Hungarian Federation and the Christian Democratic Union of Central Europe, whose leaders criticized the "creeping pro-Communist elements" in Canadian newspapers, such as the "red [Toronto] Daily Star" and the "red *Globe and Mail*" the recent trip by *Star* writer George Bryant to Russia, and the decision of the Royal Bank of Canada and United Church of Canada to call for recognition of China.

56. No Peace Without Freedom for All Nations and Individuals, Anticommunist Demonstration at Massey Hall, Toronto, 26 Nov. 1950, Speeches and Conclusions (14 pages).

57. Ibid. On other rallies, see, for example, Eric Geiger, "New Canadians" column, "Exiled Ukraine President Visits Toronto for Rally," *Toronto Star*, 2 June 1956.

58. From the rise of the forced labour camp system in the 1920s, through to the disappearances and party purges of the Great Terror of the 1930s, and the wartime prisoners and labour armies, millions of men and women were victimized or eliminated under Stalinist totalitarianism. Millions more were persecuted or killed after the war, as the regime imprisoned or executed many of the repatriated nationals and created an expanding population of "political" and "criminal" prisoners in the various labour camps, special settlements and colonies (for certain groups, such as scientists), and the prisons of the Gulag. The estimates vary considerably for all three periods, including for the period under review, but one estimate is that by the summer of 1950 the Gulag population had reached a peak number of 2.8 million inmates. Drawing on more recently opened Soviet archives, which suggest that the camp inmate populations grew even larger after the Second World War, Galina Mikhailovna Ivanova suggests that, overall, about 20 million Soviet citizens moved through the camps of the Gulag from the 1930s to their dismantling in the 1950s, of whom about one-third were political prisoners and 10 to 15 per cent were criminal recidivists, while millions of others were subjected to forced labour and other discriminatory policies or punishments. She is reluctant to provide a figure for deaths in camps and colonies, except for the war years – two million between 1941 and 1944 – and notes that during the same period about one million prisoners were released to fight on the front and another five million were conscripted into the wartime industry labour camps. My discussion draws from several works, including: J. Arch Getty, Gabor T. Rittersporn, and Viktory N. Zemskov, "Victims of the Soviet Penal System in the Pre-war Years: A First Approach on the Basis of Archival Evidence," *American Historical Review* October 1993; Galina Mikhailovna Ivanova, *Labor Camp Socialism: The Gulag in the Soviet Totalitarian System* (Armonk, N.Y. and London 2000), and from conversations with Soviet historian Lynne Viola, who generously fielded my questions and directed me to sources, including those just cited, which can also be read against Alexander Solzhenitsyn, *The Gulag Archipelago 1918–1956* (London 1973). See also Helene Celmins, *Women in Soviet Prisons* (New York 1985).

59. Katie Pickles discusses the mix of British imperialism, Canadian patriotism, and fighting communism "U.S. style" in Pickles, *Female Imperialism and National Identity: Imperial Order Daughters of the Empire* (Manchester, Eng. 2002), ch. 7, "Defending Cold War Canada."

60. LAC, RG26, Vol. 12, File: La Ligue Anticommuniste Canadienne, "The Ugly Truth about the NAACP," by Attorney General Eugene Cook of Georgia, with the mailing address of the Latvian Information Centre in Canada, 23 Falcon St., Toronto, and noted as reference material.

61. The point should not be exaggerated, for while the IODE had lobbied hard to keep the Black Communist singer Paul Robeson from entering Canada, it did not appear to regularly draw on racist tracts like the anti-NAACP flyer. See also Pickles, *Female Imperialism and National Identity*, ch. 7.

62. "How to Tell a Catholic from a Communist," *Canadian Register*, 10 May 1952, 4 – a piece penned by a U.S. academic, Dr. Helen C. Potter, Department of Economics, Seton Hill College, Greensburg, Penn; LAC, MG 28 I17 (IODE), Vol. 24, File: Anti-Communist Activities, "Empire Study Questionaire: Communism," 1949. The flyer, which supplied readers with a list of questions and answers about communism, drew on a pamphlet prepared by Mrs. Ralph Silverthorn, Convener of Empire Study for the Municipal Chapter of Toronto for the IODE newsletter *Echoes*.

63. Like other alert writers, Lamb produced short pamphlets, written in plain English, and easily copied and distributed, that informed readers about Communist policies and operations and ways of combatting it. They were drawn in part on the U.S. alert services, including Alert America and Alert American Convoy. The IODE also produced radio talks for the CBC (including scripts for a Canadian Heritage Program) and articles for newspapers across Canada. To reach youth the organization printed comic books and cartoon stories dealing with communism that paralleled the Biblical comic books and ran youth programs in the schools. On Lamb, see Pickles, *Female Imperialism and National Identity*, ch. 7. For a sample of news alerts, see LAC, MG28 I17, Vol. 24, File: Anti-Communist Activities, 1948–1966, *Press Analysis* (Press Analysts [Canada]), Toronto, 1 Nov. 1957; MG 31 D, Vol. 11, M. Kos (resume), "Disruption of the Soviet Empire the Only Warrant

of a True and Lasting Peace," 26 Nov. 1951.

64. LAC, IODE Collection, MG28 I17, Vol. 24, File: Anti-Communist Activities, copy of address on "Communism" delivered by W.J. Sheridan, 22 April 1948; Marjorie Lamb, *The Canadian Peace Congress and the World Peace Movement* (1958); Pickles, *Female Imperialism and National Identity*, ch 7. For a broadsheet regarding youth, see, for example, LAC, CB, Files on New Canadian Service Bureau, January 1949: "Training the Young for Stalin (Satellite Communists use Education for Party Aims)," which notes that the Eastern bloc satellite states were seeking to control all education "in the interests of Party aims" and to produce citizens "with nothing more than technical skill and blind faith in Marxism" partly by purging non-Communist teachers and professors from schools and universities, eliminating academic freedom, indoctrinating new teachers in communism, rewriting textbooks to conform with Marxism, and denying the church a role in the training of youth.

65. For example, by asking a question about recent events in China and assessing how it was answered. LAC, IODE Collection, MG28 I17, Vol. 24, File: Anti-Communist Activities, "How to Spot a Communist" or "How Communists Operate! A Brief Memorandum on Communist Tactics," Canadian Chamber of Commerce, 1948.

66. LAC, RG26, Vol. 12, File: La Ligue Anti-Communiste Canadienne, Marjorie Lamb, "The Canadian Peace Congress and the World Peace Movement," pamphlet, published by The Alert Service, Toronto, spring 1958. It also bears a stamp saying distributed by the Latvian Distribution Centre (in Canada), Toronto.

67. Lamb, "Canadian Peace Congress and the World Peace Movement."

68. Pickles, *Female Imperialism and National Identity*, ch. 7; LAC, MG31 D69, Vol. 12, File 54-56-26, Kaye, Annual Report, Liaison Division; File (1955) 25, Minutes of Staff Meeting, 7 Feb. 1949; "Get Out of Our Seats," *Financial Post*, editorial, 1 Jan. 1958. The editorial draws on a recent Royal Bank report on the growing waistline of North American children and

their weak back and abdominal muscles. In the United States, after Sputnik, President John F. Kennedy, motivated by similar concerns, implemented a compulsory gym program into the school system.

69. The UWCA had run food and clothing drives to help refugees overseas, created student scholarships in Ukrainian institutions, and undertaken reception work for the newly arrived. By the 1940s the UWAC had established some branches outside its prairie stronghold, including in Ontario. However, despite their shared anti-communism, there were frictions between pre-war and postwar women, and the organization proved less successful than others in attracting new recruits. AO, MU2351, Minutes of Meeting, File: 1957–58, 14–16, Report of Mrs Evanetz; Swyripa, *Wedded to the Cause*. My thanks to Frances Swyripa for additional information on this group.

70. For more detail, see Iacovetta, "Remaking Their Lives.

71. "Want to Tell Them… MANY NEW CANADIANS ASK 'Why Is Communism Allowed Here?'" *Canadian Register* 5 Jan. 1957. See also the activities of the YWCA and many other groups, and their links with the CB, in LAC, MG31 D69, File (1960) 34, Report of the Canadian Citizenship Branch, Jan. 1–April 31, 1960; July 1–Dec. 31, 1960; April 1–June 30, 1960.

6 Culinary Containment? Cooking for the Family, Democracy, and Nation

1. This discussion draws on a variety of studies, including: Stephen Mennell, Anne Marcott, and Anneke H. van Otterlo, *The Sociology of Food: Eating, Diet and Culture* (London 1992); Peter Farb and George Armelagos, *Consuming Passions: The Anthropology of Eating* (Boston 1980); Harvey Levenstein, *Paradox of Plenty: A Social History of Eating in Modern America* (New York 1993); Donna Gabaccia, *We Are What We Eat: Ethnic Foods and the Making of Americans* (Cambridge 1998); Joan Jensen, *New Mexico Women: Intercultural Perspectives* (Albuquerque, N.M. 1986); Mary Ellen Kelm, *Colonizing Bodies: Aboriginal Health and Healing in British*

Columbia (Vancouver 2001); Epp, *Women without Men*; Marlene Epp, "The Semiotics of Zwieback," in Epp, Iacovetta, and Swyripa, eds., *Sisters or Strangers?*

2. "New Canadians and CPTA: We Need Each Other," *Canadian Register*, 26 Aug. 1961.

3. Doug Owram, *Born at the Right Time: A History of the Baby Boom Generation* (Toronto 1996), chs.1–3; Gleason, *Normalizing the Ideal*; essays in Parr, ed., *Diversity of Women*; Epp, *Women without Men*. On alternative models, see Farhni's discussion of Quebec-based postwar Catholic family movements that, for example, envisioned an ideal francophone, Catholic, working-class family, in Fahrni, *Household Politics*, ch. 4.

4. The vast international literature on the professionalization and medicalization of "mothercraft" and on "homemaking" includes such Canadian studies as Cynthia Comacchio, *Nations Are Built of Babies: Saving Ontario's Mothers and Children, 1900–1940* (Montreal and Kingston 1993); and Kathryn Arnup, Andrée Lévesque, and Ruth Pierson, eds., *Delivering Motherhood: Maternal Ideologies and Practices in the 19th and 20th Centuries* (London and New York 1990). Studies on First Nations, immigrants, and racialized subjects include J.R. Miller, *Shingwauk's Vision: A History of Native Residential Schools* (Toronto 1996); Gabaccia, *We Are What We Eat*; and Levenstein, *Paradox of Plenty*. Studies on post-1945 Canadian trends include Parr, ed., *Diversity of Women*; Adams, *Trouble with Normal*.

5. Canadian examples include Susan Prentice, "Workers, Mothers, Reds: Toronto's Postwar Daycare Fight," *Studies in Political Economy* 30 (1989); Veronica Strong-Boag, "Home Dreams: Canadian Women and the Suburban Experiment," *Canadian Historical Review* 72,4 (1991); Jeff Keshen, "Wartime Jitters over Juveniles: Canada's Delinquency Scare and Its Consequences, 1939–1945," in Jeffrey Keshen, ed., *Age of Contention: Readings in Canadian Social History, 1990–1945* (Toronto 1997); Pierson, *"They're Still Women After All"*; Korinek, *Roughing It in the Suburbs*.

6. Jean Bovey (Women's Voluntary Services) "'Pity U.K. Housewife,' Tells Canadians to Be Thankful," *Toronto Star* 27 Nov. 1948; "Soaring Food Prices Menace Democracy Prestige – Rabbi," *Toronto Star* 10 Jan. 1948. Other examples include: "Women Protest Lack of Subsidized Houses" (on National Council of Women) *Toronto Star* 4 June 1948.

7. Fahrni, *Household Politics*, ch. 5; Parr, *Domestic Goods*, ch. 4; Guard, "Women Worth Watching"; Julie Guard, "Canadian Citizens or Dangerous Foreign Women? Canada's Radical Consumer Movement, 1947–1950," in Epp, Iacovetta, and Swyripa, eds., *Sisters or Strangers?* On the United States, see Meyerowitz, ed., *Not June Cleaver*.

8. Laura A. Belmonte, "Mr and Mrs America: Images of Gender and the Family in Cold War Propaganda," Berkshire Conference on the History of Women, Chapel Hill, N.C., June 1996. My thanks to the author for providing a copy of her paper, which is based on her dissertation.

9. In *Canadian Register* 19 May 1962. Canadian material is thin on pathological constructions of the Communist woman in Cold War Canada, but see Guard, "Women Worth Watching," and the brief discussion of women spies in Whitaker and Marcuse, *Cold War Canada*, ch. 4.

10. Belmonte, "Mr and Mrs America"; Karal Ann Marling on the "Kitchen Debate," in Marling, *As Seen on TV: The Visual Culture of Everyday Life in the 1950s* (Cambridge, Mass. 1994), 243; May, *Homeward Bound*; Whitaker and Marcuse, *Cold War Canada*. The term "planned obsolescence" refers to the capitalist strategy of manufacturing consumer goods such as kitchen appliances with a short lifespan, thus forcing the consumer to replace them repeatedly.

11. Korinek, *Roughing It in the Suburbs*; Parr, *Domestic Goods*.

12. Korinek, *Roughing It in the Suburbs*; Franca Iacovetta and Valerie Korinek, "Jello Salads, One Stop Shopping and Maria the Homemaker: The Gender Politics of Food," in Epp, Iacovetta, and Swyripa, eds., *Sisters or Strangers?*; Alison J. Clarke, *Tupperware: The Promise of Plastic in 1950s America* (Washington, D.C. 1999). In the 1960s U.S. toaster ads showed mother using one in the living room, in front of the TV set, making a family snack without having to miss *I Love Lucy*. Marling, *As Seen on TV*, 266–67.

13. NFB Archives, File 57-602-11, Information Bulletin and Script, press release, *Arrival* (1957, 30 mins.), produced for Perspective television series and Department of Citizenship and Immigration, Information Sheet (David Bairstow, producer, Donald Ginsberg, director). The description of *Arrival* reads: "Time, patience, and understanding, we learn from Mario and Luisa, are necessary ingredients for a successful start in a new country, but the most vital is the welcome offered by native-born neighbours." See also NFB, *Mystery in the Kitchen* (1958, 23 mins.).

14. NFB Archives, File 51-214, *Canadian Notebook* (1953, 32 mins.), produced for Department of Citizenship and Immigration, Information Sheet, April 1953. On the Cold War purging of the NFB, see Whitaker and Marcuse, *Cold War Canada*, ch. 10; and on documentary filming in this era see Gary Evans, *In the National Interest: A Chronicle of the National Film Board from 1949 to 1989* (Toronto 1991).

15. NFB Archives, File 51-214, *Canadian Notebook*.

16. NFB Archives, File 57-327, *Women at Work* (1958), produced for Department of Citizenship and Immigration (Gordon Sparling, producer and director). It appears that this film was later retitled as *Careers for Women*. NFB Archives, File 57-327, "Careers for Women," Dorothy Macpherson, Liaison Officer (CCB) to Michael Spencer, NFB, 27 Dec. 1957, cc G. Sparling. The film set out to feature women "from one of the countries from which immigrant girls are recruited for these jobs, Belgium, U.K., France, Germany, Switzerland, Denmark, Norway, Sweden, Austria and the Netherlands." Sparling and the CB staffers also conferred on the making of a separate film on "Nursing." See also Marling, *As Seen on TV*, 243.

17. Stephen, *Pick One Intelligent Girl*, documents the rise of professional experts in the women's sections of the Canadian labour departments

who, equipped with their aptitude tests, training programs, and vocational tests, promised to put the right woman and job together. Although individual high-level bureaucrats, such as Fraudena Eaton or Marion Royce, used a discourse of human rights and equality of opportunity to support better equity measures for working women, including working moms, the state policies basically reflected both familialist and racialist notions of female skills and appropriate job or career categories, while the experts' individualizing processes effectively sidestepped the wider economic causes of unemployment.

18. Williams, "How to Keep Red Hands off Our New Canadians; Thelma Barer-Stein, *You Eat What You Are: A Study of Ethnic Food Traditions* (Toronto 1979), 132–37,524–32. See also Dora Wilensky (Executive Director of Jewish Family and Child Service, Toronto), "From Juvenile Immigrant to Canadian Citizen," *Canadian Welfare* 26 (January 1950).

19. Canadian medical experts said that there were not overly high rates of disease among the newcomers ("Only 4 in 10,000 Immigrants Said Victims of T.B.," *Toronto Star* 8 March 1952), but for a few examples see L.N. Ordon-Gizucki, "No Ideal Country," *Food for Thought* January 1953, 18; "An Outbreak of Typhoid Fever among New Immigrants to Canada," *Canadian Journal of Public Health* 48 (1957), 515–17.

20. Rather than specifying foods, the *Canada Food Guide* listed food groupings based on their nutritional value and then offered general guidelines for their consumption while allowing for choice and variety. (For example, "Fruit, one serving citrus fruit or tomatoes daily, or their juices; and one serving of other fruit," and "Meat and Fish: one serving of meat, fish, poultry, or meal alternates, such as fried beans, eggs, or cheese. Use liver frequently. Eggs and cheese at least 3 times a week each.) A revised 1950 version of the guide described "a new dietary standard" based on the careful study of the nutritional needs of people according to their body size, occupation, degree of activity, and other considerations. The guide was intended as a "nutritional floor" that outlined the minimal amount of food nutrients needed to maintain personal health. Because it allowed for "no margin of safety" and contained no "extras, luxuries, or non-essentials," educators warned that people who continuously consumed less than that prescribed by the standard would "endanger" their health. Nutrition Division of the Department of Health and Welfare, *Canada Food Guide* (Ottawa 1950).

21. Charles Heustis, "The Nation's Health," *Toronto Star* 5 Feb. 1949, 6; David Weiss, Executive Director, Montreal Jewish Child Bureau, "Immigrant Meets the Agency," *Social Casework* December 1952 (reprinted in *Food for Thought* January 1953).

22. Toronto Nutrition Committee, *Food Customs of New Canadians*. The guide, published with funds from the Ontario Dietetic Association, profiled fourteen ethnic groups, most of them European, and provided a detailed table of each group's food customs, including the women's cooking methods in old and new world contexts. It also discussed prenatal education and other issues. There were specific recommendations listed for each group.

23. Korinek, *Roughing It in the Suburbs*; Levenstein, *Paradox of Plenty*, ch. 12. See also Myerowitz, ed., *Not June Cleaver*.

24. For example, the supervisor of home economics for Vancouver Island had used more than two hundred copies of this guide, and five years after its original publication she was still handing it out to clients. AO, Maclean Hunter Records Series (MHRS), F-4-1-b, Box 432, Elaine Collett to DHA (Doris Anderson), LMH (Lloyd Hodgkinson), and J. Meredith, "Western Trip," 2 Oct. 1961. The first *Chatelaine Cookbook* sold 110,000 copies at a time when any Canadian book reaching sales of 10,000 copies was called a best-seller, and it was followed by *Chatelaine's Adventures in Cooking* and the *Chatelaine Diet Cookbook*. For more details, see Korinek, *Roughing It in the Suburbs*; Iacovetta and Korinek, "Jello Salads."

25. Canadian Red Cross, Ontario Division, *News Bulletin*, September-October 1945, 1, May 1946.

26. Iacovetta and Korinek, "Jello Salads."

27. Toronto Nutrition Committee, *Food Customs of New Canadians*; Korinek, *Roughing It in the Suburbs.*

28. Epp, *Women without Men*, 31.

29. Multicultural History Society of Ontario (MHSO), Oral History Collection (OHC), interviews with Amelie S-R, Lotta B., Werner B; Epp, "Semiotics of Zwieback; Epp, *Women without Men*; MHSO, OHC, interview cited in Phyllis Depoe, "Why Dutch War Brides Came to Canada and How They Survived," major research paper, Graduate History, University of Toronto, 1998, which draws on twenty-eight Dutch interviews, most of them with war brides.

30. Wyman, *DP*, 52, 54. See also Epp, "Semiotics of Zwieback"; Epp, *Women without Men*, ch. 2; Danys, *DP*, especially ch. 3.

31. Eksteins, *Walking Since Daybreak*, 169.

32. Ferguson, "Large Source of Labour in Europe's D.P.'s"; Wyman, DP, 113–17, 118; Carolyn Wyman, *Spam: A Biography* (San Diego 1999).

33. For example, see Toronto Nutrition Committee, *Food Customs of New Canadians.*

34. Danys, *DP*, 45–51

35. When I generalize from interview material, I am drawing on the following sample: thirty-five interviews in the Multicultural History Society of Ontario (MHSO), Oral History Collection (OHC), mostly conducted in the 1970s during which immigrant women or couples were asked to comment on food customs (with thanks to Martha Ophir and Renata Brun for transcribing them); several videotaped interviews with survivors that Holocaust historian Paula Draper generously shared with me; personal conversations with immigrant or ethnic Canadians; and dozens of stories from colleagues who, in response to several presentations I gave on this topic, shared their personal and family stories about experimenting with either Canadian or ethnic foodways.

36. MHSO, OHC, Interviews.

37. MHSO, OHC, Interview with Dagmar Z.

38. Personal conversation with their daughters.

39. *News Bulletin* (CRC, Ontario Division), September 1946. The "square meal" anecdote is in Baird, "British War Brides." For contrasting stories, see Hibbert, ed., *War Brides*; Butler, "Janey Canuck"; personal conversations with war brides, including Estelle Spergel (who also wrote a major research paper on the subject in the History Department at the University of Toronto in 2000).

40. "Vows Bananas Will Fatten 'Peg Hubby Freed from Japs," *Toronto Star* 23 Feb. 1946; Depoe, Why Dutch War Brides Came to Canada and How They Survived"; Barer-Stein, *You Eat What You Are*, ch. 15.

41. AO, MU3523 Series A-2, Committee Minutes 1885–1966, CCDN Minutes 12 May 1948; Danys, *DP*, chs.7–8; Christiane Harzig, "MacNamara's DP Domestics: Immigration Policy Makers Negotiate Class, Race and Gender in the Aftermath of World War Two," *Social Politics* 10,1 (Spring 2004).

42. For example, see CTA, St. Christopher House, SPC 484, IA1, Box 1, Folder 3, Minutes 1947–1948, Minutes 10 June 1948, Mrs. Donna Wood, Nursery School Report. See also UCA, Women's Missionary Society, Toronto Conference Branch, Annual Report, 1959, Box 156, File 8, Miss Mamie Gollan, Report, Queen Street, Church of All Nations; Miss Annie B. Bishop and Mrs. Pearl Budge, Report on Immigration and Community Work, and other entries on Toronto work in Annual Reports.

43. MHSO, OHC, Interview with Carol A. (who came to Canada in 1951 as a ten-year-old) and a dozen other interviews, including with Jose A., Maria A., Mr. and Mrs. Unis M., and Alfredo F. See also Iacovetta, *Such Hardworking People*; Depoe, "Why Dutch War Brides Came to Canada and How They Survived"; "Victims of Gouging Landlords," *Toronto Star* 6 Feb. 1963; Parr, "Introduction," in Parr, ed., *Diversity of Women*; Korinek, *Roughing It in the Suburbs*. The situation in Toronto would prompt struggling families to apply for low-rental housing in developments like Regent Park, but newcomers were less likely than Canadians to apply for it. Trudi Bunting and Pierre Filion, eds., *Canadian Cities in Transition: The Twenty-First Century* (Toronto 1991); Sean Purdy, "Scaffolding Citizenship: Housing Reform

and National Formation in Canada, 1900–1950," in Adamoski, Chunn, and Menzies, eds., *Contesting Citizenship*.

44. Edna Staebler, "The Other Canadians [Pillis]," *Chatelaine*, March 1965. For a contrast, see Parr, *Domestic Goods*; on Eaton's, Cynthia Wright, "Rewriting the Modern: The Death of a Department Store," *Histoire sociale/Social History* 35 (May 2000).

45. MHSO, OHC, Interviews; essays in Special Theme Issue on Toronto's People, *Polyphony* 6,1 (Spring/Summer 1984); Christiane Harzig, "When You Are a New Immigrant You Are Just Half and Half: The Process of Becoming Canadian among Post-World-War-Two German Immigrants," in Doris Eibl and Christina Strobel, eds., *Selbst und andere/s: Von Begegnungen und Grenzziehungen* (Augsburg 1998). My thanks to the author for sharing this paper with me. Also, Gabriele Scardellato and Manual Scarci, eds., *A Monument for Italian-Canadian Immigrants* (Toronto 1989); NFB Archives, *A Million and A Half of Us*, revised script, September 1958; Eric Geiger's "New Canadians" column in the *Toronto Star* includes many stories about the newcomers' cultural contributions, including culinary ones.

46. MHSO, OHC, interviews with Alfredo F., Mr. and Mrs. Unis M., and others; personal conversation with Maria Lombardi. A few husbands gained weight; see MHSO, OHC, interview with Manual Fernandes and his wife (not identified). On the lack of ethnic foods, see, for example, interviews with Iusa D-S., Raul C. (Kenora).

47. MHSO, OHC, interviews with Delkar M. They also raised two children and went into the bakery business with a friend.

48. MHSO, OHC, interviews, personal conversations; Barer-Stein, *You Eat What You Are*. This discussion, and the one following, is also informed by my research into Toronto newspapers, especially *Toronto Star*, news magazine articles, and some NFB films.

49. Toronto Nutrition Committee, *Food Customs of New Canadians*.

50. CTA, SCP, SCHO, Box 6, File 22: Interpretation, Immigrants 1958, A. Cecilia Pope to Doris Clarke, 15 April 1958, with enclosed report, "Civic Action in a Well Baby Clinic," 16 April 1958.

51. CTA, University Settlement House, SPC 24, N1, Box 1, Staff Meeting Minutes 1948–65; Minutes 28 April 1953; SPC 24C, Box 1, Annual Reports, 1 April 1949, 1953; CTA, St. Christopher House, SPC 484, IB2, Box 1, Folder 1, Reports, September 1953–56, Report of Summer Program, 1955 (29 Sept. 1955). See also AO, YWCA, MU3527, Annual Reports, 1941– 49, Report 1949,Weston Branch.

52. CTA, University Settlement House, SPC 24 N1, Box 1, Staff Meeting Minutes 1948–65, 28 April 1953; CTA, St. Christopher House, SPC 484, IB2, Box 1 Folder 1, Reports, September 1953–56, Report of Summer Program, 1955 (29 Sept. 1955).

53. Rhonda Hinther, " 'Sincerest Revolutionary Greetings: Progressive Ukrainians in Twentieth Century Canada," Ph.D. thesis, McMaster University, Hamilton, Ont., 2004, ch. 2; Swyripa, *Wedded to the Cause*, chs.4–5. The gender dynamics were discussed by older Ukrainian Canadian women at a symposium on the community organized by Nolan Reilly at the Winnipeg Ukrainian Labour Temple, Winnipeg, spring 2000. A special thank you to Larissa Stavroff for fielding several questions about Ukrainian food.

54. Personal conversations. The lower rates of citizenship among women for many groups also put them at a disadvantage vis-à-vis the Canadian state.

55. Staebler, "Other Canadians"; personal conversations with men and women who, as children, found themselves in this situation. See also Jo Marie Powers, ed., *Buon Appetito! Italian Foodways in Ontario* (Toronto 2000).

56. MHSO, OHC, interview with Helga A.; on both pre- and post-1945 Canadianization of ethnic food customs, see especially Swyripa, *Wedded to the Cause*, ch. 4.

57. MHSO, OHC, interview with Annemarie H. See also personal recollections in Powers, *Buon Appetito!*

58. MHSO, OHC, interviews; Vancy Kasper, "Use National Dishes to Build Christmas Recipes,"

Toronto Star 7 Dec. 1957; Iacovetta and Korinek, "Jello Salads"; personal conversations.

59. MHSO, OHC, interviews; personal conversations; NFB Archives, *A Million and a Half of Us*, script and video copy.

60. For example, CTA, SPC, Vol. 24, D Box 1, University Settlement House, Executive Director's Reports, 1939–1975, Head Resident's House Report, 14 Feb. 1952; Monthly Report, Executive Director's Report, 28 May 1956 on Housing and Suburbs: National Federation of Settlements Conference; St. Christopher House, SPC 484 IA1, Box 1, Folder 5, Minutes 1951– 1952: Annual Report 8 Feb. 1951; Andrew Thompson, "Victims of Gouging Landlords," *Canadian Register* 6 Feb. 1963. Later similar concerns were expressed about low-income suburbs.

61. CTA, SPC, Vol. 40, Box 6, File 15, John Haddad, Executive Director, St. Christopher House, to Miss Florence Philpott, Executive Secretary, Toronto Welfare Council, 25 April 1957.

62. The Hot Lunch quickly became incorporated into a two-year Family Life project in 1962 (see chapter 7). CTA, SPC, 40 Box 54, File 5-I,M,EG Immigration-General [1957, 1960–67, 1971] 26 April 1962, Report on Portuguese in Metropolitan Toronto, 12/62; CTA, SPC 484, IAI Box 2, Folder 4, 1962, Minutes 22 Nov. 1962, 22 Feb. 1962.

63. CTA, St. Christopher House, SPC 484, IA1, Box 1, Folder 3, minutes 1947–1948, minutes 10 June 1948, Mrs. Donna Wood, Nursery School Report. For similar food stories see, for example, UCA, WMS, Toronto Conference Branch, Annual Report, 1959, Box 156, File 8, Miss Mamie Gollan, Report, Queen Street, Church of All Nations; Miss Annie B. Bishop and Mrs. Pearl Budge, Report on Immigration and Community Work, and other entries on Toronto work in annual reports.

64. It turned out that the newcomers thought "God Save the Queen" was Canada's national anthem. (In effect, both songs had anthem status at this time.) I assume that by "pirokad" the staff meant piroshki, Russian buns filled with ground meat or vegetables and then baked or deep fried and served as an accompaniment to

bouillon. CTA, St. Christopher House, SPC 484 IA1, Box 1, Folder 6, Minutes 1953–54, 28 Jan. 1954.

65. CTA. St. Christopher House, SPC 484, 1A1, Box 1, Folder 6, minutes, report of New Canadian Adult Programme Worker, 1955.

66. A few entrepreneurs tried to cash in on the situation by creating European cooking schools or holding international food fairs in places such as the auditorium of Eaton's flagship store on College Street. See "World's Tastiest Dishes Temp Appetites at First International Cooking School," *Toronto Star* 1 Nov. 1954. Eric Geiger, "New Canadians" column, "Had 15 Cents in 1956, Buys Café," *Toronto Star*, 28 Dec. 1957, profiles Austrian-born Armand Volino, who bought a small Spadina Avenue snack bar, sinking his whole savings (earned as a waiter). Called "The Little Vienna," it was described as "an instant success," serving as many as one hundred meals a day. It served Austrian specialties such as "wiener schnitzel" and "Tyrolean knedly."

67. LAC, MG31, Citizenship Branch, D69, Col 12, File: 1950, Liaison Officer (Kaye), Report of Trip to Toronto and Hamilton, 27 Sept.–2 Oct. 1950.

68. AO, IIMT, File: Cookbook Project, "Special Greetings in Food, Christmas 1963," pamphlet.

69. LAC, MG31, D69, Vol. 12, File: 1957 Address delivered by Dr. V.J. Kaye, Sunday, 7 April 1957, Masaryk Hall, Toronto.

70. Jeannine Locke, "Can the Hungarians Fit In?" *Chatelaine*, May 1957. The readers' letters were all favourable, though for varied reasons. Mrs. M. Filwood, Toronto, really liked Katey's willingness to "iron clothes for the doctor's wife" and carry out other duties "just out of the sheer enjoyment of helping." The couple's many accommodations impressed a Nova Scotian woman who declared, "They would make better Canadians than some of us born in Canada if they were given the time and opportunity by us." A minister involved in a Hungarian resettlement project hoped that readers, "especially immigrants," would be "encouraged" by the couple's "wonderful successes

and achievements." Mrs. M. Filwood, Toronto, *Chatelaine*, July 1957; letter from a new reader, Halifax, N.S., August 1957; Rev. G. Simor, SJ, St. Elizabeth of Hungary Church, Toronto, September 1959.

71. Staebler, "Other Canadians." She became later famous for her "Schmecks" cookbook series on Mennonite and Pennsylvania German cuisine. See also Epp,"Semiotics of Zwieback"; Louise Di Iorio, "Pasta, Polenta, Ice Cream and Won Tons: Food Habits and Italian Immigrants in Postwar Toronto," History paper, York University, Toronto, April 2003.

72. Una Abrahamson, "A Streamlined System for Housekeeping," *Chatelaine*, January 1965.

73. Mimma Corno Piscitelli and Angelo Principe, "Pizza: A Worldwide Neapolitan Dish and a Success Story in Toronto," in Powers, ed., *Buon appetito!*

74. On the new left critique of U.S. food corporations in Latin America, and on sensuality, see Levenstein, *Paradox of Plenty*. I also drew on personal conversations with colleagues "of a certain age" who shared their stories of culinary and other forms of experimentation in the 1960s and 1970s.

75. Barer-Stein, "Introduction," *You Eat What You Are*.

76. Marie Holmes, "Easy-to-Make Pizza Pin Wheels" (1961), "Meals off the Shelf" (February 1955), and "Seven Dinners on the Double" (1961); Elaine Collett, "Ten New Ways of Cooking with a Pound of Hamburg" (September 1961), 47, and "98 Cent January Specials" (January 1960); all in *Chatelaine*. See also Levenstein, *Paradox of Plenty*; Gabaccia, *We Are What We Eat*.

77. AO, MU6410, IIMT, File: Cookbook Project, copy of *Discovering Canadian Cuisine: A Modern Guide to Cooking and Entertaining* (Canadian Gas Association 1966); personal conversations with elderly (and, in some cases, now deceased) Anglo-Celtic Torontonians who generously described their eating-out rituals in 1950s and 1960s Toronto. See also holiday issues of popular women's magazines such as the *Everywoman's Family Circle* 57,6 (December 1960).

78. One example is the cookbooks of homemaker Margaret Radforth (1911–92), one of the original residents of the modest middle-class planned community, Leaside, in Toronto; they included *The Joys of Jell-O* (published by General Foods, White Plains, N.Y.) and her local United Church fundraising cookbooks (in author's possession). The popularity of cookbooks and self-help books was an international phenomenon.

79. For example, AO, IIMT, File: Cookbook Project, *Special Greetings in Food, Christmas 1963*.

80. The phrase "eating the other" is from bell hooks. My discussion also draws on works dealing with cultural politics and cultural negotiations involving dominant and subordinate groups as well as readers' response or "multiple readings" approaches, as discussed, for example, in Lisa Lowe, *Immigrant Acts: On Asian American Cultural Politics* (Durham, N.C. 1996); and Lawrence Grossberg, Cary Nelson, and Paula Treichler, eds., *Cultural Studies* (London 1992).

7 Shaping the Democratic Family: Popular Advice Experts and Settlement House Workers

1. An estimated 14,000 people lived within the boundaries of St. Christopher House, located at 67 Wales Avenue. (See chapter 6, p.163 for the area's boundaries.) This vignette draws on: CTA, SPC, Vol. 24, Box 1; SPC 484, IB2, Folder 5, Beautify Our Neighbourhood Campaign 1963–64, Executive Director, John Haddad, "Rehabilitation and a Neighbourhood House," and Folder 4, United Church, 1957–1962; 1958 report to the Board of Home Missions on St. Christopher House; but mostly on the following two reports: CTA, SPC IB1, Box 2, Folder 2, "City of Toronto," 1951–53, Board requests and budgets, 1952, and SPC 484, IAI, Box 1, Folder 5, Minutes 1951–52, Annual Report, 8 Feb. 1951. The verbatim quotations are from "City of Toronto" folder except for "Communistic leanings," which is from the Feb. 8, 1951, report. My sincere thanks to Cathy James for her research into these records.

2. Margaret Finestein, "Sexuality, Mothering, and Motherhood after Auschwitz: Jewish Women as Displaced Persons in Germany, 1945–1951," paper delivered to Congress of Historical Sciences, Oslo, June 2000; Epp, *Women without Men*; Danys, *DP*; Iacovetta, *Such Hardworking People.*

3. See especially Smith, "Containments, 'Disease,' and Cold War Popular Culture."

4. AO, LCW, Minute Books, minutes of meeting, 20 May 1952, educational address to Toronto LCW, "How to Strengthen Family in Rapidly Changing World"; minutes of meeting, 19 Feb. 1952, Rev Dr. Gallagher, Canada Council of Churches, address to LCW, 19 Feb. 1952; Elinor G. Barnstead, "The Ordinary Family in Extraordinary Times," *Social Worker* 16,2 (December 1947); M.J. Henshaw, "UNRRA in the Role of Foster Parent," *Social Worker* 15,1 (September 1947); Eva Kenyon, Eileen Titus, and Alice Hall, "The Perpetual Crisis," *Social Worker*, 22, 4 (April 1954); AO, MU6474, File: Immigration, General, Dr. Robert Kreem, Director, International Institute of Metropolitan Toronto, address to IODE, St. George Chapter, Toronto, 28 March 1966; Iacovetta, "Gossip, Contest and Power."

5. Wilensky, "From Juvenile Immigrant to Canadian Citizen"; Sidney Katz, "The Redeemed Children," *Maclean's* 10 Jan. 1962; Benjamin Lappin, *The Redeemed Children* (Toronto 1963); Fraidie Martz, *Open Your Hearts: The Story of the Jewish War Orphans in Canada* (Montreal 1996); Kunzel, "Pulp Fictions and Problem Girls."

6. "Are You an Ideal Husband?" *Canadian Register* 15 Aug. 1953; Dr. Rev. Edgar Schmjedeler, "Wedding Ring" columns, "Father Is Recognized Head of the Family" and "Rules for Developing a Happy Marriage," *Canadian Register* 16 Feb. 1946; Belmonte, "Mr and Mrs America"; Thomas Waugh, "Monkey on the Back: Canadian Cinema, Conflicted Masculinities, and Queer Silences in Canada's Cold War," in Cavell, ed., *Love, Hate and Fear in Canada's Cold War*; Robert Rutherdale, "We Had a '65 Dodge: Fathers on Canada's Roads Since 1945," paper presented to Car in History:

Business, Space and Culture Conference, Toronto, 2005. See also Marling, *As Seen on TV*; Owram, *Born at the Right Time.*

7. For example, "Training the Young for Stalin" (see chapter 5, n.64). See also Gleason, *Normalizing the Ideal*; Smith, "Containments, 'Disease,' and Cold War Culture"; Smith, "National Security and Personal Isolation"; Gary Kinsman and Patrizia Gentile, *"In the Interests of the State": The Anti-gay, Anti-lesbian National Security Campaign in Canada, A Preliminary Research Report* (Sudbury 1998); Pierson, *"They're Still Women After All."* On the United States, see Michael B. Kassel, "Father Knows Best: U.S. Domestic Comedy," and Peter Orlick, "Leave It to Beaver: U.S. Situation Comedy," Museum of Broadcast Communications <http://www. musem.tv/archives/etv>; May, *Homeward Bound*; Meyerowitz, ed., *Not June Cleaver*; Margaret Marsh, "Suburban Men and Domesticity, 1870–1915," *American Quarterly* 40 (June 1988).

8. Eric Geiger's "New Canadians" column mainly dispensed practical advice about jobs and social services, but some people wrote about family problems. As for the women's columns, identifying racial-ethnic identity or status from the published letters is, of course, tricky, but the self-identified newcomers came from across Europe, and a few beyond, with the majority being British writers, whose letters reinforced the familiar theme that contrary to conventional wisdom they too faced serious adjustment problems. The new Canadians could write letters in their own language, and the final version and response appeared in English. If writers did not want their letter to appear, they could send a self-addressed envelope and receive the response in the mail. All four columns were published in *Toronto Star.*

9. *Toronto Star* 18 Aug. 1951; see also 8 March 1958.

10. For example, *Toronto Star* 21 Dec. 1946, 26 June 1948, 17 March 1951, 17 Oct. 1953, 20 Nov. 1954, 22 Sept. 1956, 6 Oct. 1956, 13 Oct. 1956, 20 Oct. 1956, 3 Nov. 1956, 5 Oct. 1957.

11. *Toronto Star* 9 March 1957.

12. *Toronto Star* 26 June 1948, 17 March 1951, 10 Sept. 1955, 20 Sept. 1958, 13 Dec. 1958.

13. *Toronto Star* 10 Sept. 1955; see also 12 April 1955, 5 May 1956.

14. Ironically, a good deal of their letters came from mixed marriages, usually between a Canadian and European partner. On Starr's concerns about mixed marriages, see *Toronto Star* 9 Oct. 1948, 23 Oct. 1948, 8 Jan. 1949, 11 Oct. 1958.

15. Also, the readers could attach their own meanings to what they read, and their reading was influenced by various factors, including the advice expert's responses and their own class, social, and political backgrounds. On readers response theory and popular media and culture texts, see, for example, on Canada, Korinek, *Roughing It in the Suburbs.*

16. Lash, "Sponge Spouse Gone Could Be a Blessing," *Toronto Star* 27 Jan. 1955.

17. Lash, "Pay Visit to Family Court Counsellor," *Toronto Star* 4 April 1959 ("Broken Hearted"). See also "Could Afford Car, Trip but Not Divorce," *Toronto Star* 20 Sept. 1958.

18. Mary Starr, column, *Toronto Star* 10 Sept. 1955.

19. *Toronto Star*, B.M.L. 13 Dec. 1958; "Can't Yet Divorce Beast," 25 Nov. 1958, signed N.J.F.; "International Group May Help!" 27 June 1959, signed C.N.

20. Margaret Little, *No Car, No Radio, No Liquor Permit: The Moral Regulation of Single Mothers in Ontario, 1920–1977* (Toronto 1998).

21. *Toronto Star*, L.K., 27 Jan. 1959, "New Start for 'Friendly' Mother Could Restore Her Two Children"; Responses: I.K. 12 Feb. 1959. See also response to self-identified English immigrant alcoholic, "AA Transforms Life," 10 Jan. 1959, 52.

22. Lash, "Wife Left, Took Furniture, 'You've Had It' Lawyer Said," *Toronto Star* 18 Nov. 1958.

23. Zay, "Adaptation of the Immigrant," 25–29; see also Schlesinger, "Socio-Cultural Elements." See also Adams, *Trouble with Normal*; Mariana Valverde, "Building Anti-Delinquent Communities: Morality, Gender and Generation in a City," in Parr, ed., *Diversity of Women*; Franca Iacovetta, "Delinquent Girls, Parents, and Family Court Intrusions into Working-Class Life," in Iacovetta and Mitchinson, eds., *On the Case.*

24. For the area covered by St. Christopher House, see p.163. The boundaries of University Settlement (15 Grange Rd.) were College Street in the north, the Waterfront in the south, University Avenue in the east, and Spadina Avenue in the west. The Central Neighbourhood House (349 Sherbourne St.) area was bounded by Bloor Street in the north, Queen Street East in the south, the Don River in the east, and Yonge Street in the west; the House was located near Regent's Park, a housing project that drew mostly Anglo-Torontonian families, and it had far fewer immigrants within its precinct than did St. Christopher House and University Settlement. But on newcomers, see CTA, SPC 484 IB2 Box 1, Folder 2, St. Christopher Reports, 1957–1962, Report 26 Feb. 1959.

   On the history of settlements, see, for example, on Canada: Sara Burke, *Seeking the Highest Good: Social Service and Gender at the University of Toronto, 1888–1937* (Toronto 1996); Cathy James, "Gender, Class and Ethnicity in the Organization of Neighbourhood and Nation: The Role of Toronto's Settlement Houses in the Formation of the Canadian State," Ph.D. thesis, OISE/Toronto, 1996; Irving, Parsons, and Bellamy, eds., *Neighbours*; Chunn, *From Punishment to Doing Good*; Graham, "History of the Toronto School of Social Work"; and Wills, *Marriage of Convenience*. On the United States, see, for example: Anthony Platt, *The Child Savers: The Invention of Delinquency* (Chicago 1969); Ellen Ryerson, *The Best-Laid Plans: America's Juvenile Court Experiment* (New York 1979); and the extensive literature dealing with Jane Addams and Hull House, including *Jane Addams, Twenty Years at Hull House* (New York 1910); Martha Vicinus, *Independent Women: Work and Community for Single Women, 1850–1920* (Chicago 1985); Rivka Shpak Lissak, *Pluralism and Progressives: Hull House and the New Immigrants, 1890–1919* (Chicago 1989).

25. CTA, St. Christopher House, SPC 484, Vol. 5 D, File 52, Annual Reports, 1945, *St. Christopher*

House: A Neighbourhood Meeting Place for Young and Old (with a Foreword by H.W. Crossin); Marion O. Robinson, *The Heart of the City* (1946).

26. (Bishop) Fulton J. Sheen, "Family Life Key to Delinquency," *Toronto Star* 7 Dec. 1957.

27. CTA, SPC 484, IB2, Box 1, Folder 1, Annual Reports, September 1953–56, Report, 27 Oct. 1955. The same information is contained in the annual reports of the other settlement houses.

28. For example, at University Settlement House in October 1954, the University of Toronto students in residence included a Masters of Social Work student, a law student, a Master's student in Zoology from Newfoundland, a Ph.D. student in Zoology, and two foreign students, one described as "a most charming woman doctor from Bombay" doing postgraduate work in biology, and the other a Nigerian political science student "who is our problem child," which is never explained. CTA, SPC 24 D, Box 1, Executive Director's Reports, 1939–1975, Head Resident's Report, October 1954.

29. CTA, St. Christopher House, SPC 484, IB2, Box 1, Folder 2, Reports 1957–62, House Report, October 1959; Folder 4, "A Review of the Religious Significance of the Program at St. Christopher House," October 1960; CTA, University Settlement, SPC 24 D, Box 1, Executive Director's Reports, 1939–1975, Head Resident's Report, April and May 1954.

30. CTA, St. Christopher House, SPC 484, IB2, Box 1, Folder 2, Reports, 1957–1962, Report 28 February 1957 (New Canadian Department).

31. Graham, "History of the Toronto School of Social Work"; Avison, *Research Compendium 1942–1962*; Josie Svanhuit, "Multi-Problem Family or Multi-Problem Agency?" *Social Worker* 31, 4 (October 1963), 14–16. See also Struthers, *Limits of Affluence*. U.S. examples include Gordon, *Heroes of Their Own Lives*.

32. CTA, University Settlement, SPC 24, C Box 1, Annual Reports, Head Resident's Report (K. Gorrie) April 1952; *St. Christopher House: A Neighbourhood Meeting Place for Young and Old.*

33. CTA, St. Christopher House, CTA, SPC 484, IB2, Box 1, Folder 2, Reports, 1957–1962, House Report, 22 Jan. 1959.

34. CTA, St. Christopher House, SPC 484, IB2, Box 1, Folder 2, Reports, 1953–56, report (Director John Haddad), report, 24 Feb. 1955; Reports 1957–1962, report, 26 Feb. 1959; Head of New Canadian Department Report, 1958.

35. CTA, St. Christopher House, SPC 484, IB2, Box 1, Folder 2, Reports 1957–1962, house report, May 1958; CTA, SPC 484, IB2, Box 1, Folder 4, United Church, 1957–1962, "A Review of the Religious Significance of the Program at St. Christopher House," October 1960.

36. *Toronto Star* 28 Aug. 1948, 11 Dec. 1948, 6 Aug. 1949, 3 Feb. 1950, 18 Oct. 1950, 24 Feb. 1951, 31 Mar 1951, 17 Oct. 1953, 25 April 1956.

37. *Toronto Star*, 13 Aug. 1949; Iacovetta, "Gossip, Contest and Power"; Foucault, *History of Sexuality*, Vol. 1 (London 1979); Adams, *Trouble with Normal*, ch. 4.

38. H.W. Crossin, Foreword, *St. Christopher House: A Neighbourhood Meeting Place for Young and Old*; Irving, Parsons, and Bellamy, eds., *Neighbours*, 162–65. For a critique of how an initially promising postwar liberal-democratic recreation movement in Ontario failed to revise gender hierarchies, see Tillotson, *Public at Play*.

39. CTA, University Settlement, SPC 24 C Box 1, Annual Reports, Annual Report, April 1949 (by A.F. Donaldson); Irving, Parsons, and Bellamy, eds., *Neighbours*, 162–65.

40. CTA, University Settlement, SPC 24 C, Box 1, Annual Reports, Head Resident's Report for 1950 (K. Gorrie).

41. CTA, St. Christopher House, SPC 484, IA3, Folder 13, Annual Report 1948; SPC 484, IB2, Box 1, Folder 2, Reports 1957–1962, including house report, May 1957.

42. Schlesinger, "Socio-Cultural Elements."

43. Katz, "How Mental Illness Is Attacking Our Immigrants"; CTA, University Settlement, SPC 24 C Box 1, Annual Reports, Annual Report, April 1949, Nursery School (the fifty children, aged two to five years, represented these nationalities: Hungarian, Polish, Ukrainian,

Finnish, Japanese Canadian, Negro, French Canadian, Jewish, British, Canadian).

44. This approach replaced what Gorrie called an earlier "permissive" approach that had failed, but she did not explain the meaning of the term. CTA, SPC 24 C, Box 1, Annual Reports, head resident's report (K. Gorrie), 1950.

45. Schlesinger, "Socio-Cultural Elements."

46. Eva-Lis Wuorio, "Two Years Later," *Maclean's*, 15 May 1950.

47. For example, CTA, St. Christopher House, SPC IB1, Box 2, Folder 2, "City of Toronto" 1951–53; SPC 484, IA3, Folder 13, Annual Report 1948; SPC 484 IB2, Box 1, Folder 2, Reports 1957–1962, summer program 1959; SPC 484, IB2, Box 1 Folder 2, Reports 57-62, house report, October 1959.

48. CTA, St. Christopher House, SPC 484, IB2, Box 1, Folder 1, Reports, September 1953–56, board report, 1953–56; Reports, 1957–1962, report, 28 Feb. 1957; "City of Toronto" 1951–53, St. Christopher board report.

49. CTA, St. Christopher House, SPC 484, IB2, Box 1, Folder 2, Reports 57-62, report, April 1957, 59 (Barbara Chisholm); see also April 1959.

50. CTA, SPC 40, Box 6, File 2, IMEG, Hungarian Relief Program, Victoria Day Nursery, Jarvis St., 29 March 1957, Viola G. Gifillan, Executive Director, Victoria Day Nursery, to Florence Philpott, Executive Secretary, Welfare Council of Toronto and District.

51. CTA, St. Christopher House, SPC 484, IB2, Box 1, Folder 2, Reports 1957–1962, house monthly report, February 1958, April 1958.

52. CTA, St. Christopher House, SPC 484, IB2, Box 1, Folder 2, Reports, 1957–1962, report, 28 Feb. 1957.

53. Frieda Held, casework instructor, University of Toronto School of Social Work, cited in John Graham, "History of the Toronto School of Social Work."

54. CTA, University Settlement, SPC 24 W, Box 1, File 7: Mental Health 1951–57 (Walter).

55. My working definition of "moral panic" is borrowed from moral regulation theorists and historians of sexuality, who suggest that professional and popular discourses, including public pronouncements by leading professionals and media overreporting, can help to create the impression that certain "folk devils" or dangerous tendencies, usually involving a sexual component, are threatening a society's moral order to a degree out of all proportion to the challenges or changes being discussed. Cohen, *Folk Devils and Moral Panics*; Weeks, *Sex, Politics and Society*; Hall et al., *Policing the Crisis*; Foucault, *History of Sexuality*, Vol. 2.

56. Gleason, *Normalizing the Ideal*, ch. 1; Adams, *Trouble with Normal*; Tillotson, *Public at Play*; Christabel Sethna, "The Facts of Life: Sex Education, Moral Regulation and Venereal Disease in Ontario, 1900–1950," book manuscript.

57. CTA, SPC 484, 1A1, Box 1, Folder 8, Minutes 1956 (Board of Directors), 23 Feb. 1956.

58. CTA, St. Christopher House, SPC IB1, Box 2, Folder 2, "City of Toronto," St. Christopher Board; SPC 484, IB2, Box 1, Folder 2, Reports 1957–1962, house report, January 1957, report 25 April 1957.

59. CTA, St. Christopher House, SPC 484 IB2, Box 1, Folder 2, Reports, September 1953–56, house report, 26 May 1953.

60. Crossin, Foreword, *St. Christopher House: A Neighbourhood Meeting Place for Young and Old*.

61. CTA, University Settlement, SPC 24 W, Box 1, File 15, Community Research Project 1948–1950, "Research Problems"; summer teen program; St. Christopher House, SPC 484, IB2, Box 1, Folder 2, Reports 1957–1962, summer program, September 1959. On efforts to deal with the boys' fears that political events in Europe might have adverse effects on them and provoke fights, see University Settlement, SPC 24 C, Box 1, Annual Reports, annual report, 1947.

62. CTA, St. Christopher House, SPC 484, IA1, Box 1, Folder 5, Minutes 1951–1952, annual report, 8 Feb. 1951.

63. CTA, St. Christopher House, SPC 484, IB1, Folder 1, Reports, September 1953–56, program

report, February 1954 (John Haddad); Irving, Parsons, and Bellamy, eds., *Neighbours*, 156, 170–72.

64. CTA, St. Christopher House, SPC 484, IB1, Box 2, Folder 2, "City of Toronto" 1951–53, St. Christopher Board; SPC 484, 1A1, Box 1, Folder 8, Minutes 1956, Board of Directors, 23 Feb. 1956.

65. CTA, St. Christopher House, SPC 484 IB2, Box 1, Folder 2, Reports 1957–1962, summer teen program, September 1959; house report, 23 Oct. 1958; report to board, January 1958; report, 26 Feb. 1959. See also Box 1, Folder 7, Minutes 1955, 26 May 1955, 25 April 1957; Box 53, File 5, A-IIAS, 1960–62, reports for April and May 1961 (J.C. Pedoni); Box 1, Folder 8, Minutes 1956 (Board of Directors), 23 Feb. 1956. See also University Settlement, SPC 24, Box 1, File 15, Community Research Project 1948–1950, "Research Problems," 1948; Box 1, Annual Reports, head resident's report, 7 April 1954; executive director's reports, 1939–1975; monthly report, 28 May 1956.

66. CTA, St. Christopher House, SPC 484, IB2, Box 1, Folder 2, Reports 1957–1962, house report, January 1957.

67. CTA, St. Christopher House, SPC 484, IB2, Box 1, Folder 2, Reports 1957–1962, house report, May 1957. See also SPC 484, IA1 Box 1, Folder 7, Minutes 1955, 26 May 1955; SPC 484, IB2 Box 1, Folder 1, Reports September 1953–56, house report, September 1954 (J. Haddad). See also SPC 484, IB2, Box 1, Folder 2, Reports 1957–1962, report, 25 April 1957.

68. CTA, St. Christopher House, SPC 484, IB2 Box 1, Folder 2, Reports 1957–1962, house report, May 1957; Phyllis Haslam, "The Damaged Girl in a Distorted Society," *Canadian Welfare* 15 March 1961, 81–85. On occasion the settlements joined forces with parents, schools, and the Big Brothers or Big Sisters organizations and family court to force a delinquent teenage boy or girl to live with a greater degree of supervised play, individualized case work procedures, and even mental testing, but these youth do not appear in the settlements' reports on their public efforts to use recreation

and community projects to fight family disorganization and delinquency. See, for example, University Settlement, SPC 24 W, Box 1, File 7, Mental Health 1951–57.

69. CTA, St. Christopher House, SPC 484, IB2, Box 1, Folder 2, Reports 1957–62, program evaluation 1961–62. (There are many statistical reports on memberships; the New Canadian Department had about four hundred members during the late 1950s.)

70. CTA, St. Christopher House, SPC 484 IA1, Box 1, Folder 7, Minutes 1955, report, 26 May 1955; Folder 8, Minutes 23 May 1956; see also Social Planning Council Questionnaire to one hundred organizations.

71. CTA, St. Christopher House, SPC 484, IB2, Box 1, Folder 2, Reports 1957–1962, report, April 1959. See also SPC, Vol. 40, Box 53, File 3, on International Institute of Metropolitan Toronto, Parkdale Branch, 1961–63, report of Branch Director to Project Committee of the International Institute, 15 May 1963.

72. CTA, St. Christopher House, SPC 484 IB2, Box 1, Folder 6, "Briefs and Reports 1962–1970," draft presentation to the Select Committee on Youth," October 1964. In the brief, he also noted that "when the needs of families are adequately met the children mature into healthy productive youth" and one of the "greatest needs" is for day-care centres for working mothers.

73. CTA, St. Christopher House, SPC 484 IB2, Box 1, Folder 1, Reports, September 1953–56, house report, 24 Feb. 1955; summer program and new Canadians – nursery and camp; Folder 2, 1957–1962, summer program, September 1959; Box 2, Folder 5, Minutes 1963, 28 Nov. 1963.

74. Schlesinger said that it made good sense for social workers to develop a working vocabulary in the language of their most numerous clients.

75. CTA, St. Christopher House, SPC 484 IB2, Box 1, Folder 6, Briefs and Reports 1962–1970, "Draft Presentation to the Select Committee on Youth," October 1964.

76. CTA, St. Christopher House, SPC 484, IAI, Box 2, Folder 4, 1962 Minutes, 22 Nov. 1962, 22 Feb. 1962; SPC 40, Box 54, File 5-I,M,E,G

Immigration-General (1957, 1960–67, 1971), "Report on Portuguese in Metropolitan Toronto," December 1962; SPC 40, Box 53, File 1 A – International Institute 1961–63 (1956-63).

8 From Newcomers to Dangerous Foreigners: Containing Deviant and Violent Men

1. On Griffin and his colleagues, see also chapter 3 here. On long-standing racial-ethnic stereotypes, see, for example, the essays by Lorna McLean and Marilyn Barber (on the Irish), Lisa Mar (on Asians), and Barrington Walker (Blacks) in Epp, Iacovetta and Swyripa, eds., *Sisters or Strangers?*; Frances Swyripa "Negotiating Sex and Gender in the Ukrainian Bloc Settlement: East Central Alberta Between the Wars," *Prairie Forum* 20,2 (Fall 1995); Karen Dubinsky and Franca Iacovetta, "Murder, Womanly Virtue and Motherhood: The Case of Angelina Napolitano, 1911–22," *Canadian Historical Review* 72,4 (1991).

2. Kimmel and Robinson, "Queer Career of Homosexual Security Vetting in Cold War Canada"; Kinsman, "'Character Witnesses' and 'Fruit Machines.'"

3. I consider both the public and confidential discourses while being mindful that these were not entirely separate spheres. The professional experts whose approaches were popularized in the English-Canadian press also intervened directly in the private lives of the offending men and their families. By focusing on European men, I am not suggesting that they alone were cast as emotionally scarred, mentally tenuous, and potentially dangerous. So too, were many others, including Canadian veterans and gays and lesbians. Nor do I mean to disparage any family names in my discussion of the press coverage of crimes or the popular stereotyping of deviant male behaviour.

4. Cohen, *Folk Devils and Moral Panics*; Weeks, *Sex, Politics and Society*; on the media's role, Hall et al., *Policing the Crisis*; Richard V. Erickson, Patricia M. Baranek, and Janet B.L. Chan, *Visualizing Deviance: A Study of News Organizations* (Toronto 1987); Mark Fishman, *Manufacturing the News* (Texas 1980).

5. For example, see the coverage of an Italian man who drowned himself near Toronto's Centre Island in order to punish an unfaithful wife. "'Wish is Granted, I'll be Dead' Believed Suicide Note to Wife," *Toronto Star* 11 June 1955. (The "believed" suicide note was in his shirt pocket.)

6. "Find Red Data in Box after Man Suicides," *Toronto Star* 24 Jan. 1952, 1.

7. Howard Sommerville, "Butchers Man and Wife, Insane DP Kills Self in Chicken Coop Home," *Toronto Evening Telegram*, 1 June 1950.

8. Walter Skol, "Nab Hardrock Miner as Landlord, Wife Stabbed to Death," *Toronto Star* 2 Feb. 1957. A photo caption states: "This Dagger Killed Two, Razor Sharp Commando Type."

9. "DP Stabbed, Hold Hubby Ex-Cop Knifed in Brawl," *Toronto Star* 28 April 1951. In his Hamilton, Ont., study, *Crimes, Constables, and Courts: Order and Transgression in a Canadian City, 1816–1970* (Montreal and Kingston 1995), John Weaver notes that the stiletto stereotype has some basis in truth insofar as a significant percentage of Italian criminals have used knives.

10. "Fires 100 Shots at Police, Flees Tear-Gas-Filled Shack with Bride," *Toronto Star* 7 Jan. 1956.

11. "Immigrant Hangs Jan. 25 for Strangling of Wife," *Toronto Star*, 6 Nov. 1954. Capital punishment was outlawed in Canada in 1976.

12. Elise Chenier, "Seeing Red: Immigrant Women and Sexual Danger in Toronto's Postwar Daily Newspapers," in Special issue, "Whose Canada Is It?" *Atlantis* 24,2 (Spring 2000). Chenier examined the *Toronto Star, Toronto Telegram*, and *Globe and Mail*. My thanks to her for bringing media critic sources to my attention.

13. On the history of this topic, see Maynard, "*On the Case* of the Case"; Strange, "Stories of Their Lives"; Stephen, "'Incorrigible,' the 'Bad,' and the 'Immoral'"; White, "Expert Witness Discourse"; Valverde, "Social Facticity and the Law."

14. LAC, MG 31, D69, Press Clippings, 1955 *Globe and Mail* columnist J.V. McAree (8, 20, 22 Jan.

1955), published "opinions directed against the newcomers to Canada."

15. LAC, RG26, Vol. 75, File 1-5-11, Pt. 1, Department of Citizenship and Immigration, Citizenship Branch, Foreign Language Press Review Service, Translation of Dr. Curt Borchardt's column, "With Pick and Shovel," 29 Nov. 1957; Brian Cahill, "Do Immigrants Bring a Mental Health Problem to Canada?" *Saturday Night*, 22 June 1957. The newcomers were aware that ethnic Canadians wondered about their mental health. Already wracked with guilt about having lived when so many died, Jewish survivors had to endure the suspicions of Canadians, gentile and Jewish, who wondered if they had done something sinister to save themselves as millions perished. Tulchinsky, *Branching Out*.

16. Stephen Paulik, president of the Ukrainian branch of the Canadian Legion, and others are cited in "Hunt Is Urged for Strangler by Vigilantes," *Toronto Star* 16 Dec. 1954.

17. LAC, MG 31, D69, Press Clippings, 1955, copy of "An Answer on Behalf of New Canadians," *Nasha Meta* 26 Feb. 1955 (translated), signed by executive members of the International Lawyers Association, Jan Aleksandrowicz and Dr. Joseph Glaug; *Globe and Mail* 5 Feb. 1955, English translation.

18. Cited in press clipping, *Globe and Mail*, 5 July 1955, and typed version in LAC, MG31, D69, Vol. 11, File: V. Kaye, Liaison Office.

19. Chenier, "Seeing Red."

20. See Iacovetta, "Making New Canadians."

21. Erickson, Baranek, and Chan, *Visualizing Deviance*, 3. See also Fishman, *Manufacturing the News*; Hall et al., *Policing the Crisis*.

22. Erickson, Baranek, and Chan, *Visualizing Deviance*, 6.

23. For a contemporary example, see the discussion of the Jamaican-born Canadian convicted of killing the young Greek-Canadian woman at the Just Desserts restaurant, Toronto, in Cynthia Wright, "Nowhere at Home: Gender, Race, and the Making of Anti-Immigrant Discourse in Canada," in Special Issue, "Whose Canada Is It?" *Atlantis* 24,2 (Spring 2000).

24. For historical treatments of this phenomenon in the Canadian past, see, for example, Karen Dubinsky and Adam Givertz, "'It Was Only a Matter of Passion': Masculinity and Sexual Danger," in Kathryn McPherson, Cecilia Morgan, and Nancy Forestell, eds., *Gendered Pasts: Historical Essays on Masculinity and Femininity in Canada* (Toronto 1999); Madge Pon, "Like a Chinese Puzzle," in Joy Parr and Mark Rosenfeld, eds., *Gender and History* (Toronto 1996). For a recent example, see Wright's discussion of the Toronto police efforts to solicit more support for tough methods by drawing dubious links between Latino gangs in Los Angeles and ethnic gangs in Toronto, and resorting to racial-ethnic profiling of crime in "Nowhere at Home."

25. "Meant No Reflection on New Canadians, Magnone Explanation," editorial, *Toronto Star*, 29 Oct. 1955.

26. Cahill, "Do Immigrants Bring a Mental Health Problem to Canada?; Griffin, "Problem of Mental Health in Canada," 3-10. See also Terry Copp and Bill McAndrew, *Battle Exhaustion: Soldiers and Psychiatrists in the Canadian Army, 1939–1945* (Montreal and Kingston 1990).

27. Katz, "How Mental Illness Is Attacking Our Immigrants." See also Gleason, *Normalizing the Ideal*; Kinsman, *Regulation of Desire*; Kinsman and Gentile, *"In the Interests of the State."*

28. Sidney Katz, "Sex Criminals," *Maclean's* 1 July 1947; J.D. Ketchum, "The Prude Is Father to the Pervert," *Maclean's* 15 Jan. 1948; June Callwood, "The Parents Strike Back Against Sex Criminals," *Maclean's* 23 July 1955. On the Parents' Action League, see Elise Chenier, "Take a Telephone and Stir: Women and the Parents' Action League," paper presented to the Canadian Historical Association, Sherbrooke, P.Q., 1999. See also the articles written by legal experts, such as W.C.J. Meredith, Q.C., "Law and the Sex Criminals," *Saturday Night* 18 Oct. 1952.

29. Some of the same authorities and studies were cited a year previously in Cahill, "Do Immigrants Bring a Mental Health Problem to Canada?"

30. The historiography reflects the deep division between those who saw the 1956 revolt as a

genuine revolt against Stalinism and those who dubbed it a bourgeois counter-revolution. However, many accounts note that when prisons were opened to free political opponents of the regime, a small proportion of the released inmates were common or hard-core criminals, although specialists looking into Hungarian immigration to Canada have not closely scrutinized the subject or estimated the numbers. For a range of positions, see Nandor F. Dreiziger's very preliminary "The Impact of the Revolution on Hungarians Abroad: The Case of Hungarian Canadians," in Bela K. Kiraly, Barbara Lotie, and Nandor F. Dreiziger, eds., *The First War between Socialist States: The Hungarian Revolution of 1956 and Its Impact* (New York 1984); Peter Fyer, *Hungarian Tragedy* (London 1997); Francois Fejto, *Behind the Rape of Hungary* (New York 1957); Bela K. Kiraly and Paul Jonas, eds., *The Hungarian Revolution in Retrospect* (New York 1977); and Reg Gadney, *Cry Hungary! Uprising 1956* (London 1986).

31. Cited in Katz, "How Mental Illness Is Attacking Our Immigrants."

32. "Boys at Stag Dances," *Toronto Star* 28 April 1956. She was responding most directly to a letter, 24 April 1956, "Puzzled by Girls," signed by A. Kupreisis.

33. Confidential conversation with a former child probation official; MHSO, Oral History Collection, Interview with Jose M.

34. She conducted at least two reports. LAC, RG26, Vol. 80, File 1-19-5 Pt. 2, Citizenship Branch, Research Division, 10-2-19; Mrs. N. Elgie, Research Division to the Director, Report on Sidney Katz, "How Mental Illness Is Attacking Our Immigrants."

35. LAC, RG26, Vol. 80, File 1-19-5, Pt. 2, Director, Citizenship Branch to Deputy Minister, Dr. Laval Fortier, Immigration and Citizenship, Re World Conference on Mental Health, 4 June 1958.

36. "Mailbox," *Maclean's* 18 Jan., 1, 15 Feb. 1958, for letters from Henry Oersen, Victoria; Gary Campbell, Cowley, Alta.; East Allwood, Montreal; Denise Lefebrve, Montreal.

37. This discussion of Canadian postwar psychiatry and newcomers relies on: Katz, "How Mental Illness Is Attacking Our Immigrants"; Griffin, "Problem of Mental Health in Canada"; Shorter, ed., *TPH*; Gleason, *Normalizing the Ideal*; Kinsman, *Regulation of Desire*; and Collins, *In the Sleep Room*.

38. Burns, "Allan Memorial Institute of Psychiatry"; Prosser, "Community Psychiatric Clinic and the *Social Worker*"; Christopher Dooley, "'What's in a Name?' Nursing in the Saskatchewan Mental Health Services, 1944–1973," paper presented to the Toronto Labour Studies Group, winter 2005.

39. AO, IIMT Collection, Restricted Material, Confidential Case Files (database of 1,105 case files), 75. To ensure anonymity, I do not provide precise citation of individual files, which have been reorganized into the database, and I have modified some details. The database contains information on each client (for example, age, nationality, sex, date of arrival), overall case file statistics (for example, by nationality, years in Canada, gender) and other features (for example, caseload, domestic violence, unemployment), and I have detailed notes on five hundred files. I am indebted to Stephen Heathorn for creating the database.

A tiny fraction of the Institute's cases (about 3 per cent) deals with men who were considered to be both mentally unstable and violent, and whose victims were their partners. In a few cases the men were described as suffering from psychosomatic disorders (stomach pains, throat problems) and paranoia. The small number of cases involving real or perceived mental illnesses reflects the Institute's mandate as a social welfare agency (and employment agency), not a psychiatric facility.

The database includes fifty-five cases involving men described as suffering from deep-seated depression, paranoia, excessive guilt, persecution complexes, or even brain disorders. Almost all of these men were not accused of being violent or cruel. Because the Institute was part of a large network of voluntary, government, and publicly funded agencies, many of its case files track people's movements and referrals from a family agency to a social welfare office, from a Children's Aid Society to family court, and so on. Although we should not merely accept at face value the caseworkers' psychiatric labelling of clients, the files are revealing in that they sometimes describe the client's "strange" behaviour or contain views that were corroborated by other caseworkers.

40. AO, IIMT Collection, Restricted Material, Confidential Case Files, 296. On the more common pattern (that is, Institute cases that began as something else, usually job placement, but eventually unmasked a domestic abuse situation), see Iacovetta, "Making New Canadians."

41. The mother's allowance cheque (or baby bonus) was made legally out to the mother, which meant that only she could legitimately cash it and use it for her child's needs.

42. On this pattern, consult historical studies of wife abuse, such as Annalee Golz, "Uncovering and Reconstructing Family Violence: Ontario Criminal Case Files," in Iacovetta and Mitchinson, eds., *On the Case*; Gordon, *Heroes of Their Own Lives.*

43. The typed copy in the file is in English, but because the brother's psychiatrist was Hungarian-speaking the original might well have been written in Hungarian.

44. Here we might keep in mind a certain irony: that the Communist authorities in Hungary, as a way of discrediting the revolutionaries, exaggerated the numbers of dangerous and deranged criminals freed in the 1956 revolt, and thus involved in the refugee streams. My thanks to Carmela Patrias for fielding my questions.

45. Elizabeth Janeway, *Powers of the Weak* (New York 1980); James C. Scott, *Weapons of the Weak: Everyday Forms of Peasant Resistance* (New Haven, Conn. 1985); Gordon, *Heroes of Their Own Lives*. See also George Chauncey, *Gay New York: Urban Culture, Gender, and the Makings of the Gay Male World, 1890–1940* (New York 1994); Little, *No Car, No Radio, No Liquor Permit.*

46. See also my first treatment of this topic based on a much smaller database (320) of Institute

files in my "Making New Canadians." The verbatim text from the file is precisely that.

47. I am not suggesting that Canadian experts did not acknowledge that dominant majority Canadian men were never violent or ill, but rather that those working primarily with minorities tended to focus on insular explanations that prioritized ill-adjustment and backward cultures.

9 The Sexual Politics of Survival and Citizenship: Social Workers, Damaged Women, and Canada's "Moral" Democracy

1. For a contemporary critique, see, for example, Bosworth, "What's Behind the Immigration Wrangle?" On immigrant histories that deal with women and moral regulation, see Iacovetta, "Manly Militants, Cohesive Societies and Defiant Domestics."

2. I place quotation marks around verbatim text, but readers should assume quotation marks around ideologically loaded terms such as bad, fit, and proper mother. The theoretical and historical literature on the normalizing of bourgeois ideals is now extensive; the much-cited work of moral regulation theorists such as Michel Foucault, Antonio Gramsci, and Philip Corrigan inform many recent Canadian gender histories, including Valverde, ed., *Studies in Moral Regulation*; Little, *No Car, No Radio, No Liquor Permit*; essays in Iacovetta and Mitchinson, eds., *On the Case.*

3. This discussion draws on studies of gender and nation, including the essays in Epp, Iacovetta, and Swyripa, eds., *Sisters or Strangers?*; Adamoski, Chun, and Menzies, eds., *Contesting Canadian Citizenship*; Bannerji, *Dark Side of the Nation*; Abigail Bakan and Daiva Stasiulus, *Not One of the Family: Foreign Domestic Workers in Canada* (Toronto 1997); Fraser and Gordon, "Civil Citizenship against Social Citizenship."

4. More recently, in what amounts to a major shift in thinking, civilian populations have been singled out as the primary victims of war, genocidal policies, and military occupations – a recognition of the horrific implications

of warfare for women, who have experienced and continue today to experience war as direct casualties, refugees, and victims of sexual and domestic violence. Still, although an estimated 80 per cent of the world's refugees are women and children, receiving nations such as Canada continue to accept more men than women refugees.

5. On situational morality, see Epp, *Women without Men*, 61–69; Annemarie Troger, "Between Rape and Prostitution: Survival Strategies and Chances of Emancipation for Berlin Women after World War II," in Judith Friedlander et al., eds., *Women in Culture and Politics: A Century of Change* (Bloomington, Ill. 1986); Lawrence Langer, *Holocaust Testimonies: The Ruins of Memory* (New Haven, Conn. 1991).

6. Cynthia Cockburn, *The Space Between Us: Negotiating Gender and National Identities in Conflict* (London and New York 1998); Cynthia Enloe, *Bananas, Beaches, and Bases: Making Feminist Sense of International Politics* (Berkeley, Cal. 1989); Wenona Giles, Helene Moussa, and Penny Van Esterick, eds., *Development and Diaspora: Gender and the Refugee Experience* (Dundas, Ont. 1996); Special Issue, "Women in Conflict Zones," *Canadian Woman Studies* 19,4 (Winter 2000), including Margaret D. Stetz, "Woman as Mother in a Headscarf: The Woman War Refugee and the North American Media"; Wenona Giles et al., eds., *Feminists under Fire: Exchanges across War Zones* (Toronto 2003); Joan Ringwold, "Gender and Genocide: A Split Memory," in Ronit Lentin, ed., *Gender and Catastrophe* (London 1997); Judith Tydor Baumel, *Double Jeopardy: Gender and the Holocaust* (London 1998); Ellen Cole, Oliva M. Espin, and Esther D. Rothblum, eds., *Refugee Women and Their Mental Health: Shattered Societies, Shattered Lives* (Binghamton, N.Y. 1992); Epp, *Women without Men*; Draper, "Surviving Their Survival"; Dalia Ofer and Lenore J. Weitzman, eds., *Women in the Holocaust* (New Haven, Conn. 1998); Finestein, "Sexuality, Mothering, and Motherhood after Auschwitz."

7. Epp, *Women without Men*, 56–69; Troger, "Between Rape and Prostitution," 99; Antony

Beevor, *Berlin–The Downfall 1945* (New York 2002); Tulchinsky, *Branching Out*. For a moving memoir of wartime rape, see Agate Nesaule, *A Woman in Amber: Healing the Trauma of War and Exile* (New York 1997).

8. MHSO, Oral History Collection, interview with C. R. and cited in Phyllis Depoe, "Why Dutch War Brides Came to Canada and How They Survived."

9. Epp, *Women without Men*, 58; Finestein, "Sexuality, Mothering, and Motherhood after Auschwitz."

10. Cited in Epp, *Women without Men*, 60, which sees these patterns as continuing survival strategies.

11. Gerda Frieberg, taped presentation to the Ontario Women's History Network (OWHN), Annual Meeting, Ontario Institute for Studies in Education (OISE), Toronto, February 1991, with introduction by Paula Draper; Frieberg cited in Al Sokol, "Remember Us," *Toronto Star* 27 Oct. 1992; Finestein, "Sexuality, Mothering, and Motherhood after Auschwitz"; Draper, "Surviving Their Survival"; Troger, "Between Rape and Prostitution," 101–4.

12. Antina Grossman, "Trauma, Memory, and Motherhood: Germans and Jewish Displaced Persons in Post-Nazi Germany, 1945–1949," *Archiv fur Sozialgeschichte* 38 (1998); Finestein, "Sexuality, Mothering, and Motherhood after Auschwitz"; Elizabeth Heineman, "The Hour of the Woman: Memories of Germany's 'Crisis Years' and West German National Identity," *American Historical Review* 101 (1996); Eksteins, *Walking Since Daybreak*. As Eksteins notes (166), the *Trummerfrauen*, or woman of the rubble, many of whom were also rape victims, came to represent the German experience and achieved a kind of sainthood.

13. However, the exact numbers are not known. Epp, *Women without Men*, 64-65.

14. Frieberg, taped presentation, OWHN.

15. Ibid. Like Frieberg, many of them were young women who had been robbed of their adolescence. She had never gone out with boys, was terrified of soldiers and other men in uniform, and still knew little about sex and pregnancy.

16. Since the Allied commanders neither advocated nor condoned rape and had greater control over their troops, rapes by Western soldiers were less common, though they did occur. For the latter point, Finestein draws on Georgia M. Gabor's account of being raped by a Jewish male survivor in Gabor, *My Destiny: Survivor of the Holocaust* (Arcadia, Cal. 1981), 142–44, cited in Finestein, "Sexuality, Mothering, and Motherhood after Auschwitz."

17. Stephanie W. Bellini, "The Kitchen Table Talks: Italian Immigrant Domestic Workers in Toronto's Postwar Years," M.A. thesis, Memorial University, St. John's, Nfld., 2001, 115–19; Miriam Halpern, "Parenthetical Memories: An Exploration of World War II Trauma and Italian Women's Fiction after 1968," thesis, Italian Studies, New York University, 2003; Alaine Polcz, *One Woman in the War: Hungary 1944–1945* (Budapest, Hungary 2002).

18. Finestein's research reveals valuable examples of this change in behaviour, including that of a woman who admonished the young DP "girls" living in her house for using sex in utilitarian ways, even threatening to kick them out if they continued. As told by Erna F. Rubenstein in her memoir *After the Holocaust: The Long Road to Freedom* (North Haven, Conn. 1995), 35, cited in Finestein, "Sexuality, Mothering, and Motherhood after Auschwitz," 12.

19. These liberation encounters created confusion or stress for some women, including survivors like Fanya Gottesfeld Heller, whose teenage memoir speaks powerfully on the topic, and suggests they were not in touch with their sexuality. Heller, *Strange and Unexpected Love: A Teenage Girl's Holocaust Memoirs* (Hoboken, N.J. 1993). Finestein directed me to this compelling source.

20. One of them left when told there were children asleep in the next room; the other ran off when the woman began screaming. Rubenstein, cited in Finestein, "Sexuality, Mothering, and Motherhood after Auschwitz," 16.

21. MHSO, Oral History Collection, Interview with Caterina A. This interview is part of a set of interviews conducted by Nancy Jones as part of a larger project on the Dutch war brides. Alas, very few of the interviews say much about sexuality, in part, it appears, because the interviewer seems to stick closely to a list of questions on a predetermined questionnaire that deals with relations between liberators and liberated but in which women's lives, or sexuality issues more generally, do not figure prominently. See also Depoe, "Why Dutch War Brides Came to Canada and How They Survived," 5–7.

22. Eksteins, *Walking Since Daybreak*, 167; Harzig, "MacNamara's DP-Domestics."

23. Eksteins, *Walking Since Daybreak*, 167.

24. Leland Stowe, "Post-war Europe Baffling to Visitor and Old-Timer," *Toronto Star* 10 Aug. 1946.

25. Similar observations were later made of the refugee camps that held Hungarian 56ers in 1956–57 and various asylum-seeking refugees from the Eastern bloc countries.

26. A female friend had relayed to Rubenstein that to experience with another person such "an exhilarating emotional high" and "release" of long-suppressed feelings made her "feel free at last." Another woman, from Kibbutz Buchenwald, wrote that becoming romantic had made the young folk cheerful and free. Rubenstein, cited in Finestein, "Sexuality, Mothering, and Motherhood after Auschwitz," 9.

27. Finestein, "Sexuality, Mothering, and Motherhood after Auschwitz."

28. Ibid. Finestein cites from several male memoirs. See also Wyman, *DP*. Many Jewish DPs disapproved of Jewish men having sex with German women, no matter what form it took, considering it morally repellent or a form of betrayal. At Kibbutz Buchenwald, the rabbis and the newspapers denounced or expelled men who slept with German women.

29. Some gravitated towards those from their home towns or regions, with whom they could share memories of peoples and places. Others renewed friendships first forged in the ghettos and concentration camps. Still others met only in the aftermath of war, often marrying only months later. Finestein, "Sexuality, Mothering, and Motherhood after Auschwitz"; Wyman, *DP*.

30. Harzig, "MacNamara's DP-Domestics"; Wyman, *DP*. On DP and immigrant domestics, see also

Danys, *DP*, chs. 7-8; Franca Iacovetta, "Primitive Villagers and Uneducated Girls: Canada Recruits Domestics from Italy, 1951–52," *Canadian Woman Studies* 7,4 (Winter 1986). My thanks to Alexander Freund for sharing with me some of the valuable doctoral research on German immigration to Canada, including the point that placement agents, whether out of lack of sympathy or sensitivity, sometimes placed German women domestics with Canadian Jewish families.

31. MHSO, interview, Mrs. C. Rhyzak; also cited in Depoe, "Why Dutch War Brides Came to Canada and How They Survived," 18.

32. The example is from my database of confidential case files culled from the Public Archives of Ontario, International Institute of Metropolitan Toronto, 106. (She eventually left her husband.) For other examples, see Epp, *Women without Men*.

33. By "these outrages," it meant specifically "the present inhuman treatment accorded loyal Greek subjects who become victims of these [rebel] forces in raids on Greek territory, especially the kidnapping and outraging of women and girls as a regular practise, according to this communication." The IODE had received its information from a Polish refugee priest at an Ontario Catholic seminary, a man who was lobbying government and non-governmental organizations to lend their support to calls to have the charges investigated. LAC, IODE Collection, RG28, Vol. 7, File 1946–47, National Executive Minutes, 3 April 1946–2 July 1947, held in different locale each year (the first example is from 19 June 1946); LAC, IODE Collection, RG28, Vol. 7, File 10, National Executive Minutes, September 1947–4, Dec. 1950, 3 March 1948.

34. In response Ottawa had asked women's groups, including the YWCA, Catholic Women's League, and the IODE, to do something positive for the girls to "offset" the influences of these communists.

35. Since the woman had come to the National Employment Service office to meet an aunt supposedly interested in hiring her, the explanation may have been an insufficient one.

36. "Hysterical D.P. Girl on Forty-Foot Perch Rescued by Firemen, *Toronto Star* 2 May 1949, 1; AO, YWCA, MU3523, Box 7, Series A-2, Committee Minutes 1885–1966. Additional suicide examples include an Italian newcomer mother accused of petty theft and an ethnic Canadian mother, a Doukhobor widow with the radical Sons of Freedom who was despondent over the children's forced location to the public school system. See, for example, "Star Brings Aid to Italian Family after Mother's Tragic Death," *Toronto Star*, 19 Oct. 1955; editorial, "How Inhuman Can Canadians Be? *Toronto Star* 27 July 1957.

37. "'Didn't Kill Him' Girl, 24, Weeps, Put in Army Care," *Toronto Star* 20 Dec. 1947, 1, and 29 Dec. 1947.

38. Battle over TV Set," *Toronto Star*, 11 April 1959, 1, with large photo of two women. For other examples, see "'Drinking Rent Money' Blamed in Fatal Fight in Parliament St. Home," *Toronto Star* 12 June 1948, 1; "Woman Is Charged with Axe Murder," *Toronto Star* 12 June 1948; "Woman Killed at Party for Freed Prisoner–Police," *Toronto Star* 31 July 1948.

39. Epp, *Women without Men*.

40. AO, IIMT Collection, Restricted Material, Confidential Case Files, 51.

41. Little, *No Car, No Radio, No Liquor Permit*.

42. Miss D. is AO, IIMT Collection, Restricted Material, Confidential Case Files, 81.

43. Miss E is in AO, IIMT Collection, Restricted Material, Confidential Case Files, 71. On postwar Italian Slovenes, see Anne Urbancic, "Italo-Slovenian Immigrants in Toronto: Doubled Ethnicities," in Scardellato and Scarci, eds., *Monument for Italian Canadians*. The racial-ethnic tensions between domestic workers and Canadian employers were not uncommon, including between Canadian Jewish families and German domestic recruits (many of whom had been in the Hitler Youth leagues), and speaks to the complicated character of postwar ethnic relations in Canada. Nor was it unusual for either Canadian families or domestic recruits to express their ethnic preferences or prejudices. Canadian selection agents also

had their own quiet racial quotas, which almost always worked against Jews. Their reasoning was often contradictory; for example, they generally exhibited a preference for Protestants yet considered the Baltic DPs, most of whom were Catholic and susceptible to accusations of Nazi collaboration, as among the most preferred recruits. Harzig, "MacNamara's DP-Domestics." Thanks to Alex Freund for his translation of his thesis research; see also his "Nationalism, Oral History, and German and German Jews," article-length manuscript.

44. AO, IIMT Collection, Restricted Material, Confidential Case Files 71. For example, when he first phoned her about the clinic, she asked him for money and when he said he had none to give, she said she did not feel well enough to travel and could not afford the streetcar fare.

45. See, for example, Betty K. Isserman, "The Case Work Relationship in Work with Unmarried Mothers," *Social Worker* 17,1 (June 1951). See also Kunzel, *Fallen Women, Problem Girls*.

46. On Canada, Draper, "Surviving Their Survival," 400; Paula Draper, Holocaust Survivors, Videotaped Interviews – with thanks to her for sharing some of her research; many of the women stressed that a key motive for doing the interviews was to pass on the history not only their tragic past but of their surviving it, to their children and grandchildren; Tulchinsky, *Branching Out*; Epp, *Women without Men*. U.S. examples include see Nesaule, *Woman in Amber* (who, many years after settling in the United States, and long after being a witness, as a young girl, to the rape and torture of Latvian and other women at the hands of both the Russians and Germans, wrote a healing memoir).

I also base this analysis on a sample of more than one hundred (transcribed) interviews with postwar European newcomers in the Oral History collection at the Multicultural History Society of Ontario.

47. Frieberg, taped presentation to the Ontario Women's History Network Annual Meeting.

48. Personal conversations with the adopted child of survivors who did not know whether their daughter was or was not Jewish by birth but raised her as a Jewish-Canadian daughter.

49. See also Giles et al., *Feminists Under Fire*.

10 Guarding the Nation's Security: On the Lookout for Femmes Fatales, Scam Artists, and Spies

1. This discussion draws on a number of works, including Whitaker and Marcuse, *Cold War Canada*; Kinsman, Steedman, and Buse, eds., *Whose National Security?*; Larry Hannant, *That Infernal Machine: Investigating the Loyalty of Canadian Citizens* (Toronto 1995); Scher, *Un-Canadians*; Merrily Weisbord, *The Strangest Dream: Canadian Communism, the Spy Trials and the Cold War* (Toronto 1983); Kinsman and Gentile, *"In the Interests of the State"*; Philip Gerrard, "From Subversion to Liberation: Homosexuals and the Immigration Act, 1952–1977," *Canadian Journal of Law and Society* 2 (1987), and, on the first red scare, Gregory S. Kealey, "1919: The Canadian Labour Revolt," reprinted in Kealey, *Workers and Canadian History* (Montreal 1995), and Kealey, "State Repression of Labour and the Left in Canada."

2. Blair Fraser, "How Racketeers Sold Entry in Canada," *Maclean's* 15 March 1952. See also the coverage of the search for Olga Leikues, the "beautiful blonde secretary and fellow countrywoman" of Latvian-born refugee Alfred Valdmanis, who, as director-general of economic development in Newfoundland, bilked the provincial government of an estimated $150,000 in connection with the prosperity grants received as part of the terms of Newfoundland entering Confederation in 1949, in Jack Gale, "Hold Valdmanis' Cash as Blonde Secretary Sought across Nation," *Toronto Star* 5 June 1954.

3. For Drane, *Canadian Register* 19 May 1962. For Pauker, "Has Armoured Car, 2 Homes, Woman Communist Is Boss," *Toronto Star* 8 Nov. 1947.

4. "Moscow Sold out for Dior Shares," *Toronto Star* 30 May 1959; Aline Mosby, "Russian Women Veto Sack Dress," *Toronto Star* 27 June 1959.

5. On occasion the news of an exceptional woman like Valentina Tereshkova, the famous "blonde"

cosmonaut who in 1963 became the first woman in space, and of educated Soviet women who appeared to have successfully combined careers and family, attracted the envy of at least some middle-class North American women who felt that they had had to choose between one or the other. Robert L. Griswold, "Russian Blonde in Space." See also Gentile, "'Government Girls' and 'Ottawa Men'"; Korinek, "'It's a Tough Time to Be in Love.'"

6. "German Girl Returns to Fight Spy Accusations," *Toronto Star* 17 July 1954, 11; on Mata Hari, see Martina Bexte, "Who Was Mata Hari?" <http://sc.essortment.com/whowasmatahar_rhrc.htrr>; Michael Duffy, "Who's Who: Mata Hari" <http://www.firstworldwar.com/bio/matahari.htm, 2000-05>; "Mata Hari," in Thomas B Allen, *Spy Book: The Encyclopedia of Espionage* (New York 1997).

7. LAC, RG26, Memorandum to the Minister from Laval Fortier, Ottawa, 31 March 1955. The memo was drawn up in response to a request for a report on the statements made by lawyers Andrew Bevin and Eugene Forsey at a Race Relations Conference organized by the CCF Joint Labour Committee for Human Rights; they raised the possibility of racial discrimination with respect to the deportation order of two South Asians born in the British West Indies and thus British subjects. See also James Walker, *Race, Rights and the Law in the Supreme Court of Canada: Historical Case Studies* (Waterloo, Ont. 1997).

8. Whitaker, *Double Standard*, Introduction, passim, and, on Brent case, 204–6. See also Kelley and Trebilcock, *Making of the Mosaic*, 324–27.

9. C.F. Bosworth, "What's Behind the Immigration Wrangle?" He noted that the controversy raised other big questions, including whether Canada had a moral obligation to help countries like the British West Indies and Italy, which had severe population problems. The article included a large photo of Brent "being hustled out" of court.

10. Bosworth, "What's Behind the Immigration Wrangle?"; Whitaker, *Double Standard*, 204-6.

11. For example, an Italian-Canadian man who had smuggled newly arrived Italians over the U.S.

border admitted to having enlisted the help of his attractive girlfriend, who had diverted the border guards with her charm and helped establish their alibi as tourists – but, being gallant, he refused to reveal the mystery woman's identity. See LAC, Department of Citizenship and Immigration (DCI), RG26, Vol. 85, File 1-37-8, Pt. 1, Reports of Investigations, including Re: Smuggling Aliens into Canada, 23 Nov. 1954. On other groups, see, in the same file, Report of Investigations, Re: Amitié Canadienne-Française (travel agency), 31 Jan. 1955; "Arrest 111 Chinese in Raid on Club, to Be Test Case," *Toronto Star* 22 April 1950, 1.

12. LAC, DCI, RG26, Vol. 85, File 1-37-8, Pt. 1, Ottawa, 23 Nov. 1953.

13. LAC, DCI, RG26, Vol. 85, File 1-37-8, Pt. 1, Report of Investigation, Administrative Branch of DIC Re: Alleged Sheltering of Seamen Deserters – Toronto, 10 and 11 Nov. 1953, assisted by Constable A. Skagfeld (RCMP Toronto).

14. Ibid.

15. RG26, Vol. 85, File 1-37-8, Pt. 2, Turner, SI Report of Investigation Re: Mrs George Z., 1954.

16. For example, see Iacovetta, "Primitive Villagers and Uneducated Girls."

17. RG26, Vol. 85, File 1-37-8, Pt. 1, 2, L.V. Turner, SI Report of Investigation Re: Earl W.C. and Rita G.N., Immigration Act (51) Montreal, 27 Jan. 1954; also, Re: Vifro M., 1953–1954.

18. June Callwood, *Emma: Canada's Unlikely Spy* (Toronto 1984); J.L. Granatstein, *Canada 1957–1967: The Years of Uncertainty and Innovation* (Toronto 1986); J.L. Granatstein and David Stafford, *Spy Wars: Espionage and Canada from Gouzenko to Glasnost* (Toronto 1990); Robert Bothwell, Ian Drummond, and John English, *Canada Since 1945: Power, Politics and Provincialism* (Toronto 1981).

19. Korinek, "'It's a Tough Time to Be in Love,'" describes the few articles on the Gouzenkos, including John Clare's 1954 article, "What's It Like to be Mrs. Gouzenko?" 170–73.

20. Roy Lindsay Kellock and Robert Taschereau, *Royal Commission on Espionage* (Ottawa 1946).

The detainees included twelve Canadians and one Briton, atomic scientist Alan Nunn May, who was sent back to England to stand trial.

21. Gregory S. Kealey, "Spymasters, Spies, and Their Subjects: The RCMP and Canadian State Repression," in Kinsman, Buse, and Steedman, eds., *Whose National Security?* 18; Cavell, *Love, Hate and Fear in Canada's Cold War*, 6-7. See also Clarke, "Debilitating Divisions"; Whitaker and Marcuse, *Cold War Canada*, chs. 2-4; Ellen Schreker, *Many Are the Crimes: McCarthyism in America* (Boston 1998); Weisbord, *Strangest Dream*.

22. This discussion draws largely on Whitaker and Marcuse, *Cold War Canada*. The events did arouse the indignation of the fledgling civil liberties movement: see Clarke, "Debilitating Divisions."

23. Whitaker and Marcuse, *Cold War Canada*, ch. 3.

24. Canada did very little atomic research. One of the main weapons about which information came from Canada was RDX, a conventional explosive used in the war.

25. Whitaker and Marcuse, *Cold War Canada*, ch. 3.

26. The quotation and the description of Ottawa at this time are from Callwood, *Emma*, ch 9.

27. Callwood, *Emma*, ch. 9. The British atomic scientist Alan Nunn May, in England, got the longest sentence, ten years. Whitaker and Marcuse, *Cold War Canada*, ch. 3.

28. The *Toronto Star*'s front-page coverage had photos of the women and Mazerall. "Moscow Had Quebec Pipeline. They Face Charges Betraying Canada's Secrets," *Toronto Star* 5 March 1946.

29. For the various examples, LAC, June Callwood Collection, MG 31, Vol. 21 (Series K-24), File 21-3, biographical notes on accused, spies, reference materials, 1946–1984, newspaper clippings and typed transcripts of clippings, Marjorie Earl, "Montreal, 26 March 1946; Ross Harkness, *Toronto Star* 11, 13, 20, 26 March 1946, and Callwood, *Emma*. After her release from prison, the Saskatoon *Star-Phoenix* described Woikin as being still youthful and

pretty: LAC, June Callwood Collection, MG 31, Vol. 21 (Series K-24), File, 21-3, clipping, 7 Dec 1948.

30. Callwood, *Emma*, and quoted in Ross Harkness, *Toronto Star* 14 March 1946.

31. Cited in "Miss Willsher Spy Witness over Protests of Defence," *Toronto Star* 25 April 1946.

32. Whitaker and Marcuse, *Cold War Canada*, ch. 3; Callwood, *Emma*.

33. LAC, MG 31, Vol. 21 (Series K-24), File 21-3, biographical notes on accused, spies, reference materials, 1946–1984, newspaper clippings and typed transcripts of clippings; "2 ½ Years for Woikin, First Convicted Spy," *Globe and Mail* 31 April 1946; "Mrs Woikin Gets 2 ½ years, Toronto *Evening Telegram*.

34. This discussion draws on Callwood, *Emma*.

35. LAC, MG 31, Vol. 21 (Series K-24), File 21-1, correspondence notes, reference materials, typed transcript of Callwood interview with Marjorie Earl, 11 May 1983. See also Callwood, *Emma*.

36. LAC, MG 31, Vol. 21 (Series K-24), File 20-18, correspondence notes, reference material, "Red Faces around the D.V.A.," *The Gazette* (Montreal), 11 Oct 1947; Callwood, *Emma*.

37. The quotation is from LAC, MG 31, Vol. 21 (Series K-24), File 21-1, correspondence notes, reference materials, typed letters, Emma to Brother Alex, 10 Jan. 1947, and the following: 8 Sept. 1946, 14 Oct. 1946, 5 Jan. 1947, 16 Feb. 1948. On this theme, she wrote, in a 3 Aug. 1947 letter to brother Alex, that some relatives had visited and described her reaction: "I could never express exactly how much it means for one in my position. It reminds you that you are a human being, an individual, that once you were a child, and that you are not just a poisonous toadstool in surroundings of darkness and gloom." See also Callwood, *Emma*.

38. LAC, MG 31 (Series K-20), Vol. 20, File 20-18, corrected notes, reference materials (2), 1939–1983, notes on Emma Woikin in prison; also, File 20-17, interview with Louie Sawula (Lucas); Callwood, *Emma*.

39. LAC, MG 31 (K-24), Vol. 21, File 21-3, biographical notes on accused spies, reference materials,

1946–1984, notes on Willsher, with references to British MI5 agents.

40. LAC, MG 31 (K-24), Vol. 21, File 21-3, *Star-Phoenix* (Saskatoon), clipping, 7 Dec 1948.

41. LAC, MG 31 (K-24), Vol. 20, File 20-17, typed transcripts of interviews with Dr. David Boyd, A.C. Cuelenaere, Marie Klassen, Dave Beaubier, Louie Sawula, autopsy report; Callwood, *Emma*. My thanks to June Callwood for a valuable conversation and for directing me to her papers at Library and Archives Canada.

42. This section draws largely on Deborah Van Seters's excellent "The Munsinger Affair: Images of Espionage and Security in 1960s Canada," *Intelligence and National Security* 13,2 (Summer 1998). Both the Munsinger and Profumo affairs have been the subject of films; see Brenda Longfellow, *Gerda*, National Film Board, 1995. See also Honourable Mr. Justice Wishart Flett Spence, *Report of the Commission of Inquiry into Matters Relating to one Gerda Munsinger* (Ottawa 1966).

43. Duiker, *Twentieth-Century World History*, ch. 9; Whitaker and Marcuse, *Cold War Canada*, Pt. 1-2; Finkel, *Our Lives*, chs. 1, 4.

44. The Liberals had first learned about Gerda Munsinger in 1964, when, finding themselves under fire for their handling of a narcotics dealer, they asked the RCMP for any files from the previous decade that involved investigations of any MPs or cabinet ministers. But they had kept it more or less under wraps. Cardin's initially cryptic reference in March 1966 to what he erroneously called "the Monseigneur case" created some confusion as to whether the Catholic Church had been involved in some security scandal; and, later, when confirming rumours of a sex and scandal case involving a call-girl-spy and Tory ministers, he called her Olga

Munsinger, adding, also incorrectly, that she had since died of leukemia in Germany. She was alive and well and living in Munich at the time.

45. Van Seters, "Munsinger Affair"; Politics, Sex and Gerda Munsinger," CBC Archives on-line <http://archives.cbc.ca>. See also the studies, cited above, by Canadian historians and political scientists, who generally agree that the event marked a low point in Canadian history.

46. Van Seters, "Munsinger Affair."

47. There were also inconsistencies; for instance, at one point Delorme conveyed Gerda's quip, made to her on a phone call from Germany, that Gerda was "too dumb to be a spy" – a comment that did not easily fit with the image of the sophisticated European woman that Delorme, Sévigny, and Hees were trying to draw.

48. Van Seters, "Munsinger Affair."

49. Longfellow supports this portrait in her film *Gerda*.

50. Van Seters, "Munsinger Affair."

51. Cited in Whitaker and Marcuse, *Cold War Canada*, 72.

11 Peace and Freedom in Their Steps

1. For a similar critique, see Rick Salutin, "Diverse Till Proven Monolithic," *Globe and Mail* 23 June 2006. Salutin notes that the discourse about Muslims betraying "Canadian values" ignores the critical point that, far from being universal, positive values, such as gender equity, have emerged out of the struggles of different generations of Canadians to challenge the status quo of their day.

2. For further discussion of these themes see, for example, Tania Das Gupta and Franca Iacovetta, editors, Special Theme Issue, "Whose Canada Is It?" *Atlantis: A Woman's Studies Journal* 24,2 (Spring 2000).

Bibliography

Primary Sources

Archival
Archives of Ontario (AO)
International Institute of Metropolitan Toronto
YWCA and YMCA Collection
Local Council of Women (LCW) Toronto
Provincial Council of Women of Ontario
Multicultural History Society of Ontario Photo Collection

City of Toronto Archives (CTA)
Social Planning Council (SPC) Collection
Central Neighbourhood House
St. Christopher House
University Settlement House

**Immigration Research Center,
St. Paul, Minnesota**
Nicholas V. Montalto. "The International Institute Movement: A Guide to Records of Immigrant Service Agencies in the United States." 1978

Library and Archives Canada (LAC), Ottawa
Canadian Association of Social Workers
Department of Citizenship and Immigration
    Immigration Branch, Canadian Citizenship Branch
Department of Labour
Imperial Order Daughters of the Empire

National Film Board (NFB) of Canada Archives, Montreal
Films produced for the Department of Citizenship and Immigration:
    A Million and a Half of Us: European Integration, 1958, Frontiers, director Julian Biggs
    Arrival, 1957, director Donald Ginsberg
    Canadian Notebook: A Cross-Section of Life and Work in Four Key Industries 1953, director David Bennett

Women at Work (previously *Careers for Women in Canada*) 1958, director Gordon Sparling

**University of Toronto,
Thomas Fisher Rare Books**
Robert S. Kenny Collection

**United Church Archives (UCA),
University of Toronto**
Women's Missionary Society Collection

**York University Archives,
Toronto**
Toronto Telegram Photo Collection

Oral History Collections and Interviews
Multicultural History Society of Ontario (MHSO), Oral History Collection (OHC)
Transcribed interviews with post-1945 newcomers from Europe

Paula Draper, Holocaust Survivors, Videotaped Interviews

Gerda Frieberg, Taped Presentation to the Ontario Women's History Network Conference, Ontario Institute for the Study of Education (OISE), University of Toronto, 1991

Personal conversations with 60 living subjects

Newspapers
Toronto Daily Star
The Globe and Mail (Toronto)
Toronto Star Weekly
Toronto Telegram

Periodicals
Food for Thought (Canadian Association of Adult Education)
Canadian Business
Canadian (Catholic) Register, The

Canadian Journal of Public Health
Canadian Unionist (Canadian Congress
  of Labour)
Canadian Welfare
Chatelaine
Echoes
Financial Post
Maclean's
News Bulletin (Canadian Red Cross [CRC],
  Ontario Division)
Trades and Labour Congress Journal
Saturday Night
Social Casework, Journal of
Social Worker, The

University of Toronto School of Social Work

Avison, Margaret. *The Research Compendium
  1942–1962: Review and Abstracts of Graduate
  Research.* 1964 (in author's possession)

Published Primary Sources

Allen, G.P. "Helping Immigrants Belong." *Canadian
  Welfare* 37 (15 May 1961).
Allen, Ralph. "The Untroublesome Canadians."
  Maclean's 7 March 1964.
Armour Stuart. "Getting Immigrants May Be
  Harder Than We Imagine." *Saturday Night*
  26 Oct. 1946.
Baird, Joan. "British War Brides." Script of a
  Canadian Broadcasting Corporation broadcast,
  Halifax, 25 Oct. 1944. Canadian Red Cross
  (CRC) Publications, National Headquarters,
  Ottawa.
Balla, Brigitta L. "With a Hungarian Accent." *Social
  Worker* 1 Oct. 1957.
Barkway, Michael. "How Many Immigrants Do We
  Want?" *Saturday Night* 14 Feb. 1950.
——. "Drastic Check to Immigration." *Saturday
  Night* 26 July 1952.
——. "We Can Still 'Save Face' with Our Refugee
  Policy." *Financial Post* 29 Dec. 1956.
——. "The Human Side." *Financial Post* 29 Dec.
  1956.
——. "Is Canada Botching the Refugee Job?"
  Financial Post 22 Dec. 1956.
——. "Are We Botching the Biggest Immigration?"
  Financial Post 30 March 1957.

Barnstead, Elinor G. "The Ordinary Family in
  Extraordinary Times." *Social Worker* 16,2
  (December 1947).
Bishop, Dorothy. "Moving Ahead in Medical
  Social." *Social Worker* 14,4 (April 1946).
Bosworth, C. F. "What's Behind the Immigration
  Wrangle?" *Maclean's* 14 May 1955.
Burns, Margaret M. "The Allan Memorial Institute
  of Psychiatry." *Social Worker* 15,2 (December
  1946).
Cahill, Brian. "Do the Immigrants Bring a Mental
  Health Problem to Canada?" *Saturday Night* 22
  June 1957.
Callwood, June. "The Parents Strike Back against
  Sex Criminals." *Maclean's* 23 July 1955.
—— (as told by Peter Keresztes). "We Are Hiding
  from Bad Men in the Forest." *Maclean's* 15 Nov.
  1957.
Canadian Broadcasting Corporation and Canadian
  Association for Adult Education, Citizens'
  Forum. *The Family in a Changing World.*
  Ottawa, January 1961.
Canadian Chamber of Commerce. *How Communists
  Operate! A Brief Memorandum on Communist
  Tactics.* 1948.
Canadian Citizenship Branch Publications,
  Citzenship Series. *How to Become a Canadian
  Citizen; Our Land; Our History; Our History
  of Government; The Citizen as Parent, The
  Citizen as Community Member; The Citizen as a
  Member of the World Community.*
Canadian Gas Association. *Discovering Canadian
  Cuisine: A Modern Guide to Cooking and
  Entertaining.* 1966.
Chamberlain, Frank. "Work's 'Have' Nations Must
  Aid 12 Million." *Saturday Night* 4 Oct. 1947.
Coldwell, M.J. "Canada's Immigration Policy."
  Canadian Unionist September 1953.
Collette, Elaine. "98 Cent January Specials."
  Chatelaine January 1960.
——. "South Seas to Enchant Your Natives."
  Chatelaine May 1963.
——. "Ten New Ways of Cooking with a Pound of
  Hamburg." *Chatelaine.* September 1961.
Council on Social Work Education. *Socio-Cultural
  Elements in Casework: A Case Book of Seven
  Ethnic Case Studies.* New York 1955.

Cross, Austin. "They Chose Canada!" *Canadian Business* 21 July 1950.

Defrates, John. "Refugees." *Canadian Welfare* 30 (June 1954).

Department of Health and Welfare. *Canada Food Guide*. Ottawa 1950.

Earl, Fraser. "The Making of Citizenship." *Food for Thought* 13,4 January 1953.

Edwards, Samuel. "Insights of Domesticity." *Food for Thought* 13,4 (January 1953).

Feinberg, Rabbi Abraham L. "Recent Jewish Orphan Projects." *Canadian Welfare* 25 (1 March 1950).

Ferguson, Edith. "Large Source of Labour in Europe's D.P.'s." *Saturday Night* 13 Dec. 1947.

Fine, Charles. "Canadian and American Ethnic Viewpoints: A Study in Contrast." *Social Worker* 29 (4 Oct. 1961).

Fitzpatrick, Anne L. "Volunteers, a Source of Strength." *Canadian Welfare* 30,3-4 (September 1954).

Foulds, Frank. "The Canadian Citizenship Branch." *Canadian Welfare* 25,1-2 (April/June 1950).

Frank, Lawrence K. "Psycho-Cultural Approach." *Intercultural Education News* June 1946.

Fraser, Blair. "How Racketeers Sold Entry in Canada." *Maclean's* 15 March 1952.

Fraser, Dorothy. "Immigration." *Saturday Night* 7 Jan. 1964.

Friedmann, W.G. "Our Growing Immigration Is Everyone's Business." *Saturday Night* 16 Feb. 1952.

Garner, Hugh. "An 'Old' Canadian Assesses the 'New' Canadians' Case against Us." *Maclean's* 18 July 1959.

Gellner, John. "So They're 'Reds'?" *Canadian Commentator* 1 (1 June 1957).

General Foods. *The Joys of Jell-O: Gelatin Dessert*. 9th ed. White Plains, N.Y. nd.

Genkind, Ethel Ostry. "Children from Europe." *Canadian Welfare* 25,1-2 (April-June 1949).

Gilbertson, F.S. "'Operation DP': A Gamble That Paid Off." *Industrial Canada* April 1950.

Goodman, Eileen. "Why We Can Take More Immigrants." *Canadian Business* June 1957.

Griffin, J.D. "The Problem of Mental Health in Canada." *Social Worker* 15,1 (September 1946).

Haslam, Phyllis. "The Damaged Girl in a Distorted Society." *Canadian Welfare* 15 March 1961.

Held, Frieda. "Social Workers and Volunteers as Partners." *Canadian Welfare* 15,1 (September 1946).

Henshaw, M.J. "UNRRA in the Role of Foster Parent." *Social Worker* 15,1 (September 1947).

Hill, Mary. "Displaced Persons – or New Canadians?" *Canadian Business* 23 (September 1950).

Holmes, Maria. "Meals off the Shelf." *Chatelaine* February 1955.

Huggard, Jean. "From Emigrants to Immigrants: Hungarians in a European Camp." *Canadian Welfare* 33 (1 Feb. 1958).

I.O.D.E. "Communism and the Canadian Woman." Released by Special IODE Committee to Study Ways and Means of Combatting Communism. *Echoes* Spring 1948.

Isserman, Betty (Kobayashi). "The Case Work Relationship in Work with Unmarried Mothers." *Social Worker* 17,1 (June 1951).

Jamieson, Robert. "Does Canada Really Want Immigrants?" *Saturday Night* 23 May 1959.

Johnson, J.G. "Immigrant Meets Teacher." *Food for Thought* 13,4 (January 1953).

Jordan, Isabel. "Canada – Land of Promises?" *Food for Thought* 13,4 (January 1953).

Kage, Joseph. "Immigration and Social Services." *Canadian Welfare* 24,3 (March 1949).

——. "The Jewish Immigrant Aid Society of Canada (JIAS) Social Services for Immigrants." *Social Worker* 18,3 (February 1950).

——. "From Bohunk to New Canadian." *Social Worker* 29,4 (October 1961).

Kaye, Vladimir. "Like Seeks Like." *Food for Thought* 13,4 (January 1953).

Katz, Sidney. "How Mental Health Is Attacking Our Immigrants." *Maclean's* 4 Jan. 1958.

——. "The Redeemed Children." *Maclean's* 10 Jan. 1962.

——. "Sex Criminals." *Maclean's* 1 July 1947.

Kenyon, Eva, Eileen Titus, and Alice Hall. "The Perpetual Crisis." *Social Worker* 22,4 (April 1954).

Ketchum J.D. "The Prude Is Father to the Pervert." *Maclean's* 15 Jan. 1948.

King, Dorothy. "Trends in Schools of Social Work." *Social Worker* 15,3 (February 1947).

Kirkconnell, Watson. *Canadians All: A Primer of National Unity*. Ottawa, 1941.

Lamb, Marjorie. *The Canadian Peace Congress and the World Peace Movement*. The Alert Service, Toronto, 1958.

Laudy, Marion. "Europeans Want to Leave Home and Canada Is Promised Land." *Saturday Night* 18 Oct. 1947.

Locke, Jeannine. "Can the Hungarians Fit In? *Chatelaine* May 1957.

MacDonald, Donald. "Canadian Labour and Immigration." *Canadian Unionist* December 1953.

——. "Congress Policy on Immigration." *Canadian Unionist* July-August 1955.

Maclean, John P. "And Reds Can't Get Them Back." *Financial Post* 8 Dec. 1956.

Marjoribanks, Robert. "Immigrants: Gold Mine of a Market." *Financial Post* 52 (24 Feb. 1959).

McCaul, Christina. "Working Wives Are Here to Stay." *Chatelaine* 1961.

McCarthur, Arthur. "The Young Idea in Immigration." *Canadian Business* 1 May 1948.

McCarthur, Jack. "Industry Likes New Canadians." *Financial Post* 24 April 1954.

McCarthy, Joseph, "Speech at Wheeling, West Virginia." In William H. Chafe and Harvard Sitkoff, eds., *A History of Our Time: Readings in Postwar America*. 2nd ed. New York, 1987.

Meredith, W.C.J. "Law and the Sex Criminals." *Saturday Night* 18 Oct. 1952.

Milling, G.B. "Immigrant Meets the Union." *Food for Thought* 13,4 (January 1953).

Moon, Barbara. "The Welcome Enemies." *Maclean's* 10 Feb. 1962.

Newman, Peter C. "The Hungarians." Special *Maclean's* Album, "What They Mean to Canada," *Maclean's* 16 Feb. 1957.

——. "The Big Battle for Our Citizens' Minds." *Financial Post* 1 Nov. 1952.

——. "Are New Canadians Hurting Canada?" *Maclean's* 18 July 1959.

——. "Are We Doing Enough? *Financial Post* 2 Aug. 1952.

Ordon-Gizucki, L.N. "No Ideal Country." *Food for Thought* 13,4 (January 1953).

Orlikow, David. "Labour and Immigration." *Canadian Labour* 9 Feb. 1964.

Parsons, J.E. "Christmas with My New Canadians." *Saturday Night* 24 Dec. 1960.

Prosser, R.R. "The Community Psychiatric Clinic and the Social Worker." *Social Worker* 19,4 (4 April 1951).

Reaume, Geoffrey. *A Classified Bibliography on the History of Psychiatry and Mental Health Services in Canada*. Toronto, 1998.

Sandwell, B.K. "It's Easy for Officials." *Saturday Night* 26 April 1952.

Schlesinger, Benjamin. "The Socio-Cultural Elements in Casework: The Canadian Scene." *Social Worker* 30,1 (January 1962).

——. *Families: A Canadian Perspective*. Toronto: McGraw Hill-Ryerson 1972.

——. *Families: Canada*. Toronto: McGraw Hill 1979.

—— and Rachel Schlesinger. *Canadian Families in Transition: A Workbook*. Toronto: Canadian Scholars Press 1992.

Schaffer, Alice C. "Drinking Milk and Learning Much." *Canadian Welfare* 30 (15 June 1954).

Shapiro, Pauline. "The Better Sort of Emigrants and Refugees." *Saturday Night* 17 May 1941.

Spector, Esther. "Successful Experiment with Volunteers." *Social Worker* 14,4 (April 1946).

Spence, Justice Wishart Flett. *Report of the Commission of Inquiry into Matters Relating to One Gerda Munsinger*. Ottawa, 1966.

Staebler, Edna. "The Other Canadians." *Chatelaine* March 1965.

Svanhuit, Josie. "Multi-Problem Family or Multi-Problem Agency?" *Social Worker* 31,4 (October 1963).

Toronto Nutrition Committee. *Food Customs of New Canadians*. Toronto: Ontario Dietetic Committee nd.

Van Heuven, G.J. Goedhart. "Refugee Problem Concerns Everybody." *Canadian Unionist* October 1955.

——. "No Need for the Displaced to Displace Canadians." *Trades and Labour Congress Journal* March 1948.

Waengler, Ernest. "The New Canadian Market Deserves Your Attention." *Industrial Canada* 59 (November 1958).

Weiss, David. Executive Director, Montreal Jewish Child Bureau. "Immigrant Meets the Agency." *Social Casework* December 1952.

Wilensky, Dora. "From Juvenile Immigrant to Canadian Citizen." *Canadian Welfare* 26 Jan. 1950.

——. "War's Impact on Family Life." *Canadian Welfare* 21,5 (Oct. 1945).

Williams, Ronald. "How to Keep Red Hands off Our New Canadians: Commie Hucksters Haven't a Chance with DP's in Town's Crusade for Democracy." *Financial Post* 43,3 (December 1949).

Wilson, Leslie. "Universities Step up First with Refugee Help Offers." *Financial Post* 29 Dec. 1956.

——. "Business Bids Fast to Get Entire Hungarian Colleges." *Financial Post* 15 Dec. 1956.

Wuorio, Eva-Lis. "We Can't Go Back." *Maclean's* 1 June 1948.

——. "Two Years Later." *Maclean's* 15 May 1950.

Zay, Nicholas. "Adaptation of the Immigrant." *Canadian Welfare* 28,7 (February 1953).

Secondary Sources

Books

Abella, Irving. *Nationalism, Communism and Canadian Labour: The CIO, the Communist Party and the Canadian Congress of Labour, 1935–1956.* Toronto: University of Toronto Press, 1973.

—— and Harold Troper. *None Is Too Many: Canada and the Jews of Europe.* Toronto: Lester & Orpen Dennys 1986.

Adamoski, Robert, Dorothy E. Chunn, and Robert Menzies, eds. *Contesting Canadian Citizenship: Historical Readings.* Peterborough, Ont.: Broadview Press 2002.

Addams, Jane. *Twenty Years at Hull House: with Autobiographical Notes.* New York: Bedford/St Martin's 1999 (1910).

Adams, Mary Louise. *The Trouble with Normal: Postwar Youth and the Making of Heterosexuality.* Toronto: University of Toronto Press 1997.

Allen, Richard, ed. *The Social Gospel in Canada.* Ottawa: National Museums of Canada 1975.

Allen, Thomas B. *Spy Book: The Encyclopaedia of Espionage.* New York: Random House 1997.

Anderson, Benedict. *Imagined Communities: Reflections on the Origin and Spread of Nationalism.* London:Verso 1991.

Anderson, Grace and David Higgs. *A Future to Inherit: The Portuguese Communities of Canada.* Toronto: McClelland and Stewart 1976.

Arnup, Katherine. *Education for Motherhood: Advice for Mothers in Twentieth-Century Canada.* Toronto: University of Toronto Press 1994.

——, Andrée Lévesque, and Ruth Pierson, eds. *Delivering Motherhood.* London and New York: Routledge1990.

Aun, Karl. *The Political Refugees: A History of Estonians in Canada.* Toronto: McClelland and Stewart 1985.

Avery, Donald. *Reluctant Host: Canada's Response to Immigrant Workers 1896–1994.* Toronto: Oxford University Press 1995.

——. *Dangerous Foreigners: European Immigrant Workers and Labour Radicalism in Canada, 1896–1932.* Toronto: McClelland and Stewart 1979.

Bakan, Abigail and Daiva Stasiulus. *Not One of the Family: Foreign Domestic Workers in Canada.* Toronto: University of Toronto Press 1997.

Bannerji, Himani. *The Dark Side of the Nation: Essays on Multiculturalism, Nationalism and Gender.* Toronto: Canadian Scholars Press 2000.

Barer-Stein, Thelma. *You Eat What You Are: A Study of Ethnic Food Traditions.* Toronto: McClelland and Stewart 1979.

Barthes, Rolande, ed. *The Pleasure of the Text.* New York: Noonday Press 1989.

Baumel, Judith Tydor. *Double Jeopardy: Gender and the Holocaust.* London: Vallentine Mitchell 1998.

Beevor, Antony. *Berlin – The Downfall, 1945.* New York: Viking 2002.

Bodnar, John. *The Transplanted: A History of Urban Immigrants in America.* Bloomington: Indiana University Press 1985.

Bothwell, Robert, Ian Drumond, and John English. *Canada Since 1945: Power, Politics and Provincialism*. Toronto: University of Toronto Press 1989.

Breines, Wini. *Young, White and Miserable: Growing Up Female in the Fifties*. Boston: Beacon 1992.

Brower, Daniel R. *The World in the Twentieth Century: The Age of Global War and Revolution*. New York: Prentice Hall 1996.

Bunting, Trudi and Pierre Filion, eds. *Canadian Cities in Transition: The Twenty-First Century*. Toronto: Oxford University Press 1991.

Burke, Sarah. *Seeking the Highest Good: Social Service and Gender at the University of Toronto, 1887–1937*. Toronto: University of Toronto Press 1996.

Callwood, June. *Emma: Canada's Unlikely Spy*. Toronto: Stoddart 1984.

Carniol, Ben. *Case Critical: Challenging Social Work in Canada*. 5th ed. Toronto: Between the Lines 2005.

Cavell, Richard, ed. *Love, Hate, and Fear in Canada's Cold War*. Toronto: University of Toronto Press 2004.

Celmins, Helene. *Women in Soviet Prisons*. New York: Paragon 1985.

Chauncey, George. *Gay New York: Urban Culture, Gender, and the Makings of a Gay Male World, 1890–1940*. New York: Basic Books 1994.

Chilton, Paul A. *Security Metaphors: Cold War Discourse from Containment to Common House*. New York: P. Lang 1996.

Chimbos, Peter. *The Canadian Odyssey: The Greek Experience in Canada*. Toronto: McClelland and Stewart 1980.

Chunn, Dorothy E. *From Punishment to Doing Good: Family Courts and Socialized Justice in Ontario, 1880–1940*. Toronto: University of Toronto Press 1992.

Churchill, Winston. *Triumph and Tragedy*. Vol 6. Boston: Houghton Mifflien Company 1953.

Clarke, Alison J. *Tupperware: The Promise of Plastic in 1950s America*. Washington, D.C: Smithsonian Institute 1999.

Cockburn, Cynthia. *The Space Between Us: Negotiating Gender and National Identities in Conflict*. London and New York: Zed Books 1998.

Cohen, Sam. *Folk Devils and Moral Panics*. London: MacGibbon and Kee 1972.

Cole, Ellen, Olivia M. Espin, and Esther D. Rothblum, eds. *Refugee Women and Their Mental Health: Shattered Societies, Shattered Lives*. Binghamton, N.Y.: Haworth Press 1992.

Collins, Anne. *In the Sleep Room: The Story of the CIA Brainwashing Experiments in Canada*. Toronto: Lester & Orpen Dennys 1988.

Comacchio, Cynthia. *Nations Are Built of Babies: Saving Ontario's Mothers and Children, 1900–1940*. Montreal and Kingston: McGill-Queen's University Press 1993.

Copp, Terry and Bill McAndrew. *Battle Exhaustion: Soldiers and Psychiatrists in the Canadian Army,1939–1945*. Montreal and Kingston: McGill-Queen's University Press 1990.

Corrigan, Philip and Derek Sayer. *The Great Arch: English State Formation as Cultural Revolution*. Oxford: Basil Blackwell 1985.

Dahlie Jorgen and Tissa Fernando, eds. *Ethnicity, Power and Politics in Canada*. Toronto: Methuen 1981.

Danys, Milda. DP: *Lithuanian Immigration to Canada after the Second World War*. Toronto: Multicultural History Society of Ontario 1986.

Das Gupta, Tania and Franca Iacovetta, eds., Special Theme Issue, "Whose Canada Is It?" *Atlantis: A Woman's Studies Journal* 24,2 (Spring 2000).

Diner, Hasia. *Hungering for America: Italian, Irish, and Jewish Foodways in the Age of Migration*. Cambridge, Mass.: Harvard University Press 1998.

Donzelot, Jacques. *The Policing of Families*. New York: Hutchinson 1979.

Dreisziger, N.F. *The Hungarian-Canadian Experience*. Toronto: McClelland and Stewart 1982.

Duiker, William J. *Twentieth-Century World History*. 2nd ed. Belmont Cal.: Wadsworth Publishing 2002.

Eksteins, Modris. *Walking Since Daybreak: A Story of Eastern Europe, World War II and the Heart of Our Century*. New York: Houghton Mifflin Company 1999.

Elliot, Mark. *Pawns of Yalta: Soviet Refugees and America's Role in Their Repatriation*. Urbana: University of Illinois Press 1982.

Enloe, Cynthia. *Bananas, Beaches, and Bases: Making Feminist Sense of International Politics*. Berkeley: University of California Press 1989.

Epp, Marlene. *Women without Men: Mennonite Refugees of the Second World War*. Toronto: University of Toronto Press 2000.

——, Franca Iacovetta, and Frances Swyripa, eds. *Sisters or Strangers? Immigrant, Ethnic and Racialized Women in Canadian History*. Toronto: University of Toronto Press 2004.

Erickson, Richard V., Patricia M. Baranek, and Janet B.L. Chan. *Visualizing Deviance: A Study of News Organizations*. Toronto: University of Toronto Press 1987.

Etzioni, Amitai, ed. *The Semi-Professions and Their Organizations: Teachers, Nurses, Social Workers*. New York: Free Press 1969.

Farb, Peter and George Armelagos. *Consuming Passions: The Anthropology of Eating*. Boston: Washington Square Press 1980.

Fahrni, Magda. *Household Politics: Montreal Families and Postwar Reconstruction*. Toronto: University of Toronto Press 2005.

Fetjo, Francois. *Behind the Rape of Hungary*. Foreword by J.P. Sartre. New York: D.Mackay Co. 1957.

Fieldhouse, Paul. *Food and Nutrition: Customs and Culture*. 2nd ed. London: Chapman and Hall 1995.

Finkel, Alvin. *Our Lives: Canada after 1945*. Toronto: Lorimer 1997.

Fishman, Mark. *Manufacturing the News*. Austin: University of Texas Press 1980.

Fiske, John. *Media Matters: Everyday Culture and Political Change*. Minneapolis: University of Minnesota Press 1996.

Fryer, Peter. *Hungarian Tragedy*. Expanded revised ed. London: Index Books 1997.

Foucault, Michel. *History of Sexuality*. Vols. 1–2. Trans. Hurley. London: Allan Lane 1979.

——. *Discipline and Punishment: The Birth of the Prison*. Trans. A. Sherida. London 1977.

——. *Power/Knowledge: Selected Interviews and Other Writings, 1972–1977*. London: Pantheon Books 1980.

Gabaccia, Donna. *We Are What We Eat: Ethnic Foods and the Making of Americans*. Cambridge, Mass.: Harvard University Press 1998.

——. *Immigration and American Diversity*. Malden, Mass: Blackwell Publishers 2002.

Gadney, Reg. *Cry Hungary! Uprising 1956*. London: Weidenfeld and Nicolson 1986.

Gay, Peter. *Modern Europe*. New York: Harper Row 1973.

Ganzevoort, Herman. *A Bittersweet Land: The Dutch Experience in Canada, 1890–1980*. Toronto: McClelland and Stewart 1988.

—— and Mark Boekelman, eds. *Dutch Immigration to North America*. Toronto: Multicultural History Society of Ontario 1983.

Gilbert, Martin. *The Routledge Atlas of the Holocaust*. London: Routledge 2002.

Giles, Wenona. *Portuguese Women in Toronto: Gender, Immigration and Nationalism*. Toronto: University of Toronto Press 2002.

——, Helene Moussa, and Penny Van Esterick, eds. *Development and Diaspora: Gender and the Refugee Experience*. Dundas, Ont.: Artemis Enterprises 1996.

—— et al., eds. *Feminists Under Fire: Exchanges across War Zones*. Toronto: Between the Lines 2003.

—— et al., eds. Special Issue, "Women in Conflict Zones." *Canadian Woman Studies* 19,4 (Winter 2000).

Gleason, Mona. *Normalizing the Ideal: Psychology, Schooling, and the Family in Postwar Canada*. Toronto: University of Toronto Press 1999.

Gordon, Linda. *Heroes of Their Own Lives: The Politics and History of Family Violence, Boston, 1880–1960*. New York: Penguin Books 1989.

——. *Pitied but Not Entitled: Single Mothers and the History of Welfare, 1890–1935*. Cambridge, Mass.: Harvard University Press 1994.

——, ed. *Women, the State, and Welfare*. Madison: University of Wisconsin Press 1990.

Gramsci, Antonio. *Letters from Prison*. Trans. Lynne Lawner. New York: Cape 1973.

Granatstein, J.L. *Canada 1957–1967: The Years of Uncertainty and Innovation*. Toronto: McClelland and Stewart 1986.

—— and David Stafford. *Spy Wars: Espionage and Canada from Gouzenko to Glasnost*. Toronto: Key Porter 1990.

Green, Alan. *Immigration and the Post-War Canadian Economy*. Toronto: Macmillan of Canada 1976.

Grossberg, Lawrence, Cary Nelson, and Paula Treichler, eds. *Cultural Studies*. London: Routledge 1992.

Hall, Stuart. *Policing the Crisis: Mugging, the State, and Law and Order*. London: Macmillan 1978.

Hallowell, Gerald, ed. *The Oxford Companion to Canadian History*. Don Mills, Ont.: Oxford University Press 2004.

Hannant Larry. *The Infernal Machine: Investigating the Loyalty of Canadian Citizens*. Toronto: University of Toronto Press 1995.

Harney, Robert., ed. Special Theme Issue on Toronto's People, *Polyphony* 6,1 (Spring/Summer 1984).

——, ed. Special Theme Issue on Ukrainians in Ontario, *Polyphony* 10,1-2 (1998).

——, ed. *The Gathering Place: Peoples and Neighbourhoods of Toronto, 1834–1945*. Toronto: Multicultural History Society of Ontario 1985.

Harper, Elise D. *The Past Is Prelude: Fifty Years of Social Action in the YWCA*. New York: YWCA 1963.

Harris, Richard. *Creeping Conformity: How Canada Became Suburban, 1900–1960*. Toronto: University of Toronto Press.

Hawkins, Freda. *Canada and Immigration: Public Policy and Public Concern*. 2nd ed. Montreal and Kingston: McGill-Queen's University Press 1988.

——. *Critical Years in Immigration: Canada and Australia Compared*. Montreal and Kingston: McGill-Queen's University Press 1989.

Heron, Craig. *Booze: A Distilled History*. Toronto: Between the Lines 2003.

Hibbert, Joyce, ed. *The War Brides*. Toronto: Peter Martin Associates 1978.

Higgs, David, ed. *Portuguese Migration in Global Perspective*. Toronto: Multicultural History Society of Ontario 1990.

Higonnet, Margaret Randolph et al., eds. *Behind the Lines: Gender and the Two World Wars*. New Haven, Conn.: Yale University Press 1987.

Hillmer, Norman, Bohdan Kordan, and Lubomyr Luciuk, eds. *On Guard for Thee: Ethnicity and the Canadian State, 1939–1945*. Ottawa: Committee for the History of the Second World War 1988.

Hoerder, Dirk. *Creating Societies: Immigrant Lives in Canada*. Montreal and Kingston: McGill-Queen's University Press 1999.

hooks, bell. *Talking Back: Thinking Feminism, Thinking Black*. Toronto: Between the Lines 1989.

Hryniuk, Stella and Lubomry Luciuk, eds. *Canada's Ukrainians: Negotiating an Identity*. Toronto: University of Toronto Press 1991.

Iacovetta, Franca. *Such Hardworking People: Italian Immigrants in Postwar Toronto*. Montreal and Kingston: McGill-Queen's University Press 1992.

——, Roberto Perin, and Angelo Principe, eds. *Enemies Within: Italian and Other Wartime Internees in Canada and Beyond*. Toronto: University of Toronto Press 1998.

—— and Wendy Mitchinson, eds. *On the Case: Explorations in Social History*. Toronto: University of Toronto Press 1998.

—— and Mariana Valverde, eds. *Gender Conflicts: New Essays in Women's History*. Toronto: University of Toronto Press 1992.

Irving, Allan, Harriet Parsons, and Donald Bellamy, eds. *Neighbours: Three Social Settlements in Downtown Toronto*. Toronto: Canadian Scholars Press 1995.

Ivanova, Galina Mikhailovna. *Labour Camp Socialism: The Gulag in the Soviet Totalitarian System*. Ed. Donald J. Raleigh, trans. Carol Flath. New York and London: M.E. Sharpe 2000.

Janeway, Elizabeth. *Powers of the Weak*. New York: Morrow 1980.

Jensen, Joan. *New Mexico Women: Intercultural Perspectives*. Albuquerque: University of New Mexico Press 1986.

Judt, Tony. *Postwar: A History of Europe Since 1945.* New York: Penguin 2005.

Kaplan, William. *Belonging: The Meaning and Future of Citizenship.* Montreal and Kingston: McGill-Queen's University Press 1993.

Kalback, Warren. *The Impact of Immigration on Canada's Population.* Ottawa: Dominion Bureau of Statistics 1970.

Kapscis, Sandor. *In the Name of the Working Class: The Inside Story of the Hungarian Revolution.* Trans. Daniel and Judy Stoffman. Toronto: Lester & Orpen Dennys 1986.

Kealey, Gregory S. and Reg Whitaker, eds. *RCMP Security Bulletins.* 4 Vols. St. John's, Nfld.: Canadian Committee on Labour History 1989–1997.

Kelley, Ninette and Michael Trebilcock. *The Making of the Mosaic: A History of Canadian Immigration Policy.* Toronto: University of Toronto Press 1998.

Kelm, Mary Ellen. *Colonizing Bodies: Aboriginal Health and Healing in British Columbia.* Vancouver: UBC Press 1998.

Kingston, Anne. *The Edible Man: Dave Nichol, President's Choice and the Making of Popular Taste.* Toronto: McFarlane, Walter and Ross 1994.

Kinsman, Gary. *The Regulation of Desire: Homo and Hetero Sexualities.* 2nd ed. Montreal: Black Rose Books 1996.

—, Dieter K. Buse, and Mercedes Steedman, eds. *Whose National Security? Canadian State Security and the Creation of Enemies.* Toronto: Between the Lines 2000.

— and Patrizia Gentile. *"In the Interests of the State": The Anti-gay, Anti-lesbian National Security Campaign in Canada: A Preliminary Research Report.* Sudbury: Laurentian University 1998.

Kiraly, Bela K. and Paul Jonas, eds. *The Hungarian Revolution of 1956 in Retrospect.* New York: East European Quarterly, distributed by Columbia University Press 1977.

Knowles, Valerie. *Strangers at Our Gates: Canadian Immigration and Immigration Policy, 1540–1990.* Toronto: Dundurn Press 1992.

Kolasky, John. *The Shattered Illusion: History of Ukrainian Pro-Communist Organizations in Canada.* Toronto: PMA Books 1979.

Kordan, Bohdan. *Canada and the Ukrainian Question, 1939–45: A Study in Statecraft.* Montreal and Kingston: McGill-Queen's University Press 2001.

Korinek, Valerie J. *Roughing It in the Suburbs: Reading Chatelaine Magazine in the Fifties and Sixties.* Toronto: University of Toronto Press 2000.

Kunzel, Regina. *Fallen Women, Problem Girls: Unmarried Mothers and the Professionalization of Social Work, 1890–1945.* New Haven, Conn. and London: Yale University Press 1993.

Kymlicka, Will. *Multicultural Citizenship: A Liberal Theory of Minority Rights.* London: Clarendon Press 1985.

—— and Wayne Norman, eds. *Citizenship in Diverse Societies.* New York: Oxford University Press 2000.

Langer, Lawrence L. *Holocaust Testimonies: The Ruins of Memory.* New Haven, Conn.: Yale University Press 1991.

Lappin, Ben. *The Redeemed Children: The Story of the Rescue of War Orphans by the Jewish Community of Canada.* Toronto: University of Toronto Press 1963.

Leiby, James. *A History of Social Welfare and Social Work in the United States, 1815–1972.* New York: Columbia University Press 1987.

Lemon, James. *Toronto Since 1918: An Illustrated History.* Toronto: Lorimer 1985.

Lévesque, Andrée. *Madelaine Parent: Activist.* Toronto: Sumach Press 2005.

Levenstein, Harvey. *Paradox of Plenty: A Social History of Eating in Modern America.* New York: Oxford University Press 1993.

—— *Revolution at the Table: The Transformation of the American Diet.* New York: Oxford University Press 1988.

Lindstrom, Varpu. *Defiant Sisters: A Social History of Finnish Women in Canada, 1880–1930.* Toronto: Multicultural History of Ontario 1988.

Little, Margaret. *No Car, No Radio, No Liquor Permit: The Moral Regulation of Single Mothers in Ontario, 1920–1977.* Toronto: Oxford University Press 1998.

Lissak, Rivka Shpak. *Pluralism and Progressives: Hull House and the New Immigrants, 1890–1919*. Chicago: University of Chicago Press 1989.

Lowe, Lisa. *Immigrants Acts: On Asian American Cultural Politics*. Durham, N.C.: Duke University Press 1992.

Luciuk, Lubomyr. *Searching for Place: Ukrainian Canadian Displaced Persons, Canada, and the Migration of Memory*. Toronto: University of Toronto Press 2000.

Lupul, Manoly, ed. *A Heritage in Transition: Essays in the History of Ukrainians in Canada*. Toronto: McClelland and Stewart 1982.

Margolian, Howard. *Unauthorized Entry: The Truth about Nazi War Criminals in Canada, 1946–1956*. Toronto: University of Toronto Press 2000.

Marling, Karal Ann. *As Seen on TV: The Visual Culture of Everyday Life in the 1950s*. Cambridge, Mass.: Cambridge University Press 1994.

Martz, Fraidie. *Open Your Hearts: The Story of the Jewish War Orphans in Canada*. Montreal: Véhicule Press 1996.

Marrus, Michael. *The Unwanted: European Refugees in the Twentieth Century*. New York: Oxford University Press 1985.

May, Elaine Tyler. *Homeward Bound: American Families in the Cold War Era*. New York: Basic Books 1988.

Meachen, Standish. *Toynbee Hall and Social Reform, 1880–1914: The Search for Community*. New Haven, Conn. and London: Yale University Press 1987.

McPherson, Kathryn, Cecilia Morgan, and Nancy Forestell, eds. *Gendered Pasts: Historical Essays on Masculinity and Femininity in Canada*. Toronto: University of Toronto Press 1999.

Mennell, Stephen, Anne Marcott, and Anneke H. Van Otterlo. *The Sociology of Food: Eating, Diet and Culture*. London: Sage Publications 1992.

Meyerowitz, Joanne J. *Women Adrift: Independent Wage Earners in Chicago, 1880–1930*. Chicago: University of Chicago Press 1988.

——, ed. *Not June Cleaver: Women and Gender in Postwar America 1945–1960*. Philadelphia: Temple University Press 1994.

Miller, J.R. *Shingwauk's Vision: A History of Native Residential Schools*. Toronto: University of Toronto Press 1996.

Moffat, Ken. *Poetics of Social Work: Personal Agency and Social Transformation in Canada, 1920–1939*. Toronto: University of Toronto Press 2001.

Morley, David and Kuan-Hsing Chen. *Stuart Hall: Critical Dialogues in Cultural Studies*. London: Routledge, 1997.

Nesaule, Agate. *A Woman in Amber: Healing and the Trauma of War and Exile*. New York: Soho Press 1995.

Ofer, Dalia and Lenore J. Weitzman, eds. *Women in the Holocaust*. New Haven, Conn. Yale University Press 1998.

Owram, Doug. *Born at the Right Time: A History of the Baby Boom Generation*. Toronto: University of Toronto Press 1996.

Parr, Joy. *Domestic Goods: The Material, the Moral and the Economic in the Postwar Years*. Toronto: University of Toronto Press 1999.

——, ed. *A Diversity of Women: Ontario, 1945–1980*. Toronto: University of Toronto Press 1995.

—— and Mark Rosenfeld, eds. *Gender and History in Canada*. Toronto: Copp Clark 1996.

Perry, Adele. *On the Edge of Empire: Gender, Race, and the Making of British Columbia 1849–1871*. Toronto: University of Toronto Press 2001.

Peiss, Kathy. *Cheap Amusements. Working Women and Leisure in Turn-of-the-Century New York*. Philadelphia: Temple University Press 1986.

Pickles, Katie. *Female Imperialism and National Identity: Imperial Order Daughters of the Empire*. Manchester: Manchester University Press 2002.

Pierson, Ruth Roach. *"They're Still Women After All": The Second World War and Canadian Womanhood*. Toronto: McClelland and Stewart 1986.

—— and Nupur Chaudhuri, eds. *Nation, Empire, Colony: Historicizing Gender and Race*. Bloomington, Ill.: Indiana University Press 1998.

Platt, Anthony. *The Child Savers: The Invention of Delinquency*. Chicago: University of Chicago Press 1969.

Polcz, Alaine. *One Woman in the War: Hungary 1944–1945*. Budapest, Hungary: Central University Press 2002.

Powers, Jo Marie. *Buon Appetito! Italian Foodways in Ontario*. Toronto: Ontario Historical Society 2000.

Pratt, Mary Louise. *Imperial Eyes: Travel Writing and Transculturation*. London and New York: Routledge 1992.

Proudfoot, Malcolm Jarvis. *European Refugees, 1939–1952: A Study in Forced Population Movement*. Evanston, Ill: Northwestern University Press 1956.

Radecki, Henry and Benedykt Heydenkorn. *A Member of a Distinguished Family: The Polish Group in Canada*. Toronto: McClelland and Stewart 1976.

Radforth, Ian. *Bushworkers and Bosses: Logging in Northern Ontario, 1900–1980*. Toronto: University of Toronto Press 1987.

Rasporich, Anthony. *For a Better Life: A History of Croatians in Canada*. Toronto: McClelland and Stewart 1992.

Radway, Janice A. *Reading the Romance: Women, Patriarchy and Popular Literature*. Berkeley: University of California Press 1991.

Ramazanoglu, Caroline, ed. *Up Against Foucault: Explorations of Some Tensions between Foucault and Feminism*. London: Routledge 1993.

Richmond, Anthony. *Post-war Immigrants in Canada*. Toronto: University of Toronto Press 1967.

——. *Immigrants and Ethnic Groups in Metropolitan Toronto: A Preliminary Study*. Toronto: Institute for Behavioural Research, York University 1967.

Rooke, P.T. and R.L. Schnell. *Discarding the Asylum: From Child Rescue to the Welfare State in English Canada 1800–1950*. Lanham, N.M.: University Press of America 1983.

——. *No Bleeding Heart: Charlotte Whitton, A Feminist on the Right*. Vancouver: UBC Press 1987.

——, eds. *Studies in Childhood History: A Canadian Perspective*. Calgary: Detselig Enterprises 1982.

Rose, Nicholas. *Governing the Soul: The Shaping of the Private Self*. London: Free Association Books 1999.

Ryerson, Ellen. *The Best Laid Plans: America's Juvenile Court System Experiment*. New York: Hill and Wang 1979.

Schrecker, Ellen. *Many Are the Crimes: McCarthyism in America*. Boston: Little, Brown and Co. 1998.

Scher, Len. *The Un-Canadians: True Stories of the Blacklist Era*. Toronto: Lester Publishing 1992.

Scott, James C. *Weapons of the Weak: Everyday Forms of Peasant Resistance*. New Haven, Conn.: Yale University Press 1985.

Shorter, Edward, ed. *TPH: History and Memories of the Toronto Psychiatry Hospital, 1925–1966*. Toronto: Wall and Emerson 1996.

Shtohryn, Dmytro, ed. *Ukrainians in North America: A Biographical Directory of Noteworthy Men and Women of Ukrainian Origin in the United States and Canada*. Champaign, Ill: Association for the Advancement of Ukrainian Studies 1975.

Solinger, Ricki. *Wake Up Little Susie: Single Pregnancy and Race before Roe v Wade*. London: Routledge 1992.

Solzhenitsyn, Alexander. *The Gulag Archipelago 1918–1956*. Trans. Thomas P. Whitney. London: Collins/Fontana 1973.

Steedman, Mercedes, Peter Suschnigg, and Dieter K. Buse, eds. *Hard Lessons: The Mine-Mill Union in the Canadian Labour Movement*. Toronto: Dundurn Press 1995.

Stephen, Jennifer. *Pick One Intelligent Girl: Employability, Domesticity and the Gendering of Canada's Welfare State, 1940s–1950s*. Toronto: University of Toronto Press, forthcoming 2007.

Strange, Carolyn. *Toronto's Girl Problem: The Perils and Pleasures of the City 1880–1930*. Toronto: University of Toronto Press 1995.

Strong-Boag, Veronica et al., eds. *Painting the Maple: Essays on Race, Gender and the Construction of Canada*. Vancouver: UBC Press 1998.

Struthers, James. *The Limits of Affluence: Welfare in Ontario, 1920–1970*. Toronto: University of Toronto Press 1994.

Swyripa, Frances. *Wedded to the Cause: Ukrainian Women and Ethnic Identity, 1891–1991*. Toronto: University of Toronto Press 1993.

—— and John Herd Thompson. *Loyalties in Conflict: Ukrainians in Canada during the Great War*. Toronto: Canadian Institute of Ukrainian Studies Press 1983.

Tannahill, Reay. *Food in History*. 4th ed. New York: Stein and Day 1984.

Taylor, Charles. *Reconciling the Solitudes: Essays on Federalism and Nationalism*. Montreal and Kingston: McGill-Queen's University Press 1993.

Taylor, Molly Ladd and Lauri Umani, eds. *Bad Mothers and the Politics of Blame in Twentieth-Century America*. New York 1998.

Terry, Jennifer. *An American Obsession: Science, Medicine and Homosexuality in Modern Society*. Chicago: University of Chicago Press 1999.

Tillotson, Shirley. *The Public at Play: Gender and the Politics of Recreation in Post-War Ontario*. Toronto: University of Toronto Press 2000.

Tolstoy, Nikolai. *Victims of Yalta*. London: Corgi 1977.

Troper, Harold and Morton Weinfeld. *Old Wounds: Jews, Ukrainians and the Hunt for Nazi War Criminals in Canada*. Markham, Ont.: Penguin 1989.

Tulchinsky, Gerald. *Branching Out: The Transformation of the Canadian Jewish Community*. Toronto: Stoddart 1998.

Valverde, Mariana. *The Age of Light, Soap and Water: Moral Reform in English Canada*. Toronto: McClelland and Stewart 1991.

——. *Diseases of the Will: Alcohol and the Dilemmas of Freedom*. Cambridge: Cambridge University Press, 1998.

——, ed. *Studies in Moral Regulation*. Toronto: Centre of Criminology, University of Toronto 1994.

Van Den Bergh, Nan and Lynne Cooper, eds. *Feminist Visions for Social Work*. New York: National Association of Social Workers 1986.

Visser, Margaret. *Much Depends on Dinner*. Toronto: McClelland and Stewart 1986.

——. *The Rituals of Dinner*. Toronto: HarperCollins 1991.

Walker, James. *Race, Rights and the Law in the Supreme Court of Canada: Historical Case Studies*. Waterloo, Ont.: Wilfrid Laurier University Press 1997.

Walkowitz, Judith. *City of Dreadful Delight: Narratives of Sexual Danger in Late-Victorian London*. Chicago: University of Chicago Press 1992.

Watney, Simon. *Policing Desire: Pornography, AIDS, and the Media*. Minneapolis: University of Minnesota Press 1989.

Weaver, John. *Crimes, Constables, and Courts: Order and Transgression in a Canadian City, 1816–1970*. Montreal and Kingston: McGill-Queen's University Press 1995.

Weeks, Jeffrey. *Sex, Politics and Society: The Regulation of Sexuality Since 1800*. London and New York: Longman 1989.

Weisbord, Marilyn. *The Strangest Dream: Canadian Communists, the Spy Trials, and the Cold War*. Toronto: Lester & Orpen Dennys 1983.

Whitaker, Reg. *Double Standard: The Secret History of Canadian Immigration*. Toronto: Lester & Orpen Dennys 1987.

—— and Gary Marcuse. *Cold War Canada: The Making of a National Insecurity State, 1945–1957*. Toronto: University of Toronto Press 1994.

Wicks, Ben. *Promise You'll Take Care of My Daughter: The Remarkable War Brides of World War II*. Toronto: Stoddart 1992.

Wills, Gale. *A Marriage of Convenience: Business and Social Work in Toronto, 1918–1957*. Toronto: University of Toronto Press 1995.

Wsevelod, Isajiw, ed. *Identities: The Impact of Ethnicity on Canadian Society*. Toronto: Peter Martin 1977.

——. *Definitions of Ethnicity*. Toronto: Multicultural History Society of Ontario 1979.

Wyman, Mark. *DP: Europe's Displaced Persons, 1945–1951*. Philadelphia: Balch Institute Press 1989.

Yuval-Davis, Nira. *Gender and Nation*. London: Sage Publishing 1997.

Articles

Brands, H.W. "The Age of Vulnerability: Eisenhower and the National Insecurity State." *American Historical Review* 94 (October 1989).

Callister, Agnes. "Canada's Immigration Policy and Domestics from the Caribbean: The Second Domestic Scheme." In Jesse Vorst et al., eds., *Race, Class and Gender: Bonds and Barriers.* Toronto: Between the Lines 1989.

Carter, Sarah. "First Nations Women and Colonization on the Canadian Prairies 1870s–1920s." In Veronica Strong-Boag, ed., *Rethinking Canada: The Promise of Women's History.* 4th ed. Toronto: Oxford University Press 2002.

Chenier, Elise. "Seeing Red: Immigrant Women and Sexual Danger in Toronto's Postwar Daily Newspapers." Special Theme Issue, "Who's Canada Is It?" ed. Tania Das Gupta and Franca Iacovetta, *Atlantis: A Woman's Studies Journal* 24,2 (Spring 2000).

Conzen, Kathleen Neils, David A. Gerber, Ewa Morawska, George E. Pozzetta, and Rudolph Vecoli. "The Invention of Ethnicity: A Perspective from the U.S.A." *Journal of American Ethnic History* 12 (1992).

Draper, Paula. "Surviving Their Survival: Women, Memory and the Holocaust." In Epp, Iacovetta, and Swyripa, eds., *Sisters or Strangers?*

Dreiziger, Nandor F. "The Impact of the Revolution on Hungarians Abroad: The Case of Hungarian Canadians." In Bela K. Kiraly, Barbara Lotie, Nandor F, Dreiziger, eds., *The First War Between Socialist States: The Hungarian Revolution of 1956 and Its Impact.* New York: Social Science Monographs 1984.

Dubinsky, Karen and Franca Iacovetta. "Murder, Womanly Virtue and Motherhood: The Case of Angelina Napolitano." *Canadian Historical Review* 72,4 (1991).

Epp, Marlene. "The Memory of Violence: Soviet and East European Mennonite Refugees and Rape in the Second World War." *Journal of Women's History* 9,1 (Spring 1997).

Fiske, Joanne. "Child of the State, Mother of the Nation: Aboriginal Women and the Ideology of Motherhood." *Culture* 13 (1993).

Fraser, Nancy and Linda Gordon. "Civil Citizenship against Social Citizenship." In Bart von Steenbergen, ed., *The Condition of Citizenship.* Thousand Oaks, Cal.: Sage Publishing 1994.

Gebhard, Krzstof. "Handbooks for Postwar Polish Immigrants." *Polyphony* 3 (Winter 1981).

Getty, J. Arch, Gabor T. Ritterspoon, and Viktory N. Zemskov. "Victims of the Soviet Penal System in the Pre-War Years: A First Approach on the Basis of Archival Evidence." *American Historical Review* October 1993.

Girard, Philip. "From Subversion to Liberation: Homosexuals and the Immigration Act, 1952–1977." *Canadian Journal of Law and Society* 2 (1987).

Golz, Annalee. "The Canadian Family and the State in the Postwar Period." *Left History* 1,2 (1993).

Grossman, Anita. "Trauma, Memory, and Motherhood: Germans and Jewish Displaced Persons in Post-Nazi Germany, 1945–49." *Archiv fur Sozialgeschichte* 38 (1998).

Harney, Robert. "Montreal's King of Italian Labour: A Case Study of Padronism." *Labour/Le Travailleur* 4 (1979).

——. " 'So Great a Heritage as Ours': Immigration and the Survival of the Canadian Polity." *Daedalus* 117,4 (Fall 1988).

Harzig, Christiane. "MacNamara's DP-Domestics: Immigration Policy Makers Negotiate Class, Race, and Gender in the Aftermath of World War Two." *Social Politics* 10,1 (Spring 2004).

——. "When You Are a New Immigrant You Are Just Half and Half: The Process of Becoming Canadian among Post-World-War-Two German Immigrants." In Doris Eibl, Christina Strobel, eds., *Selbst und andere/s: Von Begegnungen und Grenzziehungen.* Beitrage zur Kanadistik Band 7. Augsburg: Wibner Verlag 1998.

Heineman, Elizabeth. "The Hour of the Woman: Memories of Germany's 'Crisis Years' and West German National Identity." *American Historical Review* 101 (1996).

Iacovetta, Franca. "Manly Militants, Cohesive Communities, and Defiant Domestics: Writing about Immigrants in Canadian Historical Scholarship." *Labour/Le Travail* 36 (Fall 1995).

——. "Gossip, Contest, and Power: The Making of Suburban Bad Girls, Toronto, 1940s–1950s." *Canadian Historical Review* 80,4 (December 1999).

——. "Primitive Villagers and Uneducated Girls: Canada Recruits Domestics from Italy, 1951–52." *Canadian Woman Studies* 7,4 (Winter 1986).

——. "Post-Modern Ethnography, Historical Materialism, and De-centring the (Male) Authorial Voice: A Feminist Conversation." *Histoire Sociale/Social History* 32,64 (November 1999).

——. "Recipes for Democracy? Gender, Family, and Making Female Citizens in Cold War Canada." *Canadian Woman Studies* 20,2 (Summer 2000).

——. "Gendering Trans/National Historiographies: Feminists Rewriting Canadian History." *Journal of Women's History* 18,1 (Spring 2006).

——. "The Personal, Political, and Intellectual in Left Feminist History." *Left History* 11,1 (Spring 2006).

Jenson, Jane and Susan Phillips. "Regime Shift: New Citizenship Practices in Canada." *International Journal of Canadian Studies* 14 (Fall 1996).

Kealey, Gregory S. "State Repression of Labour and the Left in Canada, 1914–1920: The Impact of the First World War." *Canadian Historical Review* 73,3 (1992).

——. "1919: The Canadian Labour Revolt." In Kealey, *Workers and Canadian History*. Montreal and Kingston: McGill-Queen's University Press 1995.

Keshen, Jeffrey. "Wartime Jitters over Juveniles: Canada's Delinquency Scare and Its Consequences, 1939–1945." In Jeffrey Keshen, ed., *Age of Contention: Readings in Canadian Social History, 1990–1945*. Toronto: Harcourt Canada 1997.

Kimmel, David and Daniel Robinson. "The Queer Career of Homosexual Security Vetting in Cold War Canada." *Canadian Historical Review* 73,3 (1994).

Kinsman, Gary. " 'Character Witnesses' and 'Fruit Machines': Toward an Analysis of the Anti-Homosexual Security Campaign in the Canadian Civil Service." *Labour/Le Travail* 35 (Spring 1995).

Kunzel, Regina. "Pulp Fictions and Problem Girls: Reading and Rewriting Single Pregnancy in the Postwar United States." *American Historical Review* 100 (December 1995).

Marsh, Margaret. "Suburban Men and Domesticity, 1870–1915." *American Quarterly* 40 (June 1988).

Papp, Susan. "Hungarian Immigration after 1945." *Polyphony* 2 (1979–80).

Perin, Roberto. "Clio as an Ethnic: The Third Force in Canadian Historiography." *Canadian Historical Review* 64 (1983).

Prentice, Susan. "Workers, Mothers, Reds: Toronto's Postwar Daycare Fight." *Studies in Political Economy* 30 (1989).

Ringwold, Joan. "Gender and Genocide: A Split Memory." In Ronit Lentin, ed., *Gender and Catastrophe*. London: Zed Books 1997.

Kimmel, David and Daniel Robinson. "The Queer Career of Homosexual Vetting in Cold War Canada." *Canadian Historical Review* 75,3 (September 1994).

Ross, Becki L. "Destaining the Tatooed Delinquent Body: The Practises of Moral Regulation at Toronto's Street Haven, 1965–69." *Journal of the History of Sexuality* 7,4 (April 1997).

Sauer, Angelika. "A Matter of Domestic Policy? Canadian Immigration Policy and the Admission of Germans, 1945–50." *Canadian Historical Review* 74,2 (June 1993).

Smith, Geoffrey S. "National Security and Personal Isolation: Sex, Gender and Disease in the Cold War United States." *International History Review* 14 (May 1992).

——. "Containments, 'Disease,' and Cold War Culture." In Brian J.C. McKercher and Michael Hennessy, eds., *War in the Twentieth Century: Reflections at Century's End*. Westport, Conn.: Praeger 2003.

Stephen, Jennifer. "The "Incorrigible," the "Bad," and the "Immoral." In Louis A. Knafla and Susan W.S. Binnie, eds., *Law, Society and the State: Essays in Modern Legal History*. Toronto: University of Toronto Press 1995.

Stetz, Margaret D. "Woman as Mother in a Headscarf: The Woman War Refugee and the North American Media." In Special Theme Issue, "Women in Conflict Zones," ed. Winona Giles et al., *Canadian Woman Studies* 19,4 (Winter 2000).

Strong-Boag, Veronica. "Home Dreams: Canadian Women and the Suburban Experiment." *Canadian Historical Review* 72: 4 (1991).

Swyripa, Frances. "Negotiating Sex and Gender in the Ukrainian Bloc Settlement: East Central Alberta between the Wars." *Prairie Forum* 20,2 (Fall 1995).

Troger, Annemarie. "Between Rape and Prostitution: Survival Strategies and Chances of Emancipation for Berlin Women after World War II." In Judith Friedlander, Blanche Wiesen Cook, Alice Kessler-Harris, and Carroll Smith Rosenberg, eds., *Women in Culture and Politics: A Century of Change*. Bloomington: Indiana University Press 1986.

Tulchinsky, Gerald. "Joe Salsberg: Towards a Preliminary Biography." Paper presented to Canadian Historical Association, Winnipeg, 2004.

Urbancic, Anne. "Italo-Slovenian Immigrants in Toronto: Doubled Ethnicities." In Gabriele Scardellato and Manuela Scarci, eds., *A Monument for Italian Canadians*. Toronto: York University 1999.

Valverde, Mariana. "Social Facticity and the Law: A Social Expert's Eyewitness Account of Law." *Social and Legal Studies* 5,2 (1996).

Van Seters, Deborah. "The Munsinger Affair: Images of Espionage and Security in 1960s Canada." *Intelligence and National Security* 13,2 (Summer 1998).

Wakewich, Pamela and M. Lock. "Nerves and Nostalgia: The Expression of Loss among Greek-Canadian Immigrants in Montreal." *Canadian Family Physician* 36 (1990).

Wark, Wesley. "Security Intelligence in Canada, 1864–1945: The History of the National Insecurity State." In Keith Neilson and B.J.C. McKercher, eds., *Go Spy the Land: Military Intelligence in History*. Westport, Conn.: Praeger 1992.

Wright, Cynthia. "Nowhere at Home: Gender, Race, and the Making of Anti-Immigrant Discourse in Canada." Special Theme Issue, "Whose Canada Is It?" *Atlantis: A Woman's Studies Journal* 24,2 (Spring 2000).

——. "Rewriting the Modern: The Death of a Department Store." *Histoire sociale/Social History* 35 (May 2000).

Web On-line

Bexte, Martina. "Who Was Mata Hari?" <http://www.sc.essortment.com/whowasmatahar_rhrc.htm>.

CBC Archives. "Politics, Sex and Gerda Munsinger <wysiwyg://archives.cbc.ca/IDD-I-74-69>.

Duffy, Michael. "Who's Who: Mata Hari <http://www.firstworldwar.com/bio/matahari.htm> 2000–5.

Leibman, Nina. "Ozzie and Harriet." The Museum of Broadcast Communications <http://www.museum.tv/archives/etv>.

Kassel, Michael B. "Father Knows Best: US Domestic Comedy." <http://www.museum.tv/archives/etv>.

Orlick, Peter. "Leave It to Beaver: US Situation Comedy." <http://www.museum.tv/archives/etv>.

Films

Fernie, Lynne and Aerlyn Weissman. *Forbidden Love: The Unashamed Stories of Lesbian Lives*. National Film Board of Canada, Studio D 1993.

Longfellow, Brenda. *Gerda*. Gerda Film Productions 1992.

Unpublished Secondary Sources

Bellini, Stephanie W. "The Kitchen Table Talks: Italian Immigrant Domestic Workers in Toronto's Postwar Years." M.A. thesis, Memorial University, St. John's, Nfld., 2001.

Belmonte, Laura. "Mr and Mrs America: Images of Gender and the Family in Cold War Propaganda." Berkshire Conference on the History of Women, Chapel Hill, North Carolina, June 1996.

Butler, Cheryl A. "'Janey Canuck': Experiences of World War II British War Brides Who

Emigrated to Canada." M.A. thesis, University of Toronto, 1995.

Chenier, Elise. "Take a Telephone and Stir: Women and the Parents' Action League." Paper presented to the Canadian Historical Association, Sherbrooke, Quebec, 1999.

Depoe, Phyllis. "Why Dutch War Brides Came to Canada and How They Survived." Major research paper, Department of History, University of Toronto, 1996.

Di Iorio, Louise. "Pasta, Polenta, Ice Cream and Won Tons: Food Habits and Italian Immigrants in Postwar Toronto." Paper, Department of History, York University, 2003.

Dooley, Christopher. " 'What's in a Name?': Nursing in the Saskatchewan Mental Health Services, 1944–1973." Paper presented to the Toronto Labour Studies Group, Winter 2005.

Draper, Paula. "Lost Children: Child Survivors and the Toronto Jewish Family and Child Service, The Early Years." Article-length manuscript.

Finestein, Margaret. "Sexuality, Mothering, and Motherhood after Auschwitz: Jewish Women as Displaced Persons in Germany, 1945–1951." Paper presented to the Congress of Historical Sciences, Oslo, Norway, June 2000.

Graham, John. "A History of the Toronto School of Social Work." Ph.D. thesis, University of Toronto, 1995.

Griswold, Robert L. "Russian Blonde in Space: Americans View the Soviet Woman in the Early Cold War." Article-length manuscript.

Halpern, Miriam. "Parenthetical Memories: An Exploration of World War II Trauma and Italian Women's Fiction after 1968." Thesis, Italian Studies, New York University, 2003.

Hill, Daniel G. "The Negroes in Toronto: A Sociological Study of a Minority Group." Ph.D. thesis, University of Toronto, 1960.

Hinther, Rhonda. "Sincerest Revolutionary Greetings: Progressive Canadians in Twentieth Century Canada." Ph.D. thesis, McMaster University, Hamilton, Ont., 2004.

James, Cathy. "Gender, Class and Ethnicity in the Organization of Neighbourhood and Nation: The Role of Toronto's Settlement Houses in the Formation of the Canadian State, 1902 to 1914." Ph.D. thesis, University of Toronto, 1996.

McPhee, Debra M. "The Child Protection System: Organization Responses to Child Abuse and the Social Construction of Social Problems." Social Work, University of Toronto, 1998.

Miranda, Susanna. "Cleaning 'Ladies,' Working Women: Portuguese Immigrant Women and Domestic Day Cleaning in 1960s and 1970s Toronto." M.A research paper, York University, Toronto, 2003.

Ophir, Martha. "Defining Ethnicity in Postwar Canada: The International Institute of Metropolitan Toronto." Major research paper, Department of History, University of Toronto, 1993.

Reiter, Ester, "The Purging of the United Jewish People's Order from the Canadian Jewish Congress." Paper presented to Toronto Labour Studies Group, Spring 2005.

Rutherdale, Robert. " 'We Had a '65 Dodge: Fathers on the Road since 1945." Paper presented to Car in History: Business, Space and Culture in North America Conference, University of Toronto, 2005.

——. "New 'Faces' for Fathers: Memory, Life-Writing, and Fathers as Providers in the Postwar Consumer Era." Article-length manuscript.

Sethna, Christabel. "The Facts of Life: Sex Education, Moral Regulation and Venereal Disease in Ontario, 1900–1950." Book manuscript in review.

Smith, Cheryl. "Stepping Out: The Emergence of Professional Ballet in Canada, 1938–1963." Ph.D. thesis, University of Toronto, 1998.

Smith, Cherly. "The Show Did Not Go On: An Episode in Canada's Red Scare." Article-length manuscript.

Spergel, Estella. "British War Brides, World War II: A Unique Experiment for Unique Immigrants – The Process That Brought Them to Canada." Department of History, University of Toronto, 1997.

Taylor, Molly Ladd. "Sterilizing the Feeble-Minded in Inter-War Minnesota." Paper presented to the Berkshire Conference on the

History of Women, University of Connecticut, June 2002.

Tulchinsky, Gerald. "Joe Salsberg: Towards a Biography." Paper presented to Canadian Historical Association, Winnipeg, 2004.

Valverde, Mariana. "Symbolic Indians: Domestic Violence and the Ontario Liquor Board's 'Indian List', 1950–1990." Paper presented to the Berkshire Conference on the History of Women," University of Connecticut, June 2002.

White, Elizabeth Muir. "Expert Witness Discourse: C.K. Clarke and the Rise of the Pyschiatric 'Expert' in Canada, 1880–1920." M.A. research paper, Criminology, University of Toronto, 1996.

Index